K. Baedeker

**London and its Environs**

Handbook for Travellers

K. Baedeker

**London and its Environs**
*Handbook for Travellers*

ISBN/EAN: 9783337180904

Printed in Europe, USA, Canada, Australia, Japan

Cover: Foto ©ninafisch / pixelio.de

More available books at **www.hansebooks.com**

# LONDON

### AND ITS

# ENVIRONS.

## HANDBOOK FOR TRAVELLERS

### BY

## K. BAEDEKER.

WITH 3 MAPS AND 15 PLANS.
**SEVENTH REVISED EDITION.**

LEIPSIC: KARL BAEDEKER, PUBLISHER.
LONDON: DULAU AND CO., 37 SOHO SQUARE W.
1889.

'Go, little book, God send thee good passage,
And specially let this be thy prayere
Unto them all that thee will read or hear.
Where thou art wrong, after their help to call,
Thee to correct in any part or all.'

# PREFACE.

The chief object of the Handbook for London, like that of the Editor's other European and Oriental guide-books, is to enable the traveller so to employ his time, his money, and his energy, that he may derive the greatest possible amount of pleasure and instruction from his visit to the greatest city in the modern world.

As several excellent English guide-books to London already existed, the Editor in 1878 published the first English edition of the present Handbook with some hesitation, notwithstanding the encouragement he received from numerous English and American correspondents, who were already familiar with the distinctive characteristics of 'Baedeker's Handbooks'. So favourable a reception, however, was accorded to the first edition that the issue of a second became necessary in little more than a year, while a third, a fourth, a fifth, a sixth, and a seventh have since been called for. The present volume embodies the most recent information, down to the month of July, 1889, obtained in the course of personal visits to the places described, and from the most trustworthy sources.

In the preparation of the Handbook the Editor has received most material assistance from several English friends who are intimately acquainted with their great Metropolis. His grateful acknowledgments are specially due to the REV. ROBERT GWYNNE, B. A., who has contributed numerous valuable corrections and interesting historical and topographical data.

Particular attention has been devoted to the description of the great public collections, such as the National Gallery, the British Museum, and the South Kensington Museum, to all of which the utmost possible space has been allotted. The accounts of the pictures in the National Gallery, Buckingham Palace, Hampton Court, the Dulwich Gallery, and the various private collections, are from the pen of DR. JEAN PAUL RICHTER of Florence.

The Introduction, which has purposely been made as comprehensive as possible, is intended to convey all the information, preliminary, historical, and practical, which is best calculated to make a stranger feel at home in London, and to familiarise him with its manners and customs. While the descriptive part of the work is topographically arranged, so that the reader may see at a glance which of the sights of London may be visited together, the introductory portion classifies the principal sights according to their subjects, in order to present the reader with a convenient index to their character, and to facilitate his selection of those most congenial to his taste. As, however, it has not been the Editor's purpose to write an exhaustive account of so stupendous a city, but merely to describe the most important objects of general interest contained in it, he need hardly observe that the information required by specialists of any kind can only be given to a very limited extent in the present work. The most noteworthy sights are indicated by asterisks.

The list of Hotels and Restaurants enumerated in the Handbook comprises the most important establishments and many of humbler pretension. Those restaurants which the Editor believes to be most worthy of commendation are denoted by asterisks. The same system, however, has not been extended to the hotels, those enumerated in the Handbook being generally unexceptionable. The hotels at the West End and at the principal railway-stations are the most expensive, while the inns in the less fashionable quarters of the Metropolis generally afford comfortable accommodation at moderate charges.

The Maps and Plans, upon which the utmost care has been bestowed, will also, it is hoped, be found serviceable. Those relating to London itself (one clue-map, one large plan, four special plans of the most important quarters of the city, and a railway plan) have been specially revised for this edition, and are placed at the end of the volume in a separate cover, which may if desired be severed from the Handbook altogether. The subdivision of the Plan of the city into three sections of different colours will be found greatly to facilitate reference, as it obviates the necessity of unfolding a large sheet of paper at each consultation.

The Routes to places of interest in the Environs of London, although very brief, will probably suffice for the purposes of an ordinary visit. Some of the longer excursions that appeared in earlier editions have now been transferred to *Baedeker's Handbook to Great Britain*.

# CONTENTS.

## Introduction.

| | Page |
|---|---|
| 1. Money. Expenses. Season. Passports. Custom House. Time | 1 |
| 2. Routes to and from London. Arrival | 2 |
| 3. Hotels. Boarding Houses. Private Lodgings | 6 |
| 4. Restaurants. Dining Rooms. Oyster Shops. Confectioners | 11 |
| 5. Cafés. Billiard Rooms | 16 |
| 6. Reading Rooms. Libraries. Newspapers | 17 |
| 7. Baths | 18 |
| 8. Shops, Bazaars, and Markets. The Co-operative System | 19 |
| 9. Cabs. Omnibuses. Tramways. Coaches | 28 |
| 10. Railways | 32 |
| 11. Steamboats | 38 |
| 12. Theatres | 39 |
| 13. Concerts and other Amusements | 43 |
| 14. Races, Sports, and Games | 46 |
| 15. Embassies and Consulates. Bankers | 49 |
| 16. Divine Service | 50 |
| 17. Post and Telegraph Offices. Parcels Companies. Commissionnaires. Lady Guides | 53 |
| 18. Outline of English History | 56 |
| 19. Historical Sketch of London | 62 |
| 20. Topography and Statistics | 66 |
| 21. General Hints | 71 |
| 22. Guilds. Charities. Societies. Clubs | 72 |
| 23. Preliminary Ramble | 75 |
| 24. Disposition of Time | 78 |
| 25. Books relating to London | 80 b |

## Sights of London.
### I. The City.

| | |
|---|---|
| 1. St. Paul's Cathedral | 81 |
| 2. General Post Office. Christ's Hospital. Newgate. Holborn | 90 |
|     Paternoster Row. Peel's Statue. General Telegraph Office. Central Criminal Court. Holborn Viaduct. St. Sepulchre's Church | 90 |
|      | 93 |
|     Ely Chapel | 94 |
| 3. St. Bartholomew's Hospital. Smithfield. Charterhouse | 94 |
|     St. Bartholomew the Great | 95 |
|     Central London Meat Market. St. Giles, Cripplegate | 96 |
|     St. John's Gate | 97 |
|     Bunhill Fields. Honourable Artillery Company | 98 |
| 4. Guildhall. Cheapside. Mansion House | 98 |
|     Gresham College. Goldsmiths' Hall | 100 |

## CONTENTS.

|   |   | Page |
|---|---|---|
| | Bow Church. Mercers' Hall | 101 |
| | Grocers' Hall. Armourers' Hall. St. Stephen's Church | 102 |
| 5. | The Bank of England. The Exchange | 103 |
| | Bankers' Clearing House. Stock Exchange. **Drapers' Hall**. Dutch Church. | 104 |
| | Merchant Taylors' Hall | 105 |
| | Crosby Hall. St. Helen's Church | 106 |
| | Cornhill. Leadenhall Market. St. Andrew's Undershaft. | 107 |
| | Corn Exchange. St. Olave's Church. **Toynbee** Hall. **People's** Palace | 108 |
| 6. | London Bridge. The Monument. Lower Thames **Street** | 109 |
| | Fishmongers' **Hall**. St. Magnus the Martyr's. Billingsgate. | 111 |
| | Custom House. Coal Exchange. Tower Bridge. | 112 |
| 7. | Blackfriars **Bridge**. Thames Embankment. Queen Victoria Street. Cannon Street | 112 |
| | Cleopatra's Needle | 114 |
| | Office of the Times | 115 |
| | Bible Society. **Heralds'** College | 116 |
| | London Stone. Southwark Bridge | 117 |
| 8. | The Tower | 117 |
| | Trinity House | 124 |
| | All Hallows, Barking. Royal Mint | 125 |
| | Tower Subway. City of London Subway | 126 |
| 9. | The Port and Docks | 126 |
| | St. Katherine's Docks. London Docks | 126 |
| | Thames Tunnel | 127 |
| | Commercial Docks. Regent's **Canal**. **West** India Docks. East India Docks. Millwall Docks. **Victoria** and Albert Docks | 128 |
| 10. | Bethnal Green Museum. **National** Portrait Gallery. Victoria Park | 128 |
| 11. | Fleet Street. The Temple. Chancery Lane. Royal Courts of Justice | 134 |
| | St. Bride's | 134 |
| | St. Dunstan's in the West. New Record Office | 135 |
| | Temple Church | 136 |
| | Lincoln's Inn | 138 |
| | Gray's Inn | 139 |
| | Temple Bar. Child's Bank | 140 |

### II. The West End.

| | | |
|---|---|---|
| 12. | Strand. Somerset House. Waterloo Bridge | 141 |
| | St. Clement Danes | 141 |
| | Roman Bath. King's College. St. Mary le Strand | 142 |
| | Savoy Chapel. **Society** of Arts. National Life Boat Institution | 144 |
| | Eleanor's Cross. **The** Watergate | 145 |
| 13. | Trafalgar Square | 145 |
| | Nelson Column | 145 |
| | St. Martin's in the Fields | 146 |
| | Charing Cross | 147 |
| 14. | The National Gallery | 147 |
| 15. | Royal College of Surgeons. Soane Museum | 177 |
| | Floral Hall. Bow Street Police Court | 179 |
| | Covent Garden Market. St. Paul's. Garrick Club | 180 |
| 16. | Whitehall | 181 |
| | Royal United Service Museum | 182 |
| | Horse Guards. Government Offices | 183, 184 |
| | Montague House. Whitehall Gardens | 184 |

## CONTENTS.

| | Page |
|---|---|
| 17. Houses of Parliament and Westminster Hall | 184 |
|     St. Margaret's Church | 191 |
|     Westminster Bridge | 192 |
| 18. Westminster Abbey | 193 |
|     Westminster Column. Westminster School | 217 |
|     Westminster Hospital. Royal Aquarium | 218 |
| 19. Pall Mall and Piccadilly | 218 |
|     Haymarket. Waterloo Place. Crimean Monument | 218 |
|     York Column. St. James's Square | 219 |
|     Marlborough House. St. James's Street. Burlington House | 220 |
|     Royal Society. Royal Academy | 221 |
|     London University. St. James's Church. Geological Museum | 222 |
|     Leicester Square | 223 |
| 20. Regent Street. Oxford Street. Holborn | 224 |
|     Hanover Square. Cavendish Square | 224 |
|     Trinity College. All Saints' Church | 225 |
|     Doré Gallery. St. Giles-in-the-Fields. Russell Square | 226 |
|     University College. St. Pancras' Church. Islington. Highbury. Holloway. Camden Town. Kentish Town. Canonbury | 227 |
|     Foundling Hospital | 228 |
| 21. Regent's Park | 228 |
|     Zoological Gardens | 229 |
|     Botanic Gardens | 232 |
|     Primrose Hill. Lord's Cricket Ground | 233 |
| 22. The British Museum | 233 |
| 23. St. James's Palace and Park. Buckingham Palace | 255 |
|     Green Park | 259 |
| 24. Hyde Park. Kensington Gardens and Palace. Holland House | 259 |
|     Holly Lodge. St. George's Cemetery | 263 |
| 25. Private Mansions around Hyde Park and St. James's | 264 |
|     Grosvenor House | 264 |
|     Stafford House. Bridgewater House | 265 |
|     Dudley House | 266 |
|     Lansdowne House. Apsley House | 267 |
|     Bath House. Dorchester House. Hertford House | 268 |
|     Devonshire House | 269 |
| 26. Albert Memorial. Albert Hall. Imperial Institute. Natural History Museum | 270 |
|     Gore House. Royal College of Music | 271 |
|     School of Art Needlework. School of Cookery | 272 |
| 27. South Kensington Museum. India Museum | 275 |
|     Exhibition Galleries | 288, 289 |
|     Brompton Oratory | 291 |
| 28. Belgravia. Chelsea. Kensal Green Cemetery | 291 |
|     Millbank Penitentiary. Chelsea Hospital. Royal Military Asylum | 292 |
|     Chelsea Church | 293 |

### III. The Surrey Side.

| | |
|---|---|
| 29. St. Saviour's Church | 295 |
|     Barclay and Perkins' Brewery. Guy's Hospital | 296 |
|     Southwark Park | 297 |
| 30. Lambeth Palace. Bethlehem Hospital. Battersea Park | 297 |
|     St. Thomas's Hospital | 297 |
|     St. George's Cathedral | 299 |

CONTENTS.

## Excursions from London.

|   |   | Page |
|---|---|---|
| 31. | Greenwich Hospital and Park | 301 |
| 32. | Woolwich | 304 |
| 33. | The Crystal Palace at Sydenham | 305 |
| 34. | Dulwich | 312 |
| 35. | Hampton Court. Richmond. Kew | 315 |
| 36. | The Thames from London Bridge to Hampton Court | 323 |
| 37. | Hampstead. Highgate | 327 |
| 38. | Epping Forest. Waltham Abbey. Rye House | 329 |
|   | From Rye House to Hertford | 331 |
| 39. | St. Albans | 331 |
|   | Harrow on the Hill | 332 |
|   | From St. Albans to Luton and Dunstable | 334 |
| 40. | Windsor. Eton | 334 |
|   | From Slough to Stoke Poges and Burnham Beeches | 336 |
|   | Runnimede. Holloway College | 336 |
| 41. | Gravesend. Chatham. Rochester | 342 |
|   | Eltham | 345 |
|   | Cobham Hall. Gadshill. Chalk | 346 |
| Index | | 347 |
| List of Eminent Persons | | 357 |
| Index to Plan of London in the Appendix. | | |

### List of Maps and Plans.

1. Railway Map of England, before the title-page.
2. Map of the Environs of London, between pp. 300 and 301.
3. Key-Plan of London.
4. Plan of London in three sections.
5. Special Plan of the West End from Baker Street to Soho.
6. „ „ „ Holborn, Fleet Street, and Strand.
7. „ „ „ the City.
8. „ „ „ the West End from Hyde Park and Belgravia to the Thames.
9. Railway Map of London.
10. St. Paul's Cathedral, p. 83; 11. the Tower, p. 119; 12. Houses of Parliament, between pp. 184 and 185; 13. Westminster Abbey, p. 194; 14. Zoological Gardens, between pp. 228 and 229; 15. British Museum, between pp. 232 and 233; 16. South Kensington Museum (two sections), pp. 276 and 285; 17. Crystal Palace, p. 306; 18. Windsor Castle, p. 336.

In the Cover after the Index.

### Abbreviations.

M. = Engl. mile; hr. = hour; min. = minute; r. = right; l. = left; N. = north, northwards, northern; S. = south, etc.; E. = east, etc.; W. = west, etc.; R. = room; B. = breakfast; D. = dinner; A. = attendance; L. = light. The letter d, with a date, after a name indicates the year of the person's death.

Asterisks are used as marks of commendation.

# INTRODUCTION.

## 1. Money. Expenses. Season. Passports. Custom House. Time.

**Money.** In England alone of the more important states of Europe the currency is arranged without much reference to the decimal system. The ordinary English *Gold* coins are the sovereign or pound ($l.$ = livre) equal to 20 shillings, and the half-sovereign. The *Silver* coins are the crown (5 shillings), the half-crown, the florin (2 shillings), the shilling *(s.)*, and the six-penny and three-penny pieces. The *Bronze* coinage consists of the penny ($d.$, Lat. denarius), of which 12 make a shilling, the halfpenny, and the farthing ($1/4\,d.$). The *Guinea*, a sum of 21$s.$, though still used in reckoning, is no longer in circulation as a coin. A sovereign is approximately equal to 5 American dollars, 25 francs, 20 German marks, or 10 Austrian florins (gold). The *Bank of England* issues notes for 5, 10, 20, 50, and 100 pounds, and upwards. These are useful in paying large sums; but for ordinary use, as change is not always readily procured, gold is preferable. The number of each note should be taken down in a pocket-book, for the purpose, in the event of its being lost or stolen, of stopping payment of it at the Bank, and thus possibly recovering it. *Foreign Money* does not circulate in England, and should always be exchanged on arrival. French copper coins, though still occasionally met with in London, are liable to refusal. A convenient and safe mode of carrying money from America or the Continent is in the shape of letters of credit, or circular notes, which are readily procurable at the principal banks. A larger sum than will suffice for the day's expenses should never be carried on the person, and gold and silver coins of a similar size (*e.g.* sovereigns and shillings) should not be kept in the same pocket.

**Expenses.** The cost of a visit to London depends of course on the habits and tastes of the traveller. If he lives in a first-class hotel, dines at the table d'hôte, drinks wine, frequents the theatre and other places of amusement, and drives about in cabs or flys instead of using the economical train or omnibus, he must be prepared to spend 30-40$s.$ a day or upwards. Persons of moderate requirements, however, will have little difficulty, with the aid of the information in the Handbook, in living comfortably and seeing the principal sights of London for an expenditure of 15-20$s.$ a day or even less.

**Season.** The 'London Season' is chiefly comprised within the months of May, June, and July, when Parliament is sitting, the aristocracy are at their town residences, the greatest artistes in the world are performing at the Opera, and the Picture Exhibitions open. Families who desire to obtain comfortable accommodation had better be in London to secure it by the end of April; single travellers can, of course, more easily find lodgings at any time.

**Passports.** These documents are not necessary in England, though occasionally useful in procuring delivery of registered and *poste restante* letters (comp. p. 53). A *visa* is quite needless. American travellers, who intend to proceed from London to the Continent, should provide themselves with passports before leaving home. Passports, however, may also be obtained by personal application at the American Consulate in London (p. 49). The *visa* of the American ambassador, and that of the minister in London of the country to which the traveller is about to proceed, are sometimes necessary.

**Custom House.** Almost the only articles likely to be in the possession of ordinary travellers on which duty is charged are spirits and tobacco, but a flask of the former and $^1/_2$lb. of the latter are allowed for private use. Three pounds of tobacco may be passed on payment of a duty of 5s. per pound, and (in the case of cigars) a slight fine for the contravention of the law forbidding the importation of cigars in chests of fewer than 10,000. Foreign reprints of copyright English books are liable to confiscation. The custom-house examination is generally lenient.

**Time.** Uniformity of time throughout the country is maintained by telegraphic communication with Greenwich Observatory (p. 303).

## 2. Routes to and from London. Arrival.

It may not be out of place here to furnish a list of the principal oceanic routes between the New World and England, and also to indicate how Transatlantic visitors may continue their European travels by passing from London to the Continent. An enumeration of the routes between the Continent of Europe and London may also prove serviceable to foreigners coming in the reverse direction. It should, however, be borne in mind that the times and fares mentioned in our list are liable to alteration.

**Routes to England from the United States** of America and **Canada.** The traveller has abundant room for choice in the matter of his oceanic passage, the steamers of any of the following companies affording comfortable accommodation and speedy transit.

*Inman Line.* Every Wednesday from New York to Liverpool. Cabin 80, 90, or 110 dollars; return-ticket (available for 12 months) 130 or 150 dollars. From Liverpool also every Wednesday. Fare 12-50*l.*; return 22-90*l.* The finest steamers of this line are the *City of New York* and the *City of Paris*, the latter of which made the quickest passage on record from land to land (5 days, 23 hrs.,

## 2. PASSAGE.

7 min.) in May, 1889. London offices, 13 Pall Mall. S.W., and Eives and Allen, 99 Cannon Street, E.C.

*Cunard Line.* A steamer of this company starts every Saturday and every second Wednesday from New York and every Saturday from Boston for Queenstown and Liverpool. Cabin fare 60, 80, 100, or 125 dollars, according to accommodation; return-ticket (available for 12 months) 120, 144, 180, or 220 dollars. Steamers from Liverpool for New York every Saturday and every second Tuesday, for Boston every Thursday. Fare 12, 15, 18, or 21 guineas, or 26*l.*; return-ticket 25, 30, or 35 guineas, or 45*l.* The *Etruria* and the *Umbria* are considered the best Cunarders. The former held the record for the quickest ocean passage before the above-mentioned feat of the Inman liner. London offices at 6 St. Helen's Place, Bishopsgate Street, and 28 Pall Mall.

*White Star Line.* Steamer every alternate Wednesday from New York to Queenstown and Liverpool. Cabin 60 or 140 dollars; steerage 20 dollars. From Liverpool to New York every Wednesday. Cabin 12-22*l.*, return (available for one year) 24-40*l.*; second cabin 7-8*l.* The *Germanic* and *Britannic* are at present the largest vessels of this line, but two fine new steamers, the *Majestic* and *Teutonic*, will very soon be added to the White Star fleet. London office, 34 Leadenhall Street, E.C.

*American Steamship Company.* From Philadelphia to Liverpool every Thursday, and from Liverpool to Philadelphia every Wednesday. Cabin 10 to 18*gs.*; return-ticket 20 to 30*gs.*; intermediate 6*l.* London office, Keller, Wallis, & Co., 5 and 7 Fenchurch Street, E.C.

*North German Lloyd Line.* Between New York and Southampton twice weekly; first saloon 16-23*l.*, second saloon 10*l.* 10*s.* and 13*l.* From New Orleans to Southampton, and *vice versâ*, once a month; cabin 155, steerage 40 dollars. The newest and finest boats of this company are the *Trave*, *Lahn*, *Saale*, and *Aller*. London offices, 5 & 7 Fenchurch Street, E. C., and 32 Cockspur Street, W.C.

*National Steamship Company.* Steamers from Liverpool and also from London direct to New York every Wednesday. Cabin fare 8-15*gs.*; returns at reduced rates. From New York to Liverpool every Saturday, and from New York to London weekly. Cabin 50 to 100 dollars. London offices at 36 Leadenhall Street and 57 Charing Cross.

*Anchor Line.* Steamer between Liverpool and New York monthly. Saloon 12-25*l.*; returns 22-44*l.* Also weekly mail-steamer between New York and Glasgow. Saloon from 9*gs.*, second cabin 6*gs.*, steerage 4*l.* London address, Henderson Brothers, 18 Leadenhall Street, E. C., and 8 Regent Street, S. W.

*Alban Line.* From Liverpool every Thursday to Halifax and Portland, and every alternate Tuesday to St. John's, Halifax, and Baltimore. Saloon 10-18*gs.*; intermediate 6*gs.* London address, 103 Leadenhall Street. Also to New York weekly (Wilson Hill Line).

1*

*Guion Line.* Weekly steamers between New York and Liverpool. Cabin fare 10-25*l.*; children under 12 years, half-fare. London office, 5 Waterloo Place.

*State Line.* Weekly steamers between New York and Glasgow. Saloon 6 to 8*gs.*

*Dominion Line.* Weekly steamers from Liverpool to Halifax and Portland; fortnightly from and to Bristol. Saloon 10-15*gs.*; intermediate 6*gs*. London address, Sewell & Crowther, 18 Cockspur Street, W.C.

*Monarch Line.* Regular communication between London and New York. Saloon 12 or 15*gs.*; second cabin 7*gs.*; steerage 4*l.* 5*s.* Office, 6 Fenchurch Avenue, E.C.

*Great Western Steamship Line.* Regular communication between Bristol and New York, and Bristol and Montreal. Saloon 12*gs.*; return 21*gs.*

The average duration of the passage across the Atlantic is 7-10 days. The best time for crossing is in summer. Passengers should pack clothing and other necessaries for the voyage in small boxes or portmanteaus, such as can lie easily in the cabin, as all bulky luggage is stowed away in the hold. State-room trunks should not exceed 3 ft. in length, 2 ft. in breadth, and 1½ ft. in height. Dress for the voyage should be of a plain and serviceable description, and it is advisable, even in midsummer, to be provided with warm clothing. A deck-chair, which may be purchased at the dock or on the steamer before sailing (from 7*s.* upwards), is a luxury that may almost be called a necessary. It may be left in charge of the Steamship Co.'s agents until the return-journey. On going on board, the traveller should apply to the purser or chief steward for seats at table, as the same seats are retained throughout the voyage. It is usual to give a fee of 10*s.* (2½ dollars) to the table-steward and to the state-room steward, and small gratuities are also expected by the boot-cleaner, the bath-steward, etc. The state-room steward should not be 'tipped' until he has brought all the passenger's small baggage safely on to the landing-stage or tender.

Landing at Liverpool is generally effected with the aid of a steam-tender, to which passengers and luggage are transferred from the Transatlantic steamer. The passengers remain in a large waiting-room until all the baggage has been placed in the custom-house shed. Here the owner will find his property expeditiously by looking for the initial of his surname on the wall. The examination is generally soon over (comp. p. 2). Porters then convey the luggage to a cab (3*d.* for small articles, 6*d.* for a large trunk). — Baggage may now be 'expressed' from New York to any city in Europe. Agents of the English railway companies, etc., also meet the steamers on arrival at Liverpool and undertake to 'express' baggage on the American system to any address given by the traveller.

FROM LIVERPOOL TO LONDON, by railway, the traveller may proceed by the line of one of four different companies (202-238 M. according to route, in 4½-8 hrs.; fares by all trains 29*s.*, 21*s.* 9*d.*, 16*s.* 6*d.*; no second class by Midland Railway). The *Midland Railway* to St. Pancras runs by Matlock, Derby, and Bedford. The route of the *London and North Western Railway* (to Euston Square Station) goes viâ Crewe and Rugby. By the *Great Western Railway* to Paddington we may travel either viâ Chester, Birmingham, Warwick, and Oxford; or viâ Hereford and Gloucester; or viâ Worcester. Or, lastly, we may take a train of the *Great Northern Rail-*

*way* to King's Cross Station, passing Grantham and Peterborough (with a fine cathedral). Should the traveller make up his mind to stay overnight in Liverpool he will find any of the following hotels comfortable: *North Western Hotel*, Lime Street Station; *Adelphi*, near Central Station; *Grand*, Lime Street; *Alexandra*, Dale Street; *Laurence's Temperance Hotel*, Clayton Square.

FROM SOUTHAMPTON TO LONDON, by *South Western Railway* to Waterloo Station (79 M. in $2^1/_3$-3 hrs.; fares 15s. 6d., 11s., 6s. 6d.). Hotels at Southampton: *South Western; Radley's; Royal; Dolphin*.

FROM PLYMOUTH TO LONDON, by *Great Western Railway* to Paddington Station, or by *South Western Railway* to Waterloo Station (247 M., in $6^1/_2$-$11^1/_2$ hrs.; fares 46s. 6d., 32s. 10d., 18s. 8d.). Hotels at Plymouth: *Grand; Duke of Cornwall; Royal; Harvey's; Globe*.

For fuller details of these routes, see *Baedeker's Great Britain*.

**Routes from England to the Continent.** The following are the favourite routes between London and the Continent: —

From *Dover* to *Calais* thrice a day, in $1^1/_4$-$1^3/_4$ hr.; cabin 8s. 6d., fore-cabin 6s. 6d. (Railway from London to Dover, or *vice versâ*, in 2-4 hrs.; fares 20s. or 18s. 6d., 15s. or 13s. 6d., 6s. 9d. or 6s. $2^1/_2$d.)

From *Folkestone* to *Boulogne*, twice a day, in 2-3 hrs.; cabin 8s., fore-cabin 6s. (Railway from London to Folkestone in 2-4 hrs.; fares same as to Dover, except 3rd class, which is 6s.)

From *Dover* to *Ostend*, thrice a day, in 3-5 hrs.; cabin 15s., fore-cabin 10s.

From *London* to *Boulogne*, 5 times weekly, in 10 hrs.; 10s. or 7s.

From *London* to *Ostend*, twice a week, in 12 hrs. (6 hrs. at sea): 18s. or 14s.

From *London* to *Calais*, twice a week, in 10 hrs.: 12s. or 8s. 6d.

From *London* to *Rotterdam*, thrice a week, in 18-20 hrs. (9-10 hrs. at sea); 20s. or 16s.

From *Harwich* to *Rotterdam*, daily (Sundays excepted), in 11-12 hrs.; railway from London to Harwich in 2-3 hrs. (fares 13s. 3d., 10s., 5s. $11^1/_2$d.); fare from London to Rotterdam, 26s. or 15s.

From *London* to *Antwerp*, thrice a week, in 16 hrs. (8-9 hrs. of which are on the open sea); 21s. or 16s.

From *Harwich* to *Antwerp*, daily (Sundays excepted), in 12-13 hrs. (train from London to Harwich in 2-3 hrs.); 21s. or 15s. (from London).

From *Harwich* to *Hamburg*, twice weekly (Wed. & Sat.; train from London in 2-3 hrs.); 22s. 6d., 17s. 6d. (from London 27s. 6d., 25s., 20s.).

From *London* to *Bremerhafen*, twice a week, in 36-40 hrs.; 2l. or 1l.

From *London* to *Hamburg*, five times a week, in 36-40 hrs.; 2l. 5s. or 1l. 9s.

From *Queenborough* to *Flushing*, twice daily, in 8 hrs. (5 hrs. at sea); train from London to Queenborough in $1^1/_2$ hr., from Flushing to Amsterdam in 6-9 hrs.; through-fare 33s. 6d. or 20s. 11d.

From *Newhaven* to *Dieppe*, twice daily, in 6-8 hrs.; 16s. or 11s. 6d. (Rail from London to Newhaven, or *vice versâ*, in 2-3 hrs; fares 13s. 9d. or 11s. 3d., 10s. 6d. or 7s. 10d., and 4s. $8^1/_2$d.)

On the longer voyages (10 hrs. and upwards), or when special attention has been required, the steward expects a gratuity of 1s. or more, according to circumstances. Food and liquors are supplied on board all the steamboats at fixed charges, but the viands are often not very inviting.

**Arrival.** Those who arrive in London by water have sometimes to land in small boats. The tariff is 6d. for each person, and 3d. for each trunk. The traveller should take care to select one of the watermen who wear a badge, as they alone are bound by the tariff.

There is still much room for improvement in the arrangements for landing in small boats.

Cabs (see p. 28) are in waiting at most of the railway-stations, and also at the landing-stages. The stranger had better let the porter at his hotel pay the fare in order to prevent an overcharge. At the more important stations *Private Omnibuses*, holding 6-10 persons, may be procured on previous application to the Railway Co. (fare 1s. per mile, with a minimum of 3s.).

## 3. Hotels. Boarding Houses. Private Lodgings.

**Hotels.** Charges for rooms in the London hotels vary according to the situation and the floor. A difference is also made between a simple *Bed Room* and a bedroom fitted up like a *Sitting Room*, with writing-table, sofa, easy-chairs, etc., a higher charge being, of course, made for the latter. Most of the rooms, even in the smaller hotels, are comfortably furnished. The continental custom of locking the bedroom door on leaving it is not usual, but visitors should make their door secure at night, even in the best houses. Private sitting-rooms are generally expensive. The dining-room is called the *Coffee Room*. In some hotels the day of departure is charged for, unless the rooms are given up by noon.

Breakfast is generally taken in the hotel, the continental habit of breakfasting at a café being almost unknown in England. The meal consists of tea or coffee with meat, fish, and eggs, and is charged for by tariff. Tea or coffee with bread and butter alone is, of course, cheaper.

A fixed charge per day is also made for attendance, beyond which no gratuity need be given. It is, however, usual to give the 'boots' (i.e. boot-cleaner and errand man) a small fee on leaving, and the waiter who has specially attended to the traveller also expects a shilling or two. — In most hotels smoking is prohibited except in the *Smoking Rooms* provided for the purpose. — An assortment of English newspapers is provided at every hotel, but foreign journals are rarely met with.

The ordinary charges at London hotels are as follows: — Bed-room 3-10s., Sitting-room 5-20s., Attendance 1s. 6d., Breakfast 1-4s., Dinner 2s. 6d.-10s. Lights (*i.e.* candles or gas) are seldom charged for. Persons who make a prolonged stay at a hotel are recommended to ask for their bills every two or three days to prevent mistakes, whether accidental or designed.

Numerous as the London hotels are, it is often difficult to procure rooms in the Season, and it is therefore advisable to apply in advance by letter or telegram.

The large TERMINUS HOTELS, which have sprung up of late years at the different railway-stations, and which belong to com-

## 3. HOTELS.

panies, are handsomely fitted up, and have a fixed scale of charges. Rooms may be obtained in them at rates to suit almost every purse. They are, however, more suitable for passing travellers, who wish to catch an early train, than for those making a prolonged stay in London. The following are the chief station hotels: —

*Great Western Hotel*, Paddington Station.
*Euston Hotel*, Euston Square Station.
*Great Northern Railway Hotel*, King's Cross Station.
*Cannon Street Hotel*, Cannon Street Station.
*Grand Midland Railway Hotel*, St. Pancras Station, Euston Road.
*Great Eastern Hotel*, Liverpool Street Station.
*Terminus Hotel*, London Bridge Station.
*Charing Cross Hotel*, Charing Cross Station.
*Grosvenor Hotel*, Victoria Station, Pimlico.
*Holborn Viaduct Hotel*, Holborn Viaduct Station.

The South Western Railway station at Waterloo is still in want of a terminus hotel.

Other extensive hotels belonging to companies are: —

*Alexandra Hotel*, 16-21 St. George's Place, Hyde Park Corner.
*Langham Hotel*, Portland Place, a great American resort.
*Grand Hotel*, Charing Cross, on the site of Northumberland House (p. 141).
*Hôtel Métropole*, Northumberland Avenue, a large new house, elaborately fitted up; table-d'hôte breakfast 3*s.* 6*d.*, plain breakfast 2*s.*, table d'hôte dinner (6-8.30) 5*s.*, R. from 3*s.* 6*d.*, A. 1*s.* 6*d.*
*Hôtel Victoria*, Northumberland Avenue, opened in 1887, a still more extensive establishment than the Métropole, in a similar palatial style.
*Buckingham Palace Hotel*, Buckingham Palace Gate.
*Westminster Palace Hotel*, Victoria Street, Westminster.
*Hôtel Windsor*, Victoria Street, Westminster.
*Inns of Court Hotel*, High Holborn, grand entrance from Lincoln's Inn Fields.
*First Avenue Hotel*, Holborn, lighted throughout with the electric light ('pension' 15-25*s.* per day).

Some of the first-class hotels at the WEST END only receive travellers when the rooms have been ordered beforehand, or when the visitors are provided with an introduction.

*Claridge's Hotel*, 49-55 Brook Street, Grosvenor Square, long considered the first hotel in London, and patronised chiefly by royalty, ambassadors, and the nobility, is very expensive. — Other well-conducted hotels of a similar character are the *Albemarle*, 1 Albemarle Street; the *York*, 9-11 Albemarle Street; *Pulteney's*, 13 Albemarle Street; *Buckland's*, 43 Brook Street. At No. 2 Albemarle Street is *Berles' Private Hotel*.

At the W. end of Oxford Street, in Hyde Park Place, near the Marble Arch (p. 251), is the *Hyde Park Hotel*. — In Piccadilly,

## 3. HOTELS.

at the corner of **Berkeley Street**: *Berkeley Hotel* (No. 77; 'pension' 10s. 6d.). — *Bath Hotel*, 25 Arlington Street. — In Dover Street: *Brown's Hotel* (No. 24); *Cowan's Hotel* (No. 26); *Batt's* (No. 41); *Holloway's* (Nos. 47, 48). — *Sackville Hotel*, 28 Sackville Street.

The following, in Jermyn Street, Piccadilly, are all good: — *British Hotel* (No. 82); *Waterloo Hotel* (No. 85); *Brunswick Hotel* (Nos. 52, 53); *Cox's Hotel* (No. 55); *Rawlings's* (Nos. 37, 38); *Cavendish* (No. 81).

*Park Hotel*, 10 Park Place, St. James's Street, is a comfortable family house.

Near Bond Street are the following: — *Almond's Hotel*, Clifford Street; *Burlington*, 19 and 20 Cork Street; *Coburg Hotel*, 14 Carlos Street, Grosvenor Square; *Thomas's Hotel*, 25 Berkeley Square; *Bristol Hotel*, Burlington Gardens.

In or near Regent Street: — *Hôtel Continental*, 1 Regent Street; *Edwards's Hotel*, 12 A George Street, Hanover Square; *Marshall Thompson's Hotel*, 28 Cavendish Square; *United Hotel*, 24 Charles Street; *Ford's Hotel*, 13 Manchester Street, Manchester Square; *Limmer's Hotel*, 2 George Street, Hanover Square. — *Portland Hotel*, 95-99 Great Portland Street, Portland Place.

*Queen's Gate Hotel*, 98 Queen's Gate, near Hyde Park. — *South Kensington Hotel* (opened in 1887), Queen's Gate Terrace.

*Cadogan Hotel*, 75 Sloane Street, Cadogan Place, near Hyde Park. *Bailey's Hotel*, Gloucester Road Station.

*Norris's Hotel*, 48-53 Russell Road, Kensington, facing Addison Road Station.

All these West End hotels are good in every respect, but their terms are high: Bedroom 3s. 6d.-10s., Breakfast 3-4s., Dinner 5-10s., Attendance 1s. 6d. — Charges for the best rooms are equally high at the terminus hotels, but the attendance is inferior.

Hotels in the CITY: —

*De Keyser's Royal Hotel*, New Bridge Street, Blackfriars, conducted in the continental fashion, is well situated; R. and A. 5s. and upwards, B. 2-3s., table d'hôte (at 6 p.m.) 4s., 'pension' 12-20s. Foreign newspapers provided.

Near St. Martin's le Grand (General Post Office): *Castle and Falcon*, 5 Aldersgate Street, R. & A. 3s. 6d., B. 2s., D. 3s. 6d.

*Manchester Hotel*, corner of Aldersgate Street and Long Lane. *The Albion*, 172 Aldersgate Street.

*Green Dragon*, 188 Bishopsgate Without, old-fashioned but comfortable; *City of London*, 11 Bishopsgate Street Within.

*Metropolitan Hotel*, South Place, near the Great Eastern Railway Station.

*Seyd's Hotel*, 39 Finsbury Square, R. & B. 5s. 6d.

*Bücker's Hotel*, Christopher Street, Finsbury Square.

In SOUTHWARK and LAMBETH, on the right bank of the Thames:

## 3. HOTELS.

— *Bridge House Hotel*, 4 Borough High Street, London Bridge; *Piggott's Hotel*, 166 Westminster Bridge Road.

In or near FLEET STREET: — *Anderton's Hotel*, 162 Fleet Street; *Peele's Hotel*, 177 Fleet Street; *Salisbury Hotel*, Salisbury Square, Fleet Street. — *Cathedral Hotel*, 48 St. Paul's Churchyard.

In LEICESTER SQUARE, at the West End, a quarter much frequented by **French** visitors: — *Hôtel Sablonnière et de Provence* (Nos. 17, 18); *Hôtel de Paris et de l'Europe* (Nos. 7, 9).

Near Leicester Square: — *Hôtel de Halifax*, 1 and 2 Leicester Street, Leicester Square.

*Hôtel Solferino*, 7 Rupert Street, Coventry Street; *Hôtel Royal*, No. 60 in the same street.

*Wedde's Hotel*, 12 Greek Street, Soho Square.

The stranger is cautioned against going to any unrecommended house near Leicester Square, as there are several houses of doubtful reputation in this locality.

Near COVENT GARDEN: —

*Hummums*, and *Tavistock Hotel* (R., B., & A. 7s. 6d.), both in the Piazza, Covent Garden, for gentlemen only.

*Bedford Hotel*, also in the Piazza, Covent Garden, comfortable.

*Covent Garden Hotel*, corner of Covent Garden and Southampton Street.

*Mona Hotel*, 13 Henrietta Street, Covent Garden.

In the STRAND, a favourite neighbourhood for visitors: —
*Somerset Hotel* (No. 162); *Haxell's Royal Exeter Hotel* (Nos. 371-375), adjoining Exeter Hall.

*Golden Cross Hotel*, 452 Strand, opposite the Charing Cross Hotel (p. 7).

The streets leading from the Strand to the Thames contain a number of quiet family hotels, which afford comfortable accommodation at a moderate cost. Among these are the following: — *Johnston's Hotel*, 7, 8, and 9 Salisbury Street; *Craven Hotel*, 43-46 Craven Street (R. from 2s. 6d., board 10s. 6d.); *Barrett's Hotel*, 8-11, 16, 25 Cecil Street (R. & A. from 3s. 6d., B. 1s. 6d.–3s., D. 3-6s.); *Adelphi Hotel*, 1-4 John Street, Adelphi; *Caledonian Hotel*, 10 Adelphi Terrace, with a good view of the Thames.

Then, to the E. of Waterloo Bridge: —

In Surrey Street: *Lay's Hotel* (Nos. 5, 6, 8, and 9); *Royal Surrey Hotel* (Nos. 14 and 15); *Norfolk* (No. 30); *Bunyard's Private Hotel* (No. 31); *Hutchinson's* (No. 24); *Parker's* (Nos. 27-29).

In Norfolk Street: *Slaughter's Private Hotel* (Nos. 16, 28); *Pelham's Private* **Hotel** (No. 9); *Bunyard's* **Private** *Hotel* (No. 10); *Kent's* (No. 31); *Bond's* (No. 25; private).

In Arundel Street: — *Arundel Hotel* (No. 19; R., B., & A. from 6s., 'pension' from 8s. 6d.), pleasantly situated on the Embankment; *Jones* (No. 7; private); *Temple Hotel* (No. 28; frequented by Swedes and Germans).

## 3. PRIVATE APARTMENTS

Near TRAFALGAR SQUARE: —
*Morley's Hotel*, Trafalgar Square, pleasantly situated, and much frequented by Americans.

The *Grand Hotel*, the *Hôtel Métropole*, and the *Hôtel Victoria* have been already mentioned at p. 7.

*Panton Hotel*, 28 Panton Street, Haymarket.

*Previtali's Hotel*, 14-19 Arundell Street, Haymarket.

In TOTTENHAM COURT ROAD: *The Horseshoe* (No. 264) and the *Bedford Head* (No. 235; moderate), two commercial houses, suited for gentlemen.

In BLOOMSBURY, near the British Museum: *Burr's Hotel*, 11 Queen Square (R. 2s. 6d., 'pension' in winter 6-7s., in summer 8s.); *Rowland's*, 14 Queen Square ('pension' 5-7s.).

On the N. side of HOLBORN, near the Farringdon Street Metropolitan Station, and a few hundred paces from St. Paul's: — *Ridler's*, *Wood's*, in Furnival's Inn (very quiet; good wine). *First Avenue Hotel*, see p. 7. — On the Holborn Viaduct, the *Imperial Hotel*, and the *Holborn Viaduct Hotel*. — A little to the N. of this point, quietly situated in Charterhouse Square, are *Cocker's Hotel* (No. 19) and *Kershaw's Private Hotel* (No. 14).

The following is a small selection of the best-known TEMPERANCE HOTELS in London: —

*West Central Hotel*, 97-103 Southampton Row, Russell Square (R. from 1s. 6d., 'pension' 6s. 8d.); *Devonshire*, Bishopsgate Without; *Armfield's South Place Hotel*, South Place, Finsbury (R. & A. from 2s. 9d.); *Ling's*, South Street, Finsbury; *Insull's*, Burton Crescent, Brunswick Square, W. C.; *Wild's*, 30-40 Ludgate Hill; *Tranter's*, 7 Bridgewater Square, Barbican, E. C. (R. from 1s. 6d., R. & board 5s. 6d.).

**Boarding Houses.** The visitor will generally find it more economical to live in a *Boarding House* than at a hotel. For a sum of 30-40s. per week or upwards he will receive lodging, breakfast, luncheon, dinner, and tea, taking his meals and sharing the sitting-rooms with the family and other guests. This arrangement, however, is more suitable for persons making a prolonged sojourn in London than for those who merely intend to devote two or three weeks to seeing the lions of the English metropolis. To a visitor of the latter class the long distances between the different sights of London make it expedient that he should not have to return for dinner to a particular part of the town at a fixed hour. This independence of action is secured, more cheaply than at a hotel, by taking —

**Private Apartments**, which may be hired by the week in any part of London. Notices of '*Apartments*', or '*Furnished Apartments*', are generally placed in the windows of houses where there are rooms to be let in this manner, but it is safer to apply to the nearest house-agent. Rooms in the house of a respectable private family may often be obtained by advertisement or otherwise, and are gener-rally much more comfortable than the professed lodging-houses. The dearest apartments, as well as the dearest hotels, are at the West End, where the charges vary from 2l. to 15l. a week. The best are in the streets leading from Piccadilly — Dover Street, Half Moon Street, Clarges Street, Duke Street, and Sackville Street, — and in those leading out of St. James's Street, such as Jermyn Street, Bury Street, and King Street. Good, but less expensive lodgings may also be obtained in the less central parts of the West End, and in the streets diverging from Oxford Street and the Strand. In Bloomsbury (near the British Museum) the average charge for one room is 15-21s. per week, and breakfast is provided for 1s. a day. Fire and light are usually extras, sometimes also boot-cleaning and washing of bed-linen. It is advisable to have a clear understanding on all these points. Still cheaper apartments, varying in rent according to the amenity of their situation and their distance from the centres of business and pleasure, may be obtained in the suburbs. The traveller who desires to be very moderate in his expenditure may even procure a bedroom and the use of a breakfast-parlour for 10s. a week. The preparation of plain meals is generally understood to be included in the charge for lodgings, but the sightseer will probably require nothing but breakfast and tea in his rooms, partaking of luncheon and dinner at one of the pastrycooks' shops, oyster-rooms, or restaurants with which London abounds.

Though attendance is generally included in the weekly charge for board and lodging, the servants expect a small weekly gratuity, proportionate to the trouble given them.

Money and valuables should be securely locked up in the visitor's own trunk, as the drawers and presses of hotels and boarding-houses are frequently by no means inviolable receptacles. Large sums of money and objects of great value, however, had better be entrusted to the keeping of the landlord of the house, if a person of known respectability, or to a banker in exchange for a receipt. It is hardly necessary to point out that it would be unwise to make such a deposit with the landlord of private apartments or boarding-houses, which have not been specially recommended.

## 4. Restaurants. Dining Rooms. Oyster Shops. Confectioners.

English cookery, which is as inordinately praised by some epicures and *bons vivants* as it is abused by others, has at least the merit of simplicity, so that the quality of the food one is eating is not so apt to be disguised as it is on the Continent. Meat and fish of every kind are generally excellent in quality at all the better restaurants, but the visitor accustomed to continental fare may discern a falling off in the soups, vegetables, and sweet dishes.

At the first-class restaurants the cuisine is generally French; the charges are high, but everything is sure to be good of its kind.

## 4. RESTAURANTS.

At the smaller restaurants it is usual to find out from the waiter what dishes are to be had, and to order accordingly.

The dinner **hour** at the best restaurants is 4-8 p. m., after which **some** of them **are closed**. At less pretentious establishments dinner 'from the joint' is **obtainable** from 12 or 1 to 5 or 6 p.m. Beer, on draught or in bottle, **is supplied at** almost all the restaurants, and is the beverage most frequently drunk. The *Grill Rooms* **are** devoted to chops, steaks, **and** other dishes cooked on a gridiron. *Dinner from the Joint* is a plain **meal** of meat, potatoes, vegetables, and **cheese**. At many of the following restaurants, particularly those in the City, **there** are luncheon-bars, where **from** 11 to 3 a chop or small plate of hot meat with bread and vegetables **may** be obtained for 6-8d. Customers usually take these 'snacks' standing **at the** bar. In dining *à la carte* **at** any **of the** foreign restaurants one portion will often be found sufficient for **two persons**.

Good wine in England is expensive. *Sherry* is most frequently drunk, **but** *Port*, *Claret* (Bordeaux), and *Hock* (a corruption of Hochheimer, used **as a** generic term for Rhenish wines) **may** also be obtained **at** most of the restaurants.

**The traveller's** thirst can at all times be conveniently quenched at a *Public House*, **where a** glass of bitter beer, ale, stout, or 'half-and-half' (i. e. **ale or beer, and** stout or porter, mixed) is **to** be had for $1\frac{1}{2}$-2d. (6d. or **8d. per quart)**. Good German *Lager Bier* (3-6d. per glass) is now very generally **obtainable at** the larger restaurants, **in** some of which it has almost entirely supplanted the heavier English ales. Wine (not recommended) may also be obtained. Many of the more important streets also contain *Wine-stores* or '*Bodegas*', where a good glass of wine may be obtained for **2-6d.**, a pint **of** Hock or Claret for 8d.-1s. 6d., and **so on**, and a **few taverns (such** as *Short's*, 333 Strand) have acquired a special reputation **for their** wines.

### Restaurants at the West End.

In and near the STRAND: —

*Simpson's Dining Rooms*, **in the busiest part** of the Strand (Nos. 101-103); ladies' room upstairs; **dinner** *à la carte*.

*Imperial Café-Restaurant (Gatti & Rodersano)*, 166 Strand.

**Gaiety Restaurant* (*Spiers & Pond*), **at the** Gaiety Theatre, 343 and 344 Strand; table d'hôte from **5.30 till 8** p.m., 3s. 6d.

*Hazell's Hotel Restaurant*, **371 Strand**.

*Tivoli Restaurant and Music Hall*, **69 Strand**, opposite the Adelphi Theatre **(German** beer; **at present rebuilding**).

*Windsor*, **427 Strand**.

The *Courts Restaurant*, **222** Strand, **opposite** the **Law Courts**.

*Romano's Café-Restaurant*, 399 Strand (French).

**Gatti's Restaurant and Café*, Adelaide Street, with **a** second **entrance** at 436 Strand.

**Grand Hotel*, Charing **Cross (see p. 7); table** d'hôte at 6 p.m. 5s.; also buffet and grill-room.

*Ship Restaurant*, 45 Charing Cross.

*Darmstätter's Beer Saloon*, 395 Strand (German cuisine and beer).

*Old Drury Tavern*, 50 Catherine Street, near Drury Lane Theatre (p. 40).

The *Albion*, 26 **Russell Street**, opposite Drury Lane Theatre, frequented by actors and authors (not by ladies); dinner from the joint.

In LEICESTER SQUARE: —

## 4. RESTAURANTS. 13

*The Cavour*, 20 Leicester Square, hotel and café, French cuisine and attendance; table d'hôte from 6 to 9, 3s.

*Hôtel de Paris*, 7 & 9 Leicester Square.

**Near Leicester Square:** —

\**Kettner's Restaurant du Pavillon*, French house, 29 & 30 Church Street, Soho (somewhat expensive).

*Wedde*, German house, 12 Greek Street, Soho.

*Hôtel de Solferino*, 7 & 8 Rupert Street.

There are many cheap and good foreign restaurants in Soho.

In PALL MALL: —

*Epitaux*, in the Opera Arcade, **near the corner of Haymarket.**

In PICCADILLY, REGENT STREET, and the vicinity: —

*The Criterion (Spiers and Pond)*, Regent Circus, Piccadilly, spacious, sumptuously fitted up, and adorned with tasteful decorative paintings by eminent artists; theatre, see p. 41. — Table d'hôte from 5.30 to 8 p.m. 3s. 6d., attendance 3d., accompanied by glees and songs performed by a choir of men and boys; dinner from the joint 2s. 6d. Grill-room, café and American bar, etc.

*Piccadilly Restaurant*, in the building of **the Pavilion Music Hall.**

\**Monico's*, 15 Tichborne Street, handsomely fitted up, with restaurant, grill-room, café, luncheon bar, and concert room (see p. 43).

*Hôtel Previtali*, 14-18 Arundell Street (p. 10), with table d'hôte.

*Berkeley Hotel*, Piccadilly.

\**Bellamy's Dining Rooms*, 2 Piccadilly Place, Piccadilly, opposite St. James's Church, moderate.

\**The Burlington (Blanchard's)*, 169 Regent Street, corner of New Burlington Street; dinners on first and second floors, ground-floor reserved for luncheons. Ladies' rooms. Dinners at 5s., 7s. 6d., and 10s. 6d.; also à *la carte*.

\**St. James's Hall Restaurant*, 69-71 Regent Street, and 25, 26, and 28 Piccadilly. Ladies' rooms and grill-room. Concert dinner, with lady orchestra, 4s. 6d.

\**Kühn*, 21 Hanover Street, café downstairs, restaurant upstairs, expensive.

\**Verrey*, 229 Regent Street, French cuisine, somewhat high charges (bouillabaisse to order).

\**Grand Café Royal*, 68 Regent Street; French dinner 5s.

The table d'hôte at the *Hôtel Continental*, 1 Regent Street, is good but high-priced (7s. 6d.); déjeuner from 12 to 3 p.m. 4s.

\**Blanchard's Restaurant*, 1-7 Beak Street, Regent Street (ladies not after 5 p.m.); dinner 3s. 6d.; à *la carte*, dearer. Good wines.

In and near OXFORD STREET and HOLBORN: —

\**The Pamphilon*, 17 Argyll Street, Oxford Street, near Regent Circus, with ladies' rooms; unpretending, moderate charges.

*The Star and Garter (Pecorini)*, 98 New Oxford Street.

\**Frascati*, 26 Oxford Street, near **Tottenham Court Road** and not far from the British Museum; luncheon 2s. 6d., dinner 5s.

*Dorothy Restaurant* (for ladies), 448 Oxford Street.
*The Radnor*, 73 Chancery Lane and 311-312 High Holborn.
**The Horseshoe**, 264-267 Tottenham Court Road, not far from the British Museum, luncheon-bar, grill-room, and dining-rooms; table d'hôte 5.30 to 8.30 p.m., 2s. 6d.
*Inns of Court Restaurant*, in Lincoln's Inn Fields, N. side.
\**The Holborn Restaurant*, 218 High Holborn, an extensive and elaborately adorned establishment, with grill-room, luncheon buffets, etc.; table d'hôte at separate tables in the Grand Salon from 5.30 to 9 p.m., with music, 3s. 6d.
\**Gray's Inn Tavern*, 19 High Holborn, near Chancery Lane.
*Spiers and Pond's Buffet*, Holborn Viaduct Station.
Table d'hôte at the *First Avenue Hotel* (p. 7) from 5.30 to 8.30 p.m., 5s; also restaurant, grill-room, and luncheon-buffet.
\**Veglio*, 314 Euston Road, near the end of Tottenham Court Road (moderate).

## In the City.

In FLEET STREET: —
*The Cock*, 22 Fleet Street (chops, steaks, kidneys; good stout); with the fittings of the famous Old Cock Tavern, pulled down in 1886.
\**The Rainbow*, 15 Fleet Street (good wines); dinner from the joint, chops, steaks, etc.
*Old Cheshire Cheese*, 16 Wine Office Court, Fleet Street (steak and chop house; beefsteak puddings on Saturdays).
Near ST. PAUL'S: — Table d'hôte in *De Keyser's Royal Hotel* (p. 8), the charge for which to persons not residing in the hotel is 6s. (without wine).
*Spiers and Pond's Restaurant*, Ludgate Hill Station.
*The Cathedral Hotel*, 48 St. Paul's Churchyard, dinner at 1 and 5 p.m., 2s.; also à la carte.
*Salutation Tavern*, 17 Newgate Street (fish).
*Grand Café-Restaurant de Paris*, 74 Ludgate Hill, table d'hôte from 5 to 9, with 1/2 bottle of claret, 3s. 6d.
Near the BANK: —
*The Palmerston*, 34 Old Broad Street. — *The Lombard*, 2 Lombard Court, Lombard Street.
In Cheapside: — *Lake and Turner* (No. 49), and *Read's* (No. 94), good houses, with moderate charges; *Cyprus Restaurant* (Nos. 1 and 2); *Queen Anne* (No. 27); *Sweeting's* (No. 158; fish).
In Gresham Street: — *Gresham Restaurant* (No. 58); *The Castle* (No. 40); *Guildhall Dining Rooms* (Nos. 81-83), opposite the Guildhall.
*City Restaurant*, 34 Milk Street.
In the Poultry: — \**Pimm's* (Nos. 3, 4, 5).
In Bucklersbury, near the Mansion House: \**Reichert's* (*Bargen's*; No. 4); *Lake & Turner* (No. 21), moderate.

## 4. RESTAURANTS.

*Spiers and Pond's Buffet*, Mansion House (Metropolitan) Station. In Gracechurch Street: *Morrell* (No. 13); *Colonial Tavern* (No. 20); *Half Moon* (No. 88).

\**London Tavern*, formerly *King's Head*, 53 Fenchurch Street. Queen Elizabeth here took her first meal after her liberation from the Tower.

\**Crosby Hall* (p. 106), Bishopsgate Street (waitresses). These last two are very handsomely fitted up and contain smoking and chess rooms.

*International Restaurant*, 39 Bishopsgate Street Within.
*Three Nuns*, adjoining Aldgate Metropolitan Station.
*Wilkinson*, 59 Leadenhall Street.
*Ship and Turtle*, 129 Leadenhall Street, noted for its turtle.
*Bargen*, 37 and 48 Coleman Street.
*Ruttermann*, 41 and 42 London Wall.

In or near Cornhill: — *Birch's (Ring & Brymer)*, 15 Cornhill, the principal purveyors to civic feasts; *Purssell's Restaurant*, 2-5 Finch Lane (chess); *Woolpack*, 6 St. Peter's Alley.

*White Hart Inn*, 63 Borough High Street, Southwark, described by Dickens in 'Pickwick'.

*Three Tuns Tavern*, at Billingsgate Fish Market (p. 111), the famous 'Fish Ordinary'. Table d'hôte (upstairs) from 4 to 5 p.m., with 4-5 varieties of fish, besides meat and cheese, for 2s. Beer 6d. per pint, claret 1s. 6d. per bottle, large glass of punch (good but dear) 1s. 6d., small glass 1s., waiter 2-3d. For gentlemen only. — Fish-dinners at Greenwich, see p. 301.

Waiters in restaurants expect a gratuity of about 1d. for every shilling of the bill, but 6d. per person is the most that need ever be given. If a charge is made in the bill for attendance the visitor is not bound to give anything additional, though even in this case it is customary to give the waiter a trifle for himself.

Special mention may be made of the temperance *Eating Rooms* opened by the *People's Café Company* at 61 St. Paul's Churchyard, 1 Ludgate Circus Buildings, and 61 Gracechurch Street. Excellent plain meals may be procured in these houses at moderate rates, without the necessity of ordering anything to drink. Gratuities to the attendants are forbidden. — Among the chief VEGETARIAN RESTAURANTS in London are the *Orange Grove*, St. Martin's Lane, W.C.; *Wheatsheaf*, 13 Rathbone Place, Oxford Street; *Alpha*, 23 Oxford Street; *Queen Victoria*, 303 Strand; *Bouverie*, 63 Fleet Street.

### Oyster Shops.

\**Scott (Edwin)*, 18 Coventry Street, exactly opposite the Haymarket (also steaks), in the evening for gentlemen only; \**Rule*, 35 Maiden Lane, Covent Garden; *Smith*, 357 Strand; *Pimm*, 3 Poultry-City; *Lynn*, 70 Fleet Street, City; \**Lightfoot*, 3 Arthur Street East, 22 Lime Street, 39 Old Change, all three in the City.

The charge for a dozen oysters is usually from 2s. to 3s. 6d., according to the season and the rank of the house. Small lobster 1s. 6d.; larger lobster 2s. 6d. and upwards. Snacks of fish 2-6d. Oysters, like pork, are out of season in the month that have no R in their name, *i. e.* those of summer.

### Confectioners.

*Petrzywalski*, 62 Regent Street, good Vienna pastry and ices; *Charbonnel & Walker*, 173 New Bond Street; *Bonthron*, 106 Regent Street; *Duclos*, 178 Oxford Street; *Blatchley*, 167 Oxford Street; *Buszard*, 197 Oxford Street; *Beadell*, 8 Vere Street; *Gunter & Co.*, 7 Berkeley Square, good ices; *Wolff*, 55 Ludgate Hill.

## 5. Cafés. Billiard Rooms.

### At the West End.

*Simpson's Cigar Divan*, 101-103 Strand, second floor, café for gentlemen, containing a large selection of English and foreign newspapers (see below), and a favourite resort of lovers of chess (admission 6d., or, including cigar and cup of coffee, 1s.). *Gatti's Café*, Adelaide Street and 436 Strand, large French café, good ices (also a restaurant, p. 12); *Carlo Gatti*, Villiers Street, Strand; *Grand Café Royal*, 68 Regent Street (also a restaurant, see p. 13); \**Kühn*, 21 Hanover Street, Regent Street (restaurant upstairs, p. 13); *Verrey*, corner of Regent Street and Hanover Street, noted for ices (also a restaurant, p. 13); *R. Gunter*, 23 Motcomb Street and 15 Lowndes Street, Belgrave Square; *Gentlemen's Café*, Criterion (p. 13); *Monico*, 15 Tichborne Street (p. 13); \**Vienna Café*, corner of Oxford Street and Hart Street, near the British Museum.

### In the City.

*Peele's*, 177 Fleet Street; *Brown*, 16 Ludgate Hill; *Café de Paris*, Ludgate Hill; *Holt*, 63 St. Paul's Churchyard; *Stephen*, 51 Cheapside; *Baker's Coffee House*, 1 Change Alley, Cornhill; *Wolff's Konditorei*, 55 Ludgate Hill.

The *People's Café Company*, the *Coffee Palace* Company, *Lockhart's Cocoa Rooms*, the *Kiosk and Coffee Stall* Company, and others of a similar kind, have established a large number of cheap cafés in all parts of London. Many of these contain first-class rooms (at increased charges) and rooms for ladies. The shops of the *Aërated Bread Company* are also much frequented for tea, coffee, etc.

#### Billiard Rooms.

'*Horseshoe*', 264-267 Tottenham Court Road; *W. Cook*, 99 Regent Street; *Stradwick*, 182 Fleet Street; *Gatti's Café*, see above; *Carlo Gatti*, Villiers Street; *Veglio*, Euston Road; *Monico*, 15 Tichborne Street; *Yardley (Kettle)*, 6-10 Burleigh Street, Strand. The usual charge is 1s. per hour (1s. 6d. by gas-light), or 6d. per game of fifty.

## 6. Reading Rooms.
*Circulating Libraries. Newspapers.*

**Reading** Rooms. Besides the above-mentioned *Cigar Divan*, the following reading-rooms, most of which are supplied with English and foreign newspapers, may be mentioned: *American Traveller Office*, 4 Langham Place, Regent Street; *Gilligs United States Exchange*, 9 Strand, also with American newspapers (4s. per week, 8s. per month, or 3l. per annum); *American Register Office*, 446 Strand; *Colonial Institute*, Northumberland Avenue (subs. 1-2 guineas per annum; comp. p. 76); *Guildhall Free Library*; *Temple News Rooms* (adm. 1d.), 172 Fleet Street; *Central News Agency*, 402 Strand, next the Vaudeville Theatre (adm. 2d.); *City News Rooms*, Ludgate Circus Buildings; *City Central News Rooms*, 1 Philpot Lane, Fenchurch Street, E. C. (adm. 1d.); *Commissioners of Patents Library*, 25 Southampton Buildings, Chancery Lane; *Deacon's*, 154 Leadenhall Street; *Street's Colonial & General Newspaper Offices*, 30 Cornhill and 5 Serle Street, Lincoln's Inn; also at 54 New Oxford Street (adm. 2d.).

**Circulating Libraries.** *Mudie's Select Library* (Limited), 30-34 New Oxford Street, a gigantic establishment possessing hundreds of thousands of volumes (minimum quarterly subscription, 7s.); branches at 241 Brompton Road and 2 King Street, Cheapside. *London Library*, 14 St. James's Square, with nearly 100,000 vols. (annual subscription 3l., introduction by a member necessary); *Rolandi*, 20 Berners Street, Oxford Street, for foreign books (single books obtainable on deposit of a sum equal to their value); *W. H. Smith & Son*, 183-7 Strand; *Cawthorne*, Cockspur Street.

Among the principal public libraries in London are the following. *British Museum Library*, see p. 255; *Sion College Library*, on the Thames Embankment, the most valuable theological library in London, containing portraits of Laud and other bishops; *Dr. Williams' Library*, 16 Grafton Street, Tottenham Court Road, containing a large collection of Puritan theology and fine portraits of Baxter and other divines; *London Institution Library*, Finsbury Circus, with 100,000 vols.; *Lambeth Palace Library*, p. 208; *Allan Library*, Wesleyan Conference Office, 2 Castle St., Finsbury, with a fine collection of Bibles and theological works (p. 98); *Guildhall Library*, p. 99.

**Newspapers.** No fewer than 400 newspapers are published in London and its environs. The principal morning papers are the *Times* (3d.), in political opinion nominally independent of party (printing-office, see p. 115); then the *Daily News* (1d.; a leading Liberal journal), *Daily Telegraph* (1d.), *Standard* (1d.; a strong Conservative organ), *Morning Post* (1d.; organ of the court and aristocracy), *Morning Advertiser* (3d.; the property and organ of the licensed victuallers), and *Daily Chronicle* (1d.). The leading evening papers are the *Pall Mall Gazette* (1d.), the *St. James's Gazette* (1d.), *Evening Standard* (1d.), *Globe* (1d.; the oldest evening paper, dating from 1803), *Evening Post* (1d.), *Star* ($1/_2$d.; T. P. O'Connor's paper), *Evening News* ($1/_2$d.), and *Echo* ($1/_2$d.).

All of these are sold at the principal railway-stations, at newsmen's shops, and in the streets by newsboys. The oldest paper in the country is the *London Gazette*, the organ of the Government, established in 1642 and published twice weekly. The *City Press* contains city and antiquarian notices; the *Public Ledger* (first published in 1759) is important for its market reports and shipping register. Among the favourite weekly journals are the comic papers *Punch* and *Fun*; the illustrated papers, *Illustrated London News*, *Graphic*, *Illustrated Times*, *Pictorial World*, *Sporting and Dramatic News*, and *Queen* (for ladies); and the superior literary journals and reviews, *Athenaeum*, *Academy*, *Spectator*, and *Saturday Review*. The *Weekly Dispatch*, the *Observer* (4d.), *Lloyd's*, *Reynolds'*, the *Sun*, and the *Referee* (a sporting and theatrical organ) are Sunday papers.

The *Field* (weekly) is the principal journal of field-sports and other subjects interesting to the 'country gentleman'; and next is *Land and Water*, also weekly. *Bell's Life in London* and the *Sporting Times* are the chief organs of the racing public, and the *Era* of the theatrical world.

Science and Art Journals: *Journal of the Society of Arts*, *Popular Science Review*, *Nature*, *Science Gossip*, *Knowledge*, *The Electrician*, *Science and Art*, *Scientific and Literary Review*, *Journal of Photography*, *Chemical News*, organ of the *Inventors' Institute*. — Journals and Transactions of the Geological, Astronomical, and other learned societies.

Commercial and Professional Journals (weekly): The *Economist*, the leading commercial and financial authority; *Agricultural Gazette*; *Corn Trade Journal*; *Farmer*; *Mark Lane Express*, mainly relied upon for market prices; *Capital and Labour*, patronised by trades-unions, mechanics, etc.; *Engineer*, *Engineering Journal*, for mechanics, surveyors, and contractors; *Builder*, devoted to building, designs, sanitation, and domestic comfort; *Architect*; *Colliery Guardian*; *Mining Journal*; *Gardeners' Chronicle*; *Bullionist*; *Investor's Guardian*; *Metropolitan*, devoted to London borough and parish interests, gas and water supply, rates, improvements; *Railway Journal*; *Money Market Review*; *Joint Stock Companies Journal*; *Public Health*.

The *Anglo-American Times* (26 Basinghall Street; 4d.), the *American Traveller* (4 Langham Place), and the *American Register* (146 Strand; 3d.) are weekly American papers, published in London. The following are the London offices of a few leading American papers: — *New York Herald*, 33 Cornhill; *New York Tribune*, 26 Bedford Street, W. C.; *New York Associated Press*, 62 Gresham Street, E. C.; *American Press Association*, 34 Throgmorton Street, E. C., and 153 Fleet Street; *Boston Daily Herald*, 146 Strand; *Toronto Mail*, 146 Strand; *Toronto Globe*, 86 Fleet Street.

## 7. Baths.

(Those marked † are or include Turkish baths.)

*Albany Baths*, 83 York Road, Westminster Bridge Road.

† *Argyll Baths*, 10A Argyll Place, Regent Street, and 5 New Broad Street.

*Battersea Baths* (public), Battersea.

† *Bell's Baths*, 119 Buckingham Palace Road; Turkish bath 3s.

*Bermondsey Baths* (public), 39 Spa Road, Bermondsey.

*Bloomsbury and St. Giles Baths* (public), with swimming bath, Endell Street.

† *Bryning's*, 191 Blackfriars Road.

† *Burton's*, 182 and 184 Euston Road.

## 7. BATHS.

† *Charing Cross Baths*, Northumberland Avenue.
*Chelsea Swimming Baths*, 171 King's Road, Chelsea.
*City of London Baths*, 100-106 Golden Lane.
*Crown Swimming Baths*, Kennington Oval.
† *Earl's Court Baths*, Earl's Court.
† *Faulkner's Baths*, 26 Villiers Street, by Charing Cross Station; 50 Newgate Street, E.C.; 8 Little Bridge Street, E. C., close to Ludgate Hill Station; at Fenchurch Street Station. These establishments, with lavatories, hair-cutting rooms, etc., are convenient for travellers arriving by rail.
† *Ford's*, 48½ Kensington High Street.
*Galvano-Electric Baths*, 54 York Terrace, Regent's Park.
† *Grosvenor Baths*, 119 Buckingham Palace Road.
*Hampstead Baths* (public), Finchley Road, N.W.
† *King's Cross Turkish Baths*, 9 Caledonian Road, King's Cross.
*Lambeth Baths* (public), 156 Westminster Bridge Road.
† *London and Provincial Turkish Baths* ('The Hammam'), 76 Jermyn Street.
*Metropolitan Baths*, with swimming bath, 89 Shepherdess Walk, City Road.
*Old Roman Bath* (adjoining bath, see p. 142), 5 Strand Lane (famous for the coldness of its water).
*Paddington Baths* (public), Queen's Road, Bayswater.
*St. George's Baths* (public), 8 Davies Street, Berkeley Square, and 88 Buckingham Palace Road.
*St. James's Baths* (public), 16-18 Marshall Street, Golden Square.
*St. Martin's Baths* (public), Orange Street, Leicester Square.
*St. Marylebone Baths* (public), 181 Marylebone Road.
*St. Pancras Baths* (public), 70 A King Street, Camden Town.
† *Savoy Turkish Baths*, Savoy Street, Strand.
† *Terminus Turkish Baths*, 19 Railway Approach, London Bridge.
† *Turkish Baths*, 23 Leicester Square.
*Wenlock Baths*, with swimming bath, Wenlock Road, City Road.
*Westminster Baths* (public), 34 Great Smith Street, Westminster.
*Whitechapel Baths* (public), Goulston Square, Whitechapel.

Hot and cold baths of various kinds may be obtained at the baths above mentioned at charges varying from 6d. upwards. The Public Baths, which are plainly but comfortably fitted up, were instituted chiefly for the working classes, who can obtain cold baths here for as low a price as 1d., from which the charges rise to 6d. or 8d. Most of these establishments include swimming baths. Many of the private baths have most elegant appointments.

## 8. Shops, Bazaars, and Markets.
### The Co-operative System.

Shops abound everywhere. In the business-quarters usually visited by strangers, it is rare to see a house without shops on the ground-floor. Prices are almost invariably fixed, so that bargaining

## 8. SHOPS.

is unnecessary. Some of the most attractive shops are in Regent Street, Oxford Street, Piccadilly, Bond Street, the Strand, Fleet Street, Cheapside, St. Paul's Churchyard, and Ludgate Hill.

The following is a brief list of some of the best (and, in many cases, the dearest) shops in London; it is, however, to be observed that other excellent shops abound in all parts of London, in many cases no whit inferior to those here mentioned. Besides shops containing the articles usually purchased by travellers for their personal use, or as presents, we mention a few of the large depôts of famous English manufactures, such as cutlery, pottery, and water-colours.

AGRICULTURAL IMPLEMENTS: — *Burgess & Co.*, 51 Holborn Viaduct and 51 Farringdon Street; *Clayton & Shuttleworth*, 78 Lombard Street; *Ransomes, Sims, & Jefferies*, 9 Gracechurch Street.

ARTISTS' COLOURMEN: — *Ackermann*, 191 Regent Street (water-colours); *Newman*, 24 Soho Square; *Rowney & Co.*, 64 Oxford Street; *Winsor & Newton*, 37 Rathbone Place.

BONNETS, LADIES', see Milliners and Hatters.

BOOKBINDERS: — *Bedford*, 91 York Street, Westminster; *Kelly*, 7 Water Street, Strand; *Rivière*, 15 Heddon Street, Regent Street; *Zaehnsdorf*, 36 Catherine Street, and 14 York Street, Covent Garden; *Bookbinders' Co-operative Society*, 17 Bury Street, Bloomsbury.

BOOKSELLERS: — *Hatchards*, 187 Piccadilly; *Bumpus*, 350 Oxford Street; *Butterworth & Co.* (law books), 7 Fleet Street; *Stevens* (law books), 119 Chancery Lane; *Harrison & Sons*, 59 Pall Mall; *Griffith & Farran*, 2 Ludgate Hill; *Goodman*, 407 Strand; *Glaisher*, 95 Strand; *Stanford*, 26 Cockspur Street, Charing Cross (maps, etc.); *Bain*, 1 Haymarket; *Bickers & Son*, 1 Leicester Square; *Gilbert & Field*, 67 Moorgate Street; *Gilbert & Co.*, 18 Gracechurch Street, City; *Stoneham*, 78 & 129 Cheapside, 44 Lombard Street, 129 Fenchurch Street, 39 Walbrook, etc.; *Sotheran & Co.*, 36 Piccadilly and 136 Strand. — FOREIGN BOOKSELLERS: — *Dulau & Co.*, 37 Soho Square; *Trübner & Co.*, 57-59 Ludgate Hill; *Williams & Norgate*, 14 Henrietta Street; Covent Garden; *Hachette*, 18 King William Street, West Strand; *Nutt*, 270 Strand; *Thimm*, 24 Brook Street, Hanover Square; *Barthès & Lowell*, 14 Great Marlborough Street; *Rolandi*, 20 Berners Street; *Quaritch*, 15 Piccadilly; *Roques*, 64 New Bond Street; *Siegle*, 30 Lime Street; *Dorrell & Son*, 15 Charing Cross. — SECONDHAND BOOKSELLERS: — *Quaritch* (probably the most extensive buyer of rare books in the world), see above; *Toorey*, 177 Piccadilly; *Sotheran*, see above; *Reeves & Turner*, 196 Strand; *Stevens*, 115 St. Martin's Lane; *Jones*, 77 Queen Street, Cheapside; *Pickering & Chatto*, 66 Haymarket.

BOOTMAKERS, see Shoemakers.

CARPETS: — *Gregory & Co.*, 212-216 Regent Street, and 44-46 King Street, Golden Square; *Hampton & Sons*, 8-10 Pall Mall East; *Shoolbred & Co.*, 154-158 Tottenham Court Road, and 34-45 Grafton Street; *Marshall & Snelgrove*, 334-348 Oxford Street;

*Lapworth*, 22 Old Bond Street; *Waugh & Son*, 6 and 8 Goodge Street; *Cardinal & Harford* (Turkish carpets), 108 and 109 High Holborn; *Graham & Grossmith*, 32 Newgate Street; *Tyler & Son*, 21 Garrick Street; *Bontor & Co.*, 35 Old Bond Street.

CHEMICAL APPARATUS: — *Griffin & Sons*, 22 Garrick Street, Covent Garden; *Horne & Thornthwaite*, 416 Strand.

CHEMISTS. *Prichard*, 10 Vigo Street, Regent Street; *Wilkinson*, 270 Regent Street; *Cooper*, 66 Oxford Street; *Squire & Sons*, 413 Oxford Street; *Bell & Co.*, 225 Oxford Street; *Challice*, 34 Villiers Street, Strand; *Corbyn, Stacey, & Co.*, 300 High Holborn and 86 New Bond Street; *Pond*, 68 Fleet Street; *Nurthen & Co.*, 390 Strand; *Savory & Moore*, 143 New Bond Street; *Thomas*, 7 Upper St. Martin's Lane (moderate prices).

*Messrs. Burroughs, Wellcome, & Co*, Manufacturing Chemists. Snow Hill Buildings, Holborn Viaduct, prepare portable drugs in the form of tabloids, which will be found exceedingly convenient by travellers. Their small and light pocket-cases contain a selection of the most useful remedies in this form. These tabloid drugs may be obtained of all chemists.

### CHINA, see Glass.

CIGARS: — *Cigar Divan*, 102 Strand; *Carreras*, 7 Wardour Street, and 98 Regent Street; *Fribourg & Treyer*, 34 Haymarket, and 3 Leadenhall Street; *Ponder*, 48 Strand; *Marcovitch & Co.*, 11 Air Street, Regent Street; *Benson*, 296 Oxford Street; *Benson & Hedges*, 13 Old Bond Street; *Carlin*, 145 Regent Street; *Wolff, Phillips, & Co.*, 77 Regent Street.

Cigars in London are rather an expensive luxury, as at least 6*d.* must be paid to obtain a really good one, while 3*d.* is the lowest price that will secure a tolerable 'weed'. Fair Manilla cheroots, however, may be obtained for 2*d.* or 3*d.* Smoking is not so universal in England as in America or on the Continent, and is prohibited in many places where it is permitted in other countries.

### CLOCKS, see Watchmakers.

CUTLERY: — *Asprey & Son*, 166 New Bond Street, and 22 Albemarle Street; *Holtzapffel & Co.*, 64 Charing Cross, and 127 Long Acre; *Lund*, 25 Fleet Street, and 56-57 Cornhill; *Mappin Brothers*, 67 King William Street, City, and 220 Regent Street; *Mappin & Webb*, 158-162 Oxford Street, and Mansion House Buildings, corner of the Poultry and Queen Victoria Street; *Verinder*, 79 St. Paul's Churchyard; *Rodgers & Sons*, 4 Cullum Street, City; *Weiss & Son*, 62 Strand; *Benetfink*, 89 Cheapside. Travelling-bags, writing-cases, dispatch-boxes, etc., are also sold at most of these shops.

DENTISTS: — *Ritchie & Duplock*, 9 Cranbourn Street, Leicester Square; *G. H. Jones*, 57 Great Russell Street; *Coffin* (American), 94 Cornwall Gardens; *Pierrepoint* (American), 22 Old Burlington Street, Bond Street; *Eskell* (American), 445 Strand; *E. A. Jones*, 129 Strand; *Eskell & Sons*, 58 Ludgate Hill; *Stone & Dominy*, 35 St. Martin's Lane; *Stent*, 5 Coventry Street, Haymarket; *Crucefix Canton*, 40 St. Martin's Lane; *B. L. Moseley*, 312 Regent Street; *Browning*, 133 Oxford Street; *Gabriel*, 57 New Bond Street.

## 8. SHOPS.

DRAPERS, see Haberdashers.
DRUGGISTS, see Chemists.
ENGRAVINGS : — *Colnaghi & Co.*, 13 and 14 Pall Mall East; *Graves*, 6 Pall Mall; *Boussod, Valadon, & Co.* (successors of *Goupil & Co.*), 116 & 117 New Bond Street; *R. Dodson*, 147 Strand; *Maclean*, 7 Haymarket; *Lefèvre*, 1A King Street, St. James's Square; *Ackermann*, 191 Regent Street; *Leggatt*, 62 Cheapside; *Agnew & Son*, 39b Old Bond Street.
FURRIERS : — *Back*, 241 Regent Street; *International Fur Store*, 163 Regent Street; *Jeffs*, 244 Regent Street; *Swan & Edgar*, 39-53 Regent's Quadrant; *Marshall & Snelgrove*, 334-348 Oxford Street; *Nicholay*, 170 Oxford Street; *Poland*, 190 Oxford Street; *Peter Robinson*, 216-226 Oxford Street; *Russ*, 70 New Bond Street; *Court Fur Stores*, 352 Strand ; *Phillips*, 52 Newgate Street (moderate); *Maishman*, 14 Cheapside.
GLASS AND PORCELAIN: — *Phillips*, 155 New Bond Street; *Copeland & Sons*, 12 Charterhouse Street; *Mortlock & Sons*, 18 Regent Street; *Daniell & Co.*, 129 New Bond Street; *Pellatt & Wood*, 25 Baker Street; *Standish*, 58 Baker Street; *Osler*, 100 Oxford Street; *Phillips*, 175-179 Oxford Street; *Grimes*, 83 New Bond Street; *Green*, 107 Queen Victoria Street; *Gardner*, 453 Strand ; *Pearce*, 39 Ludgate Hill; *Salviati*, 213 Regent Street (mosaics).
GLOVES : — *Dent, Allcroft, & Co.* (celebrated firm, wholesale only; Dent's gloves are obtainable at all the retail shops), 97-99 Wood Street; *Wheeler*, 16 and 17 Poultry, and Queen Victoria Street, City. Also at all the haberdashers' and hosiers' shops.
GOLDSMITHS AND JEWELLERS: — *Emanuel*, 45 Albemarle Street; *Gass & Co.*, 166 Regent Street; *Howell, James, & Co.*, 5, 7, and 9 Regent Street; *Garrard & Co.*, 25 Haymarket; *Lambert & Co.*, 10-12 Coventry Street, Haymarket, *Hancocks & Co.*, 38 and 39 Bruton Street; *Hunt & Roskell*, 156 New Bond Street; *Streeter & Co.*, 18 New Bond Street; *Elkington & Co.*, 22 Regent Street and 42 Moorgate Street (electro-plate); *Packer*, 76 Regent Street; *Goldsmiths' Alliance*, 11 and 12 Cornhill; *Watherston & Son*, 12 Pall Mall East; *Crouch* (Scottish jewellery), 264 Regent Street; *Hancock*, 152 New Bond Street.
GUN AND RIFLE MAKERS : — *Westley Richards*, 178 New Bond Street; *Rigby & Co.*, 72 St. James's Street; *Purdey*, Audley House, South Audley Street; *Henry*, 118 Pall Mall; *Dougall*, 8 Bennet Street, St. James's Street; *Grant*, 67A St. James's Street; *Colt's Fire Arms Company*, 14 Pall Mall.
HABERDASHERS : — *Hitchcock & Co.*, 69-74 St. Paul's Churchyard ; *Lewis & Allenby*, 193-197 Regent Street; *Marshall & Snelgrove*, 334-348 Oxford Street; *Redmayne & Co.*, 19-20 New Bond Street; *Russell & Allen*, 17-20 Old Bond Street; *Shoolbred & Co.*, 151-158 Tottenham Court Road, and 34-45 Grafton Street; *Waterloo House* and *Swan & Edgar*, 39-53 Quadrant, Regent Street, and 9-11

Piccadilly; *Howell, James, & Co.*, **5** Regent Street; *Peter Robinson*, 216-226 Oxford Street; *Wallis & Co.*, 7 Holborn Circus; *Capper*, 69, 70 Gracechurch Street, City; **Liberty (Oriental fabrics)**. 142 & 218 Regent Street; *Debenham & Freebody*, 27-33 Wigmore Street, Cavendish Square; *Whiteley*, Westbourne Grove, Bayswater; *Jay*, mourning warehouse, 243-253 Regent Street; *Scott Adie*, for Scotch goods, 115 Regent Street; *Coulson & Co.*, 11 Pall Mall East; *Mrs. Washington Moon*, 16 New Burlington Street (baby linen); *Edmonds*, 47 **Wigmore Street (children)**; *Swears & Wells*, Regent Street **(children)**; *Locke & Co.*, 8 Savile Row; *Hamilton & Co.*, 326 Regent Street; *Co-operative Needlewomen*, **34** Brooke Street, Holborn.

HATTERS: — *Lincoln & Bennett*, 1-3 Sackville Street and 40 Piccadilly; *Heath*, 107 Oxford Street; *Cole*, 156 Strand; *Cater & Co.*, **56** Pall Mall; *Christy & Co.*, 35 Gracechurch Street, City; *Truefitt*, 14 Old **Bond Street and 20** Burlington Arcade. — LADIES' HATTERS: — *Mrs. Heath*, 25 St. George's Place, **Hyde Park Corner**; *Miss Lockwood*, 36 South Audley Street.

INDIA-RUBBER WARES, see Waterproof Goods.

JEWELLERS, see Goldsmiths.

LACE AND LADIES' UNDERCLOTHING: — *Steinmann*, 18 Piccadilly; *Mrs. Addley-***Bourne**, 174 Sloane Street; *Colman*, 172 Regent Street.

LEATHER GOODS (dressing-cases, **dispatch-boxes. etc.**): — *Needs*, 128 Piccadilly; *Leuchars*, 38 Piccadilly; **West**. 9 King Street, St. James's Street. Comp. Cutlery.

MAP SELLERS: — *E. Stanford* (agent for **the Ordnance Survey Maps**), **26 Cockspur** Street, Charing Cross; *C. Smith & Son*, 63 Charing Cross; *Bacon & Co.*, 127 Strand; *Wyld*. 11 Charing Cross; *Dorrell & Son*, 15 Charing Cross.

MEDICINE, see Chemists.

MILLINERS: — *Elise*, **170 Regent Street**; *Louise*, 210 and 266 Regent Street; *Moret*, **68 New Bond Street**; *Pauline*, 259 Regent Street; *Perryman*, 20 Brook Street; *Michard*, 2 Hanover Square; *Mrs. Stratton*, 104 Piccadilly; *Worth et Cie.*, 134 New Bond Street.

MUSIC-SELLERS: — *Boosey & Co.*, 295 Regent Street; *Chappell & Co.*, 49-52 New Bond Street; *Cocks & Co.*, 6 New Burlington Street; *Cramer & Co.*, 199-209 Regent Street; *Novello, Ewer, & Co.*, 1 Berners Street, Oxford Street; *Hammond & Co.*, 5 Vigo Street, Regent Street; *Metzler & Co.*, 40-43 **Great Marlborough** Street; *Augener*, 86 Newgate Street; **Keith & Prowse**, 48 Cheapside, and Northumberland Avenue, Charing Cross.

OPTICIANS: — *Elliott Brothers*, **101** St. Martin's Lane; *Dallmeyer*, 19 Bloomsbury Street; *Horne & Thornthwaite*, 416 Strand; *Negretti & Zambra*, Holborn Viaduct, Charterhouse Street, 45 Cornhill, and 122 Regent Street; *Callaghan*, 23a New Bond Street; *Dollond & Co.*, 1 Ludgate Hill; *Cox*, 98 Newgate Street.

PERFUMERS: — Atkinson, 24 Old Bond Street; *Bayley & Co.*, 17 Cockspur Street; *Piesse & Lubin*, 2 New Bond Street; *Rimmel*, 96 Strand, 128 Regent Street, and 24 Cornhill; *Gattie & Peirce*, 14 Old Bond Street; *Breidenbach*, 157 New Bond Street.

PHOTOGRAPH-SELLERS: — *J. Gerson*, 5 Rathbone Place (photographs of the pictures in the National Gallery, etc.); *Autotype Fine Art Gallery*, 74 New Oxford Street; *Mansell*, 271-273 Oxford Street; *Marion* (photographic materials), 23 Soho Square; *London Stereoscopic Company*, 54 Cheapside and 108 Regent Street; *Spooner*, 379 Strand.

PIANOFORTE-MANUFACTURERS: — *Broadwood & Sons*, 33 Great Pulteney Street, Golden Square; *Collard & Collard*, 16 Grosvenor Street, 26 Cheapside, and Oval Road, Regent's Park; *Erard*, Warwick Road, Kensington, and 18 Great Marlborough Street; *Hopkinson*, 95 New Bond Street.

PRESERVES, etc. ('Italian Warehouses'): — *Crosse & Blackwell*, 20 and 21 Soho Square, and 77 Dean Street (noted firm for pickles; wholesale); *Fortnum, Mason, & Co.*, 181-183 Piccadilly; *Castell & Brown*, 33-41 Wardour Street (wholesale); *Hedges & Butler*, 155 Regent Street; *Cobbett & Son*, 18 Pall Mall.

PRINTSELLERS, see Engravings.

SHOEMAKERS. For gentlemen: — *Deroy*, 74 Regent Street and 166 Fenchurch Street; *Dowie & Marshall*, 455 Strand; *Fuchs*, 54 Conduit Street; *Bowley & Co.*, 53 Charing Cross; *Parker*, 145 Oxford Street; *Peal*, 487 Oxford Street; *Medwin*, 86 Regent Street; *Hoby*, 20 Pall Mall; *Tuczek*, 109 New Bond Street; *Hall*, 6 Wellington Street, Strand; *Waukenphast*, 60 Haymarket; *Francis*, 40 Maddox Street. — For ladies: — *Hook, Knowles, & Co.*, 66 New Bond Street; *Bird*, 180 Oxford Street; *Gundry & Sons*, 174 New Bond Street; *Hubert*, 292 Regent Street; *Thierry*, 70 Regent Street. — Boots and shoes in London are rather dear but of excellent quality.

SILK MERCERS, see Haberdashers.

STATIONERS: — *Parkins & Gotto*, 54-62 Oxford Street; *Partridge & Cooper*, 192 Fleet Street; *Macmichael*, 42 South Audley Street; *Coram*, 205 Sloane Street; *Webster & Larkin*, 60 Piccadilly.

SURGICAL INSTRUMENT MAKERS: — *Weiss & Son*, 62 Strand; *Krohne & Sesemann*, 8 Duke Street, Manchester Square, W.; *Mayer & Meltzer*, 71 Great Portland Street; *Arnold & Son*, 35-36 West Smithfield.

TAILORS: — *Poole & Co.*, 36-39 Savile Row, Regent Street (introduction from former customer required); *Miles*, 21 Old Bond Street; *Parfitt, Roberts, & Parfitt*, 75 Jermyn Street; *Kerslake & Co.*, 12 Hanover Street, Hanover Square; *Nicoll*, 114-120 Regent Street; *Blamey & Son*, 62 Charing Cross; *Kimpton*, 105 Strand; *Ralph & Son*, 150 Strand; *Hobson & Co.*, 148 Regent Street; *Meyer & Mortimer*, 36 Conduit Street; *Brown & Son*, 10 Princes Street, Hano-

## 8. SHOPS.

ver Square; *Burn*, 6 Suffolk Street, Pall Mall; *Stohwasser & Co.*, 39 Conduit Street; *Stulz, Wain, & Co.*, 10 Clifford Street; *Doré*, 73 Piccadilly and 25 Conduit Street (ready money tailors, moderate charges); *Wray & Roby*, 78 Queen Street, Cheapside. — CLERICAL TAILORS: — *Pratt*, 23 Tavistock Street, Covent Garden, and 14 Southampton Street; *Cox & Buckley*, 28 Southampton Street; *Seary*, 13 New Oxford Street. — LADIES' TAILORS: — *Redfern*, 26 Conduit Street; *Doré*, 13 George Street, Hanover Square. — Ready-made clothes may be obtained very cheaply in numerous large shops (prices usually affixed).

TEA MERCHANTS: — *Ridgway*, 4 and 5 King William Street, City; *Strachan & Co.*, 131 Finsbury Pavement; *Twining & Co.*, 216 Strand; *Dakin & Co.*, 1 St. Paul's Churchyard, and 240 Oxford Street; *Cooper & Co.*, 268 Regent Circus, and 35 Strand.

TOY MAKERS: — *Burlington Arcade, Piccadilly*; *Lowther Arcade*, Strand; *Cremer*, 210 Regent Street; *Kindergarten Emporium*, 57 Berners Street.

TRUNK MAKERS: — *Allen*, 37 West Strand; *Asprey & Son*, 166 New Bond Street, and 22 Albemarle Street; *Southgate*, 75 and 76 Watling Street; *Millard*, 6 Lisle Street, Leicester Square; *Trunk Makers' Society*, 9 Sherwood Street, Golden Square. — (Strangers should be on their guard against the temptation of purchasing trunks and portmanteaus in inferior leather marked 'second hand' — a common form of fraud in houses of a lower class.)

UMBRELLAS AND PARASOLS: — *Sangster & Co.*, 94 Fleet Street, 140 Regent Street, 75 Cheapside, and 10 Royal Exchange; *Martin*, 64-65 Burlington Arcade; *Brigg*, 23 St. James's Street.

WATCHMAKERS: — *Bennett*, 64 and 65 Cheapside; *Barraud & Lunds*, 49 Cornhill; *Benson*, 25 Old Bond Street, and 62 and 64 Ludgate Hill; *E. Dent & Co.*, 61 Strand; *M. F. Dent & Co.*, 33 Cockspur Street; *Frodsham & Co.*, 84 Strand.

WATERPROOF GOODS: — *Macintosh & Co.*, 19 St. Bride Street, E. C. (wholesale only); *Bax*, 28 Cockspur Street; *Matthews & Son*, 58 Charing Cross; *Piggott*, 117 Cheapside; *Edmiston*, 14 Cockspur Street; *Cording*, 125 Regent Street; *Walkley*, 5 Strand.

WINE MERCHANTS. — There are about 2500 wine merchants in London, most of whom can supply fairly good wine at reasonable prices. Visitors who occupy private apartments should procure their wine from a dealer. The wines at hotels are generally dear and indifferent. The following are good houses: — *Cockburn & Co.*, 8 Lime Street, City; *Hedges & Butler*, 155 Regent Street; *Gilbey*, Pantheon, 173 Oxford Street, besides other offices (with a very extensive trade in low-priced wines; Claret from 1s. per bottle, Hock and Moselle from 1s. 6d.); *Fortnum & Mason*, 181-183 Piccadilly; *Carbonell & Co.*, 182 Regent Street; *G. Tanqueray & Co.*, 5 Pall Mall East; *Basil Woodd & Sons*, 34 New Bond Street; *Law, Holloway, & Co.*, 22 Finch Lane, City; *Payne & Sons*,

## 8. BAZAARS.

61 St. James's Street. Most of the best-known continental wine-firms have agencies in London, the addresses of which may be ascertained from the Post Office Directory. Claret and other wines may also be obtained from most of the grocers.

**Bazaars.** These emporiums afford pleasant covered walks between rows of shops abundantly stocked with all kinds of attractive and useful articles. The most important are the *Soho Bazaar*, 4-7 Soho Square and 58 Oxford Street; *Baker Street Bazaar*, 58 Baker Street; *Opera Colonnade*, adjoining Her Majesty's Theatre, Haymarket; *Burlington Arcade*, Piccadilly; *Lowther Arcade*, Strand (chiefly for toys and other articles at moderate prices); *Royal Arcade*, 28 Old Bond Street. — Among these the Soho Bazaar is *facile princeps*. It has been in existence for half a century, and is conducted on very strict principles. A rental of twelve shillings per week is paid for each stall; some holders rent three or four contiguous stalls.

**Markets.** The immense market traffic of London is among the most interesting and impressive sights of the Metropolis, and one with which no stranger should fail to make himself acquainted. The chief markets are held at early hours of the morning, when they are visited by vast crowds hastening to supply their commissariat for the day.

The chief *Vegetable, Fruit, and Flower Market* is **Covent Garden** (p. 180), where all kinds of vegetables, fruits, ornamental plants, and cut flowers are displayed in richest profusion. The best time to visit this market is about sunrise.

*Billingsgate* (p. 111), the great fish-market, as interesting in its way as Covent Garden, though pervaded by far less pleasant odours, is situated in Lower Thames Street, City, near London Bridge. The covered market is a handsome building lately erected, with an open front towards the street and a façade on the river. Along the quay lie fishing boats, whence the fish are landed in baskets, and sold first to the wholesale, and afterwards to the retail dealers. Oysters and other shell-fish are sold by measure, salmon by weight, and other fish by number. Large quantities of fish are also conveyed to Billingsgate daily by railway; salmon chiefly from Scotland, cod and turbot from the Doggerbank, lobsters from Norway, soles from the German Ocean, eels from Holland, and oysters from the mouth of the Thames and the English Channel. The market commences daily at 5 a. m.

*Smithfield Market*, Newgate Street, City, is the great meat-market of London. The covered market, opened in 1868, is most admirably fitted up (comp. p. 96). Subterranean lines connect it with the Metropolitan Railway, and thence indirectly with the Metropolitan Cattle Market. It was once the chief cattle market of London, and the famous *Bartholomew Fair* was held here down to 1853. A large *Poultry Market* was added to the meat-market in 1876, and *Vegetable* and *Fish Markets* have also been built (comp. p. 96).

The *Metropolitan Cattle Market*, Copenhagen Fields, between

Islington and Camden Town, is the largest in the world. The principal markets are held on Mondays and Thursdays, but on other days the traffic is also very considerable. Around the lofty clock tower are grouped a post-office, a telegraph station, banks, an enquiry office, shops, etc. At the sides are interminable rows of well-arranged stalls for the cattle. — At *Deptford* is a great *Foreign Cattle Market*, for cattle imported from the Continent.

Among the other important markets of London are *Leadenhall Market* (p. 107), Leadenhall Street, for poultry and game; *Farringdon Street Market*, at which watercress is one of the chief articles sold; *Great Eastern Railway Market*, for fish and vegetables; the *Elephant and Castle Market*, for fish; and the *Shadwell Market*, East of London Docks, also for fish. *Columbia Market*, Bethnal Green, was erected by the munificence of the Baroness Burdett Coutts, at a cost of 200,000*l.*, for supplying meat, fish, and vegetables to one of the poorest quarters of London.

The largest Horse Market is *Tattersall's*, Knightsbridge Green, where a great number of horses are sold by auction on every Monday throughout the year, and in spring on Thursdays also. Tattersall's is the centre of all business relating to horse-racing and betting throughout the country, — the Englishman's substitute for the continental lotteries. *Aldridge's*, St. Martin's Lane, is another important horse-mart.

**The Co-operative System.** The object of this system may be described as the furnishing of members of a trading association, formed for the purpose, with genuine and moderately-priced goods on the principle of ready-money payments, the cheapness being secured by economy of management and by contentment with small profits. Notwithstanding the opposition of retail and even of wholesale dealers, it has of late years made astonishingly rapid progress in London, where there are now about thirty 'co-operative stores', carrying on an immense trade. The chief companies are the *Army and Navy Co-operative Stores*, Victoria Street, Westminster, and the *Civil Service Supply Association*.

The Civil Service Supply Association consists of shareholders, of members belonging to the Civil Service, and of outsiders (who, however, must be friends of member or shareholders), who pay 5*s.* the first year and 2*s.* 6*d.* in subsequent years. The association now employs 1170 persons, who receive salaries amounting in all to 102,000*l.* annually. The cost of the string, paper, and straw used in packing goods for customers amounts to 12,000*l.* a year, and upwards of 26,000*l.* is spent annually for carriage and booking. The sales in 1888 reached the enormous sum of 1,760,000*l.*, the net profit being about 2½ per cent. The articles sold comprise groceries, wines, spirits, provisions, tobacco, clothing, books, stationery, fancy goods, drugs, and watches. The premises of the association in Queen Victoria Street (No. 136) cost 27,000*l.*, while it has others in Bedford Street, Strand, and in Tavistock Street, Covent Garden. — The sales of the Army and Navy Stores reach a still higher total, amounting to 2,620,000*l.* per annum.

Strangers or visitors to London are, of course, unable to make purchases at a co-operative store except through a member.

**Co-operative Working Societies.** Another application of the co-operative system is seen in the various associations established on the principle of the Co-Partnership *of the* Workers.

Among meritorious societies of this kind the following may be mentioned: *Bookbinders' Co-operative Society*, 17 Bury Street, Bloomsbury; *Trunk and Bag Makers' Society*, 9 Sherwood Street, Golden Square; *Hamilton & Co.* (shirt makers), 326 Regent Street; *Women's Printing Society*, 21 B Great College Street, Westminster; *Mrs. Alison* (Co-operative Needlewomen; shirts, etc.), 34 Brooke Street, Holborn; *Miss M. Hart* (Decorative Co-operators' Association), 105 Oxford Street; *Bag Manufacturing Supply Association*, 11 Moor Lane, E. C.; *Co-operative Printers*, Salisbury Court, Fleet Street.

## 9. Cabs. Omnibuses. Tramways. Coaches.

**Cabs.** When the traveller is in a hurry, and his route does not coincide with that of an omnibus, he **had** better at once engage a cab at one of the numerous cab-stands, **or** hail one of those passing along the street. The '*Four-wheelers*', which are small and uncomfortable, **hold** four persons inside, while a fifth can be accommodated beside the driver. The two-wheeled cabs, called *Hansoms*, from the name of their inventor, have seats for two persons only (though often used by three), and drive at a much quicker rate than the others. Persons without much luggage will therefore prefer a hansom. The driver's seat is at the back, so that he drives over the heads of the passengers sitting inside. Orders are com**municated** to him through a small trap-door in the roof. — There are now about 10,000 cabs in London, employing about 18,000 horses.

Fares are reckoned by distance, unless the cab is expressly hired by time. The charge for a drive of 2 M. or under is 1s.; for each additional mile or fraction of a mile 6d. For each person above two, 6d. additional is charged for the whole hiring. Two children under 10 years of age are reckoned as one adult. For each large article of luggage carried outside, 2d. is charged; smaller articles are free. The cabman is not bound to drive more than 6 miles. Beyond the 4-mile radius from **Charing Cross the fare is 1s. for every mile or** fraction of a mile. The charge **for waiting is** 6d. for each completed 1/4 hr. for four-wheelers, and 8d. **for** hansoms. The fare *by time* for the first hour or part of an hour is 2s. for four-wheelers, and 2s. 6d. for hansoms. For each additional 1/4 hr., 6d. and **8d.** Beyond the 4-mile radius the fare is 2s. 6d. for the first hour, **for both 2-wheel and 4-wheel vehicles**, and for each additional 1/4 hr. 8d. The **driver may** decline to drive for **more than one full hour,** or **to** be hired by **time between** 8 p. m. and 6 a. m.

**Whether the hirer knows the proper fare or** not, he is recommended to come **to** an agreement with the **driver** before starting.

Each driver is bound **to** possess **a copy** of the authorised Book of Distances, and to produce **it** if required.

In **cases** of attempted im**position** the passenger should demand the cabman's number, or order him to drive to the nearest police court or station.

The driver is bound to deposit any articles left in the cab at the nearest police station within twenty-four hours**, to** be claimed by the owner at **the** Head Police Office, Scotland **Yard.**

The *Fly* **is a vehicle** of a superior description, resembling the **Parisian** *Voiture de remise*, and is admitted to the parks more freely **than the cabs. Flys** must be specially ordered from a livery stable **keeper, and the charges** are of course higher. These vehicles are **recommended in preference** to cabs for drives into the country.

## Cab Fares from the chief railway stations to

| | Broad Street & Liverpool Street | Charing Cross | Euston Square | Fenchurch Street | King's Cross and St. Pancras | London Bridge | Paddington | Victoria | Waterloo |
|---|---|---|---|---|---|---|---|---|---|
| | s. d. | s. d. | s. d. | s. d. | s. d. | s. d. | s. d. | s. d. | s. d. |
| Bank of England | 1 - | 1 - | 1-6 | 1 - | 1-6 | 1 - | 2-6 | 2 - | 1 - |
| Bond Street, Piccadilly | 1-6 | 1 - | 1 - | 1-6 | 1-6 | 1-6 | 1-6 | 1 - | 1 - |
| British Museum | 1-6 | 1 - | 1 - | 1-6 | 1 - | 1-6 | 1-6 | 1-6 | 1 - |
| Covent Garden | 1-6 | 1 - | 1 - | 1-6 | 1 - | 1-6 | 1-6 | 1 - | 1 - |
| Grosvenor Square, N.W. | 2 - | 1 - | 1 - | 2 - | 1-6 | 2 - | 1 - | 1 - | 1-6 |
| Hyde Park Corner | 2 - | 1 - | 1-6 | 2 - | 2 - | 2 - | 1-6 | 1 - | 1-6 |
| Leicester Square | 1-6 | 1 - | 1 - | 1-6 | 1-6 | 1-6 | 1-6 | 1 - | 1 - |
| London Bridge | 1 - | 1-6 | 2 - | 1 - | 1-6 | | 2-6 | 1-6 | 1 - |
| Ludgate Hill | 1 - | 1 - | 1-6 | 1 - | 1 - | 1 - | 2 - | 1-6 | 1 - |
| Marble Arch | 2 - | 1 - | 1-6 | 2 - | 1-6 | 2 - | 1 - | 1 - | 1-6 |
| Oxford Circus | 1-6 | 1 - | 1 - | 1-6 | 1 - | 2 - | 1 - | 1 - | 1 - |
| Piccadilly, Haymarket | 1 - | 1 - | 1 - | 1-6 | 1-6 | 1-6 | 1-6 | 1 - | 1 - |
| Post Office | 1 - | 1 - | 1-6 | 1 - | 1 - | 1 - | 2 - | 2 - | 1 - |
| Regent Street, Piccadilly | 1-6 | 1 - | 1 - | 1-6 | 1-6 | 1-6 | 1-6 | 1 - | 1 - |
| St. Paul's | 1 - | 1 - | 1-6 | 1 - | 1 - | 1 - | 2-6 | 1-6 | 1 - |
| South Kensington Museum | 2-6 | 1-6 | 2 - | 2-6 | 2-6 | 2-6 | 1-6 | 1-6 | 2 - |
| Strand (Wellington Street) | 1-6 | 1 - | 1 - | 1-6 | 1 - | 1 - | 2 - | 1 - | 1 - |
| Temple Bar | 1 - | 1 - | 1 - | 1 - | 1 - | 1 - | 2 - | 1-6 | 1 - |
| Tower | 1 - | 1-6 | 2 - | 1 - | 2 - | 1 - | 2-6 | 2 - | 1-6 |
| Trafalgar Square | 1-6 | 1 - | 1 - | 1-6 | 1-6 | 1-6 | 1-6 | 1 - | 1 - |
| Westminster Palace | 1-6 | 1 - | 1-6 | 1-6 | 1-6 | 1-6 | 2 - | 1 - | 1 - |
| Zoological Gardens | 2 - | 1-6 | 1 - | 2-6 | 1 - | 2-6 | 1-6 | 2 - | 2 - |

**Omnibuses,** of which there are about 200 lines, cross the Metropolis in every direction from eight in the morning till midnight. The destination of each vehicle (familiarly known as a '*bus*'), and the names of some of the principal streets through which it passes, are usually painted on the outside. As they always keep to the left in driving along the street, the intending passenger should walk on that side for the purpose of hailing one. To prevent mistakes, he had better mention his destination to the conductor before entering.

The first omnibuses plying in London were started by Mr. George Shillibeer in 1829. They were drawn by three horses yoked abreast, and were much heavier and clumsier than those now in use. At first they were furnished with a supply of books for the use of the passengers. The London service of omnibuses is now mainly in the hands of the London General Omnibus Co. and the London Road Car Co. Within the last year or two a number of small one-horse omnibuses have been started which ply for short distances for a fare of 1½d. These vehicles have no conductor, and passengers place their fares in a box. Omnibuses of this kind run from Charing Cross over Westminster Bridge, from Oxford Street to Euston Road, from Farringdon Street Station over Blackfriars Bridge, etc. Special railway omnibuses ply between different railway-stations, as from Portland Road (Metropolitan Railway) to Charing Cross, from Baker Street to Piccadilly Circus, etc. In point of comfort the vehicles generally still leave much to be desired.

The principal points of intersection of the omnibus lines are (on the N. of the Thames) the Bank, Charing Cross, Piccadilly Circus, Oxford Circus, and the junction of Tottenham Court Road and Oxford Street. The chief point in Southwark is the hostelry called the Elephant and Castle.

Those who travel by omnibus should keep themselves provided with small change to prevent delay and mistakes. The fare varies from ½d. to 6d., and is in a few cases 9d. For a drive to Richmond, the Crystal Palace, and other places several miles from the City the usual fare is 1s. A table of the legal fares is placed in the inside of each omnibus.

OMNIBUS LINES. The following is a list of a few of the principal routes:—

| Name | Colour | Route |
|---|---|---|
| Atlas | Light green | St. John's Wood, Baker Street, Oxford Street, Regent Street, Charing Cross, Westminster Bridge, Camberwell Gate; every 10 min. |
| Bayswater | Green | Bayswater, Oxford Street, Holborn, Cheapside, Bank, London Bridge, every 3-4 min.; Bayswater to Whitechapel, every 8 min.; to Broad Street and Liverpool Street Stations every hour. |
| Bow and Regent Circus | Dark green | Stratford and Bow, Whitechapel, Cornhill, Cheapside, Fleet Street, Strand, Regent Street, Oxford Street; every 10 min. |
| Brompton | White | Walham Green, Piccadilly, Charing Cross, Strand, Fleet Street, Cheapside, Bank, Broad Street; every 20 min. |
| Camberwell Gate | Yellow | Camberwell, Walworth Road, Borough, London Bridge, Gracechurch Street, Shoreditch; every 7 min. |
| Camden Town | Yellow | Kentish Town, Haverstock Hill, Camden Town, Tottenham Court Road, St. Martin's Lane, Charing Cross, Victoria; every 3-5 min. |
| Charing Cross and Kilburn | Red | Kilburn, Edgeware Road, Oxford Street, Regent Street, Charing Cross; every 15 min. |
| Chelsea | Chocolate | Chelsea, Sloane Street, Piccadilly, Strand, Fleet Street, Bank, and then by Bishopsgate Street and Bethnal Green Road to Old Ford, or by Moorgate Street to Hoxton; every 20 min. |
| City Atlas | Dark green | Swiss Cottage, St. John's Wood, Oxford Street, Holborn, Bank; every 7 min. |
| Clapham | Chocol., red, or green | Clapham, Stockwell, Kennington, London Bridge, Gracechurch Street; every 10-12 min. |
| Clapton and Oxford Circus | Dark green | Clapton, Hackney Road, Bishopsgate Street, Bank, Cheapside, Holborn, Oxford Street; every 20 min. |
| Favorite | Dark green | Holloway, Pentonville Road, Chancery Lane, Strand, Westminster Abbey, Victoria Station; every 8 min. |
| Favorite | Dark green | Holloway, Highbury, Islington, City Road, Bank, King William Street, London Bridge; every 8 min. |
| Victoria & King's Cross | White | Victoria, Piccadilly, Long Acre, Great Queen Street, Russell Square, King's Cross; every few minutes. |
| Hammersmith | Red | Hammersmith, Shaftesbury Avenue, Charing Cross Road, Tottenham Court Road, King's Cross; every few minutes. |
| London Road Car Co. | Brown | West Kensington, Shaftesbury Avenue, Charing Cross Road, Oxford Street, Liverpool Street Station; every few minutes. |

| Name | Colour | Route |
|---|---|---|
| Favorite | Blue | Holloway, Islington, Euston Road, Regent Street, Piccadilly, Brompton; every 15 min. |
| Favorite | Red | Holloway, Islington, Goswell Road, Bank; every 10-15 min. |
| Favorite | Dark green | Stoke Newington, Essex Road, Chancery Lane, Charing Cross, Westminster, Victoria Station; every 20 min. |
| Hampstead | Yellow | Haverstock Hill, Camden Town, Tottenham Court Road, Charing Cross Road, Piccadilly Circus; every 20 min. |
| Islington and Kent Road | Dark green | New North Road, City Road, Moorgate Street, London Bridge, Borough, Old Kent Road; every 7 min. |
| Kennington to Charing Cross | Red | Kennington Park and Road, Westminster Bridge, Parliament Street; every 6 min. |
| Kilburn | Dark green | Edgeware Road, Oxford Street, Holborn, Cheapside, Cornhill, Leadenhall Street, Aldgate; every 8 min. |
| Kilburn and Victoria Station | Red | Edgeware Road, Park Lane, Victoria Station; every 12 min. |
| King's Cross | Light green | Great College Street, King's Cross, Gray's Inn Road, Chancery Lane, Fleet Street, Blackfriars Bridge, Kennington; every 9 min. |
| Kingsland | Green or chocol. | Dalston, Kingsland Road, Shoreditch, Bishopsgate Street, Gracechurch, London Bridge, Borough, Elephant and Castle; every 5 min. |
| Old Ford | Yell. or chocol. | Old Ford, Bethnal Green Road, Shoreditch, Bishopsgate, Exchange; every 5 min. |
| Paddington | Yellow | Kensal Green, Paddington, Edgeware Road, Oxford Street, Holborn, Cheapside, London Bridge; every ½ hr. |
| Paddington | Yellow | Paddington, Edgeware Road, Oxford Street, Holborn, Newgate Street, Cheapside, London Bridge; every 5 min. |
| Paddington via New Road | Light green | Westbourne Grove, Edgeware Road, Marylebone Road, King's Cross, Islington, City Road, Moorgate Street, King William Street, London Bridge; every 8 min. |
| Piccadilly and St. Thomas's Hospital | Yellow | Piccadilly Circus, Charing Cross, Westminster Bridge, St. Thomas's Hospital; every 7 min. |
| Putney Bridge | White | Putney Bridge, Fulham, Brompton, Piccadilly, Strand, Fleet Street, St. Paul's, Cannon Street, London Bridge; every 20 min. |
| Royal Blue | Dark blue | Victoria Station, Piccadilly, Bond Street, Oxford Circus; every 5 min. |
| Royal Oak and Charing Cross | Red | Archer Street (Bayswater), Edgeware Road, Oxford Street, Regent Street, Charing Cross; every 8 min. |
| Royal Oak and Victoria Station | Red | Praed Street, Edgeware Road, Park Lane, Victoria Station; every 12 min. |
| South Hackney | Red | Victoria Park, Hackney Road, Shoreditch, Bank; every 10 min. |
| Waterloo | Blue | Camden Town, York and Albany, Regent Street, Waterloo Bridge, Elephant and Castle, Camberwell Gate; every 7 min. |
| Westbourne Grove and Camden Town | Brown | Paddington, St. John's Wood, Regent's Park, Camden Town; every 15 min. |
| Westminster | Brown | Bank, Cheapside, Fleet Street, Strand, Westminster, Pimlico; every 6 min. |

Tramways. Since 1870 several lines of tramways have been in operation in the outlying districts of London. The cars are comfortable, and the fares moderate (1-4d.)
The cars of the *South London Tramways Co.* run from Westminster Bridge and London Bridge to Wandsworth, and from Chelsea Bridge to Lavender Hill and Clapham Junction. Those of the *London Tramways Co.* run from Westminster Bridge to Brixton, Clapham, New Cross, Greenwich, and Peckham; from Blackfriars Bridge to Brixton, Peckham, and Greenwich; and from Victoria Station to Vauxhall Bridge and Camberwell. The *London Street Tramways Co.* runs cars from King's Cross to Kentish Town, from Euston Road to Kentish Town, Holloway, and Highgate, and from Holborn viâ Grey's Inn Road and Kentish Town to Hampstead Heath. The lines of the *North Metropolitan Tramways Co.* extend from Moorgate Street to Finsbury Park, Stamford Hill, Clapton, Highbury, New Park, Canonbury, and Highgate; from Aldersgate Street to Hackney and Dalston, and to Highgate Archway; from Holborn to Goswell Road, Dalston, and Stamford Hill; from Canning Town Station to Green Gate; from Stratford to Manor Park and Leytonstone; from King's Cross to Finsbury Park; from Bloomsbury to Hackney, Dalston Lane, Lea Bridge, and Poplar; and from Aldgate to Well Street, Victoria Park, Stratford, and Poplar. The cars of the *London Southern Tramways Co.* run from Stockwell to Camberwell Green and Norwood, and from Brixton to Loughborough Junction. The *Southall, Ealing, and Shepherd's Bush Tramway Co.* runs cars from Uxbridge Road to Shepherd's Bush and Acton. The lines of the *Harrow Road and Paddington Tramways Co.* extend from Amberley Road, Paddington (near Royal Oak Station), to Harlesden Green, Willesden, with a branch running towards the Paddington Recreation Ground and Maida Vale.

The *Highgate Steep Gradient Cable Tramway*, the first of the kind in Europe, opened in 1884, ascends Highgate Hill from Highgate Archway; the cars start every 5 min. (fares 2d. up, 1d. down; halfway up 1d.). The motive power is supplied by an endless wire rope, placed in a tube below the surface of the road and kept in motion by a stationary engine at one end of the line. Connection between the car and the rope is effected by means of a 'gripping attachment', passing through a slit in the middle of the track. The rope runs between the jaws of the 'gripper', which the driver closes when he wishes to start the car, reversing the operation and applying the brakes when he wishes to stop. The system works with great effectiveness and a pleasant freedom from noise or dirt.

Coaches. During the summer months well-appointed stage coaches run from London to *Bentley Priory* (near Harrow), *Guildford*, *St. Albans*, *Virginia Water*, *Dorking*, *Sevenoaks*, *Hampton Court*, *Hertford*, *Maidenhead*, *Brighton*, etc. Most of them start from the White Horse Cellar, Piccadilly (where particulars may be learned), between 10 and 11.45 a.m. The fares vary from 2s. 6d. to 14s.; return-fares one-half or two-thirds more; box seats usually 2s. 6d. extra. Some of these coaches are driven by the gentlemen who own them. They afford better opportunities in many respects for viewing the scenery than railway-trains, and may be recommended in fine weather. On the more popular routes seats have often to be booked several days in advance.

## 10. Railways.

The principal Railway Stations in London are fourteen in number. Many of them are now lighted by the electric light. On the left (N.) bank of the Thames are the following: —

I. **Euston Square Station**, the terminus of the LONDON AND NORTH WESTERN RAILWAY, Euston Square, near Euston Road and Tottenham Court Road. Trains for *Rugby, Crewe, Chester, Bangor, Holyhead* (whence steamers to *Ireland*); *Birmingham, Shrewsbury; Stafford,* **Leicester,** *Derby, Nottingham,* Lincoln, Leeds, Hull; Liverpool, Manchester; Carlisle, Glasgow, Edinburgh, etc.

II. **St. Pancras Station**, Euston Road, to the W. of King's Cross Station, the terminus of the MIDLAND RAILWAY. Trains for *Camden Road, Kentish Town, Haverstock Hill, Hendon; Bedford, Leicester, Nottingham, Derby, Chesterfield, Normanton, Hull, York, Leeds, Newcastle, Lancaster; Glasgow, Edinburgh,* etc.

III. **King's Cross Station**, Euston Road, terminus of the GREAT NORTHERN RAILWAY. Trains for the N. and N.E.: *York, Newcastle, Edinburgh; Hull, Leeds, Sheffield, Manchester, Liverpool; Cambridge, Bedford, Hertford, Lincoln;* suburban trains to *Highgate, Hornsey, Alexandra Park, Barnet,* and *Edgware.*

IV. **Paddington Station**, terminus of the GREAT WESTERN RAILWAY for the W. and S.W. of England (trains start from the W. side of the station). Trains to *Berkshire, Oxfordshire, Wiltshire, Somersetshire, Devonshire, Cornwall, Gloucestershire, South Wales; Windsor, Reading, Cheltenham, Gloucester, Bath, Bristol, Exeter; Oxford, Birmingham, Liverpool, Manchester,* etc.

V. Liverpool **Street Station**, near Bishopsgate Street, terminus of the GREAT EASTERN RAILWAY and EAST LONDON LINE. Trains to *Chelmsford, Colchester, Harwich, Ipswich, Norwich, Lowestoft, Yarmouth; Cambridge, Ely, Peterborough, Lincoln,* etc.; *Bethnal Green, Hackney, Clapton, Old Ford, Stratford, Epping Forest, Tilbury, Southend;* and through the Thames Tunnel to *New Cross, Peckham Rye,* etc.

VI. **Charing Cross Station**, on the site of Old Hungerford Market, close to Trafalgar Square, terminus of —

1. The SOUTH EASTERN RAILWAY viâ *Redhill, Tunbridge,* and *Ashford,* to *Folkestone* and *Dover.*

2. The GREENWICH RAILWAY, a viaduct borne by brick arches, viâ *London Bridge Station, Spa Road,* and *Deptford,* to *Greenwich.*

3. The MID and NORTH KENT LINES to *New Cross, Lewisham, Beckenham, Bromley, Blackheath, Woolwich, Dartford, Erith, Gravesend, Rochester.*

VII. **Cannon Street Station**, Cannon Street, City, near the Bank and St. Paul's Cathedral, City terminus for the same lines as Charing Cross. Trains from Charing Cross to Cannon Street, and *vice versâ,* every 10 minutes.

VIII. **Victoria Station**, the West End terminus of the LONDON, CHATHAM, AND DOVER RAILWAY, in Victoria Street, near Buckingham Palace and Westminster. — The following lines issue from this station —

1. The LONDON, CHATHAM, AND DOVER RAILWAY, to *Clapham, Brixton, Herne Hill, Dulwich, Sydenham Hill, Beckenham, Bromley, Bickley, Rochester, Chatham, Faversham, Canterbury, Dover, Herne Bay, Margate, Broadstairs, Ramsgate.*

2. The CRYSTAL PALACE branch of the London, Chatham, and Dover Railway; stations, *Clapham, Brixton, Denmark Hill, Peckham Rye, Honor Oak, Lordship Lane, Crystal Palace (High Level Station).*

3. The METROPOLITAN EXTENSION, to *Ludgate Hill* and *Holborn Viaduct Station*, via *Grosvenor Road, Battersea Park, York Road, Wandsworth Road, Clapham* and *North Stockwell, Brixton and South* **Stockwell**, *Loughborough* **Junction**, *Camberwell New Road,* **Walworth Road, Elephant and** *Castle,* and *Borough Road.*

4. The WEST LONDON EXTENSION, via *Battersea, Chelsea, West* **Brompton**, and **Kensington (Addison Road),** to *Willesden Junction.*

5. The BRIGHTON AND SOUTH COAST RAILWAY, via *Clapham Junction* (a most important station for South London), *Wandsworth Common,* **Balham, Streatham Hill**, *West Norwood, Gipsy Hill,* and *Crystal Palace (Low Level Station)*, to *Norwood Junction* (see p. 35), or by *Clapham Junction, Wandsworth Common, Balham, Streatham Common, Norbury, Thornton Heath,* and *Selhurst* to *Croydon* (see p. 35). At Norwood Junction and Croydon **the line** joins the London Bridge and Brighton Line.

6. The SOUTH LONDON LINE, via *Grosvenor Road, York Road, Wandsworth Road, Clapham Road, Loughborough Junction, Denmark Hill, Peckham Rye, Queen's Road, Old Kent Road,* and *South Bermondsey,* to *London Bridge.*

IX. Broad Street Station, terminus of the NORTH LONDON RAILWAY. Trains to *Shoreditch, Haggerston,* and *Dalston,* where the line forks. The rails to the W. run to *Mildmay Park, Canonbury, Islington &* **Highbury, Barnsbury,** *Camden Town, Kentish Town, Gospel Oak* (for Highgate), **Hampstead** *Heath, Finchley Road, West End Lane, Brondesbury, Kensal* **Green,** *Willesden Junction* (an important station for North London, stopped **at by all the** express **trains** of **the N.W. railway), Acton, Hammersmith,** *Gunnersbury, Kew Bridge, Kew Gardens, Richmond,* **and Kingston.** The line to the E. goes **to Hackney,** *Homerton, Victoria* **Park, Old** *Ford, Bow,* and *Poplar.* Trains also run every ¼ hr. from Broad Street to *Camden Town* (as **above**) and *Chalk Farm,* on the L. N. W. railway.

X. Ludgate Hill **Station,** near St. Paul's Cathedral and Blackfriars Bridge, City terminus of the METROPOLITAN EXTENSION (see above), and also of the London, Chatham, and Dover Railway.

XI. Holborn Viaduct Station, Holborn Viaduct, **for the same** trains as **Ludgate Hill** Station.

XII. St. Paul's Station, Queen Victoria Street, a terminus of **the** London, Chatham, and Dover Railway.

XIII. Fenchurch **Street** Station, **near the** Bank, on the S. side of Fenchurch Street, **terminus of the BLACKWALL RAILWAY to** *Shadwell, Stepney, Limehouse, West India Docks, Poplar,* and *Blackwall*, and of the TILBURY, GRAVESEND, AND SOUTHEND RAILWAY.

On the right (S.) bank of the Thames: —

XIV. London **Bridge Station**, the terminus of the BRIGHTON AND SOUTH COAST RAILWAY, viâ *New Cross, Brockley, Forest Hill, Sydenham (Crystal Palace), Penge, Norwood Junction* (see p. 34), *Croydon* (where the main L. B. S. C. line from Victoria joins; see also (p. 34), *Purley* (junction for *Caterham*), *Red Hill Junction* (branch to the W. for *Reigate, Box Hill,* and *Dorking*; to the E. for *Dover*), *Three Bridges* (for *Arundel*), and *Hayward's Heath* (junction for *Lewes* and *Newhaven*), to *Brighton*. Also to *Chichester* and *Portsmouth* for the *Isle of Wight*.

XV. **Waterloo Station**, Waterloo Road, Southwark, terminus of the SOUTH WESTERN RAILWAY, consists of two parts —

1. The NORTHERN (entrance on the E. and N.E.), for the line to *Reading* by *Vauxhall, Clapham Junction, Wandsworth, Putney,* and *Barnes*. At Barnes the line forks; the branch to the right (N.) leads to *Chiswick, Kew, Brentford, Isleworth,* and *Hounslow;* that to the left to *Mortlake, Richmond, Twickenham, Kingston,* and *Windsor*.

2. The SOUTHERN (entrance on the S. side), for the line to *Southampton, Portsmouth (Isle of Wight), Exeter, Plymouth,* etc. The nearest stations to London on this line are *Vauxhall, Clapham, Wimbledon, Coombe-Malden, Surbiton* (for *Kingston*), *Thames Ditton,* and *Hampton Court*.

On all **the English lines the first-class** passenger is entitled to carry 112lb. of luggage free, **second-class** 80lb., and **third-class** 60lb. The companies, however, **rarely make any** charge for overweight unless the excess is exorbitant. On **all inland routes** the traveller should see that his luggage is duly labelled **for his destination, and put** into the right van, as otherwise the railways **are not responsible for its transport**. Travellers to the Continent require **to book their luggage and obtain a ticket for it, after which it gives them no farther trouble. The railway porters are nominally forbidden to accept gratuities**, but it is a common custom to give 2-6d. to the porter who **transfers the luggage from the cab to the train** or vice versâ.

Travellers accustomed to the formalities of Continental railway officials may perhaps consider that in England they are **too much left to themselves. Tickets** are not invariably checked **at the beginning of a journey,** and travellers should therefore make sure that **they** are in the **proper compartment. The names** of the stations are **not always so conspicuous as they should be** (especially at night); and **the way in which the porters call them** out, laying all the stress **on the last syllable, is seldom of much assistance**. The officials, however, are generally civil in answering questions and giving information. In winter foot-warmers with hot water are usually provided. **It is 'good form' for a** passenger **quitting a railway-carriage where there are other travellers to close the door behind him,** and to pull up the window **if he has had to let it down**.

SMOKING is forbidden in **all the carriages except the 'smoking compartments'**, under a penalty of 10s.

*Bradshaw's Railway Guide* (monthly: 6d.) is the most complete; **but** numerous others (the *ABC Railway Guide*, etc.), claiming to be easier of reference, are also published. Each of the great railway-companies publishes a monthly guide **to its own system (price 1-2d.)**.

## 10. RAILWAYS.

### Metropolitan or Underground Railways.

An important artery of 'intramural' traffic is afforded by the *Metropolitan* and *Metropolitan District Railways*. These lines, which for the most part run under the houses and streets by means of tunnels, and partly also through cuttings between high walls, form a complete belt (the 'inner circle') round the whole of the inner part of London, while various branch-lines diverge to the outlying suburbs. The Midland, Great Western, Great Northern, and other railways run suburban trains in connection with the Metropolitan lines. The Metropolitan Railway Company now conveys about 81 million passengers annually, or upwards of $1^1/_2$ million per week, at an average rate of about twopence per journey. Over the quadruple part of the line, between Farringdon street and Moorgate street, 1406 trains run every week-day. The stations on the underground lines are the following (see Railway Map): —

**Mark Lane**, for the Tower of London, the Mint, Corn Exchange, Billingsgate, and the Docks.

**Aldgate**, Houndsditch, corner of Leadenhall and Fenchurch Streets, for Mincing Lane, Whitechapel, Minories, and the East End.

From Aldgate the line is extended to *Aldgate East*, *St. Mary's* (Whitechapel), and *Whitechapel* (Mile End), whence the District Company's trains run on to *Shadwell*, *Wapping*, *Rotherhithe*, *Deptford Road*, and *New Cross*, on the East London Railway. Through trains now run between New Cross and many of the District and Metropolitan stations.

**Bishopsgate**, near the Liverpool Street (Great Eastern; subway) and Broad Street (North of London) stations.

**Moorgate Street**, close to Finsbury Circus, 5 min. from the Bank, chief station for **the City**.

**Aldersgate Street**, Long Lane, near the General Post Office and Smithfield Meat Market (branch-line to the latter, see p. 26); change for Ludgate Hill, Crystal Palace, and London, Chatham, and Dover Railway.

**Farringdon Street**, in Clerkenwell, $^1/_4$ M. to the N. of Holborn Viaduct, connected with *Holborn Viaduct* and *Ludgate Hill* stations (see p. 34); trains to and from the latter (London, Chatham, and Dover Railway) every 10 min.

**King's Cross**, corner of Pentonville Road and Gray's Inn Road, connected with the Great Northern and Midland Railways.

**Gower Street**, near Euston Square (North Western) Terminus and about $^1/_2$ M. from the British Museum.

**Portland Road**, Park Square, at the S.E. angle of Regent's Park, $^1/_2$ M. from the S. entrance of the Zoological Gardens (by the Broad Walk); omnibus to Oxford Circus (1 d.) and Charing Cross Station (2 d.) in connection with the trains.

**Baker Street**, corner of York Place, another station for the Botanic and Zoological Gardens. A little to the E., in Marylebone Road, is Madame Tussaud's (**p. 44**). Railway omnibus to Piccadilly Circus (1 d.).

Branch Line to *St. John's Wood Road* (for Lord's Cricket Ground), *Marlborough Road, Swiss Cottage, Finchley Road, West Hampstead, Kilburn-Brondesbury, Willesden Green, Kingsbury-Neasden* (with the extensive works of the Metropolitan Railway), *Harrow, Pinner, Rickmansworth,* and *Chesham* (the last extension opened in July, 1889).

**Edgware Road**, Chapel Street.

Branch Line to *Bishop's Road, Royal Oak, Westbourne Park, Notting Hill* (the last two stations are both near Kensal Green Cemetery). *Latimer Road, Shepherd's Bush , Hammersmith* (trains every ¼ hr.); also to *Turnham Green* (Bedford Park Estate), *Gunnersbury, Kew Gardens, Richmond* (trains every half-hour, from Bishop's Road to Richmond in 28 min.) — From Latimer Road branch-line to the left to *Uxbridge Road, Addison Road* (Kensington; for Olympia, p. 44). *Earl's Court,* and *Brompton (Gloucester Road),* see below; trains every ½ hr. — Omnibus to Kilburn.

**Praed Street (Paddington)**, opposite the Great Western Hotel and the Paddington Station.

**Queen's Road (Bayswater)**, N. side of Kensington Gardens.

**Notting Hill Gate**, Notting Hill High Street, for the E. part of Notting Hill.

**Kensington High Street**, Kensington, ⅓ M. from Holland House and Park.

**Brompton (Gloucester Road)**.

Branch Lines to *West Brompton, Addison Road, Earl's Court, Putney Bridge, Wimbledon* (new extension-line, opened in June, 1889), *Acton, Ealing, Kew* and *Richmond,* etc.

**South Kensington**, Cromwell Road, for South Kensington Museum (3 min. to the N.), Natural History Museum, Albert Hall (subway, see p. 271), Albert Memorial, and the Imperial Institute.

**Sloane Square**, near Chelsea Hospital, station for Battersea Park.

**Victoria**, opposite Victoria Terminus (London, Chatham, and Dover and Brighton Railways), with which it is connected by a subway, and ¼ M. from Buckingham Palace.

**St. James's Park**, Tothill Street, near Birdcage Walk, to the S. of St. James's Park, the station for the Panorama of Niagara.

**Westminster Bridge**, Victoria Embankment, at the W. end of Westminster Bridge, station for the Houses of Parliament, Westminster Abbey, etc.

**Charing Cross**, for Charing Cross, Trafalgar Square, National Gallery, and West Strand.

**Temple**, between Somerset House and the Temple, below Waterloo Bridge, station for the new Law Courts, Somerset House, and the London School Board Office.

**Blackfriars**, Bridge Street, adjacent to Blackfriars Bridge, connected by a covered way with the St. Paul's Station of the London, Chatham, & Dover Railway, and near Ludgate Hill Station (p. 34). From Westminster to Blackfriars the line runs below the Victoria Embankment (p. 113).

**Mansion House**, corner of Cannon Street and Queen Victoria Street, station for St. Paul's. Omnibus to Liverpool Street Station.

**Cannon Street**, below the terminus of the South Eastern Railway, the station nearest the Bank and the Exchange.

**The Monument**, at the corner of Eastcheap, station for the Monument, London Bridge, the Coal Exchange, and the new Electric Railway Subway under the Thames.

Trains run on the main line (inner circle) in both directions from 6 a.m. to nearly midnight, at intervals of 5-10 min. during the day, and of 15 min. before 8 a.m. or after 8 p.m.

The stations generally occupy open sites, and are lighted from above, many of them being roofed with glass. At night some of them are now lighted with electric light. The carriages are comfortable and roomy, and are lighted with gas. The booking-office is generally on a level with the street, at the top of the flight of stairs leading down to the railway. The official who checks the tickets points out the right platform, while the tickets themselves are marked with a large red O or I (for 'outer' and 'inner' line of rails), corresponding with notices in the stations. After reaching the platform the traveller had better enquire whether the train for his destination is the first that comes up or one of those that follow, or consult the telegraph-board on which the destination of the next train is indicated. It may, however, be useful to know that the trains of the 'inner circle' have one white light on the engine; trains between Hammersmith and New Cross have one white and one blue light, between Hammersmith and Aldgate two blue lights, and between Richmond and Aldgate two white lights. The terminus towards which the train is travelling is also generally placarded on the front of the engine. Above the platforms hang boards indicating the points at which the different classes of carriage are drawn up; the first-class carriages are in the middle of the train. The names of the stations are called out by the porters, and are always painted at different parts of the platform and on the lamps, though frequently difficult to distinguish from the surrounding advertisements. As the stoppages are extremely brief, no time should be lost either in taking seats or alighting. Passengers leave the platform by the 'Way Out', where their tickets are given up. Those who are travelling with through-tickets to a station situated on one of the branch-lines show their tickets at the junction where carriages are changed, and where the officials will indicate the proper train. — Comp. the time-tables of the companies.

The fares are extremely moderate, seldom exceeding a shilling even for considerable distances. Return-tickets are issued at a fare and a half. At first, in order to make himself acquainted with the Metropolis, the stranger will naturally prefer to make use of omnibuses and cabs, but when his first curiosity is satisfied he will probably often avail himself of the easy, rapid, and economical mode of travelling afforded by the Metropolitan Railway.

## 11. Steamboats.

The VICTORIA STEAMBOAT COMPANY, established in 1888, practically commands the whole route from Hampton Court towards the west to Southend and Sheerness on the east. On this great length of river, with all its sinuosities, there are about 45 piers or landing-places, the larger half of which are on the north or left bank. Above Vauxhall Bridge are *Nine Elms*, **Pimlico**, *Battersea Park*, *Chelsea*, *Wandsworth*, *Putney*, **Hammersmith**, *Kew*, *Richmond*, *Teddington*, and *Hampton Court*. Between **the bridges**, as the reach between Vauxhall Bridge on the west and London Bridge on the east is sometimes called, are the piers at *Millbank*, *Lambeth*, *Westminster*, **Charing Cross**, *Waterloo*, *Temple*, *Blackfriars*, *St. Paul's Wharf*, and two at **London Bridge** (one on each bank). Below all the bridges are *Cherry Gardens* (in no sense corresponding with its name), *Thames Tunnel, Globe Stairs, Limehouse, West India Docks, Commercial Docks, Millwall, Greenwich,* **Isle of** *Dogs, Cubitt* **Town,** *Blackwall,* **Charlton,** *Woolwich,* **North Woolwich,** *Erith, Greenhithe, Rosherville, Gravesend, Southend,* and *Sheerness,* where the Nore **light-ship is reached,** and **the estuary of the Thames expands into the German Ocean.** Some of the larger steamers from **London Bridge** extend their trips to *Margate, Ramsgate,* **Clacton-on-Sea, Walton-on-the-Naze,** *Harwich,* and *Ipswich.*

Steamers ply every ten minutes between **London** *Bridge* **and** **Chelsea,** calling at intermediate stations (fares 1, 2d., according to distance), every ½ **hr.** between *Greenwich* and *Westminster* (fare 3d.), and every ½ **hr.** between *Chelsea* (Cadogan Pier) and *Kew* (fare 6d.). The longer trips (fares 6d.-3s 6d.) are advertised from time to time in the newspapers. The steamers may also be hired for excursion-parties at prices ranging from 10l. to 65l. per day.

On Sundays and holidays the fare is raised for most of the shorter trips. Although the steamers cannot all be described as comfortable, they at any rate afford **an** excellent survey of the traffic on the Thames 'below bridge' and of the **smiling** beauties of its banks 'above'.

## 12. Theatres.

The performance at many of the **London theat**res begins about 7.30 or 8 and **lasts** till 11 p.m.; but the latter part of the **representation is apt to be** more of a fatigue **than** a pleasure.

London possesses **65** theatres and about 500 music halls, which are visited by 325,000 **people** nightly or nearly 100,000,000 yearly. A visit to the whole of the **theat**res of London, which, however, could only be managed in the course of a prolonged sojourn, would give the traveller a capital insight into the social life of the people throughout all its gradations. Copies of the play are often sold **at the theatres for** 6d. **or** 1s. each, enabling the spectator to appreciate the performance more thoroughly. At some of the better theatres all extra fees have been abolished, **but many of them still maintain the** objectionable **custom of charging for programmes,** the care of wraps, etc. *French* (late **Lacy**), 89 **Strand, is the chief thea**trical bookseller.

The best seats **are** the *Stalls,* next to **the Orchestra, and the** *Dress Circle.* On the occasion of popular **performances tickets for these places** are often not to be had at the door on **entering, but must be secured** previously at the *Box Office* of the theatre, **when an extra fee of** 1s. **for** booking is sometimes charged. The office always **contains a plan of the** theatre, showing **the** positions of the seats. Tickets **for the opera and** for most of the theatres may also be obtained at *Mitchell's,* **33 Old Bond Street;** *Lacon & Ollier,* 168 New Bond Street; *Ollivier,* 38 Old **Bond Street;** *Hays,* 4 Royal Exchange Buildings; *Keith, Prowse, & Co,*, 48 **Cheapside,** 218 High Holborn, Langham Hotel, 148 Fenchurch Street, **2 Army and Navy Buildings,** Victoria Street, and Hôtel Métropole, Northumberland Avenue, Charing Cross; *Cramer,* Regent Street; *Austin's Ticket Office,* 81. **James's** Hall, Piccadilly, and elsewhere, at charges somewhat higher as a rule **than** at the theatres themselves, but occasionally **lower.** Single box seats **can** generally be **obtained** at the door as well **as at the** box-office, except when the boxes are let for the season.

Those who have not taken their tickets in advance should be at the door half-an-hour before the beginning of the performance, with, if possible, the exact price of their ticket in readiness. (This is scarcely ever necessary in regard to the dearest seats.) The ticket office is usually opened half-an hour before the commencement **of** the performance. All the theatres are closed on Good Friday and Christmas Day, and many of them throughout the whole of Passion Week.

Evening dress is not now compulsory in any of the London theatres, but is customary in the stalls and dress circle and *de rigueur* in most parts of the opera-houses during the opera season.

The chief London theatres are the following, but many of them are closed in August and September.

HER MAJESTY'S THEATRE, or OPERA HOUSE, corner of Haymarket and Pall Mall. This theatre, originally erected by Vanbrugh in 1705, was burned down in 1789, rebuilt by Novosielski the following year, and extended by Nash and Repton in 1816-18. The interior was again destroyed by fire in December 1867, but since then the theatre has been entirely restored. Italian operas are performed here. Private boxes from 1*l*. 1*s*. to 10*l*. 10*s*.; stalls 12*s*. 6*d*., first two rows of dress circle 10*s*., other rows of dress circle 7*s*. 6*d*., first circle 5*s*. & 6*s*., second circle 3*s*. & 4*s*., pit 2*s*. 6*d*. Doors open at 7.30; performance commences at 8 p.m. Winter season at reduced prices. Often closed.

ROYAL ITALIAN OPERA, or COVENT GARDEN THEATRE, on the W. side of Bow Street, Long Acre, the third theatre on the same site, was built in 1858 by Barry. It accommodates an audience of 3500 persons, being nearly as large as the Scala at Milan, and has a handsome Corinthian colonnade. This house was originally sacred to Italian opera, but is now used for promenade concerts in autumn and as a circus in winter. Boxes $2^1/_2$-7 guineas, orchestra stalls 21*s*., amphitheatre stalls 10*s*. 6*d*. and 5*s*, amphitheatre 2*s*. 6*d*. Performance commences at 8 or 8.30 p.m. Operas have also been given here at 'theatre' prices — *i.e.* about 50 per cent. lower than those just mentioned. In winter, stalls 6*s*., stage stalls 4*s*., grand circle 2*s*. 6*d*., balcony stalls 2*s*., promenade 1*s*. Doors open at 7.30, performance commences at 8 p.m.

DRURY LANE THEATRE, between Drury Lane and Brydges Street, near Covent Garden, where Garrick, Kean, the Kembles, and Mrs. Siddons used to act. Shakspeare's plays, comedies, spectacular plays, English opera. etc. Pantomime in winter. Stalls 10*s*., dress circle 7*s*. & 6*s*., first circle 5*s*. and 4*s*., balcony 3*s*., pit 2*s*., gallery 1*s*., second gallery 6*d*. No fees. Begins at 7.30 p.m. The vestibule contains a statue of *Kean* as Hamlet, by Carew, and others.

LYCEUM THEATRE, Strand, corner of Wellington Street. Shakspearian pieces, comedies, etc. (Mr. Henry Irving and Miss Ellen Terry). Stalls 10*s*. 6*d*., dress circle 6*s*. 6*d*., upper circle 4*s*., pit 2*s*., gallery 1*s*. Performance begins at 7.30 p.m. No fees.

HAYMARKET THEATRE, at the S. end of the Haymarket. English comedy. Stalls 10*s*., dress circle 7*s*., first circle 4*s*. & 5*s*., upper circle 2*s*., gallery 1*s*. Begins at 7.45 p.m. No fees.

ST. JAMES'S THEATRE, King Street, St. James's Square. Comedies. Stalls 10*s*. 6*d*., dress circle 6*s*. 6*d*., boxes 4*s*., pit 2*s*. 6*d*., gallery 1*s*. No fees. Commences at 8 p.m.

SAVOY THEATRE, Savoy Place, Strand (electric light). Gilbert and Sullivan's operettas. Stalls 10s. 6d., balcony 7s. 6d., first circle 4s., **pit 2s. 6d.**, amphitheatre 2s., gallery 1s. No fees. Begins at 8 p.m.

PRINCESS'S THEATRE, **150 Oxford Street, between** Oxford Circus and Tottenham **Court Road. Comedies, operettas,** etc. Stalls 10s., dress circle 6s., boxes 3s., pit 2s., amphitheatre **1s.** 6d., **gallery 1s.** Begins **at** 8 p.m.

**ROYAL ADELPHI** THEATRE, 411 Strand (N. side), near **Bedford Street. Melodramas** and farces. Stalls 10s., balcony stalls 6s., **upper circle 3s., pit** 2s., gallery 1s. Begins at 7.15 p.m.

ROYAL STRAND THEATRE, Strand, near Somerset House. Comedies, opera-bouffes, and burlesques. Stalls **10s. 6d., dress** circle 6s., boxes 4s., pit 2s., amphitheatre 1s. **Begins** at 8 p.m.

**GAIETY** THEATRE, **345 Strand. Comedies, operettas, farces.** Orchestra stalls 10s. 6d., balcony stalls **6s. & 7s., upper boxes** 4s., pit 2s. 6d., gallery **1s. Begins at 8 p.m. No fees.**

OPÉRA COMIQUE, **299 Strand. Operettas, etc. Stalls 10s.,** balcony stalls 7s. 6d. and 6s., boxes 4s., **first circle 2s., gallery** 1s. Commences at 8 p.m. **This theatre is built end to end with the** Globe (see below), and like it is partly **below the level of the street.**

VAUDEVILLE THEATRE, 404 Strand. Comedies (Sheridan), farces, **and burlesques.** Stalls 10s., balcony stalls 6s., boxes 4s., **upper** circle 2s. 6d., pit 2s., **gallery 1s.** Begins at 8 p.m.

GLOBE THEATRE, Newcastle Street, Strand. Operettas, comedies, etc. Stalls **10s.** 6d., dress circle 6s., upper **boxes 3s.,** pit 2s., gallery 1s. and 6d. Begins at 8 p.m. No **fees.**

**ROYAL COURT THEATRE,** Sloane Square, Chelsea. **Comedies, farces, etc.** Stalls 10s. 6d., dress circle **7s. 6d., upper circle** 4s., pit 2s. 6d., gallery 1s. No fees. **Commences at 8 p.m.**

CRITERION THEATRE, Piccadilly **East. Comedies, farces,** etc. **(Mr.** Charles Wyndham). **Stalls** 10s. **6d., dress circle 7s., family** circle 3s. Begins at 8 p.m.

TOOLE'S THEATRE, King William **Street, Strand.** Burlesques, etc. **(Mr.** Toole). Stalls 10s., dress circle 4s. & 6s., upper circle 3s., **pit** 2s. 6d., gallery **1s.** Begins **at 7.30** p.m.

GARRICK **THEATRE,** Charing Cross Road. Comedies and dramas (Mr. John Hare). Stalls 10s. 6d., dress circle **7s., upper boxes** 4s., pit 2s. 6d., gallery **1s.** Begins at 8.15 **p.m.**

SHAFTESBURY THEATRE, **Shaftesbury Avenue.** Comedies, **etc.** Stalls 10s., balcony stalls 6s., upper **circle 3s., pit 2s.,** amphitheatre 1s. 6d., gallery 1s.

LYRIC THEATRE, Shaftesbury Avenue. Comedy-operas. Stalls **10s.** 6d., balcony stalls 7s. 6d. and 6s., circle 4s., pit 2s. 6d., gallery 1s.

TERRY'S THEATRE, 105 Strand. Comedies, domestic dramas, etc. (Mr. Edward Terry). Stalls 10s. 6d., **dress circle** 7s. **6d.** and 6s., **upper** boxes 4s., pit **2s. 6d., gallery** 1s.

Avenue Theatre, Northumberland Avenue. Operettas. Stalls 10s. 6d., dress circle 7s. 6d. and 6s. (last row 4s.), upper boxes 3s., pit 2s., **gallery** 1s. Begins at 8.15 p.m.

Prince of Wales Theatre, **Coventry** Street, Haymarket. **Comedies.** Stalls 10s. 6d., pit 2s. 6d., gallery 1s. Begins at 7.30 p.m.

Royal Olympic Theatre, **Wych** Street, Strand. Comedies, **farces,** and extravaganzas.

Royal Comedy Theatre, Panton Street, Haymarket. Comic operas. Begins at 8 p.m. Prices from 1s. to 4l. 4s.

Royalty Theatre, 73 Dean Street, Soho. Burlesques, farces, and opera-bouffes. **Stalls** 12s. 6d., dress circle 10s. 6d. and 7s. 6d., upper boxes 6s. and 5s., pit 2s. 6d., amphitheatre 1s. 6d. Performance begins at 7.30 p.m.

Novelty Theatre, Great Queen Street, Lincoln's Inn Fields.

Grand Theatre, High Street, Islington. Comedies, melodramas, operettas, etc.; pantomime in winter. Stalls 3s., pit stalls 1s. **6d.,** pit 1s., gallery 6d. Commences at 7.30 p.m.

National Standard Theatre, 204 Shoreditch High Street. Popular pieces. Stalls 4s., balcony 3s., lower circle 2s., upper boxes 1s. 6d., pit stalls 1s., gallery 6d. Begins at 7 p.m.

Marylebone Theatre, Church Street, near Edgware Road Station. **Dramas and farces.** Begins at 7 p.m.

Pavilion Theatre, Whitechapel, with accommodation for nearly **4000** persons. Nautical dramas, melodramas, farces. Admission 1s. 6d., 1s., 6d., and 4d. Begins at 7.15 p.m.

Imperial Theatre, Royal Aquarium, Westminster (see p. 218). Comedies, burlesques, and farces. Stalls 7s., dress circle 5s., boxes 3s., pit 2s., amphitheatre 1s. Begins at 8 p.m.

New Sadler's Wells Theatre, **St.** John Street Road, **Clerkenwell.** Standard plays. Stalls 4s., **dress circle 3s., boxes and pit 1s.,** gallery **6d.** Begins at 7.30 p.m. No fees.

Sanger's **Amphitheatre,** Westminster Bridge Road, Lambeth, built in 1805 of the wood of an old man-of-war, burned down in 1841, and re-erected in 1850. Equestrian performances, spectacles, **and** farces. Dress circle 4s., orchestra stalls 2s. 6d., boxes 2s., pit 1s., gallery 6d. Begins at 7.30 p.m.

Royal Surrey Theatre, 124 Blackfriars Road. Melodramas **and farces.** Stalls 3s., dress circle 2s., boxes 1s., pit 6d., gallery **4d.** Begins at 7 p.m.

Britannia Theatre, Hoxton Street, in the N.E. **of** London, holding nearly **3400 persons.** Melodramas. Admission 2s., 1s., 6d., **and 3d. Commences at 7 p.m.**

Elephant and Castle Theatre, New Kent Road. Popular performances. Prices 3d. to 2s.

Many of **the** theatres also **give afternoon** performances.

## 13. Concerts and other Amusements.

*Concerts.*

WILLIS'S ROOMS, formerly called *Almack's* (see p. 220), King Street, St. James's, for **concerts and balls.**

ST. JAMES'S HALL, with entrances from the Regent Street Quadrant and Piccadilly, used for concerts, balls, and public meetings. Among the concerts given here are the *Philharmonic Concerts*, those of the *Musical Union*, those of the *Sacred Harmonic Society* (oratorios) and the favourite *Monday and Saturday Popular Concerts*, held every Monday evening at 8 o'clock and every Saturday afternoon at 3 o'clock during the season, at which classical music is performed by eminent artistes. Admission to the last-named concerts: stalls 5s., front gallery 3s., other parts of the hall 1s.

ROYAL ALBERT HALL, South Kensington (p. 270), for musical fêtes and concerts on a large scale, but at uncertain intervals.

CRYSTAL PALACE, Sydenham (p. 305); numerous concerts by a good orchestra and celebrated artistes.

ALEXANDRA PALACE, Muswell Hill (p. 316); **concerts and theatrical performances.**

AGRICULTURAL HALL, Islington. Occasional concerts, which are advertised in the daily papers.

ST. GEORGE'S HALL, 4 Langham Place, W.

STEINWAY HALL, **Lower** Seymour **Street,** Portman **Square.**

STORE STREET HALL, **Store** Street, **Bedford** Square.

PRINCESS'S CONCERT ROOM, at the **back of the** Princess's Theatre (p. 41); **occasional** concerts.

ALBERT **PALACE,** on the S. side of Battersea Park.

PRINCE'S HALL, Piccadilly, opposite Sackville Street.

INTERNATIONAL HALL, **above** the Café Monico (p. 13).

*Music Halls, Public Gardens, Concerts and Comic Operas, and Circuses.*

ALHAMBRA, **Leicester Square (elaborate ballets). Begins at** 7.30 p.m. Fauteuils 5s., stalls and promenade 3s., pit stalls 1s.

EMPIRE THEATRE OF VARIETIES, Leicester Square (also with good ballets). Prices 5s., 3s., 2s., 1s., 6d.

LONDON PAVILION, Piccadilly. Begins at 7.30 p.m. Prices 1s., 1s. 6d., 3s., 5s.

CANTERBURY THEATRE OF VARIETIES, 143 Westminster Bridge Road. Entertainment begins at 7.30 p.m. Adm. from 6d.

TROCADERO (late *Argyll Rooms*), Great Windmill Street, Shaftesbury Avenue. Admission 1s., 2s., 3s. Performance at 7.30 p.m.

ROYAL VICTORIA COFFEE MUSIC HALL, Waterloo Bridge Road, Lambeth, formerly the Victoria Palace Theatre. Open at 7 p.m. Prices from 3d. to 10s. 6d. (private box).

FORESTERS' HALL, 93 **Cambridge** Road, E.

## 13. ENTERTAINMENTS.

METROPOLITAN MUSIC HALL, 267 Edgware Road.
THE OXFORD, 14 Oxford Street, near Tottenham **Court** Road.
PARAGON **THEATRE** OF VARIETIES, Mile End Road. Begins at
**7.30 p.m.** Admission from 6d. upwards.
PECKHAM THEATRE OF VARIETIES, Commercial Road, Peckham, S.E.
CAMBRIDGE HALL OF VARIETIES, 136 Commercial Street, E. Adm. from 3d.
SOUTH LONDON PALACE OF AMUSEMENTS, 92 London Road, St. George's Fields, near the Elephant and Castle. Concerts, ballets, etc. This is the largest concert room in London, seating 5000 persons. Admission 2s., **1s. 6d.**, 1s., 6d., and 3d.
ROSHERVILLE GARDENS, Gravesend. Music, dancing, theatre, zoological collection. Admission 6d. Reached by rail or steamer. Open in summer **only.**
HENGLER'S **CIRCUS, 7A** Argyll Street, Oxford Circus. Begins at
**8 p.m. Prices 1-5s.**
**There are also** various public dancing rooms in different parts **of the town, the** company at which is far from select.

*Exhibitions and Entertainments.*

MADAME TUSSAUD'S WAXWORK EXHIBITION, Marylebone Road, **near Baker** Street Station, a well-known and interesting collection of wax **figures** of ancient **and** modern notabilities. The best time for visiting it is in the **evening, by** gaslight. Admission 1s. — At the **back** (6d. extra) is a **room with** various memorials of Napoleon I. **(including his** travelling carriage, captured by the Prussians at **Genappe,** and bought by Madame Tussaud for 2500l.), and also the **'Chamber** of Horrors', containing casts and portraits of executed **criminals,** the guillotine which decapita**ted** Louis XVI. and Marie Antoinette, **and other articles of a** like ghastly nature.
  *Mme. Tussaud*, **a Swiss by birth, came to London** in 1802, lost her **first collection of waxworks by shipwreck on the** way to Ireland, started a new one, **and died in** London **in** 1850 at the age of ninety. The exhibition is still **under** the management **of her** great-grandson.
  MR. AND MRS. **GERMAN** REED'S DRAMATIC AND MUSICAL ENTER**TAINMENT, St. George's Hall,** 4 Langham Place. Adm. 1-5s.
  **EGYPTIAN HALL, Piccadilly,** opposite **Burlington** Arcade. Mas**kelyne and Cooke's conjuring** and illusionary performances (at 3 **and** 8 p.m.; **5s., 3s., 2s., 1s.), concerts, art** exhibitions, etc.
  MOORE AND BURGESS **MINSTRELS** (Christy Minstrels), St. James's Hall, Regent Street and Piccadilly. Adm. 5s., 3s., 2s. and 1s. At 8 p.m. daily; and on Mondays, Wednesdays, and Saturdays at 3 p.m. also.
  ROYAL AQUARIUM AND SUMMER AND WINTER GARDEN, Broad Sanctuary, Westminster (p. 217). Theatre, concerts, ballets, acrobatic, pantomimic, and conjuring performances. Adm. 1s.
  NATIONAL AGRICULTURAL HALL (OLYMPIA), opposite the Addison **Road Station, Kensington, a huge amphitheatre,** holding 10,000

people, for equestrian and spectacular performances, shows, exhibitions, etc. Adm. 1s., 1s. 6d., 2s. 6d., 5s.

AGRICULTURAL HALL, Liverpool Road, Islington. Cattle shows, military tournaments, lectures, dioramas, concerts, etc.

PICCADILLY HALL, exhibitions, etc.

NIAGARA IN LONDON, York Street, Westminster (near St. James's Park Station). A cycloramic representation of the Falls of Niagara, by *Phillippoteaux*; open daily 10-10 (adm. 1s.).

The large open space between West Kensington, Earl's Court, and West Brompton stations (see Pl. G, 1, 2) is used for Exhibitions of various kinds (In 1889 the *Spanish Exhibition*).

## Exhibitions of Pictures.

ROYAL ACADEMY OF FINE ARTS, Burlington House, Piccadilly (p. 221). Exhibition of the works of modern English painters and sculptors, from first Monday in May to first Monday in August. Open daily 8-7; admission 1s., catalogue 6d. Exhibition of the works of Ancient Masters in January and February. Diploma galleries, open throughout the year (see p. 221; entrance to the right of the main entrance).

GROSVENOR GALLERY, 137 New Bond Street. Summer and winter exhibitions. Admission 1s.

THE NEW GALLERY, 121 Regent Street. Summer and winter exhibitions. Admission 1s. Paintings by *Mr. Burne Jones*, *Mr. Watts*, *Mr. William Morris*, and others.

EXHIBITION OF THE ROYAL SOCIETY OF PAINTERS IN WATER-COLOURS, 5 Pall Mall East. Open from Easter to the end of July, and from December to March; admission 1s., catalogue 1s.

ROYAL INSTITUTE OF PAINTERS IN WATER-COLOURS, Piccadilly Galleries, 191 Piccadilly. Exhibitions from Easter to the end of July (9-6; 1s.) and from 1st Dec. to end of Feb. (10-4; 1s.).

DUDLEY GALLERY, Egyptian Hall, Piccadilly. Various exhibitions.

ROYAL SOCIETY OF BRITISH ARTISTS, 6 Suffolk Street, Pall Mall. Exhibitions from 1st April to 1st Aug. (9-6) and from 1st Dec. to 1st March (9-5). Admission 1s.

SOCIETY OF LADY ARTISTS. Summer exhibition in the Egyptian Hall, Piccadilly; admission 1s., catalogue 6d.

DORÉ GALLERY, 35 New Bond Street (p. 226). Open daily from 10 to 6; admission 1s.

There are also in winter and spring various **exhibitions of** French, Belgian, German, and other paintings at 120 Pall Mall (French Gallery), **39** Old Bond Street (Agnew's), 47 New Bond Street (Hanover Gallery), 116 & **117** New Bond Street, 148 New Bond Street, 5 Haymarket (Mr. Tooth), the Conduit Street Galleries (Nineteenth Century Art Society), the **St. James's** Gallery, King Street (Mr. Mendoza), etc. Usual charge 1s.

## 14. Races, Sports, and Games.

Horse-Racing. The principal race-meetings taking place within easy distance of London are the following: —

1. The *Epsom Summer Meeting*, at which the *Derby* and *Oaks* are run. The former invariably takes place on a Wednesday, and the latter on a Friday, the date being generally within a fortnight before or after Whitsuntide.

The Derby was instituted by the Earl of Derby in 1780, and the value of the stakes now sometimes exceeds 6000l. The length of the course is 1½ M., and it was gone over by Kettledrum in 1861 in 2 min. 45 sec., the shortest time on record. Both horses and mares are allowed to compete for the Derby (mares carrying 3lb. less weight), while the Oaks is confined to mares. In both cases the age of the horses running must be three years. To view these races London empties itself annually by road and rail, even Parliament suspending its sitting on Derby Day, in spite of the ever recurring opposition. The London and Brighton Railway Company (London Bridge and Victoria stations) have a station at Epsom close to the course, and this is the most convenient route. It may also be reached by the London and South Western Railway from Waterloo. The increased facilities of reaching Epsom by train have somewhat diminished the popularity of the road; but the traveller who would see the Derby Day and its characteristic sights thoroughly will not regret his choice if he select the latter. A decently appointed open carriage and pair, holding four persons, will cost 8-10l., everything included. A hansom cab can be had for rather less than half that amount, but an arrangement should be made with the driver on the previous day. The appearance of Epsom Downs on Derby Day, crowded with myriads of human beings, is one of the most striking and animated sights ever witnessed in the neighbourhood of London, and will interest the ordinary visitor more than the great race itself.

2. The *Ascot Week* is about a fortnight after the Derby. The Gold Cup Day is on Thursday, when some members of the Royal Family usually drive up the course in state, attended by the master and huntsmen of the Royal Buckhounds. The course is reached by train from Waterloo; or the visitor may travel by the Great Western Railway (Paddington Station) to Windsor and drive thence to Ascot.

3. At *Sandown*, near Esher, and at *Kempton Park*, Sunbury, races and steeplechases are held several times during the year.

4. The *Epsom Spring Meeting*, lasting for three days, on one of which the City and Suburban Handicap is decided.

Besides the above there are numerous smaller race-meetings near London, but with the exception of that at *Croydon* they will hardly repay the trouble of a visit, as they are largely patronised by the 'rough' element. The stranger should, if possible, attend races and other public gatherings in company with a friend who is well acquainted with the best method of seeing the sport. Much trouble and disappointment will be thereby avoided.

*Newmarket*, the headquarters of racing, is situated on the Great Eastern Railway, at some distance from London. As the accommodation of the town is limited, beds and living rise to famine prices during race times, and even then are not always obtainable. A better plan is to stay at Cambridge and to drive over, but this involves no little expense. All the races at Newmarket are run on the Heath, but not, as in other places, over the same ground. The spectator has to move about from place to place, and this, on foot, is tiring work. In short, racing at Newmarket is a business, and does not offer the same attractions to a visitor as at

Epsom or **Ascot** (comp. *Baedeker's Great Britain*). — *Goodwood Races*, see *Baedeker's Great Britain*.

**Hunting.** This **sport is carried on** throughout England **from autumn** to spring. **Cub-hunting** generally begins in September and continues until **31st Oct.** Regular **fox-hunting** then takes its place and lasts till **about** the middle **of April. Hare-hunting** lasts from 28th Oct. **to 27th Feb.**, and **buck-hunting begins on 14th** Sept. Should **the traveller be staying in the country he will probably have** but little **difficulty in seeing a meet of a pack of fox-hounds. The** Surrey **fox-hounds are** the nearest **to London. There is a pack of** harriers **at Brighton.** The Royal **Buckhounds often meet in the** vicinity **of Windsor, and** when **this is** the case the **journey can be easily made from London. The quarry** is a stag, **which is allowed** to escape from a cart. The huntsmen **and** whippers-in **wear a** scarlet and gold **uniform.** The followers of the hounds wear **scarlet, black,** and indeed **any** colour, **and** this diversity, coupled **with the** large attendance in carriages, on foot, **and** on horseback, **makes the scene a very lively one. For** meets **of** hounds, **see the** *Field* or *Bell's Life*.

**Fishing** (roach, **perch, gudgeon, pike, barbel, and trout**) can be indulged in at all places on the *Thames* between Richmond **and** Wallingford. No permission is required, **except** in private waters. The services of a fisherman, who will furnish a punt and all tackle, can be secured at **a** charge **of** about 10s. per day, the hirer providing him with dinner and beer. The *Lea* (p. 317), **Darent,** *Brent, Colne*, etc., also afford good opportunities to the London angler. See the *Angler's Diary* (Field Office, 346 Strand; 1s. 6d.) or *Dickens's Dictionary of the Thames* (1s.), and compare pp. **317,** 318.

**Cricket.** *Lord's* at St. John's Wood (p. 233), the headquarters of the Marylebone Club, **is the** chief cricket **ground** in London. Here are played, in June and July, the Eton **and Harrow, and the** Oxford and Cambridge **matches,** besides many others. The *Kennington Oval* (p. 292) the headquarters of the Surrey County Club, is also an important cricket-centre. RACKET and TENNIS COURTS are attached to both these grounds.

**Athletics.** The chief scene of athletic sports of **all kinds is** *Stamford Bridge*, on the Fulham Road, where the *London Athletic Club* has its headquarters. **The** Amateur Championships of the United Kingdom are decided here when these sports are **held in** London (every third year). The University Sports, **between** Oxford and Cambridge, take place at Queen's Ground, Kensington, in the Boat Race week (p. 48). The card comprises nine 'events', and the university whose representatives secure the majority is the winner. The *German Gymnastic Society*, 26 Pancras Road, King's Cross, takes the lead among all gymnastic clubs; about half of its 7-800 members are English. The *Amateur Athletic Association* consists of representatives of the leading athletic clubs.

## 14. RACES, SPORTS, GAMES.

**Boxing.** Among the chief boxing clubs in London are the *West London Boxing Club* and the *Cestus Boxing Club*, and there are also boxing clubs in connection with the German **Gymnastic** Society, the London Athletic Club, etc. Most of these are affiliated to the *Amateur Boxing Association*. A competition for amateur boxers is held yearly, the prizes being handsome challenge cups presented by the Marquis of Queensberry.

**Lawn Tennis.** The governing and controlling body for this pastime is the *Lawn Tennis Association* (sec., Mr. H. Chipp), established in 1888. The Lawn Tennis Championship of the World is competed for early in July on the ground of the *All England Lawn Tennis Club*, Wimbledon, and other important competitions take place at Stamford Bridge, Hyde Park (Covered Court Championship), etc. Courts open to strangers are found at the Crystal Palace, Battersea Park, and other public gardens, drill-halls, etc., but as a rule this game cannot be enjoyed to perfection except in club or private grounds.

**Cycling.** There are now a great many bicycling and tricycling clubs in London, the oldest of which was founded in 1870. The chief bicycle race-meetings are held at the Alexandra Park, Stamford Bridge, Surbition, and the Crystal Palace. The annual muster of the clubs sometimes attracts thousands of cyclists.

The headquarters of the *National Cyclists' Union* are at 57 Basinghall Street, E. C. (sec., Mr. Finlay Macrae), and those of the *Cyclists' Touring Club* are at 139 Fleet Street (sec., Mr. E. R. Shipton). The chief consul for the foreign district of the latter club is Mr. S. A. Stead, 19 Tabley Road, Holloway. An exhibition of **bicycles**, tricycles, and their accessories, called the *Stanley Show*, is held in London annually. Compare the *Cycling Times* (Whitefriars Street) or the *Monthly Gazette* of the Cyclists' Touring Club.

**Aquatics.** The chief **event in the year is** the *Oxford and Cambridge Boat Race*, rowed on the second Saturday before Easter. The course is on the Thames, from Putney **to Mortlake; the** distance is just over $4\frac{1}{4}$ M., and the time **occupied in rowing it varies from just under** 20 min. to 23 min., **according to the state of the wind and tide.** The Londoners pour **out to see** the boat-race **in** almost as great **at crowds as to** the Derby, sympathetically exhibiting in some portion **of their attire** either the dark blue colours of Oxford or the light blue of the sister university. There are also several regattas held upon the **Thames.** The best are **those** at *Henley* (at the end of **June** or the beginning **of** July), *Marlow*, *Staines*, and *Walton*. To Henley crews are usually sent from the universities of Oxford, Cambridge, and Dublin, by Eton College, and by the London Rowing **Club,** the Leander, the Thames Club, and other clubs of more or less note. Crews from American universities sometimes take part in the proceedings. On **Aug.** 1st a boat-race takes place among young **Thames** watermen for *Doggett's Coat and Badge*, a prize founded by Doggett, the comedian, in 1715. **Yacht** races are held at the mouth of the Thames during summer. See the *Rowing Almanack*

(1s.; Field Office, 346 Strand) or *Dickens's Dictionary of the Thames* (1s.).

**Swimming.** Of the numerous swimming clubs in London, most of which belong to the *Swimming Association of Great Britain* (see., Mr. Barron, Goswell Hall, Goswell Road, E.C.), the most important are the *Ilex*, *Otter*, and *Serpentine*. The races for the amateur championship of Great Britain take place at the Welsh Harp, Hendon (p. 332), and those for the professional championship in the Thames at Putney. The races are swum in 'university costume', and may be witnessed by ladies.

## 15. Embassies and Consulates. Bankers.
### Embassies.

*America, United States of.* Legation, 123 Victoria Street, S.W. (office-hours 11-3); minister, Hon. Robert T. Lincoln. Consulate (office), 12 St. Helen's Place, Bishopsgate, E.C.

*Austria.* Embassy, 18 Belgrave Square. Consulate, 11 Queen Victoria Street, E.C.

*Belgium.* Legation, 36 Grosvenor Gardens, S.W. Consulate, 118 Bishopsgate Street Within, E.C.

*Brazil.* Legation, 32 Grosvenor Gardens, S.W. Consulate, 6 Great Winchester Street, E.C.

*China.* Legation, 49 Portland Place, W.

*Denmark.* Legation, 19 Grosvenor Square. Consulate, 5 Muscovy Court, Tower Hill, E. C.

*France.* Embassy, Albert Gate House, Hyde Park. General Consulate, 38 Finsbury Circus.

*Germany.* Embassy, 9 Carlton House Terrace. General Consulate, 5 Blomfield Street, London Wall, E. C.

*Greece.* Legation, 5 St. James Street, S.W. Consulate, 19 Great Winchester Street, E.C.

*Italy.* Embassy, 20 Grosvenor Square, W. General Consulate, 31 Old Jewry.

*Japan.* Legation, 9 Cavendish Square, W. Consulate, 84 Bishopsgate Street Within, E. C.

*Netherlands.* Legation, 40 Grosvenor Gardens. Consulate, 40 Finsbury Circus, E. C.

*Persia.* Legation, 80 Holland Park, W. Consulate, 1 Drapers' Gardens, Throgmorton Avenue, E. C.

*Portugal.* Embassy, 12 Gloucester Place, Portman Square, W. Consulate, 3 Throgmorton Avenue, E. C.

*Russia.* Embassy, Chesham House, Belgrave Square. Consulate, 17 Great Winchester Street, City.

*Spain.* Embassy, 46 Portland Place, W. Consulate, 21 Billiter Street, E. C.

*Sweden and Norway.* Legation, 47 Charles Street, Berkeley Square, W. Consulate, 24 Great Winchester Street, E. C.

*Switzerland.* Consulate, 25 Old Broad Street.
*Turkey.* Embassy, 1 Bryanston Square. Consulate, Union Court, Old Broad Street, E. C.

### Bankers.

PRIVATE BANKS: — Messrs. *Barclay, Bevan, & Co.*, 54 Lombard Street; *Lloyd, Barnett, & Bosanquet*, 72 Lombard Street; *Child.* 1 Fleet Street; *Coutts*, 56-59 Strand; *Drummond*, 49 Charing Cross; **Herries**, *Farquhar, & Co.*, 16 St. James's Street; **Hoare & Co.**, 37 Fleet Street; *Prueds & Co.*, 189 Fleet Street; *Ransom, Bouverie, & Co.*, 1 Pall Mall East; *Robarts, Lubbock, & Co.*, 15 Lombard Street; *Smith, Payne, & Smiths*, 1 Lombard Street; **Williams, Deacon, & Co.**, 20 Birchin Lane, etc.
JOINT STOCK BANKS: — *London and County*, 21 Lombard Street; *London Joint Stock*, 5 Prince's Street, Bank; *London and Provincial*, 7 Bank Buildings; *London and South Western*, 168 Fenchurch Street; **London and** *Westminster*, 41 Lothbury; *Union Bank of London*, 2 Prince's Street, Mansion House, E. C.; *Glyn, Mills, & Co.*, 67 Lombard Street, etc.
AMERICAN BANKS: — *Brown, Shipley, & Co.*, Founders Court, Lothbury, E. C.; *Baring Brothers*, 7-9 Bishopsgate Street Within, E.C.; **J. S.** *Morgan & Co. (Drexel & Co.)*, 22 Old Broad Street, E. C.; **Knauth**, *Nachod, & Kühne*, at the Alliance Bank, Bartholomew Lane, E. C.

All the banking **companies** have branch-offices in different parts of London, some as **many as** fifteen or twenty.

MONEY-CHANGERS. *Osborne & Gall*, 264 Strand; *Reinhardt & Co.*, 14 Coventry Street; **Whiteley**, 31-61 Westbourne Grove; *Smart*, 19 Westbourne Grove; *Cook's Tourist Offices*, Ludgate Circus, 445 Strand, 35 Piccadilly, 82 Oxford Street, Euston Road (in front of St. Pancras Station), and at the corner of Gracechurch Street and Leadenhall Street; *Gaze's Tourist Office*, 142 Strand; *United States Exchange* (p. 17); *Lady Guide Association* (p. 55).

## 16. Divine Service.

To enable visitors belonging to different religious denominations to attend their respective places of worship, a list is here given of the principal churches in London. The denominations are arranged in alphabetical order. The chief edifices of the Church of England are noticed throughout the Handbook, but it may not be invidious here to specify *Canon Farrar* of Westminster Abbey, **Canon Liddon** of St. Paul's Cathedral, and *Dean Vaughan* of the Temple, **as** among the **most eminent preachers in** London.

There are about 800 churches of the Church of England in London or its immediate vicinity, of which 100 are parish churches in the City, 50 parish churches in the Metropolitan district beyond, and 250 ecclesiastical **parish or** district churches or chapels, **some** connected with asylums, missions, etc. Of the Nonconformist churches, which amount to about 600 in all, 240 are Independent, 130 Baptist, 150 Wesleyan, and 50 Roman Catholic. — The hours named after each church are those of divine service on Sundays; when no hour is specified it is understood that the hours of the regular Sunday services are 11 a.m. and 6.30 p.m. Many of the Saturday morning and evening papers give a list of the principal preachers on Sunday.

BAPTIST CHAPELS: — *Metropolitan Tabernacle*, Newington Butts, close to the Elephant and Castle (p. 78); *Rev. C. H. Spurgeon* (general public admitted to all vacant seats 5 min. before the beginning of service; strangers may obtain early admission by applying at the doors for an envelope, in which they are requested to place a donation for the Tabernacle). — *Bloomsbury Chapel*, Bloomsbury Street, Oxford Street; services at 11 and 7. — *Park Square Chapel*, Regent's Park; services at 11 and 7.

CATHOLIC APOSTOLIC CHURCHES: — Gordon Square, Euston Road; services at 6, 10, 2, 4.15, 5, and 7. — College Street, Chelsea; services at 6, 10, 5, and 7. — Duncan Street, Islington.

CONGREGATIONALISTS or INDEPENDENTS: *City Temple*, Holborn Viaduct *(Dr. Parker)*; services at 11 and 7 (lecture on Thurs. at noon). — *Union Chapel*, Islington *(Dr. Allon)*. — *Westminster Chapel*, James Street, Westminster. — *Whitefield Tabernacle*, Tottenham Court Road. — *Kensington Chapel*, Allen Street, Kensington. — *Christ Church*, Westminster Bridge Road *(Rev. Newman Hall)*.

FRIENDS or QUAKERS: — Meeting-houses at 52 St. Martin's Lane, Trafalgar Square, and Devonshire House, 12 Bishopsgate Street; services at 11 and 6.

INDEPENDENTS, see Congregationalists.

IRVINGITES, see Catholic Apostolic Churches.

JEWS: — *Great* Central Synagogue, 129 Great Portland Street. — *New Synagogue*, Great St. Helen's, St. Mary Axe, Leadenhall Street. — *West London Synagogue*, 34 Upper Berkeley Street, Edgware Road. — *Great Synagogue* (German), 52 New Bond Street, City. — *Bayswater Synagogue*, St. Petersburg Place, Bayswater Road. — Service begins at sunset on Fridays.

METHODISTS. a. Wesleyan Methodists: — *Wesley's Chapel*, 47 City Road; *Great Queen Street Chapel*, Lincoln's Inn Fields; *Finsbury Park Chapel*, Wilberforce Road; *Hinde Street Chapel*, Manchester Square; *Mostyn Road Chapel*, Brixton Road; *Peckham Chapel*, Queen's Road, Peckham; *Welsh Wesleyan Chapel*, 57 City Road. — b. Other Methodists: — *Brunswick Chapel* (New Connexion), 156 Great Dover Street, Southwark; *Elim Chapel* (Primitive Methodists), Fetter Lane, Fleet Street; *United Methodist Free Chapel*, Willow Street, Tabernacle Square, Moorgate; *United Free Chapel*, Queen's Road, Bayswater.

NEW JERUSALEM or SWEDENBORGIAN CHURCHES: — Palace Gardens Terrace, Kensington. — Argyle Square. King's Cross. — Camden Road, Holloway. — *College Chapel*, Devonshire Street, Islington. — Flodden Road, Camberwell. Services at 11 and 7.

PRESBYTERIANS: — *Scottish National Church* (Church of Scotland), Pont Street, Belgravia. — *Regent Square Church*, Regent's Square, Gray's Inn Road *(Rev. J. MacNeil)*; services at 11 and 7. — *Marylebone Church*, Upper George Street, Bryanston Square, Edgware Road *(Dr. Donald Fraser).* — *St. John's Wood Presbyterian Church*, Marlborough Place, St. John's Wood *(Dr. Munro Gibson).* — *Welsh Calvinist Chapel*, Cambridge Circus, Charing Cross Road.

ROMAN CATHOLICS: — *St. George's Cathedral*, Westminster Bridge Road (see p. 299); various services. — *Pro-Cathedral*, Newland Terrace, Kensington Road; services at 8, 9, 10, 11, 3, and 7. — *Oratory*, Brompton Road; various services. — *Berkeley Mews Chapel* (Jesuits), Farm Street, close to Berkeley Square. — *St. Mary's Chapel*, Moorfields. — *St. Mary of the Angels*, Westmoreland Road, Bayswater. — *St. Etheldreda's*, Ely Place, Holborn; principal services at 11 and 7. — *St. Patrick's*, Sutton Street, Soho Square. — High Mass usually begins at 11 a.m., and Vespers at 7 p.m.

SWEDENBORGIANS. see New Jerusalem Churches.

UNITARIANS: — *Bedford Chapel*, Bloomsbury Street *(Rev. Stopford Brooke);* services at 11 and 7. — *Little Portland Street Chapel (Rev. P. H. Wicksteed); Unity Church*, Islington *(Rev. I. W. Freckelton), Rosslyn Hill Chapel*, Hampstead *(Dr. Sadler); Mall Chapel*, Notting Hill; *Wandsworth Chapel.*

WESLEYANS, see Methodists.

The services of the *South Place Ethical Society (Dr. Stanton Coit)* are held at the South Place Institute at 11.15 a.m. — The lectures of the *Ethical Society* are held in Essex Hall, Essex Street, Strand, at 7.30 p.m.

Foreign Churches: — *Bavarian Chapel* (Roman Catholic), 12 Warwick Street, Regent Street; services at 8, 9, 10, 11.15, 3.30, and 7. — *Danish Church* (Lutheran), King Street, Poplar; service at 10.30 a.m. — *Dutch Church* (Reformed Calvinist), 6 Austin Friars, near the Bank; service at 11 a.m. — *French Protestant*, Athenæum Hall, 73 Tottenham Court Road (pending the erection of a new church); services at 11 and 7. — *French Protestant Evangelical Church*, Monmouth Road, Westbourne Grove, Bayswater; services at 11 and 7. — *French Protestant Anglican Church*, 36 Bloomsbury Street, Oxford Street; services at 11 and 3.30. — *French Roman Catholic* Chapels, Little George Street, King Street, Portman Square, and at Leicester Place, Leicester Square; various services. — *German Lutheran Church* (lately in the Savoy), 43 Cleveland Street, Fitzroy Square; services at 11 and 6.45. — *German Lutheran Church*, Dalston. — *German Church* at Forest Hill. — *German Evangelical Church*, Fowler Road, Islington. — *German Methodist Church (Böhlerkirche)*, Commercial Road; services at 11 and 6.30. — *German Roman Catholic Chapel*, 9 Union Street, Whitechapel; services at 9, 11, 3, and 7. — *German Synagogue*, see Jews. — Greek *Chapel* (Russian), 32 Welbeck Street, Cavendish Square; service at 11 a.m. — *Greek Church* (St. Sophia), Moscow Road, Bayswater; service at 11.15 a.m. — *Italian Roman Catholic Church*, Clerkenwell Road, E.C. — *Spanish Roman Catholic Chapel*, Spanish Place, Manchester Square; numerous services. — *Swedish Protestant Church*, Prince's Square, St. George's Street, Shadwell; service at 11 a.m. — *Swiss Protestant Church*, 78 Endell Street, Long Acre; service at 11 a.m.

## 17. Post and Telegraph Offices. Parcels Companies. Commissionnaires. Lady Guides.

Post Office. The English Post Office undertakes the transmission of letters, newspapers, book-packets, patterns and samples, printed or lithographed circulars or notices, and telegrams. The GENERAL POST OFFICE is in St. Martin's le Grand (p. 90). The *Poste Restante Office* is on the S. (right) side of the portico (p. 90), and is open from 10 a.m. to 4 p.m. There is also a Poste Restante Office at the Charing Cross Station. Poste Restante letters, which should have the words 'to be called for' added to the address, are delivered to applicants on the production of their passports or other proof of identity, but it is better to give correspondents a private address. Letters addressed to persons who have not been found are kept for a month, and then sent to the *Dead Letter Office* for return to the writer, or for destruction. The value of enclosures in such letters amounts in some years to more than 200,000*l*.

Unprepaid letters are charged double postage, but may be refused by the addressee. The postage for the whole of Great Britain, Ireland, and the islands in the British seas, is 1*d*. for letters not exceeding 1 oz. The fee for registration for a letter or other packet is 2*d*.; special registered-letter envelopes are supplied at $2^{1}/_{4}$ - 3*d*. each (according to size), to which the ordinary postage must be added. For letters to the United States, Europe, and various other places included in the postal union the rate is $2^{1}/_{2}d$. for letters under $^{1}/_{2}$ oz. Newspapers are transmitted to any part of Great Britain and the adjoining islands for $^{1}/_{2}d$. each. Newspapers for abroad ($^{1}/_{2}d$. per 2 oz.) must be posted within eight days of publication, otherwise book postage rates must be paid. For *Book Packets*, *Patterns*, and *Samples* $^{1}/_{2}d$. per 2 oz. is charged for Great Britain and the countries of the postal union. No inland book packet may exceed 18 in. in length, 9 in. in width, and 6 in. in depth, or 5 lbs. in weight. *Postcards* for use in the British Islands are issued at $5^{1}/_{2}d$. or 6*d*. per packet of ten (thin and thick); for countries included in the postal union, at 1, $1^{1}/_{2}$, or 2*d*. each; reply post-cards may be had at double these rates. Envelopes of three sorts, with embossed 1*d*. stamps, and newspaper wrappers with impressed $^{1}/_{2}d$. or 1*d*. stamps, are also sold by the post office.

The number of daily deliveries of letters in London varies from six to twelve according to the distance from the head office at St. Martin's le Grand. On Sundays there is no delivery, but letters posted in the pillar boxes within the town limits and in some of the nearer suburbs are collected in time for the general day mails and for the first London district delivery on the following day. Letters for the evening mails must be posted in the pillars before 5.30 p.m., in the central districts before 6 p.m., or at the General Post Office, with an additional $^{1}/_{2}d$. stamp, up to 7.45 p.m. Foreign

## 17. POST AND TELEGRAPH OFFICES.

letters may be posted at the General Post Office till 7 p.m. with an additional 1d. stamp; till 7.15 with 2d. extra; till 7.30 with 3d. **extra**; and at the termini for Continental trains till 8 p.m. with 4d. **extra.** The head district offices are open on Sunday for **two hours.** Comp. the *Post Office Guide*, published quarterly (6d.), or the *Post Office Handbook* (half-yearly; 1d.).

**London is** divided into eight POSTAL DISTRICTS. — the Eastern, **Northern, North** Western, Western, South Western, South Eastern, **East** Central, and West Central, — which are designated by the capital letters E., N., **N.W., and** so on. Each has its district post-office, from which letters are distributed to the surrounding district. At these chief district offices letters may be posted about $1/_2$ hr. later than at the branches or pillars. The delivery of London letters is facilitated by the addition to the address of the initials of the **postal district. The number** of offices and pillars in London is upwards of **2000 and** the number of people employed by the post-office is about 11,000.

PARCEL POST. **The parcel post** was introduced into England in **1883. The rate of postage for** an inland parcel is 3d. for a weight **not exceeding 1lb.; each** additional pound $1^1/_2d$. The maximum **length allowed for such a parcel is 3** ft. 6 in., and the length and **girth combined must not exceed 6** ft.; the maximum weight is **11lbs. Insurance and compensation (up to 10l.)** are allowed. — A *Parcel Post Service*, **at various rates, is also establ**ished between **the United Kingdom and several foreign countries (not including the U**nited States) **and British colonies.**

POST OFFICE ORDERS are issued **for sums** not exceeding 10l. at the numerous *Money Order Offices* **connected with** the post-office, at least one of which is to be found in every post town in the United Kingdom. For sums under 1l. the charge for transmission is 2d.; over 1l. and under 2l., **3d.;** over **2l.** and under 4l., 4d.; over 4l. and under 7l., 5d.; over 7l. and not exceeding 10l., 6d. *Foreign Money Orders*, payable in the countries of the postal union, are issued at **a charge of 6d. up** to 2l., 1s. up to 5l., 1s. 6d. **up to 7l., and 2s.** up to 10l.

POSTAL ORDERS, **of the value of 1s.,** 1s. 6d., 2s., 2s. 6d., 3s., 3s. 6d., **4s., 4s. 6d., 5s., 7s. 6d., 10s., 10s. 6d., 15s.,** and 20s., are issued at a small **charge varying from $1/_2d$. to 2d., and** pass from hand to hand like ordi**nary money. They are payable at an**y Money Order Office **in the** United **Kingdom. If not presented for** payment within **three** months from the **last day of the month** of issue, a fresh commission is charged equal to **the original cost. By the use of n**ot more than five 1d. stamps, affixed to **the face of** the **order, any broken** amount may be made up.

TELEGRAPHS. **At one time** there were no fewer than 35 different **telegraph companies in Great** Britain, but in 1870 the whole telegraph **graph** system, with **the sole exception of** wires for the private use of the railway companies, **was taken over by** Government (p. 91). The present tariff for the transmission **of** messages by telegraph throughout the United Kingdom, **which came** into force in 1885, is $1/_2d$. per word, with a minimum charge of 6d.; the addresses **are counted as part of** the telegram. The charge for telegrams to **the United States** varies from **6d. to** 1s. per word, address included. Telegrams are received at all railway-stations and almost all post-offices throughout the country. London and its suburbs contain 300 telegraph offices, open from 8 a.m. to 8 p.m. The following seven are always open: Central Station, St. Martin's le Grand (corner of Newgate Street); St. Pancras Station; Paddington Station; Victoria Station; King's Cross Station; West Strand; Willesden Junction Station. There are in Great Britain 175,000 miles of telegraph wires.

Telephones. The telephonic communication of London is mainly in the hands of the *United Telephone Co.*, the head office of which is in Oxford Court, Cannon Street, City. In July, 1889, between 30 and 40 call-rooms were open in and near London; and arrangements have been made to open about 80 more in the shops of the Aërated Bread Co.

Parcels Companies. Parcels for London and the environs are transmitted by the *London Parcels Delivery Company*, which has 120 receiving offices distributed throughout London, usually in shops indicated by notices. The head office is in Rolls Buildings, Fetter Lane, Fleet Street. Within a radius of 3 M. a parcel under 4lbs. is sent for 3*d*., under 14lbs., 6*d*., under 28lbs., 8*d*., and so on up to 112lbs. for 1*s*. 2*d*.; beyond 3 M. the charges are from 4*d*. upwards. Parcels for all the chief towns of England are conveyed by *Pickford & Co.* (57 Gresham Street, E.C.) or *Carter, Paterson, & Co.* (126 Goswell Road, E.C.), but the Post Office forms the best carrier for packages not exceeding 11lbs. in weight. (A card with C. P. in large letters, conspicuously exhibited in the window, secures the stopping of the first of Carter & Paterson's vans which happens to pass the house.) Parcels for the Continent are forwarded by the *Continental Daily Parcels Express* (53 Gracechurch Street and 34 Regent Circus) and the *Globe Parcels Express* (20 St. Paul's Churchyard and 13 Woodstock Street, Oxford Street), which work in connection with the continental post-offices. Parcels for America are forwarded by *Stareley & Co.'s American European Express* (H. Starr & Co.), 19 Australia Avenue, Barbican, E.C.; the *American Express*, 99 Cannon Street, E.C.; and the *American & European Express*, 52 Lime Street, E.C., and 113A. Regent Street. *Pitt & Scott*, 23 Cannon Street, City, and 7 Carlton Street, Regent Street, are general shipping and parcel agents for all parts of the world.

Commissionnaires. These are a corps of retired soldiers of good character, organised in 1859 by Captain Sir Edward Walter of the 'Times' newspaper, and form convenient and trustworthy messengers for the conveyance of letters or small parcels. Their head office is at Exchange Court, 419A Strand, but they are also to be found in most of the chief thoroughfares, where they may be recognised by their green uniform and metal badge. Their charges are 3*d*. per mile or 6*d*. per hour; the rate is a little higher if the parcel to be carried weighs more than 11lbs. The charge for a day is about 3*s*. 6*d*., and they may also be hired by special arrangement for a week or a longer period. — The *Army and Navy Pensioners Employment Society*, 4 Charing Cross, is a similar organisation.

The **Lady Guide Association**, 121 Pall Mall (temporary office; Managing Directress, Miss Davis), established in 1889, provides ladies qualified to act as guides to the sights of London, as interpreters, as travelling companions, as aids in shopping, etc. It also keeps a register of boarding and lodging houses, engages rooms at hotels, exchanges money, provides railway and other tickets, and generally undertakes to give all the information and assistance required by a stranger in London. The charge for the guides, who are arranged in three classes and may be engaged by the hour, day, or month, varies from 4*s*. to 8*s*. 6*d*. **per day.**

## 18. Outline of English History.

The **visitor to the** metropolis of Great Britain, whether from the western **hemisphere**, from the antipodes, or from the provinces of that **country** itself, will at almost every step meet with interesting **historical** associations; **and it is to** a great extent on his acquaintance with these **that the enjoyment** and **instruction** to be derived from **his** visit **will depend. We therefore** give a brief table **of the chief events in** English **history, which** the tourist will often **find convenient** as an aid to his memory. In the following section **will be found a sketch of the rise and** progress of London itself.

| | |
|---|---|
| B.C. 55-445 A.D. | ROMAN PERIOD. |
| B.C. 55-54. | **Of Britain** before its first **invasion by Julius Cæsar in** B.C. **55 there** is no authentic history. **Cæsar** repeats his **invasion in** B.C. **54,** but makes no **permanent** settlement. |
| 43 A.D. | Emp. Claudius undertakes the **subjugation of Britain.** |
| 78-85. | Britain, with **part of Caledonia, is overrun by the Roman general Agricola,** and reduced **to the form of a province.** |
| 412. | **Roman legions** recalled **from Britain by Honorius.** |
| 445. | The Britons, deprived **of their Roman protectors, are** unable to resist **the attacks of the** *Picts*, **and summon the** *Saxons*, **under** *Hengist* **and** *Horsa*, **to their aid.** |
| 445-1066. | ANGLO-SAXON PERIOD. |
| 445-585. | The Saxons, **re-inforced by the** *Angles*, *Jutes*, and other Germanic tribes, **gradually overcome** Britain on their own account, until the whole **country, with** trifling exceptions, is **divided** into the seven **kingdoms of** the Saxon **Heptarchy** (585). **To** this period belong **the** semi-mythical exploits of *King Arthur* and **his knights.** |
| | Christianity re-introduced by *St. Augustine* (597). The *Venerable Bede* (d. 735). *Caedmon* (about 680). |
| 835-871. | Contests **with the** *Danes* and *Normans*, **who repeatedly** invade **England.** |
| 871-901. | **Alfred the Great** defeats the Danes, **and** compels them **to make peace. Creates navy, establishes** militia, **revises laws, reorganises institutions, founds university** of Oxford, **is a patron of learning, and himself an author.** |
| 979-1016. | **Ethelred the Unready** draws down upon England the **vengeance of the Danes by a massacre** of those who had settled in England. |
| 1013. | The Danish king *Sweyn* con**quers** England. |
| 1017-1035. | *Canute the Great*, the son **of Sweyn,** reigns over England. |
| 1035-1040. | *Harold Harefoot*, illegitima**te son** of Canute, usurps the throne. |
| 1040-1042. | *Hardicanute*, son of Canute. — The Saxon line is restored **in the person of** — |

## 18. OUTLINE OF ENGLISH HISTORY. 57

1042-1066. **Edward the Confessor**, who makes London the capital of England, and builds Westminster Abbey (see p. 193). His brother-in-law and successor —

1066. **Harold** loses his kingdom and his life at the *Battle of Hastings*, where he opposed **the invasion** of the Normans, under William the Conqueror.

1066-1154. ### NORMAN DYNASTY.

1066-1087. **William the Conqueror**, of Normandy, establishes himself as King of the English. Introduction of Norman (French) **language and customs.**

1087-1100. **William II.**, surnamed *Rufus*, after a tyrannical **reign, is accidentally** shot by Sir Walter Tyrrell while out **hunting.**

1100-1135. **Henry I.**, *Beauclerc*, defeats his elder brother **Robert**, Duke of Normandy, at the battle of *Tenchebrai* (1106), **and** adds Normandy to the possessions of the English crown. **He leaves his kingdom to his daughter** *Matilda*, **who, however, is unable to wrest it from** —

1135-1154. **Stephen**, *of Blois*, grandson of the Conqueror. David, **King** of Scotland, **and uncle** of Matilda, is defeated and **taken**
1138. prisoner at the *Battle of the Standard*. Stephen appoints as his successor Matilda's son, Henry of Anjou or Plantagenet (from **the** *planta genista* or broom, the badge of this family).

1154-1485. ### HOUSE OF PLANTAGENET.

1154-1189. **Henry II.** Strife with *Thomas Becket*, Archbishop **of** Canterbury, over the respective spheres **of the civil** and ecclesiastical powers. The Archbishop excommunicates the
1170. King's **followers**, and is murdered by five knights at
1172. Canterbury. Ireland is **conquered by De Coucy.** *Robin Hood*, the forest outlaw, flourishes.

1189-1199. **Richard I.**, *Coeur de Lion*, takes a prominent part in the Third Crusade, but **is captured on his way home, and imprisoned in Germany for upwards of a year.** He carries on war with Philip II. of France.

1199-1216. **John**, surnamed *Lackland*, is defeated at *Bouvines* by Philip II. **of France, and** loses Normandy. *Magna Charta*, **the groundwork of the** English constitution, is extorted from him by his Barons (comp. pp. 186, 336).

1216-1272. **Henry III.**, by his misrule, becomes involved in a war with his Barons, headed by *Simon de Montfort*, **and is defeated at** *Lewes*. His son Edward gains the battle of *Evesham*, where De Montfort is slain. *Hubert de Burgh* defeats the French at sea. *Roger Bacon*, the philosopher.

1272-1307. **Edward I.**, *Longshanks*, conquers the Welsh under *Llewellyn*, and annexes North Wales. **The** heir apparent to the English throne thenceforward bears the title of *Prince of*

## 18. OUTLINE OF ENGLISH HISTORY.

| | |
|---|---|
| 1308. | *Wales. Robert Bruce* and *John Baliol* struggle for the **crown** of Scotland. Edward espouses the cause of the latter (who swears fealty **to** England), and overruns Scotland. The Scots, led by *Sir William Wallace*, offer a determined **resistance.** Wallace executed at London. The Scots defeated at *Falkirk* and *Methuen*, and the country subdued. **Establishment of the** English Parliament **in its modern** form. |
| 1307-1327. 1314. | **Edward II.** is signally **defeated at** *Bannockburn* **by the** Scots under *Robert Bruce* the younger, and is forced to retire to England. The Queen and her paramour *Mortimer* join with **the Barons in** taking up arms against the King, who is deposed, **and shortly** afterwards murdered in prison. |
| 1327-1377. 1364. | **Edward III.** defeats the Scots at *Halidon Hill* and *Neville's Cross*. Lays claim to the throne of France, and invades that country, thus beginning the hundred years' war between France and England. Victories of *Sluys* (naval), *Crécy* (1346), **and** *Poitiers* (1356). **John** the **Good of France,** taken prisoner by **the** *Black* **Prince,** dies in **captivity. After the** death of the Black Prince, **England loses all her** French possessions, except Calais and Gascony. Order of the Garter founded. Movement against the pretensions and corruption of the clergy, headed by the early reformer *John Wycliffe*. House of Commons holds its meetings apart from the House **of Lords.** |
| 1377-1399. | **Richard II.** Rebellion **of** *Wat Tyler*, occasioned by increase of taxation (see **p.** 96). Victory over the Scots at *Otterburn* or *Chevy Chase*. *Henry of Bolingbroke, Duke* **of** *Lancaster*, leads an army against the King, takes him captive, and according to popular tradition, starves him to death in Pontefract Castle. *Geoffrey Chaucer*, the father of English poetry, flourishes. |
| 1399-1461. 1399-1413. | HOUSE OF LANCASTER. **Henry IV.,** *Bolingbroke*, **now secures** his election **to the** crown, in **right of** his descent **from** Henry III. Outbreak of the nobility, **under the** *Earl of Northumberland* and his son |
| 1403. | *Henry (Percy Hotspur),* **is** quelled by the victory of *Shrewsbury*, at which **the** latter is slain. |
| 1413-1422. | **Henry V.** renews the claims of England to the French **crown, wins the battle of** *Agincourt*, and subdues the N. of France. Persecution of the *Lollards*, or followers of Wycliffe. |
| 1422-1461. | **Henry VI.** is proclaimed King of France at Paris. The *Maid of Orleans* defeats the English and recovers French possessions. Outbreak of the civil contest called the '*Wars of the Roses*', between **the houses of** Lancaster (red rose) and York (white rose). Henry becomes insane. *Richard, Duke of York*, grandson of Edward III., lays claim to the |

## 18. OUTLINE OF ENGLISH HISTORY. 59

throne, **joins** himself with *Warwick*, the 'King-Maker', and wins the battle of *Northampton*, but is defeated and slain at *Wakefield*. His son *Edward*, however, is appointed King. Rebellion of *Jack Cade*.

1461-1485.
1461-1483.

### House of York.

Edward IV. wins the battles of *Towton, Hedgley Moor*, and *Hexham*. Warwick takes the part of *Margaret of Anjou*, wife of Henry VI., and forces Edward to **flee to** Holland, whence, however, he soon returns and wins the victories of *Barnet* and *Tewkesbury*. Henry VI. dies sud-

1471. denly **in the** Tower. Edward's brother, the *Duke of Clarence*, is said to have been drowned in a butt of malmsey.

1483. Edward **V.**, the youthful son of Edward IV., is declared illegitimate, **and murdered in the Tower**, along with his brother (p. 120), by his uncle, the *Duke of Gloucester*, who takes possession of the throne as —

1483-1485. Richard III., but is defeated and slain at *Bosworth* by *Henry Tudor, Earl of Richmond*, a scion of the House of Lancaster.

1485-1603.
1485-1509.

### House of Tudor.

Henry VII. marries *Elizabeth*, daughter of Edward IV., and **so puts an end to** the Wars of the Roses. The pretenders *Lambert Simnel* and *Perkin Warbeck*.

1509-1547. Henry VIII., married six times (to *Catherine of Arragon, Anne Boleyn, Jane Seymour, Anne of Cleves, Catherine Howard*, and *Catherine Parr*). Battles of the *Spurs* and *Flodden*. Separation of the Church of England from that of Rome. Dissolution of monasteries and persecution of the Papists. *Cardinal Wolsey* and *Thomas Cromwell*, all-powerful ministers. Whitehall and St. James's Palace built.

1547-1553. Edward VI. encourages the Reformed faith.

1553-1558. **Mary I.** causes *Lady Jane Grey*, whom Edward had appointed his successor, to be executed, and imprisons her own sister *Elizabeth* (pp. 123, 182). Marries *Philip of Spain*, and restores Roman Catholicism. Persecution of the Protestants. Calais taken by the French.

1558-1603. Elizabeth. Protestantism re-established. Flourishing state of commerce. *Mary, Queen of Scots*, executed after a

1587. long confinement in England. Destruction of the Spanish

1588. 'Invincible Armada'. *Sir Francis Drake*, the celebrated circumnavigator. Foundation of the East India Company. Golden age of English literature: *Shakspeare, Bacon, Spenser, Jonson, Beaumont, Fletcher, Marlowe, Drayton*.

## 18. OUTLINE OF ENGLISH HISTORY.

1603-1714.  HOUSE OF STUART.

1603-1625.  **James I.**, King of Scots, and son of Mary Stuart, **unites by his accession** the two kingdoms of England and **Scotland**. Persecution of the **Puritans** and Roman Catholics. Influence of *Buckingham*. Gunpowder Plot. Execution of *Sir Walter Raleigh*.

1625-1649.  **Charles I.** imitates his father in the arbitrary nature of his rule, quarrels with Parliament on questions of taxation, dissolves it repeatedly, and tyrannically arrests five leading members of the House of Commons (*Hampden*, *Pym*, etc.). Rise of the *Covenanters* in Scotland. *Long Parliament*. Outbreak of civil war between the King and his adherents (*Cavaliers*) on the one side, and the Parliament and its friends (*Roundheads*) on the other. The King defeated by *Oliver Cromwell* at *Marston Moor* and *Naseby*. He takes refuge in the Scottish camp, but is betrayed to the Parliamentary leaders, tried, and executed at Whitehall (p. 182).

1649-1653.  **Commonwealth.** The Scots rise in favour of Charles II., but are defeated at *Dunbar* and *Worcester* by Cromwell.

1653-1660.  **Protectorate.** Oliver Cromwell now **becomes Lord Protector of England, and by his vigorous and wise government makes England** prosperous **at home and respected abroad.** *John Milton*, the poet, *Thomas Hobbes*, **the** philosopher, and *George Fox*, the founder of the Quakers, live at this period.

1658.  On Cromwell's death, he is succeeded by his son **Richard**, who, however, soon resigns, whereupon Charles II. is restored by *General Monk*.

1660-1685.  **Charles II.** General amnesty proclaimed, a few of the regicides only being excepted. Arbitrary government. The *Cabal*. Wars with Holland. Persecution of the Papists after the pretended discovery of a *Popish Plot*. Passing **of the** *Habeas Corpus Act*. Wars with the Covenanters. **Battle of** *Bothwell Bridge*. *Rye House Plot*. Charles a pensioner of France. Names *Whig* and *Tory* come into use. *Dryden* **and** *Butler*, the poets; *Locke*, the philosopher.

1685-1688.  **James II.**, a Roman Catholic, soon alienates the people by his love for that form of religion, is quite unable to resist the invasion of *William of Orange*, and escapes **to** France, where he spends his last years at St. Germain.

1688-1702.  **William III. and Mary II.** William of Orange, with his wife, the eldest daughter of James II., now ascends the throne. The *Declaration of Rights*. Battles of *Killiecrankie* and *The Boyne*. *Sir Isaac Newton*.

1702-1714.  **Anne**, younger daughter of James II., completes the fusion of England and Scotland by the union of their parliaments. *Marlborough's* victories of *Blenheim*, *Ramilies*,

## 18. OUTLINE OF ENGLISH HISTORY.

*Oudenarde*, and *Malplaquet*, in the Spanish War **of Succession**. Capture of *Gibraltar*. The poets *Pope*, *Addison*, *Swift*, *Prior*, and *Allan Ramsay*.

### HANOVERIAN DYNASTY.

1714-1727. **George I.** succeeds in right of his descent from James I. Rebellion in Sctland (in favour of the *Pretender*) quelled. *Sir Robert Walpole*, prime minister. *Daniel Defoe*.

1727-1760. **George II.** Rebellion in favour of the Young Pretender, *Charles Edward Stuart*, crushed at *Culloden*. *Canada* taken from the French. *William Pitt*, *Lord Chatham*, prime minister; *Richardson*, *Fielding*, *Smollett*, *Sterne*, novelists; *Thomson*, *Young*, *Gray*, *Collins*, *Gay*, poets; *Hogarth*, painter.

1760-1820. **George III.** American War of Independence. War with France. Victories of *Nelson* at *Aboukir* and *Trafalgar*, and of *Wellington* in *Spain* and at *Waterloo*. The younger *Pitt*, prime minister; *Shelley* and *Keats*, poets.

1820-1830. **George IV.** Roman Catholic Emancipation Bill. *Daniel O'Connell*. The English aid the Greeks in the War of Independence. Victory of *Navarino*. *Byron*, *Sir Walter Scott*, *Wordsworth*, *Coleridge*, *Southey*.

1830-1837. **William IV.** Abolition of slavery. Reform Bill.

The present sovereign of Great Britain is —
**Victoria,** born 24th May, 1819; ascended the throne in 1837; married, on 10th Feb., 1840, her cousin, Prince Albert of Saxe-Coburg-Gotha (d. 14th Dec., 1861).
The children of this marriage are: —
(1) Victoria, born 21st Nov., 1840; married to the Crown Prince of Germany, 25th Jan., 1858.
(2) Albert Edward, Prince of Wales, Heir Apparent to the throne, born 9th Nov., 1841; married Alexandra, Princess of Denmark, 10th Mar., 1863.
(3) Alice, born 25th April, 1843; married to the Grand-Duke of Hessen-Darmstadt, 1st July, 1862; died 14th Dec., 1878.
(4) Alfred, Duke of Edinburgh, born 6th Aug., 1844; married the Grand Duchess Marie of Russia, 23rd Jan., 1874.
(5) Helena, born 25th May, 1846; married to Prince Christian of Schleswig-Holstein-Sonderburg-Augustenburg, 5th July, 1866.
(6) Louise, born 18th March, 1848; married to the Marquis of Lorne, eldest son of the Duke of Argyll, 21st March, 1871.
(7) Arthur, Duke of Connaught, born 1st May, 1850; married Princess Louise Margaret, daughter of Prince Frederick Charles, nephew of the German Emperor, 13th March, 1879.
(8) Leopold, Duke of Albany, born 7th April, 1853; married Princess Helen of Waldeck-Pyrmont, 27th April, 1882; died 28th March, 1884.
(9) Beatrice, born 14th April, 1857; married Prince Henry of Battenberg, 23rd July, 1885.

## 19. Historical Sketch of London.

The most populous city in the world (which London unquestionably is) cannot fail to have had an eventful history, in all that concerns race, creed, institutions, culture, and general progress. At what period the Britons, one branch of the Celtic race, settled on this spot, there is no authentic evidence to shew. The many forms which the name assumes in early records have led to much controversy; but it is clear that 'London' is derived from the Latin *Londinium*, the name given it in Tacitus, and that this is only an adaptation by the Romans of the ancient British name *Llyn*, or *Lin*, a pool, and *din* or *dun*, a high place of strength, a hill fort, or city. The 'pool' was a widening of the river at this part, where it makes a bend, and offered a convenient place for shipping. Whether the 'dun' or hill was the high ground reached by Ludgate Hill, and on which St. Paul's now stands, or Cornhill, near the site of the Mansion House, it is difficult to decide*. Probably both these elevations were on the 'pool'. The etymology of the first syllable of London is the same as that of 'Lin' in Lincoln, which was called by Ptolemy Lindon (Λίνδον), and by the Romans Lindum, the second syllable of the modern form of the name representing the word 'Colonia'. The present British or Welsh name of London is *Llundain*; but it was formerly also known to the Welsh as *Caer-ludd*, the City of Lud, a British king said to have ruled here just before the Roman period, and popularly supposed to be commemorated in Lud-gate†, one of the gates of the old walled city, near the junction of Ludgate Hill and Farringdon Street.

London, in the days of the Britons, was probably little more than a collection of huts, on a dry spot in the midst of a marsh, or in a cleared space in the midst of a wood, and encompassed by an artificial earthwork and ditch. That there was much marsh and forest in the immediate vicinity is proved by the character of the deep soil when turned up in digging foundations, and by the small subterranean streams which still run into the Thames, as at Dowgate, formerly *Dourgate* ('water gate', from Celtic *dwr*, water), at the Fleet Ditch, at Blackfriars Bridge, etc. Such names as *Fenchurch Street* (see p. 107) are reminiscent of the former character of the neighbourhood.

After the settlement of the Romans in Britain, quite early in the Christian era, London rapidly grew in importance. In the time of the Emperor Nero (62 A.D.), the city had become a resort of merchants from various countries and the centre of a considerable

---

\* The latter alternative is that of the Rev. W. J. Loftie London's latest and probably best historian (see p. 80).

† In his 'History' Mr. Loftie suggests that Ludgate may mean 'Fleet' or 'Flood' gate, but he now informs us that when he wrote this passage he was not aware that Ludgate is the Anglo-Saxon word for a postern, and merely indicates that this was one of the smaller gates of the city.

## 19. HISTORICAL SKETCH OF LONDON. 63

maritime commerce, **the river Thames** affording ready **access for shipping**. It suffered terribly **during the** sanguinary struggle between the Romans and the British **queen Boadicea**, and was in later centuries frequently attacked and plundered by piratical bands **of Franks**, Norsemen, Picts, Scots, **Danes, and Saxons**, who crossed **the seas to reap a ruthless** harvest **from a city which** doubtless **possessed much commercial** wealth; **but it speedily recovered from the** effects of these **visitations. As a** Roman **settlement London was frequently** named *Augusta*, but it was **never raised to the dignity of being a municipium like** *Verulamium* (p. 333) **or** *Eboracum* (York), **and was not regarded as the capital of** Roman Britain. **It extended from the site of the present Tower of London** on **the E. to Ludgate on the W., and inland from the Thames as far** as the marshy **ground known in later times as Moorfields and Finsbury or Fensbury. Watling Street perpetuates the name of one among many roads made through London by the Romans. Relics are still found almost annually of the foundations of Roman buildings of a substantial and** elegant character. **Fragments of the Roman wall are also discernible. This wall was maintained in parts until** modern **times, but** has almost entirely disappeared **before the alterations and improvements** which **taste and the** necessities **of trade** have introduced. The most prominent **remaining** piece of the **Roman** wall is in London Wall, between Wood **Street and** Aldermanbury, **where an** inscribed **tablet calls attention to it. Another** fragment **may be** seen in **the adjacent churchyard of** St. Giles, Cripplegate **(see p. 96).**

The gates of Roman London, whose **walls are believed to have been first built on** such **an extended scale as to include the abovementioned limits** by the Emperor **Constantine in the fourth century, were in after** times called **Lud-gate, Dour-gate, Belins-gate, Postern-gate, Ald-gate, Bishops-gate, Moor-gate, Cripple-gate, Alders-gate and New-gate, all of which are still commemorated in names of streets, etc., marking the localities. Roman London from the Tower to Ludgate was about a mile in length, and from the Thames to 'London Wall' about half a mile in breadth. Its remains at Cheapside and the Mansion House are found at about 18 feet below the present surface. The Roman city as at first enclosed must, however, have been smaller, as Roman sepulchres have been found in Moorgate Street, Bishopsgate, and Smithfield, which must then have lain beyond the walled city. The Saxons, who seldom distinguished themselves as builders, contributed nothing to the fortification of London; but the Normans did much, beginning with the erection of the Tower. During the earlier ages of Saxon rule, the great works left here** by the **Romans — villas, baths, bridges, roads, temples, statuary,** — were **either** destroyed or **allowed to fall into decay, as was the** case, indeed, all **over** Britain.

London became the capital **of one of the** Anglo-Saxon **kingdoms, and continued to** increase in size **and** importance. **The sites of two** of modern London's most prominent buildings — Westminster Abbey and St. Paul's Cathedral — were occupied as early as the beginning of the 7th cent. by the modest originals of these two stately churches. Bede, at the beginning of the 8th cent., speaks of London as a great market frequented by foreign traders, and we find it paying one-fifth of a contribution exacted by Canute from the entire kingdom. From William the Conqueror London received a charter* in which he engaged to maintain the rights of the city, but the same monarch erected the White Tower to overawe the citizens in the event of disaffection. At this time the city probably contained 30-40,000 inhabitants. A special promise is made in Magna Charta, extorted from King John, to observe all the ancient privileges of London; and we may date the present form of its Corporation, consisting of Mayor, Aldermen, and Common Councilmen, from a somewhat earlier period †. The 13th and 14th centuries are marked in the annals of London by several lamentable fires, famines, and pestilences, in which many thousands of its inhabitants perished. The year 1380 witnessed the rebellion of Wat Tyler, who was slain by Lord Mayor Walworth at Smithfield. In this outbreak, and still more in that of Jack Cade (1450), London suffered severely, through the burning and pillaging of its houses. During the reigns of Henry VIII. (1509-1547) and his daughter Mary (1552-1558), London acquired a terrible familiarity with the fires lighted to consume unfortunate 'heretics' at the stake, while under the more beneficent reign of Elizabeth (1558-1603), the capital showed its patriotic zeal by its liberal contributions of men, money, and ships, for the purpose of resisting the threatened attack of the Armada.

A map of London at this time would show the Tower standing on the verge of the City on the E., while on the W., the much smaller city of Westminster would still be a considerable distance from London. The Strand, or river-side road connecting the two cities, would appear bordered by numerous aristocratic mansions, with gardens extending into the fields or down to the river. Throughout the Norman period, and down to the times of the Plantagenets and the Wars of the Roses, the commonalty lived in poor and mean wooden dwellings; but there were many good houses for the merchants and manufacturers, and many important religious houses and hospitals, while the Thames was provided with numerous convenient quays and landing-stages. The streets, even as lately as the 17th cent., were narrow, dirty, full of ruts and holes, and ill-adapted for traffic. Many improvements, however, were made at the period we have now reached (the end of the 16th cent.), though these still left London very different from what we now see it.

---

* The following is the text of this charter as translated by Bishop Stubbs: — 'William king greets William bishop and Gosfrith portreeve, and all the burghers within London, French and English, friendly; and I do you to wit that I will that ye be all lawworthy that were in King Edward's day. And I will that every child be his father's heir after his father's day; and I will not endure that any man offer any wrong to you. God keep you'.

† A deed among the archives of St. Paul's mentions a 'Mayor of the City of London' in 1193.

## 19. HISTORICAL SKETCH OF LONDON.

In the Civil Wars, London, which had been most exposed to the exactions of the Star Chamber, naturally sided with the Roundheads. It witnessed Charles I. beheaded at the Palace of Whitehall in 1649, and Oliver Cromwell proclaimed Lord Protector of England in 1653; and in 1660 it saw Charles II. placed on the throne by the 'Restoration'. This was a period when England, and London especially, underwent dire suffering in working out the problem of civil and religious liberty, the successful solution of which laid the basis of the empire's greatness. In 1664-1666 London was turned into a city of mourning and lamentation by the ravages of the Great Plague, by which, it is calculated, it lost the enormous number of 100,000 citizens. Closely treading on the heels of one calamity came another — the Great Fire — which, in September, 1666, destroyed 13,000 houses, converting a great part of the eastern half of the city into a scene of desolation. This disaster, however, ultimately proved very beneficial to the city, for London was rebuilt in a much improved form, though not so advantageously as it would have been if Sir Christopher Wren's plans had been fully realised. Among the new edifices, the erection of which was necessitated by the fire, was the present St. Paul's Cathedral. Of important buildings existing before the fire, Westminster Abbey and Hall, the Temple Church, and the Tower are now almost the only examples.

Wren fortunately had his own way in building the fifty odd City churches, and the visitor to London should not fail to notice their great variety and the skill with which they are grouped with St. Paul's. A good panorama of the entire group is obtained from the tower of St. Saviour's, Southwark; the general effect is also visible from Blackfriars Bridge (p. 112).

It was not, however, till the reign of Queen Anne (1702-1714), that London began to put on anything like its present appearance. In 1703 it was visited by a fearful storm, by which houses were overthrown, the ships in the river driven on shore, churches unroofed, property to the value of at least 2,000,000*l.* destroyed, and the lives of several hundreds of persons sacrificed. The winter of 1739-1740 is memorable for the Great Frost, lasting from Christmas to St. Valentine's Day, during which a fair was held on the frozen bosom of the Thames. Great injuries were inflicted on the city by the Gordon No-Popery Riots of 1780. The prisons were destroyed, the prisoners released, and mansions were burned or pillaged, thirty-six conflagrations having been counted at one time in different quarters: and the rioters were not subdued till hundreds of them had paid the penalty of their misdeeds with their lives.

Many of the handsomest streets and finest buildings in London date from the latter half of last century. To this period belong the Mansion House, the Horse Guards, Somerset House, and the Bank. During the 19th cent. the march of improvement has been so rapid as to defy description. The Mint, the Custom House, Waterloo Bridge, London Bridge, Buckingham Palace, the Post Office, the British Museum, the Athenæum Club, the York Column, the National

Gallery, the Houses of Parliament, the new Law Courts, and the whole of Belgravia and the West End beyond, have all arisen during the last 50 years. An important event in the domestic history of the city was the commencement of gas-lighting in 1807. (Before 1716 the provisions for street-lighting were very imperfect, but in that year an act was passed ordering every householder to hang out a light before his door from six in the evening till eleven.) From that time to the present London has been actively engaged, by the laying out of spacious thoroughfares and the construction of handsome edifices, in making good its claim to be not only the largest, but also one of the finest cities in the world. The electric light has hitherto been used comparatively little in the London streets; but in 1889 this question was definitely taken in hand by the Board of Trade and the County Council, and it seems probable that the development of systematic lighting by electricity will now be steady and rapid.

No authentic estimate of the population of London can be traced farther back than two centuries. Nor is it easy to determine the area covered by buildings at different periods. At one time the 'City within the Walls' comprised all; afterwards was added the 'City without the Walls'; then the city and liberties of Westminster; then the borough of Southwark, S. of the river; then numerous parishes between the two cities; and lastly other parishes forming an encircling belt around the whole. All these component elements at length came to be embraced under the name of 'London'. The population was about 700,000 in the year 1700, about 900,000 in 1800, and 1,300,000 in 1821. Each subsequent decennial census included a larger area than the one that preceded it. The original 'City' of London, covering little more than 1 square mile, has in this way expanded to a great metropolis of fully 120 square miles, containing, in 1881, a population of 3,814,571 persons (see p. 69). Extension of commerce has accompanied the growth of population. Statistics of trade in past centuries are wanting; but at the present time London supplies half the total customs-revenue of the kingdom. One fourth of the whole ship tonnage of England, and one fourth of the entire exports, are centred in the port of London. (For fuller statistical information, see below, Section 20.)

## 20. Topography and Statistics.

Topography. The city of London is built upon a tract of undulating clay soil, which extends irregularly along the valley of the Thames from a point near Reading to Harwich and Herne Bay at the mouth of the river, a distance of about 120 miles. It is divided into two portions by the river *Thames*, which, rising in the Cotswold Hills in Gloucestershire, is from its source down to its mouth in the German Ocean at Sheerness 230 M. in length, and is navigable for a distance of 50 M. — The southern and less important part of London (*Southwark* and *Lambeth*) lies in the counties of *Surrey* and *Kent*; the northern and principal portion in *Middlesex* and *Essex*. The latter part of the immense city may be divided, in accordance with its general characteristics, into two great halves (not taking into account the extensive outlying districts on the N. and the N.E., which are comparatively uninteresting to strangers): —

## 20. TOPOGRAPHY AND STATISTICS.

I. The *City* and the *East End*, consisting of that part of London which lies to the E. of the Temple, form the commercial and money-making quarter of the metropolis. It embraces the Port, the Docks, the Custom House, the Bank, the Exchange, the innumerable counting-houses of merchants, money-changers, brokers, and underwriters, the General Post Office, the printing and publishing offices of the Times, the legal corporations of the Inns of Court, and the Cathedral of St. Paul's, towering above them all.

II. The *West End*, or that part of the town to the W. of the Temple, is the quarter of London which spends money, makes laws, and regulates the fashions. It contains the Palace of the Queen, the Mansions of the aristocracy, the Clubs, Museums, Picture Galleries, Theatres, Barracks, Government Offices, Houses of Parliament, and Westminster Abbey; and it is the special locality for parks, squares, and gardens, for gorgeous equipages and powdered lackeys.

Besides these great divisions, the following districts are distinguished by their population and leading occupations: —

I. On the LEFT BANK of the Thames: —

(a) To the E. of the City is the so-called *Long Shore*, which extends along the bank of the Thames, and is chiefly composed of quays, wharves, store-houses, and engine-factories, and inhabited by shipwrights, lightermen, sailors, and marine store dealers.

(b) *Whitechapel*, with sugar-bakeries and their German workmen.

(c) *Houndsditch* and the *Minories*, the quarters of the Jews.

(d) *Bethnal Green* and *Spitalfields* to the N., and part of *Shoreditch*, form a manufacturing district, occupied to a large extent by silk-weavers, partly descended from the French Protestants (Huguenots) who took refuge in England after the Revocation of the Edict of Nantes in 1685.

(e) *Clerkenwell*, between Islington and Hatton Garden, the district of watch-makers and metal-workers.

(f) *Paternoster Row*, near St. Paul's Cathedral, the focus of the book-trade.

(g) *Chancery Lane* and the *Inns of Court*, the headquarters of barristers, solicitors, and law-stationers.

II. In *Surrey*, on the RIGHT BANK of the Thames: —

(a) *Southwark* and *Lambeth*, containing numerous potteries, glass-works, machine-factories, breweries, and hop-warehouses.

(b) *Bermondsey*, famous for its tanneries, glue-factories, and wool-warehouses.

(c) *Rotherhithe*, farther to the E., chiefly inhabited by sailors, ship-carpenters, coalheavers, and bargemen.

By the Redistribution Bill of 1885 London is divided for parliamentary purposes into the City Proper, returning two members of parliament, and 27 metropolitan boroughs, comprising 59 single member districts. London University also returns one member.

## 20. TOPOGRAPHY AND STATISTICS.

The *City Proper*, which strictly speaking forms a county of itself and is neither in Middlesex nor Essex, is bounded on the W. by the site of Temple Bar and Southampton Buildings; on the N. by Holborn, Smithfield, Barbican, and Finsbury Circus; on the E. by Bishopsgate Without, Petticoat Lane, Aldgate, and the Minories; and on the S. by the Thames.

The City is divided into 26 *Wards* and 108 parishes, has a separate administration and jurisdiction of its own, and is presided over by the Lord Mayor. At the census of 1881 it consisted of 6493 inhabited houses with 50,526 inhabitants (21,371 less than in 1871). The *resident* population is steadily decreasing on account of the constant emigration to the West End and suburbs, the ground and buildings being so valuable for commercial purposes as to preclude their use merely as dwellings. More than 1000 houses are left empty every night under the guardianship of the 800 members of the City police force (p. 60). The *day* population of the City in 1881 was 261,061, and the number of houses or separate tenements in which persons were actively employed during the day was 25,143. The rateable value of property in 1887 was 3,767,000*l*. or about 300,000*l*. more than that of Liverpool. Sites for building in the City sometimes realise no less than 20-70*l*. per square foot. The annual revenue of the City of London is about 500,000*l*. In 1881 an attempt was made to estimate the number of persons and vehicles entering the City precincts within 24 hours. Enumerators were stationed at 60 different inlets, and their returns showed the enormous totals of 797,563 foot-passengers and 71,893 vehicles.

*Westminster*, to the W. of the City, bounded on the N. by Bayswater Road and Oxford Street, on the W. by Chelsea, Kensington, and Brompton, and on the S. by the Thames, comprises three of the parliamentary boroughs (Westminster Proper or the Abbey District, the Strand District, and the District of St. George's, Hanover Square), each returning one member to the House of Commons. It contains 25,312 houses and 228,932 inhabitants.

The remaining parliamentary boroughs are *Battersea*, *Bethnal Green*, *Camberwell*, *Chelsea*, *Clapham*, *Deptford*, *Finsbury*, *Fulham*, *Greenwich*, *Hackney*, **Hammersmith**, *Hampstead*, *Islington*, *Kensington*, **Lambeth**, *Lewisham*, **Marylebone**, **Newington**, *Paddington*, *St. Pancras*, *Shoreditch*, **Southwark** (including Bermondsey and Rotherhithe), **Tower Hamlets**, **Wandsworth**, **West Ham**, and **Woolwich**. The population, area, and boundaries of these new boroughs are given in a map published by Philip, 32 Fleet Street (6*d*.).

**Statistics.** The City, the West End, and the Borough, together with the suburban villages which have been gradually absorbed, form the great and constantly extending metropolis of London — a city which, in the words of Tacitus (*Ann.* 14, 33), was and still is 'copiâ negotiatorum et commeatuum maxime celebre'. It has doubled in size within the last half-century, being now, from Stratford and Blackwall on the E. to Kew Bridge and Acton on the W., 14 M. in length, and from Clapham and Herne Hill on the S. to Hornsey and Highgate on the N., 8 M. in breadth, while it covers an area of 122 square miles. This area is, at a rough estimate, occupied by 7800 streets, which if laid end to end would form a line 3000 M. long, lighted by a million gas-lamps consuming daily 28,000,000

## 20. TOPOGRAPHY AND STATISTICS. 69

cubic feet of gas. The 528,794 buildings of this gigantic city include 1400 churches of various denominations, 7500 public houses, 1700 coffee-houses, and 500 hotels and inns. The Metropolitan and City Police District, which extends 12-15 M. in every direction from Charing Cross, embraces an area of 690 sq. M., with streets and roads measuring 7000 M. in aggregate length. The annual value of house property was estimated in 1886 at nearly 34 millions sterling. According to the census of 1881, the population of London consisted of 3,814,571 souls (or within the bounds of the Metropolitan Police District 4,766,661; now considerably above 5,000,000), showing an increase of 562,660 over that of 1871. The annual increase is about 70,000. Among these there are about 3000 master-tailors, 2800 bakers, 2400 butchers (besides many thousands of men and women in their employ), and 300,000 domestic servants. The number of paupers was 141,770. The population of London has been almost exactly doubled within the last forty years (pop. in 1841, 1,948,417), and within the same period about 2000 M. of new streets have been constructed. There are in London more Scotsmen than in Edinburgh, more Irish than in Dublin, more Jews than in Palestine, and more Roma Catholics than in Rome.

Statistics as to the consumption of food in this vast hive of human beings are not easily obtained; but we may state approximately that there are annually consumed about 2,000,000 quarters of wheat, 400,000 oxen, 1,500,000 sheep, 130,000 calves, 250,000 swine, 8 million head of poultry and game, 40 million pounds of fish, 500 million oysters, 1,200,000 lobsters, and 3,000,000 salmon. The butcher-meat alone is valued at 50,000,000*l*. The Londoners wash down this vast annual repast by 180 million quarts of porter and ale, 8 million quarts of spirits, and 31 million quarts of wine, not to speak of the 150 million gallons of water supplied every day by the nine water-companies. About 1000 collier-vessels yearly bring 4,000,000 tons of coal into London by the river, while the railways supply about as much more. The sum of money spent by the whole population each year may be estimated as at least 200,000,000*l*. The number of vessels which annually enter the port of London is about 20,000, while the average value of exports from the Thames is not less than one hundred millions sterling.

Between 1856 and 1889 the important METROPOLITAN IMPROVEMENTS, undertaken for the facilitation of traffic and for the sanitary benefit of the population, were superintended by the *Metropolitan Board of Works*. This body, however, ceased to exist on March 31st, 1889, and all its powers and duties have been transferred to the LONDON COUNTY COUNCIL, a new body called into existence by an Act of Parliament passed in 1888. Various new powers have also been conferred on the Council. The new '*Administrative County of London*' includes the City of London and parts of the counties of Middlesex, Essex, Surrey, and Kent. Its electoral divisions coincide with the parliamentary boroughs mentioned at p. 68, two Councillors being elected by the borough franchise for each division. With the 19 Aldermen appointed by the Council itself, the total number of members is thus 137.

Though the Metropolitan Board of Works never exactly met the idea of a popular elective body and though it had practically lost the public confidence before its extinction, it is yet impossible to deny that it accomplished many public works of great magnificence and utility. The expenses connected with these works — the construction of new streets, the extension of old ones, and so on — were of course enormous, and as much as 900,000*l.* has been paid for a single acre of ground. Half a million sterling was paid for Northumberland House, by Charing Cross, removed for the purpose of opening up the short new street to the Thames, named Northumberland Avenue. The most important work of the Board was the new system of *Interceptive Main Drainage*, begun in 1859 under the superintendence of Sir Joseph Bazalgette, and carried out at a cost of 6,500,000*l.* Formerly all the drainage of London was conducted directly into the Thames, to the amount of 10,000,000 cubic feet on the N. and 4,000,000 cubic feet on the S. side, with the virtual result of converting the river into a huge, offensive, and pernicious cess-pool (especially in summer). The new system consists of large sewers or tunnels, constructed nearly parallel with the Thames as far as Barking Creek, 14 M. below London, on the left bank of the river, and to Crossness on the right, where the drainage is made to flow into the Thames at high water with the view of its being carried out to sea by the ebb-tide. Great complaints have been made, however, that the more solid parts of the sewage are not carried out to sea, but form thick deposits at the bottom of the river; and though the sewage is now subjected to an elaborate chemical process of deodorisation before its discharge into the river, it can hardly be asserted that the drainage problem has been finally solved. It is worthy of remark that this pollution of the most important river in Britain is at present made legal by an exceptional clause in the River Pollution Prevention Act. The main sewers, of which there are three on the N. side of the Thames, independent of each other and at different levels, consist of tunnels lined with brick, 11 ft. wide and 10 ft. high. Their aggregate length amounts to 85 M. — The new *Thames Embankment*, described at p. 113, is another and scarcely less important undertaking of the Board of Works. — Among the new *Streets* formed by the Board are Clerkenwell Road, Great Eastern Street, Queen Victoria Street (p. 115), Charing Cross Road (p. 147), and Shaftesbury Avenue (p. 147), while several important street-improvements are still in progress. — All the *Bridges* over the Thames on which toll was levied have been made free by the Board at a cost of 1½ million sterling. — The acquisition and opening of *Parks* and other *Open Spaces* were also among the Board's duties.

The London Fire Brigade, a well-equipped force of 600 men, is under the control of the County Council. It is maintained at an annual cost of upwards of 115,000*l.*

The elementary **education of London is** attended to by the London School Board, consisting of 55 members, elected by the City and the ten other districts into which London is divided for the educational franchise. In the City the electors are the voters for Common Councilmen, in the other divisions the rate-payers. The annual income of the Board, exclusive of loans, is over 1,500,000*l.*, about 87 per cent of which is derived from taxation and 13 per cent from fees. The 400 schools provided by the board accommodate nearly 400,000 children, out of a total of 628,000 upon the roll of efficient schools. The office of the board is on the Victoria Embankment, near the Temple Station (see p. 113).

## 21. General Hints.

Some of the following remarks may be deemed superfluous by many readers of this Handbook; but a few observations on English or London peculiarities may not be unacceptable to the American, the English-speaking foreigner, or the provincial visitor.

In England, Sunday, as is well known, is observed as a day of rest and of public worship. Shops, places of amusement, galleries, and the City restaurants are closed the whole day, while other restaurants are open from 1 to 3, and from 6 to 11 p.m. only. Many places of business are closed from 1, 2. or 3 p.m. on Saturday till Monday morning. Among these are all the banks and insurance offices and practically all the wholesale warehouses.

Like 's'il vous plait' in Paris, 'if you please' or 'please' is generally used in ordering refreshments at a café or restaurant, or in making any request. The English forms of politeness are, however, by no means so minute or ceremonious as the French. For example, the hat is raised to ladies only, and is worn in all public places, such as shops, cafés, music halls, and museums.

The fashionable hour for paying visits in London is between 4 and 6 p.m. The proper mode of delivering a letter of introduction is in person, along with the bearer's visiting-card and address; but when this is rendered inconvenient by the greatness of distance or other cause, the letter may be sent by post, accompanied by a polite explanation.

The usual dinner hour of the upper classes varies from 6 to 8 or even 9 p.m. It is considered permissible for guests invited to a dinner-party to arrive a few minutes late, but they should take care never to be before the time. Gentlemen remain at table, over their wine, for a short time after the ladies have left.

Foreigners may often obtain, through their ambassadors, permission to visit private collections which are not open to the ordinary English tourist.

We need hardly caution new-comers against the artifices of pickpockets and the wiles of impostors, two fraternities which are very numerous in London. It is even prudent to avoid speaking to strangers in the street. All information desired by the traveller may be obtained from one of the policemen, of whom about 14,000 (500 mounted) perambulate the streets of the metropolis. If a policeman is not readily found, application may be made to a postal letter carrier, to a commissionaire, or at a neighbouring shop. A considerable degree of caution and presence of mind is often requisite in crossing a crowded thoroughfare, and in entering or alighting from a train or omnibus. The 'rule of the road' for foot-passengers in busy streets is to keep to the right. Poor neighbourhoods should be avoided after nightfall. Strangers are also warned against *Mock* **Auctions**, a specious trap for the unwary, and indeed should neither buy nor sell at any auction in London without the aid of an experienced friend or a trustworthy broker.

Addresses of all kinds may be found in *Kelly's* **Post Office Directory**, a thick volume of 3000 pages, or in *Morris's Directory*, a less extensive work, one or other of which may be seen at all the hotels and cafés and at most of the principal shops. The addresses of residents at the West End and other suburbs may also be obtained from *Boyle's Court Guide*, *Webster's Royal Red Book*, the **Royal Blue Book**, or *Kelly's Suburban Directory*, and those of city men and firms in *Collingridge's City Directory*.

A useful adjunct to most houses in the central parts of London is a *Cab Whistle*, one blast upon which summons a four-wheeler, two a hansom.

Among the characteristic sights of London is the *Lord Mayor's Show* (9th Nov.), or the procession in which — maintaining an ancient and picturesque, though useless custom — the newly-elected Lord Mayor moves, amid great pomp and ceremony, through the streets from the City to the new Courts of Justice, in order to take the oath of office. It is followed by the great dinner in the Guildhall (p. 99).

## 22. Guilds, Charities, Societies, Clubs.

**Guilds.** The City Companies or Guilds of London were once upwards of one hundred in number, about eighty of which still exist, though few exercise their ancient privileges. About forty of them possess halls in which they transact business and hold festivities; the others meet either in rooms lent to them at Guildhall, or at the offices of the respective clerks. All the companies except five are called *Livery Companies*, and the members are entitled, on ceremonial occasions, to wear the liveries (gowns, furs, etc.) of their respective guilds. Many of the companies possess vast estates and revenues, while others possess neither halls nor almshouses, neither estates nor revenues, — nothing but ancient charters to which they reverentially cling. Some of the guildhouses are among the most interesting buildings in London, and are noticed throughout the Handbook. The Twelve Great Companies, wealthier and more influential than the rest, are the *Mercers*, *Grocers*, *Drapers*, *Fishmongers*, *Goldsmiths*, *Skinners*, *Merchant Taylors*, *Haberdashers*, *Salters*, *Ironmongers*, *Vintners*, and *Clothworkers*. Some of the companies represent trades now quite extinct, and by their unfamiliar names strikingly illustrate the fact how completely they have outlived their original purpose. Such are the *Bowyers*, *Broderers*, *Girdlers*, *Horners*, *Loriners* (saddler's ironmongers), *Patten Makers*, and *Scriveners*.

**Charities.** The charities of London are on a scale commensurate with the vastness of the city, being no fewer than 2000 in number. They comprise hospitals, dispensaries, asylums; bible, tract, missionary, and district visiting societies: provident homes, orphanages, etc. A tolerably complete catalogue will be found in *Low's Handbook of the Charities of London*, *Howe's Classified Directory of Metropolitan Charities* (1s.), or *Dickens's Dictionary of London*. In 1885 the total voluntary subscriptions, donations, and bequests to these charities amounted to 4,447,000*l*., or more than 1*l*. for each man, woman, and child in the capital. The institution of 'Hospital Sunday', on which collections are made in all the churches for the hospitals, produces a yearly revenue of about 40,000*l*. Non-church-goers have a similar opportunity afforded them on 'Hospital Saturday', when about 750 ladies station themselves at street-corners to receive contributions; this produces about 10,000*l*. more. The following is a brief list of the chief general hospitals, besides which there are numerous special hospitals for cancer, smallpox, fever, consumption, eye and ear diseases, and so forth.

*Charing Cross*, Agar Street, Strand. — *French Hospital*, Shaftesbury Avenue. — *German*, Dalston. — *Great Northern*, Caledonian Road. — *Guy's*, St. Thomas Street, Southwark. — *King's College*, Carey Street, Strand. — *London*, Whitechapel Road. — *Metropolitan Free*, 81 Commercial Street, Spitalfields. — *Middlesex*, Mortimer Street, Berners Street. — *University College*, or *North London*, Gower Street. — *Royal Free*, Gray's Inn Road. — *St. Bartholomew's*, Smithfield. — *St. George's*, Hyde Park Corner. — *St. Mary's*, Cambridge Place, Paddington. — *St. Thomas's*, Albert Embankment. — *West* London, Hammersmith Road. — *Westminster*, Broad Sanctuary.

**Societies.** The societies for the encouragement of industry, art, and science in London are extremely numerous, and many of them possess most ample endowments. The names of a few of the most important may be given here, some of them being described at length in other parts of the Handbook: —

*Royal Society, Royal Academy, Society of Antiquaries, Geological Society, Royal Astronomical Society, Linnaean Society, Chemical Society*, all in Burlington House, Piccadilly. — *Royal Archaeological Institute*, Oxford Mansions, Oxford Street. — *Royal Academy of Music*, 4 Tenterden Street, Hanover Square. — *Royal College of Music*, near the Albert Hall. — *Royal College of Physicians*, Pall Mall East. — *Royal College of Surgeons*, Lincoln's Inn Fields. — *Royal Geographical Society*, 1 Savile Row, Burlington Gardens. — *Royal Asiatic Society*, 22 Albemarle Street, Piccadilly. — *Royal Society of Literature*, 21 Delahay Street, Westminster. — *Society for the Encouragement of Arts, Manufactures, and Commerce*, generally known as the *Society of Arts*, John Street, Adelphi, Strand. — *Trinity College* (music and arts), 13 Mandeville Place, Manchester Square. — *Heralds'* College, Queen Victoria Street. — *Institution of Civil Engineers*, 25 Great George Street, Westminster. — *Institute of British Architects*, 16 Lower Grosvenor Street, Grosvenor Square. — *Sanitary* Institute *of Great Britain* (Museum of Hygiene), 74A Margaret Street, Cavendish Square. — *School of Electrical Engineering and Submarine Telegraphy*, 12 Prince's Street, Hanover Square. — *Royal Institution*, 21 Albemarle Street, Piccadilly. Popular lectures on science, art, and literature are delivered here on Friday evenings during the Season (adm. by a member's order). Six lectures for children, illustrated by experiments, are given after Christmas. — *City and Guilds of London Institute*, Exhibition Road, South Kensington, for the advancement of technical education.

The **Clubs** are chiefly devoted to social purposes. Most of the club-houses at the West End, particularly those in or near Pall Mall, are very handsome, and admirably fitted up, affording every possible comfort. To a bachelor in particular his 'club' is a most serviceable institution. Members are admitted by ballot, but candidates are rejected by a certain small proportion of 'black balls' or dissentient votes. The entrance fee varies from 5*l*. 5*s*. to 40*l*. (usually about 25*l*.), and the annual subscription is from 3*l*. 3*s*. to 15*l*. 15*s*. The introduction of guests by a member is allowed in some, but not in all of the clubs. The cuisine is usually admirable. The wine and viands, which are sold at little **more than** cost price, often attain a pitch of excellence unequalled **by the most** elaborate and expensive restaurants.

We append an alphabetical list of the most important **clubs**:—

*Albemarle*, 25 Albemarle Street, for ladies and gentlem**en.**
*Alexandra*, 12 Grosvenor Street, W., **for** ladies only.
**Alpine Club**, 8 St. Martin's Place, Trafalgar Square.
*Army and Navy Club*, **36-39 Pall Mall**, N. side, corner of George Street; **2350** members.
*Arthur's Club*, 69 St. James's Street.
*Athenaeum Club*, 107 Pall Mall, **the** club of the *literati*; **1200 members.** (**Distinguished strangers visiting** London may be elected **honorary members of the A**thenæum during their temporary residence **in London.**)
*Badminton Club*, Piccadilly (sporting and coaching club).
*Boodle's Club*, 28 St. James's **Street** (chiefly **for** country gentlemen).
*Brooks's Club*, 60 St. James's Street.
*Burlington Fine Arts Club*, 17 Savile Row.
*Carlton Club*, 94 Pall Mall, the chief Conservative club; **1600 members.**
*Cigar Club*, 6 Waterloo Place.
*City Carlton Club*, 24 St. Swithin's Lane.
*City Liberal Club*, Walbrook.
*City of* **London Club**, 19 Old Broad Street, City.
*Conservative Club*, **74 St.** James's Street; 1200 members.
*Constitutional Club* (**Conservative**), Northumberland Avenue; 6500 **members.**
*Devonshire Club*, 50 St. James's Street; 1500 members.
*East India United Service Club*, 16 St. James's Square.
*Empire Club* (Colonies and India), 4 Grafton Street, Piccadilly.
*French National Society Club*, Adelphi Terrace, Strand.
*Garrick Club*, 13 and 15 Garrick Street, Covent Garden, for lit**erary men and actors.**
*German Athenaeum Club*, 93 Mortimer Street, W.
*Gresham Club*, 1 Gresham Place, City.
*Grosvenor Club*, 135 New Bond Street.
*Guards' Club*, 70 Pall Mall.
*Isthmian Club*, 150 **Piccadilly.**
*Junior Army and Navy* **Club**, 10 St. James's Street.
*Junior Athenaeum Club*, 116 Piccadilly.
**Junior Carlton Club**, 30-35 Pall Mall; 2100 members.
**Junior Constitutional Club**, 14 Regent Street.
**Junior United Service Club**, corner of Regent Street and Charles Street; 2000 **members.**
*Kennel Club*, 29a Pall Mall; for improving the breed of dogs.
*National Club*, 1 Whitehall Gardens.
*National Conservative Club*, 9 Pall Mall.

## 22. CLUBS.

*National Liberal Club*, corner of Northumberland Avenue and Whitehall Place; 6500 members.
*National Union Club*, 23 **Albemarle** Street, W.
*Naval and Military Club*, 94 Piccadilly; 2000 members.
*New University Club*, 57, 58 St. James's Street.
*Northbrook* **Club**, 3 Whitehall Gardens (for **Indian** gentlemen and others interested in Indian affairs).
*Oriental Club*, 18 Hanover Square.
*Orleans Club*, 29 King Street, St. James's (see also p. 326).
*Oxford and Cambridge Club*, 71-76 Pall Mall. (Those only who have studied at Oxford or Cambridge are eligible as members.)
*Pall Mall Club*, 7 **Waterloo Place.**
*Prince's Club*, Knightsbridge (mainly for racquets, tennis, etc.).
*Raleigh Club*, 16 Regent Street; 1400 members.
*Reform Club*, the chief Liberal club, 104 Pall Mall; 1400 members.
*St. George's Club*, Hanover Square, with which is combined the *Imperial and American Club*; 3000 members.
*St. James's Club*, 106 Piccadilly; for the diplomatic service.
*St. Stephen's Club*, 1 Bridge Street, Westminster; 1500 members.
*Savage Club*, Savoy Place, Strand.
*Savile Club*, 107 Piccadilly.
*Scottish Club*, 39 Dover Street, Piccadilly.
*Somerville Club*, 231 Oxford Street; for ladies only.
*Thatched House* **Club**, 86 St. **James's Street.**
*Travellers' Club*, 106 Pall Mall. (Each member must have travelled at least 500 M. from London.)
*Turf Club*, 47 Clarges Street, Piccadilly.
*Union Club*, Trafalgar Square, corner of Cockspur Street.
*United Service Club*, 116 Pall Mall; 1600 members. (Members must not hold lower rank than that of major in the army, or commander in the navy.)
*United University Club*, Pall Mall East, corner of Suffolk Street.
*Whitehall Club*, 47 Parliament Street.
*White's Club*, 38 St. James's Street. (This club was formerly celebrated for its high play.)
*Windham Club*, 11 St. James's Square.

The *Royal Colonial Institute*, Northumberland Avenue, founded in 1868 for the purpose of 'providing a place of meeting for all gentlemen connected with the Colonies and British India', offers many of the advantages of a good club.

## 23. Preliminary Ramble.

Nothing is better calculated to afford the traveller some insight **into the** labyrinthine topography of London, **to** enable him to **ascertain his** bearings, and to dispel the first oppressive feeling of solitude and insignificance, **than a drive** through the principal quarters of the town.

The outside of an omnibus affords a **much** better view than a cab (fares, see p. 28), and, moreover, has the advantage of cheapness. If the driver, beside whom the stranger should sit, **happens to be** obliging (and a small gratuity will generally make him so), **he will** afford much useful information about the buildings, monuments, and other sights on the route; but care should be taken not to distract his attention in crowded parts. Even without such assistance, however, our plan of the city, if carefully consulted, will supply all necessary information. If ladies are of the party, an open *Fly* (see p. 28) is the most comfortable conveyance.

Taking *Hyde Park* Corner, at the W. end of Piccadilly, **as a convenient starting-point,** we mount **one of the numerous** omnibuses which ply to the Bank and London Bridge and traverse nearly the whole of the quarters lying on the N. bank of the Thames. Entering Piccadilly, we first pass, on the right, the Green Park, beyond which rises Buckingham Palace (p. 257). A little farther to the E., in the distance, we descry the towers of Westminster Abbey (p. 193) and the Houses of Parliament (p. 184). In Regent Street on the right, at some distance off, rises the York Column (p. 219). Passing Piccadilly Circus, we drive to the right through the Haymarket, at the end of which, on the left, is the theatre of that name (p. 40), and, on the right, Her Majesty's Opera House (p. 40). We now come to Trafalgar Square, with the Nelson Monument (p. 145) and the National Gallery (p. 147). On the right, in the direction of Whitehall, we observe **the old statue of** Charles I. Passing **Charing Cross,** with the large **Charing** Cross Hotel (p. 7) on the right, we enter the Strand, where the Adelphi, Lyceum, Gaiety, **and other theatres lie on our left, and the Savoy, Terry's, and** Strand theatres **on our right (p. 41).** Through Salisbury Street, on the right, a glimpse is obtained of Cleopatra's Needle (p. 114). Farther on, on the left is Southampton Street, leading to Covent Garden (p. 180), and on the right Wellington Street, with Somerset House (p. 142) near the corner, leading to Waterloo Bridge (p. 143). Near the middle of the Strand we reach the churches of St. Mary le Strand (p. 142) and St. Clement Danes (p. 141). On the left we see the extensive new Law Courts (p. 139). Passing the site of Temple Bar (recently **removed; see p. 140), we now enter the City** proper (p. 66). On the right of Fleet Street are several entrances to the Temple (p. 136), while on the left rises the church of St. Dunstan in the West (p. 135). At the end of Farringdon Street, diverging on the left, we notice the Holborn Viaduct Bridge (p. 93); on the right, in New Bridge Street, is the Ludgate Hill Station. We **next drive** up Ludgate Hill, pass St. Paul's Cathedral (p. 84) on **the left,** and turn to the left to Cheapside, noticing the monument of Sir Robert Peel (p. 90), a little to the N. of which is the General

Post Office (p. 90). In Cheapside we observe Bow Church (p. 101) on the right, and near it the Guildhall (p. 98) at the end of King Street on the left. Quitting Cheapside, we enter the Poultry, in which the Mansion House (p. 102) rises on the right. Opposite the Mansion House is the Bank of England (p. 103), and before us is the Royal Exchange (p. 104), with Wellington's Statue in front. We then drive through King William Street, with the Statue of William IV., observing the Monument (p. 110) on the left.

We now quit the omnibus, and, after a walk across London Bridge (p. 109) and back, pass through part of Gracechurch Street on the right, and follow Fenchurch Street to the station of the *London and Blackwall Railway*. A train on this line carries us to Blackwall, whence we ascend the Thames by one of the *Greenwich Steamers*, passing London Docks (p. 126), St. Katherine's Docks (p. 126), the Tower (p. 117), the Custom House (p. 112), and Billingsgate (p. 111), to London Bridge. Here we may disembark, and take an omnibus back to Hyde Park Corner, or, continuing in the same boat, may pass under the Cannon Street Station Railway Bridge, Southwark Bridge (with St. Paul's rising on the right), the Chatham and Dover Bridge, and Blackfriars Bridge. Between Blackfriars Bridge and Westminster runs the Victoria Embankment (p. 113). On the right are the Temple and Somerset House (p. 142). The steamer then passes under Waterloo Bridge (p. 113), beyond which, to the right, on the Embankment, stands Cleopatra's Needle (p. 114). We alight at Charing Cross Pier, adjacent to the Charing Cross Railway Bridge, and re-embark in a *Chelsea Boat*, which will convey us past Montague House (p. 184), Richmond Terrace, Westminster Bridge, and the Houses of Parliament (p. 184), behind which is Westminster Abbey (p. 193). On the left is the Albert Embankment, with St. Thomas's Hospital (p. 297); and, farther on, Lambeth Palace (p. 297) with the Lollards' Tower, Lambeth Bridge, and, on the right, Millbank Penitentiary (p. 292). We then reach Vauxhall Bridge. From Vauxhall the traveller may walk or take a tramway car to Victoria Station, whence an omnibus will convey him to Oxford Street.

In order to obtain a view of the quarters on the right (S.) bank of the Thames, or Surrey side, we take a light-green *Atlas* omnibus (*not* a City Atlas) in Regent Circus, Oxford Street (Plan R, 23), and drive through Regent Street, Regent's Quadrant, Regent Circus (Piccadilly), Regent Street (continued), Waterloo Place (with the Crimean Monument and the York Column), Pall Mall East, and Charing Cross to (right) Whitehall. Here we observe on the left Scotland Yard, the chief police-station of London, and Whitehall Chapel (p. 181), and on the right the Admiralty, the Horse Guards (p. 183), and the Government Offices. Our route next lies through Parliament Street, beyond which we pass Westminster Abbey (p. 193) and the Houses of Parliament (p. 184) on the right. The omnibus then crosses Westminster Bridge, with the Victoria Embankment on the left, and the Albert Embankment and St. Thomas's Hospital on the right. Traversing Westminster Bridge Road, we observe at the end of it, on the right, Christchurch and Hawkstone Hall, occupying the site of the recently removed Orphan Asylum. In Lambeth Road we perceive the Church of St. George's, the Roman Catholic Cathedral of Southwark, and, opposite to it, Bethlehem Hospital. On the W. side of Circus Place, with its obelisk, rises the Blind Asylum. A little to the S. of this point, we arrive at the Elephant and Castle (on the right), where we alight, to resume our journey on a blue Waterloo omnibus. This takes us through London Road to Waterloo Road, to the right of which are the Surrey Theatre (Blackfriars Road), Magdalene Hospital, and the Victoria Music Hall (p. 43), and on the left the South Western Railway Station. We then cross Waterloo Bridge, drive along Wellington Street, passing Somerset House, and turn to the left into the Strand, which leads us to Charing Cross.

Our first curiosity having thus been gratified by a general survey of London, we may now devote our attention to its collections, monuments, and buildings in detail.

## 24. Disposition of Time.

The most indefatigable sight-seer will take at least three weeks to obtain even a superficial acquaintance with London and its objects of interest. A plan of operations, prepared beforehand, will aid him in regulating his movements and economising his time. Fine days should be spent in visiting the docks, parks, gardens, and environs. Excursions to the country around London, in particular, should not be postponed to the end of one's sojourn, as otherwise the setting in of bad weather may altogether preclude a visit to the many beautiful spots in the neighbourhood. Rainy days had better be devoted to the galleries and museums.

The following list shows the days and hours when the various collections and other sights are accessible. The early forenoon and late afternoon hours may be appropriately spent in visiting the principal churches, many of which are open the whole day, or in walking in the parks or in the Zoological and the Botanical Gardens, while the evenings may be devoted to the theatres. The best time for a promenade in Regent Street or Hyde Park is between 5 and 7 o'clock, when they both present a remarkably busy and attractive scene. When the traveller happens to be near London Bridge he should take the opportunity of crossing it in order to obtain a view of the Port of London and its adjuncts, with its seagoing vessels arriving or departing, the innumerable river craft of all sizes, and the vast traffic in the docks. A trip to Gravesend (see p. 315) should by all means be taken in order to obtain a proper view of the shipping, no other port in the world presenting such a sight.

The following data, though carefully revised down to 1889, are liable to frequent alteration. The traveller is therefore recommended to consult one of the principal London newspapers with regard to the sights of the day. Our list does not include parks, gardens, and other places which, on all week-days at least, are open to the public gratis.

## 24. DISPOSITION OF TIME.

*Academy of Arts* (p. 221), exhibition of paintings and sculpture, from May to the first Monday in August, open daily 10-7 (1s.).

*Bethnal Green Museum* (p. 128), open free on Mondays, Tuesdays, Thursdays, Fridays, and Saturdays, 10 a.m. to 10 p.m.; on Wednesday, 10-4, 5, or 6, admission 6d.

\*\**British Museum* (p. 233), daily from 10 a.m. till 4, 5, or 6 p.m. according to the season (on Mondays and Saturdays in summer till 7 or 8 p.m.); the reading-room is open to readers daily from 9 a.m. The Museum is closed on Good Friday and Christmas Day.

*Chelsea Hospital* (p. 292), daily, 10-1 and 2-7.

\**Crystal Palace, Sydenham* (p. 305), open daily, Sundays excepted, from 10 a.m. till the evening, sometimes as late as 10 or 11 p.m. Admission 1s.; Saturday occasionally 2s. 6d.; special days dearer; children half-price.

\**Dulwich Gallery* (p. 312), daily, Sundays excepted, 10-5, in winter 10-4.

\**Foundling Hospital* (p. 228), Mon. 10-4, and Sun. after morning service.

*Geological Museum* (p. 222), Mon. and Sat. 10-10, Tues., Wed., and Thurs. 10-5; closed 10th Aug. to 10th Sept.

*Greenwich Hospital* (p. 301), daily from 10 a.m. (Sun. from 2 p.m.) to 4, 5, or 6 p.m.

*Guildhall Museum* (p. 99), daily, summer 10-5; winter 10-4.

\**Hampton Court Gallery* (p. 317), daily, except Fridays, 10-6; in winter 10-4 (Sundays 2-6 or 2-4).

\**India Museum* (p. 289), daily, 10 to 4, 5, or 6; free.

\**Kew Gardens* (p. 322), daily, 12-6; Sundays 1-6 p.m.

\*\**National Gallery* (p. 147), Mondays, Tuesdays, Wednesdays, and Saturdays, 10 to 4, 5, 6, or 7, according to the season, free; Thursdays and Fridays, after 11 o'clock, 6d.

\*\**National Portrait Gallery* (p. 129), now in Bethnal Green Museum (see above).

\**Natural History Museum* (p. 273), daily from 10 to 4, 5, or 6 (closed on Sundays, Good Friday, and Christmas Day).

\**Parliament, Houses of* (p. 184), on Saturday, 10-4, by tickets obtained gratis at the office of the Lord Chamberlain.

*Royal College of Surgeons* (p. 177), Mondays, Tuesdays, Wednesdays, and Thursdays, 12-5 in summer, and 12-4 in winter; by special permission.

\*\**Saint Paul's Cathedral* (p. 81), daily, 9-5, except Sundays and the hours of divine service (admission to the crypt, etc., see p. 84).

*Soane Museum* (p. 178), Tues., Wed., Thurs., and Sat. in April, May, June, July, and August, and Tues. and Thurs. in Feb. and March, from 11 to 5.

*Society of Arts* (p. 144), daily, except Wednesdays, 10-4 p.m.

\*\**South Kensington Museum* (p. 275), Mondays, Tuesdays, and Saturdays, 10 a.m. to 10 p.m., gratis; Wednesdays, Thursdays,

and Fridays, **10 a.m. to 4, 5. or 6 p.m.** according to **the** season, admission 6d.
*Temple Church* (**p.** 136), daily, **10-1** and 2-4 o'clock, Saturday excepted (free). **The** rotunda is open **to the** public on Sundays **during** divine service.
**\*Tower** (**p.** 117), daily, 10-4, **except** Sundays; Mondays and Saturdays free; other days, Armoury **6d. and Crown** Jewels 6d.
*United Service Museum* (p. 182), **daily,** except Fridays and Sundays, 11-5, in winter 11-4 p.m.
*\*\*Westminster Abbey* (p. 193), **daily,** except Sundays, 9 a.m. till dusk. Admission to the chapels 6d.; on Mondays and Tuesdays free. Divine service **on** Sundays.
*\*Zoological Gardens* (p. 229), daily, except Sundays **(when members only are** admitted); **admission** 1s., Mondays 6d.
The royal palaces, the mansions **of** the nobility and gentry, the Bank, the Mint, the Times Printing Office, **and** other objects **of** interest for which a special permission is required, **can be** visited only **on** the days and at the hours indicated **in the order.**

### Diary.
(To be compared with the above alphabetical list.)

*Sundays.* Hampton Court, Picture Gallery **2-6,** in **winter 2-4**; Gardens from 2 till dusk. — Kew **Gardens, 1-6.** — Greenwich Hospital, **Pictures, 2 to 4, 5, or 6 p.m.** — Foundling Hospital, after morning service.

*Mondays.* **Tower, 10-4 (10-6 in** summer), free. — Temple Church, 10-4 **and 2-4, free.** — Westminster Abbey, 9-3, in summer 9-6 also, free. — National **Gallery, 10-6, in** winter 10-5. — Royal College of **Surgeons, by permission, 12-5, in** winter 12-4. — St. Paul's **Cathedral, 9-5 (crypt, clock, bell, whispering** gallery, etc., **various fees).** — South Kensington Museum, **10 a.m. to 10 p.m.,** gratis. — **Bethnal Green** Museum **and National** Portrait Gallery, 10-10, gratis. — Geological Museum, **10-10.** — British Museum, 10 to 4-5. — United Service Museum, **11-5, in** winter 11-4, by permission. — India Museum, 10-6, free. — Foundling Hospital, 10-4. — **Greenwich Hospital,** 10 to 4-6. — Chelsea Hospital, 10-4 **and 2-7.** — **Society of Arts, 10-4.** — Guildhall Museum, 10 to 4 or 5. — **Zoological Gardens, from 9 a.m.** (6d.). — Kew Gardens, 12-6. — Dulwich Gallery, 10-5, in winter 10-4. — Hampton Court, 10-6. — Crystal Palace at Sydenham, **10 a.m. till dusk** (1s.).

*Tuesdays.* Tower, 10-4 **(armouries 6d.,** crown jewels 6d.). — Temple Church, 10-4 **and 2-4 (free).** — Westminster Abbey, 9-3, in summer 9-6, free. — **St. Paul's Cathedral,** 9-5 (crypt, etc., various fees). — National Gallery, **10-6.** — Royal College of **Surgeons,** 10 to 4 or 5. — **South** Kensington Museum, 10 a.m. to 10 p.m., gratis. — Bethnal **Green** Museum and National Portrait Gallery, 10-10, gratis. — British Museum, 10 to 4, 5, or 6. — Geological Museum, 10-5. — United Service Museum, 11-5, in winter

11-4. — India Museum, 10-6, **free**. — Soane Museum, by card obtained within, from Feb. to Aug., 11-5. — Guildhall Museum, 10 to 4 or 5. — Zoological Gardens, from 9 a.m. (1s.). — Kew Gardens, 12-6. — Dulwich Gallery, 10-5, in winter 10-4. — Hampton Court, **10-6**. — Crystal Palace at Sydenham, 10 a.m. till dusk (1s.). — Greenwich Hospital, **10 till 4-6**. — **Chelsea** Hospital, **10-1 and 2-7**. — Society of Arts, 10-4.

*Wednesdays.* Tower, 10-4 (armouries, etc., 1s.). — Temple Church, 10-1 and 2-4 (free). — Westminster Abbey, **9-3**, and in summer 4-6 (chapels 6d.). — **St. Paul's** Cathedral, 9-5 (various fees). — National Gallery, 10-6. — Royal College of Surgeons, 12 to 4 or 5. — South Kensington Museum, 10 a.m. till dusk (6d.). — Bethnal Green **Museum** and National Portrait Gallery, 10 to **4, 5, or 6** (6d.). — India Museum, 10-6, **free**. — Guildhall Museum, 10 to 4 or 5. — Geological Museum, 10-5. — British Museum, 10 to 4, 5, or 6. — Soane Museum, by card obtained within, from **April to Aug.**, **11-5**. — **United Service Museum, 10-5, in winter 11-4**. — Zoological Gardens, from 9 a.m. (1s.). — Dulwich Gallery, 10-5, in winter 10-4. — Hampton Court, 10-6. — **Crystal Palace, Sydenham, 10 a.m. till dusk** (1s.). — Kew Gardens, 12-6. — Greenwich Hospital, **10 to 4-6**. — Chelsea **Hospital, 10-1 and 2-7**.

*Thursdays.* Tower, 10-4 (armouries, etc., 1s.). — Temple Church, 10-1 and 2-4 (free). — Westminster Abbey, 9-3, and in **summer 4-6 also** (chapels 6d.). — St. Paul's Cathedral, 9-5 (**various fees**). — National Gallery, 11 to 5 or 6 (6d.). — South Kensington Museum, 10 a.m. till dusk (**6d.**). — Bethnal Green **Museum** and National Portrait **Gallery, 10 to 10**, gratis. — British **Museum, 10 to 4, 5, or 6**. — Geological **Museum, 10-5**. — Soane Museum (**Feb. to Aug.**), **11-5**. — Guildhall Museum, 10 to 4 or 5. — United Service Museum, **11-5**, in winter 11-4. — India Museum, 10-6, free. — Zoological Gardens, from 9 a.m. (1s.). — Dulwich Gallery, 10-5, in winter 10-4. — Hampton Court, 10-6. — Crystal Palace at Sydenham, 10 a.m. till dusk. (1s.). — Kew Gardens, 12-6. — Greenwich Hospital, 10 till 4, 5, or 6. — Chelsea Hospital, 10-1 and 2-7. — Society of Arts, 10-4.

*Fridays.* Tower, 10-4 (armouries, etc., 1s.). — Temple Church, 10-1 and 2-4 (free). — Westminster Abbey, 9-3, and in summer 4-6 also (chapels 6d.). — St. Paul's Cathedral, 9-5 (various fees). — National Gallery, 11 to 5 or 6 (6d.). — South Kensington Museum, 10 a.m. till dusk (**6d.**). — Bethnal Green **Museum** and National Portrait Gallery, **10 to 10**, gratis. — Guildhall Museum, 10 to 4 or 5. — British Museum, **10 to 4, 5, or 6**. — India Museum, 10-6, free. — Greenwich Hospital, **10** to dusk. — Chelsea Hospital, **10-2 and 2-7**. — — Kew Gardens, 12-6. — Society of Arts, 10-4. — Zoological Gardens, from 9 a.m. (1s.). — Dulwich Gallery, 10-5, in winter 10-4. — Crystal Palace, 10 a.m. till dusk (1s.).

*Saturdays.* Houses of Parliament, 10-4. — Tower, 10-4 (10-6

## 1. ST. PAUL'S CATHEDRAL.

by a tax on coal. Sir Christopher Wren received during the building of the cathedral a salary of 200*l*. a year.

The church, which resembles St. Peter's at Rome, though much smaller, is in the form of a Latin cross. It is 500 ft. in length and 118 ft. broad, and the transept is 250 ft. long. The inner dome is 225 ft., the outer, from the pavement to the top of the cross, 364 ft. in height. The diameter of the dome is about 112 ft. (27 ft. less than that of St. Peter's at Rome). In the original model the plan of the building was that of a Greek cross, having over the centre a large dome, supported by eight pillars; but the court party, which was favourable to Roman Catholicism, insisted, notwithstanding Wren's opposition, on the erection of the cathedral with a long nave and an extensive choir, suitable for the Romish ritual.

The church is so hemmed in by streets and houses that it is difficult to find a point of view whence the colossal proportions of the building can be properly realised. The best idea of the majestic dome, allowed to be the finest known, is obtained from a distance, *e.g.* from Blackfriars Bridge. St. Paul's is the third largest church in Christendom, being surpassed only by St. Peter's at Rome and the Cathedral of Milan.

EXTERIOR. The *West Façade*, towards Ludgate Hill, was brought better to view in 1873 by the removal of the railing which formerly surrounded the whole church. In front of it rises a *Statue of Queen Anne*, with England, France, Ireland, and America at her feet; the present statue, by *Bell*, erected in 1886, is a replica of the original by *Bird* (1712). The façade, 180 ft. in breadth, is approached by a flight of 22 marble steps, and presents a double portico, the lower part of which consists of 12 coupled Corinthian pillars, 50 ft. high, and the upper of 8 Composite pillars, 40 ft. high. On the apex of the pediment above the second row of pillars, which contains a relief of the Conversion of St. Paul by *Bird*, rises a statue of St. Paul 15 ft. in height, with St. Peter and St. James on his right and left. On each side of the façade is a *campanile* tower, 222 ft. in height, with statues of the four Evangelists at the angles. The one on the N. side contains a fine peal of 12 bells, hung in 1878, and the other contains the largest bell in England ('Great Paul'), hung in 1882 and weighing more than 16 tons. Each arm of the transept is terminated by a semicircular portico, adorned with five statues of the Apostles, by *Bird*. Over the S. portico is a phœnix, with the inscription 'Resurgam', by *Cibber*; over the N. portico, the English arms. In reference to the former it is related, that, when the position and dimensions of the great dome had been marked out, a labourer was ordered to bring a stone from the rubbish of the old cathedral to be placed as a guide to the masons. The stone which he happened to bring was a piece of a gravestone with nothing of the inscription remaining save the one word 'Resurgam' in large letters. This incident was regarded as a

# 1. ST. PAUL'S CATHEDRAL.

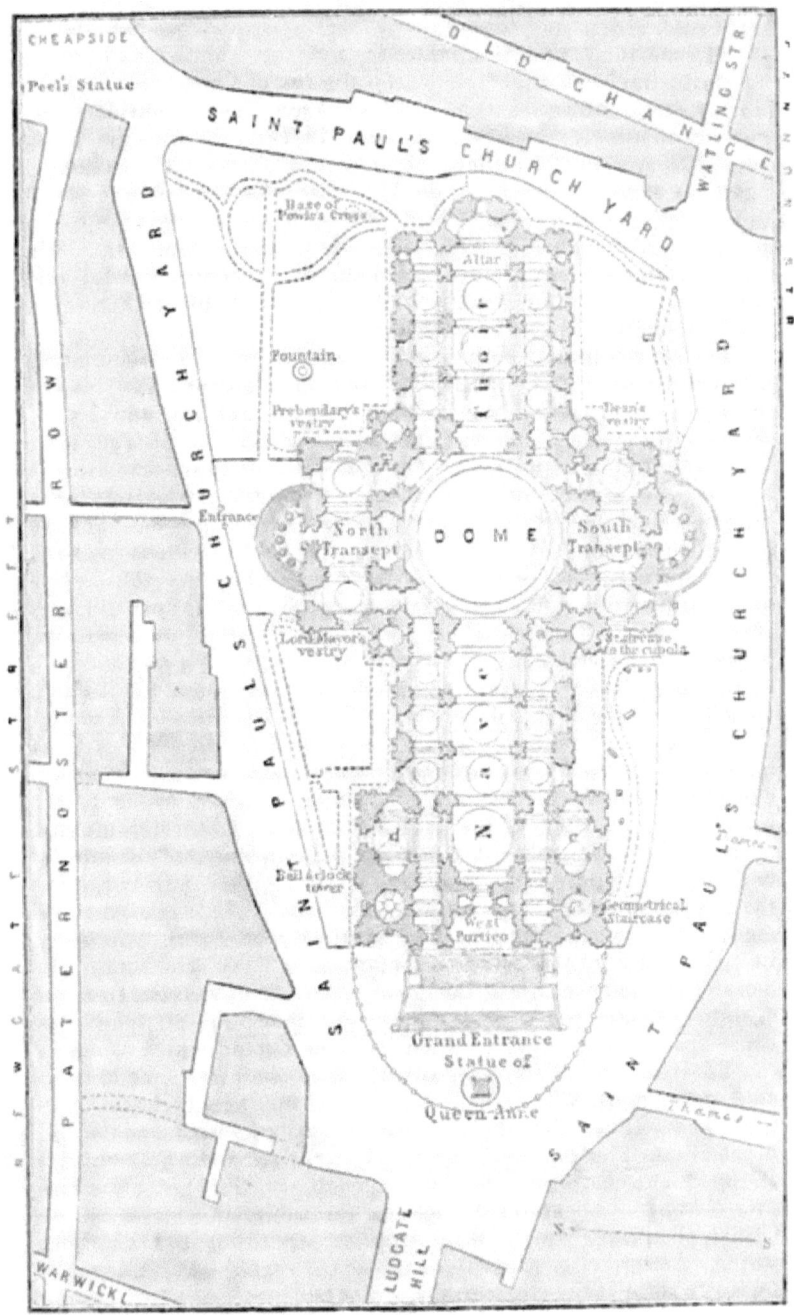

## 1. ST. PAUL'S CATHEDRAL.

favourable omen, and the word accordingly adopted as a motto. At the E. end the church terminates in a circular projection or apse. The balustrade, about 9 ft. high, on the top of the N. and S. walls was erected contrary to the wishes of Wren, and is considered by modern architects a mistake. A drum in two sections, the lower embellished with Corinthian, the upper with Composite columns, bears the finely-proportioned double *Dome*, the outer part of which consists of wood covered with lead. The *Lantern* above it is supported by a hollow cone of brickwork resting upon the inner dome. On the top of the lantern is a ball, surmounted by a cross, the ball and cross together weighing 8960 pounds. The ball is 6ft. in diameter, and can hold ten or twelve persons.

The church is open daily from 9 a.m. to 5 p.m. The monuments may be inspected, free of charge, at any time, except during divine service, which takes place daily at 10 a.m. (choral) and 4 p.m. (choral) in the choir, and on Sundays at 8 a.m., 10. 30 a.m. (fine music), 3. 15 p.m., and 7 p.m. On week-days daily services are also held at 8 a.m. and 8 p.m. in the chapel in the crypt, and Holy Communion celebrated at 8 a.m. and a short sermon preached at 1.15 p.m. in the chapel at the end of the N. aisle. The choir is closed except during divine service, but the verger from time to time admits visitors who wait at the gate of the N. ambulatory. Tickets admitting to the Library, Clock, the Whispering Gallery, and the Stone Gallery (6d.) and to the *Crypt and Vaults (6d.) are obtained in the S. transept. At present no one is admitted to the Golden Gallery or to the Ball.

The usual ENTRANCES are on the W. and N. The INTERIOR is imposing from the beauty and vastness of its proportions, but strikes one as bare and dark. Recently, however, mainly owing to the praiseworthy exertions of the late Dean Milman, a considerable sum of money has been subscribed for the embellishment of the interior with marble, gilding, mosaics, and stained glass; but at present the scheme makes little or no progress. The dome is adorned with eight scenes from the life of St. Paul in grisaille by *Thornhill*, restored in 1854, but hardly visible from below (see p. 88). The three large mosaics in the spandrils of the dome, executed by *Salviati* from the designs of *Watts*, represent Isaiah, St. Matthew, and St. John. The other spaces have yet to be filled in. The *Organ*, which is one of the finest in Great Britain, is divided into two parts, one on each side of the choir, with connecting mechanism under the choir flooring. The builder, *Mr. Willis*, in constructing it, used some of the pipes of the old organ by *Father Smith* or *Schmitz*, which dated back to 1694. The choir contains some admirable wood-carving by *Grinling Gibbons*. Above the N. door is the tablet in memory of Sir Christopher Wren, with the inscription containing the celebrated words, '*Lector, si monumentum requiris, circumspice*'. This tablet formerly stood at the entrance to the choir.

The numerous monuments of celebrated Englishmen (chiefly naval and military officers), which make the church a kind of national Temple of Fame (though second to Westminster Abbey, p. 193), are very rarely of artistic value, while many are remarkable for egregiously bad taste. The most interesting are the following, beginning to the left of the door of the N. TRANSEPT: —

L. *Sir Charles James Napier* (d. 1853); statue by *Adams*, 'a prescient General, a beneficent Governor, a just Man' (comp. p. 146).

R. *Admiral Lord Duncan* (d. 1804), who defeated the Dutch in the naval battle of Camperdown; statue by *Westmacott*.

L. *General Sir William Ponsonby* (d. 1815), 'who fell gloriously in the battle of Waterloo', by *Baily*; a nude dying hero, crowned by the Goddess of Victory, with a falling horse in the rear.

L. *Admiral Charles Napier* (d. 1860), commander of the English Baltic fleet in 1854, with portrait in relief.

L. *Henry Hallam* (d. 1859), the historian; statue by *Theed*.

L. \**Dr. Samuel Johnson* (d. 1785), statue by *Bacon*.

We have now arrived at the entrance to the CHOIR, the most conspicuous object in which is the new *Reredos*, an elaborate marble structure in the Italian Renaissance style, designed by *Messrs. Bodley & Garner* and erected in 1888. The sculptures, by *Guellemin*, represent the chief events in the life of Christ; at the top are statues of the Risen Saviour, the Virgin and Child, St. Paul, and St. Peter. The verger also shows an elaborate altar-frontal worked in embroidered silk.

Along the S. wall of the ambulatory are the following five monuments: —

*Reginald Heber*, Bishop of Calcutta (d. 1826); a kneeling figure in episcopal robes, by *Chantrey*. The relief on the pedestal represents the prelate confirming converted Indians.

*John Jackson*, Bishop of London (d. 1884); by *Woolner*.

*Charles J. Blomfield*, Bishop of London (d. 1857); sarcophagus with recumbent figure, by *G. Richmond*.

*Henry Hart Milman*, Dean of St. Paul's (d. 1868); sarcophagus and recumbent figure, by *Williamson*.

*Dr. Donne*, the poet, Dean of St. Paul's from 1621 till his death in 1631, a sculptured figure in a shroud, in a niche in the wall, by *Nicholas Stone* (the only uninjured monument from old St. Paul's).

Leaving the passage round the choir, we pass, at the entrance, on the left, a handsome pulpit of coloured marbles, erected to the memory of *Captain Fitzgerald*. Then —

In the S. TRANSEPT: —

L. *John Howard* (d. 1790), the philanthropist; statue by *Bacon*. On the scroll in the left hand are written the words '*Plan for the improvement of prisons and hospitals*'; the right hand holds a key. He died at Cherson in the S. of Russia, while on a journey which he had undertaken 'to ascertain the cause of and find an efficacious remedy for **the plague'**. This monument was the first admitted to St. Paul's.

L. *Admiral Earl Howe* (d. 1799), by *Flaxman*. Behind the statue of the hero is Britannia in armour; to the left Fame and Victory; on the right reposes the British lion. — Adjoining —

L. *Admiral Lord Collingwood* (d. 1810), Nelson's companion in arms (p. 88), by *Westmacott*.

L. *Joseph Mallord William Turner* (d. 1851), the celebrated painter; statue by *Macdowell*.

Opposite the door of the S. transept, in the passage to the nave, against the great piers: —

L. \**Admiral Lord Nelson* (d. 1805), by *Flaxman*. The **want** of the right arm, which Nelson lost at Cadiz, is concealed by the cloak; the left hand leans upon an anchor supported on a coiled up cable. The cornice bears the inscription 'Copenhagen — Nile — Trafalgar', the names of the Admiral's chief victories. The pedestal is embellished with figures in relief representing the German Ocean, the Baltic Sea, the Nile, and the Mediterranean. At the foot, to the right, couches the British lion; while on the left is Britannia inciting youthful sailors to emulate the great hero.

R. *Marquis Cornwallis* (d. 1805), Governor-General of Bengal, in the dress of a knight of the Garter; at the base, to the left, Britannia armed, to the right two Indian rivers, by *Rossi*.

In the S. transept to the W. of the door: —

L. *Sir Astley Paston Cooper* (d. 1842), the surgeon, by *Baily*.

L. *Lieutenant-General Sir John Moore* (d. 1809), by the younger *Bacon*. The general, who fell at Corunna, is being interred by allegorical figures of Valour and Victory, while the Genius of Spain erects his standard over the tomb.

L. *Lieutenant-General Sir Ralph Abercromby* (d. 1801), by *Westmacott*. The general, mortally wounded, falls from his rearing horse into the arms of a Highland soldier. The Sphinxes at the sides are emblematical of Egypt, where Sir Ralph lost his life.

L. *Sir William Jones* (d. 1794), the orientalist, who, in Dean Milman's words, 'first opened the poetry and wisdom of our Indian Empire to wondering Europe'; statue by *Bacon*.

In the S. AISLE: —

L. *Thomas Fanshaw Middleton* (d. 1822), the first English bishop in India, by *Louth*. The prelate is represented in his robes, in the act of blessing two young heathen converts.

A little farther on is a recess, formerly used as the Ecclesiastical or Consistory Court of the Diocese, and now containing the \***Monument to the *Duke of Wellington*, by *Stevens*. The bronze figure of Wellington rests on a lofty sarcophagus, overshadowed by a rich marble canopy, with 12 Corinthian columns. Above is a colossal group of Valour overcoming Cowardice. This imposing monument loses much of its effect by the confined dimensions of the chapel in which it stands, and wants the equestrian effigy with which the sculptor intended it to be crowned. The bas-reliefs on the walls of the chapel are by *Calder Marshall* (E. end) and *Woodington* (W. end). The wooden screen between the chapel and the nave was carved by *Grinling Gibbons*.

At the end of the nave is the *Crimean Monument*, to the memory of the officers of the Coldstream Guards who fell at Inkerman in 1854, a relief by *Marochetti*, with the colours of the regiment hung above.

We now reach the Grand Entrance (W.), which is a favourable point for a survey of the whole length of the nave. The new reredos also looks well from this point. Passing the entrance, we come to the Morning Chapel, which is handsomely decorated with marble. The mosaic, representing the Risen Saviour, was executed by *Salviati*, and commemorates Archdeacon Hale. The stained-glass window is a memorial of *Dean Mansel* (1868-71). Then to the left, in the N. AISLE: —

L. *The Crimean Cavalry Monument*, in memory of the officers and men of the British cavalry who fell in the Crimean war (1854-56).

L. *Major-General Sir Herbert Stewart*, who died in 1885 of wounds received at the battle of Abu-kru, Egypt; bronze medallion and reliefs by *Boehm*.

L. *Major-General Charles George Gordon*, killed at Khartoum in 1885; sarcophagus-tomb, with bronze effigy by *Boehm*.

L. *Lord William Melbourne* (d. 1848) and *Lord Frederick Melbourne* (d. 1853), by *Marochetti*. Two angels guard the closed entrance to the tomb. — On each side is a brass plate, on which are inscribed the names of the officers and crew (484 in number) of the ill-starred line-of-battle ship *Captain*, which foundered with all hands off Cape Finisterre on 7th Sept., 1870.

In the N. TRANSEPT (W. side): —

L. *Sir Joshua Reynolds* (d. 1792), the celebrated painter, statue by *Flaxman*. Upon the broken column to his left is a medallion-portrait of Michael Angelo.

L. *Admiral Lord Rodney* (d. 1792), by *Rossi*. At his feet, to the left, is History listening to the Goddess of Fame (on the right), who recounts the Admiral's exploits.

L. *Lieutenant-General Sir Thomas Picton* (killed at Waterloo in 1815), by *Gahagan*. In front of his bust is a Goddess of Victory presenting a crown of laurels to a warrior, upon whose shoulder leans the Genius of Immortality.

R. *Admiral Earl St. Vincent* (d. 1823), the victor at Cape St. Vincent; statue by *Baily*.

L. *General William Francis Patrick Napier* (d. 1860), the historian of the Peninsular War, by *Adams*.

In the S. aisle, near the S. transept (Pl. a), is the entrance to the UPPER PARTS of the church (admission, see p. 84). Ascending about

110 steps, we reach a gallery (above the S. aisle), a room at the end of which contains the *Library* (9000 volumes; portrait of the founder, Bishop Compton). The flooring consists of artistically executed **mosaic in wood.** The large, self-supporting, winding staircase, **called the** *Geometrical Staircase,* is interesting only on account of its **age.** The *Great Bell* (cast in 1716; 88 steps) and the large *Clock* (constructed in 1708; 13 steps more), in the N.W. tower, are scarcely **interesting enough to repay the** fatigue of ascending to them. The **minute hand of the clock is nearly 10 ft. long.**

The *Whispering Gallery,* in the interior of the cupola, reached by a flight **of steps from the library** (260 steps from the floor of the church), is remarkable **for a curious** echo, which resembles that of the Salle d'Echo in the Conservatoire des Arts et Métiers at Paris. **A slight whisper uttered** by the **wall on one** side of the gallery is distinctly audible to an ear near the wall on the other side, a dis**tance of 108 ft. in a** direct line, or 160 ft. round the semicircle. **This is the best point of view for** Thornhill's ceiling-paintings, and from it we also obtain a fine survey of the interior of the church.

From this point a flight of 118 steps leads to the \*Stone Gal*lery,* **an outer gallery, enclosed by a stone parapet, which runs round the foot of the outer dome. This gallery commands an admirable view of the city. The survey is** still more extensive from the outer *Golden Gallery* above the dome and at the foot of the lantern, to **which a winding staircase ascends** in the inside of the roof. **The** *Ball* **(p. 84) on the lantern is 45 ft.** higher (616 steps from the tesselated pavement of the church). Visitors, however, are not at **present admitted to either the** Golden Gallery or the Ball.

At the S. end of the transept is the door leading down into the \*CRYPT **(Pl. b). Here we are first conducted to the** left into a **chamber lighted by four candelabra** of polished **granite, in the centre of which stands the** sarcophagus of *Wellington* (d. 1852), **consisting of a huge block of** porphyry, resting on a granite base. Adjacent **is the sarcophagus of** *Sir Thomas Picton* (p. 87), who fell **at Waterloo in 1815. Farther on, exactly** under the centre of the **dome, is the black marble sarcophagus of** *Nelson* (d. 1805), con**taining an inner coffin made of** part of the mainmast of the French **flag-ship L'Orient,** which was blown up **at** Aboukir. **This sarcophagus, said to be the work of** Torregiano (p. 209), was originally **ordered by** Card. Wolsey for himself (comp. p. 338). The smaller **sarcophagus on the S. is that** of Nelson's comrade, *Admiral Collingwood* **(d. 1810), while on the** N. is that of the *Earl of Northesk*.

We next notice two tabular monuments in memory of two **officers who fell at Trafalgar in** 1805, placed here recently to **make room for the** reconstruction of the organ at the entrance to the **choir.** In a chamber behind Nelson's sarcophagus is the hearse **used at** the Duke of Wellington's **funeral,** with its trappings. It **was cast from guns captured in the victories of the** 'Iron Duke'.

In a straight direction from the staircase we reach the vaults, which contain busts and fragments of monuments from the earlier building (*i.e.* **prior to** 1666). The flooring **consists of memorial** slabs of celebrated artists and others. Among these are *John Rennie*, builder of Waterloo Bridge; *Robert Mylne*, who built several other London bridges; *Benjamin West; Sir Joshua Reynolds; Sir Thomas Lawrence; Sir* **Edwin Landseer;** *John Opie; J. M. W. Turner* (buried, **at his own dying** request, **near** Reynolds); *Thos. Newton*, Dean of the Cathedral; and *Dean Milman. Sir Christopher Wren*, the **architect of St.** Paul's, **and his wife,** *Samuel Johnson. William Babington. Sir Astley Cooper. George Cruikshank, Sir Bartle Frere,* and *Sir William Jones* also repose here. A space at the E. end of the crypt, used as a morning chapel, possesses a fine mosaic pavement.

In May an annual festival is held in St. Paul's for the benefit of the sons of deceased clergymen. Admission by tickets, procured at the Corporation House, 2 Bloomsbury Place, Bloomsbury Square, W.C. The Charity School Festivals formerly held in St. Paul's have been discontinued on account of the interruption to the services caused by the erection of the necessary scaffolding.

The clerical establishment of the cathedral consists of the Dean, four Canons. 30 Prebendaries. 12 Minor Canons, and 6 Vicars Choral. *Sydney Smith* and *R. H. Barham*, author of the 'Ingoldsby Legends', were canons of St. Paul's. — For a full account of this noble church, see Dean Milman's 'Annals of St. Paul's'.

The street round the cathedral, called *St. Paul's Churchyard*, has been much improved by the removal of the railings before the western front of the Cathedral, which has widened the street and facilitated the passage of pedestrians, as well as given a better view of the building. On the three other sides the church is still surrounded by high and heavy railings, but the stone walls supporting them have recently been lowered with advantage to a height of eighteen inches. In the 16th cent. St. Paul's Churchyard was open to Paternoster Row, with a few intervening buildings, all belonging to the precincts. These disappeared in the Great Fire.

¦ Celebrated coffee-houses in the Churchyard, where authors and booksellers used to meet, were St. Paul's Coffee-House, near the archway leading to Doctors' Commons; Child's Coffee-House, a great resort of the clergy and *literati;* and the Queen's Arms Tavern, often visited by Dr. Johnson. They were also frequented by the lawyers of Doctors' Commons. Among the famous eighteenth century publishers of St. Paul's Churchyard may be mentioned Johnson, Hunter, Newbery, and Rivington. For Newbery, the site of whose shop (rebuilt in 1885), at the corner next Ludgate Hill, is now occupied by Griffith and Farran, Goldsmith is said to have written 'Goody Two Shoes', amongst other books.

## 2. General Post Office. Christ's Hospital. Newgate. Holborn.

*Paternoster Row. Peel's Statue. Central Criminal Court. St. Sepulchre's. Holborn Viaduct.*

Leaving St. Paul's Churchyard, on the N. side of the church, we enter **Paternoster Row** (so called from the prayer-books formerly sold in it), the chief seat of the publishers and booksellers. To the W., in Stationers' Hall Court, off Ludgate Hill, is situated Stationers' **Hall**, the guild-house of the booksellers and stationers.

This company is one of the few London guilds the majority of whose members actually practise their nominal craft. The society lost its monopoly of publishing almanacks in 1771, but still carries on this business extensively. The company distinguished itself in 1631 by printing a Bible with the word 'not' omitted in the seventh commandment. Every work published in Great Britain must be registered at Stationers' Hall to secure the copyright. The hall contains portraits of Richardson, the novelist (Master of the Company in 1754), and his wife, Prior, Steele, Bunyan, and others; also *West's* painting of King Alfred sharing his loaf with the pilgrim St. Cuthbert.

At the E. end of Paternoster Row, at the entrance to Cheapside (p. 101), rises the **Statue of Sir Robert Peel** (d. 1850), by *Behnes*. Immediately to the N., on the E. side of St. Martin's le Grand, is the **General Post Office East** (Pl. R, 39, and III; comp. p. 53), built in the Ionic style in 1825-29, from designs by *Smirke*. In this building, 390 ft. in length, *Letters* and *Newspapers* are dealt with and all the ordinary business of a postal-telegraph office carried on. *Parcels* are received here, but are at once sent on to the Parcel Post Office at Mount Pleasant, Farringdon Road (formerly Coldbath Fields Prison). To the S. of the portico is the 'Poste Restante' Office. This is the headquarters of the London Postal District, and the vast City correspondence is all dealt with here. The *Returned Letter Office* is in Moorgate Street Buildings, off Moorgate Street, where boards are exhibited with lists of persons whose addresses have not been discovered.

POSTAL TRAFFIC. The number of *letters* transmitted by post in the United Kingdom in 1874 was 962,000,000, in 1876 it was 1,019,000,000, and in 1885-86 no less than 1,403,547,900, or 39 letters per head of population. Besides letters, 259,000,000 *book-packets* and newspapers, and 79,000,000 *post-cards*, were delivered in 1874; 298,000,000 newspapers and book-packets, and 93,000,000 post-cards, in 1876; and 189,928,500 newspapers and book-packets, and 171,290,000 post-cards, in 1885-86. About 23 per cent of the letters and other postal packets received from abroad come from the United States, while 20 per cent of those dispatched from the United Kingdom are addressed to that country. In the same period the Parcel Post forwarded 26,417,422 parcels. The sums of money sent by *post-office orders*, notwithstanding the universal practice of transmitting money by cheque, and the limitation of the orders to ten pounds, are very considerable. Thus in 1874 there were issued 15,100,562 inland post-office orders representing a sum of 26,296,441*l*. The introduction of postal orders diverted part of this stream of money, and in 1885-6 the number of post office orders had sunk to 10,358,000. In that year 25,790,369 *postal orders* were also issued, amounting in value to 10,788,940*l*. The *Post Office Savings Banks*, established in 1861, hold at present about 51,000,000*l.* on deposit. The profits of the English Post Office Department in 1885-86 amounted to 2,708,882*l.*

Opposite to the General Post Office East stands the **General Post Office West**, containing the *Administrative Offices* and the *Telegraph Department*. This imposing building was erected in 1870-73 at a cost of 485,000*l*. The large Telegraph Instrument Galleries, extending the whole length of the building and measuring 300 by 90 ft., should be visited (admission by request from a banker or other well-known citizen). They contain 500 instruments with their attendants. On the sunk-floor are four steam-engines of 50 horse-power each, by means of which messages are forwarded through pneumatic tubes to the other offices in the City and Strand district. The number of telegrams conveyed in the year ending 31st March, 1886, was 39,235,900.

The vast and ever-growing business of the General Post Office has long found itself straitened for room even in these huge buildings, and extensive additions have been begun to the N. To secure a site for these the Queen's Hotel, the Bull & Mouth Hotel, the French Protestant Church, and numerous other buildings have been pulled down.

To the N. of the Post Office lies *Aldersgate Street*, a little to the E. of which is *Monkwell Street* (reached by Falcon Street and Silver Street), containing the *Barber-Surgeons' Court Room*. Among the curiosities preserved here are a valuable portrait of Henry VIII. by Holbein, and one of Inigo Jones by Vandyck. — Milton once lived in Aldersgate Street, and afterwards in Jewin Street, a side-street on the right.

To the W. of the General Post Office is NEWGATE STREET, a great omnibus thoroughfare, leading to Holborn and Oxford Street. This neighbourhood has long been the quarter of the butchers. In *Panyer Alley*, the first cross-lane to the left, once inhabited by basket-makers, is an old relief of a boy sitting upon a 'panier', with the inscription:

'When ye have sought the city round,
Yet still this is the highest ground.
August the 27th, 1688'.

Farther on, opposite the site of old Newgate Market, is a passage on the right leading to —

**Christ's Hospital** (Pl. R, 39; *III*), a school for 1200 boys and 100 girls, founded by Edward VI., with a yearly income from land and funded property of 60,000*l.*, not all of which, however, is devoted to educational purposes. It occupies the site of an ancient monastery of the Grey Friars, founded in the 13th cent., and once the burial-place of many illustrious persons. The general government of the school is in the hands of a large 'Court of Governors', consisting of noblemen and other gentlemen of position; but the internal and real management is conducted by the President, Treasurer, and 'Committee of Almoners', fifty in number. The original costume of the boys is still retained, consisting of long blue gowns, yellow stockings, and knee-breeches. No head-covering is worn even in winter. The pupils (*Blue Coat Boys*), who are admitted between the ages of eight and ten, must be the children of parents whose income is insufficient for their proper education and maintenance. They are first sent to the preparatory school at Hertford, whence they are transferred according to their progress to the city establishment. Their education, which is partly of a commercial nature, is completed at the age of sixteen. A few of the more talented pupils are, however, prepared for a university career, and form the two highest classes of the school, known as the *Grecians* and *Deputy-Grecians*. There are also 40 *King's Boys*, forming the mathematical school founded by Charles II. in 1672. The school possessed many ancient privileges, some of which it still retains. On New Year's Day the King's Boys used to appear at Court; and on Easter Tuesday the entire school is presented to the Lord Mayor, at the Mansion House, when each boy receives the gift of a coin fresh from the Mint. A line in the swimming-bath marks the junction of three parishes. In the *Hall*, which was erected by *Shaw* in 1825-29, the head-pupils annually deliver a number of public orations. The 'suppings in public' on each Thursday in Lent, at 7 p.m., are worth attending (tickets from governors). Among the pictures on the walls are the Founding of the Hospital by Edward VI., ascribed to *Holbein;* Presentation of the King's Boys at the Court of James II., a very large work by *Verrio;* Portraits of the Queen and Prince Albert, by *Grant*. Among the celebrated men who were educated here we may mention William Camden, Stillingfleet, Middleton, Dyer, Samuel Richardson, S. T. Coleridge, Charles Lamb, Leigh Hunt, and Sir Henry Sumner Maine (d. 1888).

Opposite Christ's Hospital is *Warwick Lane*, leading out of Newgate Street. On the wall of the first house from Newgate Street on the right is a curious relief of 1668, representing Warwick, the 'King-maker'.

At the W. end of Newgate St., at the corner of Old Bailey, stands **Newgate Prison** (Pl. R. 35: *II*), once the principal prison of London, now used as a temporary house of detention for prisoners awaiting trial at the Old Bailey Court. The present building, which was begun in 1770 by *George Dance*, was partly destroyed in 1780, before its completion, by the Gordon rioters, but was restored in 1782. The principal façade, looking towards the Old Bailey, is 300 ft. in length. The interior was rebuilt in 1858 on the separate cell system. Permission to inspect the prison, which has accommodation for 192 prisoners, is granted by the Secretary of State for the Home Department, the Lord Mayor, and the Sheriffs. The public place of execution, which was formerly at Tyburn near Hyde Park, was afterwards for a long period in front of Newgate, but criminals are not now hanged in public. Among the famous or notorious prisoners once confined in old Newgate were George Wither, Daniel Defoe, Jack Sheppard, Titus Oates, and William Penn. Old London Wall had a gateway at the bottom of Newgate Street, by Newgate Prison.

Adjoining Newgate is the **Central Criminal Court**, consisting of two divisions; *viz.* the *Old Court* for the trial of grave offences, and the *New Court* for petty offences. The trials are public, but as the courts are often crowded, a fee of 1-5*s.*, according to the interest of the case, must generally be given to the door-keeper to secure a good seat. At great trials, however, tickets of admission are usually issued by the aldermen and sheriffs.

No. 68 Old Bailey, near Ludgate Hill, was the house of the infamous thief-catcher, Jonathan Wild, himself hanged in 1725.

A little to the W. of Newgate begins the *Holborn **Viaduct*** (Pl. R, 35, 36; *II*), a triumph of the art of modern street-building, designed by *Haywood*, and completed in 1869. Its name is a reminiscence of the '*Hole-Bourne*', the name given to the upper course of the *Fleet* (p. 134), from its running through a deep hollow. This structure, 465 yds. long and 27 yds. broad, extending from Newgate to Hatton Garden, was constructed in order to overcome the serious obstruction to the traffic between Oxford Street and the City caused by the steep descent of Holborn Hill. Externally the viaduct, which is constructed almost entirely of iron, is not visible, as rows of new buildings extend along either side. Beneath the roadway are vaults for commercial purposes, and subways for gas and water pipes, telegraph wires, and sewage, while at the sides are the cellars of the houses. At the E. extremity, to the right, stands *St. Sepulchre's Church*, with its square tower, where a knell is tolled on the occasion of an execution at Newgate. At one time a nosegay was presented at this church to every criminal on his way to execution at Tyburn. On the S. side of the choir lie the remains of the gallant *Captain John Smith* (d. 1631), 'Sometime Governour of Virginia and Admirall of New England'. The first line of the now nearly illegible epitaph runs thus: —

'Here lies one conquer'd that hath conquer'd kings!'

*Roger Ascham*, author of 'The Scholemaster' and teacher of Lady Jane Grey, is also buried here.

Obliquely opposite, to the left, is the *Holborn Viaduct Station* of the London, Chatham, and Dover Railway (p. 33), and near it is the *Imperial Hotel* (p. 10). The iron *Bridge over Farringdon Street (which traverses Holborn Valley, p. 134) is 39 yds. long and is supported by 12 columns of granite, each 4 ft. in diameter. On the parapet are bronze statues of Art, Science, Commerce, and Agriculture; on the corner-towers, statues of famous Lord Mayors. Flights of steps descend in the towers to Farringdon Street.

To the left, beyond the bridge, are the *City Temple* (Congregational church; Dr. Joseph Parker; see p. 51) and *St. Andrew's Church*, where Lord Beaconsfield was christened, the latter erected in 1686 by Wren. Nearly opposite the church is the entrance to *Ely*

*Place*, formerly the site of the celebrated palace of the bishops of Ely, **where John** of Gaunt, brother of the Black Prince and father of Henry IV., **died** in 1399. The chapel of the palace, known as *Ely Chapel* (St. Etheldreda's; see p. 52), escaped the fire of 1666 **and has been** recently restored. It is a good specimen of 14th cent. architecture and retains its original oaken roof. The noble E. and W. windows are splendid examples of tracery, and the former is filled with fine stained glass. The crypt is also worth visiting, and the **quaint** cloister, planted with fig-trees, forms a strangely quiet nook amid the roar of Holborn. A little farther on is Holborn Circus, **embellished with** an *Equestrian Statue of Prince Albert*, by *Bacon*, with allegorical figures and reliefs on the granite pedestal. The new and wide **Charterhouse Street** leads hence in a N.E. direction to *Smithfield* (**p.** 95) **and the** *Farringdon Street Station* of the Metropolitan Railway (p. 36). On the W. side of the Circus begins *Holborn*, **leading to** Oxford **Street and** Bayswater; see p. 225. On the N. side **of Holborn** are the *Black Bull* and the *Old Bell*, two survivals **of the old-fashioned inns**, with galleried court-yards, and *Furnival's Inn*, formerly an inn of chancery (comp. p. 139), entirely rebuilt **in 1818.** Charles Dickens was living at Furnival's Inn, when he began the 'Pickwick Papers'. **On the** opposite **side of** the street are *Barnard's Inn* and *Staple Inn*, two quaint and picturesque old **inns of chancery (comp. p.** 139), celebrated by Dickens.

### 3. St. Bartholomew's Hospital. Smithfield. St. Giles, Cripplegate. Charterhouse.

**St.** Bartholomew's Hospital (Pl. R, 40; II), in Smithfield, **to the** N. of Christ's Hospital, is the oldest and one of the wealthiest **benevolent** institutions in London. In 1123 Rahere, a favourite of Henry I., **founded here a priory and hospital of St. Bartholomew**, which **were enlarged by Richard Whittington**, Lord Mayor of London. The **hospital was refounded by Henry** VIII. on the suppression of the monasteries **in 1547. The present** large quadrangular edifice was **erected by** *Gibbs* **in 1730-33, and has two entrances. Above the** W. **gate, towards** Smithfield, **built in** 1702, **is a statue of Henry** VIII., **with a sick man and a cripple at the sides. An inscription on the external wall commemorates the burning of** three **Protestant martyrs in the reign of Queen** Mary **(p.** 95). Within the gate is the church of *St. Bartholomew the Less*, originally built by Rahere, but re-erected in 1823. The hospital enjoys a yearly **revenue of 40,000***l.***, and contains 676** beds, in which 6000 **patients are annually attended. Relief is** also given to about 140,000 out-patients. **Cases of accident are taken in** at any **hour** of the **day or** night, **and** receive immediate **and gratuitous attention.**

**The** Medical School connected with **the hospital is famous.** It has numbered **among its teachers Harvey, the discoverer** of the circulation of the blood, Abernethy, and other renowned physicians. The lectures are delivered in the *Anatomical Theatre*, built in 1842. There are also *Museums of Anatomy* and *Botany*, a well-furnished *Library*, and a *Chemical Laboratory*. The medical school has recently been rebuilt and enlarged.

The great hall contains a few good portraits, among which we notice an old portrait of Henry VIII. (*not* by Holbein); **Dr. Radcliffe**, physician to Queen Anne, by *Kneller*; Perceval **Pott**, for 42 years surgeon to the Institution, by *Sir Joshua Reynolds*; **Abernethy**, the physician, by *Sir Thomas Lawrence*. **The paintings on** the grand staircase, the Good Samaritan, the **Pool of Bethesda**, Rahere as founder of the Hospital, and a Sick man borne **by** monks, are the work of *Hogarth*, who executed them **gratuitously,** and was in return made a Governor for **life**.

The neighbouring *Church of St. Bartholomew the Great, chiefly **in the** Anglo-Norman style, **restored** in 1865-69 **and again in** 1886, merits attention (keys at 1 Church Passage, **Cloth Fair**). **With the exception of the chapel in the Tower (p. 120),** which **is 20 years earlier, this is the oldest church in the City of** London. **Like the** Hospital (p. **94) it was founded by** Rahere in 1123, **sixty years before the foundation of the Temple Church** (p. 136).

The existing church, consisting **merely of the** choir, the crossing, and one bay of the nave of the **original Priory** Church, **is mainly pure Norman work as left by** Rahere. Other portions of the church **were alienated or destroyed by Henry** VIII. **From Smithfield we pass through an arched gateway, with** line **dog-to-**othed **moulding, which formed the entrance either to the nave or to an inner court, now the graveyard. Here may be seen some remains of the E.E. piers of the nave, which was somewhat later than the choir. In the 14th cent. the apsidal end of the choir was replaced by a square ending, with one large window, the jambs of which still remain. The clerestory was rebuilt at the same time and a fine Lady Chapel thrown out to the E. of the high-altar. This chapel was long used as a fringe manufactory, being mutilated almost beyond recognition, but was repurchased in 1886 for 6500l. *Prior Bolton* made farther alterations in the 16th cent. and his rebus (a 'bolt' through a 'tun') may be seen at the base of the beautiful oriel on the S. side of the choir and on the doorway at the E. end of the S. ambulatory. The present apse was built in the recent restoration, and has restored the choir to something of its original beauty. Funds, however, are still needed to remove the blacksmith's forge which occupies the N. transept and to complete the restoration of other parts of the church (photographs of the church sold by the verger, prices 6d.-2s.; description of the church 1s.).**

**The *Tombs* are worthy of attention. That of the founder, on the N. side of the** sanctuary, **with its rich canopy, is much later than the effigy of** Rahere resting upon it. **In the S. ambulatory is the handsome tomb, in** alabaster, of Sir Walter Mildmay **(d. 1589), Chancellor of the Exchequer to** Queen Elizabeth and founder of **Emmanuel College, Cambridge. Many of the** epitaphs are curious. At the **W. end of the church is a tasteful oaken screen**, erected in 1889.

Among the notable men **who** have lived in **Bartholomew Close are** Milton, Franklin, Hogarth **(who** was baptized **in the existing font), Dr.** Caius, and Washington **Irving**.

The adjoining **market-place of Smithfield** (Pl. R, 36, 40; *II*), a **name** said **to have been originally** *Smooth-field*, **was formerly a tournament ground, and lay outside the walls of London. Here**

## 3. CENTRAL LONDON MEAT MARKET.

Bartholomew Fair, with its revels, was held for many ages. Sham-fights, tilts, tricks of acrobats, and even miracle-plays were exhibited. Wat Tyler was slain here in 1381 by the then Lord Mayor, Sir William Walworth; and here in the reign of 'Bloody Mary' many of the persecuted Protestants, including Rogers, Bradford, and Philpot, suffered death at the stake, while under Elizabeth several Nonconformists met with a similar fate. Smithfield was the place of public execution before Tyburn, and in 1305 witnessed the beheading of the Scottish patriot, William Wallace. Subsequently, during a long period, Smithfield was the only cattle-market of London. The space having at length become quite inadequate, the cattle-market was removed to Copenhagen Fields (comp. p. 27) in 1855, after much opposition from the Corporation, and in 1862-68 the *Central London Meat Market was erected here. The building, designed by *Horace Jones*, is in a pleasing Renaissance style, with four towers at the corners. It is 630 ft. long, 245 ft. broad, and 30 ft. high, and covers an area of $3\frac{1}{2}$ acres. The roof is of glass and iron. A broad carriage-road intersects the market from N. to S.

Below the building is an extensive Railway Depôt, belonging to the Great Western Co., and connected with several underground railways, from which the meat is conveyed to the market by a lift. In the centre of Smithfield is a small garden, with a handsome fountain. The road winding round the garden leads down to the subterranean area below the market, which is a sufficiently curious specimen of London underground life to repay the descent.

To the W. of the Meat Market is the new *Market for Pork, Poultry, and Provisions*, which was opened for business in 1876. It is by the same architect and in the same style as the Meat Market, and measures 260 by 245 ft. Still farther to the W. (on the E. side of Farringdon Street) stands another market, erected in 1883 as a fish-market at a cost of 435,000l., but now being converted into a *Fruit and Vegetable Market*. A new *Fish Market* has been erected in Snow Hill, immediately to the S. Smithfield Market affords a sight not easily paralleled, and deserves a visit.

*Charterhouse Street*, a broad and handsome thoroughfare, leads to the W. from Smithfield to Holborn (p. 94).

A little to the E. of Smithfield is the church of **St. Giles** (Pl. R. 40), Cripplegate, built in 1545 (approached by an archway in Red Cross Street).

It contains the tombs of John Milton (d. 1674), who wrote 'Paradise Lost' in a house in this parish, now pulled down; Foxe (d. 1587), the martyrologist; Frobisher (d. 1594), the voyager; and Speed (d. 1629), the topographer. Oliver Cromwell was married in this church (Aug. 22nd, 1620), and the parish register contains an entry of the burial of Daniel Defoe (d. 1731). Milton is commemorated by a good bust, by *Bacon*, and a stained-glass window has been erected to his memory by Mr. G. W. Childs of Philadelphia. Comp. *J. J. Baddeley's* 'Account of the Church and Parish of St. Giles' (1888).

In the churchyard is an old bastion of London Wall, and close by, in *London Wall*, is a small part of the churchyard of St. Alphage, containing another large and interesting fragment of the old wall (p. 63).

To the E. of St. Giles, running N. from Fore Street to Chiswell Street, is *Milton Street*, better known as the 'Grub Street' of Pope and his contemporaries.

To the N.E. of Smithfield we traverse Charterhouse **Square** to the **Charterhouse** (corrupted from Chartreuse), formerly a Carthusian monastery, or priory of the Salutation (whence the name of the Salutation Tavern in Newgate **Street**), founded **in 1371 on the site of a burying-field for persons dying of the plague. After** its dissolution by Henry VIII. in 1537, the monastery **passed** through various hands, including those of Lord North and Thomas Howard, Duke of Norfolk, who made it the town-house of the Howards. Queen Elizabeth made a stay of five days a**t the Charterhouse awaiting** her coronation, and her successor James I. kept court **here for** several days on entering London. The property **was purchased in** 1611 by *Thomas Sutton*, a wealthy merchant, for his '**Hospital**', *i.e.* a school for 40 'poor boys' and a home for 80 'poor **men**'. **The school was transferred in 1872 to Godalming in Surrey, where large and handsome buildings were erected for it. The** part of the **property** thus vacated was sold to the Merchant Taylors' Company **for their** ancient school, now containing 500 **boys. The** Charterhouse **School,** which is attended by 440 boys **besides 60 on** the **foundation, boasts among its** former **scholars the names of Barrow, Lovelace, Steele,** Addison, **Blackstone, Wesley, Grote, Thirlwall, Leech, Havelock,** and Thackeray. **Visitors are shown over the buildings by the porter.**

The ancient buildings date chiefly from the early part of the 16th cent., but have been modified and added to by Lord North, the Duke of Norfolk, and others. The *Great Hall* is considered one of the finest specimens of a 16th cent. room in London. The *Great Staircase* and the *Great Chamber* upstairs are, with the exception of the W. window of the latter, just as the Duke of Norfolk left them three centuries ago. Part of the original *Chapel* (1371) remains, but it was altered by the monks about 1500 and greatly enlarged by the Trustees of Thomas Sutton in 1612, when it received its present Jacobean appearance. It is approached by a cloister with memorials of Thackeray, Leech, Havelock, John Hullah, etc., and contains a fine alabaster monument of Sutton (1611) and the monuments of the first Lord Ellenborough by Chantrey and of Dr. Raine by Flaxman. The two quadrangles in which the Pensioners and some of the officials reside were built about 1825-30.

The *Master's Lodge* contains several portraits: Sutton, the founder of the institution; Charles II.; George Villiers, second Duke of Buckingham (one of *Kneller*'s best portraits); Duke of Monmouth; Lord Chancellor Shaftesbury; Lord Chancellor Somers; William, Earl of Craven; Archbishop Sheldon; Talbot, Duke of Shrewsbury; and the fine portrait of Dr. Burnet, also by *Kneller*.

A little to the W. of the Charterhouse is *St. John's Lane*, in which is situated **St. John's Gate** (Pl. R, 36), an interesting relic **of an old priory** of the knights of St. John, with lateral **turrets, erected in the** late-Gothic **style** in 1504. The knights **of St. John were** suppressed **by** Henry **VIII.,** restored **by Mary, and finally** dispersed by Elizabeth. The rooms above **the gate were once occupied by Cave, the** founder of the 'Gentleman's **Magazine'** (1731)**, to which** Dr. Johnson contributed **and** which has a representation **of St. John**'s Gate on the cover; they now contain some interesting **historical** relics, including the chair of the great lexicographer. **The Norman crypt** of *St. John's Church* is part of the old priory church. In the little graveyard are buried the grandfather and other relatives of Wilkes Booth, the murderer of President Lincoln. The neighbouring **district** of *Clerkenwell*, now largely inhabited by watchmakers, goldsmiths, and opticians, derives its name from the 'Clerks' Well' once situated here, to which the parish clerks of London annually resorted for the celebration of miracle plays, etc.

To the E. of the Charterhouse, adjoining Bunhill Row, is the **Bunhill Fields Cemetery** (Pl. R, 40, 44), once the chief burial-place for Nonconformists, but now disused It contains the tombs of **John Bunyan** (d. 1688), Daniel Defoe (d. 1731), Dr. Isaac Watts (d. 1748). Susannah Wesley (d. 1742; the mother of John and Charles Wesley), William Blake (d. 1827), Henry, Richard, and William Cromwell, etc. Immediately to the S. of the cemetery are the headquarters and drill-ground of the **Honourable Artillery Company**, the oldest military body in the kingdom.

The H. A. C., as it is generally called, received its charter of incorporation, under the title of the Guild or Fraternity of St. George, from Henry VIII. in 1537, and its rights and privileges have been confirmed by upwards of 20 royal warrants. The officers of the Trained Bands and the City of London Militia were formerly always selected from members of this Company. Since 1660 the Captain-General and Colonel has always been either the King or the Prince of Wales. The Company, which has occupied its present ground since 1642, consists of light cavalry, a battery of field artillery, and a battalion of infantry. It is the only volunteer corps which includes horse-artillery. See the *History* of the Company, by *Lt. Col. Raikes*.

In Castle Street (Pl. R, 44), to the E. of Bunhill Fields, is the **Allan Wesleyan Library** (p. 17), containing one of the finest collections of Biblical and theological works in England. In Blomfield Street, London Wall (Pl. R, 43, 44), is the *Museum of the London Missionary Society* (open 10 to 3 or 4 on Tues., Thurs., & Sat.)

A little to the E. of the Hon. Artillery Company's ground, in Curtain Street, is the *Church of St. James* which probably stands on or near the site of the old *Curtain Theatre*, where, according to tradition, 'Hamlet' was first performed. It is not unlikely that Shakespeare acted here in his own plays. To commemorate this association a stained glass **window** was erected in 1880 at the W. end of the church by Mr. Stanley Cooper.

Immediately to the S.E. of the Charterhouse, in Goswell Road, at the corner of Long Lane, is the *Aldersgate* **Street** *Station* (Pl. R, 40) of the Metropolitan Railway (p. 36). *Aldersgate Street* leads hence to St. Martin's le Grand and St. Paul's (p. 81).

## 4. Guildhall. Cheapside. Mansion House.

*Gresham College. Goldsmiths' Hall. St. Mary le Bow. Mercers' Hall. Armourers' Hall. St. Stephen's, Walbrook.*

To the N. of Cheapside, **at the end** of King Street (p. 101), rises the **Guildhall** (Pl. R, 39; *III*), or Council-hall of the city. The building was originally **erected in 1411-31** for the sittings of the magistrates and municipal corporation, which had formerly been held **at Aldermanbury. It was** seriously injured by the great fire of 1666, but immediately restored. The unpleasing front towards **King Street** was erected in 1789 from designs by the younger *Dance*, and various improvements were effected in 1865-68, including the **construction of a new roof.** Above the porch are the arms of the city, with the motto, *Domine dirige nos*. The *Great Hall* (open to visitors), 153 ft. long, 48 ft. broad. and 55 ft. high, is now used for various municipal meetings, the election of the Lord Mayor and members of parliament, and public meetings of the citizens of London to consider questions of great social or political interest. The open timber roof is very handsome. The stained-glass window at the E. end was presented by the Lancashire operatives in acknowledgment of the City of London's generosity during the Cotton Famine; that at the W. end is a memorial of the late Prince Consort. The two colossal and fanciful wooden figures on the W. side, carved by *Saunders* in 1708, are called *Gog* and *Magog*, and were formerly carried in the Lord Mayor's procession. By the N. wall are monuments to Lord Chatham, by *Bacon*; Wellingtons by *Bell*; and Nelson, by *Smith*. On the S. wall are monuments to William Pitt by *Bubb*, and Lord Mayor Beckford by *Moore* (bearing on the pedestal the mayor's famous address to George III., which some writers affirm was never actually delivered). — Every 9th of November the Lord Mayor, on the occasion of his accession to office, gives a great public dinner here to the members of the Cabinet, the chief civic dignitaries, and others, which is generally attended by nearly 1000 guests. The speeches made by the Queen's Ministers on this and other civic occasions are scanned attentively, as often possessing no little political significance. The expense of this banquet is shared jointly by the Lord Mayor and the Sheriffs.

To the N. of the Great Hall is the new *Common Council Chamber*, erected from the plans of Sir Horace Jones in 1885. It contains a statue of George III. by *Chantrey*, and in the passage leading to it are busts of Derby, Palmerston, and Canning. The *Aldermen's Room* contains a ceiling painted by *Thornhill*, and stained-glass windows exhibiting the arms of various Lord Mayors. The interesting old *Crypt* of the Guildhall, borne by clustered columns of Purbeck marble, is now, with the porch, almost the sole relic of the original edifice of 1411-31.

THE FREE LIBRARY OF THE CORPORATION OF THE CITY OF LONDON (open daily, 10-9, to all-comers; no introduction necessary) contains in its handsome hall, built in the Tudor style in 1871-72, above 60,000 volumes, including several good specimens of early printing, and a large and valuable collection of works on or connected with London, its history, antiquities, and famous citizens. The special collections include the library of the old Dutch church in Austin Friars (p. 104; with valuable MSS. and original letters of Reformers), a carefully selected Hebrew library (new catalogue), etc. It also possesses a very fine collection of maps and plans of London, and a series of English medals. In 1888 the library was visited by 396,720 persons. On the right is the *Reading Room*. In the room at the top of the staircase to the museum is an interesting collection of ancient chronometers, **clocks**, watches, and watch-movements, made by members of the Clockmakers' Company, whose library is also deposited at the Guildhall.

The \*Museum (open from 10 to 4 or 5), on the sunk floor, contains a collection of Roman antiquities found in London: a group of the Dea Matres, found at Crutched Friars; hexagonal funeral column, from Ludgate Hill; **Roman** tesselated pavement, from Bucklersbury (1869); sarcophagus of the 4th cent., from Clapton; **statue of a** Roman warrior and some architectural antiquities **found in** a bastion of the old Roman wall in Bishopsgate; a curious **collection** of old London shop-signs (17th cent.), including that **of the Boar's** Head in Eastcheap (mentioned by Shakspeare); a large **collection of** smaller antiquities, terracotta figures, lamps, vases, **dishes, goblets, trinkets, spoons,** pins, needles, etc. There are also two sculptured slabs from Nineveh. Two glass-cases in the centre contain **autographs, including a very valuable one** of Shakspeare, dated 10 Mar., **1613 (purchased for 147** *l.*)**; also those of Cromwell,** Wellington, and Nelson. In two other cases are impressions of the great seals of England from 757 down to the present time.

The **Corporation Art Gallery**, on the right of the entrance to the Guildhall, opened in **1886**, contains the chief historical portraits and other paintings belonging to the Corporation, collected here from the old council chamber and committee-rooms, and also a few recent donations. Among the busts are those of Cobden, Gladstone, Beaconsfield, Granville Sharp (by Chantrey), and Nelson.

The numerous pigeons which congregate in the nooks and crannies of the Guildhall, or fly about the yard, will remind the traveller of the famous pigeons of St. Mark at Venice. The London pigeons, unlike their Venetian compeers, are generally left to cater for themselves, and to judge from their numbers and plumpness do so with perfect success.

At the corner of Basinghall Street, which flanks the Guildhall on the E., stands **Gresham College**, founded by *Sir Thomas Gresham* (comp. p. 104) in 1579 for the delivery of lectures by seven professors, on law, divinity, medicine, rhetoric, geometry, **astronomy, and music.**

The lectures were delivered in Gresham's house in Bishopsgate Street until 1843, when the present hall was erected out of the accumulated capital. The lecture theatre can hold 500 persons. According to Gresham's will, the lectures were to be delivered in the middle of the day, and in Latin, but the speakers now deliver their courses of four lectures each in English, at 6 p.m.

To the W. of the Guildhall, in Foster Lane, behind the General Post Office, rises **Goldsmiths' Hall**, re-erected in the Renaissance style by *Hardwick* in 1835 (visitors must be introduced by a member). Chief objects of interest in the interior: Grand Staircase, with portraits of George IV., by *Northcote*; William IV., by *Hayter*; George III. and his consort Charlotte, by *Ramsay*; in the Committee Room (first floor), the remains of **a** Roman altar **found in** digging the **foundations of the present hall**; portrait of Lord Mayor Myddelton, who provided **London with water** by the construction of the New River (1644), by *Jansen*; portrait **of Lord Mayor Sir** Martin Bowes (1545), with the goblet which he bequeathed to **the** Goldsmiths' **Company** (out of which Queen Elizabeth is said to have drunk at her coronation, and which is still preserved); portraits of Queen Victoria, by *Hayter*; Prince Albert, by *Smith*; Queen Adelaide, by *Shee*; busts of George III., George IV., and William IV., by *Chantrey*; statues of Cleopatra and the Sibyl, by *Story*. — The Company, incorporated in 1327, has the privilege of assaying and stamping most of the gold and silver manufactures of England, for which it receives a small percentage.

From Goldsmiths' Hall, Foster Lane leads southwards to the W. end of **Cheapside** (Pl. R, 39, and *III;* from the Anglo-Saxon *cyppan*, 'to buy', 'to bargain'), one of the busiest streets in the city, rich in historical reminiscences, and now lined with handsome shops (to the right is *Peel's Statue*, p. 90). Its jewellers and mercers have been famous from a time even earlier than that of honest John Gilpin, under whose wheels the stones rattled 'as if Cheapside were mad'. Cheapside Cross, one of the memorials erected by Edward I. to Queen Eleanor, stood here till destroyed by the Puritans in 1643; and the neighbourhood was frequently the scene of conflicts between the pleasure-loving and turbulent apprentices of the various rival guilds. To the right and left diverge several cross-streets, the names of which probably preserve the position of the stalls of the different tradespeople in the far back period when Cheapside was an open market. Between Friday Street and Bread Street, on the right, once stood the Mermaid Tavern, rendered famous by the social meetings of Shakspeare, Beaumont, Fletcher, Dr. Donne, and other members of the club founded here by Ben Jonson in 1603. John Milton was born in Bread Street in 1608, and Sir Thomas More (b. 1480) first saw the light in Milk Street, on the opposite side. — On the right (S.) side of Cheapside, farther on, is the church of **St. Mary le Bow**, or simply *Bow Church* (so named after an earlier church on the same site borne by stone *arches*), one of *Wren's* best works, with a tower 235 ft. high. The tower, at the top of which is a dragon is 9 ft. long, is especially admirable; 'no other modern steeple', says Fergusson, 'can compare with this, either for beauty of outline or the appropriateness with which classical details are applied to so novel a purpose'. Under the church is a fine old Norman crypt. Persons born within the sound of Bow-bells are popularly called *Cockneys*, *i.e.* true Londoners.

A curious old rhyming couplet foretold that: —
'When the Exchange grasshopper and dragon from Bow
Shall meet — in London shall be much woe.'
This improbable meeting actually took place in 1832, when the two vanes were sent to the same yard for repairs.
The ecclesiastical *Court of Arches* takes its name from having originally met in the vestry of this church.

To the E. of St. Mary le Bow, *King Street*, on the left (N.), leads to *Guildhall* (p. 98), and *Queen Street*, on the right (S.), to *Southwark Bridge* (p. 117.)

Farther to the E. in Cheapside, on the N. side of the street, between Ironmonger Lane and Old Jewry, rises **Mercers' Hall, the guild-house of the silk** mercers, rebuilt in 1884. The interior (otherwise uninteresting) contains portraits of Dean Colet, founder of St. Paul's School, and Sir Thomas Gresham, founder of the Exchange, as well as a few relics of Sir Richard Whittington. The chapel, which is adorned with modern frescoes of Becket's Martyrdom and the Ascension, occupies the site of the house in which Thomas Becket was born in 1119, and where a hospital and chapel were erected to his memory about the year 1190. Henry VIII. afterwards granted the hospital to the Mercers, who had been incorporated in 1393. — *Saddlers' Hall*, 143 Cheapside, possesses a fine large hall and a good gateway.

*Old Jewry*, to the E. of Mercers' Hall, derives its name from the synagogue which stood here prior to the persecution of the Jews in 1291. On its site, close to the Bank, now stands the *Grocers' Hall*, the guild-house of the Grocers, or, as they were once called, the '*Pepperers*', with a fine stained-glass window. This company is one of the oldest in London. Old Jewry is continued towards the N. by *Coleman Street*, in which, on the right, is situated the *Armourers' Hall* (Pl. R, 39; *III*), founded about 1450, and spared by the fire of 1666. It contains an interesting and valuable collection of armour and old plate.

The continuation of Cheapside towards the E. is called the POULTRY, once the street of the poulterers, at the farther end of which, on the right, rises the Mansion House (Pl. R, 39, *III*), the official residence of the Lord Mayor during his year of office, erected by *Dance* in 1739-52. Lord Burlington sent in a design by **the** famous Italian architect Palladio, which was rejected **on** the naive question of one of the aldermen — 'Who was Palladio — **was he a freeman of the city?**' The building is preceded by a Corinthian hexastyle portico. The tympanum contains an allegorical group in relief by *Sir Robert Taylor*.

In the interior, to the left of the entrance, is the Lord Mayor's police-court, open to the public daily from 12 to 2. The long suite of state and reception rooms are only shown by the special permission of the Lord Mayor. The principal room is the *Egyptian Hall*, in which the Lord Mayor gives his banquets and balls, said to be a reproduction of the hall described under that name by Vitruvius. It contains several pieces of modern English sculpture: 'Caractacus and the nymph Egeria, by *Foley;* Genius and the Morning Star, by *Baily;* Comus, by Lough; Oriselda, by *Marshall.*

The interior of **St. Stephen's Church**, Walbrook, behind **the** Mansion House, with its graceful dome supported by Corinthian columns, is considered one of *Wren's* masterpieces. Altarpiece by *West*, Stoning of St. Stephen.

*Queen Victoria Street*, 1/3 M. in length, one of the great modern improvements of London, constructed at vast expense, leads directly from **the** Mansion House to Blackfriars Bridge (see p. 112).

### 5. The Bank of England. The Exchange.

*Stock Exchange. Merchant Taylors' **Hall**. Crosby Hall. St. Helen's Church. Cornhill. Leadenhall Market. **St**. Andrew's Undershaft. Corn **Exchange**. Toynbee Hall. People's **Palace**.*

Opposite the Mansion House, and bounded on the S. by Threadneedle Street, on the W. by Prince's Street, on the N. by Lothbury, and on the E. by Bartholomew Lane, stands the **Bank of England** (Pl. R, 39, 43 ; *III*), an irregular and isolated building of one story, the W. part of which was designed by *Sir John Soane* in 1788. The external walls are entirely devoid of windows, the Bank being, for the sake of security, lighted from interior courts. The only attractive portion of the architecture is at the N.W. angle, which was copied from the Temple of the Sibyl at Tivoli. The edifice covers an area of about four acres.

The Bank was founded in 1691 by William Paterson, a Scotsman. It is a joint stock bank, and was the first of the kind established in the kingdom. Having exclusive privileges in the metropolis, secured by Royal Charter, it continued to be the only joint stock bank in London till 1834, when the London and Westminster Bank, soon to be followed by many others, was established. The Bank of England is still the only bank in London which has the power of issuing paper money. Its original capital was 1,200,000*l*., which has since been multiplied more than twelvefold. It now employs 900 persons at salaries varying from 50*l*. to 1,200*l*. (in all 210,000*l*.). The vaults usually contain 15-20 million pounds sterling in gold and silver, while there are 20-25 millions of pounds sterling of the Bank's notes in circulation. The Bank receives 200,000*l*. a year for managing the national debt (now amounting to about 700,000,000*l*.), besides which it carries on business like other banks in discounting bills, receiving deposits, and lending money. It is bound to buy all gold bullion brought to it, at the rate of 3*l*. 17*s*. 9*d*. per oz. The average amount of money negociated in the Bank per day is over 2,000,000*l*.

The business offices of the Bank are open to the public daily from 9 to 3 ; the Printing, Weighing, and Bullion Offices are shown only by the special order of the Governor or Deputy-Governor, to whom an introduction must be obtained.

The account-books of the Bank are ruled and cut in the *Ruling Room*, and bound in the *Binding Room*. The Bank also contains a general *Printing Room*, and a special *Bank-note Printing Room*, where 15,000 new banknotes are produced daily. Many notes of 1000*l*. are printed, and cases have been known of the issue of notes for as large sums as 50,000*l*. or 100,000*l*. The Bank pays above 70,000*l* annually to the Stamp Office for stamps on notes; and it is estimated that its losses, from forgeries, etc., have amounted at times to more than 40,000*l*. annually. The note printing-press is exceedingly interesting. In the *Old Note Office* the halves of old **bank-notes are** kept for a period of ten years. All notes paid into the Bank **are at once** cancelled, so that in some cases the active life of a **bank-note** may not be longer than **a single day**. The cancelled notes, however, are kept for ten years, **in case they may** be required as testimony in a court of law. Every month the notes received in the corresponding month ten years ago are burned; and the furnace provided for this purpose, 5 ft. in height and 10 ft. in diameter, is said to be completely filled on each occasion. The stock of paid notes for five years amounts to about 80 millions; if the notes were joined end to end they would form a ribbon 13,000 M. long, while their superficial extent would almost equal that of Hyde Park. The *Bank-Note Autograph Books* contain the signatures of various royal and distinguished personages. A bank-note for 1,000,000*l*. is also exhibited to the curious visitor. The *Weighing Office* contains a machine for weighing sovereigns (33 per minute), which throws those of full weight into one compartment and the light ones into another. The *Bullion Office* is the treasury for the precious metals. The Bank is protected at night by a small garrison of soldiers.

In Post Office Court, Lombard Street, is the *Bankers' Clearing House*, a useful institution through which bankers obtain the amount of cheques and bills in their hands without the trouble of collecting them at the various banks on which they are drawn. The bills and cheques received by the various bankers during the day are here compared, and the difference settled by a cheque on the Bank of England. The amount changing hands here is enormous, reaching in the year ending Dec. 31st., 1857, the sum of 6,077,097,000*l*.

In Capel Court, opposite the Bank, is the Stock Exchange, the headquarters of the *Stock-brokers* and *Stock-jobbers* (about 900 in number), each of whom pays an annual subscription of 10*l*. Strangers are not admitted. The Stock Exchange has recently been much enlarged by an extension on the E. side, between Throgmorton Street and Old Broad Street.

In Throgmorton Street, to the N. of the Stock Exchange, is the *Drapers' Hall*, containing a portrait of Nelson by *Sir William Beechey*, and a picture of Mary, Queen of Scots, and her son James I, attributed to *Zucchero*. Adjoining is the *Drapers' Garden*, containing one or two old mulberry-trees.

The *Dutch Church* in Austin Friars, behind the Drapers' Hall, dates from the 14th cent. and is one of the few ecclesiastical edifices which escaped the fire of 1666. It contains numerous more or less interesting graves of the 14-16th centuries.

The **Royal Exchange** (Pl. R, 43; *III*), built in 1842-44 by *Tite*, a successor to the first Exchange erected in 1564-70 by Sir Thomas Gresham, is preceded by a Corinthian portico, and approached by a broad flight of steps. The group in the tympanum is by *Westmacott*: in the centre is Commerce, holding the charter of the Exchange in her hand; on the right the Lord Mayor, municipal officials, an Indian, an Arab, a Greek, and a Turk; on the left English merchants, a Chinese, a Persian, a Negro, etc. On the architrave below is the inscription: 'The Earth is the Lord's and the fulness thereof'.

The interior of the Exchange forms a quadrangular covered court surrounded by colonnades. In the centre is a statue of Queen Victoria, by *Lough*; in the N.E. and S.E. corners are statues of Queen Elizabeth, by *Watson*, and Charles II. The walls of the colonnades bear the armorial bearings and products of the different countries of Europe and America, in encaustic painting. The

## 5. MERCHANT TAYLORS' HALL.

tesselated pavement of Turkey stone is the original one of Gresham's Exchange, opened by Queen Elizabeth on June 23rd, 1571. The chief business hour is from 3.30 to 4.30 p.m., and the most important days are Tuesdays and Fridays. On the E. side rises a campanile, 180 ft. in height. On the front (E.) of the tower is a statue of Sir Thomas Gresham, and at the top is a large gilded vane in the shape of a grasshopper (Gresham's crest). The shops on the outside of the Exchange greatly disfigure the building. Nearly opposite the Exchange is No. 15 Cornhill, occupied by Messrs. Birch, confectioners, and said to be the oldest shop in London.

At the E. end of the Exchange a staircase ascends to *Lloyd's Subscription Rooms*, the central point of every kind of business connected with navigation, maritime trade, marine insurance, and shipping intelligence. The vestibule is adorned with statues of Prince Albert by *Lough*, and Huskisson by *Gibson*. On the wall is a tablet to the 'Times' newspaper, erected in recognition of the public service it rendered by the exposure of a fraudulent financial conspiracy of gigantic character. The first room is used by Underwriters, the second by Merchants, and the third by Ship-Captains.

The space in front of the Bank and the Exchange is the chief point of convergence of the London omnibus traffic, which during business hours is enormous.

In front of the Exchange is an *Equestrian Statue of Wellington*, by *Chantrey*, erected in 1844, beside which is a handsome fountain with a female figure. On the S.E. side of the Exchange is a statue of *Sir Rowland Hill*, the inventor of the cheap postal system. Behind the Exchange, in Threadneedle Street, is a statue, in a sitting posture, of *Peabody* (d. 1869), the American philanthropist, by *Story*, erected in 1871 by public subscription.

*George Peabody*, an American merchant, who carried on an extensive business and spent much of his time in London, gave at different times upwards of half a million of money for the erection of suitable dwellings for the working classes of the metropolis. The property is managed by a body of trustees. The number of persons accommodated in the Peabody Buildings is about 20,000, each family paying an average weekly rent of about 4s., which includes the use of baths and wash-houses. The capital of the fund now amounts to about 1,000,000l. Mr. Peabody declined a baronetcy offered by the Queen, but accepted a miniature portrait of Her Majesty. He spent and bequeathed still larger sums for educational and benevolent purposes in America, the grand total of his gifts amounting to nearly 2,000,000l. sterling.

Farther along Threadneedle Street, beyond Finch Lane, on the E. side of the street, is the **Merchant Taylors' Hall**, the largest of the London Companies' halls, erected, after the Great Fire of 1666, by *Jarman* (admission on application to a member). The company was incorporated in 1466. The handsome hall contains some good portraits: Henry VIII., by *Paris Bordone*; Duke of York, by *Lawrence*; Duke of Wellington, by *Wilkie*; Charles I.; Charles II.; James II.; William III.; Queen Anne; George III. and his consort; Lord Chancellor Eldon, by *Briggs*; Pitt, by *Hoppner*.

There is also a valuable collection of old plate. The small, but interesting *Crypt* was spared by the Fire.

Near this point, in Bishopsgate Street, stands ***Crosby Hall**, built in 1466 by** Alderman Sir John Crosby, and once occupied **by the notorious** Duke of Gloucester, afterwards Richard III. The building subsequently belonged to Sir Thomas More, and **it is** mentioned by Shakspeare in his 'Richard III.' For a long **time** it was used for the reception of ambassadors, and was considered the finest house in London. During the Protectorate it was a prison; **and it afterwards became** in turn a meeting-house, a warehouse, and **a concert and lecture room. It has been** lately restored, and is now **used as a restaurant (p. 15).** Crosby Hall deserves a visit as **being one of the few** existing relics of the domestic **architecture of mediæval London, and the only one** in the Gothic style. The **present street front and many parts of** the interior do not belong **to the ancient structure. The** *Banqueting Hall* has a fine oaken roof.

**St. Helen's Church,** near Crosby Hall, called by Dean Stanley the 'Westminster Abbey of the City', once belonged to an ancient **nunnery and dates** originally from 1145-50. Among other old **monuments,** it contains those of Sir John Crosby and Sir Thomas Gresham (see p. 100). The Latin inscription on the tomb of Sir **Julius Cæsar (d.** 1636), Master **of the** Rolls in the reign of James I., **is to the effect that he had given his bond to Heaven to yield up his soul willingly when God should demand it.** His monument, in **the Chapel of the Holy Ghost, is** by *Nicholas Stone.* Over the **picturesque 'Nuns' Gate'** is a recent inscription to Alberico Gentile**, the Italian jurist, and professor of** civil law at Oxford, who **was buried near it. A** stained-glass window was erected in 1884 **to the memory of Shakspeare, who was a** parishioner in 1598 **and is rated in the parish books for 5*l*. 13*s*. 4*d*.** See 'Annals of **St. Helen's, Bishopsgate', by** *Rev. J. E. Cox*, **D.D.** (1876). — In **St. Helen's Place is the modern** *Hall of the Leathersellers*, a com**pany incorporated at the end of the 14th** century. The building is **erected over the old crypt of St. Helen's** Nunnery.

**On the W. side of Bishopsgate Street** Without (No. 168) is the **picturesque old house (now a tavern)** of *Sir Paul Pindar* (d. 1650), **one of the merchant-princes of his time.**

The *National Provincial Bank of England*, 112 Bishopsgate **Street, is worth visiting for** the beautiful interior of its large hall, **a remarkable** specimen of the Byzantine-Romanesque style, with **polished** granite **columns and polychrome decoration.**

**Shoreditch, the continuation** of Bishopsgate Street, leads to the chief goods depôt (once **the** Shoreditch or Bishopsgate terminus) of the Great Eastern Railway, **and** beyond it to *Kingsland* and to *Dalston*, where the *German Hospital* is situated.

In Cornhill, the **street** which leads to the E. straight past the S. side of the **Exchange, rises** on the right (S.) *St. Michael's*

Church, with a large late-Gothic tower, built by Wren, and lately restored by *Sir G. G. Scott*. Farther on is *St. Peter's Church*, which according to a groundless tradition was originally built by the ancient Britons. Gray, the poet (1716-71), was born in the house which formerly occupied the site of No. 41 Cornhill.

In *Leadenhall Street*, which continues Cornhill, stands, on the right and near the corner of Gracechurch Street, **Leadenhall Market**, one of the chief marts in London for poultry, game, and hides (see p. 27); large additions have recently been made to this market. Farther on, to the left, is the small church of **St. Andrew Undershaft** (*i. e.* under the maypole, as the maypole which used to be erected here was higher than the tower of the church); the turreted late-Gothic tower dates from 1532. At the end of the N. aisle is the tomb of Stow, the antiquary (d. 1605). Still farther on, on the same side, is the *Church of St. Catherine* **Cree**, with an interior by Inigo Jones, being the successor of an older church in which Holbein (d. 1543) is said to have been interred. The character of the services held here by Archbp. Laud in 1631 formed one of the charges in his trial. The old *House of the East India Company*, in which Charles Lamb was a clerk, stood at the corner of Leadenhall Street and Lime Street. The *New Zealand Chambers* (No. 34), nearly opposite St. Andrew Undershaft's, are one of Norman Shaw's reproductions of mediæval architecture. At the end of Leadenhall Street is the *Aldgate Station* of the Metropolitan Railway.

*Lombard Street* and *Fenchurch Street*, forming a line on the S. nearly parallel to Cornhill and Leadenhall Street, are also among the busiest thoroughfares of the city. Lombard Street has been for ages the most noted street in London for banking and finance, and has inherited its name from the 'Lombard' money dealers from Genoa and Florence, who, in the 14th and 15th centuries, took the place of the discredited and persecuted Jews of 'Old Jewry' as money lenders. Fenchurch Street reminds us by its name of the fenny character of the district when the old church was built (drained by the little stream of 'Lang bourne' running into the 'Walbrook')†. On the N. side of the street is the *Elephant Tavern* (rebuilt), where Hogarth lodged for some time, and which was once adorned with several of his works. Adjacent is the *Ironmongers' Hall*, whose company dates from the reign of Edward IV., with an interesting interior, portraits of Isaak Walton and Admiral Hood, etc. Fenchurch Street is connected with Great Tower Street by *Mincing Lane* (so called from the 'minchens', or nuns of St. Helen's, to whom part of it belonged), which is the central point of the colonial wholesale trade. The fine *Tower of All Hallows Staining* in this lane is one of the oldest of the relics which have

---

† Mr. Loftie thinks 'fen' may be a corruption of the Anglo-Saxon *foin* (hay), as 'grace' in Gracechurch Street is of *grass*.

survived the Great Fire. The *Clothworkers' Hall*, in the same street, dates originally from the 15th century. A little to the E., in *Mark Lane* (originally *Mart Lane*), is the **Corn Exchange** (Pl. R, **43**; *III*), and near it is *Fenchurch Street Station* (for the railway to **Blackwall**, p. 34). On the E. side of Mark Lane is Hart Street, with the *Church of St. Olave*, interesting as having survived the Great Fire, and as the church once frequented by Samuel Pepys (d. 1703). The picturesque interior contains **a number of** curious old tombs, including those of Pepys and his wife. A bust of Pepys was placed on the S. wall in 1884. Many persons who died of the plague in 1665 are buried in the churchyard. In the same street once stood **a monastery of the 'Crossed Friars'**, a reminiscence of whom **still exists** in the adjoining street of Crutched Friars.

On the E. margin of the City proper lie WHITECHAPEL, a district **chiefly inhabited by** artisans, and HOUNDSDITCH, the quarter of Jew **brokers and second-hand** dealers, whence the *Minories* lead south**wards to the Tower and** the Thames. In the Minories rises the old **Church of the Trinity**, once belonging to a Minorite nunnery, and **containing the head of the** Duke of Suffolk (beheaded, 1554) and **several curious old monuments.**

The main thoroughfare traversing this E. London district is *Whitechapel Road*, continued by *Mile End Road*, leading to Bow and Stratford (comp. p. 316). To the left, about ¼ M. beyond Aldgate Station (p. 36), diverges *Commercial Street*, in which stands *St. Jude's Church* (Pl. R, 47; *III*), containing copies of four of the **principal works** of *Mr. G. F. Watts*, finished off by that artist **himself ('Love and Death'**, 'Messenger of Death', 'Death crown**ing Innocence'**, 'The Good Samaritan'). The exterior is adorned **with a fine mosaic after** *Watts*.

Adjoining the church is **Toynbee Hall**, named after *Arnold Toynbee*, **who died in the prime of youth (in 1883)**, while actively engaged in **lecturing on political economy to the** working-men of London. The hall, **which is a 'hall'** in the academic sense, contains rooms for about 20 residents, **chiefly** Oxford and Cambridge graduates desirous of sharing the life **and experiences** of the E. end poor. It also contains drawing, dining, reading, **and lecture** rooms, a library, etc., in which numerous social meetings are **held for the** people of the neighbourhood. Those interested in work **of this** kind should apply to the Warden (Rev. S. Barnett, **vicar of St. Jude's**). Toynbee Hall is also one of the centres of the 'University **Extension Lectures'** scheme. — *Oxford House*, Bethnal Green, **is a** similar institution.

A *Loan Exhibition of Pictures*, established by Mr. **and** Mrs. Barnett in 1880, is held for a fortnight every Easter (10-10; free) in the schoolrooms adjoining St. Jude's. It generally contains some of the best works of modern English artists, and now ranks among the artistic 'events' of the year.

In Mile End Road, about ½ M. farther on, is the **People's Palace for East London**, a large institution for the 'recreation and amusement, the intellectual and material advancement of the vast artisan population **of** the East End'. Its form was suggested by the 'Palace of Delight' **described in** Mr. **Walter** Besant's novel, 'All Sorts and Conditions **of Men'; and the** nucleus of the 100,000*l*.

required for **its erection was furnished** by an endowment of *Mr. J. F. Barber Beaumont* (d. **1841**). This has been largely supplemented by voluntary public subscriptions, including **60,000l.** from the Drapers' Company. The large \**Queen's Hall*, opened by Queen Victoria in May, 1887, is adorned with statues of the Queens of England by F. **Verheyden. When complete the** Palace will comprise **technical and trade schools, a reference library**, reading-rooms, a covered garden and promenade, an open-air garden and **recreation ground, swimming-**baths, **gymnasia,** schools of **cookery and needlework, etc. Exhibitions, concerts, and entertainments of various kinds are held here; and the evening classes are attended by about 3000 students.**

## 6. London Bridge. The Monument. Lower Thames Street.

*Fishmongers' Hall. St. Magnus the Martyr's. Billingsgate. Custom House. Coal Exchange.*

*King William Street*, a wide thoroughfare with handsome buildings, leads S.E. from the Bank to London Bridge. Immediately on the left, at the corner of Lombard Street, is the church of *St. Mary Woolnoth*, erected in 1716, by *Hawksmoor*. It contains a tablet to the memory of Newton, the friend of Cowper the poet, with an epitaph by himself. Farther on, at the point where King William Street, Gracechurch Street, Eastcheap, and Cannon Street (p. 116) converge, on a site once occupied by Falstaff's 'Boar's Head Tavern', rises the *Statue of William IV.*, by Nixon. Adjacent is the *Monument Station* of the Underground Railway (p. 38). To the left, in Fish Street Hill, is the *Monument* (see p. 110). On each side of the first arch of London Bridge, which crosses *Lower Thames Street* (p. 111), are flights of stone steps descending to the street below.

**London Bridge** (Pl. R, 42; *III*), until a century ago the only bridge over the Thames in London, and still the most important, connects the City, the central point of business, with the *Borough*, a densely populated, chiefly manufacturing district, on the Surrey (S.) side of the river (see p. 293).

The Saxons, and perhaps the Romans before them, erected various wooden bridges over the Thames on the site of the present London Bridge, but these were all at different periods carried away by floods or destroyed by fire. At length in 1176 Henry II. instructed *Peter*, chaplain of the church of St. Mary Cole, to construct a stone bridge at this point, but the work was not completed till 1209, in the reign of Henry's son, John. A chapel, dedicated to St. Thomas of Canterbury, was built upon the bridge, and a row of houses sprang up on each side, so that the bridge resembled a continuous street. It was terminated at both banks by fortified gates, on the pinnacles of which the heads of traitors used to be exposed.

In one of the houses dwelt Sir John Hewitt, Lord Mayor in the time of Queen Elizabeth, whose daughter, according to the romantic story, fell into the river, and was rescued by Edward Osborne, his apprentice. The brave and fortunate youth afterwards married the young lady and founded the family of the present Duke of Leeds.

The present London Bridge, 33 yds. higher up the river than the old bridge (removed in 1832), **was** designed by *John Rennie*, a Scotch engineer, begun in 1825 under the superintendence of his sons, *Sir John* and *George Rennie*, and completed in 1831. The total outlay, including the cost of the approaches, was about 2,000,000*l.* The bridge, 928 ft. long and 54 ft. broad, is borne by five granite arches, of which **that in** the centre has a span of 152 ft. The lamp-posts **on the bridge are cast of the** metal of French cannon captured **in the** Peninsular **War**.

It is estimated that 15,000 vehicles and about 100,000 pedestrians cross London Bridge daily, a fact which **may** give the stranger some idea of the prodigious traffic carried on in this part of the city. New-comers should pay a visit to London Bridge on a weekday during business hours to see this busy scene and hear the almost deafening noise of the traffic. Stoppages or 'blocks' in the stream of vehicles, of course, sometimes take place; but, thanks **to the skilful management of the** police, such interruptions are seldom of long duration. One of the police regulations is that slow-moving **vehicles travel at the sides,** and quick ones in the middle. **London Bridge divides London into 'above'** and 'below' bridge. Looking *down* the river we survey the *Port of London,* the part immediately below the bridge being called the *Pool*. To this portion of the river sea-going vessels of the largest **size have** access, there being as yet no bridge below this point. On the right and left, **as far as the eye can penetrate** the smoky atmosphere, **are** seen **forests of masts; while high above** and behind the houses on both **banks rises the** rigging of large vessels in the **various docks.** *Above* bridge the **traffic is carried on** chiefly by penny steamboats and coal **barges. Among the** buildings visible from the bridge are, on the **N. side of the river, the Tower,** Billingsgate Market, the **Custom House, the Monument, St. Paul's,** a great number of other **churches, and the Cannon Street** Station, while on the Surrey side **lie St. Saviour's** Church, Barclay and Perkins's Brewery, and the ex**tensive double station of the** South Eastern and Brighton Railways.

**An admirable** survey of the traffic on the bridge as well as on the river is obtained from **The Monument** (Pl. R, 43; *III*), in Fish Street **Hill, a little to the north. This** consists of a fluted column, 202 ft. in height, designed by **Wren, and was** erected in 1671-77 in commemoration of the Great Fire of London, which, on 2-7th Sept., 1666, destroyed 460 streets with 89 churches and 13,200 houses, valued at 7,335,000*l.* The height of the column is said to equal **its** distance from the house in Pudding Lane in which the fire broke out. A winding staircase of 345 steps (adm. 3*d.*) ascends the column to a platform enclosed by an iron cage (added to put a stop to suicides from the monument), above which rises a gilt urn with blazing flames, 42 ft. in height. The pedestal bears inscriptions and allegorical reliefs.

Immediately to the W. of London Bridge, at the lower end of *Upper Thames Street*, stands **Fishmongers' Hall**, a guild-house erected in 1831 on the site of an older building. The Company of Fishmongers existed as early as the time of Edward I. It originally consisted of two separate trades, that of the *Salt-Fishmongers* and that of the *Stock-Fishmongers*, which were united to form the present body in the reign of Henry VIII. The guild is one of the richest in London, possessing an annual revenue of 20,000*l*. In politics it has usually been distinctively attached to the Whig party, while the Merchant Taylors are recognised as the great Tory company. On the landing of the staircase is a statue of Lord Mayor Walworth (a member of the company), who slew the rebel Wat Tyler (p. 95). Among the objects of interest in the interior are the dagger with which that rebel was slain; a richly embroidered pall used at Walworth's funeral; a chair made out of part of the first pile driven in the construction of Old London Bridge, supposed to have been submerged in the Thames for 650 years; portraits of William III. and his queen by *Murray*, George II. and his consort by *Shackleton*, and Queen Victoria by *Herbert Smith*.

LOWER THAMES STREET runs eastwards from London Bridge to the Custom House and the Tower. Chaucer, the 'father of English poetry', is said to have lived here in 1379-85. Close to the bridge, on the right, stands the handsome church of **St. Magnus the Martyr**, with a cupola and low spire, built by *Wren* in 1676. It contains the tomb of Miles Coverdale, Bishop of Exeter, author of the first complete printed English version of the Bible (1535).

Farther to the E., on the Thames, is **Billingsgate** (so called from a gate of old London, named, as tradition says, after Belin, a king of the Britons), the chief *fish-market* of London, the bad language used at which has become proverbial. In the reign of Elizabeth this was a market for all kinds of provisions, but since the reign of William III. it has been used for fish only. Fish has been landed and sold here from time immemorial. In the reign of Edward I. the prices of fish were as follows: soles, per doz., 3*d*.; oysters, per gallon, 2*d*.; four whitings 1*d*.; four best salmon 5*s*.; eels, per quarter of a hundred, 2*d*.; and so on. The best fish is bought at the beginning of the market by the regular fishmongers. After them come the costermongers, who fill their barrows at lower prices, and are said to sell a third of the fish consumed in London. Billingsgate wharf is the oldest on the Thames. The present market, with a figure of Britannia on the apex of the pediment, was designed by *Horace Jones*, and opened in July, 1877. The market begins daily at 5 a.m., and is one of the sights of London (see p. 26). At one corner of the market is the *Three Tuns Tavern*, noted for its fish dinners (p. 15).

Adjacent to the fish-market is the **Custom House**, built by *Laing* in 1814-17, with an imposing façade towards the Thames, 490 ft. in length, by *Sir R. Smirke*. The customs-dues levied at the port of London amount to above 12,000,000*l.* a year, equalling that of all the other English sea-ports put together. The London Custom House employs more than 2200 officials; in the *Long Room* (190 ft. in length by 66 in breadth) no fewer than 80 clerks are at work. Confiscated articles are stored in a warehouse reserved for this **purpose, and are disposed of at** quarterly sales by auction, which **take place in Mark Lane**, and yield 5000*l.* per annum. **Attached to the Custom House is** a Museum containing curious contrivances **for smuggling, etc.** Between the Custom House and the Thames is a broad quay, which affords a fine view of the river and shipping.

The **Coal Exchange**, opposite the W. wing of the Custom House, erected in 1849 from plans by *Bunning*, is in the Italian style, and has a **tower 106 ft. in** height. Adjoining it on the E. is a *hypocaust*, or **stove of masonry** belonging to a Roman bath, discovered when the foundations were being dug (shown on application to one of the attendants). The circular hall, with glass dome and triple gallery, is adorned with **frescoes by** *F. Sang*, representing the formation of coal and process **of mining.** The flooring is inlaid with **40,000 pieces** of **wood, arranged** in the form of a mariner's compass. The sword in the municipal coat-of-arms is said to be formed of the wood of a mulberry-tree planted by Peter the **Great** in 1698, **when he was** learning the art of ship-building at Deptford. — The amount of coal annually consumed in London alone at present averages upwards of 8,000,000 tons (comp. p. 69).

A huge new **Bridge has** been begun by the Corporation below the Tower, but as yet nothing **but** the piers and the approaches have been constructed. The novel principle on which the bridge is to be built will be best understood from **an** inspection of the model exhibited in the grounds of the Crystal Palace (see p. 311). The bridge is expected to be finished in 1890 or 1891, at a total cost **of 750,000***l*.

## 7. Blackfriars Bridge. Thames Embankment. Queen Victoria Street. Cannon Street.

*Cleopatra's Needle. Times' Publishing Office. Bible Society. Heralds' College. London Stone. Southwark Bridge.*

**Blackfriars Bridge** (Pl. R, 34, 35; *II*), an iron structure, built by *Cubitt*, and opened in 1869, occupies the site of a stone bridge dating from 1769, the piers of which had given way. The bridge, which consists of five arches (the central having a span of 185 ft.) supported by granite piers, is 1272 ft. in length, including the abutments, and 80 ft. broad. The cost of construction amounted to

320,000*l*. The dome of St. Paul's is seen to the greatest advantage from this bridge, which also commands an excellent view otherwise. Just below Blackfriars Bridge the Thames is crossed by the *London, Chatham, and Dover Railway Bridge*. On the right bank of the river is the spacious *Blackfriars Bridge Station*.

The bridge derives its name from an ancient Monastery of the Black Friars, situated on the bank of the river, and dating from 1276, where several parliaments once met, and where Cardinals Wolsey and Campeggio pronounced sentence of divorce against the unfortunate Queen Catharine of Arragon in 1529 ('King Henry VIII.' ii. 4). Shakspeare once lived at Blackfriars, and in 1599 acted at a theatre which formerly occupied part of the site of the monastery, and of which the name *Playhouse Yard* is still a reminiscence. In 1607 Ben Jonson was also a resident here.

The new *Victoria Embankment leads from Blackfriars Bridge towards the W. along the N. bank of the Thames as far as Westminster. It was constructed in 1864-70, under the supervision of *Sir Joseph W. Bazalgette*, chief engineer of the late Metropolitan Board of Works (p. 69), at a cost of nearly 2,000,000*l*. It is about 2300 yds. in length, and consists of a macadamised carriage-way 64 ft. wide, with a foot pavement 16 ft. broad on the land-side, and one 20 ft. broad on the river-side. The whole of this area was once covered by the tide twice a day. It is protected on the side next the Thames by a granite wall, 8 ft. thick, for which a foundation was made by sinking iron cylinders into the river-bed as deeply as possible and filling them with concrete. Under the Embankment run three different tunnels. On the inland side is one traversed by the Metropolitan District Railway (p. 36), while on the Thames side there are two, one above the other, the lower containing one of the principal intercepting sewers (p. 70), and the upper one holding water and gas pipes and telegraph wires. Rows of trees have been planted along the sides of the Embankment, which in a few years will afford a shady promenade. At intervals are large openings, with stairs leading to the floating steamboat piers (p. 38), which are constructed of iron, and rise and fall with the tide. Part of the land reclaimed from the river has been converted into tasteful gardens. The gardens above Charing Cross Bridge are embellished with bronze statues of *General Outram*, *Sir Bartle Frere*, and *William Tyndale*, the translator of the New Testament, and those below with statues of *Robert Raikes*, the founder of Sunday schools, and *Robert Burns*. A statue of *Isambard Brunel* stands on the Embankment near Waterloo Bridge; and another, of *John Stuart Mill*, was erected near the Temple Station in 1878. Above Waterloo Bridge, at the back of the Savoy (p. 141), is the *Medical Examination Hall*, a building of red brick and Portland stone in the Italian style, erected in 1886. It contains a statue of the Queen by Williamson, unveiled in 1889. Near the Temple Station, opposite Mill's statue, is the tasteful *Office of the London School Board*, the weekly meetings of which are held here on Thursday at 3 p.m. (public admitted to the gallery; comp. 70). At the E. end of the Embankment, close to Blackfriars Bridge, is the handsome new *City of London School*, completed in 1883. To the W. of the school is the new Gothic building of *Sion College* and *Library* (see p. 17), opened in Dec., 1886. To the N., in Tudor Street, is the new *Guildhall School of Music*, a building in the Italian style, erected by the Corporation of London in 1886 at a cost of 22,000*l*. — In 1878 the Embankment was embellished by the erection on it, by the Adelphi Steps, of **Cleopatra's Needle** (Pl. R, 30; *I*), an Egyptian obelisk from Alexandria.

This famous obelisk was presented to the English Government by Mohammed Ali, and brought to this country by the private munificence of Dr. Erasmus Wilson, who gave 10,000*l*. for this purpose. Properly speaking Cleopatra's **Needle** is the name of the companion obelisk now in New York, which **stood erect at** Alexandria till its removal, while the one now in London **lay prostrate** for many years. Both monoliths were originally brought **from Heliopolis, which**, as **we are** informed by the Flaminian Obelisk **at Rome, was full** of obelisks. **The** inscription on the London obelisk **refers to Heliopolis as the** 'house **of the Phœnix'.** The obelisk, which **is of reddish granite**, measures 68½ **ft. in height, and is** 8 ft. **wide at the base. Its weight is** 180 **tons.** The **Obelisk** of Luxor at Paris is 76 **ft. in height, and** weighs 240 tons.

The **pedestal of grey** granite is 18½ **ft. high, including the steps. The inscriptions on it are as** follows. E. **Face.** 'This obelisk, quarried **at Syene, was erected at On (Heliopolis) by the** Pharaoh Thothmes III., about 1500 **B.C. Lateral inscriptions were added** nearly two centuries later by **Rameses the Great. Removed during the Greek** dynasty to Alexandria, the **royal city of Cleopatra, it was there erected in** the 8th year of Augustus **Cæsar, B.C. 23'. — W. Face. 'This obelisk,** prostrate for centuries on **the sands of Alexandria, was presented to the** British nation A. D. 1819 **by Mohammed Ali, Viceroy of** Egypt; **a** worthy memorial **of our distinguished countrymen. Nelson** and Abercromby'. — N. Face. 'Through the **patriotic zeal of** Erasmus Wilson, F. R. S., **this obelisk was brought from Alexandria** encased **in an iron** cylinder. It was abandoned during a storm in **the Bay of** Biscay, **recovered,** and erected on this spot by John Dixon C.E., **in the** 42nd year **of the reign** of Queen Victoria, 1878'. — River Face, **added at the suggestion of the** Queen. 'William Asken, James Gardiner, **Joseph Benbow, Michael Burns,** William Donald, William Patan, per**ished in a bold attempt to succour the crew** of the obelisk ship 'Cleo**patra' during the storm, October 14th, 1877'.**

Two large bronze *Sphinxes*, designed by Mr. G. Vulliamy, **have been placed at the base of the Needle.**

The **principal approaches to the Victoria Embankment** are from Blackfriars Bridge and Westminster Bridge (p. 193), from Charing Cross (p. 147), and from Arundel, Norfolk, Surrey, and Villiers Streets, all leading off the Strand.

The *Albert Embankment* (Pl. G, 29, R, 29; *IV*), completed in 1869, extending along the right bank of the Thames from Westminster Bridge to Vauxhall Bridge, a distance of about $1/5$ ths of a mile, has a roadway 60 ft. in breadth, and cost above 1,000,000*l*. Adjacent to it rises the new *Hospital of St. Thomas* (p. 297). — The *Chelsea Embankment*, on the left bank, between the Albert Suspension Bridge and Chelsea Hospital (p. 292), was opened in 1873.

In *New Bridge Street*, which leads straight to the N. from Blackfriars Bridge, immediately to the right, is the *Blackfriars* **Station** of the Metropolitan District Railway (p. 37); and farther on, beyond Queen Victoria Street (see below), is the large *Ludgate Hill Station* of the London, Chatham, and Dover Railway (p. 34), opposite which, on the left, the prison of *Bridewell* (so called from the old 'miraculous' Well of St. Bride or St. Bridget) stood down to 1864. The site of the prison was once occupied by Bridewell Palace, in which Shakspeare lays the 3rd Act of his 'Henry VIII.' New Bridge Street ends at the corner of *Fleet Street* (p. 134), the prolongation to the N. being called *Farringdon Street* (see p. 94). To the E., opposite Fleet Street, diverges *Ludgate Hill*, leading to St. Paul's Cathedral, and passing under the viaduct of the London, Chatham, and Dover Railway (p. 38).

QUEEN VICTORIA STREET, a broad and handsome thoroughfare, leads straight from Blackfriars Bridge, towards the E., to the Mansion House and the Bank. In Water Lane, to the left, stands *Apothecaries' Hall*, built in 1670, and containing portraits of James I., Charles I., and others. The company, most of whose members really are what the name implies, grants licenses to dispense medicines; and to give medical advice; and pure drugs are prepared in the chemical laboratories at the back of the Hall. On the left side of Queen Victoria Street, farther on, is the **Office of the Times** (Pl. R. 35; *II*), a handsome building of red brick. The tympanum bears an allegorical device with allusions to times past and future. Behind the Publishing Office, in Printing House Square, is the interesting *Printing Office*. Tickets of admission are issued on written application to the Manager, enclosing a note of introduction or reference. Visitors should be careful to attend at the hour named in the order, when the second edition of the paper is being printed. No fewer than 20,000 copies can be struck off in an hour by the wonderful mechanism of the *Walter* press, and about 70,000 are issued daily. The continuous rolls or webs of paper, with which the machine feeds itself, are each 4 miles in length, and of these 28 to 30 are used in one day. The finished and folded copies of the *Times* are thrown out at the other end of the machine. The type-setting machines are also of great interest. The official who conducts visitors round the works explains all the details (no gratuity). The electric light is used in the office. The *Times* celebrated its centenary in 1884.

Printing House Square stands on a corner of old London which for many ages was occupied by frowning Norman fortresses. Part of the castle of Montfiquet, a follower of the Conqueror, is said to have stood here; and the ground between the S. side of Queen Victoria Street, or Earl Street, and the Thames was the site of *Baynard's Castle* (mentioned in 'Richard III'.) with its extensive precincts, which replaced an earlier Roman fortress, and probably a British work of defence. Baynard's Castle was presented by Queen Elizabeth to the Earls of Pembroke, and continued to be their residence till its destruction in the Great Fire†.

Adjacent to the Times Printing Office on the E. rises the large building occupied by the **British and Foreign Bible Society**, erected in 1868. The number of Bibles and Testaments issued by this important society, which was founded in 1804, now amounts to more than four millions a year, printed in 286 different languages and dialects. The total number of copies issued since its foundation exceeds 116,000,000. The annual income of the society from subscriptions and the sale of Bibles is about 250,000*l*. Visitors are shown a long series of Bibles in different languages.

At the W. end of Queen Victoria Street, adjoining the Blackfriars Metropolitan Station, is the large *St. Paul's Station* of the London, Chatham, and Dover Railway.

Opposite is *Upper Thames Street*, leading on the right to London Bridge (p. 109). In *St. Bennet's Hill*, the first cross-street, was situated *Doctors' Commons Will Office*, prior to its removal in 1874 to Somerset House, in the Strand (see p. 142). To the left, in Queen Victoria Street, is **Heralds' College**, or the College of Arms (rebuilt in 1683), formerly the town house of the Earls of Derby. The library contains a number of interesting objects, including a sword, dagger, and ring belonging to James IV. of Scotland, who fell at Flodden in 1513; the Warwick roll, a series of portraits of the Earls of Warwick from the Conquest to the time of Richard III. (executed by *Rous* at the end of the 15th cent.); genealogy of the Saxon kings, from Adam, more curious than trustworthy, illustrated with drawings of the time of Henry VIII.; portrait of the celebrated Talbot, Earl of Shrewsbury, from his tomb in old St. Paul's. The college also contains a valuable treasury of genealogical records.

The office of Earl-Marshal, president of Heralds' College, is hereditary in the person of the Duke of Norfolk. The college consists of three kings-at-arms, Garter, Clarencieux, and Norroy — six heralds, Lancaster, Somerset, Richmond, York, Windsor, and Chester — and four pursuivants, Rouge Croix, Blue Mantle, Portcullis, and Rouge Dragon. The main object of the corporation is to make out and preserve the pedigrees and armorial bearings of noble and great families. It grants arms to families recently risen to position and distinction, and determines doubtful questions respecting the derivation and value of arms. Fees for a new coat-of-arms 10*l*. 10*s*. or more; for searching the records 1*l*.

A little farther on, Queen Victoria Street intersects CANNON STREET, which is the most direct route between St. Paul's Churchyard and London Bridge, and *Queen Street* (p. 101), leading from Cheapside to Southwark Bridge. Cannon Street, which is ²/₃ M. long, was constructed at a cost of 589,470*l*., and opened in 1854.

---

† This is the ordinary account, but it is disputed by Mr. Loftie, who maintains that the later house known as Baynard's Castle did not occupy the site of the original fortress of that name. See his 'London' (in the 'Historic Towns Series'; 1887).

This street contains the *Cannon Street* (p. 37) and *Mansion House* (p. 37) stations of the Metropolitan District Railway, and also the extensive *Cannon Street Station*, the City Terminus of the South Eastern Railway (p. 33; hotel, see p. 7). Opposite stands the church of *St. Swithin*, popularly regarded as the saint of the weather, into the wall of which is built the *London Stone*, an old Roman milestone, supposed to have been the *milliarium* of the Roman forum in London, from which the distances along the various British high-roads were reckoned. Against this stone, which is now protected by an iron grating, Jack Cade once struck his staff, exclaiming 'Now is Mortimer lord of the city'. In St. Swithin's Lane stands the large range of premises known as '*New Court*', occupied by Messrs. Rothschild. — Close by is *Salters' Hall*, and near it was Salters' Hall Chapel, begun by the ejected minister Richard Mayo in 1667, and long celebrated for its preachers and theological disputations. — Down to 1853 the *Steel Yard*, at one time a factory or store-house of the Hanseatic League, established in 1250, stood on the site now occupied by the Cannon Street Terminus. — Adjacent to the station, on the W., is Dowgate Hill, with the *Hall of the Skinners*, who were incorporated in 1327. The court (with its wooden porch) and interior were built soon after the Fire; the staircase and the wainscoted 'Cedar Room' are interesting.

**Southwark Bridge** (Pl. R, 38; *III*), erected by *John Rennie* in 1815-19, at a cost of 800,000*l*., is 700 ft. long, and consists of three iron arches, borne by stone piers. The span of the central arch is 240 ft., that of the side ones 210 ft. The penny toll, formerly levied here, was abolished in 1865, and the bridge purchased by the City for a sum of 218,868*l*. The traffic is comparatively small on account of the inconvenience of the approaches to the bridge, but has of late greatly increased. In Southwark, on the S. bank, lies *Barclay and Perkins's Brewery* (p. 296). The river farther down is crossed by the imposing five-arched railway bridge of the *South Eastern Railway* (terminus at Cannon Street Station, see above).

## 8. The Tower.

*Trinity House. Royal Mint. Thames Subways.*

The **Tower** (Pl. R, 46; *III*), the ancient fortress and gloomy state-prison of London, and historically the most interesting spot in England, is an irregular mass of buildings erected at various periods, surrounded by a battlemented wall and a deep moat, which was drained in 1843. It stands on the bank of the Thames, to the E. of the City, and outside the bounds of the ancient city-walls. The present external appearance of the Tower is very unlike what it originally was, perhaps no fortress of the same age having undergone greater transformations. It is possible, though very doubtful, that a fortification of some kind stood here in Roman times, but the Tower of London properly originated with William the Conqueror (see p. 64). Though at first a royal palace and stronghold, the Tower is best known in history as a prison. It is now a government arsenal, and is still kept in repair as a fortress. The ground-plan is in the form of an irregular pentagon, which covers an area of 13 acres, and is enclosed by a double line of circumvallation (the *outer* and *inner ballium* or *ward*), strengthened with towers. The square White Tower rises conspicuously in the centre. A broad quay lies between the moat and the Thames. The Tower is conveniently reached by the Underground Railway to *Mark Lane Station* (Pl. R, 42; *III*).

The Tower is provided with four entrances, viz. the *Iron Gate*, the *Water Gate*, and the *Traitors' Gate*, all on the side next the Thames; and on the W., the principal entrance, or *Lions' Gate*, so called from the royal menagerie formerly kept here. (The lions were removed to the Zoological Gardens in Regent's Park in 1834.) To the right is the *Ticket Office*, where tickets are procured for the Armoury (6d.) and the Crown Jewels (6d.). The Tower is open daily from 10 to 4 (till 6 on Mon. & Sat. in summer). Mondays and Saturdays are free days, and should be avoided on account of the crowd. Really interested visitors may sometimes obtain an order from the Constable of the Tower admitting them to parts not shown to the general public. The quaintly-attired *Warders* or *Beef-eaters*, officially designated *Yeomen of the Guard*, who are stationed at different parts of the building, are all old soldiers of meritorious service. The term Beef-eater is commonly explained as a corruption of *Buffetiers*, or attendants at the royal *Buffet*, but is more probably a nickname bestowed upon the ancient Yeomen of the Guard from the fact that rations of beef were regularly served out to them when on duty. The names of the different towers, gates, etc., are now indicated by placards, and the most interesting objects in the armouries also bear inscriptions. The *Guides to the Tower* (1d. and 6d.; the latter by W. J. Loftie) are almost unnecessary, except to those who take a special interest in old armour.

To the left of the entrance, opposite the Ticket Office, is a Turkish cannon, presented by Sultan Abdul Medjed Khan in 1857. A stone bridge, flanked by two towers (*Middle* Tower and *Byward* Tower), leads across the moat (which can still be flooded by the garrison) into the *Outer Bail* or anterior court. On the left is the *Bell Tower* (Pl. 4), adjacent to which is a narrow passage, leading round the fortifications within the outer wall. Farther on, to the right, is the *Traitors' Gate* (Pl. 6), a double gateway on the Thames, by which state-prisoners were formerly admitted to the Tower; above it is *St. Thomas's Tower* (Pl. 5). A gateway opposite leads under the *Bloody Tower* (p. 122) to the *Inner Bail*. In the centre of this court, upon slightly rising ground, stands the square

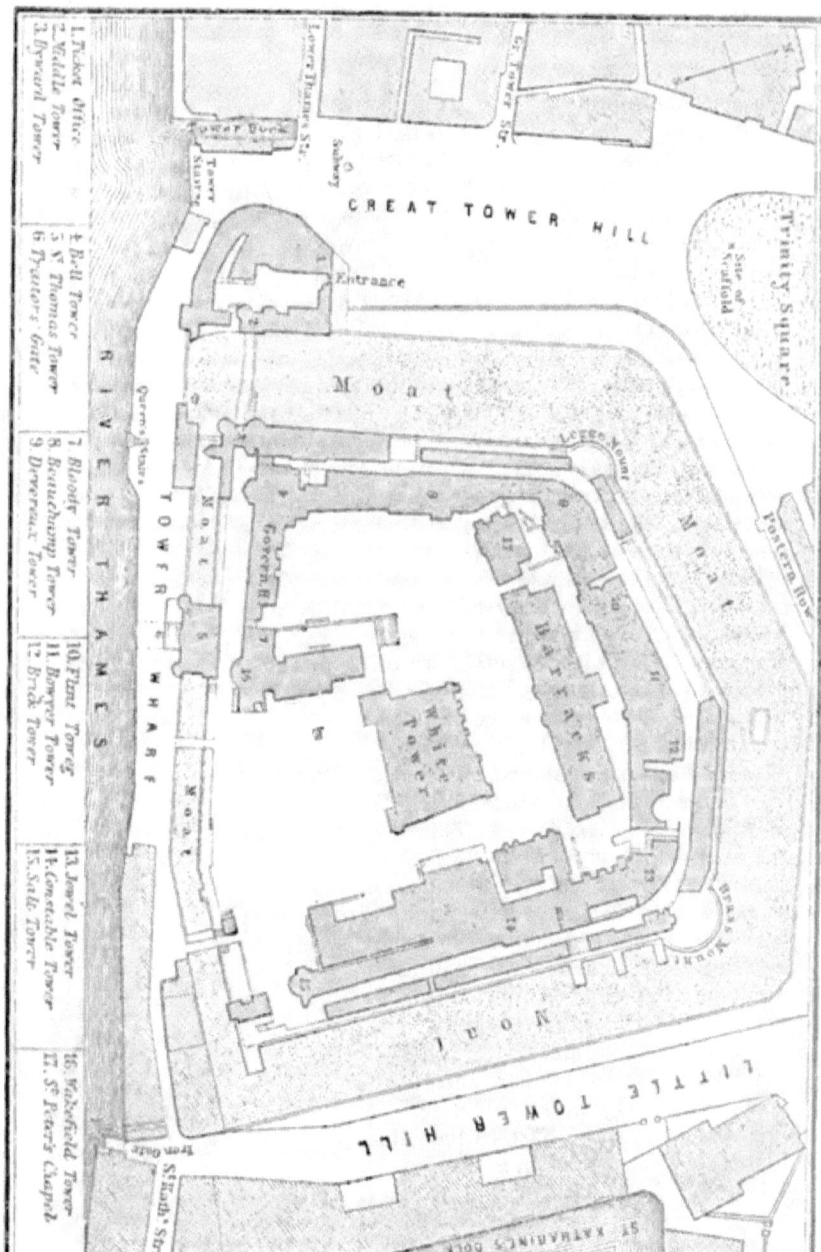

*WHITE TOWER, or *Keep*, the most ancient part of the fortress, erected by William the Conqueror in 1078, on a site previously occupied by two bastions built by King Alfred in 885 (perhaps on a Roman foundation; comp. p. 118). It measures 116 ft. from N. to S. and 96 ft. from E. to W., and is 92 ft. high. The walls are 13-15 ft. thick, and are surmounted with turrets at the angles. The armoury and military stores to the S. were removed in 1882-3, so as to leave an unimpeded view of this ancient keep. Among the many important scenes enacted in this tower may be mentioned the abdication of Richard II. in favour of Henry of Bolingbroke in 1399; and it was here that Prince James of Scotland was imprisoned in 1405. We first ascend a staircase passing through the wall of the White Tower (15 ft. thick). It was under this staircase that the bones of the two young princes murdered by their uncle Richard III. (see p. 123) were found. On the first floor are two apartments, said to have been those in which Sir Walter Raleigh was confined and wrote his History of the World (1605-17; closed). The *Chapel of St. John, on the second floor, with its massive pillars and cubical capitals, its wide triforium, its apse borne by stilted round arches (somewhat resembling those of St. Bartholomew's, p. 95), and its barrel-vaulted ceiling, is one of the finest and best-preserved specimens of Norman architecture in England. Adjacent is the *Banqueting Hall*, which contains some stands of arms, a valuable cannon cast at Malta in 1773 (with exquisite reliefs on the barrel), two chased brass guns made for the Duke of Gloucester, son of Queen Anne, who died in 1700 at the age of eleven, etc. The walls and ceilings are adorned with trophies of arms, skilfully arranged in the form of stars, flowers, coats-of-arms, and the like.

On the upper floor is the *Council Chamber*, in which the abdication of Richard II. took place. This and the adjoining room contain the *Collection of old armour, formerly in the so-called Horse Armoury, which, though not equal to the best Continental collections of the kind, is yet of great value and interest. The large stands on both sides of the central passage of the Council Chamber are occupied by a series of 22 equestrian figures in full equipment, as well as numerous figures on foot, affording a faithful picture, in chronological order, of English war-array from the time of Edward I. (1272) down to that of James II. (1688). In the Norman period armour consisted either of leather, cut into small pieces like the scales of a fish, or of flat rings of steel sewn on to leather. Chain mail was introduced from the East in the time of Henry III. (1216-1272). Plates for the arms and legs were introduced in the reign of Edward II. (1307-1327), and complete suits of plate armour came into use under Henry V. (1413-22). The glass-cases contain various smaller objects of interest.

By the N. wall is an equestrian figure of Queen Elizabeth. Suit of armour (shirt of mail), dating from the time of Edward I. (1272-1307). Suit of the time of Henry VI. (1422-61). Tournament suit of the time of Ed.

ward IV. (1461-83); adjacent a knight's suit of the time of Richard III. (1483-85), worn by the Marquis of Waterford at the Eglinton Tournament in 1839. Suit of Burgundian armour, Henry VII. (1485-1509); adjacent a second suit of the same period. Suit of richly damasceened armour, worn by Henry VIII. (1509-47). Suit worn by Charles Brandon, Duke of Suffolk (1520). Suit of Edward Clinton, Earl of Lincoln (1535).

Brown suit, with the arms of Burgundy and Granada, Edward VI. (1547-53). Suit of heavy armour of the time of Queen Mary, said to have belonged to Francis Hastings, Earl of Huntingdon (1555). Suit actually worn by Robert Dudley, Earl of Leicester (1580), the favourite of Queen Elizabeth; the armour bears his initials and crest. — Magnificent suit, of German workmanship, said to have been presented by the Emperor Maximilian to Henry VIII. on his marriage with Catharine of Arragon. Among the numerous ornaments inlaid in gold, the rose and pomegranate, the badges of Henry and Catharine, are of frequent recurrence; the other cognisances of Henry, the portcullis, fleur-de-lys, and dragon, and the initials of the royal pair connected by a true-lover's knot, also appear. On the armour of the horse are engraved scenes of martyrdom. — Suit of Sir Henry Lee, Master of the Armouries to Queen Elizabeth (1570). Suit of Robert Devereux, Earl of Essex, worn by the King's champion at the coronation of George I. Tournament suit, James I. (1605). Plain suit of armour of the same period. Suit of armour that was worn by Charles I. Suit, richly inlaid with gold, belonging to Henry, Prince of Wales (1612), the eldest son of James I. Beside it, Charles I., as Prince of Wales, on foot, with a page bearing the chanfron or head-piece of the horse-armour.

Full suit of plate armour, dating from the first half of the 17th century. Fine suit of Italian armour, said to have belonged to Count Oddi of Padua (1650; unmounted figure). Suit of bright armour, studded with brass. Pikemen of the 17th century. Suit of George Monk, Duke of Albemarle (1669). Suit of knight of the time of Charles I. The mounted figure at the S. side of the room wears a slight suit of armour that belonged to James II. (1685), after whose time armour was rarely worn.

Interspersed among the equestrian figures are numerous weapons of the periods illustrated by the suits of armour; instruments of torture; the head-piece with ram's horns of the court fool of Henry VIII.; weapons used by the rebels at Sedgemoor; assegais from Caffraria; two drums taken at Blenheim; execution-axe of the King of Oude; arbalest or crossbow; ancient matchlocks and fowling-pieces, some of them breech-loaders; Chinese arms; chain-mail of the Norman period; arms and armour from China, Persia, Japan, and Africa. Near the S. side is the block on which Lord Lovat, the last person beheaded in England, suffered the penalty of high treason on Tower Hill in 1747; and a little farther on is a heading-axe, said to be that by which the Earl of Essex was decapitated.

The glass-cases contain Etruscan, Roman, British, Anglo-Saxon, and other arms and armour; a complete suit of ancient Greek armour, discovered in a tomb at Cumæ; a spear-head found on the plain of Marathon; a very interesting collection of old weapons, ancient and Norman helmets, early fire-arms, etc.; two English long-bows of yew, recovered in 1841 from the wreck of the Mary Rose, after having been submerged for almost 300 years; a model of the Tower; Indian battle-axes, guns, and accoutrements; scimitar with jade hilt; sword with hilt of lapis lazuli; a bit of leather scale-armour; revolvers of the 16-17th cent., with beautifully inlaid stocks; Asiatic suits of armour; sword, helmet, and saddle of Tippo Sahib, Sultan of Mysore, captured at Seringapatam in 1799; helmet brought from Otaheite by Capt. Cook in 1774.

The smaller room to the E. of the Council Chamber contains ancient and modern armour of all kinds (Oriental, European, etc.). In glass-cases here are the uniform worn by the Duke of Wellington as Constable of the Tower, and the cloak on which General Wolfe died before Quebec in 1759.

At the foot of the staircase by which we leave the White Tower are some fragments of the old State Barge of the Master-General of the Ordnance (broken up in 1859), with the arms of the Duke of Marlborough and other decorations in carved and gilded oak.

Outside the White Tower is an interesting collection of old cannon, some of very heavy calibre, chiefly of the time of Henry VIII., but one going back to the reign of Henry VI. (1422-61).

The large modern buildings to the N. of the White Tower are the **Wellington** or *Waterloo Barracks*, erected in 1845 on the site of the Grand Storehouse and Small Armoury, which had been destroyed by fire in 1841. The armoury at the time of the conflagration contained 150,000 stand of arms.

The CROWN JEWELS, or *Regalia*, formerly kept in the building erected in 1842 at the N.E. corner of the fortress, are now in the Record or Wakefield Tower (see below). During the confusion that prevailed after the execution of Charles I. the royal ornaments and part of the Regalia, including the ancient crown of King Edward, were sold. The crowns and jewels made to replace these after the Restoration retain the ancient names. The Regalia now consist of the following articles, which are preserved in a glass-case, protected by a strong iron cage: —

*St. Edward's Crown*, executed for the coronation of Charles II., and used at all subsequent coronations. This was the crown stolen in 1671 by Col. Blood and his accomplices, who overpowered and gagged the keeper. The bold robbers, however, did not succeed in escaping with their booty. *Queen Victoria's Crown*, made in 1838, a masterpiece of the modern goldsmith's art. It is adorned with no fewer than 2783 diamonds; the large ruby in front, said to have been given to the Black Prince in 1367 by Don Pedro of Castile, was worn by Henry V. on his helmet at the battle of Agincourt. It also contains a magnificent sapphire. The *Prince of Wales's Crown*, of pure gold, without precious stones. The *Queen Consort's Crown*, of gold, set with jewels. The *Queen's Crown*, a golden circlet, embellished with diamonds and pearls, made for Queen Maria d'Este, wife of James II. *St. Edward's Staff*, made of gold, 4½ ft. long and about 90lbs. in weight. The orb at the top is said to contain a piece of the true cross. The *Royal Sceptre* with the Cross, 2 ft. 9 in. long, richly adorned with precious stones. The *Sceptre of the Dove*, or *Rod of Equity*. Above the orb is a dove with outspread wings. *Queen Victoria's Sceptre*, with richly gemmed cross. The *Ivory Sceptre* of Queen Maria d'Este, surmounted by a dove of white onyx. The *Sceptre of Queen Mary*, wife of William III. The *Orbs* of the King and Queen. Model of the *Koh-i-Noor* (Mountain of Light), one of the largest diamonds known, weighing 102 carats. The original, now at Windsor Castle, was formerly in the possession of Runjeet Singh, Rajah of Lahore, and came into the hands of the English in 1849, on their conquest of the Punjab. The *Curtana*, or pointless *Sword of Mercy*. The *Swords of Justice*. The *Coronation Bracelets*. The *Royal Spurs*. The *Coronation Oil Vessel* or *Ampulla*, in the form of an eagle. The *Spoon* belonging to the ampulla, thought to be the only relic of the ancient regalia. The *Salt Cellar of State*, in the form of a model of the White Tower. The silver *Baptismal Font* for the royal children. A silver *Wine Fountain* given by the Corporation of Plymouth to Charles II. Gold *Basin* used in the distribution of the Queen's alms on Maundy Thursday (see p. 182). The cases at the side contain the insignia of the *Orders of the Bath*, *Garter*, *Thistle*, *St. Michael and St. George*, and *Star of India*; also the *Victoria Cross*.

The total value of the Regalia is estimated at 3,000,000*l*.

The twelve TOWERS of the Inner Ward, at one time all used as prisons, were afterwards employed in part for the custody of the state archives. The names of several of them are indissolubly associated with many dark and painful memories. In the *Bloody Tower*

(Pl. 7) the sons of Edward IV. are said to have **been murdered**, by order of Richard III. (comp. pp 120, 210); in the *Bell Tower* (Pl. 4) the Princess Elizabeth was confined by her sister Queen Mary; **Lady Jane Grey is** said to have been imprisoned in *Brick Tower* (Pl. 12); **Lord** Guildford Dudley, husband of Lady Jane Grey, was **confined, with** his father and brothers, in *Beauchamp Tower* (Pl. 8); in the *Bowyer Tower* (Pl. 11), **the Duke** of Clarence, brother **of** Edward IV., is popularly **supposed to have been** drowned in a butt of malmsey; and Henry VI. was commonly believed to have been **murdered in** *Record (Wakefield) Tower* (Pl. 16). The *Salt Tower* (Pl. 15) **contains a curious drawing of the zodiac,** by Hugh Draper of Bristol, who was confined **here in** 1561 on a charge of sorcery. — The *Beauchamp Tower*, **built in** 1199-1216, **consists of two stories, which are reached by a narrow winding staircase. The walls of the room on the first** floor are covered **with inscriptions by former prisoners,** including those of the **Dudley family.** That **of John Dudley, Earl of** Warwick, eldest **brother of** Lord Guildford **Dudley, is on the right side of the fire-place, and is a well executed family coat-of-arms with the following lines:** —

'Yow that these beasts do wel behold and se,
May deine with ease wherefore here made they be
Withe borders wherein . . . . . . . . .
4 brothers' names who list to serche the grovnd'

Near the recess in the N.W. corner is the word JANE (repeated in the window), supposed to represent the signature of Lady Jane Grey as queen, but not inscribed by herself. Above the fire-place is a Latin inscription left by Philip Howard, Earl of Arundel, eldest son of the Duke of Norfolk who was beheaded in 1572 for aspiring to the hand of Mary, Queen of Scots. The inscriptions in the upper chamber are less interesting.

At the N.W. corner of the fortress rises the chapel of ST. PETER AD VINCULA (Pl. 17; interior not shown), erected by Edward I. on the site of a still older church, re-erected by Edward III., altered by Henry VIII., and restored in 1877. Adjoining it is a small burial-ground.

'In truth, there is **no sadder spot on earth than this** little cemetery. **Death** is there associated, **not,** as in Westminster Abbey and **St. Paul's, with genius** and virtue, with public veneration and with **imperishable** renown; not, as in our humblest churches and churchyards, **with every-thing that is most endearing in social and domestic charities; but with whatever is darkest in** human **nature and in human destiny, with the savage triumph of** implacable **enemies, with the inconstancy, the ingratitude, the cowardice** of friends, **with all the miseries of fallen greatness and of blighted fame'.** — *Macaulay.*

**The following celebrated** persons **are buried in this chapel:** Sir **Thomas More, beheaded** 1535; Queen **Anne** Boleyn, **beheaded** 1536; Thomas Cromwell, Earl of Essex, beheaded 1540; Margaret Pole, Countess of Salisbury, beheaded 1541; Queen Catharine Howard, beheaded 1542; Lord Admiral Seymour of Sudeley, beheaded 1549; Lord Somerset, the Protector, beheaded 1552; John Dudley,

Earl of Warwick and Duke of Northumberland, beheaded 1553; **Lady Jane Grey and** her husband, Lord Guildford Dudley, beheaded **1554**; Robert Devereux, Earl of **Essex,** beheaded 1601; Sir **Thomas** Overbury, poisoned in the Tower in **1613**; **Sir John Eliot**, died as a prisoner in the Tower 1632; James Fitzroy, **Duke of Monmouth, beheaded** 1685; Simon, Lord Fraser of Lovat, beheaded **1747.** The executions took place in the Tower itself only in the cases of **Anne Boleyn,** Catharine Howard, Lady Jane Grey, and Devereux, Earl of Essex; in all the other instances the prisoners were beheaded **at the public place of execution on** Tower Hill (see below).

The **list of those who were confined for** a longer or shorter period in the Tower **comprises a** great number of other celebrated persons: John Baliol, **King of Scotland, 1296;** William Wallace, the Scottish patriot, 1305; David **Bruce,** King of Scotland, 1347; King John of France **(taken prisoner at Poitiers,** 1357); **Duke of** Orleans, father **of Louis XII. of France, 1415;** Lord Cobham, the most distinguished **of the Lollards (burned as** a heretic at St. Giles in the **Fields, 1416); King Henry VI. (who is said to have been murdered in the Wakefield Tower by the Duke** of Gloucester, 1471); **Anne Askew (tortured in the Tower, and burned** in Smithfield as **a heretic, 1546); Archbishop Cranmer, 1553;** Sir Thomas **Wyatt (beheaded on Tower Hill in 1554); Earl of** Southampton, **Shakspeare's patron, 1562; Sir Walter Raleigh (see** p. 120; beheaded **at Westminster in 1618); Earl of Strafford** (beheaded 1641); **Archbishop Laud (beheaded** 1643); Viscount Stafford (beheaded **1680); Lord** William **Russell** (beheaded 1683); **Lord** Chancellor **Jeffreys, 1688; Duke of** Marlborough, 1692, etc.

On Tower Hill, N.W. of the Tower, formerly stood the scaffold for the execution of traitors (see above). William Penn (baptised 23rd Oct., 1644, in All Hallows, Great Tower Street) was born, and Otway, the poet, died on Tower Hill, and here too Sir Walter Raleigh's wife lodged while her unfortunate husband languished in the Tower. On the N. side rises **Trinity House,** a plain building, erected in 1793 from designs by *Wyatt*, the façade of which is embellished with the arms of the corporation, medallion portraits of George III. and Queen Charlotte, and several emblems of navigation. This building is the property of 'The Master, Wardens, and Assistants of the Guild, Fraternity, or Brotherhood, of the most glorious and undividable Trinity', a company founded by Sir Thomas Spert in 1515, and incorporated by Henry VIII. in 1529. The society consists of a Master, Deputy Master, 31 Elder Brethren, and an unrestricted number of Younger Brethren, and was founded with a view to the promotion **and encou**ragement of English navigation. Its rights and duties, which have been defined by various acts of parliament, com**prise** the regulation and management of lighthouses and buoys round the British coast, and the appointment and licensing of a body of efficient pilots. Two elder brethren of Trinity House assist the Admiralty in deciding all cases relating to collisions at sea. Its surplus funds are devoted to charitable objects connected with sailors. The interior of Trinity House contains busts of Admirals St. Vincent, Howe, Duncan, and Nelson; and portraits of James I. and his consort Anne of Denmark, James II., and Sir Francis Drake. There is also a large picture of several Elder Brethren, by *Gainsborough*. Many visitors will be interested in the model-chamber, containing a collection of models and designs of lighthouses and life-boats. The Duke of Edinburgh, second son of Queen Victoria, is the present Master of Trinity House, while the Prince of Wales is a 'Younger Brother'. Mr. W. E. Gladstone is an 'Elder Brother'. The annual income of Trinity House is said to be above 300,000*l*.

At the end of Great Tower Street, to the W. of the Tower, is the church of *All Hallows, Barking*, founded by the nuns of Barking Abbey, and containing some fine brasses. Archbishop Laud was buried in the graveyard after his execution on Tower Hill (1643), but his body was afterwards removed to the chapel of St. John's College, Oxford, of which he was an alumnus. The parish register records the baptism of William Penn (Oct. 23rd, 1644). The *Czar's Head*, opposite the church, is said to occupy the site of a tavern frequented by Peter the Great (see p. 141).

On the E. side of Tower Hill stands the **Royal Mint**, erected in 1811, from designs by *Johnson* and *Smirke*, on the site of the old Cistercian Abbey of St. Mary of the Graces, and so extensively enlarged in 1881-82 as to be practically a new building. The Mastership of the Mint (an office abolished in 1869) was once held by Sir Isaac Newton (1699-1727) and Sir John F. W. Herschel (1850-55). Permission to visit the Mint is given for a fixed day by the Deputy-Master of the Mint, on a written application stating the number and addresses of the intending visitors. The various processes of coining are extremely interesting, and the machinery used is of a most ingenious character. In 1882 fourteen improved presses were introduced, each of which can stamp and mill 120 coins per minute. The cases in the waiting-room contain coins and commemorative medals, including specimens of Maundy money, and gold pieces of 2*l*. and 5*l*., which were never brought into circulation. Among the other objects of interest is a skeleton cube, each side of which is $33\frac{3}{8}$ in. in length, showing the size of a mass of standard gold worth 1,000,000*l*.

In 1888 the value of the money coined at the Mint was 3,363,524*l*., including 2,277,424 sovereigns; 1,128,787 half-crowns, value 178,598*l*.; 1,517,540 florins, value 151,754*l*.; 4,526,840 shillings, value 226,942*l*.; 4,597,680 sixpences, value 104,942*l*.; 522,640 threepennies, value 6,533*l*; 5,124,960 pence, value 21,354*l*; 6,814,080 half-pence, value 14,196*l*.; and 1,886,400 farthings, value 1965*l*. In the ten years 1879-88 there were coined here 9,217,671 sovereigns, 10,347,228 half-sovereigns, 15,280,848 half-crowns, 16,915,140 florins, 40,621,680 shillings, etc. Of copper or bronze coins, most of which were made by contract at Birmingham, about 164,000,000 were issued in the same decade. The total value of the coins issued by the Mint between 1817 and 1880 was 246,000,000*l*.

On the S. side of Tower Hill is the **Tower Subway**, a tunnel constructed by *Barlow* in 1870, passing under the Thames, and leading to Tooley Street (corrupted from St. Olave Street) on the right (Southwark) bank. This gloomy and unpleasant passage consists of an iron tube 400 yds. long and 7 ft. in diameter, originally traversed by a tramway-car, but now used by pedestrians only. A winding staircase of 96 steps descends to it on each side (1/2d.). The subway was made in less than a year, at a cost of 20,000l.

The **City of London and Southwark Subway**, now in progress a little higher up the river, between a point near the Monument Station and Stockwell, is practically an *Underground Electric Railway*, consisting of two separate tunnels for the 'up' and 'down' traffic. It is expected to be finished in the course of 1889. The tunnel extends underground to King William Street on the N. bank and to the 'Swan' at Stockwell on the S., with intermediate stations at Kennington Oval, New Street, the Elephant and Castle, and Great Dover Street. At each station powerful hydraulic lifts will convey the passengers between the streets and the platforms. The total cost of this subway is estimated at 500,000l.

## 9. The Port and Docks.

*St. Katherine's Docks. London Docks. Thames Tunnel. Commercial Docks. Regent's Canal. West and East India Docks. Millwall Docks. Victoria and Albert Docks.*

One of the most interesting sights of London is the **Port**, with its immense warehouses, the centre from which the commerce of England radiates all over **the globe**. The *Port of London*, in the wider sense, extends from London Bridge to a point 6½ miles down the river, but as actually occupied by shipping may be said to terminate at Deptford, 4 miles from London Bridge. Ships bearing the produce of every nation under the sun here discharge their cargoes, which, previous to their sale, are stored, free of customs, in large bonded warehouses mostly in the Docks. Below these warehouses, which form small towns of themselves, and extend in long rows along the banks of the Thames, are extensive cellars for wine, oil, etc., while above ground are huge magazines, landing-stages, packing-yards, cranes, and every kind of apparatus necessary for the loading, unloading, and custody of goods.

To the E. of the Tower, and separated from it by a single street, called *Little Tower Hill*, are **St. Katherine's Docks** (Pl. R, 46; *III*), opened in 1828, and covering an area of 24 acres, on which 1250 houses with 11,300 inhab. formerly stood. The engineer was *Telford*, and the architect *Hardwick*. The docks admit vessels of 700 tons. The warehouses can hold 110.000 tons of goods. St. Katherine's Docks are now under the same management as the London Docks.

*St. Katherine's Steamboat Wharf*, adjoining the Docks, is mainly used as a landing-stage for steamers from the continent.

**London Docks** (Pl. R, 50), lying to the E. of St. Katherine's Docks, were constructed in 1805 at a cost of 4,000,000l., and cover an area of 120 acres. They have four gates on the Thames, and contain water-room for 300 large vessels, exclusive of lighters. Their warehouses can store 220,000 tons of goods, and their cellars 70,000 pipes (8,316,050 gallons) of wine. The Tobacco Dock and Warehouses (the *Queen's Warehouse*) alone cover an area of 5 acres of ground. At times, particularly when adverse winds drive vessels into the Thames, upwards of 3000 men are employed at these docks in one day. Every morning at 6 o'clock, there may be seen waiting at the principal entrance a large and motley crowd of labourers, to which numerous dusky visages and foreign costumes impart a curious and picturesque air. A good physique and willingness to work are the only credentials required. The capital of the London & St. Katherine's Docks Co. amounts to 13,000,000*l*. The door in the E. angle of the docks, inscribed '*To the Kiln*', leads to a furnace in which adulterated tea and tobacco, spurious gold and silver wares, and other confiscated goods, are burned. The long chimney is jestingly called the *Queen's Tobacco Pipe*. [Smuggled tobacco was also formerly burned here, but is now sent to the Broadmoor Criminal Lunatic Asylum.]

Nothing will convey to the stranger a better idea of the vast activity and stupendous wealth of London than a visit to these warehouses, filled to overflowing with interminable stores of tea, coffee, sugar, silk, tobacco, and other foreign and colonial products; to these enormous vaults, with their apparently inexhaustible quantities of wine; and to these extensive quays and landing-stages, cumbered with huge stacks of hides, heaps of bales, and long rows of casks of every conceivable description.

Permission to visit the warehouses and vaults may be obtained from the secretary of the London Dock Company, at 109 Leadenhall Street, E.C. Those who wish to taste the wines must procure a *tasting-order* from a wine-merchant. Ladies are not admitted after 1 p.m. Visitors should be on their guard against the insidious effects of 'tasting', in the heavy, vinous atmosphere of the vaults.

To the S. of the London Docks, and about 2 M. below London Bridge, lies the quarter of the metropolis called *Wapping*, from which the **Thames Tunnel** leads under the river to Rotherhithe on the right bank. The tunnel was begun in 1825, on the plans and under the supervision of *Sir Isambard Brunel*, and completed in 1843, after several accidents occasioned by the water bursting in upon the works. Seven men lost their lives during its construction. It consists of two parallel arched passages of masonry, 14 ft. broad, 16 ft. high, and 1200 ft. long, and cost 468,000*l*. The undertaking paid the Thames Tunnel Company so badly, that their receipts scarcely defrayed the cost of repairs. The tunnel was purchased in 1865 by the East London Railway Company for 200,000*l*., and is now traversed daily by about 40 trains (terminus at Liverpool Street Station, p. 33).

At Rotherhithe, to the E. of the tunnel, are situated the numerous large basins of the **Surrey** and Commercial Docks (Pl. R, 53, etc.), covering together an area of about 350 acres, and chiefly used for timber. On the N. bank of the river, at Limehouse, opposite the Commercial Docks, is the entrance to the **Regent's Canal**, which runs N. to Victoria Park, then turns to the W., traverses the N. part of London, and unites with the Paddington Canal, which forms part of a continuous water-route as far as Liverpool. The **West India Docks** (Pl. R, 62, etc.), nearly 300 acres in area, lie between Limehouse and Blackwall, to the N. of the *Isle of Dogs*, which is formed here by a sudden bend of the river. They can contain at one time as many as 460 West India merchantmen. Several of the chief lines of steamers load and discharge their cargoes in these docks. The three principal basins are called the *Import Dock*, the *Export Dock*, and the *South Dock*. The smaller **East India Docks** (Pl. R, 70, 71) are at *Blackwall*, a little lower down. The **Millwall Docks**, 100 acres in extent (35 water), are in the Isle of Dogs, near the West India Docks. Still lower down than the East India Docks, between Bow Creek, North Woolwich, and Galleon's Reach, lie the magnificent Victoria and Albert Docks, $2\frac{3}{4}$ M. in length, lighted by electricity and provided with every convenience and accommodation for sailing vessels and steamers of the largest size. The steamers of the Peninsular and Oriental, the Anchor, the National, and other important companies, put in at these docks. The *Hydraulic Lift*, for supporting vessels when undergoing repair, is worthy of inspection. The Victoria Dock Co. has been amalgamated with the London and St. Katherine's Docks Company, which has constructed a special railway, extending to Galleon's Reach and bringing the docks into direct connection with the Great Eastern Railway. The East and West India Dock Company have constructed large new docks at *Tilbury* (p. 344).

## 10. Bethnal Green Museum. National Portrait Gallery. Victoria Park.

The **Bethnal Green Museum** (Pl. B, 52), a branch of South Kensington Museum, opened in 1872, occupies a red brick building in Victoria Square, Cambridge Road, Bethnal Green. It was established chiefly for the benefit of the inhabitants of the poorer East End of London. The only permanent contents are collections of specimens of food and of animal and vegetable products, but loan collections of various kinds are also always on view. Admission on Mon., Tues., and Sat., 10 a.m. to 10 p.m., and Thurs. and Frid. 10 to 4, 5, or 6, free; on Wed., 10 a.m. to 4, 5, or 6 p.m., 6*d*. (catalogues on sale). The Resident Keeper is *Mr. Matchwick*. The number of visitors in 1887 was 409,929 and in 1888 it was 910,511, the great increase in the latter year being due to the temporary exhibition here of the Queen's Jubilee Presents.

## 10. NATIONAL PORTRAIT GALLERY.

The Museum may be conveniently **reached** by an Old Ford omnibus from the Bank; by the Metropolitan Railway to Aldgate, and thence by a Well Street tramway-car (a red car; fare 2*d*.), which passes the Museum; or by train from Liverpool Street Station to Cambridge Heath (about every 10 min.; through-booking **from** Metropolitan stations). In returning we may traverse Victoria Park to the (20 Min.) Victoria Park Station of the N. London Railway. whence there are trains every 1/4 hr. to Broad Street, City.

The space in front of the Museum is adorned with a handsome majolica *Fountain*, by *Minton* (1862). The interior of the Museum, entirely constructed of iron, consists of a large central hall, surrounded by a double gallery. To the right and left as we enter are busts of *Garibaldi* and *Cromwell*.

The extensive and well-arranged *Collection of Articles used for Food* occupies the N. side of the lower gallery. It comprises specimens of various kinds of edibles, models of others, diagrams, drawings, and so forth. On the S. side is the collection of *Animal Products*, largely consisting of clothing materials (wool, silk, leather, etc.) at different stages of their manufacture. The area of the central hall is occupied by a *Collection of Works of Ornamental Art* in gold, silver, bronze, and china, French furniture, etc., lent by Mr. and Mrs. Massey-Mainwaring and others. On screens round the hall is the *Dixon Collection* of water-colours and oil-paintings, bequeathed to the Museum in 1886. The former include examples of De Wint, Cooper, Birket Foster, David Cox, etc.; the latter are less interesting. Here too are exhibited an alto-relievo of *Mrs. Siddons* (d. 1831), by Campbell, and a bust of *Mrs. Jameson* (d. 1860), the writer on art, by Gibson, both belonging to the National Portrait Gallery (see below). The flooring of the central hall consists of a mosaic pavement formed from refuse chippings of marble, executed by female convicts in Woking Prison. The N. and S. basements are occupied by part of the Dixon Collection and by various picture, etc., on loan. In the N. basement is a plain refreshment-room.

The upper gallery, well lighted from the roof, now contains (on loan for a limited period) the \*\*National **Portrait Gallery** (formerly at S. Kensington; see p. 289), a highly valuable series of original portraits and busts of celebrated natives of Great Britain and Ireland. The director of the gallery is *Mr. George Scharf, C. B.*, who has prepared an excellent catalogue. The pictures are arranged approximately in historical sequence, beginning at the E. end of the S. Gallery. The outsides of the screens facing the central hall, however, are hung in both galleries with modern portraits. In the E. gallery are two recumbent figures, electrotype casts of the originals in Gloucester Cathedral: on the right, Edward II (d. 1327), a good piece of Gothic work; on the left, Robert, Duke of Normandy, surnamed Curthose, eldest son of William the Conqueror. Here also are various statues and busts. In the W. Gallery is a series of electrotypes of English sovereigns. The following is a list of the more important portraits, arranged roughly in chronological order.

In May, 1889, Lord Salisbury, Prime Minister of England, announced that an anonymous **private** donor had offered to build a National Portrait Gallery if Government would grant a suitable site; and a short time after an Act of Parliament authorised the erection of the new building adjoining the National Gallery (see p. 148).

Several paintings belonging to the National Portrait Gallery are at present deposited in the National Gallery (see p. 149).

PORTRAITS OF THE PLANTAGENET PERIOD (1154-1485). The portraits, executed at a later period, are of little artistic value. The best is that of *Richard III.* (d. 1483), in the act of putting a ring on his finger, probably by a Flemish artist. Facsimile of an ancient diptych representing *Richard II.* (1366-1400), at the age of fifteen, kneeling before the Virgin and Child (Arundel Society publication). Portrait of *Geoffrey Chaucer* (1340-1400). Tracings of the portraits of *Edward III.* and his family on the E. wall of St. Stephen's Chapel, Westminster (date, 1356), now destroyed.

PORTRAITS OF THE TUDOR PERIOD (1485-1603). *Henry VII.* (d. 1509), a work in the upper German style, painted, according to the Latin inscription, for Hermann Rinck (restored); *Cardinal Wolsey*, a crude performance, probably after an Italian original; several portraits of *Henry VIII.*, nearly all after Holbein; *Queen Mary I*, at the age of 28, before her accession; \**Thomas Cranmer, Archbishop of Canterbury* (1489-1556), by Gerbarus Flicius; \**Sir Thomas Gresham* (1519-1579), founder of the Royal Exchange, by Sir Anthony More, a pupil of Schoorcel; *Peter Martyr Vermilius* of Florence (1500-1562), preacher of the Reformation at Oxford, by Hans Asper of Zürich; *Sir Henry Unton* (d. 1596), a curious work with scenes from his life, by an unknown painter; portraits of *Raleigh*, *Burleigh*, *Camden*, and *George Buchanan*; several portraits of *Queen Elizabeth* and *Mary, Queen of Scots*; also the so-called Frazer-Tytler portrait of the latter, now accepted as Mary of Lorraine, her mother.

PORTRAITS OF THE STUART PERIOD (1603-1649). *Earl of Southampton* (d. 1624), the friend and patron of Shakspeare, by Mierevelt; oil-portrait of *Shakspeare* (the Chandos portrait), with an engraving from the first folio edition of the plays (1623); *Guy Fawkes* and other conspirators of the Gunpowder Plot, engraving with good portraits taken from life; *Ben Jonson* (d. 1637); *Children of Charles I.*, early copy of a well-known picture by Van Dyck; \**Endymion Porter*, confidant of Charles I. (1587-1649), an excellent work by Dobson; *James I.*, in the royal robes, by Van Somer; *Lord Bacon* (1561-1626), by Van Somer; *James VI.* of Scotland at the age of eight, by Zucchero; *Elizabeth, Queen of Bohemia* (d. 1662), by Mierevelt; *Inigo Jones*, the architect (1573-1652), by Old Stone, after Van Dyck; *W. Dobson* (1610-1646), a follower of Van Dyck and the first native English portrait-painter of any eminence, by himself; *Michael Drayton*, the poet (d. 1631); *Sir Kenelm Digby* (d. 1665), by Van Dyck.

PORTRAITS OF THE COMMONWEALTH (1649-1660) AND THE REIGN

of Charles II. (1660-85). Among the best portraits of this period are those of *Harrington* (d. 1677), the author, by Honthorst; *Thomas Hobbes*, the philosopher (d. **1679**), by J. M. Wright, and *Queen Elizabeth of Bohemia* (d. 1662), at the age of forty-six, by Honthorst. The portraits of *Nell Gwynne*, *Mary Davis*, the actress, *La Belle Hamilton*, and other beauties by Sir Peter Lely, are inferior in art value to the \*Portraits of the *Duke of Buckingham* (d. **1687**) and the *Countess of Shrewsbury* by the same artist. Portraits of *Cromwell*, *Milton* (a painting by Van der Plaas and an engraving from the life by Faithorne). *Cowley*, *Suckling*, *Andrew Marvell*, *Ireton*, *Monk*. and *Samuel Butler* are also exhibited here.

Portraits of the reigns of James II., William III., and Queen Anne (**1685-1714**). The best portrait in this section is that of \**Sir Christopher Wren*, the architect of St. Paul's Cathedral (1637-1723), by Sir Godfrey Kneller, a pupil of Rembrandt. Among the other portraits are the *Seven Bishops*, *Waller*, the poet, *Locke*, the philosopher, the *Duke of Marlborough*. *Duchess of Marlborough*, *Viscount Torrington* (d. 1733). *Lord Chancellor Jeffreys*, and the first *Duke of Bedford* (d. 1700), by Kneller. *Henry St. John*, *Viscount Bolingbroke*, the statesman (1678-1751), by H. Rigaud ; *Matt. Prior* (**1664-1721**), the poet, by Richardson ; *Joseph Addison* (**1672-1719**), two portraits, by Kneller and Dahl ; *Sir Isaac Newton* (**1642-1727**), by Vanderbank ; *Jonathan Swift* (**1667-1745**), by C. Jervas.

As we approach our own times the portraits become much more numerous, and it must suffice to give here a mere selection of those most interesting from their subject or treatment.

Portraits of the Eighteenth Century. Several portraits of *Cardinal York* (**1725-1807**), including one of him when a child by \*Largillière ; *Charles Edward Stuart* (**1720-88**), the Pretender, portraits by Largillière and Batoni ; *Simon Fraser*, Lord Lovat (p. 124), by Hogarth ; **Wm.** *Hogarth* (**1697-1764**), the painter, by himself ; *Alexander Pope* (1688-1744), in crayons, by Hoare ; *Pope* and *Martha Blount*, by **Jervas**; *Bishop Berkeley* (1684-1753), by **Smibert**; *James Thomson* (d. 1748), the poet, by Paton ; *Händel* (d. 1759), by Hudson ; *Isaac Watts* (d. 1748), the hymn-writer, by Kneller ; \**W. Pulteney, Earl of Bath* (**1682-1764**), by Reynolds, vigorously handled ; *General Wolfe* (**1726-59**), by Highmore ; *Samuel Richardson* (d. 1761), by Schaak ; *Peg Woffington* (**1720-1760**), the actress, painted as she lay in bed paralysed, by A. Pond ; *Sir Joshua Reynolds* (1723-1792), **when a** young man, **by himself** ; *Oliver Goldsmith* (1728-1774), by a pupil of Reynolds, a portrait familiar from numerous engravings; *David Garrick* (d. 1779), by Pine ; *Edmund Burke* (d. 1797), by Reynolds ; *Sir Wm.* **Blackstone** (1723-80), the **lawyer**, by Reynolds ; *William.* **Duke** *of Cumberland* (d. 1765), by **Reynolds**; *Sir William Chambers* (d. 1796), the architect of Somerset House, by Reynolds, somewhat pale in tone ; *Admiral Viscount Keppel* (**1727-1782**), by Reynolds ; *Sir William Hamilton* (1740-1803),

9\*

the diplomatist and antiquary, by Sir **Joshua** Reynolds, and another by **Allan** (1775); *Lord Clive* (d. 1774), by Dance; *Lord Chancellor Thurlow* (1732-1806), by Phillips; *William Pitt*, first Earl of Chatham (d. 1778), by Brompton; *Charles James Fox* (1794-1806), by Hickel; *Queen* (Charlotte, wife of George III., by Allan Ramsay; *Benjamin Franklin* 1706-1790), by Baricolo; *George Whitefield* (d. 1770), by Woolaston; *Robert Burns* (d. 1796), by Nasmyth, well known from engravings; *Captain Cooke* (d. 1779), by Webber; two portraits of *John Wesley* (1703-1791), one by Hone representing him at the age of 63, the other by Hamilton at the age of 85; *John Wilkes* (d. 1797), drawing by Earlom; *R. B. Sheridan* (d. 1816), by Russell.

PORTRAITS OF THE NINETEENTH CENTURY. *Warren Hastings* (1733-1818), by Sir Thomas Lawrence; *Francis Horner* (1778-1817), the politician and essayist, one of the founders of the 'Edinburgh Review', by Sir Henry Raeburn; *James Watt* (1736-1819), by C. J. de Breda; *Sir Walter Scott* (d. 1832), by Graham Gilbert; *Scott*, in his study at Abbotsford, with his deerhound Maida, by Sir Wm. Allan, the last portrait he sat for; another by Landseer; *Lord Byron* (d. 1824), in Greek costume, by T. Phillips; *Sir William Herschel* (1738-1822), by Abbott; *J. Flaxman* (d. 1826), by Romney; *W. Wilberforce*, the philanthropist (d. 1833), by Sir T. Lawrence (unfinished); *John Keats* (d. 1821), by Hilton, and another by Severn; *John Philip Kemble* (1757-1826), the tragedian, as Hamlet, by Sir Thos. Lawrence; *S. T. Coleridge* (d. 1834), by Allston; *Emma, Lady Hamilton* (d. 1815), by Romney; *Sir Philip Francis* (d. 1818; supposed author of the 'Letters of Junius'), by Lonsdale; *Sir James Mackintosh* (d. 1832), by Lawrence; *Wm. Blake* (d. 1827), the poet and painter, by Phillips. *Dr. Jenner* (d. 1823), the discoverer of the protective properties of vaccination, by Northcote; in front lies his work, 'On the Origin of Vaccine Inoculation' (1801), with a cow's hoof as letter-weight. *Lord Nelson* (d. 1805), by L. J. Abbott and H. Füger of Vienna (two portraits); *Jeremy Bentham*, the economist and political writer (d. 1832), by T. Frye and H. W. Pickersgill; *George Stephenson* (1781-1848), the first to apply the locomotive engine to railway trains, and constructor of the first railway (from Manchester to Liverpool), opened in 1830; *Rev. Ed. Irving* (1792-1834), founder of the Irvingite or Catholic Apostolic Church, drawing by Slater; *Chas. Lamb* (d. 1834), by Hazlitt; *Thos. Campbell* (d. 1844), by Lawrence; *Mrs. Siddons* (d. 1831), by Lawrence, and another by Beechey; *James Hogg*, the 'Ettrick Shepherd' (d. 1833), by Denning; *Sir David Wilkie* (d. 1841), by himself; *Benjamin West* (d. 1820), by Stuart; *Leigh Hunt* (d. 1859), by Haydon; *Admiral Sir John Ross* (1777-1856), the arctic navigator, by J. Green; *William Wordsworth* (1770-1850), by H. W. Pickersgill; *Samuel Rogers*, the poet (1762-1855), charcoal drawing by Sir T. Lawrence; *Queen Victoria*, after Angeli; the late *Prince Consort* (d. 1861), by Winterhalter; *Professor Wilson*

(*Christopher North*; d. 1854), by Gordon; *Rev. F. D. Maurice* (d. 1872), by Hayward; *Thomas de **Quincey*** (1785-1859), by Sir John Watson Gordon; *Cobden* (d. 1867), by Dickinson; *John Gibson*, the sculptor (1791-1861), by Mrs. Carpenter; *M. Faraday* (d. 1867), by Phillips; **Charles** *Dickens* (d. 1870), by Ary Scheffer; *Lord Macaulay* (d. 1859), sketch by Grant; *W. S. Landor* (d. 1864), by Fisher; *Douglas Jerrold* (d. 1857), by Macnee; *W. M. Thackeray* (d. 1863), by Lawrence; *Daniel Maclise* (d. 1870), by Ward; *E. B. Browning*, the poetess (d. 1861), a chalk drawing by Talfourd; *Geo. Grote*, the historian of Greece (1794-1871), by Stewardson; *George Eliot* (*Mrs. Cross*; d. 1880), by Sir F. Burton; *Sarah Austin*, the novelist; *Daniel O'Connell* (d. 1847), by Mulrennin; *Sir Fr. Chantrey* (d. 1841), by himself; *Lord Stratford de Redcliffe* (1788-1880), by G. F. Watts; *Adelaide Procter* (1825-1864), by Mrs. Gaggiotti Richards; *Robert Owen*, the socialist (d. 1858).

At the E. end of the N. Gallery are the following large pictures: The *First House of Commons after the Reform Bill of 1832*, with 320 portraits, by Hayter (key below); *Convention of the Anti-Slavery Society* in 1840, by Haydon, with portraits of Clarkson, Fowell Buxton, Gurney, Lady Byron, etc. In the S. gallery is a photograph of the *House of Commons in 1793*, from the original picture by Anton Hickel, now in the National Gallery (p. 149).

Among the most interesting of the busts and statues interspersed among the pictures are the following. Sitting figure of *Francis Bacon, Baron Verulam* (1561-1626); bronze busts of *Charles I.* and *Oliver Cromwell*; terracotta *Bust of *Thomas Carlyle* (1795-1881), by Boehm; a small marble bust of *Thackeray* (1811-63), by Barnard; an electrotype mask of *Keats*, from a mould taken during life; sitting statuette of the *Earl of Beaconsfield* (1804-1881), by Lord Ronald Gower; busts of *W. Hogarth* (1697-1764), by Roubiliac; *Thackeray*, by Durham; *Charles James Fox* (1749-1806), by Nollekens; *John Hampden* (1594-1643); *Garrick* (1716-1779); *William Pitt* (1759-1806), by Nollekens; *Lord George Bentinck* (1802-1848), by Campbell; *Thomas Moore* (d. 1852), by C. Moore; *Lord Jeffrey* (d. 1850), by Park; *Porson* (1759-1808), by Gangarelli; *Dr. Thomas Arnold* (1795-1842), by Behnes; *John Wesley* (1703-1791); *Lord Chancellor Eldon* (1751-1838), by Tatham; *Sir Thos. Lawrence* (d. 1830), by Baily; *Wm. Etty* (d. 1849), by Noble; *Benjamin West* (d. 1820), by Chantrey; *Sum. Lover* (d. 1868), by Foley; *George Stephenson* (d. 1848), by Pitts; *John Rennie* (d. 1821), the engineer, by Chantrey; *Chas. Knight* (d. 1873), by Durham; *Sir Robert Peel* (d. 1850), by Noble; *Cobden* (d. 1865), by Woolner; and *Lord John Russell* (d. 1878), by Francis. — The glass-cases contain interesting *Autographs*, *Miniatures*, *Medals*, etc.

To the N.E. of Bethnal Green lies **Victoria Park** (Pl. B, 55, 58, 59), covering 290 acres of ground, laid out at a cost of

130,000*l.*, and forming a place of recreation for the poorer (E.) quarters of London. The eastern and larger portion is unplanted, and is used for cricket and other games. The W. side is prettily laid out with walks, beds of flowers, and two sheets of water, on which swans may be seen disporting themselves, and pleasure boats hired. Near the centre of the park is the *Victoria Fountain*, in the form of a Gothic temple, erected by Baroness Burdett Coutts (comp. p. 27) in 1862. The park also contains open air gymnasiums. The most characteristic times to see Victoria Park are on Sat. or Sun. evenings or on a public holiday. On the N. side of the park is the large and handsome *Hospice for the Descendants of French Protestants*. — Victoria Park is most easily reached by the *North London Railway;* trains start from Broad Street Station, City (p. 34), every $1/4$ hr., and reach *Victoria Park Station*, at the N.E. extremity of the park, in 19 min. (fares 6d., 4d., 3d.; return-tickets 9d., 6d., 5d.); stations *Shoreditch*, *Haggerston*, *Dalston*, *Hackney*, *Homerton*, *Victoria Park*. Beyond Victoria Park the train proceeds to *Old Ford, Bow, Poplar,* and *Blackwall* (p. 128).

## 11. Fleet Street. The Temple. Chancery Lane. Royal Courts of Justice.

*St. Bride's. Church of St. Dunstan in the West. New Record Office. Temple Church. Lincoln's Inn. Gray's Inn. Temple Bar.*

**Fleet Street** (Pl. R, 35; *II*), one of the busiest streets in London, leads from Ludgate Hill to the Strand and the West End. It derives its name from the *Fleet Brook*, which, now in the form of a main sewer, flows through *Holborn Valley* (p. 93) and under Farringdon Street, reaching the Thames at Blackfriars Bridge. On the E. side of the brook formerly stood the notorious *Fleet Prison* for debtors, which was removed in 1844. Prisoners condemned by the Star Chamber were once confined here, and within its precincts were formerly celebrated the clandestine 'Fleet marriages' (see 'The Fleet: its River, Prison, and Marriages', by *John Ashton;* 1888). Its site (in Farringdon Street, on the right) is now occupied by the handsome Gothic *Congregational Memorial Hall*, begun in 1862, and so named in memory of the 2000 ministers ejected from the Church of England by Charles II.'s Act of Uniformity, 1667. The site of the Hall cost nearly 30,000*l.*, and the total amount expended on land and building has been 93,450*l.*

Fleet Street itself contains few objects of external interest, though many literary associations cluster round its courts and byways. It is still celebrated for its newspaper and other printing and publishing offices. To the left, but not visible from the street (entrance in St. Bride's Passage, adjoining the office of *Punch*) is **St. Bride's**, a church built by *Wren* in 1703, with a handsome tower 223 ft. in height. In the central aisle is the grave of

## 11. ST. DUNSTAN IN THE WEST. 135

Richardson, the author of 'Clarissa Harlowe' (d. 1761), who lived in Salisbury Square in the neighbourhood. The old church of St. Bride, destroyed in the Fire, was the burial-place of Sackville (1608), Lovelace (1658), and the printer Wynkin de Worde. In a house in the adjacent churchyard Milton once lived for several years. *Shoe Lane*, nearly opposite the church, leads to Holborn; while a little farther on, on the same side, are *Bolt Court*, where Dr. Johnson spent the last years of his life (1776-84), and where Cobbett afterwards toiled and fumed; *Wine Office Court*, in which is still the famous old hostelry of the *Cheshire Cheese*, where Johnson and Goldsmith so often dined, and Boswell so often listened and took notes; *Gough Square*, at the top of the Court, where Johnson laboured over his Dictionary and other works; and *Crane Court*, once the home of the Royal Society, its president being Sir Isaac Newton, and until very recently the seat of the Scottish Corporation, whose ancient Hall was burnt down in 1877. On the other side is Bouverie Street, leading to what was once the lawless *Alsatia*, immortalised by Scott in the 'Fortunes of Nigel'. In the beginning of 1883 a part of the ancient monastery of Whitefriars was discovered in this street, including a fragment of a stone tower of great thickness and strength. *Fetter Lane* and *Chancery Lane*, farther to the W., on the N. side, also lead to Holborn. At the corner of Chancery Lane, Isaac Walton, the famous angler, once occupied a shop as a hosier (1624-43). Close to it is a quaint old house with bow windows (No. 184), once occupied by Drayton, the poet (d. 1631). Between Fetter Lane and Chancery Lane rises the church of **St. Dunstan in the West**, erected by *Shaw* in 1833, with a fine Gothic tower. Over the E. door is a statue of Queen Elizabeth from the old Lud-Gate, once a city-gate at the foot of Ludgate Hill. The old clock of St. Dunstan had two wooden giants to strike the hours, which still perform that office at St. Dunstan's Villa, Regent's Park (p. 228). Near St. Dunstan's Church, at No. 183 Fleet Street, was Cobbett's book-shop and publishing office, where he issued his 'Political Register'; and on the opposite side, now No. 56, was the house of William Hone, the free-thinking publisher of the 'Everyday Book'. Opposite Fetter Lane is *Mitre Court*, with the tavern once frequented by Johnson, Goldsmith, and Boswell.

The **New Record Office** (Pl. R, 35; *II*), for the custody of legal records and state papers, in Fetter Lane, is a fire-proof edifice in the Tudor style, erected in 1851-66 by *Sir J. Pennethorne*.

The interior contains 142 rooms, between the rows of which on each floor run narrow passages paved with brick. Each room or compartment is about 25 ft. long, 17 ft. broad and $15^3{}_4$ ft. high. The floor, door-posts, window-frames, and ceilings are of iron, and the shelves of slate. Since the completion of the structure, the state papers, formerly kept in the State Paper Office, the Tower, the Chapter House of Westminster Abbey, the Rolls Chapel in Chancery Lane, at Carlton House, and in the State Paper Office in St. James's Park, have been deposited here. Here, too, are preserved the *Domesday Book*, in two parchment volumes of different sizes, containing the results of a statistical survey of England made in 1086 by order of William the Conqueror; the deed of resignation of the Scottish throne by David Bruce in favour of Edward II.; a charter granted by Alphonso of Castile on the marriage of Edward I. with Eleanor of Castile; the treaty of peace between Henry VIII. and Francis I., with a gold seal said to be the work of Benvenuto Cellini; various deeds of surrender of monasteries in England and Wales in favour of Henry VIII.; and an innumerable quantity of other records. The business hours are from 10 a.m. to 4 p.m. (on Sat. 2 p.m.), during which the Search Rooms are open to the public. Documents down to 1600 may be inspected gratis; the charge for copying is 6d.-1s. (according to date) per folio of 72 words, the minimum charge being 2s.

**Chancery Lane** (Pl. R. 32, 31, 35; *II*) leads through the quarter chiefly occupied by barristers and solicitors. On the right is *Serjeants' Inn* (p. 139). Farther up are the *Rolls Buildings*, consisting of the court of the Master of the Rolls, the Master's residence, and a chapel, containing a remarkably fine monument to Dr. John Young, Master of the Rolls, by *Torregiano* (1516). To the barristers belong the four great *Inns of Court*, viz. the *Temple* (*Inner* and *Middle*) on the S. of Fleet Street, *Lincoln's Inn* in Chancery Lane, and *Gray's Inn* in Holborn. These Inns are colleges for the study of law, and possess the privilege of calling to the Bar. Each is governed by its older members, who are termed *Benchers*.

The **Temple** (Pl. R, 35; *II*), on the S. side of Fleet Street, formerly a lodge of the Knights Templar, — a religious and military order founded at Jerusalem, in the 12th century, under Baldwin, King of Jerusalem, to protect the Holy Sepulchre, and pilgrims resorting thither, and called Templars from their original designation as 'poor soldiers of the Temple of Solomon' — became crown-property on the dissolution of the order in 1313, and was presented by Edward II. to Aymer de Valence, Earl of Pembroke. After Pembroke's death the Temple came into the possession of the Knights of St. John, who, in 1346, leased it to the students of common law. From that time to the present day the building, or rather group of buildings, which extends down to the Thames, has continued to be a school of law. Down to the reign of James I. it had to pay a tax to the Crown, but in 1609 it was declared by royal decree the free, hereditary property of the corporations of the *Inner* and the *Middle Temple*. The revenue of the Inner Temple amounts to 25,676*l.*; that of the Middle Temple to 12,240*l.*

The Inner Temple is so called from its position within the precincts of the City; the Middle Temple derives its name from its situation between the Inner and the Outer Temple, the last of which was afterwards replaced by Exeter Buildings. Middle Temple Lane separates the Inner Temple on the east from the Middle Temple on the west. The Inner and the Middle Temple possess in common the \***Temple Church, or St. Mary's Church**, situated within the bounds of the Inner Temple.

This church is divided into two sections, the *Round Church* and the *Choir*. The **Round Church**, about 58 ft. in diameter, a Norman edifice with a tendency to the transition style, and admirably enriched, was completed in 1185. The choir, in the Early English style, was added in 1240. During the Protectorate the ceiling-paintings were white-washed; and the old church afterwards became so dilapidated, that it was necessary in 1839-42 to subject it to a thorough restoration, a work which cost no less than 70,000*l*. The lawyers used formerly to receive their clients in the Round Church, each occupying his particular post like merchants 'on change'. The incumbent of the Temple Church is called the Master of the Temple, an office once filled by the 'judicious Hooker'.

A handsome Norman archway leads into the interior, which is a few steps below the level of the entrance. The choir, at the end of which are the altar and stalls (during divine service open to members of the Temple corporations and their families only), and the Round Church (to which the public is admitted) are both borne by quadrangular clustered pillars in marble. The ceiling is richly painted in arabesques resembling mosaics. The pavement consists of tiles, in which the lamb with the cross (the *Agnus Dei*), the heraldic emblem of the Templars, continually recurs. Most of the stained-glass windows are modern. In the Round Church are nine \**Monuments of Templars* of the 12th and 13th centuries, consisting of recumbent figures of dark marble in full armour. One of the four on the S. side, under whose pillow is a slab with foliage in relief, is said to be that of William Marshal, Earl of Pembroke (d. 1219), brother-in-law of King John, who filled the office of Regent during the minority of Henry III. The detached monument on the S. wall, resembling the other eight, is that of Robert de Ross (d. 1227), one of the Barons to whom England owes the Magna Charta (p. 186). The monuments are beautifully executed and admirably preserved. In a recess to the left of the altar is the white marble monument of *John Selden* (d. 1654), 'the great dictator of learning to the English nation'.

The triforium, which encircles the Round Church, contains some uninteresting old monuments, which were formerly preserved in the vaults, and belong exclusively to members of the corporations.

The Temple Church is open daily, 10-1 and 2-4 (free). Visitors knock at the door; if the verger is not in the church, the keys may be obtained at the porter's lodge, at the top of Inner Temple Lane.

Oliver Goldsmith (d. 1774), author of the 'Vicar of Wakefield', is buried in the *Churchyard* to the N. of the choir.

The *Temple Gardens*, once immediately adjacent to the Thames, but now separated from it by the Victoria Embankment, are open to the public on days and hours determined from time to time by the Benchers (ascertainable by enquiry at the gates or lodges). The gardens are well kept, but are becoming more and more circumscribed by the erection of new buildings. Here, according to Shakspeare, were plucked the *white* and *red roses* which were assumed as the badges of the houses of York and Lancaster, in the long and bloody civil contest, known as the 'Wars of the Roses'.

*Plantagenet.* Great lords, and gentlemen, what means this silence?
Dare no man answer in a case of truth?
*Suffolk.* Within the Temple hall we were too loud;
The garden here is more convenient.
. . . . . . . . . . . . . . . . . .
*Plantagenet.* Since you are tongue-tied and so loath to speak,
In dumb significants proclaim your thoughts:
Let him that is a true-born gentleman,
And stands upon the honour of his birth,
If he suppose that I have pleaded truth,
From off this brier pluck a white rose with me.
*Somerset.* Let him that is no coward, nor no flatterer,
But dare maintain the party of the truth,
Pluck a red rose from off this thorn with me.
. . . . . . . . . . . . . . . . . .
*Warwick.* — This brawl to-day,
Grown to this faction in the Temple Garden,
Shall send, between the red rose and the white,
A thousand souls to death and deadly night.
*Henry VI.*, *Part I; Act* ii. *Sc. 4.*

The **Temple Gardens** are famous for their *Chrysanthemums*, a brilliant show of which is held in November.

The fine Gothic \*HALL of the **Middle Temple**, built in 1572, and used as a dining-room, is notable for its handsome open-work ceiling in old oak. The walls are embellished with the armorial bearings of the Knights Templar, **and five large full-length** portraits of princes, including **an equestrian portrait of Charles I.** The large windows contain the **arms of members of the Temple who** have **sat in the** House of Peers. Shakspeare's 'Twelfth Night' was acted in this hall during the dramatist's lifetime. — The *Library* (30,000 vols.) is preserved in a modern Gothic building on the side next the Thames, which contains a hall 85 ft. long and 62 ft. high. — The new *Inner Temple Hall*, opened in 1870, is a handsome structure, also possessing a fine open-work roof. — Oliver Goldsmith lived and died on the second floor of **2 Brick Court**, Middle Temple Lane; Blackstone, the famous commentator on the law of England, lived **in** the rooms below him; and Dr. Johnson occupied apartments in Inner Temple Lane, in a house now taken down.

**Lincoln's Inn** (Pl. R, 31, 32; *II*), the third of the Inns of Court in importance, is situated without the City, on a site once occupied by the mansion of the Earl of Lincoln and other houses. The *Gatehouse* in Chancery Lane was built in 1518 by *Sir Thomas Lovell*, whose coat-of-arms it bears. About a century later (1617), Ben Jonson is said to have been employed as a bricklayer in constructing the **adjacent wall**; but the truth of this tradition may well be doubted, **since in 1617 Jonson was 44 years** old and had written some of his best plays. The *Chapel* was erected by *Inigo Jones* in **1621-23**, and contains good wood-carving and stained glass. Like **the Round Church** of the Temple, this chapel was once used as a **consultation room by** the barristers and their clients.

The *New Hall*, the handsome dining-hall of Lincoln's Inn, in the Tudor style, was completed in 1845 under the supervision of Mr. *Hardwick*, the architect. It contains a painting by *Hogarth*, representing Paul before Felix, a large fresco of the School of Legislation, by *G. F. Watts* (1860), and a statue of Lord Eldon, by *Westmacott*. The *Library*, founded in 1497, is the oldest in London, and contains 25,000 vols. and numerous valuable MSS.; most of the latter were bequeathed by Sir Matthew Hale, a member of the Inn. Among its most prized contents is the fourth volume of Prynne's Records, for which the society gave 335*l*. — The revenue of this inn amounts to 35,329*l*. Sir Thomas More, Shaftesbury, Selden, Oliver Cromwell, William Pitt, Lord Erskine, Lord Mansfield, and Lord Brougham were once numbered among its members. Thurloe, Cromwell's secretary, had chambers at No. 24 Old Square (to the left, on the ground-floor) in 1645-59, and the Thurloe papers were afterwards discovered here in the false ceiling. Among the preachers of Lincoln's Inn were Usher, Tillotson, Heber, and Frederick Denison Maurice. — The *Court of Chancery*, or, more correctly, under the new Judicature Act, the 'Equity Division of the High Court of Justice', formerly held some of its sittings in Lincoln's Inn.

The neighbouring establishment of **Gray's Inn** (Pl. R, 32; *II*), a little to the N. of Holborn, which formerly paid a ground-rent to the Lords Gray of Wilton, has existed as a school of law since 1371. The Elizabethan Hall, built about 1560, contains fine woodcarving. During the 17th cent. the garden, in which a number of trees were planted by Lord Bacon, was a fashionable promenade; but it is not now open to the public. The name of Lord Bacon is the most eminent among those of former members of Gray's Inn. Comp. 'Chronicles of an Old Inn', by *Andrée Hope*.

Formerly subsidiary to the four Inns of Court were the nine *Inns of Chancery*, which now, however, have little beyond local connection with them, and are let out in chambers to solicitors, barristers, and the general public. These are *Clifford's Inn*, *Clement's Inn*, and *Lyon's Inn* (now the site of the Globe Theatre), attached to the Inner Temple; *New Inn* and *Strand Inn*, to the Middle Temple; *Furnival's Inn* and *Thavies' Inn*, to Lincoln's Inn; *Staple Inn* and *Barnard's Inn* (p. 94), to Gray's Inn. *Serjeants' Inn*, Chancery Lane, was originally set apart for the use of the serjeants-at-law, whose name is derived from the 'fratres servientes' of the old Knights Templar; but the building is now used for other purposes.

To the S. of Lincoln's Inn, between Temple Bar and St. Clement Danes, at the E. end of the Strand (p. 141), rise the **Royal Courts of Justice**, a vast and magnificent Gothic pile, forming a whole block of buildings, with a frontage towards the Strand of about 500 ft. The architect was *Mr. G. E. Street*, who unfortunately died shortly before the completion of his great work; a statue of him, by Armstead, has been placed on the E. side of the central hall. The Courts were formally opened on Dec. 4th, 1882, by Queen Victoria, in presence of the Lord Chancellor, the Prime Minister, and the other chief dignitaries of the realm. The building cost about

750,000*l*. **The** principal internal feature is the large central hall, 238 ft. long, 48 ft. wide, and 80 ft. high, with a fine mosaic flooring designed by Mr. Street. The building contains in all 19 court-rooms. When the courts are sitting, the general public are admitted to the ga**lleries only**, the central hall and the court-rooms being reserved for **members** of the Bar **and persons** connected with the **cases**. During the vacation the central hall is open to the public from 11 to 3, and tickets **of admission to the courts** may **be obtained gra**tis at the superintendent's **office**.

For about a century and **a half after the** Norman Conquest, the royal court of justice followed **the King from** place to place; but one of the articles of Magna Charta **provided that the** Common Pleas, **or that** branch of **the court in which disputes between** subjects **were** settled, **should be fixed at Westminster. The Court of** King's Bench seems to have been **also held here from the time of Henry III.** The Court of Chancery sat **regularly in Westminster Hall from** about the reign of Henry VIII., **but was afterwards removed to Lincoln's Inn.** This separation **of common law and equity proved very** inconvenient **to the** attorneys **and others, and the Westminster** courts became much too small for the **business carried on in them.** It was accordingly resolved to build a **large new palace of justice to** receive all the superior courts, and the **site of the present Law Courts was** fixed upon in 1867. The work of **building actually began in 1874.** The Judicature Act of 1873 obliterated **the distinction between common** law and equity, **and** united all the **superior tribunals of the** country into a Supreme Court of Judicature, **subdivided into a court** of original jurisdiction (the High Court of Justice) **and a court of appellate** jurisdiction (the Court of Appeal).

**Temple Bar,** a gateway formerly adjoining the Temple, between Fleet Street and the Strand, was built by *Wren* in 1670. Its W. side was adorned with statues of Charles I. and Charles II., its E. side with statues of Elizabeth and James I. The heads of criminals used to be barbarously exhibited on iron spikes on the top of the gate. When the reigning sovereign visited the City on state occasions, he was wont, in accordance with an ancient custom, to obtain permission from the Lord Mayor to pass Temple Bar. The heavy wooden gates were removed a few years ago to relieve the Bar of their weight, as it had shown signs of weakness; and the whole erection was finally demolished early in 1878, to permit of the widening of the street and to facilitate the enormous traffic. In Dec., 1888, the gate was re-erected at one of the entrances of Theobalds Park, Waltham Cross, Herts, the seat of Sir H. B. Meux (see p. 330). A *Memorial* of Temple Bar, with statues of Queen Victoria and the Prince of Wales at the sides, and surmounted by the City Griffin and arms, was **erected in 1880 on the site** of the **old** gate.

Immediately adjoining the site of Temple Bar, on the S. side of Fleet **Street,** stands the **large, new building of** *Child's* Bank, which was in high repute in the **time of the Stuarts**, and is the oldest banking house in London but one. Dryden, Pepys, Nell Gwynne, and Prince Rupert were early customers of this bank. The Child family is still connected with the business. Next door to this house was the 'Devil's Tavern', noted as the home of the Apollo Club, of which Ben Jonson, Randolph, and Dr. Kenrick were frequenters. The tavern was in time absorbed by Child's Bank, which also used the room over **the** main arch of Temple Bar as a storehouse.

# II. THE WEST END.

## 12. Strand. Somerset House. Waterloo Bridge.

*St. Clement Danes. The Roman Bath. King's College. St. Mary le Strand. Savoy Chapel. Savoy Palace. Society of Arts. National Life Boat Institution. Eleanor's Cross.*

The Strand (Pl. R, 26, 31, and *II*; so named from its skirting the bank of the river, which is now concealed by the buildings), a broad street containing many handsome shops, is the great artery of traffic between the City and the West End, and one of the busiest and most important thoroughfares in London. It was unpaved down to 1532, and about this time it was described as 'full of pits and sloughs, very perilous and noisome'. At this period many of the mansions of the nobility and hierarchy stood here, with gardens stretching down to the Thames. The names of several streets and houses still recall these days of bygone magnificence, but the palaces themselves have long since disappeared or been converted to more plebeian uses. Ivy Bridge Lane and Strand Bridge Lane commemorate the site of bridges over two water-courses that flowed into the Thames here, and there was a third bridge farther to the E. The Strand contains a great many newspaper offices and theatres.

Just beyond the site of Temple Bar (p. 140), to which its name will doubtless long attach, on the (N.) right, rise the new Law Courts (p. 139). The church of St. Clement Danes, in the centre of the Strand, was erected in 1688 from designs by *Wren*. The tower, 115 ft. in height, was added by *Gibbs* in 1719. Dr. Johnson used to worship in this church, a fact recorded by a tablet affixed to one of the pillars. The church is said to bear its name from being the burial-place of Harold Harefoot and other Danes. *Wych Street*, in which the *Olympic Theatre* (p. 42) is situated, leads from this point to Drury Lane. At the entrance of this street is *Clement's Inn* (p. 139), now connected with the Temple, and named after St. Clement's Well, once situated here, but removed in 1874. The garden is embellished with the figure of a Moor (Italian, 17th cent.), bearing a sun-dial. — In Newcastle Street, a little to the N., is the *Globe Theatre* (p. 41).

*Essex Street, Arundel Street, Norfolk Street*, and *Surrey Street*, diverging to the left, mark the spots where stood the mansions of the Earls of Essex (Queen Elizabeth's favourite), Arundel, and Surrey (Norfolk) respectively; and they all lead to the Thames Embankment. Peter the Great resided in Norfolk Street during his visit to London in 1698, and William Penn once lived at No. 21 in the same street. George Sale, the translator of the Koran, as well as Congreve (d. 1729), the dramatist, lived and died in Surrey Street. Beyond Norfolk Street, on the left, is the *Strand Theatre* (p. 41). At No. 5 Strand Lane, the adjacent narrow opening on the left, is an ancient **Roman Bath**, about 13 ft. long, 6 ft. broad, and 4½ ft. deep, one of the few relics of the Roman period in London. The bricks at the side are laid edgewise, and the flooring consists of brick with a thin coating of stucco. At the point where the water, which flows from a natural spring, has washed away part of the stucco covering, the old pavement below is visible. The clear, cold water probably flows from the old '*Holy Well*', situated on the N. side of the Strand, and lending its name to the adjacent Holywell Street, which is chiefly occupied by book-shops of a low class. The Roman antiquities found here are preserved in the British Museum (**p. 252**). Close by, on the right of the passage, is another bath, said to have been built by the Earl of Essex about 1588; it is supplied by a pipe from the Roman bath. At No. 36 Holywell Street is a survivor of the ancient signs with which every shop in London used to be provided (a crescent moon with a face in the centre).

**King's College**, the large pile of buildings adjoining Strand Lane on the W., built by *Smirke* in 1828, forms the E. wing of Somerset House (see below). The *Museum* contains a collection of models and instruments, including Babbage's calculating machine.

In the Strand we next reach, on the N. side, the church of **St. Mary le Strand**, built by *Gibbs* in 1717, on the spot where stood in olden times the notorious Maypole, the May-day and Sunday delight of youthful and other idlers. It was called St. Mary's after an earlier church which had been demolished by Protector Somerset to make room for his mansion of Old Somerset House (see below). Thomas Becket was rector of this parish in the reign of King Stephen. — Drury Lane, a street much in need of improvement, and containing the theatre of the same name (p. 40), leads N. from this point to Oxford Street and the British Museum.

Farther on, on the S. side of the Strand, rises the stately façade of **Somerset House** (Pl. R, 31; *II*), 150 ft. in length. The present large, quadrangular building was erected by *Sir William Chambers* in 1776-86, on the site of a palace which the Protector Somerset began to build in 1549. The Protector, however, was beheaded (**p. 123**) before it was completed, and the palace fell to the Crown. It was afterwards the residence of Anne of Denmark, consort of James I., of Henrietta Maria, the queen of Charles I., and of Catharine of Braganza, the neglected wife of the second Charles. Inigo Jones died here in 1652. The old building was taken down in 1766, and the present edifice, now occupied by various public offices, erected in its stead. The imposing principal façade towards the Thames, 780 ft. in length, rises on a terrace 50 ft. broad and 50 ft. high, and is now separated from the river by the Victoria Embankment. The quadrangular court contains a bronze group by *Bacon*, representing George III. leaning on a rudder, with the English lion and Father Thames at his feet. The two wings of the building were erected during the present cent.: the eastern, containing King's College (p. 142), by *Smirke*, in 1828; the western, towards Wellington Street, by *Pennethorne*, in 1854-56. The sum expended in constructing the latter alone was 81,000*l.*; and the cost of the whole building amounted to 500,000*l*. At Somerset House no fewer than 900 officials are employed, with salaries amounting in the aggregate to 275,000*l*. The building is said to contain 3600 windows. The public offices established here include the *Audit Office;* the *Inland Revenue Office*, in the new W. wing, containing the presses for stamped paper, postage stamps, etc.; the *Office of the Registrar-General of Births, Deaths, and Marriages;* the *Admiralty Register;* and *Doctors' Commons Will Office (Prerogative Court)*, transferred hither from Doctors' Commons, Bennet's Hill (p. 116), in 1874. This last department is the great repository of testamentary writings of all kinds. The *Department for Literary Enquiry* in the Central Hall is open daily from 10 a. m. to 3 p. m. Here may be seen an interesting collection of wills, including those of Shakspeare, Holbein, Van Dyck, Newton, and Samuel Johnson. The will of Napoleon I., executed at St. Helena, used to be kept here, but was handed over to the French in 1853. Visitors are allowed to read copies of wills previous to 1700, from which also pencil extracts may be made. For showing wills of a later date a charge of 1*s.* is made. A fee of 1*s.* is also charged for searching the calendars. No extracts may be made from these later wills, but official copies may be procured at 8*d.* per folio page.

On the W. side of Somerset House is Wellington Street, leading to *Waterloo Bridge. This bridge, one of the finest in the world, was built by *John Rennie* for a company in 1811-17, at a cost of over 1,000,000*l*. It is 460 yds. long and 42 ft. broad, and rests upon 9 arches, each of 120 ft. span and 35 ft. high, and borne by granite buttresses. It commands an admirable view of the W. part of London between Westminster and St. Paul's, of the Thames Embankment, and of the massive but well-proportioned façade of Somerset House. In 1878 the bridge was sold to the Metropolitan Board of Works for 475,000*l*. and opened to the public toll-free.

On the N. side of the Strand we next observe several theatres, including the *Gaiety* (p. 41) and the *Lyceum* (p. 40). Beyond these, between Burleigh Street and Exeter Street (commemorating Exeter House, the residence of Queen Elizabeth's Lord Chancellor), is *Exeter Hall*, marked by its Corinthian portico, and capable of containing 5000 persons. It is the property of the Young Men's Christian Association and used for the advocacy of religious and philanthropic movements (the large annual 'May Meetings' of various religious societies being held here).

To the left is Savoy Street, leading to the **Savoy Chapel**, dedicated to St. John the Baptist, and built in the Perpendicular style in 1505-11, during the reigns of Henry VII. and Henry VIII., on the site of the ancient *Savoy Palace*.

The chapel, which is one of the Chapels Royal, was seriously injured by fire in 1864, but restored at the expense of Queen Victoria. The handsome wooden ceiling is modern. Bishop Gavin Douglas of Dunkeld (d. 1522), the poetical translator of Virgil, is buried in the chancel (with brass), and George Wither (d. 1667), the poet, was also buried here. Fine stained glass. Savoy Palace was first built in 1245, and was given by Henry III. to Peter, Count of Savoy, the uncle of his queen, Eleanor of Provence. The captive King John of France died here in 1364, and Chaucer was probably married here when the palace was occupied by John of Gaunt. It lay between the present chapel and the river, but has entirely disappeared. At the Savoy, in the time of Cromwell, the Independents adopted a Confession of Faith, and here the celebrated 'Savoy Conference' for the revision of the Prayer Book was held, when Baxter, Calamy, and others represented the Nonconformists. The German chapel which used to stand contiguous to the Savoy Chapel was removed in widening Savoy Street, which now forms a thoroughfare to the Thames Embankment The French Protestants who conformed to the English church had a chapel here from the time of Charles II. till 1737. See *Memorials of the Savoy*, by the Rev. W. J. Loftie (MacMillan; 1878).

At No. 13 Cecil Street, to the left, Sir W. Congreve (d. 1828), the inventor of the Congreve Rocket, resided and made his experiments, firing the rockets across the Thames. Near the corner of the Strand and Cecil Street is the *Savoy Theatre* (p. 41).

A little to the N. of this part of the Strand lies *Covent Garden Market* (p. 180). On the right, between Southampton Street and Bedford Street, is the *Vaudeville Theatre* (p. 41); beyond it, the *Royal Adelphi Theatre* (p. 41). In Bedford Street is the new store of the *Civil Service Supply Association* (p. 27).

To the S. of the Strand, in John Street, Adelphi (approached through Adam Street, opposite the Adelphi Theatre), rises the building of the Society **of Arts** (Pl. R, 30; *II*), an association established in 1754 for the encouragement of arts, manufactures, and commerce, which took a prominent part in promoting the Exhibitions of 1851 and 1862. The large hall (open daily, 10-4, except Wednesdays and Saturdays) contains six paintings by *Barry* (1777-83), representing the progress of civilisation. No. 14 in the same street is the headquarters of the Royal National **Life Boat** Institution, founded in 1824 and supported entirely by voluntary contributions. This society now possesses a fleet of about 300 life-boats stationed round the British coasts, and in 1888 was instrumental in saving 800 lives and 26 vessels. The total number of lives saved through the agency of the Institution from its foundation down to 1889 was above 34,000. The expenditure of the society in 1888 was 53,270*l*. The average cost of establishing a life-boat station is 1050*l*., and the annual expense of maintaining it 70*l*. In the middle of **Adelphi** Terrace, parallel with John Street on the S., David Garrick died in 1779. On the right, where King William Street joins the Strand, stands the *Charing Cross Hospital;* and in King William Street is the *Ophthalmic Hospital*. A little farther on, in the Strand, on the right hand, is the *Lowther Arcade* (p. 26), and on the left is **Coutts's Bank**, a very noted firm, at which the royal family has banked for nearly 200 years.

At the W. end of the Strand, on the left, is *Charing Cross Station* (with a large *Hotel*, p. 7), the West End terminus of the South-Eastern Railway (p. 33), built by *Barry* on the site of *Hungerford Market*, where the mansion of Sir Edward Hungerford stood until it was burned down in 1669. In front of it stands a modern copy of *Eleanor's Cross*, a Gothic monument erected in 1291 by Edward I. at Charing Cross, on the spot where the coffin of his consort was set down during its last halt on the way to Westminster Abbey. The original was removed by order of Parliament in 1647. The river is here crossed by the *Charing Cross Railway Bridge*, on each side of which is a foot-way (freed from toll in 1878). — To the E. of the station is *Villiers Street*, which descends to the *Embankment Gardens* (p. 114) and to the *Charing Cross Station* (p. 36) of the Metropolitan Railway. The *Watergate, situated close by, is an interesting relic of York House, a palace begun by *Inigo Jones* for George Villiers, the favourite of James I., and first Duke of Buckingham. — Benjamin Franklin lived at No. 7 *Craven Street* (denoted by a memorial tablet), to the W. of the station.

## 13. Trafalgar Square.

*Nelson Column. St. Martin's in the Fields. Charing Cross.*

"Trafalgar Square (Pl. R, 26; *II, IV*), one of the finest open places in London and a great centre of attraction, is, so to speak, dedicated to *Lord Nelson*, and commemorates his glorious death at the battle of Trafalgar (22nd Oct., 1805), gained by the English fleet over the combined armaments of France and Spain. By this victory Napoleon's purpose of invading England was frustrated. The ambitious Emperor had assembled at Boulogne an army of 172,000 infantry and 9000 cavalry, and also 2413 transports to convey his soldiers to England, but his fleet, which he had been building for many years at an enormous cost, and which was to have covered his passage of the Channel, was destroyed by Nelson at this famous battle. The Admiral is, therefore, justly revered as the saviour of his country.

In the centre of the square rises the massive granite Column, 145 ft. in height, to the memory of the hero. It is a copy of one of the Corinthian columns of the temple of Mars Ultor, the avenging god of war, at Rome, and is crowned with a Statue of Nelson, by *Baily*, 17 ft. in height. The pedestal is adorned with reliefs in bronze, cast with the metal of captured French cannon. On the N. face is a scene from the battle of Aboukir (1798); Nelson, wounded in the head, declines to be assisted out of his turn by a surgeon who has been dressing the wounds of a common sailor. On the E. side is the battle of Copenhagen (1801); Nelson is represented as sealing upon a cannon the treaty of peace with the conquered Danes. On the S. is the death of Nelson at Trafalgar (22nd Oct., 1805); beside the dying hero is Captain Hardy, commander of the Admiral's flag-ship. Below is Nelson's last command: 'England expects every man will do his duty'. On the W. side is a representation of Nelson receiving the sword of the Spanish commander after the battle of St. Vincent (1797).—Four colossal bronze lions, modelled by *Sir Edwin Landseer* (d. 1874) in 1867, couch upon pedestals running out from the column in the form of a cross. — The monument was erected in 1843 by voluntary contributions at a total cost of about 45,000*l*.

Towards the N. side of the square, which is paved with asphalt, are two fountains. A *Statue of Sir Henry Havelock*, the deliverer of Lucknow (d. 1857), by *Behnes*, stands on the E. (Strand) side of the Nelson Column, and a *Statue of Sir Charles James Napier*, the conqueror of Scinde (d. 1853), by *Adams*, on the other. The N.E. corner of the square is occupied by an *Equestrian Statue of George IV.*, in bronze by *Chantrey*. Between the fountains is a *Statue of General Gordon* (killed at Khartoum in 1885), by *Hamo Thorneycroft*, erected in 1888.

On the terrace on the N. side of the square rises the *National Gallery* (see next page). Near it, on the E., is the church of St. Martin in the Fields, with a noble Grecian portico, erected in 1721-26 by *Gibbs*, on the site of an earlier church, and containing a few uninteresting tombs. Nell Gwynne (d. 1687), Farquhar the dramatist (d. 1707), Roubiliac the sculptor (d. 1762), and James Smith (d. 1839), one of the authors of 'Rejected Addresses', were buried in the churchyard.

Adjoining Morley's Hotel, on the E. side of the square, is the building of the *Royal* Humane Society, founded in 1774 for the rescue of drowning persons. This valuable society possesses a model house on the N. bank of the Serpentine in Hyde Park, containing models of the best appliances for saving life, and apparatus for aiding bathers and skaters who may be in danger. It also awards prizes and medals to persons who have saved others from drowning.

Down to 1874 *Northumberland House*, the noble mansion of the Duke of Northumberland, with the lion of the Percies high above the gates, rose on the S.E. side of Trafalgar Square. It was purchased in 1873 by the Metropolitan Board of Works for 497,000*l*., and was removed to make way for Northumberland Avenue, a broad new street from Charing Cross to the Thames Embankment (comp. p. 113). The *Grand Hotel* (p. 7) occupies part of the site. Two other large hotels, the *Hôtel Métropole* and the *Hôtel Victoria*, have been built on the opposite side of Northumberland Avenue. Next door to the Grand Hotel is the *Constitutional Club*, a handsome building of red and yellow terracotta in the style of the German Renaissance, erected in 1886. At the corner of Northumberland Avenue and Whitehall Place, facing the Thames, is the magnificent new building of the *National Liberal Club*, opened in 1887. One of the most attractive features of this imposing edifice is the spacious flagged terrace overlooking the Embankment Gardens and the river.

On the W. side of Trafalgar Square, between Cockspur Street and Pall Mall East, is the *Union Club* (p. 75), adjoining which is the *Royal College of Physicians*, built by *Smirke* in 1825, and containing a number of portraits and busts of celebrated London physicians.

**Charing Cross** (Pl. R, 26, and *IV*; probably so called from the village of *Cherringe* which stood here in the 13th cent.), on the S. side of Trafalgar Square, between the Strand and Whitehall, is the principal point of intersection of the omnibus lines of the West End, and the centre of the 4 and 12 miles circles on the Post Office Directory Map. The *Equestrian Statue of Charles I.*, by *Le Sueur*, which stands here, is remarkable for the vicissitudes it has undergone. It was cast in 1633, but had not yet been erected when the Civil War broke out. It was then sold by the Parliament to a brazier, named John Rivet, for the purpose of being melted down, and this worthy sold pretended fragments of it both to friends and foes of the Stuarts. At the Restoration, however, the statue was produced uninjured, and in 1674 it was erected on the spot where *Eleanor's Cross* (p. 145) had stood down to 1647. In *Hartshorn Lane*, an adjoining street, Ben Jonson, when a boy, once lived with his mother and her second husband, a bricklayer.

Among the many street improvements which the Metropolitan Board of Works accomplished before its supersession by the County Council (see p. 69) is CHARING CROSS ROAD, a great and much needed thoroughfare from Charing Cross to Tottenham Court Road, cutting through a number of low streets and alleys to the N. of St. Martin's Church. SHAFTESBURY AVENUE, another wide street opened in 1886, runs from Regent Street to meet the first-mentioned thoroughfare at *Cambridge Circus*, and is prolonged to New Oxford Street opposite Hart Street, Bloomsbury.

## 14. The National Gallery.

Among the buildings round Trafalgar Square the principal in point of size, although perhaps not in architectural merit, is the **\*\*National Gallery** (Pl. R, 26; *II*), situated on a terrace on the N. side, and erected in 1832-38, at an original cost of 96,000*l.*, on the site of the old King's Mews. The building, designed by *Wilkins*, is in the Grecian style, and has a façade 460 ft. in length. The Gallery was considerably altered and enlarged in 1860; an extensive addition (including the central octagon) was made by Mr. E. M. Barry in 1876; and five other rooms, including a gallery 85 ft. long, were opened in 1887. The back of the National Gallery is very plain and unfinished-looking, but the new National Portrait Gallery (see p. 129) is to be erected here, with a façade towards Charing Cross Road. The central staircase leading to the new rooms is intended to be used by entering visitors, while the old staircases, to the right and left, serve as exits.

The nucleus of the Gallery, which was formed by Act of Parliament in 1821, consisted solely of the Angerstein collection of 38 pictures. It has, however, been rapidly and greatly extended by means of donations, legacies, and purchases, and is now composed of some 1300 pictures, about 1100 of which are exhibited in the 22 rooms of the Gallery, while the others are lent to provincial collections. Among the most important additions have been the collections presented or bequeathed by Robert Vernon (1847), J. M. W. Turner (1856), and Wynn Ellis (1876); and the Peel collection, bought in 1871. For a long period part of the building was occupied by the Royal Academy of Arts, which, however, was removed to Burlington House (p. 220) in 1869. The National Collection has since been wholly re-arranged, and is now entirely under one roof. (This is of course quite distinct from the national collections at South Kensington.) — In 1888 the National Gallery was visited on the free days by 550,817 persons, being a daily average of 2635, and on the students' days by 17,931 persons, besides 26,127 students.

From the number of artists represented, the collection in the National Gallery is exceedingly valuable to students of the history of art. The older Italian masters are especially important. The catalogues prepared by Mr. *Wornum* (d. 1877), the late keeper of the Gallery, and re-issued with corrections and additions by Sir F. W. Burton in 1889 (Foreign Schools 1s., abridgment 6d.; British School 6d.), comprise short biographies of the different artists. Mr. *E. T. Cook's* 'Popular Handbook to the National Gallery' (MacMillan & Co., 1888) includes an interesting collection of notes on the pictures by Mr. Ruskin and others. See also *Dr. J. P. Richter's* 'Italian Art in the National Gallery' (1883). Each picture is inscribed with the name of the painter, the year of his birth and death, the school to which he belongs, and the subject represented. The present director is *Sir F. W. Burton*, and the keeper and secretary is Mr. *Charles Eastlake*. — Photographs of the paintings, by Signor Morelli, are sold in the gallery at prices ranging from 1s. to 10s. Those taken by *Braun & Cie.*, of Dornach and Paris, and by the *Berlin Photographic Co.* are, however, better; the former (6-12s.) may be obtained at the Autotype Fine Art Gallery, 74 New Oxford Street, while the latter (1s.6d. each, 15s. per dozen) are sold by J. Gerson, 5 Rathbone Place, Oxford Street.

The Gallery is open to the public all the year, free of charge, on Mon., Tues., Wed., and Sat., from 10 to 4, 5, 6, or 7 according to the season; on Thurs. and Frid. (students' days), after 11 o'clock, on payment of 6d. It is closed for cleaning on the Thursday, Friday, and Saturday before Easter Sunday. Sticks and umbrellas are left at the entrance (no charge).

The addition of the new rooms opened in 1887 has enabled the authorities of the Gallery to arrange the pictures in schools, adhering as closely as possible to a chronological order. The main staircase facing us as we enter ascends to Room I., in which begins the series of Italian works. The staircase to the left leads to the Modern British Schools; that on the right to the Older British and the French Schools.

The **Hall** contains a marble statue of Sir David Wilkie (d. 1841), with his palette let into the pedestal, by *Joseph;* busts of the painters W. Mulready (d. 1863) and Th. Stothard (d. 1834), by *Weekes;* and busts of Samuel Johnson (by *Baily,* after *Nollekens*), Canning (also by *Baily,* after *Nollekens*), Bewick (by *Gibson*), and Newton (by *Baily,* after *Roubiliac*). On the walls are two large landscapes with cattle by *James Ward,* the Battle of the Borodino by *Jones,* a forest-scene by *Salvator Rosa,* and a cast of a bust of Mantegna by *Sperandio.* At the top of the staircase to the right are busts of Wellington by *Nollekens* and Scott by *Chantrey.*

To the left is a staircase descending to a room containing *Watercolour Drawings* from paintings by early Italian and other masters, published and lent by the Arundel Society. Other rooms contain copies of paintings by *Velazquez* at Madrid and by *Rembrandt* at St. Petersburg.

To the right is a flight of steps (with a bronze bust of Napoleon at the top) descending to the collection of *Turner's Water-Colours* (catalogue by Ruskin 1s.). Two adjoining rooms contain other water-colours (*De Wint, Cattermole,* etc.), monochrome paintings by *Rubens* and *Van Dyck,* crayon studies by *Gainsborough,* drawings by *Wm. Blake,* etc. Another room, through which we pass to reach the Turner Collection, contains several paintings belonging to the National Portrait Gallery (p. 129). Among these are two large paintings: The House of Commons in 1793, by *Karl Anton Hickel* (presented by the Emp. of Austria in 1885), and a fine *Work by Marcus Gheeraedts,* representing a group of eleven statesmen, assembled at Somerset House in 1604 to ratify a commercial treaty between England, Spain, and the Netherlands. Among the single portraits, which include specimens of *Lely, Gainsborough, Dobson, Richmond,*etc., is one of George Washington, by *Gilbert Stuart.*

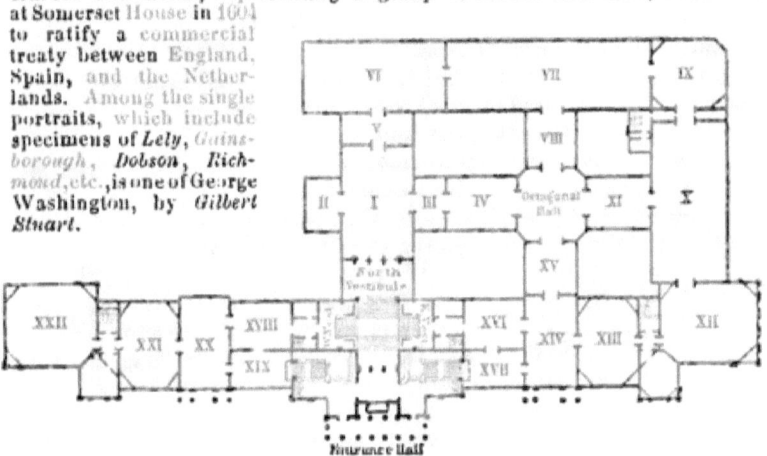

The **Vestibule of the Main Staircase** is roofed by a glass dome and embellished with marble columns and panelling, of green 'cipollino', 'giallo antico', 'pavonazzetto', etc. Here are hung several large paintings of the British School. To the left (W.): 789. *Thomas Gainsborough* (one of the most eminent of English portrait-painters; d. 1788). Family group; 1228. *Fuseli* (d. 1825), Titania and Bottom; two groups by *Reynolds,* lent by the Dilletanti Society; 677. *Sir Martin Shee* (d. 1850). Portrait of the actor Lewis as the Marquis in the 'Midnight Hour'. To the right (E.):

*143. Reynolds, Equestrian portrait of Lord Ligonier; 1146. Sir Henry Raeburn (Scottish School; d. 1823), Portrait of a lady; 144. Sir Thomas Lawrence (d. 1830), Benjamin West, the painter; 681. Reynolds, Capt. Orme; 684. Gainsborough, Dr. Schomberg. — In the North Vestibule (see Plan) are three fragments of frescoes (Nos. 1216-1216 b) by *Spinello Aretino* (Tuscan School; d. 1410), three frescoes (Nos. 766, 767, 1215) by *Domenico Veneziano* (d. 1461), and nine interesting Greek portraits of the 2nd and 3rd cent. from mummies found in the Fayoum. [A mummy with a portrait of this kind may be seen at the British Museum; p. 251.]

Room I., a handsome new room, lighted from above, is devoted to the Tuscan School. Above the doors are bronze medallions of Rubens, Titian, and Rembrandt. — To the left: 1150. Attributed to *Pontormo* (*Carucci*; d. 1557), Portrait; 21. *Cristofano Allori* (1577-1621), Portrait; *592. Ascribed to *Filippino Lippi*, Adoration of the Magi (more probably a masterpiece of *Botticelli*, but freely retouched); 727. *Pesellino* (early Florentine School; d. 1457), Trinità, the largest work of this rare master; *1282. *Jacopo Chimenti da Empoli* (1554-1640), San Zenobio restoring a dead child to life; 1143. *Ridolfo Ghirlandajo* (Florence, follower of Leon. da Vinci; d. 1561), Procession to Mt. Calvary; 17. *A. del Sarto* (the greatest Florentine colourist; d. 1531), Holy Family; 809. Ascribed to *Michael Angelo* (d. 1564; probably by *Granacci*), Madonna and Infant Christ, with John the Baptist and angels (in tempera, on wood; unfinished); 790. *Michael Angelo*, Entombment (unfinished and youthful work, very primitive in colouring).

*296. *A. Pollajuolo* (?, Florentine painter, sculptor, and engraver; d. 1498), Virgin adoring the Infant Christ.

This painting is executed with great carefulness, but the conception of the forms and proportions is hardly worthy of a master of the first rank, such as Verrocchio, to whom some critics assign the work. The utmost that we can assert with safety is that it is by a Florentine master.

704. *Bronzino*, Cosimo de' Medici; 1194. *Marcello Venusti* (d. ca. 1570), Jesus expelling the money-changers from the Temple; 652. *Francesco Rossi* (1510-63), Charity; 1227. *Venusti*, Holy Family; *593. *Lorenzo di Credi* (Florence, pupil of Verrocchio at the same time as Leonardo da Vinci; d. 1537), Madonna and Child. — *292. *Pollajuolo*, Martyrdom of St. Sebastian.

This picture was the altarpiece of the Pucci chapel, in the church of San Sebastiano de' Servi at Florence, and according to Vasari is the artist's masterpiece. The lower parts have been retouched.

648. *Credi*, Virgin adoring the Infant (in his best style); 781. School of *Verrocchio* (?), The archangel Raphael and Tobias; *293. *Filippino Lippi* (d. 1504), Madonna and Child, with SS. Jerome and Dominic, a large picture with predelle; 1035. *Franciabigio* (Florence, follower of A. del Sarto; d. 1524), A Knight of Malta. 1131. *Pontormo*, Joseph and his Brethren; according to Vasari, the boy seated on the steps, with a basket, is a portrait of Bronzino. 650. *Bronzino*, Portrait; 1124. *Filippino Lippi*, Adoration of the Magi.

*1093. *Leonardo da Vinci* (1452-1519), Madonna and Child, with John the Baptist and an angel, an altered replica of 'La Vierge aux Rochers' in the Louvre, bought from the Earl of Suffolk in 1884 for 9000*l*. (perhaps a copy by a pupil).
670. *Bronzino*, Knight of St. Stephen; 649. Ascribed to *Pontormo*, Portrait of a boy, in the style of Bronzino; *690. *Andrea del Sarto*, Portrait, a masterpiece of chiaroscuro; 698. *Piero di Cosimo* (pupil and assistant of Cosimo Rosselli; d. ca. 1521), Death of Procris, in a beautiful landscape. — 651. *Bronzino*, Venus, Cupid, Folly, and Time, an allegory, an unpleasant, cold, and stony work.

'Bronzino painted a picture of remarkable beauty, which was sent into France to King Francis. In this picture was portrayed a naked Venus together with Cupid, who was kissing her. On the one side were Pleasure and Mirth, with other Powers of Love, and on the other Deceit, Jealousy, and other Passions of Love.' — *Vasari*.

*915. *Sandro Botticelli* (d. 1510), Mars and Venus; 8. After *Michael Angelo*, A dream of human life.

On a screen: 645. *Albertinelli* (d. 1515), Madonna and Child; 275. *School of Botticelli*, Madonna and Child, a circular picture in a fine old frame; 928. *Pollajuolo*, Apollo and Daphne.

**Room II.** SIENESE SCHOOL. To the left: 1109. *Buonacorso* (14th cent.), Marriage of the Virgin; 1113. *P. Lorenzetti* (d. 1350), Legendary scene; 247. *Matteo di Giovanni da Siena* (d. 1495), Ecce Homo; 246. *Girolamo del Pacchia* (d. after 1535), Madonna and Child; 591. *Benozzo Gozzoli* (pupil of Fra Angelico; d. 1498), Rape of Helen; 1108. *Early Sienese School*, Virgin enthroned, with saints. *Duccio di Buoninsegna* (founder of the school of Siena; d. about 1339), 1140. Christ healing the blind; 1139. Annunciation. 1199. *Florentine School of the 15th cent.*, Madonna and Child, with John the Baptist and an angel; 218. *Baldassare Peruzzi* (Siena; d. 1537), Adoration of the Magi (portraits of Titian, Raphael, and Michael Angelo); 248. *School of Filippo Lippi*, Vision of St. Bernard; 227. *Rosselli* (d. 1507), St. Jerome. — 283. *Benozzo Gozzoli*, Virgin and Child enthroned, with saints.

'The original contract for this picture, dated 23d Oct. 1461, is still preserved; it was published in Florence in 1855. The figure of the Virgin is in this contract specially directed to be made similar in mode, form, and ornaments to the Virgin Enthroned, in the picture over the high altar of San Marco, Florence, by Fra Giovanni (Angelico) da Fiesole, and now in the Academy there'. — *Catalogue*.

*663. *Fra Angelico* (d. 1455), Christ with the banner of the Resurrection, surrounded by a crowd of saints, martyrs, and Dominicans, 'so beautiful', says Vasari, 'that they appear to be truly beings of Paradise'; 586. *Pupil of Fiorenzo di Lorenzo*, Madonna enthroned. — *566. *Duccio di Buoninsegna*, Madonna and Child.

'A genuine picture, which illustrates how well the master could vivify Byzantine forms with tender feeling'.

1138. *Andrea del Castagno* (early Florentine School; d. 1457), Crucifixion; 582. *Fra Angelico* (school-piece), The Magi; 1155. *Matteo di Giovanni*, Assumption; 1147. *Ambrogio Lorenzetti* (Siena;

d. ca. 1348), Heads of saints (a fragment of a fresco). *Ugolino da Siena* (14th cent.), 1188. Betrayal of Christ; 1189. Procession to Calvary. 909. *Benvenuto da Siena* (c. 1520), Madonna and Child.

**Room III.** TUSCAN SCHOOLS. To the left: 782. *Botticelli*, Madonna and Child; *666. *Fra Filippo Lippi* (Florence; d. 1496), Annunciation, painted like No. 667 for Cosimo de' Medici and marked with his crest; 598. *Filippino Lippi*. St. Francis in glory, with the stigmata; 916. *Botticelli*. Venus and Cupid; *583. *Paolo Uccello* (Florence; d. 1479), Cavalry engagement, one of the earliest Florentine representations of a secular subject; 1196. *Tuscan School*, Amor and Castitas; 1230. *Domenico Ghirlandajo* (1449-94), Portrait of a woman; 1033. *Lippi*, Adoration of the Magi; 626. *Botticelli*, Young man; no number, *Dom. Ghirlandajo*, Portrait of a lady ('the lovely Benci' of Longfellow; lent by Mr. Henry Willett). — *1034. *Botticelli*, The Nativity, to the left Magi, to the right the Shepherds, in front shepherds embraced by angels.

The subject is conceived in a manner highly mystical and symbolical. At the top of the picture is a Greek inscription to the following effect: 'This picture I, Alessandro, painted at the end of the year 1500 in the (troubles) of Italy in the half-time after the time during the fulfilment of the eleventh of St. John in the second woe of the Apocalypse, in the loosing of the devil for three years and a half. Afterwards he shall be chained and we shall see him trodden down as in this picture'.

589. *Filippo Lippi*, Madonna and Child, with an angel. — 1126. *Botticelli*, Assumption of the Virgin.

In the centre of the upper part of the picture is the Virgin, kneeling before the Saviour, while around are cycles or tiers of angels, apostles, saints, and seraphim. Below are the apostles gathered round the tomb of the Virgin, with portraits of the Palmieri, the donors of the altarpiece. The picture was probably executed by a pupil from a cartoon by Botticelli.

226. *Botticelli*, Madonna and Child, with John the Baptist and angels, with a rose-hedge in the background ('no man has ever yet drawn', says Mr. Ruskin, 'and none is likely to draw for many a day, roses as well as Sandro has drawn them'); *667. *Fra Filippo Lippi*, SS. John the Baptist, Francis, Lawrence, Cosmas, Damianus, Anthony, and Peter the Martyr, sitting on a marble bench (painted for Cosimo de' Medici 1266-1336).

'No one draws such lilies or such daisies as Lippi, Botticelli beat him afterward in roses, but never in lilies'. — *Ruskin*.

**Room IV.** EARLY ITALIAN SCHOOL. The pictures in this room are mainly of historical interest. Neither Giotto, the chief founder of Italian painting, nor his pupils are represented by authenticated works, but there are several fine works of the 14th century.

'The early efforts of Cimabue and Giotto are the burning messages of prophecy, delivered by the stammering lips of infants'. — *Ruskin*.

To the left: *School of* **T***addeo Gaddi* (d. after 1366), 215. Saints; 216. Baptism of Christ. 594. *Emmanuel* (Greek priest, who lived apparently at Venice; Byzantine School), SS. Cosmas and Damianus (one of the earliest pictures in the Gallery in point of artistic development); 573-575. *Andrea Orcagna* (Florentine School, master of Fra Angelico; d. 1376). Three small pictures belonging to the large altarpiece, No. 569; 276. Ascribed to *Giotto* (d. 1336), Heads of Apostles; 569. *Orcagna*, Coronation of the Virgin (large **altarpiece from the church of San Pietro Maggiore** in Florence; school-piece); 701. *Justus of Padua* (School of Giotto; d. 1400), Coronation of the Virgin, dated 1367 (a small triptych, of cheerful, soft, and well-blended colouring); 567. *Segna di Buonaventura* (Tuscan School; ca. 1310), Crucifixion; 576-578. *Orcagna*, Three other pictures belonging to No. 569; 580a. 579a. Terminal panels of 580 and 579 (see below); 568. *School of Giotto* (early Florentine; ca. 1330), Coronation of the Virgin; 579. *School of Taddeo Gaddi*, Baptism of Christ; 565. *Giov. Cimabue* (b. 1240; Tuscan School), Madonna and Child enthroned; 584. *Spinello Aretino*, John the Baptist, with SS. John the Evangelist and James the Less; 564. *Margaritone* (d. 1293), Virgin and Child, with scenes from the lives of the saints; 570-572. *Orcagna*, Trinity, with angels adoring, belonging to No. 569; 580. *Jacopo di Casentino* (d. ca. 1390), St. John the Evangelist lifted up into Heaven.

**Room V.** SCHOOLS OF FERRARA AND BOLOGNA. — To the left: *Cosimo Tura* (d. 1498), 905. Madonna; 773. St. Jerome in the wilderness; 772. Madonna and Child. 597. *Marco Zoppo* (end of 15th cent.), St. Dominic as Institutor of the Rosary; 82. *Mazzolino da Ferrara* (1480-1528), Holy Family; 1062. *School of Ferrara*, Battle. — *1119. *Ercole Grandi di Giulio* (Ferrara; d. 1531), Madonna enthroned, with John the Baptist and St. William; the throne is adorned with sculptural panels of Adam and Eve (a masterpiece). — *Benvenuto Tisio*, surnamed *Garofalo* (d. 1559), 642. Agony in the Garden; *81. Vision of St. Augustine; 170. Holy Family; *671. Madonna and Child enthroned, surrounded by saints. 590. *Marco Zoppo*, Dead Christ, with John the Baptist and Joseph of Arimathea (lucid in colouring); 770. *Giovanni Oriolo* (Ferrara; d. after 1461), Leonello d'Este, Marquis of Ferrara (d. 1450); 1127 *Ercole di Roberto Grandi* (d. before 1513), Last Supper. *Lorenzo Costa* (early School of Ferrara, contemporary of Francia; d. 1535), 895. The Florentine general, Francesco Ferucci; *629. Madonna enthroned, dated 1505.

*Francesco Francia* (*Raibolini*, early school of Bologna, also a goldsmith; d. 1517), *179. Virgin enthroned and St. Anne; 180. Pietà (the lunette of No. 179).

These two pictures constituted formerly one altarpiece. The composition is of a very high order, reminding us of Perugino, by whom there is a Pietà very similar to this in Florence.

771. *Bono di Ferrara* (15th cent.), St. Jerome in the desert; 169. *Mazzolino* (Ferrara; d. 1530), Holy Family; 638. *Francia*, Virgin and Child, with two saints; 73. *Ercole Grandi*, Conversion of St. Paul; 641. *Mazzolino*, The Woman taken in adultery; 640 *Dosso Dossi* (Ferrara; d. ca. 1534), Adoration of the Magi, 752. *Dalmasio* (end of the 14th cent.), Madonna and Child; 669. *Orto-*

*lano* (Ferrara; d. ca. 1525). SS. Sebastian, Rock, and Demetrius, an imitation of Garofalo and Dosso; 1234. *Dosso Dossi*, Allegorical group; 1217. *Ercole di Roberto Grandi*, Israelites gathering manna.

**Room VI.** UMBRIAN SCHOOL. To the left: 912-914. *Pinturicchio* (? School of Signorelli), Illustrations of the story of Griselda. Slight in execution, but fresh in conception and skilfully composed. The story of Griselda is the last in Boccaccio's Decameron.

*Melozzo da Forli* (Umbrian school), influenced by Piero della Francesca; d. 1494), 756. Music; 755. Rhetoric (three similar representations at Windsor Castle and at Berlin). 703. *Bernardino Pinturicchio* (d. 1513), Madonna and Child; 1103. *Fiorenzo di Lorenzo* (end of 15th cent.), Madonna and saints (lucid colouring); 1092. *Bernardino Cotignola* (ca. 1500), St. Sebastian, with a landscape in the Flemish style; 249. *Lorenzo San Severino* (second half of the 15th cent.), Marriage of St. Catharine; 769. *Fra Carnovale* (ca. 1480), St. Michael and the serpent; 1107. *Niccolò da Foligno* (*Alunno*; end of the 15th cent.), Crucifixion, a triptych; 1104. *Paolo Manni* (d. 1544), Annunciation; 702. *L'Ingegno* (*Andrea di Luigi*; 15th cent.), Madonna; 691. *Lo Spagna* (first half of the 16th cent.), Ecce Homo; 1051. *Umbrian School*, Our Lord, St. Thomas, and St. Anthony of Padua, the Donor kneeling to the right; 929. After *Raphael*, Madonna and Child, old copy of the Bridgewater Madonna; *288. *Perugino* (*Pietro Vannucci*, the master of Raphael; d. 1524), Madonna adoring the Infant, with the archangel Michael on the left and Raphael with Tobias on the right; 693. *Pinturicchio*, St. Catharine of Alexandria; 1220. *L'Ingegno*, Madonna and Child; 1032. *Lo Spagna*, Agony in the Garden.

**213. *Raphael* (*Sanzio*; 1483-1520), Vision of a knight (a youthful work, as fine in its execution as it is tender in its conception). This little gem reveals the influence of Raphael's early master Timoteo Viti, without a trace of the later manner learned from Perugino. The original 'Cartoon hangs close by.

'Two allegorical female figures, representing respectively the noble ambitions and the joys of life, appear to a young knight lying asleep beneath a laurel, and offer him his choice of glory or pleasure'. — *Passavant*.

**1171. *Raphael*, **Madonna degli** Ansidei, bought from the Duke of Marlborough in 1884 for 70,000*l*., the largest sum ever **given for a picture.**

This Holy Family was painted by Raphael in 1606 for the chapel of the Ansidei family in the Servite church at Perugia. In 1764 it was purchased by Lord Robert Spencer, brother of the third Duke of Marlborough. The two figures flanking the Virgin are those of John the Baptist and St. Nicholas of Bari, the latter represented in his episcopal robes. The small round loaves at his feet refer to his rescue of the town of Myra from famine. In the background is a view of the Tuscan hills. From the canopy hangs a rosary, recalling a similar ornament in Mantegna's Holy Family in the Louvre. — This great work, the most important example of Raphael in the country, was executed entirely by the master's own hand and is in admirable preservation.

*744. *Raphael*, Madonna, **Infant** Christ, and St. John (the 'Aldobrandini' or 'Garvagh Madonna').

'The whole has a delicate, harmonious effect. The flesh, which is yellowish in the lights, and lightish brown in the shadows, agrees extremely well with the pale broken rose-colour of the under garment, and the delicate bluish grey of the upper garment of the Virgin. In the seams and glories gold is used, though very delicately. The execution is particularly careful, and it is in an excellent state of preservation'. — *W*.

*168. *Raphael*, St. **Catharine of Alexandria**.

'In form and feeling no picture of the master approaches nearer to it than the Entombment in the Borghese Palace, which is inscribed 1507.' — *W*.

181. *Perugino*, Madonna and Child; 751. *Giovanni Santi* (Umbrian painter and poet, Raphael's father; d. 1494), Madonna; *1075. *Perugino*, Virgin and Child, a work of great depth of feeling; *27. *Raphael*, Pope Julius II. (replica of the original in Florence); 596. *Palmezzano* (pupil of Melozzo; d. after 1537), Entombment, painted under the influence of Giov. Bellini. *Signorelli* (d. 1523), 1128. Circumcision, a dramatic composition in the style of Michael Angelo, of whom Signorelli is generally considered the forerunner (the figure of the child has been spoiled by repainting); 1133. Adoration of the Holy Child (school-piece?). 908. *Piero della Francesca* (ca. 1460), Nativity (injured and retouched); 911. *Pinturicchio*, Return of Ulysses, or Lucretia and Collatinus (fresco from Siena, about 1509); 1218, 1219. *Francesco Ubertini* (d. 1557), History of Joseph. 758. *Francesca* (?more probably by *Paolo Uccello*), Portrait of a lady; 665. Baptism of Christ; 585. Portrait. 910. Ascribed to *Signorelli* (more probably by *Genga da Urbino*), Triumph of Chastity, a fresco; 282. *Lo Spagna* (? more probably by *Bertucci of Faenza*, a contemporary belonging to the Eclectic School), Madonna and Child enthroned.

**Room VII.** VENETIAN AND BRESCIAN SCHOOLS. To the left: 1098. *Bart. Montagna* (d. 1523; Venetian School), Virgin and Child; *625. *Moretto* (*Alessandro Bonvicino*, the greatest painter of Brescia; d. about 1560), Madonna and Child, with saints, 802. *Montagna*(?), Madonna and Child; 1023. *Giambattista Moroni* (portrait-painter at Bergamo, pupil of Moretto; d. 1578), Portrait of an Italian lady; *748. *Girolamo dai Libri* (Verona; d. 1556), Madonna and Child, with St. Anne, clear in colour and harmonious in tone, heralding the style of Paolo Veronese; *16. *Tintoretto (Jacopo Robusti*, Venice; d. 1594), St. George and the Dragon; 24. *Sebastian del Piombo* (Venice, follower of Michael Angelo; d. 1547), Portrait of a lady, as St. Agatha; 1105. *Lorenzo Lotto* (Treviso; d. ca. 1556), The Apostolic prothonotary Giuliano; 26. *Paolo Veronese* (d. 1588), Consecration of St. Nicholas; 1041. *Paolo Veronese*(?), St. Helena; 34. *Titian* (*Tiziano Vecellio*; 1477-1576), Venus and Adonis (an early copy of the original in Madrid); *1022. *Moroni*, Nobleman; 224. *Titian*, The Tribute Money. —*4. *Titian*, Holy Family, with adoring shepherd.

'This picture is painted in Titian's early style, and recalls at once the schooling of Giorgione and Palma'. — *Crowe* and *Cavalcaselle*, '*Titian*'.

*1. *Sebastian del Piombo*, Raising of Lazarus.

'The transition from death to life is expressed in Lazarus with wonderful spirit, and at the same time with perfect fidelity to Scripture

The grave-clothes, by which his face is thrown into deep shade, vividly excite the idea of the night of the grave, which but just before enveloped him; the eye looking eagerly from beneath this shade upon Christ his Redeemer, shows us, on the other hand, in the most striking contrast, the new life in its most intellectual organ. This is also expressed in the whole figure, which is actively striving to relieve itself from the bonds in which it was fast bound'. — *W.*

The picture was painted in 1517-19 in competition with Raphael's Transfiguration. The figure of Lazarus is quite in the spirit of Michael Angelo.

20. *Sebastian del Piombo*, Portraits of the painter with his seal ('piombo') of office in his hand, and Cardinal Ippolito de' Medici, painted after 1531. — *635. *Titian*, Madonna and Child, with SS. John the Baptist and Catharine.

'Here we are transported into a scene almost heavenly in the fulness of its pathos and loveliness, and there is true solemnity and religious grandeur in the tender feeling which enlivens a group in keeping, yet in contrast, with a landscape of delicious lines, whose enamelled greys so delicately harmonize with the rich blues, yellows, and crimsons of the dresses in the figures'. — *C. & C.*

1025. *Moretto*, Portrait of an Italian nobleman (1526). — *35. *Titian*, Bacchus and Ariadne.

'This is one of the pictures which once seen can never be forgotten .... Rich harmony of drapery tints and soft modelling, depth of shade and warm flesh all combine to produce a highly coloured glow; yet in the midst of this glow the form of Ariadne seems incomparably fair. Nature was never reproduced more kindly or with greater exuberance than it is in every part of this picture. What splendour in the contrasts of colour, what wealth and diversity of scale in air and vegetation; how infinite is the space — how varied yet mellow the gradations of light and shade!' — *C. & C.*

932. *Italian School*, Portrait of a man; 636. *Palma Vecchio* (d. 1528; pupil of Titian), Portrait of Ariosto; 846. *Cima da Conegliano* (Venice, contemporary of Bellini; about 1500), Christ appearing to St. Thomas (freely restored); *735. *Paolo Morando* (*Cavazzola*, the most important master in Verona before Paolo Veronese; d. 1522), St. Rochus with the angel, an excellent specimen of his work; 234. *Catena* (pupil of Giov. Bellini), Warrior adoring the Infant Christ; 287. *Bartolommeo Veneziano* (rare Venetian master, first half of the 16th cent.), Portrait, dated 1530 (rich in colour); 1203. *Giovanni Busi* (*Cariani*, Venetian School; d. ca. 1541), Madonna; 277. *Jacopo Bassano* (*Jacopo da Ponte*; d. 1592), The Good Samaritan; 930. *Venetian School*, Garden of Love; *697. *Moroni*, Portrait of a tailor ('Tagliapanni'). — *270. *Titian*, Christ and Mary Magdalene after the Resurrection ('Noli me tangere').

A youthful work of the master. The slenderness of the figures, which are conceived in a dignified but somewhat mundane spirit, and the style of the landscape reveal the influence of Giorgione.

632, 633. *Girolamo da Santacroce* (Venetian School; about 1530), Saints; *280. *Giovanni Bellini* (1430-1516; described by Mr. Ruskin as 'the mighty Venetian master who alone of all the painters of Italy united purity of religious aim with perfection of artistical power'), Madonna of the Pomegranate; 623. *Girolamo da Treviso*

(a follower of **Raphael**; d. 1544). Madonna and Child (mentioned by **Vasari** as the **painter's** masterpiece). — *189. *G. Bellini*, The Doge Leonardo Loredano.
    'This remarkable portrait is a singular instance of the skill with which Bellini could seize and embellish nature, reproduce the flexibility of flesh in a soft and fused golden tone, and venture at the same time into every line of detail'. — *C. & C.*

*808. *Bellini*, St. Peter Martyr (with very delicate gradations in the flesh tones); 300. *Cima da Conegliano*, Madonna and Child; *777. *Paolo Morando*, Madonna and Child, with John the Baptist and an angel, tender in conception and radiant in colour; 1123. *Venetian School* (16th cent.), Venus and Adonis; 750. *Vittore Carpaccio* (Venice, contemporary of Giov. Bellini; d. after 1522), Madonna and Child, with the Doge Giovanni Mocenigo in adoration; 699. *Lotto*, Portraits of Agostino and Niccolò della Torre (1515); 742. *Moroni*, Lawyer; 1213. *Gentile Bellini* (d. 1507), Portrait of a mathematician; 1202. *Bonifacio Veronese* (d. 1540). Madonna and Child, with saints; *268. *Paolo Veronese*, Adoration of the Magi, painted in 1573 for the church of St. Sylvester at Venice; 1130. Ascribed to *Tintoretto*, Christ washing the feet of his disciples. — *726. *Giovanni Bellini*, Christ in Gethsemane.
    This is an early work of the master, painted in 1456, and reveals the influence of Mantegna, as is proved by the resemblance to the work of that master in the possession of the Earl of Northbrook.

812. *Gior. Bellini*. Death of St. Peter Martyr (a late work); 694. *Catena* (Treviso, d. 1531 at Venice; a follower of Giov. Bellini), St. Jerome in his study; 32. *School of Titian*, Rape of Ganymede; 1024. *Moroni*, Italian ecclesiastic; *1047. *Lotto*, Family group; *299. *Moretto*, Count Sciarra Martinengo Cesaresco. — *294. *Paolo Veronese*, Family of Darius at the feet of Alexander the Great.
    In excellent condition; perhaps the only existing criterion by which to estimate the genuine original colouring of Paul Veronese. It is remarkable how entirely the genius of the painter precludes criticism on the quaintness of the treatment. Both the incident and the personages are, as in a Spanish play, romantically travestied'. — *Rumohr* (MS. notes).
    Mr. Ruskin calls this picture 'the most precious Paul Veronese in the world'... 'The possession of the Pisani Veronese will happily enable the English public and the English artist to convince themselves how sincerity and simplicity in statements of fact, power of draughtmanship, and joy in colour, were associated in a perfect balance in the great workmen in Venice'.

3. Ascribed to *Titian Vecellio*, Concert; 674. *Paris Bordone* (Treviso, celebrated for his female portraits; d. 1571), A lady of Genoa; *1031. *Giovanni Girolamo Savoldo* (Brescia, about 1480-1548), Mary Magdalene going to the Sepulchre (similar picture at Berlin); 637. *Bordone*, Daphnis and Chloe; 595. *Venetian School*, Portrait of a lady; 173. *Bassano*, Portrait of a nobleman; *297. *Il Romanino* (*Girolamo Romani*, Brescia, a rival of Moretto; d. 1560), Nativity.

ON THE STANDS: 97. *Veronese*, Rape of Europa; 1239, 1240. *Mocetto* (Venice, painter and engraver; ca. 1490-1515), Massacre of the Innocents; 1233. *Giov. Bellini*, Blood of the Redeemer.

673. *Antonello da Messina* (said to have imported painting in oil from Flanders into Italy; d. after 1493), Salvator Mundi, 1465. 'The oldest of his pictures which we now possess. It is a solemn but not an elevated mask; half Flemish, half Italian. The colour is warm but not quite clear, solid in light, brownish, uneven, and showing the ground in shade, but without the brightness or pellucid finish of a later period'. — *Crowe and Cavalcaselle*, 'History of Painting in Italy'.
*Anton. da Messina*, 1141. Portrait of a young man; 1166. Crucifixion. 631. *Bissolo* (d. about 1530), Portrait of a woman; 1121. *Venetian School* (15th cent.), Portrait of a young man. Ascribed to *Francesco Mantegna* (son and pupil of Andrea; b. about 1470), 1106. Resurrection of Christ; 639. Christ and Mary Magdalene in the Garden. 1160. *Venetian School of the 15th cent.*, Adoration of the Magi; 736. *Bonsignori* (Verona; d. 1519), Portrait of a senator, dated 1487; 1120. *Cima da Conegliano*, St. Jerome in the wilderness; \*281. *Marco Basaiti* (Venetian School; ca. 1520), St. Jerome reading.
776. *Pisano of Verona* (founder of the Veronese school, painter and medallist; d. 1451), SS. Anthony and George, with a vision of the Virgin and Child in a glory above.

In the frame are inserted casts of two of Pisano's medals. The one above represents Leonello d'Este, his patron; the other, the painter himself.

\*269. After *Giorgione* (*Giorgio Barbarelli*, a fellow-pupil of Titian under Giov. Bellini; d. 1511), Knight in armour.

A slightly altered and admirable repetition of the knight in Giorgione's altarpiece at Castelfranco.

634. *Cima da Conegliano*, Madonna and Child; 1173. *School of Giorgione*, Subject unknown; 1134. *Liberale da Verona* (b.1456, d. after 1515), Madonna; 599. *Basaiti* (?), Infant Christ asleep in the lap of the Virgin, with a pleasing landscape in the background (a good work of the school of Giov. Bellini); 695. *Andrea Previtali* (d. 1528), Monk adoring the Holy Child.

**Room VIII.** PADUAN AND EARLY VENETIAN SCHOOLS. To the left: 602. *Carlo Crivelli* (d. ca. 1495; Venice), Dead Christ supported by angels; 1145. *Andrea Mantegna* (d. 1506; School of Padua), Samson and Delilah (on the tree is carved the motto 'foemina diabolo tribus assibus est mala peior'). *Crivelli*, 807. Madonna and Child enthroned; 668. The Beato Ferretti. \*274. *A. Mantegna*, Virgin and Child, with St. John the Baptist and the Magdalen (of the master's early period; conscientiously minute in execution and of plastic distinctness in the outlines); 804. *Marco Marziale* (Venetian painter; flourished ca. 1490-1500), Madonna and Child. — \*902. *A. Mantegna*, Triumph of Scipio, or the reception of the Phrygian mother of the gods (Cybele) among the publicly recognised divinities of Rome.

In obedience to the Delphic oracle, the 'worthiest man in Rome' was selected to receive the goddess, and the choice fell upon Publius Cornelius Scipio Nasica (B.C. 204). The picture was painted for a Venetian nobleman, Francesco Cornaro, whose family claimed to be descended from the Roman *gens* **Cornelia**. It was finished in 1506, a few months before the painter's death, and is 'a tempera', in chiaroscuro. It is not so important a work of Mantegna as the series at Hampton Court (p. 319).

749. *Niccolò Giolfino* (a little-known Veronese painter; ca. 1465-1520), Portraits; 739. **Carlo Crivelli**, Annunciation, dated 1486 (the heads are pleasing and the motions graceful); 904. *Gregorio Schiavone* (the 'Slavonian', a native of Dalmatia; ca. 1470), Madonna and Child; 284. *Bartolommeo Vivarini* (end of the 15th cent.), Virgin and Child, with SS. Paul and Jerome; 906. *Crivelli*, Madonna in prayer. — *724. *Crivelli*, Madonna and Child with SS. Jerome and Sebastian.

This picture is known, from the swallow introduced, as the 'Madonna della rondine'. 'It may be said of the predella, which represents St. Catharine, St. Jerome in the wilderness, the Nativity of our Lord, the Martyrdom of St. Sebastian, and St. George and the Dragon, that Crivelli never concentrated so much power on any small composition'. — *C. & C.*

788. *Crivelli*, Madonna and saints (large altarpiece in 13 sections, painted in 1476); 803. *Marco Marziale*, The Circumcision; 907. *Crivelli*, SS. Catharine and Mary Magdalene; 1125. Ascribed to *Mantegna*, Two allegorical figures of the Seasons, in grisaille.

**Central Octagon.** VARIOUS SCHOOLS. To the left: 1241. *Pedro Campaña* (a native of Flanders, who studied in Italy and executed his best work in Seville; d. at Brussels in 1570 or 1580), Mary Magdalene led by Martha to hear the preaching of Christ (executed in Venice for Cardinal Grimani); 778. Ascribed to *Pellegrino da San Daniele* (Friuli, pupil of Bellini; about 1540), Madonna and Child (repainted); 285. *Francesco Morone* (early Veronese painter; d. 1529), Madonna and Child; 1135, 1136. *Veronese School* (15th cent.), Legend of Trajan and the widow; 1211, 1212. *Dom. Morone* (d. ca. 1508), Fêtes at the wedding of Gianfrancesco II. Gonzaga and Isabella d'Este; 1165. *Moretto*, Madonna and Child, with two saints; 1214. *Michele da Verona* (d. after 1523), Coriolanus meeting Volumnia and Veturia; 1102. *Pietro Longhi* (Venetian genre-painter; d. 1762), Andrea Tron, procurator of the church of St. Mark; 41. Ascribed to *Busi (Cariani)*, Death of Peter Martyr; 1048. *Italian School*, Portrait of a cardinal; 272. *Unknown Italian Master*, An Apostle; 931. *Veronese*, The Magdalen laying aside her jewels; 768. *Antonio Vivarini*, SS. Peter and Jerome.

ON A STAND: 630. *Schiavone*, Madonna and Child enthroned, with saints. — In the centre of the Octagon is a piece of sculpture by *Gibson*, representing Hylas and the nymphs.

**Room IX.**, adjoining Room VII. LOMBARD SCHOOLS. To the left: 806. *Boccaccio Boccaccino* (Cremona; d. after 1518), Procession to Calvary; 286. *Francesco Tacconi* (Cremona; d. after 1490), Virgin and Child enthroned (the only signed work of this master extant); 1077. *Ambrogio Borgognone*(architect and painter, Milanese School), Christ bearing the Cross, Virgin and Child, Agony in Gethsemane, a triptych, one of the master's earlier works; 298. *Borgognone*, Marriage of St. Catharine of Alexandria, to the right St. Catharine of

Siena; 729. *Vincenzo Foppa* (d. 1492), Adoration of the Magi; 700. *Lanini* (d. ca. 1578). Holy Family, with Mary Magdalene, Pope Gregory, and **St.** Paul (dated 1543); *18. *Bernardino **Luini*** (of Milan, pupil of Leonardo da Vinci), Christ disputing with the Doctors; *15. *Correggio* (*Antonio Allegri*; d. 1534), Ecce Homo; *23. *Correggio*, 'La Madonna della Cesta', **or 'La Vierge au Panier'**; 33. *Parmigiano* (**Francesco** *Maria Mazzola*; d. 1540), Vision of St. Jerome; 76. *Correggio*, Christ's Agony **in the Garden.** — *10. *Correggio*. Mercury instructing Cupid **in the presence of Venus, of the** master's **latest period.**

This picture has passed through the hands of numerous owners, chiefly of royal blood. It was bought by Charles I. of England with the rest of the Duke of Mantua's collection in 1630. From England it passed to Spain, Naples, and then to Vienna, where it was purchased by the Marquis of Londonderry, who sold it to the National Gallery. It has suffered considerable damage during its wanderings.

Mr. Ruskin, who describes Correggio as 'the captain of the painter's art as such, the master of the art of laying colour so as to be lovely', couples this picture **with Titian's** Bacchus (p. 156), as one of the two paintings in the Gallery he would last part with.

*1144. *Gior. Bazzi*, surnamed *Sodoma* (Siena, pupil of Leon. da Vinci; d. 1549), **Madonna and** Child, with St. Catharine of Siena, St. Peter, and a monk. *Andrea da Solario* (Milan; d. after 1515), *923. **Venetian senator (recalling Anton.** da Messina); *734. **Portrait, a work of much power and finish** (1505). 1201, 1200. *Macrino d'Alba* (ca. 1500), **Saints; 779, 780.** *Ambrogio Borgognone*, Family **portraits, painted on two fragments of** a silken standard, attached to wood; *728. *Gior. Ant. Beltraffio* (pupil of Leonardo at Milan; d. 1516), **Madonna and Child (an** effective, though simple and quiet composi**tion, suffused** in a cool light); 1152. *Martino Piazza* (16th cent.), John the Baptist; 1149. *Marco d'Oggionno* (Milanese School, pupil of Leonardo; d. 1549), Madonna and Child; 753. *Altobello Melone* (**Cremona; 15th** cent.), On the way to Emmaus.

Visitors who wish **to make an** unbroken survey of Italian art should now pass on to R. XIII.

Room X. **DUTCH AND** FLEMISH **SCHOOLS.** Besides works of **Rubens** and Van Dyck, **the chiefs of the Fl**emish school of the **17th cent., this room contains** good examples of Rembrandt, their **great Dutch contemporary, principally of his later period. His pupils, N. Maas and P. de Hooghe, are also well** represented. The **small pictures by Flemish masters of the 15th** cent., though **neither usually of the first class, nor** always to be attributed to the **painters whose names they bear, are yet of** great interest, **as affording a varied survey of the realistic** manner of the school.

To the left: 202. *Melchior d'Hondecoeter* (animal-painter at Utrecht; d. 1695), Poultry (**'this cock was** Hondecoeter's favourite bird, which he is said to have **taught to** stand to him in a fixed position as a model'); *1248. ***Bart.*** *van der Helst* (one of the best Dutch portrait-painters; b. **at Haarlem** in 1611 or 1612, d. 1670),

Portrait of a girl (dated 1645); 240. *Nicholas Berchem* (Haarlem; 1620-1683), Crossing the ford. *W. van de Velde* (Amsterdam, the greatest of marine-painters, in the service of Charles II.; 1633-1707), 149. Calm; 150. Blowing fresh. 140. *Bart. van der Helst* (d. 1670), Portrait of a lady; *775. *Rembrandt van Ryn* (*Harmens* or *Hermanszoon*, Amsterdam; 1607-69), Old lady (1634); 223. *Ludolf Bakhuizen* (marine-painter of Amsterdam, with a partiality for stormy scenes; d. 1708), Dutch shipping; 239. *Van der Neer* (d. ca. 1690; Amsterdam), River by moonlight; 237. *Rembrandt*. Portrait of a woman (one of his latest works, dated 1666); 1252. *Frans Snyders* (animal and fruit painter; Antwerp. 1579-1657), Fruit; 1222. *Hondecoeter*, Foliage, birds, and insects; 187. *Peter Paul Rubens* (Antwerp; 1577-1640), Apotheosis of William the Taciturn, of Holland; 954. *Cornelis Huysmans* (1648-1727; Malines and Antwerp), Landscape; *53. *Albert Cuyp* (Dort; 1605-91). Landscape with cattle and figures (with masterly treatment of light and great transparency of shadow); 981. *W. van de Velde*, Storm at sea; 1168. *Van der Vliet* (Delft; d. 1642), Portrait of a Jesuit; 38. *Rubens*, Rape of the Sabine women; 152. *Van der Neer*, Evening scene, with figures and cattle by *Cuyp*, whose name is inscribed on the pail. — *672. *Rembrandt*, His own portrait (1640).

'If Rembrandt has often chosen to represent himself in more or less eccentric costumes, he has here preferred to pose as a man of quiet and dignified simplicity.... The portrait is admirable in design and tone. A delicate and warm light shines from above on part of the forehead, cheek, and nose, and imparts a golden hue to the shirt collar, while a stray beam brings the hand into like prominence. The execution is excellent, the effect of light delicate and vigorous'. — *Vosmaer*.

*243. *Rembrandt*, Portrait of a man, dated 1657.

'This picture is one of those darkly coloured pieces which Rembrandt meant to be strongly lighted. The head alone is in the full light, the hands are in the half-light only. The most conspicuous colours are vivid brown and red. The features, with the grey beard and moustache, though heavily painted, are well defined, and look almost as if chiselled by the brush, while the effect is enhanced by the greenish tint of the colouring. The face, and the dark eyes in particular, are full of animation. The whole work is indeed a marvel of colouring, expression, and poetry'. — *Vosmaer*.

49. *Sir Anthony van Dyck* (1599-1641), Portrait of Rubens; 51. *Rubens*(?), Jewish merchant. — *1172. *Van Dyck*, Charles I. mounted on a dun horse and attended by Sir Thomas Morton.

This fine specimen of Van Dyck was acquired at the sale of the Blenheim Collection in 1884 for 17,500*l*. It was originally in Somerset House and was sold by Cromwell for 150*l*. The great Duke of Marlborough discovered and bought it at Munich.

679. *Ferd. Bol* (pupil of Rembrandt; d. 1681), Astronomer (1652); *1247. *Nicolas Maes* or *Maas* (1632-1693; figure-painter at Dort, a pupil of Rembrandt), The card-players (an exceedingly graphic group of life-size figures); 732. *A. van der Neer*, Canal scene (daylight scenes and canvases of so large a size as this were rarely executed by Van der Neer); 190. *Rembrandt*. Jewish Rabbi. — *52. *Van Dyck*, Portrait.

This portrait is generally said to represent Gevartius, the friend of Rubens; and some authorities maintain, with great probability, that it was painted by Rubens, and not by Van Dyck.

924. *Pieter Neeffs* (d. ca. 1660; Antwerp), Interior of a Gothic church. — 194. *Rubens*, Judgment of Paris.

Repetitions on a smaller scale exist in the Louvre and at Dresden. The London picture, though possibly not painted entirely by Rubens' own hand, was certainly executed under his guidance and supervision.

901. *Jan Looten* (Dutch landscape-painter in the style of Van Everdingen; d. about 1681), Landscape. — *45. *Rembrandt*, The Woman taken in adultery, dated 1644.

'The colouring of the 'Woman taken in adultery' is in admirable keeping. A subdued light, an indescribable kind of glow, illumines the whole work, and pervades it with a mysterious harmony. The idea of the work is most effectively enhanced by the magic of chiaroscuro .... The different lights, the strongest of which is thrown on the yellow robe of the woman, on the group on the stairs, and on the gilded altar, are united by means of very skilful shading. The whole of the background is bathed in dark but warm shades'. — *Vosmaer*.

1137. *Dutch School*, Portrait of a boy; *66. *Rubens*, Autumnal landscape, with a view of the Château de Stein, the painter's house, near Malines; 166. *Rembrandt*, Capuchin friar; *47. *Rembrandt*, Adoration of the Shepherds (1646); 920. *Roelandt Savery* (Courtrai, landscape and animal painter; long at the court of Emp. Rudolph II.; d. 1639), Orpheus.

289. *Gerrit Lundens* (1622-77; Amsterdam), Amsterdam Musketeers.

'This picture, although but a greatly reduced copy of the renowned work by Rembrandt in the State Museum at Amsterdam, has a unique interest as representing the pristine condition of its great original before it was mutilated on all four sides and shorn of some of its figures .... in order to suit the picture to the dimensions of a room to which it was at that time (early part of last century) removed'. — *Official Catalogue*.

238. *Jan Weenix the Younger* (Amsterdam, d. 1719), Dead game; *207. *Nicholas Maas*, The idle servant, a masterpiece, dated 1665; *794. *P. de Hooghe* (1632-81), Courtyard of a Dutch house; 72. *Rembrandt*, Landscape; 685. *Hobbema*, Landscape; 989. *Ruysdael*, Water-mills; 628, *627. *Ruysdael*, Landscapes with waterfalls; 209. *Jan Both* (Utrecht, painter of Italian landscapes in the style of Claude; d. after 1662), Landscape, with figures by *Poelenburg*; 50. *Anthony van Dyck*, Emperor Theodosius refused admission to the Church of S. Ambrogio at Milan by St. Ambrose (copied, with slight alterations, from Rubens's picture at Vienna); 948. *Rubens*, Landscape (sketch); 1096. *Jan Weenix*, Hunting-scene; 1053. *Emanuel de Witte* (d. 1692; Amsterdam). Interior of a church; 680. *Van Dyck* (after Rubens), Miraculous Draught of Fishes. *David Teniers the Younger* (genre-painter in Antwerp, pupil of A. Brouwer and Rubens; 1610-94), *805. Old woman peeling a pear; 817. Château of the painter at Perck, with portraits of himself and his family. 986. *Ruysdael*, Water-mills; 59. *Rubens*, The brazen serpent; 242. *Teniers*, Players at tric-trac or backgammon; 157. *Rubens*, Landscape; 746. *Ruysdael*, Landscape with ruins; 1008. *Pieter Potter* (?

father of Paul Potter; d. 1595), Stag-hunt; 71. *Both*, **Landscape with figures.** *Rubens*, 67. Holy Family; 279. Horrors of War, **coloured sketch for a large picture now in the Pitti Palace at Florence. 155.** *Teniers the Younger*, The misers; 57. *Rubens*, Conversion of St. Bavon; 1012. *Matthew Merian* (b. at Bâle in 1621, d. 1687; **painted portraits at Nuremberg and** Frankfort), **Portrait.**

*278. ***Rubens*, Triumph** of Julius Cæsar, **freely adapted from Mantegna's famous cartoons,** now **in Hampton Court Palace.**

'His tendency to the fantastic and grand led him to select the picture with the elephant carrying the candelabra; while his ardent imagination, ever directed to the dramatic, would not be restrained within the limits of the original. Instead of a harmless sheep, which, in Mantegna, is walking by the side of the foremost elephant, Rubens has introduced a lion and a lioness (or rather a tiger) growling angrily at the elephant. Nor is the elephant more peacefully disposed, but, with an expression of fury, is on the point of striking the lion a blow with his trunk'. — *W.*

1050. **Bakhuizen**, Shipping; 737. *Ruysdael*. **Landscape with waterfall;** 46. *Rubens*, **Peace and War (presented by the painter to Charles I. in 1630);** 955. *Corn. van Poelenburg* (d. 1667; Utrecht, imitator of the Roman School). **Ruin, with women bathing;** 1061. *Egbert van der Poel* (d. 1664; Delft), **View of Delft after the explosion of a powder-mill in 1654;** 970. *Gabriel Metsu* (Amsterdam; 1630-67), **The drowsy landlady;** *963. *Isaac van Ostade* (landscape and figure painter, pupil of his elder brother Adrian; d. 1649), **Frozen river (glowing with light, very transparent in colour, and delicate in treatment);** 1009. *Bakhuizen*, Shipping; *212. *Thos. de Keyser* (Amsterdam; about 1660), **Merchant and clerk;** *757. *Rembrandt*(?), **Christ blessing little children;** 1221. *A. de Pape* (d. 1668), **Interior;** 1255. *Jan Jansz van de Velde* (a rare Amsterdam painter; ca. 1640-56), **Still-life;** 1256. *Herman Steenwyck* (Delft), **Still-life;** 156. *Van Dyck*, Study **of horses;** *1021. *Frans Hals* (Haarlem; 1580-1666), Portrait; 994. *Jan van der Heyde* (architectural and landscape-painter at Amsterdam; **1637-1712), Street;** 1004. *N. Berchem*, Italian landscape; *797. **Attributed to** *A. Cuyp* (in the style of his father Jacob Gerritz Cuyp, an eminent portrait-painter, and perhaps by him), Portrait, dated **1649;** 1060. *Philip Wouwerman* (Haarlem; 1619-68), Vedettes, **an early work;** 154. *Teniers*, Musical party; 1095. *Jan Lievens* (1607-?1663), Portrait; 221. *Rembrandt*. **The artist at an advanced age;** 956. *Jan Both* (d. 1652; Utrecht, visited Rome), **Italian scene;** 972. *Jan Wynants* (ca. 1640-80), **Landscape;** 158. *Teniers*, **Boors regaling;** 1251. *Fr. Hals*, **Portrait.**

On Stands: 659. *Rottenhammer* (1564-1623), **Pan and Syrinx;** 1015. *Jan van Os* (d. 1808), **Fruit;** 1014. *Adam Elshaimer* (German School; d. 1620), **Martyrdom of St. Lawrence;** 998. *Godfried Schalcken* (Dutch genre-painter, famed for his candle-light effects, and a pupil of Gerard Dou; d. 1706), **Duet;** 1132. *Hendrick Steenwyck the Younger* (b. at Frankfort, worked at Antwerp and at London, where he supplied architectural backgrounds to Van Dyck's portraits; 1580-1649), **Interior.**

11*

*896. *Gerard Terburg* or *Ter Borch* (Deventer, the greatest Dutch painter of conversation pieces; d. 1681), Peace of Münster. 'This picture represents the Plenipotentiaries of Philip IV. of Spain and the Delegates of the Dutch United Provinces assembled in the Rathhaus at Münster, on the 15th of May, 1648, for the purpose of ratifying and confirming by oath the Treaty of Peace between the Spaniards and the Dutch, signed on the 30th of January previous'. (*Catalogue*). It is one of the master's very finest works.

199. *Schalcken*, Lesbia weighing jewels against her dead sparrow (Catullus, Carmen iii); 192. *Gerard Dou* or *Dow* (Leyden; 1613-1675), Portrait of himself; 796. *Jan van Huysum* (Amsterdam; 1682-1749), Flowers; *1277. *N. Maes*, Portrait (dated 1666); *680. *Van Dyck*, The Miraculous Draught of Fishes, copy of a large altarpiece by Rubens at Malines; *1114-1118. *Gonzales Coques* (Antwerp, d. 1684), The five senses, allegorical and finely executed half-lengths. *H. Sorgh* (Rotterdam, pupil of Teniers the Younger; d. 1682), 1056. Man and woman drinking; 1055. Card-players. 985. *Karel Dujardin* (pupil of Berchem, painted landscapes and animals in Holland and Italy; d. 1678), Sheep and goats, dated 1673; 1011. *Coques*, Portrait; 1002. *J. Walscappelle* (ca. 1667-1718), Flowers; 1243. *Dutch School*, Portrait; 1001. *Van Huysum*, Flowers; 1195. *Rubens*, Design for a salver; no number, *Hans Holbein* (German School; 1497-1543), Portrait of Christina, Princess of Denmark, lent by the Duke of Norfolk.

**Room XI.** EARLY GERMAN AND FLEMISH SCHOOLS, etc. The names of the artists are in many cases doubtful.

To the left: 1094, 1231. *Sir Anthony More* or *Moro* (b. at Utrecht in 1512, painted portraits in England), Portraits; 184. *Nicolas Lucidel* (ca. 1527-90; b. in Hainault, painted portraits at Nuremberg), Jeanne d'Archel (formerly ascribed to More); 719. *Henrik met de Bles* ('Henry with the forelock'; Flemish painter of the 16th cent.), Mary Magdalen; 1232. *Heinrich Aldegrever* (Westphalian School, imitator of Dürer; 16th cent.), Portrait; 706. *Master of the Lyversberg Passion* (Cologne; 15th cent.), Presentation in the Temple; 1089. *Patinir* (d. 1524), Virgin and Child, with St. Elizabeth; 291. *Cranach* (German School; d. 1553), Young lady; 664. *Roger van der Weyden the Elder* (d. 1464), Deposition in the Tomb; 295. *Quintin Matsys* (d. 1531), Salvator Mundi and Virgin Mary, replicas of two pictures at Antwerp; 687. *William of Cologne* (early Cologne painter; 14th cent.), St. Veronica with her napkin; *944. *Marinus de Zeeuw* or *Van Romerswale* (d. ca. 1570; a follower of Q. Matsys), Two bankers or usurers in their office, one inserting items in a ledger, while the other seems to recall with difficulty the particulars of some business transaction; 654. *School of Roger van der Weyden*, Mary Magdalen; 1082. *Patinir*, Visitation; 653. *Flemish Master of the 15th cent.*, Portraits; 260. *Meister von Liesborn* (15th cent.), Saints; 657. *Jac. Cornelissen* (Amsterdam; d. ca. 1560), Dutch lady and gentleman, with their patron-saints, Peter and Paul;

*Patinir*, 1717. St. John in Patmos, 1716. St. Christopher; 709. *Early Flemish School*, Virgin and Child; *J. van Schoreel* (d. 1562), 720. (?) Rest on the Flight into Egypt, 721. Portrait; 655. *Bernard van Orley* (d. 1542), Reading Magdalen; 718. *Henrik met de Bles*, Mt. Calvary; 1086. *Early Flemish School*, Christ appearing to the Virgin after his Resurrection; *707. *Master of the St. Bartholomew Altar*, SS. Peter and Dorothy, parts of an altarpiece in Munich; 774. *Flemish School of the 15th cent.*, Virgin and Child enthroned; *658. *Early German School* (formerly ascribed to Martin Schongauer), Death of the Virgin; *1045. *Gheerardt David* (early Flemish painter of Bruges; d. 1523), Wing of an altarpiece, representing Canon Bernardino di Salviatis, a Florentine merchant in Flanders, with SS. Martin, Donatian, and Bernardino of Siena, a masterpiece; 711. Ascribed to *Roger van der Weyden*, Mater Dolorosa. — *686. *Hans Memling* or *Memline* (early Flemish master of Bruges; d. ca. 1495), Virgin and Child enthroned.

This is the only authentic work of this master in the gallery, and is marked by his peculiar tenderness of conception and vividness of tints.

*222. *Jan van Eyck* (d. 1440; founder of the early Flemish School), Portrait of a man.

'This is a panel in which minute finish is combined with delicate modelling and strong relief, and a brown depth of colour'. — *Crowe and Cavalcaselle*, 'Early Flemish Painters'.

*186. *Jan van Eyck*, Portraits of Giovanni Arnolfini and Jeanne de Chenany, his wife.

'In no single instance has John van Eyck expressed with more perfection, by the aid of colour, the sense of depth and atmosphere; he nowhere blended colours more carefully, nowhere produced more transparent shadows. .... The finish of the parts is marvellous, and the preservation of the picture perfect'. — *C. & C.*

'Without a prolonged examination of this picture, it is impossible to form an idea of the art with which it has been executed. One feels tempted to think that in this little panel Van Eyck has set himself to accumulate all manner of difficulties, or rather of impossibilities, for the mere pleasure of overcoming them. The perspective, both lineal and aerial, is so ably treated, and the truthfulness of colouring is so great, that all the details, even those reflected in the mirror, seem perspicuous and easy; and instead of the fatigue which the examination of so laborious and complicated a work might well occasion, we feel nothing save pleasure and admiration'. — *Reiset*, 'Gazette des Beaux Arts', 1878 (p. 7).

The signature on this picture is 'Johannes de Eyck fuit hic' ('Jan van Eyck was here'). The inscription on No. 222 is equally modest: 'Als ich kan' ('As I can').

*290. *Jan van Eyck*, Portrait of a man, dated 1432.

'The drawing is careful, the painting blended to a fault'. — *C. & C.*

712. *Roger van der Weyden*, Ecce Homo; 747. Attributed to *Memling*, St. John the Baptist and St. Lawrence, 'very minutely and delicately worked'; 705. *Stephan Lochner* (early master of Cologne, about 1440), SS. Matthew, Catharine of Alexandria, and John; 783. *Flemish School*, Exhumation of St. Hubert; 722. *Sigismund Holbein* (?), Portrait of a woman; 1280. *Flemish Master of the 15th cent.*, Christ appearing to Mary after the Resurrection; 710. *Hugo van der Goes* (?), Portrait of a monk, a 'vivid and truth-

ful portrait'; *656. *Jan Mabuse* (*Jan Gossaert*; early Flemish portrait and historical painter; d. 1532), Portrait, drawing and colouring alike admirable; 245. **Hans** *Baldung Grien* (d. 1512; German School), Senator (with the monogram of Albrecht Dürer, probably forged); 946. *Mabuse*, Portrait. — *943. *Memling* (?), Portrait of a man, dated 1462.

The authenticated paintings of this master bear dates not earlier than 1470. Critics are not yet wholly agreed as to the authorship of this admirable work, but it is more probably by Dierick Bouts than by Memling.

1042. **Catharine van Hemessen** (portrait-painter at the Spanish court; 16th cent.), Portrait.

We now again pass through Room X. in order to reach —

**Room XII.** PEEL COLLECTION. This is a collection of Flemish and Dutch cabinet-pieces, chiefly works of the very first rank.

819. **Bakhuizen**, Off the mouth of the Thames. *W. van de Velde*. 872. Shipping; 876. Gale. *834. *P. de Hooghe*, Dutch interior (broad, full, sunlight effect); 818. *Bakhuizen*, Coast-scene; 865. *Jan van de Cappelle* (marine-painter of the 17th cent., at Amsterdam, under the influence of Rembrandt), Coast-scene.

*873. *W. van de Velde*, Coast of Scheveningen.

'The numerous figures are by Adrian van de Velde. The union of these two great masters makes this one of the most charming pictures of the Dutch school'. — *W.*

*864. **Gerard** *Terburg*, Guitar lesson.

'Terburg may be considered as the creator of what are called conversation-pieces, and is at the same time the most eminent master in that line. In delicacy of execution he is inferior to none; nay in a certain delicate blending he is superior to all. But none can be compared to him in the magical harmony of his silver tones, and in the gradations of the aerial perspective'. — *Waagen*, '*Treasures of Art in Britain*'

853. *Rubens*, **Triumph of** Silenus; *839. *Metsu*, Music-lesson; 884. **Wynants**, Landscape, with figures by *A. van de Velde*. — *852 *Rubens*, Portrait, known as the 'Chapeau de paille'.

The chief charm of the celebrated 'Chapeau de Paille' (chapeau de poil) consists in the marvellous triumph over a great difficulty, that of painting a head entirely in the shadow cast by the hat, and yet in the clearest and most brilliant tones'. — '*Kugler*', edited by *Crowe*.

*856. *Jan* **Steen** (painter of humorous conversation-pieces; Delft and the Hague; d. 1679), The music-master (an early and very carefully finished work. — *869. *A. van de Velde*, Frost-scene.

'Admirably drawn, touched with great spirit, and of a very pleasing, though, for the subject, perhaps too warm a tone'. — *W.*

829. *Jan Hackaert* (Amsterdam, 17th cent.), Stag-hunt; *870, 871. *W. van de Velde*, Sea-pieces; *849. *Paul Potter* (The Hague; 1625-54), Landscape with cattle; 833. *Meindert Hobbema* (Amsterdam, pupil of Ruysdael; 1638-1709), Forest scene. — *868. *A. van de Velde*, Ford.

'The composition is very tasteful, and the contrast between the concentrated mass of light and the clear half shadow, which is repeated in soft broken tones upon the horizon, is very attractive'. — *W.*

*826. *Dujardin*, Figures and **animals reposing**; *835. *Pieter de Hooghe*, Court of a Dutch house, 1658.

'Excites a joyful feeling of summer. In point of fulness and depth of tone and execution one of the best pictures of the master'. — W.

882. *Wouwerman*, Landscape; 827. *Dujardin*, Fording the stream, dated 1657.

*830. *Hobbema*, The Avenue, Middelharnis.

'From simple and by no means beautiful materials a picture is formed which, by the feeling for nature and the power of art, makes a striking impression on the intelligent spectator. Such daylight I have never before seen in any picture. The perspective is admirable, while the gradation, from the fullest bright green in the foreground, is so delicately observed, that it may be considered a masterpiece in this respect, and is, on the whole, one of the most original works of art with which I am acquainted'. — W.

866. *Van der Heyde*, Street in Cologne, with figures by *A. van de Velde*; 880. *Wouwerman*, On the seashore, selling fish (supposed to be his last work); 828. *Dujardin*, Landscape, with cattle. — *846. *Adrian van Ostade* (figure-painter at Haarlem, pupil of Frans Hals; d. 1685), The alchymist.

'The effect of light in the foreground, the predominant golden tone of extraordinary brightness and clearness, the execution equally careful and spirited, and the contrast of the deep cool chiaroscuro in the background have a peculiar charm'. — W.

883. *Wynants* (d. ca. 1680), Landscape, with accessories by *Lingelbach* (dated 1659).

'This landscape has, in a rare degree, that serene, cool freshness of tone, which so admirably expresses the character of northern scenery, and in which Wynants is quite unrivalled'. — W.

*832. *Hobbema*, Village, with water-mills (in a warm, summer-like tone). — *822. *Cuyp*, Horseman and cows in a meadow.

'Of exquisite harmony, in a bright cool light, unusual with him'. — W.

867. *Adrian van de Velde* (brother of Willem and pupil of Wynants at Haarlem; 1639-72), Farm cottage; 861. *Teniers*, River-scene; *836. *Phil. de Koninck* (pupil of Rembrandt; d. 1690), Landscape, figures by *A. van de Velde*; 841. *Willem van Mieris* (d. 1747), Fish and poultry shop (1713). — *825. *Gerard Dou* (d. 1675), Poulterer's shop.

'Besides the extreme finish, in which he holds the first place, it surpasses many of his other pictures in its unusual clearness and in the agreeable and spirited heads'. — W.

878. *Wouwerman*, 'La belle laitière'.

'This picture combines that delicate tone of his second period with the great force which he adopted especially toward the end of it. The effect of the dark figures relieved against the landscape is extraordinary' — W.

855. *Ruysdael*, Landscape with a waterfall. — *847. *I. van Ostade*, Village-scene in Holland.

'This delicately drawn picture combines the greatest solidity with the most spirited execution, and the finest impasto with the greatest glow and depth of tone. Paul Potter himself could not have painted the grey horse better'. — W.

*879. *Wouwerman*, Interior of a stable (very delicately finished). — 831. *Hobbema*, Ruins of Brederode Castle.

'Strongly illumined by a sunbeam, and reflected in the dark yet clear water which surrounds them'. — W.

*848. *Isaac van Ostade* (d. 1649), Canal scene in winter.
'The great truth, admirable treatment, and fresh feeling of a **winter's day** render it one of the *chefs-d'œuvre* of the master'. — *W.*

820. *Berchem*, Landscape, with ruin; 881. *Wouwerman*, Gathering faggots; 862. *Teniers*, The husband surprised; 854. *Ruysdael*, Forest-scene; 823. *Cuyp*, River-scene, with cattle; 843. *Caspar Netscher* (pupil of Terburg, settled at the Hague; d. 1684), Children blowing soap-bubbles (1670); 863. *Teniers*, Dives in torment; 954. *David Teniers the Elder* (pupil of Rubens, and also of Elshaimer at Rome; d. 1649), Playing at bowls; 1003. *Jan Fyt* (animal-painter at Antwerp in the time of Rubens; d. 1661), Dead birds; 957. *Jan Both*, Cattle and figures; 1009. *Paul Potter*, Old grey hunter; 964. *Van der Cappelle*, River-scene; 962. *A. Cuyp*, Cattle and figures; 961. *Cuyp*, Cattle and figures; 205. *J. W. E. Dietrich* (German School, court-painter at Dresden; d. 1774), Itinerant musicians; 1006. *Berchem*, Landscape; 949. *Teniers the Elder*, Rocky landscape; 1010. *Dirk van Deelen* (architectural painter in Zeeland; 17th cent.), Extensive palatial buildings of Renaissance architecture, with figures by *A. Palamedesz*; 969. *A. van der Neer*, Frost-scene; 798. *Philip de Champaigne* (d. 1674), Three portraits of Cardinal Richelieu, painted as a guide in the execution of a bust (over the profile on the spectator's right are the words, 'De ces deux profiles ce cy est le meilleur'); 991. *Ruysdael*, Prostrate tree; 992. *J. van der Heyden* (d. 1712), Gothic and classic buildings; 1017. *Unknown Flemish Master*, Landscape (signed D. D. V., 1622); 978. *Van de Velde*, River-scene; 980. *Willem van de Velde the Younger*, Dutch vessels saluting; 950. *Teniers*, Conversation (three men near the door of a house); 973. *Jan Wouwerman* (landscape-painter at Haarlem; wrongly ascribed to Wynants), Sandbank in a river; 975. *Philip Wouwerman*, Stag-hunt.

*54. *Rembrandt*, Woman bathing, dated 1654.
'Her eyes are cast down, her head inclined. Is she hesitating to enter the water in which she is mirrored? .... The charm and value of this painting lie in the brilliant touch and impasto, the warm and forcible colouring, the middle tints, and the admirable modelling'. — *Vosmaer*, '*Rembrandt, Sa Vie et ses Œuvres*'.

983. *Adrian van de Velde*, Bay horse, cow, and goat; 43. *Rembrandt*, Descent from the Cross; *159. *Maas*, The Dutch housewife, dated 1655; 974. *Philip de Koninck*, Hilly, wooded landscape, with a view of the Scheldt and Antwerp Cathedral; *995. *Hobbema*, Forest-landscape, of peculiarly clear chiaroscuro; 988. *Ruysdael*, Old oak; *153. *Maas*, Cradle. *Van der Cappelle*, 966. River-scene; 967. Shipping. 1013. *Hondecoeter*, Geese and ducks. *Ruysdael*, *990. Landscape, an extensive flat, wooded country (a *chef-d'oeuvre*); 987. Rocky landscape. — 952. *Teniers the Younger*, Village fête, dated 1643.
'An admirable original repetition of the masterly picture in the possession of the Duke of Bedford, though not equal to the Bedford picture in delicacy'. — *W.*

960. *Cuyp*, Windmills; 958. *Jan Both*, Outside the walls of Rome. — *976. *Philip Wouwerman*, Battle.

'Full of animated action, of the utmost transparency, and executed with admirable precision'. — *W.*

1005. *Berchem*, Landscape; 971. *Wynants*, Landscape; 211. *J. van Huchtenburgh* (d. 1733), Battle; 877. *Van Dyck*. His own portrait; 1074. *Dirk Hals* (younger brother of Frans; d. 1656), Merry party; 1278. *Hendrik Gerritz Pot* (d. ca. 1656), Convivial party.

On STANDS: 953. *Teniers*, The toper; 999. *G. Schalcken*, Candlelight effect; *821. *Gonzales Coques*, Family portraits, amply justifying the artist's claim to be the 'Little Van Dyck'; 968. *Gerard Dou*, The painter's wife; 997. *Schalcken*, Old woman. — *844. *Netscher*, Maternal instruction.

'The ingenuous expression of the children, the delicacy of the handling, the striking effect of light, and the warm deep harmony render this one of the most pleasing pictures by Netscher'. — *W.*

Above the cupboard at the back there hangs a small copy of Rubens' 'Brazen Serpent' in this collection (No. 59, see p. 162).

845. *Netscher*, Lady at a spinning-wheel (finished with great delicacy; 840. *Frans van Mieris* (d. 1681), Lady feeding a parrot (these two figures, of the same size and in the same dress, afford an interesting comparison of the workmanship of the two masters); *824. *A. Cuyp*, Ruined castle in a lake ('gilded by the most glowing evening sun').

*838. *Gabriel Metsu* (painter of interiors at Amsterdam; d. after 1667), The duet.

'Painted in the warm, full tone, which is especially valuable in his pictures'. — *W.*

875. *W. van de Velde*, Light breeze; 857-860. *Teniers*, The seasons; 850. *Rembrandt*, Portrait of a man (1635).

**Room XIII.** LATER ITALIAN SCHOOL. What is known as the Eclectic or Academic School of Painters arose in Italy with the foundation of a large academy at Bologna by the Carracci in 1589. Its aim was to combine the peculiar excellences of the earlier masters with a closer study of nature. The best representatives of the school are grouped together in this room, which also contains examples of the later Venetian masters.

*Annibale Carracci* (younger brother of Lodovico, and founder along with him of the Bolognese Academy; d. 1609), 93. Silenus gathering grapes; 94. Pan teaching Apollo to play on the pipe, quite in the style of the ancient frescoes. 228. *Jacopo Bassano* (Venetian painter of the late Renaissance; d. 1597), Christ driving the money-changers out of the Temple; 624. Ascribed to *Giulio Romano* (Roman School, pupil of Raphael; d. 1546), Infancy of Jupiter; 1054. *Francesco Guardi* (architectural and landscape painter, closely allied to Canaletto; d. 1793), View in Venice; 1157. *Bernardo Cavallino* (Naples; d. 1654). Nativity; 48. *Domenichino* (*Domenico Zampieri*; d. 1641), Tobias and the Angel; 22. *Guercino* (*Giovanni Francesco Barbieri*; d. 1666), Angels weeping over the dead body of Christ (a good example of this painter, resembling Caravaggio in the management of the light, and recalling the picture of the same subject by Van Dyck in the Antwerp Museum); 214. *Guido* (? probably a northern painter), Coronation of the Virgin; 198. *Ann. Carracci*, Temptation of St. Anthony, unattractive; 160. *Pietro Francesco Mola* (1612-68), Repose on the Flight into Egypt; 11. *Guido Reni* (d. 1642), St. Jerome; 936. *Bibiena* (Bologna; d. 1743), Performance of Othello in the Teatro Farnese at Parma.

*942. *Canaletto* (*Antonio Canale*, of Venice; d. 1768), Eton College in 1746, with the Thames in the foreground.

This picture was painted during the artist's visit to England in 1746-8, perhaps, as Mr. Cook points out, in the same year (1747) that Gray published his well-known 'Ode on a distant Prospect of Eton College'.

1100. *Pietro Longhi* (Venice, sometimes called the 'Italian Hogarth'; 1702-62), Domestic group; 935. *Salvator Rosa* (Neapolitan landscape-painter; d. 1673), River-scene. — 937. *Canaletto*, Scuola di San Rocco, Venice.

The picture represents 'the ceremony of Giovedì Santo or Maundy Thursday, when the Doge and officers of state with the fraternity of St. Rock went in procession to the church of St. Mark to worship the miraculous blood'. — *Catalogue*.

940. *Canaletto*, Ducal Palace and Column of St. Mark, Venice; 1101. *Longhi*, Carnival maskers at a menagerie; 25. *Ann. Carracci*, St. John in the Wilderness; 939. *Canaletto*, Piazzetta of St. Mark, Venice; 1206. *Salv. Rosa*, Landscape; 210. *Guardi*, Piazza of St. Mark, Venice; 85. *Domenichino*, St. Jerome and the Angel; 934. *Carlo Dolci* (Florentine painter of sacred subjects; d. 1686), Virgin and Child; 196. *Guido*, Susannah and the Elders ('a work', says Mr. Ruskin, 'devoid alike of art and decency'); *84. *Salv. Rosa*, Mercury and the woodman; 77. *Domenichino*, Stoning of St. Stephen; 9. *Ann. Carracci* (?), Christ appearing to St. Peter after his Resurrection (the difficulties of foreshortening have been only partly overcome); 75. *Domenichino*, Landscape with St. George and the Dragon; 200. *Sassoferrato* (*Gior. Batt. Salvi*; d. 1685), Madonna in prayer (primitive in colouring, common in form, and lighted for effect); 163. *Canaletto*, Grand Canal, Venice; 138. *Pannini* (Roman School; d. 1764), Ancient ruins. — 740. *Sassoferrato*, Madonna and Child.

The composition is not by Sassoferrato, but is from an earlier etching by Cav. Ventura Salembeni (d. 1613). See *Catalogue*.

28. *Lodovico Carracci* (d. 1619), Susannah and the Elders; *643. *Giulio Romano* (ascribed by Mr. Crowe to Giulio's pupil, *Rinaldo Mantovano*), Capture of Carthagena, and the Moderation of Publius Cornelius Scipio, colouring and drawing both excellent. — *56. *Annibale Carracci*, Landscape with figures.

'Under the influence of Titian's landscapes and of Paul Bril, who was so justly esteemed by him, Annibale acquired that grandeur of composition, and beauty of outlines, which had so great an influence upon Claude and Gaspar Poussin.' — *W.*

941. *Canaletto*, Grimani Palace, Venice; 177. *Guido Reni*,

Mary Magdalen; 174. *Carlo Maratta* (Roman painter; d. 1713), Portrait of Cardinal Cerri; 172. *Caravaggio* (Michaelangelo Amerighi, founder of the naturalistic school of Naples; d. 1609), Christ and the Disciples at Emmaus; 127. *Canaletto*, View of the Scuola della Carità, now the Accademia delle Belle Arti, Venice; 63. *Ann. Carracci*, Landscape. — 29. *Baroccio (Federigo Barocci*, a follower of Correggio; d. 1612), Holy Family ('La Madonna del Gatto', so called from the cat introduced).

'The chief intention of the picture is John the Baptist as a child, who teases a cat by showing her a bullfinch which he holds in his hand. The Virgin, Christ, and Joseph seem much amused by this cruel sport.' — *W*.

271. *Guido Reni*, Ecce Homo; 70. *Padovanino (Alessandro Varotari*, of Venice; d. 1650), Cornelia and her children (children form this artist's favourite subject); *644. Ascribed to *Rinaldo Mantovano*, Rape of the Sabine women, and Reconciliation between the Romans and Sabines (these pictures recall, in many respects, Raphael's frescoes in the Vatican); 1059. *Canaletto*, Church of S. Pietro di Castello, Venice; 88. *Ann. Carracci*, Erminia taking refuge with the shepherds (from Tasso); 938. *Canaletto*, Regatta on the Canale Grande, Venice; *191. *Guido Reni*, Youthful Christ embracing St. John, a very characteristic work, and the best picture by Guido in this collection; 1058. *Canaletto*, Canal Reggio, Venice.

**Room XIV.** FRENCH SCHOOL. The French landscape-painter Claude Lorrain, who is represented in this collection by several fine examples, is chiefly eminent for his skill in aërial perspective and his management of sunlight. Salvator Rosa and the two Poussins lived and painted at Rome contemporaneously with him (17th cent.). Nicolas Poussin, more famed as a painter of figures than of landscapes, was the brother-in-law of Gaspar Poussin (properly Gaspar Dughet), a follower of Claude.

On each side of the doorway hang a large landscape by Claude and one by Turner. To the right, as we enter from Room XIII.: *12. *Claude* (d. 1682), Landscape with figures (with the inscription on the picture itself, 'Mariage d'Isac avec Rebeca'), a work of wonderfully transparent atmosphere, recalling in its composition the celebrated picture 'Il molino' (the mill) in the Palazzo Doria at Rome, painted in 1648; *479. *Turner*, Sun rising in a mist. — To the left: 498. *Turner*, Dido building Carthage. (These two pictures were bequeathed by the artist on condition that they should be hung beside the Claudes.)

This picture (No. 498) is not considered a favourable specimen of Turner, whose 'eye for colour unaccountably fails him' (Ruskin). Mr. Ruskin comments on the 'exquisite choice' of the group of children sailing toyboats, as expressive of the ruling passion, which was to be the source of Carthage's future greatness.

The visitor will scarcely need to be referred to 'Modern Painters' (Vol. I.), for Mr. Ruskin's eloquent comparison of Turner with Claude and the other landscape-painters of the old style and for his impassioned championship of the English master.

*14. *Claude*, Embarkation of the **Queen of Sheba** (1648).
'The effect of the morning sun on the sea, the waves of which run high, and on the masses of building which adorn the shore, producing the most striking contrast of light and shade, is sublimely poetical'. — *W.*
Then, to the left: 1190. Ascribed to *Fr. Clouet* (court-painter to Francis I.; b. about 1510, d. **before** 1574), Portrait **of** a boy; 660. *Clouet*, Portrait **of** a man; 36. *Gaspard Poussin* (properly *G. Dughet*; d. 1675), Land-storm; 236. *C. J. Vernet* (grandfather of Horace Vernet; d. 1789), Castle of Sant' Angelo, Rome. *Claude*, *1018. Classical **landscape, dated 1673**; 2. Pastoral landscape with figures (reconciliation **of Cephalus and Procris**); *30. Embarkation of St. Ursula. 95. *G. Poussin*, **Landscape with Dido and Æneas**, with sky much overcast; 65. *N. Poussin* (d. 1665). **Cephalus and Aurora**; 19. *Claude*, **Landscape with figures**; 903. *Hyacinthe Rigaud* (portrait-painter under Louis XIV. and Louis XV.; d. 1743), Portrait of Cardinal Fleury. *Nicolas Lancret* (painter of 'Fêtes Galantes'; d. 1743), 101. Infancy; 102. Youth; 103. Manhood; 104. Age. 5. *Claude Lorrain*. Seaport at sunset. — *62. *N. Poussin*, Bacchanalian dance.
This is the best example of Nicholas Poussin in the gallery. The composition is an imitation of an ancient bas-relief.
61. *Claude*, Landscape; 165. *N. Poussin*, Plague among the Philistines at Ashdod. — *31. *G. Poussin*, Landscape, with **Abraham and Isaac.**
'This is the finest picture by Poussin here. Seldom, perhaps, have the charms of a plain, as contrasted with hilly forms overgrown with the richest forests, been so well understood and so happily united as here, the effect being enhanced by a warm light, broken by shadows of clouds'. — *W.*
206. *Jean Greuze* (**painter of fancy** portraits; d. 1805), Head of a girl; 58. *Claude Lorrain*, **Landscape** with goats. — 40. *N. Poussin*, **Landscape, with Phocion.**
According to Mr. Ruskin, this is 'one of the finest landscapes that ancient art has produced, — the work of a really great and intellectual mind'.
42. *N. Poussin*, Bacchanalian festival; 55. *Claude*, Landscape, with death of Procris; 1154. *Greuze*, Girl with a lamb; 161. *G. Poussin*, Italian **landscape**; *6. *Claude*, Landscape with figures (David and Saul in **the Cave of Adullam?**); 1159. *G. Poussin*, The Calling of Abraham. *N. Poussin*, 91. **Venus asleep, surprised by satyrs**; 39. Nursing of Bacchus. 1090. *François Boucher* (**1704-1770**), Pan and Syrinx. *Greuze*, *1019. Head of a girl looking up; 1020. Girl **with an apple.**

**Room XV.** SPANISH SCHOOL.

To the left: *Velazquez* (d. 1660), *232. Adoration of the Shepherds (early work, under the influence of Spagnoletto); *197. Philip IV. hunting **the wild boar.** *Bartolome Esteban Murillo* (influenced by Velazquez **and Van Dyck**; d. 1682), 1257. Nativity of **the Virgin** (said to **be a colour-sketch** for the large painting in the Louvre); *176. St. John and the Lamb; *74. Spanish peasant boy. 1229. *Morales* (**1509-86; surnamed 'the Divine'** from his love of religious subjects), Holy Family, a highly finished little work, recalling the Flemish manner; *1129. *Velazquez*, Philip IV. (bought at the Hamilton sale for 6300*l.*); 1122. *Theotocopuli* (d. 1625), surnamed *Il Greco*, Portrait of a cardinal; 230. *Zurbaran* (d. 1662), Franciscan monk. *Velazquez*, *745. Philip IV; *1148. Scourging of Christ. *13. *Murillo*, Holy Family; 235. *Ribera*, Dead Christ; 244. *Ribera*, Shepherd; 741. *Velazquez*, Dead warrior.

**Room XVI.** (adjoining R. XIV.). OLDER BRITISH SCHOOL.. To the left: *Thomas Gainsborough* (comp. p. 149), 760. Orpin, Parish Clerk of Bradford, Wiltshire; 109. The watering-place; *683. *Gainsborough*, Mrs. Siddons; 312. *Romney* (1734-1802), Lady Hamilton as a bacchante. — *Sir Joshua Reynolds*, portrait-painter and writer on art, founder and first president of the Royal Academy (1723-92). *1259. Anne, Countess of Albemarle; 888. James Boswell, the biographer of Johnson. 1068. *Romney*, The parson's daughter; 1198. *Lemuel Abbott* (d. 1803), Portrait; 305. *Reynolds*, Portrait; 928. *Gainsborough*, Landscape; 1197. Ascribed to *John Zoffany* (d. 1810), Portrait of Garrick; 1044. *Gainsborough*, Portrait. *Reynolds*, 107. The banished lord; 885. The snake in the grass; 162. Infant Samuel; 892. Robinetta, a study of the Hon. Mrs. Tollemache, painted about 1786; 106. Portrait; 306. Portrait of himself; 886. Admiral Keppel; 887. Portrait of Dr. Johnson; 891. Lady and child; 889. Portrait of himself; 307. Age of Innocence; 79. The Graces decorating a terminal figure of Hymen (portraits of the daughters of Sir. W. Montgomery); 890. George IV. when Prince of Wales; 182. Heads of angels (one of the most popular and most frequently copied pictures in the Gallery); 111. Lord Heathfield, the defender of Gibraltar in 1779-83; *754. Portraits. 308. *Gainsborough*, Musidora (from Thomson's 'Summer'). — This room also contains a few other works by Reynolds lent by the Dilletanti Society.

**Room XVII.** OLDER BRITISH SCHOOL. To the left: 119. *Sir George Beaumont* (d. 1827), Landscape with the 'Melancholy Jacques'. *William Hogarth* (d. 1764), 1161. Miss Fenton, the actress, as 'Polly Peachum' in the 'Beggars' Opera'; *1046. Sigismonda mourning over the heart of Guiscardo; 1162. Shrimp girl; 675. Portrait of his sister. 316. *Loutherbourg* (d. 1812), Lake in Cumberland; 304, 1064, 267, 303, 302, 1071, 108, 110. *Wilson* (d. 1782), Landscapes. *Samuel Scott* (d. 1772), 314. Old Westminster Bridge; 313. Old London Bridge. 309. *Gainsborough*, The watering-place; 1016. *Sir Peter Lely* (d. 1680), Portrait. *Hogarth*, 1153. Family group; 113-118. Marriage à la mode (in 1750 Hogarth received only 110*l.* for the series, which when sold again in 1794 realised 1381*l.*). *1249. *William Dobson* (1610-46; the 'English Van Dyck'). Endymion Porter, Groom of the Bedchamber to Charles I.; 1224. *Hudson* (d. 1779), Scott, the painter; 1076. *Unknown*, Portrait, supposed to be the poet Gay; 112. *Hogarth*,

Portrait of himself; 1279. *Francis Cotes* (d. 1770), Portrait of Mrs. Brocas.

To reach the next room, we cross the main staircase.

Room XVIII. BRITISH SCHOOL. To the left: *1242. *Alex. Nasmyth* (1758-1840; a painter of portraits and landscapes at Edinburgh; father of Patrick Nasmyth), Stirling Castle.

Sir David Wilkie describes Alex. Nasmyth as 'the founder of the landscape school of Scotland, and the first to enrich his native land with the representation of her romantic scenery'.

1030. *George Morland* (d. 1804). Interior of a stable (1791). 374. *Bonington* (d. 1828). Column of St. Mark at Venice; 380, 381. *Patrick Nasmyth* (1786-1831), Landscapes; 787. *John S. Copley* (b. at Boston, Mass., in 1737; d. 1815), Siege and relief of Gibraltar. *John Constable* (one of the greatest English landscape-painters, who has exercised great influence on the modern French school of landscape; 1776-1837), 1066. Barnes Common; 1235. House in which the artist was born; 1277. Landscape; 1245. Church-porch at Bergholt, Suffolk. 1110. *William Blake* (1757-1827), The Spiritual Form of Pitt guiding Behemoth (an 'iridescent sketch of enigmatic dream', symbolizing the power of statesmanship in controlling brute force); *1037. *Crome* ('Old Crome' of Norwich; d. 1821). Slate quarries. *Constable*, 1236. View on Hampstead Heath; 1276. Harwich. 1208. *Opie* (d. 1807). William Godwin; 926. *Crome*, Windmill; 725. *Joseph Wright* (Derby; d. 1797), Experiment with an air-pump; 689. *Crome*, Mousehold Heath, near Norwich; 1167. *Opie*, Portrait, supposed to be Mary Wollstonecraft (Mrs. Godwin). *Sir Thomas Lawrence* (d. 1830), 129. John Angerstein (p. 148); 1238. Sir Samuel Romilly. 1163. *Stothard* (1755-1834), The Canterbury Pilgrims; 733. *John Copley*, Death of Major Peirson; 1177. *P. Nasmyth*, Landscape; 1246. *Constable*, House at Hampstead; 1164. *Blake*, Procession from Calvary. *Gainsborough*, 1271. Portrait; 80. The market cart; *311. Rustic children. 1029. *Thos. Barker* (1769-1847), Landscape. *Copley*, 100. Last public appearance of the Earl of Chatham, who fainted in endeavouring to speak in the House of Peers on April 7th, 1778. and died a month later; 1072, 1073. Studies for No. 100. 321. *Stothard*, Intemperance (Cleopatra and Mark Antony); 310. *Gainsborough*, Watering-place; 1158. *James Ward* (d. 1859), Harlech Castle.

Room XIX. BRITISH SCHOOL. This room, which formerly contained part of the Turner Collection (comp. p. 176), has not yet been finally arranged.

*Constable*, 1275. View at Hampstead; *1273. Flatford Mill; 1272. Cenotaph erected in memory of Sir Joshua Reynolds in Coleorton Park, Leicestershire; 1274. Glebe Farm. 897. *Crome*. Chapel Fields, Norwich; 1250. *Daniel Maclise* (1811-70). Charles Dickens; 853. *Newton* (d. 1835), Yorick and the Grisette; 1176, 1183, 1178. *P. Nasmyth*, Landscapes; 343. *Sir A. Calcott* ('the English Claude', not seen to advantage in the National Gallery; d. 1844), Rustic bridge; 600. *Dyckmans* (b. 1811), Blind beggar, 400. *David Roberts* (1796-1864), Interior of Burgos Cathedral.

**Room XX.** MODERN BRITISH SCHOOL. To the left: 394. *William Mulready* (1786-1863), Fair time; 607. *Sir Edwin Landseer* (d. 1873). Highland dogs; 439. *J. Linnell* (d. 1882), Windmill; 452. *J. F. Herring* (d. 1865), The scanty meal; 407. *C. Stanfield* (d. 1867), View in Venice; 412. *Landseer*, Hunted stag; 614. *W. Etty* (d. 1849), The bather; 406. *Stanfield*, Lake of Como; 1111. *J. S. Cotman* (d. 1842), Wherries on the Yare; *1226. *Landseer*, A distinguished member of the Royal Humane Society; 395. *Mulready* (d. 1863), Crossing the ford; 1186. *J. Glover* (d. 1849), Landscape, with cattle; 443. *G. Lance* (d. 1864), Fruit; 409. *Landseer*, King Charles spaniels; 431. *E. M. Ward* (d. 1879). Disgrace of Lord Clarendon; 393. *Mulready*. The last in; 359. *Etty*, Luteplayer; 411. *Landseer*. Highland music; 426. *Webster*, The truant; 403. *Charles Leslie* (d. 1859), Uncle Toby and Widow Wadman in the sentry-box (from 'Tristram Shandy'); 444. *A. G. Egg* (d. 1863), Scene from the 'Diable Boiteux'; 404. *Stanfield*, Entrance to the Zuyder Zee; *604. *Landseer*. Dignity and Impudence; 408. *Charles Landseer* (d. 1879), Clarissa Harlowe in the spunging-house; 1040. *W. J. Müller* (d. 1845), Landscape; 410. *Landseer*, High Life and Low Life; 423. *Daniel Maclise*, Malvolio and the Countess; 427. *Webster*, Dame-school; 450. *Fred. Goodall*, Village holiday; 615. *W. P. Frith*, Derby Day; 815. *Clays*, Dutch boats in the roads of Flushing; 1205. *F. L. Bridell* (d. 1863), Chestnut woods above Varenna, Lake Como; 241. *Sir David Wilkie* (d. 1840), The Parish Beadle; 183. *Thos. Phillips* (d. 1845). Sir David Wilkie; 810. *C. Poussin*, Pardon Day in Brittany. *Constable*, *130. Corn-field; *1207. Hay-wain; *327. Valley Farm. 124. *John Jackson* (d. 1831), Rev. Wm. Holwell Carr; 398. *Sir Charles Eastlake* (d. 1865), A Greek girl; 1253. *J. Holland* (d. 1870). Hyde Park Corner in 1825; 446. *J. C. Horsley*. The Pride of the Village (from Irving's 'Sketch Book'). *Sir David Wilkie* (1785-1841), 99. Blind Fiddler; 122. Village Festival. 453. *Alex. Fraser* (d. 1865), Highland cottage; 425. *J. R. Herbert*, Sir Thomas More and his daughter in the Tower observing monks led to execution; 317. *Stothard*. Greek vintage; 1175. *James Ward*, Regent's Park in 1807; 1204. *James Stark* (d. 1859), Valley of the Yare, near Norwich; 921. *Wilkie*, Blindman's Buff (sketch).

On SCREENS; *1210. *Dante Gabriel Rossetti* (the leader of the pre-Raphaelite movement in English art; 1828-82), Annunciation ('Ecce Ancilla Domini'); 379. *W. J. Müller*, Landscape, with Lycian peasants; 563. *Thos. Seddon* (a pre-Raphaelite; d. 1856), Jerusalem and the Valley of Jehoshaphat.

**Room XXI.** BRITISH SCHOOL OF THE 19th CENTURY. To the left: 402. *Leslie*, Sancho Panza in the chamber of the Duchess; 620. *Lee* (d. 1879). River-scene, the cattle by *Cooper*; *432. *E. M. Ward*, The

South Sea Bubble; 120. *Sir William Beechey* (d. 1839). Nollekens, the sculptor; *356. *Etty*, 'Youth on the prow and Pleasure at the helm' (Gray). *E. Landseer*, 605. Defeat of Comus; 603. Sleeping bloodhound (painted in four days); *608. 'Alexander and Diogenes'. 922. *Lawrence*. Portrait of a child; 1142. *Cecil Lawson* (d. 1882), The August moon; *621. *Rosa Bonheur*, Horse-fair; 416. *Pickersgill* (d. 1875), Robert Vernon (p. 148). *Ary Scheffer* (d. 1868), 1170. SS. Augustine and Monica; 1169. Mrs. Robert Hollond, who sat for St. Monica in No. 1170. 397. *Eastlake*, Christ lamenting over Jerusalem; 401. *David Roberts* (architectural painter; d. 1864), Chancel of the church of St. Paul at Antwerp; *1209. *Fred. Walker* (d. 1875), The vagrants; 606. *Landseer*, Shoeing the bay mare; 814. *Clays*, Dutch shipping. *Sir Edwin Landseer*, 413. Peace; 414. War. 784. *Opie*, William Siddons, husband of the celebrated actress; 399. *Sir Chas. Eastlake*, Escape of the Carrara family from the Duke of Milan in 1389; 437. *Danby* (d. 1861), Landscape; 609. *E. Landseer*, The Maid and the Magpie; *430. *E. M. Ward*, Dr. Johnson in Lord Chesterfield's ante-room; 1029. *Linton* (d. 1876), Temples of Pæstum; *422. *Maclise*, Scene from Hamlet; 340. *Sir A. Callcott*, Dutch peasants returning from market; 898. *Sir Chas. Eastlake*, Byron's dream; 900. *John Hoppner* (d. 1810), Countess of Oxford; *894. *Wilkie*, John Knox preaching before the Lords of the Congregation in 1559, after his return from an exile of 13 years; 1091. *Poole* (d. 1879), Vision of Ezekiel; 616. *E. M. Ward*, James II. receiving the news of the landing of William of Orange; 785. *Sir Thos. Lawrence*, Mrs. Siddons. — On SCREENS in the middle of the room; 442. *Lance*, Little Red-cap; 917. *T. S. Good* (d. 1872), No news; 1225. *Thos. Webster* (d. 1886), His father and mother; 1112. *Linnell*, Portrait.

**Room XXII.** contains an admirable collection of paintings by *J. M. W. Turner* (1775-1851), the greatest English landscape-painter (comp. p. 166), chiefly bequeathed by the artist himself. To the left: *528. Burial at sea of Sir David Wilkie; 534. Approach to Venice; *530. Snow-storm, steamboat off Harwich making signals; 472. Calais pier, English packet arriving; 470. Tenth plague of Egypt; 476. Shipwreck; 483. View of London from Greenwich; 813. Fishing-boats in a breeze; 480. Death of Nelson; 493. The Deluge; 481. Boat's crew recovering an anchor at Spithead; 488. Apollo slaying the Python; 477. Garden of the Hesperides; 513. Vision of Medea; 516. Childe Harold's Pilgrimage; 473. Holy Family; *497. Crossing the brook; 512. Caligula's palace and bridge at Baiæ; 558. Fire at sea (unfinished); 458. Portrait of himself; *538. Rain, steam, and speed, the Great Western Railway; 501. Shipwreck at the mouth of the Meuse; 520. Apollo and Daphne; 506. Dido directing the equipment of the fleet at Carthage; *502. Richmond Hill; 508. Ulysses deriding Polyphemus; 505. Apollo and the Sibyl. Bay of Baiæ; 474. Destruction of Sodom; *492.

Frosty morning; 495. Apuleia in search of Apuleius; 559. Petworth Park; *535. The 'Sun of Venice' putting to sea; *524. The 'Fighting Temeraire' towed to her last berth to be broken up (one of the most frequently copied pictures in the whole Gallery); 486. View of Windsor; 543. Queen Mab's Grotto; 523. Agrippina landing with the ashes of Germanicus.

## 15. Royal College of Surgeons. Soane Museum.
*Floral Hall. Covent Garden Market. St. Paul's. Garrick Club.*

On the S. side of Lincoln's Inn Fields rises the **Royal College of Surgeons** (Pl. R, 31; *II*), designed by *Sir Charles Barry*, and erected in 1835. It contains an admirable museum. Visitors are admitted, through the personal introduction or written order of a member, on Mon., Tues., Wed., and Thurs. from 12 to 4 in winter, and from 12 to 5 in summer. The Museum is closed during the month of September. Application for orders of admission, which are not transferable, may be made to the secretary.

The nucleus of the museum consists of a collection of 10,000 anatomical preparations formed by John Hunter (d. 1793), which was purchased by Government after his death and presented to the College. It is divided into two chief departments, viz. the *Physiological Series*. containing specimens of animal organs and formations in a normal state, and the *Pathological Series*, containing similar specimens in an abnormal or diseased condition. There are now in all about 23,000 specimens. A *Synopsis of the Contents* is sold at the Museum, price 6d. Extended catalogues of the different departments are also distributed throughout the Museum for the use of visitors.

In the centre of the WESTERN MUSEUM, the room we first enter, is hung the skeleton of a Greenland whale; a marble statue of Hunter by Weekes, erected in 1864, stands in the middle of the floor at the S. end of the hall. The Wall Cases on the *right* side contain Egyptian and other mummies, an admirable and extensive collection of the skulls of the different nations of the earth, deformed skeletons, abnormal bone formations, and the like. The Floor Cabinets on the *right* contain anatomical preparations illustrating normal human anatomy, and also additional specimens of diseased and injured bones, including some skulls and bones injured by gun-shot wounds in the Crimean war. The first five Floor Cabinets on the *left* contain a collection illustrating the zoology of the invertebrates, such as zoophytes, shell-fish, crabs, and beetles. In the sixth cabinet are casts of the interior of crania. The Wall Cases on this side hold vegetable fossils, human crania, and human skeletons. In the case at the upper end of the room is the skeleton of the Irish giant Byrne or O'Bryan, 7ft. 7in. high; adjoining it, under a glass-shade, is that of the Sicilian dwarf, Caroline Crachami, who died at the age of 10 years, 20in. in height. Under the same shade are placed wax models of her arm and foot, and beside it is a plaster cast of her face.

The MIDDLE MUSEUM forms the palæontological section, where the antediluvian skeletons in the centre are the most interesting objects. Skeleton of a gigantic stag (erroneously called the *Irish Elk*), dug up from a bed of shell-marl beneath a peat-bog at Limerick; giant armadilloes from Buenos Ayres; giant sloth (mylodon), also from Buenos Ayres; a cast of the *Dinornis giganteus*, an extinct wingless bird of New Zealand; the huge megatherium, with the missing parts supplied. In the Wall Cases is a number of smaller skeletons and fossils. The Floor Cabinet contains in one of its trays specimens of the hair and skin of the great extinct **elephant or** mammoth, of which there **are** some fossil remains in one of the cases.

The EASTERN MUSEUM contains the osteological series. In the centre are the skeletons of the large mammalia: whales (including a spermwhale or cachalot, 50 ft. long), hippopotamus, giraffe, rhinoceros, elephant, etc. The elephant, Chunee, was exhibited for many years in England, but becoming unmanageable had at last to be shot. The poor animal did not succumb till more than 100 bullets had been fired into its body. The skeleton numbered 4506 A. is that of the first tiger shot by the Prince of Wales in India in 1876. The skeleton of 'Orlando', a Derby winner, and that of a favourite deerhound of Sir Edwin Landseer, are also exhibited here. The Cases round the room contain smaller skeletons.

Round each of the rooms run two galleries, in which are kept numerous preparations in spirit, etc., including the diseased intestines of Napoleon I. The galleries of the Western Museum are reached by a staircase at the S. end of the room, those of the Eastern by a staircase at the E. end of the room. The galleries of the Middle Room are entered from those of either of the others. A room, entered from the staircase of the Eastern Museum, contains a collection of surgical instruments.

The Museum is conspicuous for its admirable organisation and arrangement. The College also possesses a library of about 35,000 volumes. The Council Room contains a good portrait of Hunter by *Reynolds* and several busts by *Chantrey*.

At No. 13, Lincoln's Inn Fields, N. side, opposite the College of Surgeons, is the **Soane Museum** (Pl. R, 31; *II*), founded by *Sir John Soane* (d.1837), architect of the Bank of England. During April, May, June, July, and August this interesting collection is open to the public on Tues., Wed., Thurs., and Sat., from 11 to 5; in February and March on Tues. and Thurs. only. Strangers are also admitted at other times by tickets obtained from the curator, Mr. Wild. The collection, which is exceedingly diversified in character, occupies 24 rooms, some of which are very small, and is most ingeniously arranged, every corner being turned to account. Among the contents, many of which offer little attraction, are a few good pictures and a number of curiosities of historical or personal interest. A *General Description* of the contents, price 6d., may be had at the Museum.

The DINING ROOM AND LIBRARY, which the visitor first enters, are decorated in the Pompeian style, and contain a large cork-model, showing the state of the excavations at Pompeii as they were in 1820. Above it are a number of plaster models of ancient temples restored. The ceiling paintings are by *Howard*, and the principal subjects are Phœbus in his car, Pandora among the gods, Epimetheus receiving Pandora, and the Opening of Pandora's vase. On the walls are *Reynolds*' Snake in the grass, a replica of the picture at the National Gallery, and a portrait of Sir John Soane, by *Lawrence*. The Greek painted fictile vase at the S. end of the room, 2 ft. 8 in. high, and the vase and chopine on the E. side, all deserve notice.

We now pass through two diminutive rooms into a HALL containing numerous columns and statues. To the right is the PICTURE GALLERY, a room measuring 13 ft. 8 in. in length, 12 ft. 4 in breadth, and 19 ft. 6 in. in height, which, by dint of ingenious arrangement, can accommodate as many pictures as a gallery of the same height, 45 ft. long and 20 ft. broad. The walls are covered with movable shutters, hung with pictures on both sides. Among these are: *Hogarth*, The Election, a series of four pictures; *Canaletto*, Port of Venice, The Rialto at Venice, and The Piazza of St. Mark; Study of a head from one of Raphael's large cartoons, perhaps by *Giulio Romano; Calcott*, Passage Point, a landscape. — When the last shutter of the S. wall is opened we see below us a kind of small chapel with an altar and stained-glass windows, illumined by a yellow light from above, and on a beam above it a copy of a nymph by Westmacott.

From the hall with the columns we descend into a kind of crypt, containing the tombstone of Lady Soane. Here we thread our way to the left through numerous statues, both originals and casts, and relics of ancient art, to the SEPULCHRAL CHAMBER, which contains the most curious object in the whole collection. This is an Egyptian sarcophagus, found in 1817 by Belzoni in a tomb in the valley of Beiban el Maluk, near the ancient Thebes, and consisting of a piece of alabaster or arragonite, 9 ft. 4 in. long, 3 ft. 8 in. wide, and 2 ft. 8 in. deep at the head, covered both internally and externally with hieroglyphics and figures. A light placed in the sarcophagus shines through the alabaster, which is $2^1/_2$ inches in thickness. The hieroglyphics are interpreted as referring to Sethos I., father of Ramses the Great. On the E. side of this, the lower part of the Museum, is the MONUMENT COURT, with an 'architectural pasticcio', showing various styles, in the centre.

The above-mentioned chapel, which is known as the MONK'S PARLOIR, contains objects of mediæval and Renaissance art and some Peruvian antiquities. The *Oratory*, in its N.E. corner, contains a fine Flemish wood-carving of the Crucifixion. The remaining rooms on the ground-floor (to which we now re-ascend) are filled with statuary, architectural fragments, models, and bronzes, among which some fine Roman portrait-busts may be noticed. In the BREAKFAST ROOM are some choice illuminated MSS., including the °Conversion of St. Paul by Giulio Clovio after Raphael, and Stoning of St. Stephen after Giulio Romano, with fine ornamentation. Also a pistol which once belonged to Peter the Great.

The first floor contains, among numerous other articles, the celebrated series of pictures of the Rake's Progress, by *Hogarth* (8 in number), and a carved ivory and gilt table and some chairs from the palace of Tippoo Sahib at Seringapatam. Opposite the windows is a collection of exquisitely delicate miniature paintings on silk, by *Labelle*. In the second room, at the window, is a small but choice collection of antique gems, chiefly from Tarentum. It also contains a landscape by *J. van Ruysdael*; a Seapiece by *Turner*, representing Adm. Tromp's barge entering the Texel; the Cave of Despair, by *Eastlake*; and various architectural designs by Sir John Soane. In the glass-cases in the middle of the room are exhibited the first three folio editions of Shakspeare, an original MS. of Tasso's 'Gerusalemme Liberata', and two sketch-books of Sir Joshua Reynolds. On the second floor are exhibited cork-models of ancient temples, architectural drawings in water-colours, and a few pictures.

The museum also contains a collection of valuable old books and MSS., most of which are only shown to visitors by special permission of the Curator. The most interesting of them are, however, those exhibited on the first floor (see above).

The **Floral Hall** in Bow Street, adjoining the *Royal Italian Opera*, Covent Garden, a Crystal Palace in miniature, will scarcely repay a visit. It is sometimes used for concerts, in connection with the Covent Garden Theatre (p. 40). Nearly opposite is the *New Bow Street Police Court*, the most important of the 17 or 18 metropolitan police courts of London. At the corner of Bow Street and Russell Street was *Will's Coffee House*, the resort of Dryden and other literary men of the 17-18th centuries. In the vicinity, between Catherine Street and Drury Lane, is *Drury Lane Theatre* (p. 40).

**Covent Garden Market** (Pl. R, **31**; *II*), the property of the **Duke of Bedford**, is the principal vegetable, fruit, and flower market in London, and presents an exceedingly picturesque and lively scene. The best time **to** see the vegetable market is about 6 o'clock on the mornings of Tuesdays, **Thursdays,** and Saturdays, the market-days (comp. p. 26). **The show of** fruit and flowers is one of the finest in the world, **presenting a gorgeous** array of colours and diffusing a delicious fragrance; **it is seen to** full advantage from 7 **to 10 a.m. The Easter Eve flower-market is** particularly brilliant.

**The neighbourhood of Covent Garden** is full of historic memories. The name reminds us of the *Convent Garden* belonging **to the monks of Westminster,** which in Ralph Agas's Map of London **(1560) is shown walled** around, and extending from the Strand **to the present Long Acre, then in** the open country. **The** Bedford **family received these lands** (seven acres, **of the** yearly value of 6*l.* 6*s.* 8*d.*) **as a gift from the Crown** in 1552. The square was **planned by Inigo Jones; and vegetables used** to be sold here, **thus perpetuating the** associations **of** the ancient garden. In 1831 the **Duke of Bedford** erected the present market buildings, which have **recently been much** improved. The neighbouring streets, Russell, **Bedford, and** Tavistock, **commemorate the family** names of the **lords of the soil. In** the Covent Garden Piazzas, now nearly all **cleared** away, the families of Lord Crewe, Bishop Berkeley, Lord **Hollis,** Earl of Oxford, Sir Godfrey Kneller, Sir Kenelm Digby, **the Duke** of Richmond, **and** other distinguished persons used to **reside. In this square was the old** 'Bedford Coffee-house', frequented **by Garrick, Foote, and** Hogarth, where the Beef-Steak **Club was held; and here was the not** over savoury 'Old Hummums **Hotel'. Here also was 'Evans's'** (so named from a former proprietor), **a house once the abode of Sir Kenelm** Digby, **and long noted as a place for** suppers **and evening** entertainments. **It is now occupied by a** fashionable club.

**The neighbouring church of St. Paul,** a plain building erected by *Inigo Jones* at the **beginning of the** 17th cent., contains nothing of interest. **It was the first Protestant church** of any **size** erected in London. **In the churchyard are** buried *Samuel Butler* (d. 1680), the author of 'Hudibras'; **Sir Peter** *Lely* (*Vandervaes,* d. 1680), the painter; *W. Wycherley* **(d. 1715),** the dramatist; *Grinling Gibbons* (d. 1721), **the carver in** wood; *T. A. Arne* (d. 1778), the composer; *John Wolcot* **(Peter Pindar; d. 1819),** the author; and *Kynaston,* the actor.

Between Covent Garden and the Strand is old *Maiden Lane,* where Andrew Marvel, the poet, and Turner, the painter once resided, and where Voltaire lodged for some time.

The **Garrick Club**, 13 and 15 Garrick Street, Covent Garden, founded in 1831, possesses an important and valuable collection of portraits of celebrated English actors, shown on Wednesdays only, to visitors accompanied by a member.

## 16. Whitehall.

*United Service Museum. The Horse Guards. The Government Offices.*

The broad street leading from Trafalgar Square, opposite the National Gallery, to the S., towards Westminster, is called **Whitehall** (Pl. R, 26; *IV*), after the famous royal palace of that name formerly situated here, of which the banqueting hall only now remains.

At the beginning of the 13th cent., the Chief Justiciary, Hubert de Burgh, who resided here, presented his house with its contents to the Dominican monks of Holborn, who afterwards sold it to Walter Gray, Archbishop of York. Thenceforward it was the London residence of the Archbishops of York, and was long known as York House or York Palace. On the downfall of Wolsey, Archbishop of York, and favourite of Henry VIII., York House became crown property, and received the name of *Whitehall*: —

> 'Sir, you
> Must no more call it York-place, that is past;
> For, since the cardinal fell, that title's lost;
> 'Tis now the king's, and call'd — Whitehall'.
> *Hen. VIII. iv. 6.*

The palace was greatly enlarged and beautified by its new owner, Henry VIII., and with its precincts became of such extent as to reach from Scotland Yard to near Bridge Street, and from the Thames far into St. James's Park, passing over what was then the narrow street of Whitehall, which it spanned by means of a beautiful gateway designed by Holbein.

The banqueting hall of old York House, built in the Tudor style, having been burned down in 1615, James I. conceived the idea of erecting on its site a magnificent royal residence, designed by *Inigo Jones*. The building was begun, but, at the time of the breaking out of the Civil War, the *Banqueting Hall* only had been completed. In 1691 part of the old palace was burned to the ground, and the remainder in 1697; so that nothing remained of Whitehall, except the new hall, which is still standing (on the E. side of Whitehall). This fine hall, one of the most splendid specimens of the Palladian style of architecture, is 111 ft. long, $55\frac{1}{2}$ ft. wide, and $55\frac{1}{2}$ ft. high. The ceiling is embellished with pictures by *Rubens*, on canvas, painted abroad, at a cost of 3000*l.*, and sent to England. They are in nine sections, and represent the Apotheosis of James I. in the centre, with allegorical representations of peace, plenty, etc., and scenes from the life of Charles I., the artist's patron. Van Dyck was to have executed for the sides a series of mural paintings, representing the history and ceremonies of the Order of the Garter, but the scheme was never carried out.

George I. converted the banqueting-house into a *Royal Chapel*, and as such it is still used. In the lobby may be seen a large sheet showing the **design** by Inigo Jones of the entire palace as projected. On **Maundy Thursday the Queen's** 'eleemosynary bounty' **is distributed here** according to ancient custom. The public are **admitted on** application to the keeper. In *Whitehall Gardens*, **at the back** of Whitehall, stands a bronze statue of James II., by *Grinling Gibbons*, erected in 1686.

The reminiscences of the tragic episodes of English history transacted at Whitehall are much more interesting than the place itself. It was here that Cardinal Wolsey, the haughty, splendour-**loving Archbishop of Y**ork, gave his costly entertainments, and **here he** was **disgraced.** Here, too, Henry VIII. became enamoured of the unhappy Anne Boleyn, **at a** ball given in honour of the fickle and voluptuous monarch; and here he died in 1547. Holbein, the **famous painter,** occupied rooms in the palace at that period. It was from Whitehall that Elizabeth was carried as a prisoner to the Tower, **and to** Whitehall **she returned** in triumph as Queen of England. From an opening made in the wall between the upper **and lower central** windows of the Banqueting Hall (Chapel Royal), **Charles I. was** led out to the scaffold erected in the street close by. **A little later** the Protector Oliver Cromwell took up his residence **here with his** secretary, John Milton, **and here** he died on 3rd Sept., **1658.** Here Charles II., restored, held a profligate court, one of the darkest blots **on** the fame of England, and here he died in 1685. After the destruction of Whitehall Palace by fire in 1697, St. James's Palace became the royal **residence.**

In Whitehall Yard, a little to the N., is the **Royal United Service Museum,** which was founded in 1830 and contains an interesting **collection of objects** connected with the military and **naval professions, and a library.** The institution numbers 4600 **members, each of whom pays** an entrance fee of 1*l*. and a yearly **subscription of the** same amount or a life-subscription of 10*l*. Admission, **by order from a member,** daily, except Sundays and Fridays, 11-5 in **summer,** 11-4 in winter. Soldiers, sailors, and policemen in uniform are admitted without orders. — The *Auditorium,* **or Lecture Theatre,** has seats for about 500 persons.

The vestibule contains **weapons** and martial equipments from America, Africa, the South Sea Islands, **etc.** We then enter the *European Armoury,* containing specimens of **the** armour and weapons of the different European nations. In the glass-cases by the windows are the swords of Cromwell and General Wolfe, a dirk which belonged to Nelson, and other objects interesting from their historical association. The next room is the *Asiatic Armoury,* with Indian guns and armour, etc. — The following three rooms are devoted to the *Naval Collection,* including models of different kinds of vessels, ships' gear, marine machinery, and the like. In the first room is an ingenious little model of a ship, executed by a French prisoner-of-war, hung up (under glass) on one of the pillars. The second naval room contains relics of Franklin's expedition to the N. pole, and others of the Royal George, sunk at Spithead in 1782. The case in the centre contains personal relics of Drake, Nelson, Captain Cook, and other famous seamen. In the centre of the adjoining room, under glass, is a large model of the sea-fight of Trafalgar. — In a room immediately to the right of the entrance are models of ordnance and **specimens of shot and shells**, while an **apartment** beyond this contains a collection of model steam-engines.

The principal room **of the FIRST FLOOR** contains military models of various kinds: siege-operations with trenches, **lines, batteries, approaches,** and walls in which a breach **has been effected; fortifications, pioneer instruments, etc.** The other rooms contain **uniforms and equipments** of soldiers **of different countries**, fire-arms and portions of fire-arms at different **stages of their** manufacture, **and (in cases) various objects of personal interest,** such as the pistols of **Sir Ralph Abercromby, Bolivar, and Tippoo Sahib,** relics of Sir John Moore, etc.

The **SECOND FLOOR contains a** large "Model **of** the battle **of Waterloo,** by *Captain Siborne*, in which 190,000 figures are represented, giving one an admirable idea of the disposition **and** movements **of the forces on the eventful day;** relics of Napoleon **and** Wellington; the skeleton of Napoleon's charger, Marengo; *Hamilton's* **model of** Sebastopol, showing **the** position of the troops; the stuffed figure of **Bob,** the dog of **the** Scotch Fusilier Guards; trophies from the **Crimean war and from the last campaign in China.**

**Whitehall** and the neighbourhood now contain various public offices. Near Charing Cross, to the left, in *Great Scotland Yard*, is the headquarters of the Metropolitan Police; it contains in one section the 'Black Museum', a motley collection of objects connected with crime and criminals. Scotland Yard is said to have belonged to the kings of Scotland (whence its name) from the reign of Edgar to that of Henry II. At a later period, Milton, Inigo Jones, Sir Christopher Wren, and other celebrated persons resided here. Opposite, on the right side of Whitehall, is the *Admiralty*. Below the Admiralty is the **Horse Guards,** the office of the commander-in-chief of the army, an inconsiderable building with a low clock-tower, erected in 1753 on the site of an old Tilt Yard. It derives its name from its original use as a guard-house for the palace of Whitehall. Two mounted Life Guards are posted here as sentinels every day from 10 a.m. to 4 p.m., and the operation of relieving guard, which takes place hourly, is interesting. At 11 a.m. the troop of 40 Life Guards on duty is relieved by another troop, when a good opportunity is afforded of seeing a number of these fine soldiers together. The infantry sentries on the other side of the Horse Guards, in St. James's Park, are also changed at 11 a.m. A passage, much frequented by pedestrians, leads through the Horse Guards into St. James's Park, but no carriages except those of royalty and **of a few** privileged persons are permitted to pass.

The **Treasury,** a building 100 yds. in length, situated between the Horse Guards and Downing Street, originally erected during the reign of George I. and provided by Sir Charles Barry with a new façade, is the office of the *Prime Minister (First Lord of the Treasury)* and also contains the *Education Office*, the *Privy Council Office*, and the *Board of Trade*. The *Office of the Chancellor of the Exchequer* occupies a separate edifice in Downing Street.

To the S., between Downing Street and Charles Street, rise the

### 16. MINISTERIAL OFFICES.

new Public Offices, a large pile of buildings in the Italian style constructed in 1868-73 at a cost of 500,000l., from designs by Sir G. G. Scott (d. 1878). They comprise the *Home Office*, the *Foreign Office*, the *Colonial Office*, and the **India Office**. The handsomely furnished and **decorated** apartments of **the F**oreign and India Offices are shown to visitors on Fridays from 12 to 3, on application to the porter. — The **effect of the** imposing façade towards Parliament Street (the southern prolongation of Whitehall) has been greatly enhanced by **the** widening **of the** street to 50 yds., whereby, too, a view of Westminster **Abbey from** Whitehall is disclosed; but the removal of the **W. side of Parliament** Street will be necessary for **the full realisation of this effect.**

The *East India Museum*, a rich collection of Indian products and manufactures, formerly exhibited in the India Office, has been removed to South Kensington (see p. 289).

The modern edifice on the E. side of **Whitehall, in the Franco-**Scottish Renaissance style, is *Montague House*, the mansion of the Duke of Buccleuch, containing a splendid collection of miniatures and many valuable pictures.

No. 2 *Whitehall Gardens*, to the N. of Montague House, **was the** home of Benjamin Disraeli (Lord Beaconsfield) in 1873-5. No. 4 was the townhouse of Sir Robert Peel, whither he was carried to die after falling from his horse in Constitution Hill (June 29th, 1850).

## 17. Houses of Parliament and Westminster Hall.
### St. Margaret's Church. Westminster Bridge.

The *****Houses of Parliament, or** New Palace of Westminster (Pl. R, 25; *IV*), which, together with Westminster Hall, form a single pile of buildings, have been erected since 1840, from a plan by *Sir Charles Barry*, which was selected as the best of 97 sent in for competition. The previous edifice was burned down in 1834. The new building is in the richest late-Gothic (**Tudor** or Perpendicular) style, and cove**rs an area of** 8 **acres. It contains 11** courts, 100 staircases, and 1100 apartments, and **has** cost in all about 3,000,000l. Although so **costly a** national structure, some serious defects are observable: **the external stone is** gradually crumbling, and the **building** stands on so low **a level** that the basement **rooms are** said to be lower **than the Thames at high** tide. The *Clock* **Tower** *(St. Stephen's* ***Tower)***, at the N. end, next to Westminster Bridge, **is 318 ft.** high; **the** *Middle Tower* is 300 ft. high; and the S.W. *Victoria Tower*, **the largest of the** three, through which the Queen **enters** on the opening **and** prorogation **of** Parliament, attains a **height of** 340 ft. The large clock has four dials, each 23 ft. in diameter, and it takes five hours to wind up the striking parts. The great Bell of the Clock Tower, popularly known as 'Big Ben' (named **after** Sir Benjamin Hall, Chief Commissioner of Works at the time **of its erection) is one of the** largest known, weighing no less

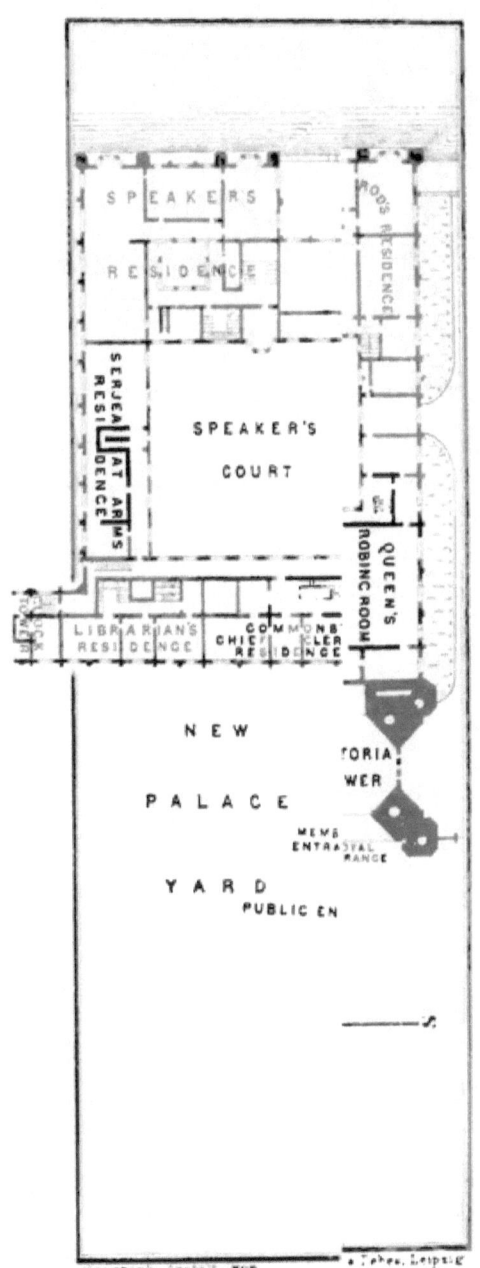

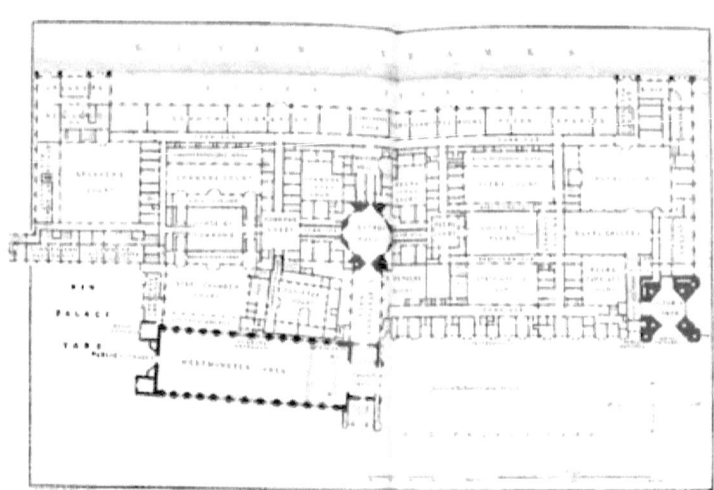

## 17. HOUSES OF PARLIAMENT.

than 13 tons. It was soon found to have a flaw or crack, and its tone became shrill, but the crack was filed open, so as to prevent vibration, and the tone became quite pure. It is heard in calm weather over the greater part of London. The imposing river front (E.) of the edifice is 940 ft. in length. It is adorned with statues of the English monarchs from William the Conqueror down to Queen Victoria, with armorial bearings, and many other enrichments. — The old Law Courts, on the W. side, have been removed.

The impression produced by the interior is in its way no less imposing than that of the exterior. The tasteful fitting up of the different rooms, some of which are adorned down to the minutest details with lavish magnificence, is in admirable keeping with the office and dignity of the building.

The Houses of Parliament are shown on Saturdays from 10 to 4, by tickets obtained gratis at the office of the *Lord Chamberlain*, to the E. of Victoria Tower. We enter on the W. side by a door adjacent to the Victoria Tower (public entrance also through Westminster Hall).

Police-constables, stationed in each room, hurry visitors through the building in a most uncomfortable fashion, scarcely giving time for more than a glance at the objects of interest. The crypt is not now shown. Handbook 1s. (unnecessary).

Ascending the staircase from the entrance door, we first reach the *Norman Porch*, a small square hall, with Gothic groined vaulting, and borne by a finely clustered central pillar. We next enter (to the right) the QUEEN'S ROBING ROOM, a handsome chamber, 45 ft. in length, the chief feature in which is formed by the fresco paintings by *Mr. Dyce*, representing the virtues of chivalry, the subjects being taken from the Legend of King Arthur. Above the fireplace the three virtues illustrated are Courtesy, Religion, and Generosity; on the N. side are Hospitality and Mercy. The fine dado panelling with carvings illustrative of Arthurian legends, the rich ceiling, the fireplace, the doors, the flooring, and the state chair at the E. end of the room are all worthy of notice. Next comes the ROYAL or VICTORIA GALLERY, 110 ft. long, through which the Queen, issuing from the Queen's Robing Room on the S., proceeds in solemn procession to the House of Peers, for the purpose of opening or proroguing Parliament. On these occasions privileged persons are admitted into this hall by orders obtained at the Lord Chamberlain's Office (see above). The pavement consists of fine mosaic work; the ceiling is panelled and richly gilt. The sides are adorned with two large frescoes in water-glass by *Maclise*; on the left, Death of Nelson at Trafalgar (comp. p. 145), and on the right, Meeting of Blücher and Wellington after Waterloo.

The PRINCE'S CHAMBER, the smaller apartment entered on quitting the Victoria Gallery, is a model of simple magnificence, being decorated with dark wood in the style for which the middle ages are famous. Opposite the door is a group in marble by *Gibson*.

representing Queen Victoria enthroned, with allegorical figures of Clemency and Justice. The stained-glass windows on the W. and E. exhibit the rose, thistle, and shamrock, the emblems of England, **Scotland**, and Ireland. Above, in the panels of the handsome **wainscot**, is a series of portraits of English monarchs and their relatives of the Tudor period (1485-1603).

These are as follows, beginning to the left of the entrance door: 1. Louis XII. of France; 2. Mary, daughter of Henry VII. of England and **wife** of Louis; 3. Charles Brandon, Duke of Suffolk, Mary's second husband; 4. Marquis of Dorset; 5. Lady Jane Grey; 6. Lord Guildford Dudley, her husband; 7. James IV. of Scotland; 8. Queen Margaret, daughter of Henry VII. of England and wife of James (through this princess the Stuarts derived their title to the English throne); 9. Earl of Angus, second **husband of Margaret, and** Regent of Scotland; 10. James V.; 11. Mary of **Guise, wife of James V., and** mother of Mary Stuart; 12. Queen Mary Stuart; **13. Francis II. of** France, Mary Stuart's first husband; 14. Lord Darnley, **her second husband;** 15. Henry VII.; 16. Elizabeth, daughter **of** Edward IV., **and wife of Henry** (this marriage put an end to the Wars of the **Roses, by uniting the** Houses of York and Lancaster); **17. Arthur,** Prince **of Wales; 18. Catharine** of Arragon; 19. Henry VIII.; 20. Anne Boleyn; **21. Jane Seymour; 22.** Anne of Cleves; 23. Catharine Howard; 24. **Catharine Parr; 25. Edward VI.;** 26. Queen Mary of England; 27. **Philip of Spain, her husband; 28. Queen Elizabeth.**

Over these portraits **runs a frieze with oak** leaves and acorns **and the armorial bearings of the** English sovereigns since the Conquest; **below, in the sections of the** panelling, are 12 reliefs in oak, **representing events in English** history (Tudor period).

Two doors lead from this room into the *HOUSE OF PEERS, which is sumptuously **decorated in the** richest Gothic style. The oblong **chamber, in** which the peers **of** England sit in council, is 90 ft. in **length 45 ft.** broad, and 45 ft. high. The floor is almost entirely occupied, with the **red leather** benches of the 434 members. The **twelve fine** stained-glass **windows** contain portraits of all the kings and **queens of** England since the Conquest. At night the House is lighted **from** the **outside through** these windows. Eighteen niches between the windows are **occupied** by statues of **the** barons who extorted the Magna **Charta from King John.** The **very** handsome walls and ceiling are decorated **with heraldic and other** emblems.

Above, **in recesses at the upper and** lower ends of the room, are six frescoes, the **first attempts on a large** scale of modern English art in this department **of** painting. That on the wall above the throne, in the centre, represents the Baptism of King Ethelbert (about 596), by *Dyce;* to the left of it, Edward III. **investing** his son, the 'Black Prince', with the Order of the Garter; **on the** right, Henry, son of Henry IV., acknowledging the authority of Judge Gascoigne, who had committed the Prince to prison for striking him, both by *Cope.* — Opposite, at the N. end of the chamber, three **symbolical** pictures of the Spirits of Religion, Justice, and Chivalry, the first by *Horsley,* the other two by *Maclise.*

At the S. **end of** the hall, raised by a few **steps,** and covered **with a richly** gilded canopy, **is the** magnificent throne of the Queen. **On the** right of it is the lower throne of the Prince of Wales, **while** on the left is that intended for the sovereign's consort. At the sides are two large gilt candelabra.

The celebrated woolsack of the Lord Chancellor, a kind of

cushioned ottoman, stands in front of the throne, almost in the centre of the hall. — At the N. end of the chamber, opposite the throne, **is the** *Bar*, **where** official communications from the Commons to the Lords are delivered, and where law-suits on final appeal are pleaded. Above the Bar are the galleries for the reporters and for strangers. Above the throne on either side are seats for foreign ambassadors and other distinguished visitors.

From the House of Lords we pass **into the** PEERS' LOBBY, another rectangular apartment, richly **fitted up, with a door on** each side. The brass foliated wings of the southern door are well worthy of examination. The corners **contain elegant candelabra of brass.** The encaustic tiled pavement, with a fine enamel inlaid **with brass in the** centre, is of great **beauty. Each peer has in this lobby his own hat-peg,** etc., provided with **his name.**

The door on the left (W.) side leads into the PEERS' ROBING ROOM (not always shown), which is decorated with frescoes by *Herbert*. Two only have been finished (Moses bringing the Tables of the Law from Sinai, and the Judgment of Daniel).

The door on the N. side opens on the PEERS' CORRIDOR, the way to the Central Hall and the House of Commons. This corridor is embellished with the following eight frescoes (beginning on the left): —
1. Burial of Charles I. (beheaded 1649); 2. Expulsion of the Fellows of a college at Oxford for refusing to subscribe to the Covenant; 3. Defence of Basing House by the Cavaliers against the Roundheads; 4. Charles I. erecting his **standard at Nottingham; 5. Speaker Lenthall** vindicating the rights **of the House of Commons against Charles I. on his attempt to arrest the five members; 6. Departure of the London train-bands to the relief of** Gloucester; **7. Embarkment of the Pilgrim Fathers for New England;** 8. Lady Russell **taking leave of her husband before his execution.**

The spacious \*CENTRAL HALL, in the middle of the building, is octagonal in shape, and richly decorated. It is 60 ft. in diameter and 75 ft. high. The surfaces of the stone-vaulting, between the massive and richly embossed ribs, are inlaid with Venetian mosaics, representing in frequent repetition the heraldic emblems of the English crown, *viz.* the rose, shamrock, thistle, portcullis, and harp. Lofty portals lead from this hall into (N.) the Corridor to the House of Commons; to (W.) St. Stephen's Hall; to (E.) the Waiting-Hall (see below); and (S.) the House of Peers (see above). Above the last door is a representation, in glass mosaic, of St. George, by *Poynter*. Here, too, are **statues of Lord John Russell (d. 1878) and Lord Iddesleigh (d. 1887).**

The niches at the **sides of** the portals bear statues **of** English sovereigns. At the W. door: **on the** left, **Edward I.,** his consort Eleanor, and **Edward II.; on the** right, Isabella, **wife** of King **John,** Henry III., and **Eleanor, his wife. At the N. door: on the** left, Isabella, wife of Edward II., Henry IV., **and Edward III.; on the right, Richard II., his** consort, Anne **of Bohemia, and Philippa,** wife of Edward III. At the E. **door: on the** left, **Jane** of Navarre, wife of Henry IV., Henry V., **and** his wife Catharine; on the right, Henry **VI.,** Margaret, his wife, and Edward VI. At the S .door **on the left, Elizabeth,** wife **of Edward IV., Edward V., and Richard III.; on the right,** Anne, wife of Richard III., Henry VII., and his consort **Elizabeth.** The niches in the windows are filled with similar statues.

## 17. HOUSES OF PARLIAMENT.

Round the handsome mosaic pavement runs the inscription (in the Latin of the Vulgate), 'Except the Lord keep the house, their labour is but lost that build it'.

A door on the E. side of the Central Hall leads to the HALL OF THE POETS, also called the UPPER WAITING HALL (not always shown). It contains the following frescoes of scenes from English poetry: — Griselda's first trial of patience, from Chaucer, by *Cope*; St. George conquering the Dragon, from Spenser, by *Watts*; King Lear disinheriting his daughter Cordelia, from Shakspeare, by *Herbert*; Satan touched by the spear of Ithuriel, from Milton, by *Horsley*; St. Cecilia, from Dryden, by *Tenniel*; Personification of the Thames, from Pope, by *Armitage*; Death of Marmion, from Scott, by *Armitage*; Death of Lara, from Byron, by *W. Dyce*.

Beyond the N. door of the Central Hall, and corresponding with the passage leading to the House of Lords in the opposite direction, is the COMMONS' CORRIDOR, leading to the House of Commons. It is also adorned with 8 frescoes, as follows (beginning on the left): — 1. Alice Lisle concealing fugitive Cavaliers after the battle of Sedgemoor; 2. Last sleep of the Duke of Argyll; 3. The Lords and Commons delivering the crown to William and Mary in the Banqueting Hall; 4. Acquittal of the Seven Bishops in the reign of James II. (comp. p. 190); 5. Monk declaring himself in favour of a free parliament; 6. Landing of Charles II.; 7. The executioner hanging Wishart's book round the neck of Montrose; 8. Jane Lane helping Charles II. to escape.

We next pass through the COMMONS' LOBBY to the —

HOUSE OF COMMONS, 75 ft. in length, 45 ft. wide, and 41 ft. high, very substantially and handsomely fitted up with oak-panelling, in a simpler and more business-like style than the House of Lords. The present ceiling, which hides the original one, was constructed to improve the lighting and ventilation. The members of the House (670 in number, though seats are provided for 476 only) enter either by the public approach, or by a private entrance through a side-door to the E. of Westminster Hall and along an arcade between this hall and the Star Chamber Court. The twelve stained glass windows are adorned with the armorial bearings of parliamentary boroughs. In the evening the House is lighted through the glass panels of the ceiling. The seat of the Speaker or president is at the N. end of the chamber, in a straight line with the woolsack in the House of Lords. The benches to the right of the Speaker are the recognised seats of the Government Party; the ministers occupy the first bench. On the left of the Speaker are the members forming the Opposition, the leaders of which also take their seats on the first bench.

In front of the Speaker's table is the Clerks' table, on which lies the *Mace*. The Reporters' Gallery is above the speaker, while above it again, behind an iron grating, are the seats for ladies.

At the S. end of the House, opposite the Speaker, are the galleries for strangers. The upper, or Strangers' Gallery, can be visited by an order from a Member of Parliament. To the lower,

## 17. HOUSES OF PARLIAMENT.

or Speaker's Gallery, **admission is granted only on the Speaker's order**, obtained by a member. The row of seats in front of the Speaker's Gallery is appropriated to members of the peerage and to distinguished strangers. The galleries at the sides of the House are for the use of members, and are considered to form part of the House.

The seats underneath the galleries, on a level with the floor of the House, but outside the bar, are appropriated to members of the diplomatic corps and to distinguished strangers.

Permission to be present at the debates of the Lower House can be obtained only from a member of parliament. The House of Lords, when sitting as a Court of Appeal, is open to the public; on other occasions a peer's order is necessary. On each side of the House of Commons is a '*Division Lobby*', into which the members pass, when a vote is taken, for the purpose of being counted. The '*Ayes*', or those who are favourable to the motion, retire into the W. lobby, to the right of the Speaker; the '*Noes*', or those who vote against the motion, retire into the E. lobby, to the Speaker's left.

Returning to the Central Hall we pass through the door at its western (right) extremity, leading to ST. STEPHEN'S HALL, which is 75 ft. long, 30 ft. broad, and 55 ft. high. It occupies the site of old St. Stephen's Chapel, founded in 1330, and long used for meetings of the Commons. Along the walls are marble statues of celebrated English statesmen: on the left (S.), Hampden, Selden, Sir Robert Walpole, Lord Chatham, his son Pitt, and the Irish orator Grattan; on the right (N.), Lord Clarendon, Lord Falkland, Lord Somers, Lord Mansfield, Fox, and Burke. The niches at the sides of the doors are occupied by statues of English sovereigns. By the E. door: on the left, Matilda, Henry II., Eleanor; on the right, Richard Cœur de Lion, Berengaria, and John. By the W. door: on the left, William the Conqueror, Matilda, William II; on the right, Henry I. Beauclerc, Matilda, and Stephen.

A broad flight of steps leads hence through St. Stephen's Porch (62 ft. in height), passing a large stained-glass window, and turning to the right, to *Westminster Hall*.

The present **Westminster Hall** is part of the ancient Palace of Westminster founded by the Anglo-Saxon kings, and occupied by their successors down to Henry VIII. The hall was begun by William Rufus, son of the Conqueror, in 1097, continued and extended by Henry III. and Edward I., and almost totally destroyed by fire in 1291. Edward II. afterwards began to rebuild it; and in 1398 Richard II. caused it to be remodelled and enlarged, supplying it with a new roof. It is one of the largest halls in the world with a wooden ceiling unsupported by columns. Its length is 290 ft., breadth 68 ft., and height 92 ft. The oaken roof, with its hammer-beams, repaired in 1820 with the wood of an old vessel in

## 17. HOUSES OF PARLIAMENT.

Portsmouth Harbour, is considered a masterpiece of timber architecture, both in point of beauty and constructive skill.

Westminster Hall, which now forms a vestibule to the Houses of Parliament, is rich in interesting historical associations. In it were held some of the earliest English parliaments, one of which declared Edward II. to have forfeited the crown; and by a curious fatality the first scene of public importance in the new hall, as restored or rebuilt by Richard II., was the deposition of that unfortunate monarch. In this hall the English monarchs down to George IV. gave their coronation festivals; and here Edward III. entertained the captive kings, David of Scotland and John of France. Here Charles I. was condemned to death; and here, a few years later (1653), Cromwell, wearing the royal purple lined with ermine, and holding a golden sceptre in one hand and the Bible in the other, was saluted as Lord Protector. Within eight years afterwards the Protector's body was rudely dragged from its resting-place in Westminster Abbey and thrust into a pit at Tyburn, while his head was exposed with those of Bradshaw and Ireton on the pinnacles of this same Westminster Hall, where it remained for 30 years. A high wind at last carried it to the ground. After some years the family of the sentry who picked it up sold it to one of the Russells, a distant descendant of Cromwell, and it passed finally into the possession of Dr. Wilkinson, one of whose descendants, living at Sevenoaks, Kent, is said now to possess it. There is some evidence, however, to the effect that the Protector's body, after its exhumation, was buried in Red Lion Square, and that another, substituted for it, was deprived of its head and buried at Tyburn. Either story serves to illustrate the horrible barbarity of that unhappy juncture.

Many other famous historical characters were condemned to death in Westminster Hall, including William Wallace, the brave champion of Scotland's liberties; Sir John Oldcastle, better known as Lord Cobham; Sir Thomas More; the Protector Somerset; Sir Thomas Wyatt; Robert Devereux, Earl of Essex; Guy Fawkes; and the Earl of Strafford. Among other notable events transacted at Westminster Hall was the acquittal of the Seven Bishops, who had been committed to the Tower for their opposition to the illegal dispensing power of James II.; the condemnation of the Scotch lords Kilmarnock, Balmerino, and Lovat; the trial of Lord Byron (grand-uncle of the poet) for killing Mr. Chaworth in a duel; the condemnation of Lord Ferrars for murdering his valet; and the acquittal of Warren Hastings, after a trial which (including numerous postponements) had lasted seven years.

The last public festival held in Westminster Hall was at the coronation of George IV., when the King's champion in full armour rode into the hall, and, according to ancient custom, threw his gauntlet on the floor, challenging to mortal combat anyone who might

## 17. ST. MARGARET'S CHURCH.

dispute the title of the sovereign. The ceremony of swearing in the Lord Mayor took place here for the last time in 1882, and is now performed in the new Law Courts (p. 139).

On the E. side of the hall are placed the following marble statues (beginning from the left): Mary, wife of William III., James I., Charles I., Charles II., William III., George IV., William IV.

From the first landing of the staircase leading to St. Stephen's Hall a narrow door to the left (E.) leads to ST. STEPHEN'S CRYPT (properly the *Church of St. Mary's Undercroft;* not now shown), a low vaulted structure supported by columns, measuring 90 ft. in length, 28 ft. in breadth, and 20 ft. in height. It was erected by King Stephen, rebuilt by Edwards II. and III., and, after having long fallen to decay, has recently been thoroughly restored and richly decorated with painting and gilding. *St. Stephen's Cloisters*, on the E. side of Westminster Hall, were built by Henry VIII. and have been lately restored. They are beautifully adorned with carving, groining, and tracery, but are not open to the public. The other multifarious portions of this immense pile of buildings include 18 or 20 official residences of various sizes, libraries, committee rooms, and dining, refreshment, and smoking rooms. The number of statues, outside and inside, is about five hundred.

On the W. side of Westminster Hall, and to the N. of the Abbey, stands St. Margaret's Church (Pl. R, 25; *IV*), which, down to 1858, used to be attended by the House of Commons in state on four days in the year, as then prescribed in the Prayer Book. It was erected in the time of Edward I. on the site of an earlier church built by Edward the Confessor in 1064, and was greatly altered and improved under Edward IV. The stained-glass window of the Crucifixion at the E. end was executed at Gouda in Holland, and is said to have been a gift from the town of Dordrecht to Henry VII. Henry VIII. presented it to Waltham Abbey. At the time of the Commonwealth it was concealed, and after various vicissitudes it was at length purchased in 1758 by the churchwardens of St. Margaret's for 400*l.*, and placed in its present position. William Caxton, whose printing-press was set up in 1476-77 in the almonry, formerly standing near the W. front of Westminster Abbey, was buried here in 1491. From the fact of a chapel existing in the old almonry, printers' work-shops and also guildmeetings of printers are still called 'chapels'. Sir Walter Raleigh, who was executed in front of the palace of Westminster in 1618, was buried in the chancel. The church, the interior of which has been lately restored, is open daily, 9-1 and 2-4.30, except Sat. afternoon (entr. by the E. or vestry door, facing Westminster Hall).

At the E. end of the S. aisle is a stained-glass window placed here by the printers in 1882 in memory of Caxton, containing his portrait, with the Venerable Bede on his right and Erasmus on his left. On a tablet below the window is a verse by Tennyson, referring to Caxton's motto,

'Fiat lux'. Adjacent is a brass memorial of Raleigh. The large and handsome window over the W. door was put up by Americans to the memory of Sir Walter Raleigh in 1882; it contains portraits of Raleigh and several of his distinguished contemporaries, and also scenes connected with the life of Raleigh and the colonisation of America. The poetic inscription on the Raleigh window was written by Mr. J. Russell Lowell. There are also windows in the S. wall in memory of Lord and Lady Hatherley, Sir **Thomas Erskine** May (d. 1886), the great authority on Constitutional Law, etc., **and also one** erected in 1887 in memory of Queen Victoria's Jubilee, **with an** inscription by Browning. The window at the W. end of the S. **aisle** commemorates Lord Frederick Cavendish, assassinated at Dublin in 1882. At the W. end of the N. aisle is a memorial window (erected by Mr. G. W. Childs) to **John** Milton, whose second wife and infant child are buried here and w**hose** banns are in the parish register; the inscription is by Whittier. In the N. wall is a window to Admiral Blake (d. 1657), 'chief founder of England's naval supremacy', who was buried in St. Margaret's churchyard after being exhumed from Westminster Abbey. Besides Raleigh and **Caxton, the** church shelters the remains of Skelton (d. 1529), the satirist, **and James** Harrington (d. 1677), author of 'Oceana'. Some of the old monuments **are** interesting.

In **Old Palace Yard**, **to** the S., between the **Houses of Parliament** and Westminster Abbey, rises an *Equestrian Statue of Richard* **Coeur de Lion, in** bronze, by *Marochetti*.

To **the N.** of St. Margaret's, in Parliament Square, opposite the **entrance** into New Palace Yard, stands the bronze *Statue of the Earl of Derby* (d. 1869), in the robes of a peer, 10 ft. high, by *Noble*, **erected in** 1874. The granite pedestal bears four reliefs in bronze, representing his career as a statesman. A little to the spectator's right **is a** bronze statue of *Lord Palmerston* (d. 1865), and on the N. side of the square is that of *Sir Robert Peel* (d. 1850). On the W. side of the square is the bronze *Statue of Canning* (d. 1827), by *Westmacott*, near which, at the corner of Great George Street, is a handsome Gothic fountain, erected in 1865 as a memorial to the distinguished men who brought about the abolition of slavery in **the** British dominions. On the S. side is a bronze *Statue of Lord Beaconsfield* (d. 1881), in the robes of the Garter, by *Raggi*, **unveiled** in April, 1883.

The visitor should not quit this spot without a glance at *King Street*, the only thoroughfare in earlier times, before Parliament Street was **made**, from Whitehall to Westminster. At the North **end of this** street, demolished to make room for the new Government **Offices, stood Holbein's** great gate. Spenser, the poet, spent his last days in this street, and he was carried hence to Westminster Abbey. Cromwell's mother lived here, often visited by her affectionate son; so did Dr. Sydenham, Lord North, Bishop Goodman, and at one time Oliver Cromwell himself. Through this street, humble as it now looks, all the pageants from Whitehall to the Abbey and Westminster Hall passed, whether for burial, coronation, or state trials. Parliament Street was only opened in 1732, long after Whitehall had ceased to be a royal residence, and was carried through the old privy garden of Whitehall.

\***Westminster Bridge** (Pl. R, 29; *IV*), erected in 1856-62, by

*Page*, at a cost of 250,000*l*., on the site of an earlier stone bridge, is 1160 ft. long and 85 ft. broad (carriage-way 53 ft., side-walks each 15 ft.). It consists of seven iron arches borne by granite buttresses, the central arch having a span of 120 ft., the others of 114 ft. The bridge is one of the handsomest in London, and affords an admirable view of the Houses of Parliament. It was the view from this bridge that suggested Wordsworth's fine sonnet, beginning 'Earth has not anything to show more fair'. Below the bridge, on the left bank, is the beginning of the *Victoria Embankment* (p. 113); above, on the right bank, is the *Albert Embankment*, with the extensive *Hospital of St. Thomas* (p. 297).

## 18. Westminster Abbey.

*Westminster Column. Westminster School. Westminster Hospital. Royal Aquarium.*

On the low ground on the left bank of the Thames, where Westminster Abbey now stands, once overgrown with thorns and surrounded by water, and therefore called *Thorney Isle*, a church is said to have been erected in honour of St. Peter by the Anglo-Saxon king Sebert about 616. With the church was connected a Benedictine religious house *(monasterium,* or *minster)*, which, in reference to its position to the W. of the Cistercian Abbey of St. Mary of the Graces (Eastminster; see p. 125), was called **Westminster Abbey** (Pl. R, 25; *IV*).

The church, after having been destroyed by the Danes, appears to have been re-erected by King Edgar in 985. The regular establishment of the Abbey, however, may be ascribed to Edward the Confessor, who built a church here which seems to have been almost as large as the present one (1049-65). The Abbey was entirely rebuilt in the latter half of the 13th cent. by Henry III. and his son Edward I., who left it substantially in its present condition, though important alterations and additions were made in the two succeeding centuries. The Chapel of Henry VII. was erected by that monarch at the beginning of the 16th cent., and the towers were added by Sir C. Wren and Hawkesmore in 1722-40. At the Reformation the Abbey, which had been richly endowed by the liberality of former kings, shared in the general fate of the religious houses: its property was confiscated, and the church converted into the cathedral of a bishopric, which lasted only from 1540 to 1550. Under Queen Mary the monks returned, but Elizabeth restored the arrangements of Henry VIII., and conveyed the Abbey to a Dean, who presided over a chapter of 12 Canons. — The title Archbishop of Westminster, recently created by the Pope, is not officially recognised in England.

Westminster Abbey †, with its royal burial-vaults and long series

---

† The best guide to Westminster Abbey is the *Deanery Guide* (illustrated) of the *Pall Mall Gazette* (price 6 d.)

## 18. WESTMINSTER ABBEY.

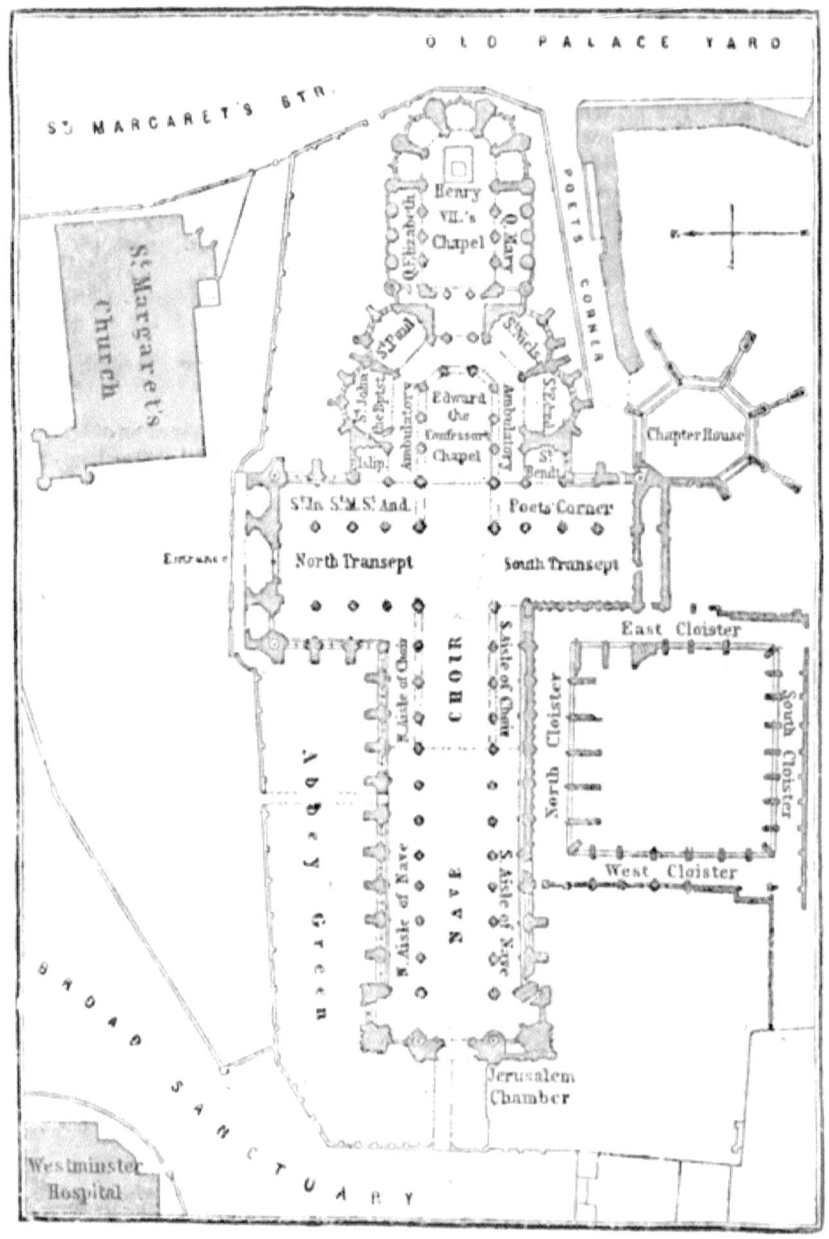

of monuments to celebrated men, is not unreasonably regarded by the English as their national Walhalla, or Temple of Fame; and interment within its walls is considered the last and greatest honour which the nation can bestow on the most deserving of her offspring. The honour has often, however, been conferred on persons unworthy of it, and even on children.

'The spaciousness and gloom of this vast edifice produce a profound and mysterious awe. We step cautiously and softly about, as if fearful of disturbing the hallowed silence of the tomb; while every footfall whispers along the walls, and chatters among the sepulchres, making us more sensible of the quiet we have interrupted. It seems as if the awful nature of the place presses down upon the soul, and hushes the beholder into noiseless reverence. We feel that we are surrounded by the congregated bones of the great men of past times, who have filled history with their deeds, and the earth with their renown'. — *Washington Irving*.

The church is in the form of a Latin cross. The much admired chapel at the E. end is in the Perpendicular style. The other parts of the church, with the exception of the unpleasing and incongruous W. towers by Wren, and a few doubtful Norman remains, are Early English. The impression produced by the interior is very striking, owing to the harmony of the proportions, the richness of the colouring, and the beauty of the Purbeck marble columns and of the triforium. In many respects, however, the effect is sadly marred by restorations and by the egregiously bad taste displayed in several of the monuments. The choir extends beyond the transept into the nave, from which it is separated by an iron screen. In front of the altar is a curious old mosaic pavement with tasteful arabesques, brought from Rome in 1268 by Abbot Ware. The fine wood-work of the choir was executed in 1848. The organ was entirely rebuilt by Mr. Hill in 1884, and stands at the two extremities of the screen between the choir and the nave. The very elaborate and handsome reredos, erected in 1867, is chiefly composed of red and white alabaster. The large figures in the niches represent Moses, St. Peter, St. Paul, and David. The recess above the table contains a fine Venetian glass mosaic, by *Salviati*, representing the Last Supper. In the S. bay of the sanctuary is a portrait of Richard II. on panel, formerly in the Jerusalem Chamber, the oldest contemporary representation of an English sovereign. Behind it is some old tapestry from Westminster School, with the names of Westminster scholars painted on its ends. The Abbey, or, as it is officially termed, the Collegiate Church of St. Peter, is now decorated with upwards of 20 stained-glass windows.

The total length of the church, including the chapel of Henry VII., is 513 ft.; length of the transept from N. to S., 200 ft.; breadth of nave and aisles, 75 ft., of transept, 80 ft.; height of the church, 102 ft., of towers, 225 ft.

The **Abbey** may be entered by the door in the N. transept, near St. Margaret's Church, by the principal portal at the W. end, or by the door in the Poets' Corner or S. transept. The nave, aisles, and transept are open gratis to the public daily (Sundays excepted), except during the hours of divine service, till 4 p.m. in winter and 6 p.m. in summer. Daily service at 8.30 (8 on Sun.), 10, and 3 o'clock. In summer there is a special Sunday service in the nave at 7 p.m. A charge of 6d. (except on Mondays and Tuesdays) is made for admission to the chapels, which are only shown to visitors accompanied by a verger. As the verger announces with a loud voice when he is about to conduct a party round the chapels, the visitor may continue to inspect the other parts of the Abbey until thus summoned. Visitors are cautioned against accepting the useless services of any of the numerous loiterers outside the church.

The following list of the most interesting monuments which do not invariably imply interment in the Abbey, begins with the N. transept, and continues through the N. aisle, the S. aisle, and the S. transept (Poets' Corner), after which we enter the chapels.

## N. Transept.

On the right, *William Pitt, Lord Chatham*, the statesman (d. 1778), a large monument by *Bacon*. Above, in a niche, Chatham is represented in an oratorical attitude, with his right hand outstretched; at his feet are sitting two female figures, Wisdom and Courage; in the centre, Britannia with a trident; to the right and left, Earth and Sea. — Opposite —

L. *John Holles, Duke of Newcastle* (d. 1711); large monument by *Bird*, in a debased style. The sarcophagus bears the semi-recumbent figure of the Duke; to the right is Truth with her mirror, on the left, Wisdom; above, on the columns and over the armorial bearings, Genii. — Adjacent —

L. *\*George Canning*, the statesman (d. 1827); statue by *Chantrey*. — Adjacent, his son —

L. *Charles John, Viscount Canning*, Governor-General of India (d. 1862), statue by *Foley*.

Close by is their relative, *Viscount Stratford de Redcliffe* (d. 1880), long British ambassador in Constantinople; statue by *Boehm*, with an epitaph by Tennyson.

Adjacent, *Lord Beaconsfield* (d. 1881), statue by *Boehm*.

R. *Lord Palmerston*, the statesman (d. 1865); statue by *Jackson*, in the costume of a Knight of the Garter. — Adjoining —

R. *William Bayne, William Blair,* and *Lord Manners*, naval officers who 'were mortally wounded in the course of the naval engagements under the command of Admiral Sir George Brydges Rodney on the 9th and 12th of April, 1782', by *Nollekens*.

L. *William Cavendish, Duke of Newcastle* (d. 1676), and his wife; a double sarcophagus, with recumbent figures in the costume of the period, under a rich canopy. — Adjacent —

L. *Sir John Malcolm*, General (d. 1833), one of the chief promoters of the English power in India; statue by *Chantrey*.

L. *\*Sir Peter Warren*, Admiral (d. 1752), by *Roubiliac*. Hercules places the bust of the Admiral on a pedestal, while Navigation looks on with mournful admiration. — Opposite —

R. *Robert, Marquis of Londonderry and Viscount Castlereagh*, the statesman (d. 1822); statue by *Thomas*. The scroll in his hand bears the (now scarcely legible) inscription, 'Peace of Paris, 1814'. Next to it —

L. *\*William, Lord Mansfield*, the statesman and judge (d. 1793), by *Flaxman*. Above is the Judge on the judicial bench, in his official robes; on the left is Justice with her scales, on the right, Wisdom opening the book of the law. Behind the bench is Lord Mansfield's motto: 'uni æquus virtuti', with the ancient representation of death, a youth bearing an extinguished torch. — Opposite, by the railing of the ambulatory —

L. *Sir Robert Peel*, the statesman (d. 1850); statue by *Gibson*.

*Henry Grattan* (d. 1820), *Charles Fox* (p. 199), and the two *Pitts* are all buried in this transept. It was the proximity here of the graves of Fox and the younger Pitt (p. 199) that suggested Scott's well-known lines: —
'Drop upon Fox's grave the tear,
'Twill trickle to his rival's bier'.

W. AISLE OF N. TRANSEPT.

R. *George Gordon, Earl of Aberdeen*, the statesman (d. 1860); bust by *Noble*.

R. *\*Elizabeth Warren* (d. 1816), widow of the Bishop of Bangor, by *Westmacott*. The fine monument represents, in half life-size, a poor mother sitting with her child in her arms, in allusion to the benevolence of the deceased. — Adjoining —

R. *Sir George Cornewall Lewis*, statesman (d. 1863); bust by *Weekes*. — Adjacent —

R. *Sir Eyre Coote*, General, Commander-in-Chief of the British forces in India (d. 1788); colossal monument by *Banks*, erected by the East India Company.

R. *Francis Horner*, Member of Parliament (d. 1817); statue by *Chantrey*. — Opposite —

L. *Sir John Balchen*, Admiral, who in 1744 was lost with his flag-ship and crew of nearly 1000 men in the English Channel; with a relief of the wrecked vessel, by *Scheemakers*.

R. *General Hope*, Governor of Quebec (d. 1789), by *Bacon*; a mourning Indian woman bends over the sarcophagus. — Above —

R. *Warren Hastings*, Governor-General of India (d. 1818); bust by *Bacon*. — Above —

*Richard Cobden*, the politician and champion of free-trade (d. 1865); bust by *Woolner*. — Adjacent —

R. *Earl of Halifax*, the statesman (d. 1771); bust by *Bacon*.

At the end of the passage, in three niches in the wall above, separated by palm-trees, is the monument of —

*Admiral Watson* (d. 1757), by *Scheemakers*. The Admiral, in a toga, is sitting in the centre, holding **a palm branch**. On the **right the town** of Calcutta on her knees presents a petition to her conqueror. On the left is an Indian in chains, emblematical of Chandernagore, also conquered by the Admiral.

### N. Aisle.

On the left. *Sir Thomas Fowell Buxton* (d. 1845), Member of Parliament, one of the champions of the movement for the **abolition of slavery**, by *Thrupp*. — Adjacent —

L. *Balfe* (d. 1870), the composer, medallion by *Mallempre*.

L. **Hugh Chamberlain**, physician (d. 1728), by *Scheemakers* and *Delvaux*; recumbent figure upon a sarcophagus; on the right and left, two allegorical figures, representing Health and Medicine.

R. Tablets to *Charles Burney* (d. 1814), the historian of music, and *John Blow* (d. 1708), the composer and organist. — Then —

R. *William Croft*, organist of Westminster Abbey (d. 1727), with a bust. On the floor are the tombstones of *Henry Purcell* (d. 1695), organist of the abbey, and *W. Sterndale Bennet* (d. 1875), the composer.

L. \*Sir Thomas Stamford Raffles*, Governor of Java (d. 1826), sitting figure, by *Chantrey*.

L. \**William Wilberforce* (d. 1833), one of the chief advocates for the emancipation of the slaves; sitting figure, **by** *Joseph*.

R. \**George Lindsay Johnstone* (d. 1815); fine monument by *Flaxman*, erected by the sister of the deceased. On a sarcophagus, with a small medallion of the deceased, is a mourning female figure.

L. **Lord John** *Thynne*, D. D., Sub-Dean of the Abbey (d. 1881), recumbent figure by *Armstead*.

To the left, at the end of the choir: —

*Sir Isaac Newton* (d. 1726), by *Rysbrack*. The half recumbent figure of Newton reposes on a black sarcophagus, beside which are two small Genii unfolding a scroll. Below is a **relief** in marble, indicating the labours of the deceased. Above is an allegorical figure of Astronomy upon a large globe.

*Charles Darwin* (d. 1882), the eminent naturalist, and *Sir John Herschel* (d. 1871), the astronomer, are buried within a few yards of Newton's tomb (memorial slabs in the floor). — The window above is a memorial of *Robert Stephenson* (d. 1859), the engineer.

In the N. aisle, farther on: —

R. *Richard Mead*, the physician (d. 1754), with bust, by *Scheemakers*. — Above, in the window: —

\**Spencer Perceval*, Chancellor of the Exchequer and First Lord of the Treasury, who was murdered at Westminster Hall in 1812, by *Westmacott*. Recumbent figure upon a sarcophagus; at the head a mourning figure of Strength, and at the foot Truth and Moderation. The bas-relief above represents the murder; the second figure to the left is that of the murderer, Bellingham.

R. *Mrs. Mary Beaufoy* (d. 1705); group by *Grinling Gibbons*.

## 18. WESTMINSTER ABBEY.

R. *Robert Killigrew*, General, killed at Almanza in Spain in 1707, by *Bird*. — In front of this monument *Ben Jonson* is buried (p. 203), with the words 'O Rare Ben Johnson!' cut in the pavement. Close by, under a modern brass, lies *John Hunter* (d. 1793), the celebrated surgeon and anatomist, brought here in 1859 from St. Martin's in the Fields. — The window above was erected to the memory of *Isambard Brunel* (d. 1859), the engineer.

R., above, *Sir Charles Lyell*, the geologist (d. 1875), bust by *Theed*.

R. *Charles James Fox*, the famous statesman (d. 1806), by *Westmacott*. The figure of the deceased lies on a couch, and is supported by the arms of Liberty; at his feet are Peace, with an olive branch, and a liberated negro slave.

R. *Captain Montagu* (d. 1794), by *Flaxman*. Statue on a lofty pedestal, crowned by the Goddess of Victory.

R. *Sir James Mackintosh*, the historian (d. 1832); bust by *Theed*.

R. *George Tierney*, the orator (d. 1830); bust by *Westmacott*.

R. *Marquis of Lansdowne* (d. 1863); bust by *Boehm*.

R. *Lord Holland*, the statesman (d. 1840); large monument, by *Baily*. Below is the entrance to a vault, on the steps to which on the left the Angel of Death, and on the right Literature and Science are posted.

R. *John, Earl Russell* (d. 1878), bust.

R. *Zachary Macaulay* (d. 1838), the father of Lord Macaulay, and a noted advocate for the abolition of slavery; bust by *Weekes*.

Having now reached the end of the N. aisle, we turn to the left (S.), where on the N. side of the principal (W.) ENTRANCE, at the end of the nave, we observe the monuments of —

*Anthony Ashley Cooper, Earl of Shaftesbury* (d. 1885), a marble statue by *Boehm*, and —

*Jeremiah Horrocks*, the astronomer (d. 1641). Above the door is the monument of —

*William Pitt*, the renowned statesman (d. 1806), by *Westmacott*. At the top stands the statue of Pitt as Chancellor of the Exchequer, in the act of speaking. To the right is History listening to his words; on the left, Anarchy in chains.

On the S. side of the door is the monument of *Admiral Sir Thomas Hardy* (d. 1732), by *Cheere*.

R. *James Cornewall*, Captain (d. 1743), a monument by *Tayler*. At the foot of a low pyramid of Sicilian marble is a grotto in white marble, with a relief of the naval battle of Toulon, in which Cornewall fell. The monument terminates above in a palm-tree with the armorial bearings.

### S. AISLE.

In the baptistery at the W. end : —

*James Craggs*, Secretary of State (d. 1721); statue by *Guelphi* with inscription by Pope.

## 18. WESTMINSTER ABBEY.

*William Wordsworth*, the poet (d. 1850); statue by *Lough*.
*Rev. John Keble* (d. 1866); bust by *Woolner*.
The baptistery also contains busts, by *Woolner*, of the *Rev. Fred. D. Maurice* (d. 1872) and the *Rev. Charles Kingsley* (d. 1875), and a bronze medallion of *Professor Henry Fawcett* (d. 1884), by *Alfred Gilbert*, with a row of small allegorical figures. The stained-glass windows were placed here by Mr. George W. Childs of Philadelphia in memory of *George Herbert* (d. 1632) and *William Cowper* (d. 1800).

We now continue to follow the S. aisle. To the right, above the door leading to the Deanery, is the *Abbot's Pew*, a small oaken gallery, constructed by Abbot Islip in the 16th century.

On the right: *William Congreve*, the dramatist (d. 1728), by *Bird*, with a medallion and a sarcophagus of Egyptian marble. The monument was erected by Henrietta, Duchess of Marlborough.

R. *William Buckland*, the geologist (d. 1856), bust by *Weekes*.

R. *Lord Lawrence* (d. 1879), Governor-General of India; bust by *Woolner*.

Then, above the door leading to the cloisters (see p. 217) —
*George Wade*, General (d. 1748), by *Roubiliac*. The Goddess of Fame is preventing Time from destroying the General's trophies, which are attached to a column.

R. Sir *James Outram*, General (d. 1863); bust by *Noble*. Below are Outram and Lord Clyde shaking hands, and between them is General Havelock. At the sides are mourning figures, representing Indian tribes. — Above, occupying the whole recess of the window —

R. *William Hargrave*, General (d. 1750), by *Roubiliac*. The General is descending from his sarcophagus, while Time, represented allegorically, conquers Death and breaks his arrow. —

Adjacent is a tablet recording the burial in the Nave of Sir *William Temple* (d. 1699) and his wife, *Dorothy Osborne* (d. 1695).

*Sidney, Earl Godolphin* (d. 1712), Lord High Treasurer, by *Bird*.

R. *Colonel Townshend*, who fell in Canada in 1759, by *Eckstein*. Two Indian warriors bear the white marble sarcophagus, which is adjoined by a pyramid of coloured Sicilian marble.

R. *John André*, Major, executed in America as a spy in 1780. Sarcophagus with mourning Britannia, by *Van Gelder*. — Opposite, in the nave, by the end of the choir: —

*James, Earl Stanhope*, ambassador and minister of war (d. 1720), by *Rysbrack*. — Then, returning to the N. aisle: —

L. *Thomas Thynne*, murdered in Pall Mall in 1682 by assassins hired by Count Koningsmarck, whose object was the hand of Thynne's wife, a wealthy heiress, by *Quellin*. The relief on the pedestal is a representation of the murder.

R. *Dr. Isaac Watts*, the famous divine and hymn-writer (d. 1748), with bust by *Banks*.

R. *John Wesley*, founder of the Methodists (d. 1791), and *Charles Wesley* (d. 1788), by *Van Gelder*, relief by *Adams-Acton*.

## 18. WESTMINSTER ABBEY.

R. *Charles Burney*, philologist (d. 1818); bust by *Gahagan*.

L. *Thomas Owen*, judge (d. 1598); an interesting old painted monument, with a life-size recumbent figure leaning on the right arm. — By the adjoining pillar —

L. *Pasquale Paoli* (d. 1807); the well-known Corsican general (buried in Corsica); bust by *Flaxman*. — Opposite —

R. *Sir Cloudesley Shovel*, Admiral (d. 1707), by *Bird*, recumbent figure under a canopy. — Above —

*Sir Godfrey Kneller*, the painter (d. 1723), by *Rysbrack*; bust under a canopy. The monument was designed by Kneller himself, who is the only painter commemorated in the abbey. He was buried in his own garden, at Kneller Hall, Twickenham.

Here is a door leading to the E. walk of the cloisters and to the chapter-house (p. 216).

L. *Sir Thomas Richardson*, judge (d. 1634), old monument by *Le Soeur*.

L. *Dr. Andrew Bell*, the founder of the Madras system of education (d. 1832), with relief representing him examining a class of boys, by *Behnes*.

In the middle of the nave lie, amongst others, *David Livingstone*, the celebrated African traveller (d. 1873), *Sir Charles Barry*, the architect (d. 1860), *Robert Stephenson*, the engineer (d. 1859), *Lord Clyde* (d. 1863), *Sir James Outram* (d. 1863; the 'Bayard of India'), *Sir George Pollock* (d. 1872), *Lord Lawrence* (d. 1879), *Sir G. G. Scott*, the architect (d. 1878; with a brass by *Street*), and *G. E. Street* (d. 1881), the architect of the New Law Courts.

We now turn to the right and enter the —

### S. Transept and Poets' Corner.

On the right: *George Grote*, the historian (d. 1871); bust by *Bacon*. — Adjacent is the monument of *Bishop Thirlwall* (d. 1875), the eminent historian of Greece.

R. *William Camden*, the antiquary (d. 1623), small statue. — Above —

*David Garrick*, the famous actor (d. 1779); large group in relief, by *Webber*. Garrick is stepping out from behind a curtain, which he opens with extended arms. Below are the comic and the tragic Muse. — Below —

*Isaac Casaubon*, the theologist (d. 1614). — Above —

*John Ernest Grabe*, the Oriental scholar (d. 1711); sitting figure by *Bird*. — Several uninteresting monuments; then —

*Isaac Barrow*, the theologian (d. 1679).

*Joseph Addison*, the essayist (d. 1719); statue by *Westmacott*. On the base are the Muses in relief.

*Lord Macaulay*, the historian (d. 1859); bust by *Burnard*.

*W. M. Thackeray*, the novelist and humorist (d. 1863); bust by *Marochetti*. — Above —

*George Frederick Händel*, the composer (d. 1759), the last work from the chisel of *Roubiliac;* life-size statue surrounded by music and instruments; above, among the clouds, a heavenly choir; in the background, an organ.

*Sir Archibald Campbell*, General (d. 1791), by *Wilton*. — Below, to the right —

*James Stuart Mackenzie*, Lord Privy Seal for Scotland (d. 1800); medallion-portrait, by *Nollekens*. — By the S. wall: —

\**John, Duke of Argyll and Greenwich* (d. 1743); a large monument by *Roubiliac*. On a black sarcophagus rests the half-recumbent, life-size figure of the Duke, supported by History, who is writing his name on a pyramid. On the pedestal, to the left, Eloquence; to the right, Valour.

Above the doorway of the chapel of St. Blaise or St. Faith (p. 216): —

*Oliver* **Goldsmith** (d. 1774), buried at the Temple (p. 137); medallion by *Nollekens*. — Then —

**John Gay**, the poet (d. 1732), by *Rysbrack*. A small Genius holds the medallion. The irreverent inscription, by Gay himself, runs: —

'*Life is a jest;* and all things show it:
I thought so once, but now I know it'.

*Nicolas Rowe*, the poet (d. 1718), and his only daughter, by *Rysbrack*. Above, the medallion of the daughter. — Then —

*James Thomson*, the poet of the 'Seasons' (d. 1748); statue by *Spang*. — Adjacent —

\**William Shakspeare* (d. 1616), designed by *Kent*, and executed by *Scheemakers*. The figure of the Poet, placed on a pedestal resembling an altar, is represented with the right arm leaning on a pile of his works; the left hand holds a roll bearing the titles of his chief writings. On the pedestal are the masks of Queen Elizabeth, Henry V., and Richard III.

Above, *Robert Burns* (d. 1796), bust by *Steell*.

*Robert Southey*, the poet (d. 1843), bust by *Weekes*.

*S. T. Coleridge*, the poet (d. 1834), bust by *Hamo Thornycroft*. — Then, opposite Addison's statue —

*Thomas Campbell*, the poet (d. 1844), statue by *Marshall*. — The grave of *Charles Dickens* (d. 1870) is between the statues of Addison and Campbell, and is surrounded by the tombs of Händel, Sheridan, and Cumberland. Garrick, Dr. Johnson, and Macaulay are also buried here.

Passing round the pillar we now enter the —

### E. Aisle of the Poets' Corner.

On the right. *Granville Sharp* (d. 1813), one of the chief advocates for the abolition of slavery, medallion by *Chantrey*. — Above:

*Charles de St. Denis, Seigneur de St. Evremont*, author, French Marshal, afterwards in the service of England (d. 1703), bust. — Below —

*Matthew* **Prior**, politician and poet (d. 1721), large monument by *Rysbrack*. In a niche is Prior's bust by *Coyzevox* (presented by Louis XIV. of France); below, a black sarcophagus, adjoined by two allegorical figures of (r.) History and (l.) Thalia. At the top are two boys, one with a torch, the other with an hour-glass. — Then —

*William Mason*, the poet (d. 1797); medallion, mourned over by Poetry, by *Bacon*. — Over it —

*Thomas Shadwell*, the poet (d. 1692), by *Bird*. — Below —

*Thomas Gray*, the poet (d. 1771); medallion, held by the Muse of poetry, by *Bacon*. — Above —

*John Milton* (d. 1674; buried in St. Giles's Church, Cripplegate), bust by *Rysbrack* (1737). Below is a lyre, round which is twining a serpent with an apple, in allusion to 'Paradise Lost'. — Below —

*Edmund Spenser* (d. 1598; buried near Chaucer), 'the prince of poets in his tyme', as the inscription says; a simple, altar-like monument, with ornaments of light-coloured marble above. — Above —

*Samuel Butler*, author of 'Hudibras' (d. 1680), with bust. — Then:

*Ben Jonson* (d. 1637), poet-laureate to James I., and contemporary of Shakspeare; medallion by *Rysbrack* (1737); on the pedestal the inscription, 'O rare Ben Johnson!' (comp. p. 198). —

*Michael Drayton*, the poet (d. 1631), with bust.

*Barton Booth*, the actor (d. 1733), an ancestor of Edwin Booth, with medallion, by *Tyler*.

*John Phillips*, the poet (d. 1708); portrait in relief.

The tomb of *Geoffrey Chaucer* (d. 1400), the father of English poetry, is on the same side, a few paces farther on, and consists of an altar-sarcophagus (supposed to be from Grey Friars Church, p. 91) under a canopy let into the wall (date, 1551). — Above it is a fine stained-glass window, erected in 1868, with scenes from Chaucer's poems, and a likeness of the poet.

*Abraham Cowley*, the poet (d. 1667), with urn, by *Bushnell*.

*H. W. Longfellow*, the poet (d. 1882), bust by *Brock*.

*John Dryden*, the poet (d. 1700); bust by *Scheemakers*.

*Archbishop Tait* (d. 1883); marble bust by *Armstead* (at the entrance to the choir-ambulatory).

*Robert South*, the preacher (d. 1716); statue by *Bird*.

*Richard Busby*, head-master of Westminster School (d. 1695); statue by *Bird*.

In the centre of the S. transept is a white slab, covering the remains of 'Old Parr' (d. 1635), who is said to have reached the age of 152 years.

To the left of the entrance to the ambulatory is an old altar-decoration of the 13th or 14th cent., below which is the old monument of the Saxon king *Sebert* (d. 616) and his wife *Athelgoda* (d. 615).

We now repair to the \*Chapels, which follow each other in the following order (starting from the Poets' Corner).

I. Chapel of St. Benedict.
1. *Archbishop Langham* (d. 1376); with recumbent figure.
2. *Lady Frances Hertford* (d. 1598).
3. *Dr. Goodman*, Dean of Westminster (d. 1601).
4. A son of Dr. Spratt.
\*5. *Lionel Cranfield, Earl of Middlesex* (d. 1645), Lord High Treasurer in the time of James I., and his wife.
6. *Dr. Bill* (d. 1561), first Dean of Westminster under Elizabeth.

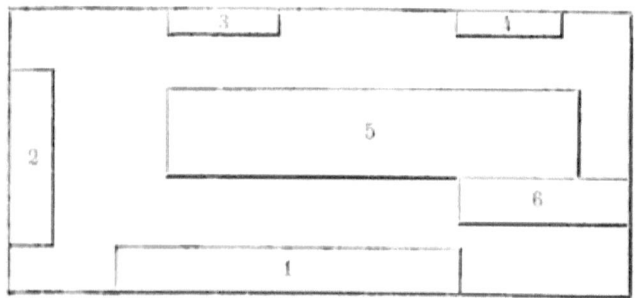

Near this is the tomb of *Ann of Cleves* (d. 1557), fourth wife of Henry VIII.

II. Chapel of St. Edmund, King of the East Anglians.
\*1. *John of Eltham*, second son of Edward II., who died in 1334 in his nineteenth year. Sarcophagus with life-size alabaster figure.
2. *Earl of Stafford* (d. 1762); slab, by *Chambers*.
3. *Nicholas Monk* (d. 1661), Bishop of Hereford, brother of the famous Duke of Albemarle (p. 208); slab and pyramid, by *Woodman*.
4. *William of Windsor* and *Blanche de la Tour* (d. 1340), children of Edward III., who both died young; small sarcophagus, with recumbent alabaster figures 20 in. in length.
5. *Duchess of Suffolk* (d. 1558), granddaughter of Henry VII. and mother of Lady Jane Grey; recumbent figure.
6. *Francis Holles*, son of the Earl of Clare, who died in 1622, at the age of 18, on his return from a campaign in Flanders, in which he had greatly distinguished himself; sitting figure, by *Stone*.
7. *Lady Jane Seymour* (d. 1560), daughter of the Duke of Somerset.
8. *Lady Katharine Knollys* (d. 1568), chief Lady of the Bedchamber to Queen Elizabeth, niece of Anne Boleyn, and grandmother of the Queen's favourite, the Earl of Essex.

## 18. WESTMINSTER ABBEY.

9. *Lady Elizabeth Russell* (d. 1601), a handsome sitting figure of alabaster, in an attitude of sleep. The Latin inscription says, 'she sleeps, she is not dead'.

10. *Lord John Russell* (d. 1584), and his son *Francis*; sarcophagus with a recumbent figure, resting on the left arm, in official robes, with the boy at the feet.

11. *Sir Bernard Brocas of Beaurepaire*, Chamberlain to Queen Anne, wife of Richard II., beheaded on Tower Hill in 1399; an interesting old monument in the form of a Gothic chapel, with recumbent figure of a praying knight; at the feet, a lion.

12. *Sir Humphrey Bourgchier*, partisan of Edward IV., who fell

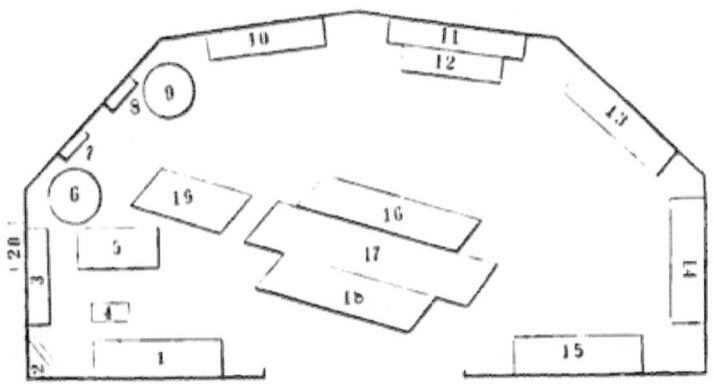

Chapel of St. Edmund.

on Easter Day, 1471, at the battle of Barnet Field. Altar monument, with the figure of a knight, the head resting on a helmet, one foot on a leopard, and the other on an eagle.

13. *Sir Richard Pecksall* (d. 1571), Master of the Buckhound; to Queen Elizabeth; canopy with three niches.

\*14. *Edward Talbot, Earl of Shrewsbury* (d. 1617), and his wife's figures lying under a canopy on a slab of black marble with a pedestal of alabaster.

15. *William de Valence, Earl of Pembroke*, who fell at Bayonne in 1296; recumbent wooden figure, overlaid with metal, the feet resting on a lion.

16. *Robert de Waldeby, Archbishop of York* (d. 1397), once an Augustinian monk and the companion of Edward the Black Prince in France, tutor to Richard II.; mediæval monument, with engraved figure.

\*17. *Eleanora de Bohun, Duchess of Gloucester*, Abbess of Barking (d. 1399), one of the most interesting monuments in the Abbey. Her husband was smothered at Calais between two feather-beds by order of Richard II., his nephew. She is represented in the dress of a nun of Barking. The inscription is in old French.

**18.** *Mary, Countess of Stafford* (d. 1693), wife of Lord Stafford, who was beheaded on Tower Hill in 1680.

**19.** *Dr. Ferne,* Bishop of Chester, Grand Almoner of Charles I. (d. 1661).

*Edward Bulwer Lytton,* the novelist (d. 1873), and *Lord Herbert* of Cherbury (d. 1678) are buried under slabs in this chapel.

III. CHAPEL OF ST. NICHOLAS, Bishop of Myra.

**1.** *Lady Cecil,* Lady of the Bedchamber to Queen Elizabeth (d. 1591).

**2.** *Lady Jane Clifford,* daughter of the Duke of Somerset (d. 1679).

**3.** *Countess of Beverley;* small tombstone with the inscription, 'Espérance en Dieu (d. 1812), by *Nollekens.*

**4.** *Anne, Duchess of Somerset* (d. 1587), widow of the Protector

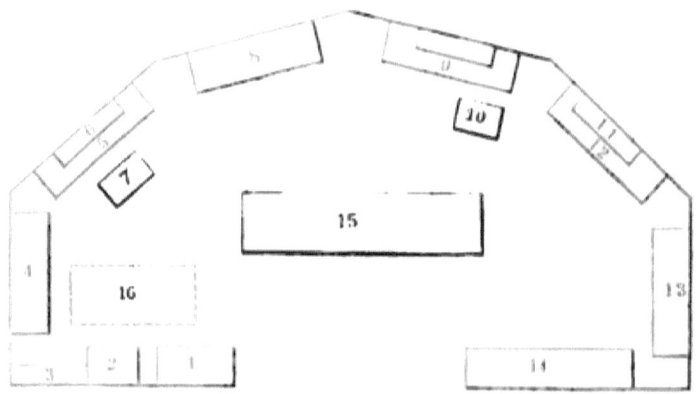

Chapel of St. Nicholas.

(beheaded on Tower Hill in 1552, see p. 123), and sister-in-law of Jane Seymour, third wife of Henry VIII.; recumbent figure.

**5.** *Westmoreland Family.* — Above —

**6.** *Baron Carew* (d. 1470) and his wife, mediæval monument, with kneeling figures.

**7.** *Nicholas Bagenall* (d. 1687), overlain by his nurse when an infant.

*****8.** *Lady Mildred Burleigh* (d. 1588), wife of Lord Burleigh, the famous minister, and her daughter *Anne.* Lady Burleigh, says the epitaph, was well versed in the Greek sacred writers, and founded a scholarship at St. John's College, Oxford. Recumbent figures.

**9.** *William Dudley,* Bishop of Durham (d. 1483).

**10.** *Anna Sophia Hurley* (d. 1604), the infant daughter of a French ambassador.

**11.** *Lady Ross* (d. 1591); mediæval monument.

**12.** *Marchioness of Winchester* (d. 1586).

**13.** *Duchess of Northumberland* (d. 1776), by *Read.*

**14.** *Philippa de Bohun, Duchess of York* (d. 1431), wife **of**

Edward Plantagenet, who fell at Agincourt in 1415. Old monument with effigy of the deceased in long drapery.

*15. *Sir George Villiers* (d. 1605) and his wife (d. 1632), the parents of the Duke of Buckingham, favourite of James I.; monument with recumbent figures, in the centre of the chapel, by Stone. — The remains of *Katherine of Valois*, wife of Henry V. (d. 1437), lay below this tomb for 350 years (comp. p. 211).

16. *Sir Humphrey Stanley* (d. 1505).

Opposite us, on leaving this chapel, under the tomb of Henry V., is a bust of *Sir Robert Aiton*, the poet (1570-1638), executed by Farelli from a portrait by Van Dyck. Aiton was secretary of two Queens Consort and a friend of Jonson, Drummond, and Hobbes. The earliest known version of 'Auld Lang Syne' was written by him.

IV. A flight of twelve black marble steps now leads into the **Chapel of Henry VII., a superb structure erected in 1502-20 on the site of an old chapel of the Virgin Mary. The roses in the decoration of the fine brass-covered gates are an allusion to the marriage of Henry VII., founder of the Tudor family, with Elizabeth, daughter of Edward IV., which united the Houses of York and Lancaster, and put an end to the Wars of the Roses (comp. p. 137). The chapel consists of nave and aisles, with five small chapels at the E. end. The aisles are entered by doors on the right and left of the main gate. On the left stands the font. The chapel contains about 100 statues and figures. On each side are carved choir-stalls in dark oak, admirably designed and beautifully executed; the quaint carvings on the 'misereres' under the seats are worthy of examination. Each stall is appropriated to a Knight of the Order of the Bath, the lower seats being for the squires. Each seat bears the armorial bearings of its occupant in brass, and above each are a sword and banner.

The chief glory of this chapel, however, is its fan tracery ceiling with its fantastic pendentives, each surface being covered with rich tret-work, exhibiting the florid Perpendicular style in its utmost luxuriance. The airiness, elegance, and richness of this exquisite work can scarcely be over-praised. The best survey of the chapel is gained either from the entrance door, or from the small chapel at the opposite extremity, behind the monument of the founder, whose portrait is to be seen in the stained-glass window above.

'On entering, the eye is astonished by the pomp of architecture, and the elaborate beauty of sculptured detail. The very walls are wrought into universal ornament, incrusted with tracery, and scooped into niches, crowded with the statues of saints and martyrs. Stone seems, by the cunning labour of the chisel, to have been robbed of its weight and density, suspended aloft, as if by magic, and the fretted roof achieved with the wonderful minuteness and airy security of a cobweb.' — *Washington Irving*.

We first turn our attention to the S. aisle of the chapel, where we observe the following monuments:

*1. *Lady Margaret Douglas* (d. 1577), daughter of Margaret, Queen of Scotland, great-granddaughter of Edward IV., granddaughter of Henry VII., niece of Henry VIII., cousin of Edward VI., sister of James V. of Scotland, mother of Henry I. of Scotland (Lord Darnley), and grandmother of James VI. Her seven children kneel round the sarcophagus; the eighth figure is her grandson, King James.

2. *Mary, Queen of Scots*, beheaded in 1587, an inartistic monument by *Stone* (d. 1607), representing a recumbent figure under a canopy, in a praying attitude. The remains of the Queen are buried in a vault below the monument. Adjacent, on the wall, hangs a photographic copy of the warrant issued by James I. in 1612 for **the removal of** his mother's body from Peterborough Cathedral to Westminster Abbey.

3. *Margaret, Countess of Richmond*, mother of Henry VII. (d. 1509): recumbent metal effigy, by *Torregiano*.

4. *Lady Walpole* (d. 1737), **first wife of** Sir Robert Walpole, executed by *Valori* after an ancient statue of Livia or Pudicitia in the Villa Mattei, Rome, and brought from Italy by her son, **Horace** Walpole.

5. *George Monk, Duke of Albemarle* (d. 1670), the restorer of the Stuarts, by *Scheemakers*. Rostral column, with life-size figure of the Duke. In Monk's vault, which is in the N. aisle, are also buried *Addison* (d. 1719) and *Secretary Craggs* (d. 1721).

In the vault in front of it are buried *Charles II., William III.* and *Queen Mary* his wife, and *Queen* Anne and her consort *Prince George of Denmark*. We now enter the nave, which contains the following monuments, beginning from the chapel on the left: —

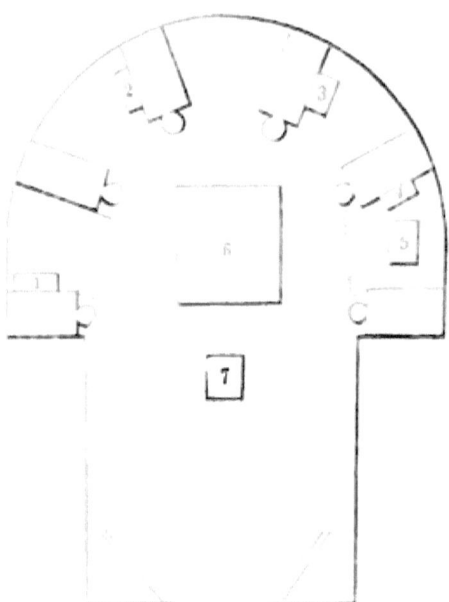

## 18. WESTMINSTER ABBEY

1. *George Villiers, Duke of Buckingham*, the favourite of James I. and Charles I., murdered in 1628 by the fanatic Felton, and his consort. The monument is of iron. At the feet of the recumbent effigies of the deceased is Fame blowing a trumpet. At the front corners of the sarcophagus are Neptune and Mars, at those at the back two mourning females, all in a sitting posture. At the top, on their knees, are the life-size children of the deceased.

2. *John Sheffield, Duke of Buckinghamshire* (d. 1720), and his wife, by *Scheemakers*. The figure of the Duke is half-recumbent, and in Roman costume. At his feet is the duchess, weeping. Above is Time with the medallions. Anne of Denmark (d. 1618), consort of James I, is interred in front of this monument.

*3. *Duke of Montpensier* (d. 1807), brother of King Louis Philippe, recumbent figure in white marble, by *Westmacott*. Dean Stanley (d. 1881; recumbent statue by *Boehm*), and his wife, Lady Augusta Stanley (d. 1876), are buried in this chapel.

4. *Esmé Stuart*, who died in 1661, in his eleventh year; pyramid with an urn containing the heart of the deceased.

In the E. chapel were interred **Oliver Cromwell** and some of his followers, removed in 1661.

5. *Lewis Stuart, Duke of Richmond* (d. 1623), father's cousin and friend of James I., and his wife. Double sarcophagus with recumbent figures. The iron canopy is borne by figures of Faith, Hope, Charity, and Wisdom. Above is a fine figure of Fame.

*6. *Henry VII.* (d. 1509) and his wife *Elizabeth of York* (d. 1502); metal monument, by *Torregiano*. It occupies the centre of the eastern part of the chapel, and is enclosed by a tasteful chantry of brass. On the double sarcophagus are the recumbent figures of the royal pair in their robes. The compartments at the sides of the tomb are embellished with sacred representations. — *James I.* (d. 1625) is buried in the same vault as Henry VII.

*George II.* and a number of members of the royal family are interred, without monuments, in front of the tomb of Henry VII. Also *Edward VI.* (d. 1553), whose monument by Torregiano was destroyed by the Republicans, and is replaced by a modern Renaissance altar (No. 7 in plan, p. 208). To the left is the tomb of *Elizabeth Claypole* (d. 1658), second daughter of Oliver Cromwell, marked by an inscription in the pavement. — Adjacent is an old pulpit of the Reformation period, probably the one in which Cranmer preached the coronation and funeral sermons of Edward VI.

The monuments in the northern aisle of this chapel are not less interesting than those in the southern.

*1. **Queen Elizabeth** (d. 1603), by *Stone*. The monument is very similar to that of her unfortunate rival Mary Stuart in the S. aisle. Here also is commemorated Elizabeth's sister and predecessor *Mary* (d. 1558), who is buried beneath.

2. *Mary*, daughter of **James I.**, **who died in** 1607 **at the age of two** years. Small altar-tomb.

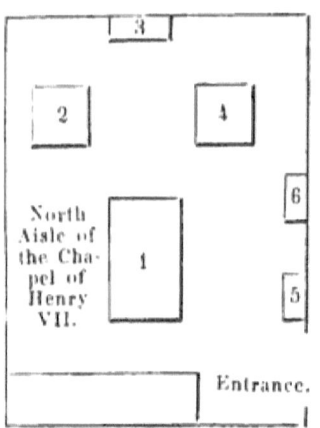

3. *Edward V.* and his brother, the *Duke of York*, the sons of Edward IV., **murdered** in the Tower when **children**, by Richard III., in 1483. Some **bones**, supposed to be those of the unfortunate boys, were found in **a chest below** a staircase in the Tower (see **p. 120**), and brought hither. Small **sarcophagus in a niche**.

4. *Sophia*, daughter of James I., **who was** born in 1607, and died when **three days old**. Small recumbent figure **in a cradle**.

5. *George Saville, Marquis of Halifax*, Lord Keeper of the Privy Seal during several reigns (d. 1695).

6. *Charles Montague, Earl of Halifax*, Lord High Treasurer (d. 1715). — The earl was the patron of *Addison* (d. **1719**), **who is commemorated by a** slab in front of **this** monument.

After quitting the Chapel of Henry VII. and descending the steps, we see in front of us the *Chantry of Henry V.* (p. 211), with its finely sculptured arch, over which is represented the coronation of that monarch (1413). A slab on the floor marks the vault of the *Earls of Clarendon*, including the distinguished historian (d. 1674).

V. Chapel of St. Paul.

1. *Sir Rowland Hill* (1795-1879), **the originator of the system of penny postage**; bust by *Keyworth*.

2. *Sir Henry Belasyse* (d. 1717), **Lieutenant-General and Governor of Galway**. Pyramid by *Scheemakers*.

3. *Sir John Puckering* (d. 1596), **Keeper of the Great Seal** under Queen Elizabeth, and his wife. Recumbent figures under a canopy.

4. *Sir James Fullerton* (d. 1630), **First Gentleman of the Bedchamber to Charles I., and his wife**. Recumbent marble figures.

5. *Sir Thomas Bromley* (d. 1587), Lord Chancellor under Queen Elizabeth. **Recumbent figure; below, his eight children**.

6. *Sir Dudley Carleton* (d. 1631), **diplomatist under James I.; semi-recumbent figure**, by *Stone*.

7. *Countess of Sussex* (d. 1589); **at her feet is** a porcupine.

8. **Lord Cottington, statesman in the reign** of Charles I. (d. 1652), **and his wife. Handsome black marble monument**, with the recumbent figure of Lord Cottington in white marble, by *Fanelli*, and, at the top, a bust of Lady Cottington (d. 1633), by *Le Soeur*.

*9. *James Watt* (d. 1819), **the improver of the steam-engine**; **colossal figure in a** sitting posture, **by** *Chantrey*.

*10. *Sir Giles Daubeney* (d. 1507), Lord-Lieutenant of Calais under Henry VII., **and his wife.** Recumbent effigies in alabaster, painted.

11. *Lewis Robsart* (d. 1431), standard-bearer of Henry V.; an interesting old monument, without an effigy.

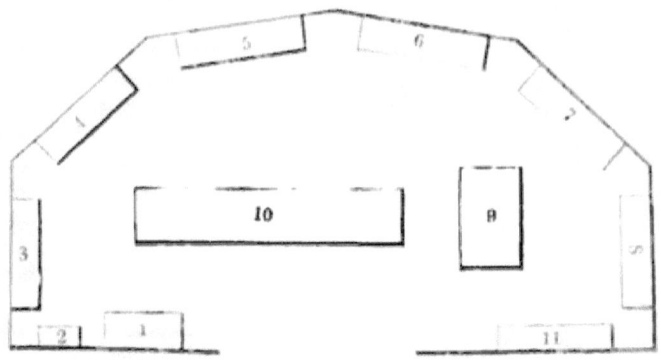

Chapel of St. Paul.

This chapel contains an ancient stone coffin found in digging the grave of Sir Rowland Hill.

To the right, on leaving this chapel, is a monument to *William Pulteney, Earl of Bath* (d. 1764), by *Wilton*; and beside it another to *Rear-Admiral Charles Holmes* (d. 1761), also by *Wilton*. Opposite is a screen of wrought iron executed by an English blacksmith in 1293.

*VI. Chapel of St. Edward the Confessor, forming the end of the choir, to which we ascend by a small flight of narrow steps. (The following chapel, No. VII., is sometimes shown before this.)

1. *Henry III.* (d. 1272), a rich and artistic monument of porphyry and mosaic, with recumbent bronze effigy of the King, by *William Torel* (1299).

2. *Queen Eleanor*, first wife of Edward I. (d. 1290), by *Torell*. The inscription is in quaint old French: — 'Ici gist Alianor, jadis reyne d'Angleterre, femme a Rey Eduard Fiz'. Recumbent metal effigy.

3. *Chantry of Henry V.* (d. 1422). On each side a life-size figure keeps guard by the steps. The recumbent effigy of the King wants the head, which was of solid silver, and was stolen during the reign of Henry VIII. In 1878 the remains of Katherine of Valois, (d. 1437) queen of Henry V. (the 'beautiful Kate' of Shakspeare's 'Henry V.') were re-interred in this chantry, whence they had been removed on the building of Henry VII.'s. Chapel. On the bar above this monument are placed the saddle, helmet, and shield said to have been used by Henry V. at the battle of Agincourt.

4. *Philippa* (d. 1369), wife of Edward III., and mother of fourteen children. She was the daughter of the Count of Hainault, and

was related to no fewer than thirty crowned heads, statuettes of whom were formerly to be seen grouped round the sarcophagus.

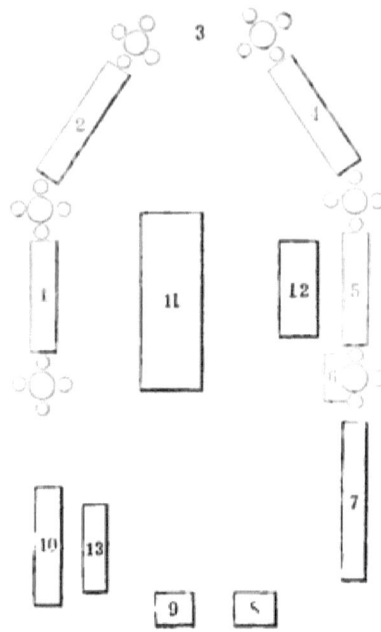

Chapel of St. Edward the Confessor.

5. *Edward III.* (d. 1377), recumbent metal figure on a sarcophagus of grey marble. This monument was once surrounded by statuettes **of the** King's children and **others.** **The** pavement in front **of it** dates from 1260.

6. *Margaret Woodville* (d. 1472), a daughter of Edward IV., who died in infancy. Monument without an **effigy.**

7. *Richard II.*, murdered on St. Valentine's Day, 1399, and his queen. The wooden canopy bears an old and curious representation **of the** Saviour and the Virgin.

8. **The** old *Coronation Chair*, **of** oak, made by Edward I., and —

9. The new *Coronation Chair*, made for Queen Mary, wife of William III., on the model of the old one. The former contains under the seat the famous *Stone of Scone*, the emblem of the power of the Scottish Princes, and traditionally said to be that once used by the patriarch Jacob as a pillow. It is a piece of sandstone from the W. coast of Scotland, and may very probably be the actual stone pillow on which the dying head of St. Columba rested in the Abbey of Iona. This stone was brought to London by Edward I. in 1297, in token of the complete subjugation of Scotland. Every English monarch since that date has been crowned in this chair. On the coronation day the chairs are covered with gold brocade and taken into the choir of the **Abbey,** on the other side of the partition in front **of** which they **now stand.** Between **the chairs are the** state sword and shield of Edward **III. (d.** 1377).

The reliefs on the screen **separating** Edward's chapel from the **choir, executed in the reign of Edward IV.,** represent the principal **events in the life of the Confessor.**

10. *Edward I.* (d. 1307), **a simple slab** without an effigy. The inscription is: — '**Eduardus** primus, Scotorum malleus, hic est (here lies Edward I., **the** hammer **of** the Scots). The body was **recently** found **to be in** remarkably **good** preservation, with a

crown of gilded tin on the head, and a copper gilt sceptre in the hand.

*11. *Edward the Confessor* (d. 1066), a large mediæval shrine, the faded splendour of which is still traceable, in spite of the spoliations of relic-hunters. The shrine was erected by order of Henry III. in 1269, and cost, according to an authentic record, 255*l*. 4*s*. 8*d*.

12. *Thomas of Woodstock, Duke of Gloucester*, murdered at Calais in 1397.

13. *John of Waltham* (d. 1395), Bishop of Salisbury, recumbent metal effigy.

Opposite the Chapel of Edward the Confessor is the entrance to the *Chapel* or *Shrine of St. Erasmus*, a picturesque archway, borne by clustered columns, dating from about 1484. Passing through this chapel, we enter the —

VII. CHAPEL OF ST. JOHN THE BAPTIST.

1. *Sir Thomas Vaughan* (d. 1483), Lord High Treasurer of Edward IV. Old monument, with a brass, which is much defaced.

2. *Colonel Edward Popham* (d. 1651), officer in Cromwell's army, and his wife. Upright figures.

3. *Thomas Carey*, son of the Earl of Monmouth, Gentleman of the Bedchamber to Charles I., who died in 1648, aged 33 years, from grief at the misfortunes of his royal master.

4. *Hugh de Bohun* and his sister *Mary* (d. 1300), grandchildren of Edward I.; tombstone of grey marble.

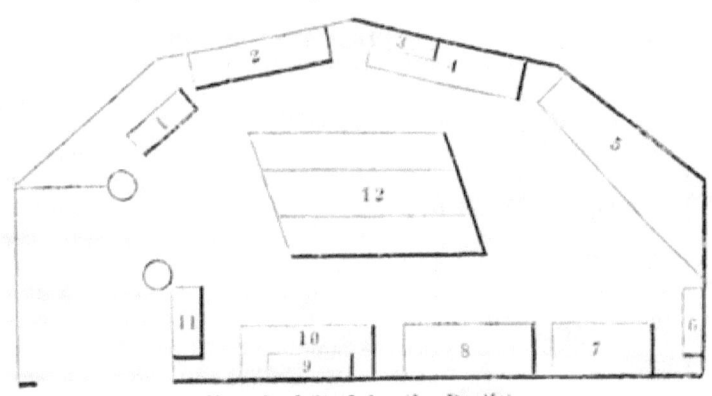

Chapel of St. John the Baptist.

5. **Henry Carey**, *Baron Hunsdon*, cousin of Queen Elizabeth (d. 1596). Rich canopy without an effigy.

6. *Countess of Mexborough* (d. 1821), small altar-tomb.

Above this monument is a slab with a mourning Genius by *Nollekens*, erected to the memory of *Lieut. Col. MacLeod*, who fell at the siege of Badajoz, at the age of 26.

7. *William of Colchester*, Abbot of Westminster (d. 1420); a mediæval stone monument with the recumbent figure of the prelate, his head supported by angels, and his feet resting on a lamb.

8. *Thomas Ruthall*, Bishop of Durham under Henry VIII., who died in 1524, leaving great wealth. Mediæval recumbent figure.

9. *Thomas Millyng*, Abbot of Westminster (d. 1492); canopy without a figure.

10. *G. Fascet*, Abbot of Westminster (d. 1500).

11. *Mary Kendall* (d. 1710); kneeling female figure.

12. *Thomas Cecil*, *Earl of Exeter* (d. 1622), Privy Councillor under James I., and his wife. His wife lies on his right hand; the space on his left was destined for his second wife, who, however, declined to be buried there, as the place of honour on the right had already been assigned to her predecessor.

VIII. The small CHAPEL OF ABBOT ISLIP is not shown. The monument of Abbot Islip (d. 1532), formerly in this chapel, was destroyed by the Roundheads, and the name of the chapel is now his only memorial. It contains the tomb of *Sir Christopher Hatton* (d. 1619) and his wife. A room above this chapel (shown on Mon. and Tues., by the order of a canon) contains the remains of the curious wax figures which were once used at the funerals of persons buried in the Abbey. Among them are Queen Elizabeth, Charles II., William III. and his wife Mary, Queen Anne, William Pitt, Earl of Chatham, and Lord Nelson.

In the ambulatory, near the chapel of Edward the Confessor, is the ancient monument of the Knight Templar, *Edmund Crouchback* (d. 1296), second son of Henry III., from whom the House of Lancaster derived its claims to the English throne. On the sarcophagus are remains of the figures of the ten knights who accompanied Edmund to the Holy Land. Adjacent is the monument of another Knight Templar, *Aymer de Valence* (d. 1323), Earl of Pembroke and cousin of Edward I., who was assassinated in France. The beautiful effigy of *Aveline, Countess of Lancaster* (d. 1273), first wife of Edmund Crouchback, on an adjoining monument (seen from the choir), merits notice.

To the right is a large marble monument, executed by *Wilton*, to *General Wolfe* (buried at Greenwich), who fell in 1759 at the capture of Quebec. He is represented sinking into the arms of a grenadier, while his right hand is pressed on his mortal wound; the soldier is pointing out to the dying man the Goddess of Fame hovering overhead. Beside this group is a mourning Highlander.

Opposite is the monument of *John, Earl Ligonier and Viscount of Inniskilling*, Field-Marshal (d. 1770), by *Moore*.

IX. CHAPELS OF ST. JOHN THE EVANGELIST, ST. MICHAEL, AND ST. ANDREW, three separate chapels, now combined.

1. *Sir John Franklin* (d. 1847), lost in endeavouring to discover the North West Passage, by *Noble*.

## 18. WESTMINSTER ABBEY.

2. *Earl Mountrath* (d. 1771), and his wife; a large monument, by *Wilton*. An angel points out to the Countess the empty seat beside her husband.

3. *Earl of Kerry* (d. 1818), and his wife; a marble sarcophagus with an earl's coronet, by *Buckham*. Altar-tomb.

4. *Telford*, the engineer (d. 1834); huge statue by *Baily*.

5. *Dr. Baillie* (d. 1823); bust by *Chantrey*.

6. *Miss Davidson*, daughter of a rich merchant of Rotterdam (d. 1767), by *Hayward*. Altar-tomb with head.

7. *Mrs. Siddons*, the famous actress (d. 1831); statue by *Chantrey*, after Reynolds's picture of her as the Tragic Muse.

8. *Sir James Simpson* (d. 1870), the discoverer of the value of chloroform as an anæsthetic; bust by *Brodie*.

9. *John Kemble* (d. 1823), the actor, in the character of Cato; statue by *Flaxman*.

\*10. *Lord Norris* (d. 1601), son of Sir Henry Norris who was executed with the ill-fated Anne Boleyn, with his wife, and six sons. The recumbent figures of Lord and Lady Norris are under a catafalque; at the sides are the life-size kneeling figures of the sons. On the S. side of the canopy is a relief of warlike scenes from the life of the deceased nobleman. At the top is a small Goddess of Fame.

11. *Mrs. Kirton* (d. 1603); altar-tomb.

12. *Sarah, Duchess of Somerset* (d. 1692). The Duchess is represented leaning on her arm under a canopy, looking towards the angels, who are appearing to her in the clouds. At the sides are two poor boys bewailing the death of their benefactress.

\*13. *J. Gascoigne Nightingale* (d. 1752), and his wife (d. 1731); group by *Roubiliac*. Death is launching his dart at the dying lady, while her husband tries to ward off the attack.

14. *Lady St. John* (d. 1614), with an effigy.

15. *Admiral Pocock* (d. 1793); sitting figure of Victory with medallion, by *Bacon*.

16. *Sir G. Holles*, nephew of Sir Francis Vere (d. 1626), by *Stone*.
*17. *Sir Francis Vere* (d. 1608), officer in the service of Queen **Elizabeth**. Four kneeling **warriors** in armour support a black marble **slab, on which** lies the armour of the deceased.

This **chapel** also contains tablets or busts in memory of *Admiral Kempenfelt*, who was drowned with 900 sailors by the sinking of the 'Royal George' in 1782 (commemorated in Cowper's well-known lines); *Sir Humphrey Davy* (d. 1829), the natural philosopher; the learned *Dr. Young* (d. 1829), and others.

Beyond this point we dispense with the services of the guide.

The *CHAPTER HOUSE, to the S.E. of the Abbey, adjoining the Poets' Corner, an octagonal room with a central pillar, was built in 1250, and from 1282 to 1547 was used for the meetings of the House of Commons, which Edward VI., in the latter year, appointed to take place in St. Stephen's Chapel, **Westminster Palace**. The Chapter House was afterwards used as a receptacle for public records, but these have now been removed to the New Record Office (p. 135).

On the wall are remains of a **mural** painting of Christ surrounded by the Christian virtues. The old tiled pavement is well executed. The Chapter House, which has recently been ably restored, contains a Roman **sarcophagus**; a **glass-case with fragments** of sculpture, coins, keys, etc., found in the neighbourhood; and another **case** with ancient documents relating to the Abbey, including the Great Charter of Edward the Confessor (1065). The stained-glass windows were erected by the Queen and a few American admirers in memory of Dean Stanley. The Chapter House is usually entered from the E. walk of the cloisters (comp. p. 201).

Adjoining the chapter-house is the *Chapel of the Pyx* (shown by special order only), which was once the *Treasury of the Kings of England*. The pyx (*i.e.* the box in which the standards of gold and silver are kept) has been removed to the Mint (p. 125).

Opposite the entrance to the Chapter House is a staircase ascending to the *Muniment Room*, or Archives of the Abbey, and to the Triforium, which affords a fine survey of the interior.

The room called the *Chapel of St. Blaise*, between the S. transept and the Chapter House, has a lofty groined roof.

In the *Jerusalem Chamber*, to the S.W. of the Abbey (shown on application **at the** porter's lodge), are frescoes of the Death of Henry IV. **and the Coronation of Queen** Victoria, some stained **glass ascribed to the period of Henry III.**, and busts of Henry IV. and Henry V. **It dates from 1376-86, and w**as the scene of the death of Henry IV.

<pre>
King Henry.   Doth any name particular belong
              Unto the lodging where I first did swoon?
Warwick.      'Tis called Jerusalem, my noble Lord.
King.         Laud be to God! even there my life must end.
              It hath been prophesied to me many years,
              I should not die but in Jerusalem;
              Which vainly I supposed the Holy Land: —
              But bear me to that chamber; there I'll lie
              In that Jerusalem shall Harry die.

              Shakspeare, King Henry IV., Part II; Act iv. Sc. 4.
</pre>

## 18. WESTMINSTER SCHOOL.

It probably derived its name from tapestries or pictures of the history of Jerusalem with which it was hung. The Upper House of Convocation of the Province of Canterbury now meets here.

The adjoining *Abbot's Refectory* or *College Hall*, where the Westminster college boys dine, contains some ancient tapestry and stained glass. The Lower House of Convocation also meets here.

The beautiful CLOISTERS, dating from the 11th-14th cent., may be entered by a door in the S. aisle of the Abbey, adjacent to the angle of Poets' Corner, whence a good view of them is obtained (see p. 201). They contain numerous tombs.

For fuller information the curious reader is referred to Dean Stanley's 'Memorials of Westminster Abbey' and Sir G. G. Scott's 'Gleanings from Westminster Abbey'.

To the W. of Westminster Abbey rises the **Westminster Column**, a red granite monument 60 ft. high, designed by *Sir Gilbert Scott*, and erected in 1854-59 to former scholars of Westminster School who fell in the Crimea or the Indian Mutiny. At the base of the column couch four lions. Above are the statues of Edward the Confessor and Henry III. (chief builders of Westminster Abbey), Queen Elizabeth (founder of Westminster School), and Queen Victoria. The column is surmounted by a group of St. George and the Dragon. It is on or near the site of Caxton's house (the 'Red Pale'), in the Almonry.

An archway, passing under the new house to the S. of the column, leads to the *Dean's Yard* and **Westminster School**, or *St. Peter's College* (Pl. R, 25; *IV*), re-founded by Queen Elizabeth in 1560. The school consists of 40 Foundationers, called *Queen's Scholars*, and about 180 *Oppidans* or *Town Boys*. Among the celebrated men educated here were Dryden, Locke, Ben Jonson, Cartwright, Bentham, Barrow, Horne Tooke, Cowley, Rowe, Prior, Giles Fletcher, Churchill, Cowper, Southey, Hackluyt the geographer, Sir Chris. Wren, Warren Hastings, Gibbon, George Herbert, Vincent Bourne, Dyer, Toplady, Charles Wesley, George Coleman, Aldrich the musician, Elmsley the scholar, Lord Raglan, J. A. Froude, and Earl Russell. Richard Busby (p. 203) was head-master here from 1638 to 1695. A comedy of Terence is annually performed at Christmas in the dormitory of the Queen's Scholars by the Westminster boys, with a prologue and epilogue alluding to current events. The old dormitory of the Abbey is now used as the great school-room, while the school-library and class-rooms occupy the site of the mediæval Misericorde, of which considerable remains are still traceable. The old tables in the dining-hall are said to be made from the timbers of the Armada. The staircase of Ashburnham House (included in the school-buildings) and the school-gateway are by Inigo Jones. — The *Royal Architectural Museum*, in Tufton Street, beyond the college (adm. daily 10-4, Sat. 10-6, free), contains Gothic, Renaissance, and Classic carvings.

In Caxton Street, leading off Victoria Street, is the new *Westminster Town Hall*, a handsome Jacobean building of red brick.

**Westminster Hospital** (Pl. R, 25; *IV*), in the *Broad Sanctuary* (formerly a sacred place of refuge for criminals and political offenders), to the N.W. of the Abbey, was founded in 1719, *Mr. Henry Hoare*, **banker**, of Fleet Street, being a leading promoter. It **was the first** of the now numerous hospitals of London supported **by voluntary** contributions. It contains beds for 200 patients.

The **Royal Aquarium**, in Victoria Street, to the W. of the hospital, a handsome red brick edifice, with an arched roof of glass **and iron**, was opened in 1876. The cost of the building, which is 600 ft. in length, **was nearly** 200,000*l*. It includes large salt and **fresh-water aquaria, a summer and** winter garden, a theatre (see p. 42), **concert-hall**, reading-room, picture-gallery, and restaurant; **and acrobatic and spectacular** performances and music-hall **entertainments of all kinds are given here.**

## 19. Pall Mall and Piccadilly.

*Waterloo Place. York Column. Marlborough House. St. James's Street. Burlington House. Geological Museum. Leicester Square.*

**Pall Mall** (Pl. R, 22, 26; *IV*), the centre of club-life (see p. 73), **and a street of** modern palaces, derives its name from the old **game** of *pail mail* (from the Italian *palla*, 'a ball', and *malleo*, a **mallet**; French *jeu de mail*), introduced into England during the **reign of** Charles I., a precursor of the **modern** croquet. In the 16th and 17th centuries Pall Mall was a fashionable suburban promenade, **but about the end** of the 17th cent. it began **to** assume the form **of a street.** Among the many celebrated persons who have resided **in this street may be mentioned** Marshal Schomberg, the scion of **a noble Rhenish family** (the Counts of Schönburg), who fell at the **Battle of the** Boyne (1690). Gainsborough, the painter, died in 1788 in the house which **had once** been Schomberg's (house next the War Office). Dodsley, the publisher, carried on business in Pall Mall under the sign of 'Tully's Head', bringing out, among other works, **Sterne's 'Tristram Shandy', and the** 'Annual Register'.

The eastern portion of the street, between Cockspur Street and Trafalgar **Square, is** called *Pall Mall East*. Here, nearly opposite the corner **of the HAYMARKET (where Addison** once resided), is a bronze statue **of *George III*., by** Wyatt, erected in 1837. On the N. side of Pall Mall East stands the *University Club* (entrance from Suffolk Street); farther to **the W.**, at the left corner of Haymarket, is **Her** *Majesty's Theatre* or **Opera-house**, rebuilt after a fire in 1867. **Farther to the N., on the right side of the** Haymarket, is the *Haymarket Theatre* (p. 40). Then in Pall Mall, to the left, at the corner of Waterloo Place, **is the** *United Service Club*, and to the right the *National Conservative Club*.

**To the N. of Waterloo Place** (Pl. R, 26, *IV*) is *Regent Street* **(p. 224), leading** to Piccadilly. In the centre of the place is the

*CRIMEAN MONUMENT, erected, from a design by *Bell*, to the memory of the 2162 officers and soldiers of the Guards, who fell in the Russian war. On a granite pedestal is a figure of Victory with laurel wreaths; below, in front, three guardsmen; behind, a trophy of guns captured at Sebastopol. On the sides are inscribed the names of Alma, Inkerman, and Sebastopol. — In the S. part of the place or square are four monuments. To the left is that of *Colin Campbell*, *Lord Clyde*, Field-Marshal (d. 1863), the conqueror of Lucknow, by *Marochetti*, consisting of a bronze statue on a circular granite pedestal, at the foot of which is Britannia, with a twig of laurel, sitting on a lion couchant. Adjacent is a similar monument (by *Boehm*) to *Lord Lawrence* (d. 1879), ruler of the Punjáb during the Sepoy Mutiny of 1857 and Viceroy of India from 1864 to 1869, erected in 1882 by his fellow-subjects, British and Indian. — To the right, opposite, is the bronze statue of *Sir John Franklin*, by *Noble*, erected by Parliament 'to the great arctic navigator and his brave companions who sacrificed their lives in completing the discovery of the North West Passage A.D. 1847-48'. On the front of the pedestal is a relief in bronze, representing the interment of the relics of the unfortunate Franklin expedition; on the sides are the names of the crews of the ships *Erebus* and *Terror*. On the right of this statue is a bronze figure of Field-Marshal *Sir John Fox Burgoyne* (d. 1871), on a pedestal of light-coloured granite, by *Boehm*.

The broad flight of steps at the S. end of Waterloo Place, known as *Waterloo Steps*, descends to St. James's Park. At the top of the steps rises the **York Column**, a granite column of the Tuscan order, 124 ft. in height, designed by *Wyatt*, and erected in 1833. It is surmounted by a bronze statue of the Duke of York (second son of George III.), by *Westmacott*. A winding staircase ascends in the interior to the platform, which affords an admirable *View of the W. portions of the great city (closed at present). — To the W. of the column, in Carlton House Terrace, is *Prussia House*, the residence of the German ambassador.

Farther on in Pall Mall (S. side) is a series of palatial clubhouses, the oldest of which dates from 1829 (see also pp. 74, 75). At the corner on the left is the *Athenæum Club* (with frieze); then the *Travellers' Club* (with its best façade towards the garden), *Reform Club*, and *Carlton Club* (with polished granite pillars; an imitation of Sansovino's Library of St. Mark at Venice). A little farther on is the *War Office*, in front of which is a bronze statue of *Lord Herbert of Lea* (d. 1861), once War Secretary, by *Foley*.

Opposite, on the right side of the street, are the *Junior Carlton Club* and the *Army and Navy Club*. ST. JAMES'S SQUARE, which is reached at this point, contains the mansions of the Duke of Norfolk, the Earl of Derby, the Bishop of London, and other members of the aristocracy, and is embellished with an *Equestrian Statue of William III.*, in bronze, by *Bacon*.

Farther on, **at the W.** end of Pall Mall, are the *Oxford and Cambridge Club*, the *Guards' Club*, and the *Unionist Club* **on** the left, and the *Marlborough Club* on the right. **Marlborough House** (Pl. R, 22; *IV*), on the S. side of Pall Mall, **was** erected by *Sir Christopher Wren*, in **1710, for the first** Duke of Marlborough, who lived here in such a **magnificent style as** entirely to eclipse the court of 'Neighbour George' in St. James's Palace. In 1817 the house was **purchased by Government as** a residence for Princess Charlotte and her husband **Prince Leopold of** Saxe-Coburg. The princess died the same year, but Leopold (d. 1865) continued to reside here till he accepted the throne of Belgium in **1831. The house** was afterwards **occupied by the Queen Dowager** Adelaide, subsequently used **as a** picture-gallery, and is now the residence of the Prince of Wales.

To **the W. of** Marlborough House, and separated **from** it by a narrow **carriage-way** only, is *St. James's Palace* (p. 255).

In ST. JAMES'S STREET, which here leads N. to Piccadilly, are situated the *Conservative Club*, *Arthur's Club*, *Brooks's Club*, *New University Club*, *White's Club* (the bow window of which has figured in so many novels), *Boodle's Club*, the *Cocoa Tree Club*, the *Junior Army and Navy Club*, the *Devonshire Club* (formerly *Crockford's*, notorious for its high play under the Regency), and others. To the right, in King Street, is *St. James's Theatre* (p. 40). *Willis's Rooms*, a little farther along King Street, were down to 1863, under the name of *Almack's* (from the original proprietor, 1765), famous for the aristocratic and exclusive balls, also called Almack's, which were held in them. The **elegantly** fitted up rooms are now used for concerts, **balls, dinners, and** other similar purposes (see p. 43). King Street **also contains** *Christie and Manson's Auction Rooms*, celebrated **for sales of valuable** art-collections. **The** chief sales take **place on Saturdays, during the Season.**

**Piccadilly** (Pl. R, 18, 22; *I*, *IV*), extending from Haymarket to Hyde Park **Corner, is nearly 1 M.** in length. The eastern portion, **with its handsome shops, is one of** the chief business streets of **the West End. The western half,** which is bordered on the S. by the *Green Park* (p. 259), **contains a** number of aristocratic and **fashionable residences, and the** *Turf* (No. 85), the *Naval and Military* (94), **Badminton** (100), *St. James's* (106), *Savile* (107), and *Junior Athenaeum* (116) **clubs.**

Turning into it to the right, we first notice, on the right side, a **few yards from the corner of** St. James's Street, the *Egyptian Hall* (p. 44). **On** the opposite **side are** *Old and New Bond Streets* (p. 226), **leading** to Oxford **Street.** Between Old Bond Street and Sackville Street rises **New Burlington House** (Pl. R, 22; *I*), to the W. **of which is** *Burlington Arcade* (p. **25**). Old Burlington House, built in 1695-1743 by Richard, Lord Burlington, with the assistance of **the** architect Kent, was purchased by Government in 1854 for the **sum of** 140,000*l*. along **with its** gardens, on which various new edifices have been built. The incongruous top story and the present façade of the old building are also new. Nearest Piccadilly is a handsome building in the Italian Renaissance style, completed in 1872 from designs by *Banks* and *Barry*, and occupied by several learned societies, to whom the rooms are granted by Government rent-free; in the E. wing are the *Royal*, *Geological*, and *Chemical Societies*, and in the W. the *Antiquarian* (with a collection of paintings, chiefly old portraits), *Astronomical*, and *Linnaean*.

The **Royal Society**, or Academy of Science, the most important of the learned bodies of Great Britain, was founded in 1660, and received its charter of incorporation from Charles II. three years later. As early as 1645, however, its germ existed in the meeting of a few men of learning, far from the turmoil of the Civil War, to discuss subjects relating to the physical and exact sciences. The first number of its fmous *Philosophical Transactions* appeared in 1665. It now comprises 750 members, each of whom is entitled to append to his name the letters F. R. S. (Fellow of the Royal Society). The *Library* of the society consists of about 50,000 vols. and 5000 MSS. The rooms contain portraits and busts of celebrated Fellows, including Sir Christopher Wren, Sir Isaac Newton, Robert Boyle, Halley, Sir Humphrey Davy, Watt, and Sir William Herschel; also a telescope which belonged to Newton, and the MS. of his 'Philosophiæ Naturalis Principia Mathematica'; and the original model of Davy's safety lamp.

An arcade leads through the building into the inner court. On the N. side is the exhibition building of the **Royal Academy of Arts** (founded in 1768), in the Renaissance style, erected by *Smirke* in 1868-9. At the top of the façade are 9 statues of celebrated artists: Phidias, Leonardo da Vinci, Flaxman, Raphael, Michael Angelo, Titian, Reynolds, Wren, and Wykeham. The Exhibition of the Royal Academy (transferred in 1869 from Trafalgar Square to Piccadilly), which takes place here every year from May to the beginning of August, attracts immense numbers of visitors (admission 1s., catalogue 1s.). It consists of paintings and sculptures by modern (mainly) British artists, which must have been finished during the previous year and not exhibited elsewhere before. The 'Private View' of the Exhibition, held by invitation of the Academicians before it is thrown open to the public, is always attended by the cream of society and is one of the events of the London Season. The Academy also organises every winter an exhibition of works of old masters belonging to private individuals. Above the exhibition-rooms three galleries (open daily 11-4, free) have been built, which contain some valuable works of early art, the diploma pictures presented by Academicians on their election, and the Gibson collection of sculpture. Among the ancient works are: \*Mary with Jesus and St. John, a relief by *Michael Angelo*; \*Madonna, Holy Child, and St. Anna, a celebrated cartoon by

## 19. MUSEUM OF GEOLOGY.

*Leonardo da Vinci*, executed in 1503 for the church Dell'Annunziata at Florence; Copy of Leonardo's Last Supper, by his pupil *Marco d'Oggionno*, from which Morghen's engraving was taken; Woman at a well, ascribed to *Giorgione* but considered by Frizzoni to be an early work of *Seb. del Piombo*; portrait by *Giorgione*. The diploma works include good specimens by Reynolds and Wilkie. The *Library*, on the first floor, contains a fine collection of books and prints.

At the back of the Academy, and facing Burlington Gardens, is the new building of **London University** (not to be confounded with University College in Gower Street), another Renaissance structure, erected in 1869 from designs by *Pennethorne*. (London University is not a teaching establishment but an examining board, granting degrees in arts, science, medicine, and law, to candidates of either sex wherever educated.)

The effective façade is decorated with a series of statues. Above the portico are those of Milton, Newton, Harvey, and Bentham (as representatives of the four Faculties), by *Durham*; over the cornice in the centre, Plato, Archimedes, and Justinian, by *Woodington*, and Galen, Cicero, and Aristotle, by *Westmacott*; in the W. wing, Locke, Bacon, and Adam Smith, by *Theed*, and Hume, Hunter, and Sir Humphrey Davy, by *Noble*; in the E. wing, Galileo, Laplace, and Goethe, by *Wyon*, and Cuvier, Leibnitz, and Linnæus, by *Macdowell*. The interior contains a spacious lecture room, a number of other apartments, in which the graduation examinations take place twice annually, and a valuable library. A marble statue of Queen Victoria, by *Boehm*, was erected here in May, 1889.

Close by, at 1 Savile Row, is the *Royal Geographical Society*. Richard Brinsley Sheridan died at 14 Savile Row in 1816.

On the N. side of Piccadilly, a little beyond Burlington House, is the *Albany*, let out in chambers, and numbering Canning, Byron, and Macaulay among quondam residents. Byron passed the first part of his married life at 139 Piccadilly, where his daughter Ada was born in Dec., 1815.

**St. James's Church** (Pl. R, 22; *I*), on the S. side of Piccadilly, built by *Wren* in 1682-84, and considered (as to the interior) one of his finest works, contains a marble font by *Grinling Gibbons*, who also executed the handsome foliage over the altar. The stained-glass windows, representing the Passion and other scenes, are modern. The vestry is hung with portraits of former rectors.

The **Museum of Practical Geology**, erected in 1850, is a little farther to the E. It is open daily, Fridays excepted, from 10 to 5 (in winter 10-4), and on Mondays and Saturday till 10 p.m.; it is closed from 10th August to 10th September. The building contains, besides the geological museum, a lecture-room for 500 hearers, and a library. Entrance by Jermyn Street (Nos. 28-32).

The HALL contains busts of celebrated geologists: on the right, Murchison, Greenough, De la Beche, Castletown, William Smith, and Jukes (behind); on the left, Buckland, Playfair, Hall, Sedgwick, and Hutton; at the pillars near the entrance, Queen Victoria and Prince Albert. At the upper end is a colossal copy of the Farnese Hercules in Portland limestone. Then English, Irish, and Scotch granite; alabaster; Portland limestone from the island of Portland, near Weymouth in Dorsetshire;

Derbyshire, Staffordshire, and Irish marbles; auriferous quartz; malachite; a large block of solid copper; and numerous varieties of limestone. These are partly in the rough, and partly polished and cut in the shape of large cubes, squares, tablets, or short columns. Also terracotta statuettes, copies of ancient statues, vases, and pieces of tesselated pavement. The mosaic pavement in the middle of the hall deserves notice.

On the FIRST FLOOR we first observe a large vase of Siberian avanturine quartz, a gift from the Emperor of Russia; a geological model of London and its vicinity; a steel salver, inlaid with gold, presented by the Russian Administration of Mines to Sir Roderick Murchison. On the S. side is a collection of porcelain, glass, enamels, and mosaics from the earliest period down to the present day. Then, in table-cases at the sides of the room, iron, steel, and copper, at different stages of their manufacture. We notice in a case on the right (E.) side a penny rolled out into a strip of copper, 10 yds. long. The cases in the form of a horse-shoe in the middle of the room contain the collection of non-metallic minerals: here are seen all kinds of crystallisations, particularly of precious stones, from quartz nodules with brilliant crystals in the interior up to the most exquisitely polished jewels. Models of the largest known diamonds, such as the Koh-i-noor and the Regent Diamond, are also exhibited in these cases. The metalliferous minerals, or ores, occupy the wall-cases. Other cabinets are filled with agates, some of which are artificially coloured with oxide of iron, and the precious metals, including a model of a huge nugget of pure gold.

In the other parts of the saloon and in the adjoining apartments are exhibited geological relief-plans and models of mines, metallurgical processes, and various kinds of machinery. The two upper galleries, running round the hall, chiefly contain fossils, which are of little interest to the ordinary visitor.

On the N. side of Piccadilly, opposite the Geological Museum, is *St. James's Hall* (p. 43), which has another entrance in the Regent Quadrant (p. 224). We next reach *Regent Circus* (p. 224), and then, on the right, the *Haymarket* (p. 218). At this point Piccadilly proper comes to an end. *Coventry Street*, its eastern prolongation, containing the *Prince of Wales Theatre* (p. 42), leads on to **Leicester Square** (Pl. R, 27; *I*), a quarter largely inhabited by French residents, and adorned in 1874 with flower-beds and a marble statue of *Shakspeare*, in the centre, bearing the inscription, 'There is no darkness but ignorance'; at the base are four waterspouting dolphins. The corners of the garden are embellished with marble busts of *Reynolds, Hunter, Hogarth*, and *Newton*, all of whom lived in or near the square. After the revocation of the Edict of Nantes (1685) this neighbourhood became a favourite resort of the more aristocratic French Protestant exiles. Leicester House and Savile House, once situated in the square, were occupied by members of the royal family during the first half of last century; and Peter the Great was entertained at Savile House by the Marquis of Carmarthen (1698). Down to the beginning of the present century the open space in the centre was a frequent resort of duellists. — The *Alhambra Theatre* (p. 43), on the E. side of the square, was burned down in 1882, but was rebuilt in 1883-84. The site of Savile House, on the N. side of the square, is occupied by the *Empire Theatre* (p. 43).

## 20. Regent Street. Oxford Street. Holborn.

*All Saints' Church. University College. St. Pancras' Church. Foundling Hospital.*

**Regent Street** (Pl. R, 23, 26; *I*), one of the finest streets in London, and containing a large number of the best shops, was laid out by *Nash* in 1813, for the purpose of connecting Carlton House, the residence of the Prince Regent, with Regent's Park. It is 1 M. in length, and extends from Waterloo Place, Pall Mall (p. 218), across Oxford Street, to Portland Place. To the right (E.), at the corner of Charles Street, stands the **Junior United Service Club**, and on the same side, at the corner of Jermyn Street (with the *Geological Museum*, p. 222), is the *Raleigh Club*. The street then reaches *Regent Circus, Piccadilly* (see p. 223; known as *Piccadilly Circus*), whence Piccadilly leads to the W., Coventry Street to the E., and the wide Shaftesbury Avenue (p. 144) to the N.E. The vacant triangle in the centre of the Circus is to be occupied by a *Memorial Fountain to Lord Shaftesbury*, by Alfred Gilbert. Beyond the Circus Regent Street describes a curve to the W., forming the so-called *Quadrant*. On the left is the entrance to *St. James's Hall* (see above). Vigo Street, at the end of the Quadrant, leads on the left to the new building of *London University* (p. 222). Farther on, to the left, we pass New Burlington Street, Conduit Street, and Maddox Street.

Between Hanover Street and Prince's Street we observe the colonnade of *Hanover Chapel*. **Hanover Square**, on the left, is embellished with a **bronze statue** of *William Pitt* (d. 1806), by *Chantrey*. On the E. side of the square is the *St. George's Club*, occupying the site of the long popular *Hanover Square Concert Rooms*; on the W. side, the *Oriental Club*; and at the N.W. angle, in Tenterden Street, the *Royal Academy of Music*. In George Street, leading out of the square on the S., is *St. George's Church*, built by *James*, with a classic portico, and three stained-**glass windows**, brought from Malines about 1520. It is the most famous church in London for fashionable weddings. Lady Mary Wortley Montagu died in George Street in 1762.

The intersection of Regent Street with Oxford Street (p. 225), which extends for a long distance in both directions, is called *Regent Circus, Oxford Street*, or simply *Oxford Circus*. The second short cross-street beyond Oxford Street (l.) leads to **Cavendish Square**, which contains an equestrian statue in marble of the *Duke of Cumberland* (the victor at Culloden in 1746), by *Chew*, and a bronze statue of *Lord George Bentinck* (d. 1848), by *Campbell*. *Harcourt House*, on the W. side of the square, is the mansion of the Duke of Portland. The old **Polytechnic Institution**, between Cavendish Square and Regent Street, has been sold to the Young Mens' Christian Institute.

Adjacent, at 13 Mandeville Place, Manchester Square, is *Trinity College*, an incorporated institution for the study of music and arts. Lord Byron was born in 1788 at 24 Holles Street, between Cavendish Square and Oxford Street; the house, however, has since been rebuilt. He was baptised in *Old Marylebone Church*, at the top of Marylebone High Street (Pl. R, 20), where Charles Wesley was buried in 1778. This was the old church (rebuilt in 1741) which figures in the 'Rake's Marriage' by Hogarth (see p. 167).

**All Saints' Church** (Pl. R, 24; *I*), in Margaret Street, to the E. of Regent Street, a brick edifice in the Early English style, built by *Butterfield* in 1850-59, is lavishly decorated in the interior with marble and gilding. The E. wall of the choir is frescoed by Dyce in the style of early Christian art.

At the N. end of Regent Street is *Langham Place*, with *All Souls' Church*, erected by Nash. The large building on the other side is the *Langham Hotel* (p. 7). From this point PORTLAND PLACE, one of the widest streets in London (120 ft.), leads to *Park Crescent, Park Square*, and *Regent's Park* (p. 228).

**Oxford Street** (Pl. R, 19, 23, 27; *I, II*), the principal artery of traffic between the N.W. quarter of London and the City, extends from the Marble Arch (at the N.E. corner of Hyde Park, p. 259) to Holborn, a distance of $1^1/_2$ M. The E. portion of this imposing street contains a number of the most important shops in London, and presents a scene of immense traffic and activity; while the W. end, with the adjoining streets and squares (particularly Grosvenor Square and Berkeley Square on the S. and Portman Square on the N.), comprises many aristocratic residences. *Edgware Road*, which begins at the W. end of Oxford Street (see Pl. R, 15), follows the line of the old Roman road to St. Albans. Many of the houses in *Grosvenor Square* and *Berkeley Square* (with its plane-trees) still have bits of fine old iron-work in front of their doors, with extinguishers for the links or torches formerly used. Horace Walpole died at 11 Berkeley Square in 1797; Clive committed suicide at No. 45 in 1774. No. 38, now the town-house of Lord Rosebery, was the house from which the daughter of Mr. Child, the banker, eloped with the Earl of Westmorland in 1782, and was afterwards the residence of their daughter Lady Jersey (d. 1867) and her husband. The 'Blue Stocking Club' met at Mrs. Montagu's (d. 1800), in the N.W. corner of *Portman Square*. At the foot of South Audley Street, which runs to the S. from the S.W. corner of Grosvenor Square, is *Chesterfield House* (Pl. R, 18; *IV*), with a fine marble staircase and the library in which the 'Chesterfield Letters' were written. In *Brook Street*, which runs E. from Grosvenor Square, is a house (No. 25) distinguished by a tablet indicating that Händel used to live here. Brook Street soon crosses *New Bond Street*, leading from Oxford Street to Piccadilly (p. 220) and containing numerous handsome shops and several picture-galleries (comp. p. 45).

## 20. ST. GILES-IN-THE-FIELDS.

The Doré Gallery, 35 New Bond Street, contains a collection of large oil-paintings and drawings by the French painter, *Gustave Doré* (b. at Strassburg, 1832; d. 1883), and should be visited (open daily 10-6; admission 1s.). Among the finest works are: 2. Christ entering Jerusalem, painted in 1875-76; *3. Christ leaving the Prætorium; 12. Massacre of the Innocents (1872); 7. Dream of Pilate's wife (1874); *4. The Brazen Serpent (1875-77); Ecce Homo; The Ascension; Gaming-table at Baden-Baden; Moses before Pharaoh; the Vale of Tears, his last work. — The Doré Gallery also contains several works by *Mr. Edwin Long, R.A.*

*Hanover Square*, *Cavendish Square*, *Regent Street*, see above. In Oxford Street, on the left, farther on, is the *Princess's Theatre* (p. 41), nearly opposite which is the *Pantheon*, which has successively been a concert-room, a theatre, and a bazaar, and is now the extensive wine warehouse of Messrs. Gilbey. Then on the right, in SOHO SQUARE, is the *Soho Bazaar* (p. 26).

Oxford Street proper ends at *Tottenham Court Road*, which runs to the N. to Euston Road, and *Charing Cross Road* (p. 144), leading to the S. to Charing Cross. In the latter is the church of *St. Mary the Virgin*, Soho, on the site of the first Greek church in London (1677), part of which is still standing (see Greek inscription over the W. door). The church, which was afterwards occupied by a French congregation, contains some old stained glass and a good Crucifixion, in marble, by Miss Grant.

The eastern prolongation of Oxford Street, extending to Holborn, and called *New Oxford Street*, was laid out in 1849 at a cost of 290,000*l.* through the 'Rookery of St. Giles', one of the most disreputable quarters of London. No. 75, to the right, belonging to *Messrs. Pears*, has a vestibule in the style of a Pompeian room, adorned with sculptures. On the left, at the corner of Hart Street, is *Mudie's Library* (p. 17). A little to the S. of New Oxford Street, in High Street, is the church of *St. Giles-in-the-Fields*, the third church on this site, completed in 1734. Chapman, the translator of Homer (tombstone against the exterior S. wall, erected by Inigo Jones), Shirley, the dramatist, and Andrew Marvell are buried here. To the E. in the churchyard is the square tomb of Pendrell, who helped Charles II. to safety after the battle of Worcester, with a quaint epitaph, now almost undecipherable, beginning 'Unparalleled Pendrell'. The *British Museum* (p. 233) lies in *Great Russell Street*, which runs off Tottenham Court Road, a little to the north. There are several squares at a short distance from the street, among the chief of which are, to the W. of the British Museum, BEDFORD SQUARE; to the E., BLOOMSBURY SQUARE and RUSSELL SQUARE, the one containing a statue of *Charles James Fox* (d. 1806), and the other one of *Francis, Duke of Bedford* (d. 1802), both by *Westmacott*.

*Gower Street*, which leads to the N. from Bedford Square, contains University College (Pl. B, 28), founded in 1828, chiefly through the exertions of Lord Brougham, for students of every religious denomination. A long flight of steps leads to the decastyle Corinthian portico fronting the main edifice, which is 400 ft. in length and surmounted by a handsome dome. It contains numerous lecture-rooms, a laboratory, and a museum with original models and drawings by **Flaxman** (d. 1826), the celebrated sculptor (open to visitors in the summer months, Sat. 10-4). A new wing was added in 1880-81. The subjects studied at the college comprise the exact and natural sciences, the classical and modern languages and literatures, history, law, and medicine. The building also contains a well-known **school for boys**. The whole is maintained without aid from Government. The number of professors is about 30, and that of students about 1600, paying nearly 30,000*l.* in fees. In Gower Street, opposite University College, and connected with it as a clinical establishment, stands the University **College Hospital**, where from 19,000 to 20,000 patients are annually treated by the medical professors of the college.

Close by, in Gordon Square, is the **Catholic Apostolic Church**, built in 1850-54, one of the largest ecclesiastical edifices in London. The INTERIOR is a fine example of modern Gothic (Early English), though unfinished towards the W. The *Choir*, with its graceful triforium and diapered spandrils, is very rich. The most beautiful part of the church is, however, the *English Chapel*, to the E. of the chancel, with its polychrome painting, stained-glass windows, and open arcade with fine carving (particularly on the three arches to the S. of the altar). In the *Morning Chapel*, to the S. of the chancel, is the altar formerly used by the Rev. Edward **Irving** (d. 1834), the founder of the Catholic Apostolic Church.

**St. Pancras' Church** (Pl. B, 28), to the N.E. of University College, in Euston Square, was built by the Messrs. Inwood in 1819 at a cost of 76,679*l.* It is an imitation of the Erechtheum at Athens; while its tower, 168 ft. in height, is a reproduction of the so-called Tower of the Winds. *Old St. Pancras' Church* (Pl. B, 27), with its historical churchyard, is situated in Old St. Pancras Road, next to the Workhouse. — A little to the W. is the *Gower Street Station* of the *Metropolitan Railway* (p. 36). To the N. is *Euston Square Station*, the terminus of the *London and North Western Railway* (p. 32), the entrance-hall of which contains a colossal statue of George Stephenson, by *Baily*. To the E. is the *St. Pancras Station*, the terminus of the *Midland Railway* (p. 33), with the terminus hotel, a very handsome building in an ornate Gothic style, by Sir G. G. Scott. Adjacent is the *King's Cross Station*, or terminus of the *Great Northern Railway* (p. 33).

To the N. of this point lie the populous but comparatively uninteresting districts of ISLINGTON, HIGHBURY, HOLLOWAY, CAMDEN TOWN, and KENTISH TOWN. In Great College Street, Camden Town, is situated the *Royal Veterinary College* (Pl. B. 23). with a museum to which visitors are admitted daily (9 to 5 or 6) on presenting their cards. *Charles Dibdin* (d. 1811), the writer of **nautical** songs, is buried in St. Martin's Burial Ground, Pratt Street, a little to the N.W. of the Veterinary College. The *Royal Agricultural Hall* (p. 45) is in Liverpool Road, Islington (Pl. B, 35), and the *Grand Theatre* (p. 42) is close by, in High Street. A little to the N.E., in Canonbury Square (Pl. B, 38), is *Canonbury Tower*, an interesting relic of the country-residence of the Priors of St. Bartholomew. The tower was probably built by Prior Bolton (p. 95), though restored at a later date, and contains a fine carved **oak room**. Oliver Goldsmith occupied **rooms** in the tower in 1762.

15 *

The eastern prolongation of New Oxford Street is **High Holborn**
(Pl. R, 32, and H; so called from the '*Hole Bourne*', or Fleet Brook,
which once flowed through the hollow near here), a street which
survived the Great Fire, and still contains a considerable number
**of old** houses. Milton once lived here, and it was by this route that
condemned criminals used to be conducted to Tyburn. The increasing **traffic** indicates that **we are** approaching the City. On the right
are several side-streets, leading to *Lincoln's Inn Fields* (with the
*Soane Museum*, etc., see pp. 177-179). Red Lion Street on the
**left**, continued **by Lamb's** Conduit Street and Lamb Street, leads
to *Guilford Street*, on the N. side of which stands the —

Foundling Hospital (Pl. R, 32), a remarkable establishment
founded by Captain Thomas Coram in 1739 for 'deserted children'.
Since 1760, however, it has not been used as a foundling hospital,
but as a home for illegitimate children, whose mothers are known.
(Neither in London nor in any other part of England are there any
foundling hospitals in the proper sense of the term, such as the
'Hospice des Enfants Trouvés' in Paris.) The number of the children
is about 500, and the yearly income of the Hospital, 13,000l.

In the *Board Room* and the *Secretary's Room* are a number of pictures,
chiefly painted about the middle of last century. They include the following: *Hogarth*, °**March to Finchley**, and Finding **of** Moses; portraits by
*Ramsay, Reynolds*, and **Shackleton**; **views** of the Foundling Hospital and
St. George's Hospital by *Wilson*; view **of** the Charterhouse by *Gainsborough*. The Board Room also contains a good portrait of Coram by
*Hogarth*. Most of the pictures were presented to the institution by the
artists themselves. (The success with which the exhibition of these pic-
**tures** was attended **is** said to have led to the first exhibition of the Royal
Academy in 1760.) **The** hospital also possesses Raphael's cartoon of the
Massacre of the Innocents, a bust of Handel and some of his musical MSS.,
a collection of coins **or** tokens deposited with the children (1741-60), etc.
The *Chapel* **is adorned with** an altarpiece by *West*, representing Christ
**blessing little children; the organ was a gift** from *Handel*. Divine ser-
**vice, at which the children are led in singing** by trained voices, is per-
**formed on Sundays at 11 a.m. and 3** p.m. The Hospital is shown to visi-
**tors on Sundays, after morning** service, and on Mondays from 10 to 4.
**The attendants are forbidden to** accept gratuities, but a contribution to
**the funds of the institution is** expected from the visitor on leaving or in
**the church-offertory.**

To the E. of Lincoln's Inn are *Chancery Lane* (p. 136) on the
right (after which we are in the City), and *Gray's Inn Road* (p. 139)
on the left. Then *Holborn Viaduct*, *Newgate*, etc., see pp. 92, 93.

## 21. Regent's Park.

*Zoological Gardens. Botanic Gardens. Primrose Hill.*
*Lord's Cricket Ground.*

**Regent's Park** (Pl. B, 15, 16, 19, 20) was laid out during the
last years of the reign of George III., and derives its name from
the then Prince Regent, afterwards George IV. It occupies the site
of an earlier park called *Marylebone Park*. The name Marylebone
is said to be a corruption of *Mary on Tyburn (Mary-le-bourne)*,

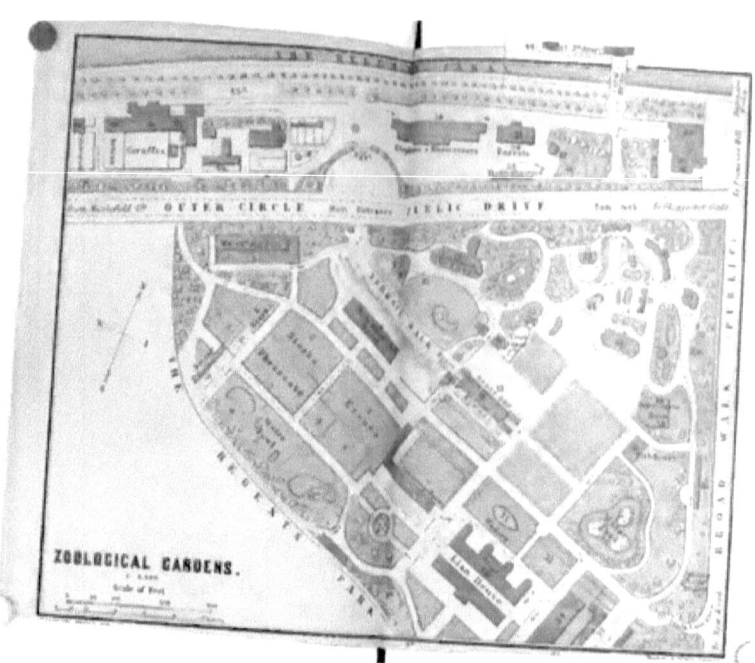

Tyburn being a small brook, coming from Kilburn and flowing into the Thames. It crossed Oxford Street a little to the E. of the Marble Arch and flowed through St. James's Park, leaving its mark upon *Brook Street*, Grosvenor Square, and notably upon '*Tyburn*', that melancholy old place of execution situated about the lower corner of Edgware Road. It has also given its name to *Tyburnia*, the quarter of London situated to the N. of Hyde Park.

In the time of Queen Elizabeth, Marylebone Park was filled with deer and game. Under the Commonwealth the land was cleared of the woods and used as pasturage. Afterwards trees were again planted, footpaths constructed, and a large artificial lake formed.

The Park, which is one of the largest in London, embraces 472 acres of ground, and extends from York Gate, Marylebone Road, to Primrose Hill. Within its precincts are situated several private residences, among which is St. Dunstan's Villa with the clock and the automatic figures from the church of St. Dunstan's in Fleet Street (see p. 135). The gardens of the *Zoological Society* (founded by Sir Humphrey Davy and Sir Stamford Raffles in 1826) occupy a large space in the N. part of the Park, which also contains the gardens of the *Botanical Society* and the *Toxopholite (Archery) Society*. The Park is surrounded by a broad drive known as the *Outer Circle*. In summer a band generally plays in the Park on Sun. afternoons in the *Kiosk* a little to the S. of the Zoological Gardens (Pl. B, 20).

The **Zoological Gardens** are bounded on the N. by the Regent's Canal and intersected by the Outer Circle, which here runs parallel with the canal. They are thus divided into two portions, which, however, communicate with each other by means of a *tunnel* constructed under the drive. The principal entrance is in the Outer Circle (the *Main Entrance* in the Plan); ingress may also be obtained from the Broad Walk, at the S.E. angle of the gardens (see Pl., *South Entrance*), or from Albert Road, Primrose Hill, on the N. side of the canal (*North Entrance* in the Plan). The Main Entrance is about $3/4$ M. from the *Portland Road Station* of the Metropolitan Railway, from which the S. Entrance is a little less remote, while both gates are about $3/4$ M. from the *Chalk Farm Station* of the North-Western and North London Railways. The *Baker Street Station* (Metropolitan) is about $3/4$ M. from the S. entrance, which is only 300 yds. from Gloucester Road, where omnibuses from all parts of London pass at frequent intervals. The *North Entrance* is $1/2$ M. from *Chalk Farm* and $3/4$ M. from *St. John's Wood Road* (Metropolitan Railway), and is passed by Camden Town and Paddington omnibuses. (Carriages may not drive along the Broad Walk.)

The Zoological Gardens are open daily from 9 a.m. to sunset, admission 1s., on Mondays 6d., children half-price except on Mondays; on Sundays only by order obtained from a member. The total number of visitors in 1888 was 608,402. The band of the Life Guards usually plays here on Saturdays at 4 p.m.

## 21. ZOOLOGICAL GARDENS.

Many of the animals conceal themselves during the day in their holes and dens, under water, or among the shrubbery; the best time to visit them, accordingly, is at the feeding-hour, when even the lethargic carnivora are to be seen in a state of activity and excitement. The pelicans are fed at 2.30, the otters at 3, the eagles at 3.30 (except Wednesdays), the beasts of prey at 4, the seals and sea-lions at 4.30, and the diving birds in the fish-house (Pl. 37) at 12 and 5 p.m. The snakes receive their weekly meal on Friday, but visitors are not admitted to this curious spectacle without the express permission of the Director of the Gardens.

Those who have not time to explore the Gardens thoroughly had better follow the route indicated on the plan by arrows, so as to see the most interesting animals in the shortest possible time, avoiding all unnecessary deviations.

On entering from the Outer Circle (Pl., *Main Entrance*), we turn to the right, and first reach the *Western Aviary* (Pl. 1), which is 170 ft. long, and contains 200 different kinds of birds, chiefly from Australia, the Indian Archipelago, and South America. Then, passing the *Crows* (Pl. 1a) and the *Cranes and Storks* (Pl. 2), we reach, on the left, the —

\*Monkey House (Pl. 3), which always attracts a crowd of amused spectators. The unpleasant odour is judiciously disguised by numerous plants and flowers. The bats are also kept here.

We next return (to the right) to the *Storks, Pheasants* (Pl. 2), and *Emeus* (Pl. 4), by which we pass to the left, and then take another turning on the right leading to the *Rodents* (Pl. 6), *Swine* (Pl. 7), and *Southern Ponds* for *Water Fowl* (Pl. 5; about 50 different kinds). We then proceed to the left, along the other side of the Southern Ponds and past the *Sheep Sheds* (Pl. 8), to the *Sea-Lions' Pond* (Pl. 9). To the right is the *Sheep Yard* (9 A), built in 1885 for the *Burrhel*, or blue wild sheep, from the Himalayas. To the S.E. of this point are the new *Wolves' and Foxes' Dens* (Pl. 9 B). We now continue our walk (see Plan) to the large *Lion House* (Pl. 10), which is 230 ft. long and 70 ft. wide. In addition to its living occupants it contains a bust of *Sir Stamford Raffles* (d. 1826), the first president of the Zoological Society.

We now retrace our steps, and pass along the open-air enclosures at the back of the Lion House to the *Antelope House* (Pl. 11). Issuing thence, we proceed straight on, past the *Bear Pit* (Pl. 14), to the southern front of the dens formerly occupied by the lions and tigers, but now containing **Hyenas** and *Bears* (Pl. 12 and 13). The terrace above affords a view of the bear-pit and the pond for the *Polar Bears*. We next turn to the right, and pass through the archway near the *Camels* (Pl. 16). Then, leaving the Clock Tower on the right and the *Eagle Owls* (Pl. 15) on the left, and passing more *Water Fowl* (Pl. 17) on the left, and the *Eastern Aviary* (Pl. 19) on the right, we reach the pavilion of the \**Pelicans* (Pl. 18).

From the pelicans we retrace our steps to the vicinity of the Clock Tower, and bear to the left to the *Northern Pond* (Pl. 20), which contains more water-fowl. By continuing to the left we reach the *Owls' Cages* (Pl. 21), at the back of which is the *Llamas' House* (Pl. 22). This should not be approached too closely on account of the unpleasant expectorating propensities of its inmates. A little farther on is the pond containing the *Mandarin Ducks* (Pl. 23). Between the two, on our left, is the entrance to the tunnel, which we pass in the meantime. Opposite, on the right, are the *Otters* (Pl. 24) and the *Kites* (Pl. 25); to the N.E., on the left, lies the *Civet House* (Pl. 26). We now turn to the right and proceed to the south.

We first reach, on the left, the *Small Mammals* (Pl. 27; the house may be entered), on the right the *Ducks* (Pl. 29); then, on the left, the *Flying Squirrels* (Pl. 28) and the *Racoons* (Pl. 30), near which is the refreshment room (see below). Continuing in a straight direction past the *Vultures* (Pl. 31) and another small aviary containing *Bateleur Eagles*, we reach the S. Entrance, which we leave on the left. Near the entrance is the new *Deer House* (Pl. 32), behind which are the *Cattle Sheds* (Pl. 34; containing, amongst other specimens, the bison, cape buffalo, zebu, and gayal). Opposite the Deer House are aviaries containing *Pheasants* and *Peacocks* (Pl. 31a). We now turn to the left, and after a few paces reach the new *Reptile House* (Pl. 33), to the E. of the Lion House. This contains an extensive collection of large serpents, lizards, alligators, and crocodiles. Here also is the *Manatee* (sea-cow or cow-whale), an interesting and recent acquisition. At this point we turn back and walk straight on, past the front of the Cattle Sheds, to the *Three Island Pond* (Pl. 36), stocked with water-fowl, among which are specimens of the black-necked swan. The path leading first to the left and then to the right, passing (opposite) more *Water Fowl* (Pl. 35), leads to the *Fish-House* (Pl. 37), containing a fine collection of fish and small aquatic birds. The *Refreshment Rooms* (Pl. 38, 39) here afford a welcome opportunity for a rest.

From the Refreshment Rooms we proceed towards the N.W. past the *Eagles' Aviaries* (Pl. 40), having on our left the *Rails* (Pl. 41), and pass through the tunnel leading into the N. section of the gardens. Here we first go straight on, across the canal-bridge, on the other side of which are the *Northern Aviary* (Pl. 42; for birds of prey); the *Tortoise House* (Pl. 43); and the new *Insectarium* (Pl. 44), containing insects, land-crustaceans, chameleons, toads, tree-frogs, terrapins, electric eels, and birds of paradise. Between the tortoise-house and the insectarium is the North Entrance, opposite which are paddocks containing *Japanese* and *Axis Deer*.

We now recross the bridge and turn to the left to the *Small Cats House* (Pl. 44a) and *Lecture Room* (Pl. 45), the latter adorned with water-colour sketches of animals. Adjoining the Lecture Room are the *Marsupials' House* (Pl. 46), containing the great ant-eater, the *\*Sloths' House* (Pl. 47), and a *Kangaroo Shed* (Pl. 48). The Sloths' **House** contains at present some of the most interesting inmates **of the** Gardens, in the form of three *Chimpanzees*, one of which ('Sally') has been here since 1883. 'Sally', who is very lively and intelligent, performs many little tricks at the command of her keeper. Opposite are another *Kangaroo Shed* (Pl. 49) and the *Wombats'* **House** (Pl. 50). Here we turn to the right and pass the *Brush Turkeys* **(Pl. 51)** and the *Markhore House* (Pl. 52) on the right, and a small *Refreshment Stall* (Pl. **53**) on the left. Opposite this stall is the **Parrot** *House* (Pl. 54), containing about ninety different species of that gaudy and harsh-voiced bird, next to which is the new *\*Elephant and Rhinoceros House* (Pl. 56), containing the African and Asiatic varieties of these animals.

No. 57 contains deer belonging to the old world; No. 59 is the *Superintendent's Office*. Proceeding in a straight direction, we reach in succession the *\*Hippopotamus and Brazilian Tapir* (Pl. 60), *\*Giraffes* (Pl. 61), *Zebras* (Pl. 62), and *Ostriches* (Pl. 63). Returning along the S. side of the houses of the animals just mentioned, we reach, on the left, the *Gazelles* (Pl. 64) and the *Beavers* (Pl. 58). A little way beyond the Beaver House we reach the *Exit*, which takes us into the Outer Circle.

Part of the southern portion of Regent's Park is occupied by the **Botanic Gardens** (Pl. B, 20), which are circular in shape, and are **enclosed** by the drive called the *Inner Circle*. Large flower-shows take place here on three Wednesdays in May and June, which are largely **attended** by the fashionable world (tickets of admission sold **at the** gate). On other occasions the gardens are open daily (Sundays **and Wednesdays** excepted) to anyone presenting an order of admission given by **a Fellow of** the Botanical Society. Strangers are generally admitted on application to the officials. The Museum and the collections of sea-weeds and orchids are very interesting.

On the E. side of the Park stands *St. Katherine's Hospital*, with its **chapel. This building** was erected in substitution of one **which** formerly **occupied the site of St.** Katherine's Docks. The property was purchased **by the Dock** Company from the Hospital trustees for a very large **sum,** part of which was laid out in the construction of the **new cluster of** buildings in the Park. The Hospital was originally intended for the shelter and succour of 'six poor bachelors and **six poor spinsters'; but is now** the *Central House for Nurses for the Poor*, **maintained by the** Jubilee gift of the women of England **to the Queen. The** income is about 7000*l.* a year. Several old monuments from the **original hospital** are preserved here.

To the S. of Regent's Park runs the MARYLEBONE ROAD, containing **the** imposing new premises of *Madame Tussaud's* wellknown waxwork exhibition (adm., see p. 44), which are close to **the Baker Street station** of the Metropolitan railway. The large

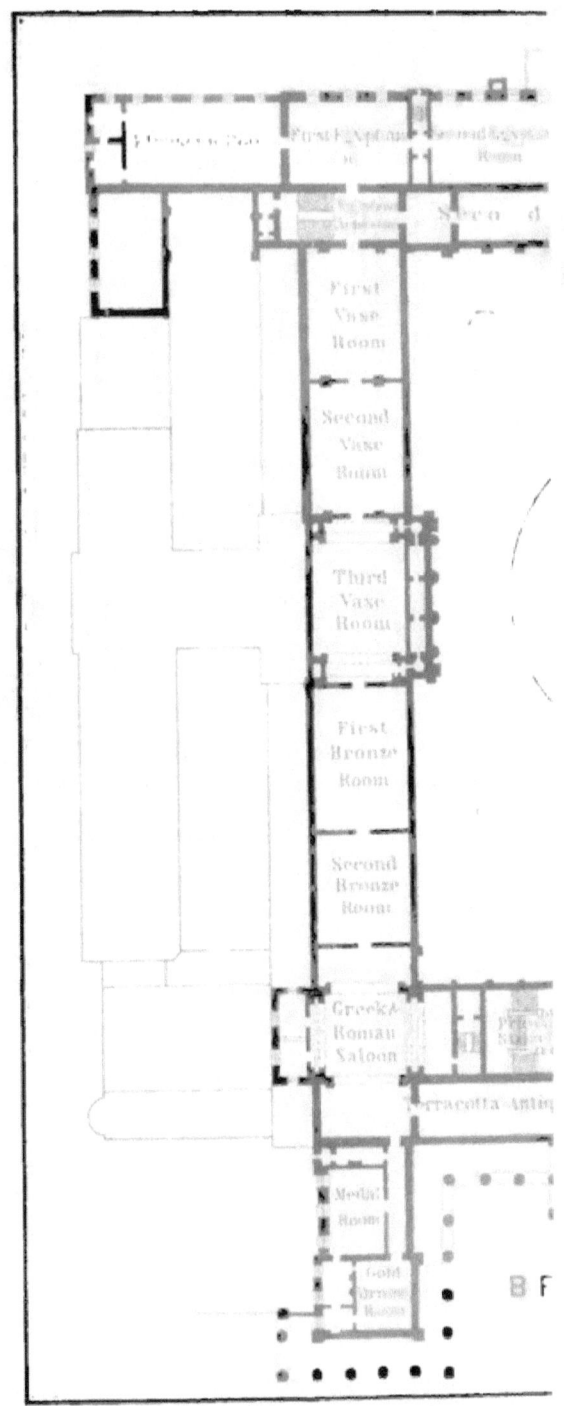

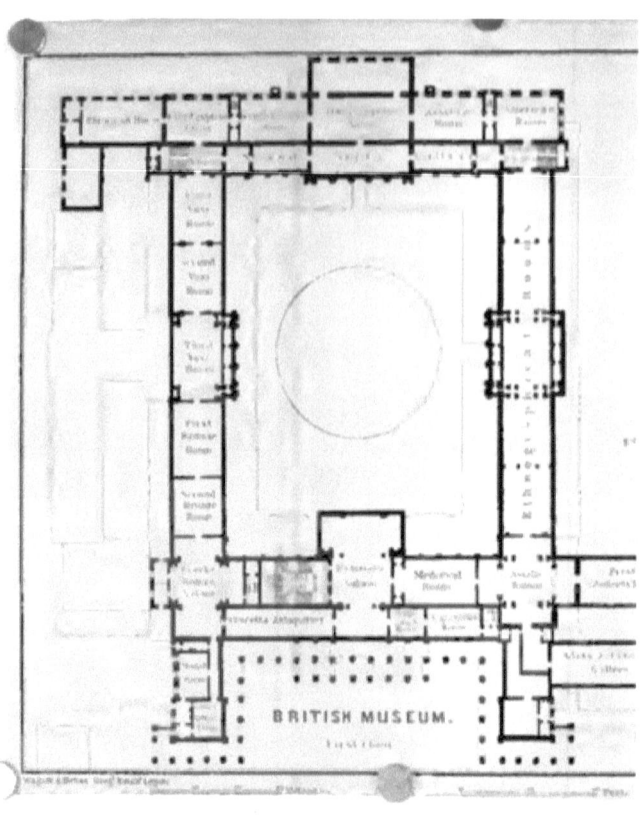

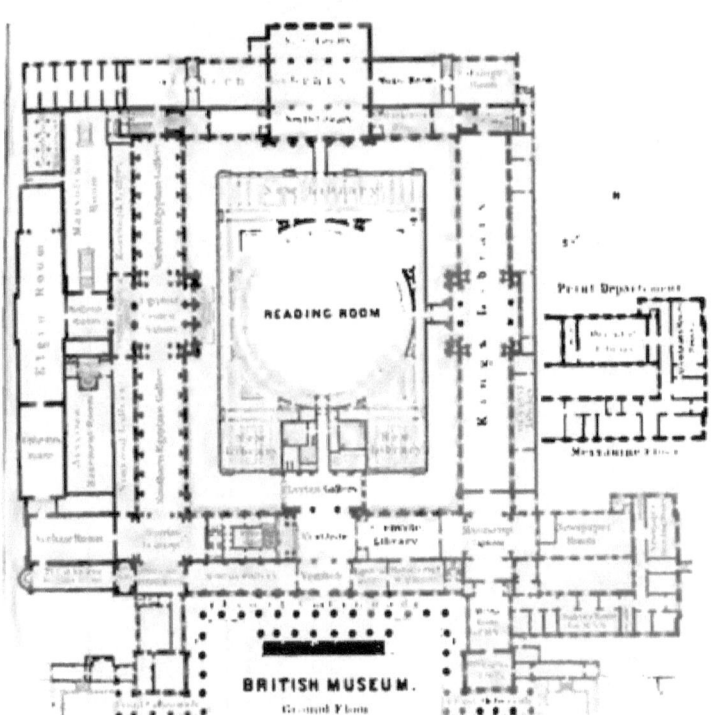

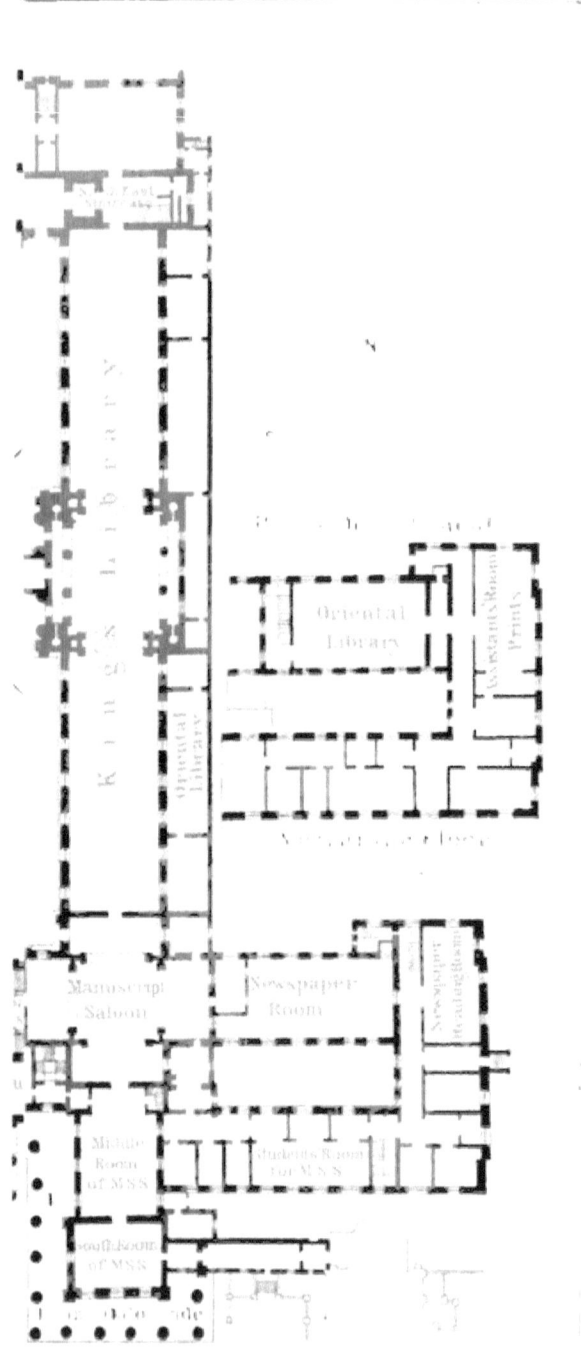

building opposite Mme. Tussaud's is the Marylebone Workhouse (see Pl. R, 20).

**The summit** of Primrose Hill (Pl. B, 14; 205 ft.), an eminence to the N. of Regent's Park, from which it is separated by the canal and **a road, commands a** very extensive view. On the E. and S., as far **as the eye can** reach, nothing **is seen but the** roofs and spires of **the stupendous city of London, while on the** N. **the green** hills of **Hampstead and Highlate form the picturesque background of** a landscape which **contrasts pleasantly** with **the dingy** buildings of the metropolis. **At the** S. **base of the hill there is an open-air gymnasium; a refreshment-room has also been opened.** A 'Shakspeare Oak' was planted **on the** S. **slope of the hill in** 1864, **on the** tercentenary celebration of **the great dramatist's birth.**

To the N.W. **in Finchley Road, near the Swiss Cottage, stands** *New College,* for **the education of ministers of the Congregational Body. Among its past professors have been some men of considerable note. It contains a good theological library. The building** was erected about 25 **years ago in the midst of what was then** green fields, and **is admired for its style and proportions.** — Farther **out in the Finchley Road (beyond Pl. B,** 5) **is the new** *Hackney Congregational College,* **erected in** 1887 **at a cost** of about 23,000l.

**Lord's Cricket Ground** (Pl. B, 12; p. 47), **in St. John's** Wood **Road, to the W. of Regent's Park, is** thronged **with a large** and **brilliant crowd of spectators on the** occasion of **the principal** cricket **matches,** particularly when Cambridge is disputing **the palm** of victory with **Oxford,** or, better **still,** Eton with Harrow; **and it then presents a** characteristic and **imposing** spectacle, **which the stranger should not** fail **to see.** Admission **on** ordinary **days** 6d.; **during great** matches, **which are always advertised beforehand,** 1s. **The ground** was **purchased by the Marylebone Cricket Club for a large sum, to prevent it from being built upon.**

## 22. The British Museum.

**The nucleus of the now vast contents of the** \*\***British Museum** (Pl. R, 28; *11* ) **was formed by the library and collection** of *Sir Hans Sloane* (d. 1753), **who in his will offered them to the** State for the **sum of** 20,000l. (**said to have been** 30,000l. less than their value). **An Act of Parliament** was at **once passed for** the acceptance of the **offer, and the collections,** along with **the** Harleian MSS. **and the** Cottonian Library, were deposited in *Montague House*, **which** was **bought for the purpose.** The presentation by George III. of a collection **of Egyptian antiquities** in 1801, **and the** purchase of the Townley **Marbles in** 1805 **and the Elgin Marbles in** 1816, made such additions **to the original contents that a new wing had** to be built for their reception. **The Museum** continued **to increase, and when** George IV. presented it in 1823 with **the King's Library**, collected by George

## 22. THE BRITISH MUSEUM.

III., old Montague House was felt to be **now** quite inadequate for its purpose, and **a new** building, designed by *Sir Robert Smirke* and completed by his younger brother *Sydney Smirke*, was erected on its site between 1823 and 1852. The new Reading Room (see p. 254) was added in 1857, and since 1879 the bequest of a large sum of money by Mr. William White has made possible the erection of a new gallery for the Mausoleum **marbles** and an entire new wing, known as the 'White **Wing', on the S.E. side of the** Museum (see p. 253). The contents of the British Museum are at present arranged in seven sections, each under the special superintendence of an Under Librarian or Keeper. These sections are as follows: Printed Books (Maps and Plans), Manuscripts, Prints and Drawings, Oriental Antiquities, British and Mediæval Antiquities and Ethnography, Greek and Roman Antiquities, and Coins and Medals. The sections of Zoology, Botany, Geology, and Mineralogy are now at S. Kensington (see p. 273). Wherever it is practicable, the names are attached to the different objects. For a thorough study of the collections the excellent official catalogues are indispensable; for a hasty visit the following directions may suffice. Courses of lectures on the various antiquities of the Museum are delivered here by experts from time to time. — The number of visitors to the British Museum in 1888, exclusive of readers and students, was 493,510.

The Museum is open free on every week-day from 10 a.m. till 4, 5, or 6 p.m. according to the season; on Mondays and Saturdays from 1st May to the middle of July it is open till 8 p.m., and from 15th July to 31st Aug. till 7 p.m. The general public are **not admitted to the** British, Mediæval, and Ethnographical departments or **to the rooms in the White Wing on Tues. and Thurs.**, these days being reserved **for students;** but strangers will obtain admission to the closed sections **without difficulty.** The Museum is shut on Good Friday **and Christmas Day. — Sticks and** umbrellas **are** left in the hall. Catalogues may be obtained in the hall, or from the attendants in the various sections. Those offered **for sale outside** are not trustworthy. Good photographs of several of the most interesting drawings and sculptures in the Museum may be purchased in the chief librarian's office.

The PRINCIPAL FAÇADE, towards (S.) Great Russell Street, with two projecting wings and a portico in the centre, **is 370 ft. in** length. In front it has an Ionic colonnade of 44 columns. The pediment above the *Portico*, which is borne by two rows of eight columns, is adorned with sculptures by *Westmacott*: on the right, Progress **of the Human Race;** on the left, allegorical figures of Mathematics, **the Drama, Poetry, Music,** and Natural Philosophy.

The ENTRANCE HALL, which in 1877 was enlarged by an extension towards the N., measures 62 ft. in length. The ceiling is embellished with encaustic painting. The statue of *Shakspeare* on the right, at the entrance to the library, chiselled by Roubiliac, was presented by Garrick, the actor. On the W. side of the hall is the principal staircase, ascending to the first floor. To the left of it is a bust of the *Duke of Marlborough*, by Rysbrack. By the door leading into the sculpture room is a statue of *Mrs. Damer*, the sculptress, by Westmacott. Various Buddhist sculptures from the Punjâb and Amravati in South India, dating from the 4th cent. A.D., are also exhibited in the hall and on the staircase. On the N. side of the hall the following Lycian sculptures are at present arranged:

To the right: Tomb of the Lycian satrap Piafa, with a pointed roof, surmounted by a ridge; the reliefs represent Bellerophon attacking the Chimæra. To the left is another large Lycian monument, behind which is a model, by Fellows, of the so-called *Nereid Monument*, to which the other sculptures in the hall belong. Double frieze (zoophorus) of the Nereid Monument: the broader frieze bears the representation of a battle of foot-soldiers, some of whom are clad in Asiatic dress, and a few horsemen; the narrower frieze represents the siege and surrender of a city. Eight Nereids, belonging to this monument, some of them much mutilated (These sculptures are soon to be removed to the Hellenic Room, p. 213.)

From the Hall we first turn to the right into the **Library**, and enter the room which contains the collection of 20,240 vols. bequeathed to the Museum by *Thomas Grenville*.

The two glass-cases on the left contain a collection of 'block-books', i.e. books printed from carved blocks of wood. Among them are several specimens of the Biblia Pauperum; Defensorium inviolatæ Virginitatis beatæ Mariæ Virginis (1470); Ars moriendi; Temptationes Demonis; Mirabilia Romæ; some old German calendars, including that of Regiomontanus printed at Nuremberg in 1474, the earliest known; Planetenbuch, or book of the planets (1470), etc.

We next enter the hall containing the **Manuscripts**, the cases in which are filled with numerous interesting autographs and treasures of a kindred nature.

CASE I. (on the left, divided into 6 sections) contains autograph writings of celebrated men, English and foreign, including Luther, Calvin, Melanchthon, Erasmus of Rotterdam; Archbishop Cranmer, Cardinal Wolsey, Sir Thomas More, John Knox, Sir Walter Raleigh, Earl of Essex, Sir Philip Sidney, Lord Burghley, Earl of Leicester; Francis Bacon, Hampden, Prince Rupert of the Palatinate, Montrose, Lord Clarendon, William Penn, Sir Christopher Wren, Sir Isaac Newton, Marlborough; Ariosto, Michael Angelo, Albert Dürer, Rubens, Rembrandt, Van Dyck, Galileo, Descartes, Leibnitz; Racine, Corneille, Molière, Despréaux, Voltaire, Prior, Swift, Addison, Dryden, Pope; Washington, Napoleon I.

CASE II. is occupied with autographs of English Sovereigns: Richard II., Henry IV., Henry V., Henry VI., Edward IV., Edward V., Henry VII. Henry VIII., Catharine of Arragon, Anne Boleyn, Edward VI., Jane Grey, Queen Mary, Queen Elizabeth, James I., Charles I., Oliver Cromwell, Charles II., James II., William III., Queen Anne, George I., George II., George III., George IV., William IV., and Queen Victoria (pencil signature written at the age of four years).

CASE III. (at right angles to the last case) contains autographs of British Statesmen and Commanders: Wolsey, Burghley, Hampden, Marlborough, Bolingbroke, Chatham, Clive, Warren Hastings, Burke, Pitt, Fox, Nelson, Wellington, Peel, Palmerston.

In the small triangular case between the last two is a Commentary on the Decretals of Pope Urban IV. in the state in which it was left after a fire at Ashburnham House, Westminster, in 1731. Beyond Case III. is Case G containing a volume of the Codex Alexandrinus and the books of Genesis and Exodus according to the Syriac Version. The former, dating from the 5th cent., ranks with the contemporary Codex Sinaiticus at St. Petersburg and the Codex Vaticanus at Rome as one of the three oldest Greek MSS. of the Bible. The Syriac MS., from the Nitrian desert, Egypt, was written at Amid in the year of the Greeks 775, A.D. 464, and is believed to be the oldest dated MS. of any entire books of the Bible now extant.

The series is continued in TABLE-CASE IV., at the S. end of the room.

22. THE BRITISH MUSEUM.

containing historical autographs: Declaration signed by 8 bishops (1588); letter of Perkin Warbeck, the pretended son of Edward IV.; autographs of several English sovereigns, Claverhouse, 'Junius;' etc. — TABLE-CASE V. contains Literary and Musical Autographs: Camden, Dr. Donne, Jeremy Taylor, Pepys Wesley, Richardson, Sterne, Goldsmith, Johnson, Boswell, Garrick, Flaxman, Turner, Gray ('Elegy'), Burns, Keats, Shelley, Coleridge, Wordsworth, Lamb, Sydney Smith, Hood, Lytton, Dickens (last letter he wrote), Händel, Beethoven, **Haydn,** Schubert, Mendelssohn, Goethe, Schiller.

We now retrace our steps to the door by which we entered, and begin our examination of the cases on the right side. The first five frames contain royal documents (charters, grants, etc.) from the 9th to the 11th cent. including an autotype copy of Magna Charta (1215); documents of Richard Coeur-de-Lion, Henry II., Henry I., Edward the Confessor, Canute the Dane, the Saxon King Edgar, etc.

CASE VI. contains autograph writings of Robert Burns (Autobiography), Walter Scott ('Kenilworth'), Torquato Tasso ('Torismondo'), Sterne, Locke, Jean Jacques Rousseau. Pope. Milton, Samuel Johnson, Chatterton, Defoe, Southey. Coleridge, Byron, Ben Jonson, and Lord Macaulay; Milton's copy of the Bible (in the triangular part of the case); some texts of Scripture in the handwriting of Edward VI.; the prayer-book of Lady Jane Grey; a book of prayers copied out by Queen Elizabeth; will of Mary, Queen of Scots; note-book of the Duke of Monmouth; original MSS. of Charles I., James I., and Frederick the Great. — In the small adjoining Case is a copy of Wycliffe's Bible (14th cent.), with illuminations. — CASE II. against the opposite pilaster, contains an illuminated copy of the Vulgate (810). Adjacent, on the pilaster, are an autograph of Edmund Spenser; the deed of sale of 'Paradise Lost', with Milton's signature; and an autotype facsimile of Shakspeare's will. — CASE K, against the N.E. pilaster, contains a double r ll of the Pentateuch, on goatskin (14th cent.).

CASES A-F, in the middle of the room, contain European and Oriental MSS., arranged to show the progress of the art of writing. A, Greek MSS., some on papyrus. B,C. Latin MSS., including illuminated Gospels, Psalters, and Hours. D. English MSS.: a unique copy of Beowulf, on vellum (ca. 1000 A.D.); Anglo-Saxon Chronicle to 1066; Piers Plowman (before 1400); poem by Occleve, with a portrait of Chaucer on the margin (early 15th cent.). E,F. Sanskrit, Pali, Cingalese, Arabic, Persian, and other Oriental MSS., some of which are of enormous value.

At the entrance to the King's Library are two glass-cases (N and O) with impressions of the Great Seals of the British sovereigns (left) and of various baronial and ecclesiastical seals (right).

In frames attached to the wainscot are exhibited several Deeds and Papyri, four of the latter, in Coptic, relating to the monastery of St. Phoebammon, near Hermonthis, Egypt.

To the S. E. of the Manuscript Saloon is the **MSS. Room for Students.** The door to the E. opens on the corridor leading to the **Newspaper Reading Room** and to the staircase ascending to the **Print Department** (see p. 253). — On the N. it is adjoined by **the King's Library,** a collection of 80,000 vols. made by George III. and presented to the nation by George IV., and arranged in a hall built expressly for the purpose, which extends along the whole breadth of the building. The collection is remarkable for the beauty and rarity of the works contained in it. Changes in the arrangements are not infrequent, and temporary exhibitions illustrating special periods are held here from time to time.

The first cases contain specimens of illumination (10-16th cent.), and another series of cases, near the N. end of the gallery, contains early printed books and prints **from China and Japan.** The first number of the *Times* (Jan. 1st, 1788) and an **Official Duplicate of** the Proclamation of the

Emancipation of the Slaves in the United States (Jan. 1st, 1863), with the signature of Abraham Lincoln, are also shown here.

Sixteen **cases** arranged on each side of the hall, and numbered III. to XVIII., **contain** typographical specimens in illustration of the history **of** printing, **in** chronological order. Cases III. and IV, on the left, are occupied by **the** earliest German printed books, including the Mazarin Bible, the first printed Bible, printed by Gutenberg and Fust (Mayence, 1455; a copy of this Bible was sold in 1873 for 3400£.); the first psalter, printed on parchme**nt** in 1457 by Fust and Schöffer (the **first** printed book bearing a date); Bible printed by **Fust** and Schöffer in 1462 (the first printed Bible bearing **a** date); Cicero **de** Officiis, of date 1465, Latin Bible, printed **at Bamberg in** 1460; Steinhoewel's **German** Chronicle (Ulm, 1473). Case V. **contains** early German **and Dutch books** (Decretum Gratiani, printed at Strassburg by Eggesteyn **in 1471).**

Case VI. contain**s** examples of Italian **typography**: Livy, print**ed** at Rome in 1469 by Schw**einheim and** Pannartz, **on vellum;** Petrarch (Fano, 1503); Lactantius, printed at **Subiaco** by Schweinheim and Pannartz in 1465; Cicero, Tusculanæ Questiones (Rome, 1469); the first printed edition of Dante (Foligno, 1472); Virgil, by **Aldus** (Venice, 1501); Æsop (Milan, 1480); Tacitus, by Da Spira (Venice, **1469);** Cicero, Epistolæ Familiares, **on** vellum (Venice, 1469); Ovid (Bologna, **1471).**

Case VII. contains Italian and French **printing**: **Valturius de re mil**itari (Verona, 1472); Le Livre du Roy Modus **et de** la Royne Racio (Chambery, 1486); Barzizius, Liber epistolarum **(Paris,** 1473), **the first book** printed in France; L'Art et Science **de Rhétorique, copy belonging to** Henry VII. (Paris, 1493); Fazio, **Dita Mundi (Vicenza, 1474).**

**In** Case VIII. are specimens **of** English printing: **Recuyell of the** Historyes of Troye, by Le Fevre, printed abroad by Caxton about 1475 (the first book printed in English); the original French of the **same** work, also printed by Caxton (the first book printed in French); The **Game and** Playe of the Chesse, printed by Caxton **about** 1475; The Dictes or Sayengis **of** the Philosophres, printed by Caxton **at Westminster in** 1477 (the first book printed in England); St. Bonaventura, Speculum vitæ Christi, printed on vellum by Caxton in 1488; Prayer-book, printed by Caxton at Westminster in 1490 (unique); the first printed edition of Chaucer's Canterbury Tales, by Caxton, about 1477; Terence, printed at London by Pynson in 1497 (the first classic printed in England); 'The Book of St. Albans', a book of the chase, printed at the Abbey **of** St. Albans **in** 1486.

Case IX. contains specimens of fine **and** sumptuous printing: Theuerdank, composed by Melchior Pfinzing **on the** marriage of the Emperor Maximilian with Mary **of Burgundy,** and printed at Nuremberg by Schœnsperger in 1507; Petrarch, **on vellum,** printed by Aldus (Venice, 1501), once the **property** of Isabella Gonzaga, Countess of Mantua; Dante, printed in 1502, **also by** Aldus at Venice, and the first book which bore the anchor, the distinguishing mark of the Aldine Press; Horace, first edition, from the Aldine press (Venice, 1501); Bourassé, La Touraine (Tours, Mame, 1855; the **cost** of printing this handsome work was 600£.).

In Case X. **are** specimens of illuminations and sumptuous printing: Euclid, printed by **Ratdolt** (Venice, 1482); Martial, Aldus (Venice, 1501); Boccaccio, Verard **(Paris,** 1493); Breviaries, missals, and hours; Virgil, printed by Aldus **on vellum** (1501); **Aulus Gellius, Noctes** Atticæ, on vellum (Florence, **1513).**

Case XI. contains works illustrated with wood-cuts and engravings. Bettini, El Monte Sancto di Dio (Florence, 1477), **the** first book with copper engravings; Ariosto (London, 1591), with engravings; Book of the Passion (Wittenberg, 1521), illustrated by Cranach; old playing cards (Augsburg, Nuremberg, 1588); first edition of Holbein's Dance of Death (Lyons, 1539); Breydenbach's Journey to the Holy Land (Mayence, 1486), illustrated.

Case XII. contain**s** books bearing the autographs of the authors or early owners: Wittenberg Bible of 1541, with Luther's signature; autographs **of** Calvin, Lord Bacon, Melanchthon, Michael Angelo, Tasso, Voltaire, Ben Jonson, Catharine Parr. There is also a collection of broadsides, including Luther**'s** 95 Theses against the Indulgence of 1517.

Case XIII. is assigned to typographical and literary curiosities: Queen Elizabeth's prayer-book; miniature breviary (beginning of 16th cent.); Horace, printed in microscopic type (Didot, Paris, 1828); the first edition of the **Book of Common** Prayer (1549); first editions of several of **Shakspeare's** works; also of Cervantes, Milton, Defoe, and many **others**.
Case XIV. contains specimens of Japanese block-printing **in** colours.
Cases XV., XVI., XVII., and XVIII. are filled with bound books, many of which are very beautiful **specimens of** the art of bookbinding, including some by Grolier.
Case XXI. contains various maps, including a facsimile of General Gordon's map of his route from Souâkin to Berber and Khartûm, drawn by him at Khartûm on Mar. 17th, 1874.
Case XXII. contains specimens of early printed music.
Case XXIII. contains a facsimile (by Rev. F. T. Havergal) of the Mappa Mundi in Hereford Cathedral (1290-1310; see *Baedeker's Great Britain*).
Cases XXIV-XXVIII. contain good relief maps of **Palestine**, Mont Blanc, the Western Alps, Mt. Vesuvius, and Mt. Etna.
Near the middle of the hall stands a large celestial globe by Coronelli (Paris, 1693), the constellations on which are very finely engraved.

At the end of the King's Library is a staircase, leading to the collections of oriental art and ethnography (comp. p. 249). In the meantime, however, we retrace our steps to the entrance hall, and pass out of it, to the left, into the \***Sculpture Gallery.** The first room we enter is the —

**Roman Gallery.** On the left side are Roman antiquities found in England. The compartments below the windows contain rough-hewn sarcophagi, while by the intervening pilasters are specimens of old Irish characters (Oghams). Above, on the walls to the right and left, are fragments of Roman **mosaic pavements,** discovered in England. On the right (N.) side of the room is ranged a collection of Roman **portrait busts** and statues (the numbering begins at the W. end of the gallery): 2. Julius **Cæsar**; 3. The youthful Augustus; 4. Augustus; 5. Tiberius; 7. **Drusus**; 8. Caligula; 9. Statue of a Roman consul wearing the toga; 11. Nero; 12. Otho; 14. Domitia (?); 15. Trajan (of Greek marble); 17, 18. **Hadrian**; 20. Antinous, favourite of Hadrian; 21. **Julia** Sabina, Hadrian's consort; 19. Statue of Hadrian in military costume (legs and arms restored); 23. Hadrian in civil costume; \*24. Antoninus **Pius**; 25, 26, 27. Marcus Aurelius; 28. Faustina, his spouse; 30. **Lucius Verus**; 34. Crispina, consort of Commodus; 35. Pertinax; 36. Septimius Severus; 37. Caracalla; then on a shelf above, near the W. end, 55 and 56. Demosthenes; 58. Epicurus; 77. **Olympias**; 78-81. Heads of Roman children. — In the centre of the floor: 1. Bust of Cornelius Lentulus Marcellinus, Proprætor of Cyrene; \*45. Equestrian statue, representing Caligula; 46. Torso of the statue of a Roman emperor; Two sarcophagi with alto-reliefs, the one representing scenes from the life of Achilles, the other the labours of Hercules. — We next reach the —

First Græco-Roman **Room.** This and the two following rooms contain sculptures, executed in Italy, but chiefly by Greek artists or from Greek models; also perhaps a few Greek originals.

L.: 109. Satyr playing with the infant Bacchus (from the Palazzo Farnese at Rome); 110. Youthful Bacchus (from Cyrene); 111. Head of Juno; 112. Statue of Diana; 113. Bust of Diana; *114. Apollo Citharœdus (replica of the statue in the Capitol at Rome); 116. Statue of Venus; 117. Bust of Homer; *118. Dancing Satyr (from the Palazzo Rondanini at Rome); 119. Bust of an unknown Greek poet; Head of Venus, with remains of flesh colour on the face and neck; 122. Head of Jupiter; 123. Head of Athena; 124. Jupiter; 126. Athena (the eyes, which were of coloured stone, are wanting); 127. Sitting figure of Hades, with the attributes of Zeus; 128. Bust of Athena (the bronze helmet and drapery are modern); 130. Statue of the triple-bodied Hecate; 131. Bust of Jupiter Serapis; 132. Statue of Apollo; 133. Ceres as Isis (time of Hadrian); 134. Heroic figure (limbs restored). — In the centre of the gallery is a *Greek cratera from the Villa of Hadrian, round the upper part of which are reliefs of Satyrs making wine.

**Second Græco-Roman Room.** In the recess on the left: *136. The Townley Venus, found at Ostia; opposite, *135. Discobolus, or the 'quoit-thrower' (ancient copy of the statue by Myron). Round the room are several heads: 156. Muse; *137. Dione (?); 138. Apollo Giustiniani (late-Romanesque replica of the head of the Apollo Belvedere); 97. Hercules; 139. Bearded head (of a Macedonian king?); *140. Apollo Musegetes.

Third Græco-Roman **Room**. On the right (N.) side: *141. Colossal **head** of Hercules; 143. Sleeping Cupid, with the attributes of Hercules; 144. Hercules subduing the Cerynæan stag (archaic **relief**); 145, 146. Cupid bending his bow; 147. Relief of a youth holding a horse; 148. Endymion asleep; **149. Iconic female bust (the so-called Clytie), perhaps of a Roman empress; 150. Head of a wounded Amazon; *151. Head of hero (Greek original), restored by Flaxman; *155. Statue of the Muse Thalia, from Ostia; 157. Relief of Nessus and Dejanira(?); 159. Apotheosis of Homer, relief with the name of **the** sculptor, Archelaus **of Priene** (found at Bovillæ, of the time of Tiberius); 160. Head of woman in Asiatic costume; 161. Bust of unknown person (bust and nose restored); 162. Youth in Persian costume, restored as Paris; 163. Mithras sacrificing a bull; 165. Actæon devoured by his dogs (from Lanuvium); 166. Head of Venus; 169. Relief, Victory sacrificing to Apollo. — West side, *171. Mercury; *Boy extracting thorn from his foot, found on the Esquiline Hill (marble, under glass); 35. Head of Mercury from **Tivoli**. — South side: 176. Relief, Bacchus visiting Icarius; 177. Midas(?); 179. Part of a Bacchic Thiasus; 172. Torso of Venus; 188, 190. Fauns; Diana in the archaistic style of the 1st cent.; 183, 184. Satyrs; **185. Venus** (from Ostia); 178. Satyr, freely restored; 189. Bacchus and Ambrosia; 186. Part of a group of two boys quarrelling at play; 191. Relief of Ariadne (? Penelope, from Cumæ); **193**. Youthful Bacchus; 195. Bacchic relief with two sitting satyrs;

196. Girl playing with astragali; 198. Ariadne with the panther; 199. Head of youthful Hercules; 201. Eros asleep; 200. Relief representing Apollo, Latona, and Diana, with three worshippers; 202. Head of Venus; 204. Head **of youthful** Hercules.

The door on the right **leads into the Archaic Room**; the staircase at the extreme end descends to **the** —

**Græco-Roman Basement** Room, which contains Greek and Roman **sculptures of various kinds**: sarcophagi, reliefs, vases, fountain basins, candelabra, table supports, animals, etc. The floor is decorated with a mosaic from a Roman villa at Halicarnassus, 40 ft. long and 13½ ft. broad, at the upper end of which is represented **Amphitrite with two Tritons.** On the E. wall is a mosaic from **Carthage of a colossal head of** Neptune. Adjacent are two sacrificial **groups in marble, and** a relief of two gladiators struggling with a **bull.** — **The annex contains the** heavier objects belonging to the **Etruscan collection (p. 251),** other sculptures, and miscellaneous objects.

The door on the right in the Third Græco-Roman **Room leads** into the —

Archaic Room, **which chiefly contains archaic remains from Asia Minor.** In the centre: \*Reliefs from the '*Harpy Tomb*' at Xanthus (at the sides sacrificial scenes; at the ends forms like **sirens, bearing away** small figures intended to represent departed **souls, whose gestures** indicate that they are trying to propitiate their captors and gain their compassion). At the W. end of **the** room are ten sitting figures, a lion, and a sphynx, of very early date (580-520 B.C.), which once formed part of the Sacred Way leading to the Temple of Apollo at Branchidæ. On the N. wall is an archaic marble frieze from Xanthus **in Lycia,** above which are **plaster casts** of four metopes from Selinus in Sicily. Plaster casts **of works** of art found in the recent German excavations at Pergamus **and** Olympia. Among the other works in this room are: \*32. Apollo, a celebrated archaic work from the Choiseul-Gouffier collection; **30, 31.** Other archaic figures of Apollo; 45. Bull, pro**bably from a** sepulchral stele at Athens; several archaic inscriptions, etc.

**The Greek Ante-Room,** a small chamber to the N., contains, on the right, **a** sitting figure of Demeter (Ceres); on the left, two swine (sacred **to** Proserpine), and other sculptures, found in 1858 **at the** Temple of **the Infernal Deities at** Cnidus, a head (eyes of enamel lost), a statuette of Persephone (under glass), and a discus **with relief of Apollo** and Artemis slaying **the** children of Niobe. Here also are two cases **with statuettes,** small heads, and sculptured fragments from Cyrene.

The **Ephesus Room** contains **fragments** of the celebrated *Temple of Diana,* found by Mr. **J.** T. Wood in the course of excavations at Ephesus in 1869-74. The remains consist chiefly of the drums and capitals **of columns**, and fragments of bases and cornices. Among them is the **lowest** drum of a column with lifesize reliefs of Hermes, Victoria, and a warrior. In this room are placed casts of the Olympian Hermes by Praxiteles, the Venus of Milo (Louvre), and the Venus de' Medici. To the right is the lower half of a statue of Lucius Verus from Ephesus. proved by the inscription to have been erected before A. D. 161. We now reach the —

\*\***Elgin Room**, containing the famous *Elgin Marbles*, being the remains of the sculptures executed by Phidias to adorn the Parthenon at Athens, and considered the finest specimens of the plastic art in existence. They were brought from Athens in 1801-3 by Lord Elgin, at that time British ambassador at Constantinople, at a cost of 70,000*l*., and sold to the English Government in 1816 for half that sum. The Parthenon, the Temple of Pallas Athena on the Acropolis of Athens, was built by Ictinos, about B.C. 440, in the time of Pericles, the golden age of Athens and of Hellenic art. It was in the Doric order of architecture, and occupied the site of an earlier temple of Athena, which had been destroyed in the Persian war. It was adorned with sculptures under the supervision of Phidias. A statue of Athena, formed of gold and ivory, stood in the interior of the cella. The sculptures preserved here consist of the frieze round the exterior of the cella, 15 metopæ, and the relics of the two pediments, unfortunately in very imperfect preservation. The figures of the deities represented are most nobly conceived, admirably executed, and beautifully draped.

The remains of the E. PEDIMENT, representing the Birth of Athena, who, according to Greek mythology, issued in full armour from the head of Zeus, are arranged on the W. (left) side of the room.

In the left angle of the tympanum we observe two arms and a mutilated human head, in front of which are two spirited horses' heads, also considerably damaged. These are considered to represent a group of Helios, the god of the rising sun, ascending in his chariot from the depths of the ocean, his outstretched arms grasping the reins of his steeds. Next comes Theseus (or Hercules?), who, leaning in a half recumbent posture on a rock covered with a lion's hide, seems to be greeting the ascending orb of day. This figure, the only one on which the head remains, is among the best preserved in the two pediments. Next to Theseus is a group of two sitting female figures in long drapery, who turn with an appearance of lively interest towards the central group — perhaps the Attic Hours, Thallo and Auxo (or Ceres and Proserpine?). Then comes the erect female figure of Iris, messenger of the gods, whose waving robes betoken rapid motion; the upper part of her body is turned towards the central group, and she seems to have barely waited for the birth of the Goddess before starting to communicate the glad tidings to the inhabitants of earth.

The central group, which probably represented Minerva surrounded by the gods, is entirely wanting. The space occupied by it, indicated here by an opening in the middle of the sculptures (partly filled by a Doric capital from the Parthenon), must have measured 33-40 ft. in length.

Next comes, on the right, a torso of Victory. Then a noble group of two sitting female forms, in the lap of one of which reclines a third female, probably representing Aglauros, Herse, and Pandrosos, the three daughters of Cecrops (or perhaps the three Fates). Adjacent, in the angle of the tympanum, the torso **of Selene** (the goddess of the moon), as a charioteer and by her side the head of one of her coursers. This portion of the frieze is thought to have shown the Moon sinking into the sea at the approach of Day. The horse's head is in good preservation.

The remains of the WEST PEDIMENT are on the opposite side of the room. They are by no means so well preserved as those from the East Pediment, and we can only form an idea of their meaning and connection from a drawing executed by the French painter Carrey in 1671, which contains several groups that are now wanting. The subject of the sculptures is the Strife of Minerva and Neptune for the soil of Athens. By a stroke of his trident Neptune caused a salt-spring to gush forth from the soil, but his gift was outdone by that of Minerva, who produced the olive-tree, and was adjudged the possession of the city. The moment chosen for representation is that, after the decision of the contest, when the two deities part from each other in anger. In the left angle we observe the torso of a recumbent male figure, probably the river god Cephissus. Next to it is a cast of a group of two figures (the original is in Athens), supposed to be Hercules and Hebe; the male figure is in a semi-recumbent posture, propped upon his left arm, the female kneeling beside him has her right arm round his neck. Next, the torso of a man, perhaps Cecrops, the first King of Attica. The relics of the central group are exceedingly scanty. Of Minerva only the upper part of the head, the right shoulder with part of the armour, and a piece of the ægis are preserved. The eyes, which were made of coloured gems, are lost. The cheeks, on close examination, still show traces of painting. A much mutilated torso, consisting of the shoulders alone, is all that remains of the rival deity, Neptune. The proportions of these two statues, which, as the central figures, occupied the highest part of the tympanum, are on a much larger scale than those of the others.

Next comes a female torso, perhaps Amphitrite; then the lower part of a sitting female form, probably Latona; then the cast of a semi-recumbent male figure, perhaps the river god Ilissus. Lastly, at the end of the tympanum, is the torso of a recumbent female form, supposed to represent the nymph Callirrhoë.

Around the whole of the hall, at a height of about 4½ ft. from the ground, we observe the *FRIEZE (about 175 yds. long), which ran round the outside of the cella (or inner sanctuary) under the colonnade enclosing the Parthenon. It forms a connected whole, and represents, chiefly in very low relief, the festive procession which ascended to the Acropolis at the end of the Panathenæa, for the purpose of presenting to the Goddess a peplos, or robe, woven and embroidered by Athenian virgins. The priests with sacrificial bulls and horses, the virgins, the warriors on horseback, on foot, and in chariots, and the thronging worshippers of all kinds are executed with admirable taste and skill. The slabs are arranged as far as possible in their original order, the points of the compass being indicated above them. 'On the east side, the side of entrance, Phidias arranged an august assembly of the gods, in whose presence the peplos is delivered to the guardians of the temple (slabs numbered 17-24). These are attended by officials and heralds, followed by trains of noble Attic maidens. The procession is continued along the north and south sides, proceeding in both towards the entrance porch, as though on the west side it had been divided into two. Bulls and lambs for sacrifice follow with their leaders, interspersed with groups of men and women; some bearing gifts in baskets and beautiful vessels on their shoulders. To these are added players on the lute and cithern, who march in front of a train of men and chariots, probably the victors in the contests. The procession is terminated on the two long sides by Athenian youths on horseback, and on the west side we find others still engaged in preparations, in bridling, restraining, and mounting horses'. — *Lübke, History of Sculpture.* — Most of the pieces of this frieze are but slightly damaged, while some of them are perfectly preserved. A few of the slabs are merely casts of portions of the frieze at Paris and Athens.

Above the frieze on the W. wall of the room are 15 METOPÆ and a cast of another from the Parthenon, being the sculptures which filled the intervals between the triglyphs of the external frieze. They represent the battle of the Centaurs and Lapithæ, and are executed in much higher relief than the sculptures of the inner frieze; some of the figures are almost entirely detached, being connected with the background or the adjoining figures at a few isolated points only.

On the E. wall are plaster casts from the external frieze of the Temple of Theseus at Athens, representing battle-scenes, partly of the contests of the Greeks with the Centaurs, and three metopæ from the same temple with sculptures of the feats of Theseus.

Towards the N. end of the room is one of the beautiful *Canephoræ from the Erechtheum (5th cent. B.C.); near it are an Ionic column from the same building, which is the purest existing type of the Ionic style, and a colossal owl.

Among the numerous other sculptures in the Elgin Room are casts of two marble chairs from the theatre of Dionysos at Athens (one on each side of the entrance); a head of Pericles (apparently a Roman copy of a Greek original); a head of Hera from Agrigentum; a draped *Torso of Æsculapius from Epidauros; a colossal sitting figure of Dionysos from the Choragic Monument of Thrasyllos at Athens; fragments of columns from the Temple of Diana at Ephesus; the capital of a Doric column from the Propylæum, the magnificent entrance to the Acropolis; a statue of a youth, probably Eros, from Athens.

This room also contains a model of the Acropolis and another representing the Parthenon as it appeared after its bombardment by the Venetian General Morosini in 1687.

The hall continuing the Elgin Room on the N. contains a colossal lion from an eminence at Cnidus, originally surmounting a pyramidal Doric monument, which was perhaps erected to commemorate the naval victory of Conon, the Athenian, over the Spartans in B.C. 394.

We now pass through the door in the centre of the E. side, and enter the —

**Hellenic Room**, which at present contains marble sculptures from every part of Greece and the Grecian colonies except Athens and Attic settlements, and also plaster casts. [The Nereid Monument from the entrance-hall is soon to be transferred to this room, and most of its present contents will be shifted to other parts of the Museum. The frieze of the Temple of Apollo Epicurius at Bassa has already been removed to the Phigaleian room (p. 244).]

The bust to the right of the door is Æschines, that on the left an unknown philosopher. On the pedestals arranged round the room are a colossal torso of a heroic figure, found at Elæa; a Diadumenos (a replica of the celebrated work of Polycletus); two other athletes; a bust of Euripides; head of Alexander the Great, from Alexandria. To the right of the E. door: Colossal head of Hercules; to the left, Statue of Dionysos (Indian Bacchus) from Posilipo; Ionic female figure from the temenos of Demeter, Cnidus; *Head of youth with a fillet.

On the S. wall are plaster casts of a pediment of the Temple of Athena at Ægina, the original of which is at Munich. Lower down, round the walls, are ranged sculptural and architectural remains, among which may be noticed the fragment of a recumbent satyr at the entrance door.

We now descend the steps on the left to the **Mausoleum Room**, added in 1882, containing remains from the **\*\*Mausoleum at Halicarnassus**, discovered by Newton in 1857.

This celebrated monument (whence the modern generic term 'mausoleum' is derived) was erected by Artemisia in B.C. 352, in honour of her husband Mausolus, King of Caria, and was reckoned among the Seven Wonders of the World. The tomb stood upon a lofty basement, and was surrounded by 36 Ionic columns. Above it was a pyramid rising in steps (24 in number), surmounted by a colossal statue of Mausolus. The monument was in all about 140 ft. in height, and was embellished by a number of statues, lions, and other pieces of sculpture. Among the remains of it preserved in the British Museum are the following: Wheel from the chariot of Mausolus, restored in harmony with the fragments that have been found; fore and hind quarters of one of the colossal horses attached to the chariot of Mausolus; a female figure found under the ruins of the pyramid; \*Statue of Mausolus, restored from 77 fragments. Near it is a head of Æsculapius from Melos. Frieze (zoophorus) from the Mausoleum, representing the contest of the Greeks with the Amazons. Among other fragments is a frieze, in bad preservation, representing races and the battle of the Greeks with the Centaurs. Female torso; eight lions; fragment of an equestrian figure in Persian garb; part of a colossal ram; fragments of columns from the Mausoleum. The room also contains a cast of a metope, the Sun God in his chariot, from the Doric temple of Ilium Novum, presented by Dr. Schliemann in 1872; a number of marbles from the Temple of Athene Polias at Priene, including the dedication of the Temple by Alexander, a colossal arm, hand, foot, and female head, and a draped female torso. At the N. end of the room is a reproduction of the cornice of the Mausoleum.

The door at the N.W. corner of the Mausoleum Room leads to two new rooms, one above the other. The upper room, which forms a gallery in continuation of the Elgin Room, is to contain the marbles from Phigaleia and from the Temple of Victory at Athens, as well as the finest of the Greek sepulchral stelæ. In the room below will be placed sepulchral monuments of Græco-Roman origin. The arrangements are still incomplete.

Among the most beautiful of the *Greek Sepulchral Monuments* are the tombstones of two young athletes found at Athens, in one of which the athlete hands his strigil to his slave, while the other stands alone holding the strigil. Another represents two ladies of Smyrna, to whom the city had voted honorary crowns. Curious relief of a Greek physician and his patient. Stele from Rhodes with a family group. Sepulchral tablet with a skeleton, and an inscription asking the passer-by if he can now tell whether the deceased had been a Hylas (beautiful) or a Thersites (ugly). — *Roman Works.* Tomb-reliefs with portrait-busts, one found in the Thames. Bas-relief of a Roman marriage, apparently the work of a Greek artist, in Italy about the time of Hadrian. Friezes of children. Sarcophagus reliefs. The Sepulchral Urns include one dedicated by a slave to his master, one in the form of the façade of a temple, etc.

We now return across the N. end of the Mausoleum Room to the Assyrian and Egyptian collections, which, next to the Elgin Room, are the most important parts of the British Museum. The **Assyrian Gallery** comprises three long narrow rooms, called the *Kouyunjik Gallery*, the *Nimroud Central Saloon*, and the *Nimroud Gallery*; the *Assyrian Transept*, adjoining the last of these three; the *Phoenician Room* and *Assyrian Basement Room*; and finally a room (p. 249) on the second floor. Its contents are chiefly the yield of the excavations of Sir H. A. Layard in 1847-50 at Kouyunjik, the ancient Nineveh, and at Nimroud, the Biblical Calah, but include the collection made by Mr. George Smith in Mesopotamia, as well as contributions from other sources.

The **Kouyunjik Gallery** contains bas-reliefs dating from B.C. 721-625, and belonging to the royal palace of Sennacherib (d. B.C. 710) at Nineveh, afterwards occupied by Sennacherib's grandson, Assurbanipal or Sardanapalus. The older reliefs, dating from the time of Sennacherib, are executed in alabaster, the others in hard, light-grey limestone.

We begin our examination at the S.E. corner. No. 1. Esarhaddon, cast from a bas-relief cut in the rock, at the mouth of the Nahr el Kelb river, near Beirût; 2. Galley with two banks of oars; 4-8. Row of fragments (upper part damaged), representing Sennacherib's advance against Babylon; 15-17. Return from battle with captives and spoil; 18-19. Procession of warriors; 20-29. Siege of a fortified town (on slab No. 25 is the city itself, while 27-29 represent the triumph of the victors). Nos. 34-43. Series of large reliefs, which decorated the walls of a long passage between the palace and the Tigris; on one side, descending the slope, are 14 horses, held by attendants; on the other, ascending, servants with dishes for a feast. The figures, rather under life-size, are beautifully designed. No. 44. Monumental tablet; 45-50. Triumph of Sardanapalus over the Elamites (in limestone, well preserved). Nos. 51-52. Removal of a winged bull on a sledge by means of wooden rollers and levers; to the right, construction of a lofty embankment. Nos. 53-56. Similar scenes in better preservation; 57-59. Sennacherib besieging a city situated on a river (quaintly represented), and receiving the spoil and prisoners; 60. Figure with the head of a lion, bearing a knife in the right hand, which is held up.

In the middle of the hall is a white limestone obelisk, found by Mr. Rassam, and near it the upper part of another. At the S. end of the room is a black marble obelisk, adorned with five rows of reliefs; the inscriptions, in cuneiform characters, record events from the history of Shalmaneser. The glass-cases contain smaller objects, such as seal-cut stones, cylindrical writing rolls, fragments of cuneiform characters, necklaces, bracelets, statuettes, iron and bronze ornaments, etc. We now enter the —

Nimroud **Central** Saloon, containing the sculptures (dating from B.C. 880-630), discovered by Mr. Layard at Nimroud, on the Tigris, situated about 18 M. below Nineveh. They are from the palace built by Esarhaddon, the successor of Sennacherib, but some of them are of a much earlier date than that monarch, who used the fragments of older buildings. The reliefs on the left are from a Temple of the God of War.

We begin to the left of the entrance from the Kouyunjik Gallery. Large relief, representing the evacuation of a conquered city; below, the triumphal procession of a king in his war-chariot. Inscribed stone, with records of Merodach Baladan I., King of Babylonia (B.C. 1320). Colossal head of a winged man-headed bull; adjacent, another similar, but smaller head. At the central pillars, two statues of the god Nebo. At the entrance to the Nimroud Gallery, on the right, a colossal winged °Lion; on the left, a colossal winged bull, both with human heads; adjacent on each side, reliefs of two winged male figures sacrificing. Then bas-reliefs, evacuation of a conquered town. Monolith (figure in relief with cuneiform inscription) of Assur-Nasir-Pal (B.C. 880); monolith of Shalmaneser (B.C. 850). Statue of Assur-Nasir-Pal. At the entrance to the Kouyunjik Gallery, a colossal lion from the side of a doorway (B.C. 880). Between this room and the Egyptian Central Saloon is the Hittite Monument, of basalt, 6 ft. high, from Jerâbis, the supposed site of Karkemish; on one side is a sculptured figure, probably of a priest, and on the other is an inscription in hieroglyphics. Also other Hittite fragments. The tablecases contain clay tablets.

**Nimroud Gallery.** On the left, colossal bas-reliefs; 18. Winged figure with ibex and ear of corn; 19. Foreigners bringing apes as tribute; 20. King Assur-Nasir-Pal in a richly embroidered dress, with sword and sceptre; *23-26. The king on his throne surrounded by attendants and winged figures with mystic offerings; 28, 29. Winged figure with a thunderbolt, chasing a demon; 36. Lion hunt; 31-41. Representation of religious service; then various martial and hunting scenes. The slabs with the larger reliefs bear inscriptions running horizontally across their centres. The glass-cases in the middle of the room contain bronze dishes with engraved and chased decorations, admirably executed, other bronze articles of different kinds, weights in the form of lions conchant, weapons, domestic utensils, etc. Cases D, C are occupied by a collection of ivory Carvings, with Egyptian figures. In the centre of the room is a broken obelisk of Assur-Nasir-Pal and at the N. end is a monolith of Samsi Rammânu, son of Shalmaneser II. (B.C. 826-812). — The door in the N W. corner of this room leads into the —

**Phœnician Room**, which contains monuments from Phœnicia, Palestine, Carthage, and Cyprus. In the middle of the room is a cast of the *Moabite Stone*, which was discovered by the Rev. F. Klein in the land of Moab in 1868. The inscription gives an account of the wars of Mesha, king of Moab, with Omri, Ahab, and Ahaziah, kings of Israel. Soon after Mr. Klein had obtained an impression of the stone, it was broken in pieces by the Arabs; most of the fragments have, however, been recovered and are now preserved in the Louvre. Adjacent are a *Maṣṣebâh*, or monument of alabaster from Larnaca, erected to the god Eshmun about B.C. 380, and a colossal marble head of a sarcophagus from Sidon. To the left are Hebrew gravestones. Cases 1-6 contain Phœnician inscriptions from the site of ancient Carthage. In Cases 7-12 are Hebrew and Phœnician inscriptions from Palestine and the Dugga stone from Numidia, with a bilingual inscription in Libyan and Phœnician. Cases 13-19 contain Phœnician inscriptions and a cast of the Siloam Inscription (ca. B.C. 700), found in 1880 at the Pool of Siloam.

We now descend the staircase to the **Assyrian** Basement **Room**, containing reliefs from Kouyunjik, excavated by Messrs.

Rassam and Loftus. These reliefs, belonging to the latest period of Assyrian art, are throughout superior to those in the upper rooms, both in design and execution. (The numbers begin in the central part of the room.)

Nos. 1-8. Scenes of war; Bringing home the heads and spoil of conquered enemies; Warriors preparing their repast. Nos. 33-53. Lion hunt; 51-62. Plundering of a city; 63-74. Return from the hunt (sequel to Nos. 33-53); 83-90. Wars of Sardanapalus; 91-94. Hostile army fleeing past an Assyrian fortress; 95. Beheading of the King of Susiana; 101-119. Three rows of scenes of gazelle, wild ass, and lion hunting, admirably executed; 120. Captives at their repast; 121. Sardanapalus and his wife banqueting in an arbour; 122. Lion hunt. In the middle are three glass cases containing smaller objects. Near them is a piece of pavement from the palace of Sardanapalus. By the door is a cast of the Sarcophagus of Eshmunâzâr (ca. B.C. 360; original in the Louvre).

The Nimroud Gallery is adjoined on the S. by the **Assyrian Transept**, which in its western half is a continuation of the Nimroud Gallery (monuments from the time of Assur-Nasir-Pal), while the eastern part contains antiquities from Khorsabad (about B.C. 720), from the excavations of Messrs. Rawlinson and Layard.

In the middle of the W. side is the monolith of Assur-Nasir-Pal, with a portrait in relief. In front of it is an altar, which stood at the door of the Temple of the God of War. At the sides are two colossal winged Lions, with human heads and three horns, from the sides of a doorway. At the sides of the entrance from the Nimroud Gallery are two torsos with inscriptions. On the wall are reliefs and inscriptions from the palace of the Persian kings at Persepolis (B.C. 500) and casts of Pehlevi inscriptions from Hadji Abad (near Persepolis). The glass-cases in the centre contain a collection of archaic sculptures, heads, statues, and inscriptions from Idalium (Dali), in Cyprus, excavated in 1870. — In the E. or Khorsabad section, two colossal animals with human heads, adjacent to which are two colossal human figures. Within the recess thus formed are fragments of various kinds; heads and figures of warriors and horses; to the right, opposite the window, a relief of a hunting scene in black marble. In the middle are two cases containing antiquities from Idalium. In the centre is a black basalt figure of Shalmaneser in a sitting posture, much injured. To the left of the doorway leading into the Egyptian gallery are two heads in the Egyptian style and the upper part of a draped statue of a deity with a wreath, from Idalium; and to the right are several small statues from the same place.

The collection of \***Egyptian Antiquities** fills three halls on the ground-floor, and four rooms in the upper story. The antiquities, which embrace the period from B.C. 3000 to A.D. 640, are arranged in chronological order. The Southern Gallery, which we enter first, is devoted to antiquities of the latest period.

**Southern Egyptian** Gallery. Section 1: monuments of the period of the Roman dominion. Section 2: time of the Ptolemies. In the middle is the celebrated '**Stone of** Rosetta', a tablet of black basalt with a triple inscription. It was found by the French near the Rosetta mouth of the Nile, but passed into the possession of the English in 1802. One of the inscriptions is in the hieroglyphic or sacred character, the second in the enchorial, demotic, or popular character, and the third in Greek. It was these inscriptions which led **Young** and Champollion to the discovery of the hieroglyphic language of ancient Egypt. The remaining part of the gallery contains monuments from the 5th to the 19th Dynasty (beginning about B.C. 1200). To the left are fragments of green basalt with reliefs; to the left, sarcophagus of King Nectanebo I. (about B.C. 360), with reliefs; to the right, sarcophagus of a priest of Memphis; right and left, two obelisks from the temple of Thoth at Memphis. — To the left, granite sarcophagus from Cairo; to the right, 'Sarcophagus of the Queen of Amasis II. (from Thebes); to the left, Psammeticlus I. sacrificing, a relief in basalt. — To the left, statue of the Nile; to the right, Apries; right and left, two sitting figures of the goddess Sekhet or Bast (with the head of a cat), between which is a colossal scarabæus in granite. — To the right, sitting figures of a man and a woman, in sandstone; to the left, King Menephtah II. on his throne. The —

**Central Egyptian Saloon**, chiefly contains antiquities of the times of Ramses the Great, the Sesostris of the Greeks. In the middle is a colossal fist from one of the statues in front of the Temple of Ptah, Memphis; to the left, two colossal heads, the one a cast from a figure of Ramses at Mitrahineh, the other in granite from the Memnonium at Thebes. To the right, a statue of the king in black basalt. Between the columns, at the entrance to the Northern Gallery, on the right, granite statue of Ramses II., from Thebes; to the left, a wooden figure of King Sethos I.

[To the E. of the Central Egyptian Saloon, opposite the entrance to the Hellenic Room (p. 243), is the **Refreshment Room** (poor).]

**Northern Egyptian Gallery**, chiefly containing antiquities of the time of the 18th Dynasty, under which Egypt enjoyed its greatest prosperity. On the left and right, statues of King Horus in black granite, and two lions in red granite (from Nubia). In the centre is a colossal ram's head from Karnak. To the right and left are sitting figures of King Amenophis III., in black granite, from Thebes. On the left is a tablet recording the Ethiopian conquests of Amenophis III. Opposite is a colossal head of Amenophis III., called by the Greeks Memnon (B.C. 1500); De Quincey speaks of this head as uniting 'the expressions of ineffable benignity with infinite duration'. On the left, column with a capital of lotus leaves. To the right and left are two colossal heads, found near the 'Vocal Memnon', at Thebes. Several repetitions of the statue of the goddess Bast, which is distinguished by the cat's head (in accordance with the Egyptian custom of representing deities with the heads of the animals sacred to them). Black granite figure of Queen Mautemua seated in a boat. In the middle is the colossal head of King Thothmes III., found at Karnak, adjoining which on the right is one of the arms of the same figure. On the right is a monument, the four sides of which are covered with figures of Thothmes III. and gods. To the left, small sandstone figure of an Egyptian prince. — The glass-cases at the sides are filled with smaller antiquities of granite, basalt, alabaster, and other materials. A hieroglyphical papyrus of Mutnetem, a queen of the 21st dynasty, is also exhibited on a stand in the middle of the room. The —

**Northern Egyptian Vestibule** contains antiquities of the period embraced by the first twelve dynasties, and particularly that of the fourth dynasty (about 3000 B.C.), when Egypt enjoyed a very high degree of civilisation. Above the door is a plaster cast of the head of the northern colossal figure of Ramses at Ipsamboul.

Opposite the Northern Vestibule is a staircase leading to the UPPER FLOOR. On the wall of the staircase are Mosaics from Halicarnassus, Carthage, and Utica. The ante-room at the top of the stairs is empty at present. To the left are four rooms filled with smaller Egyptian antiquities. [The order followed below will very soon be altered, as the old Etruscan Room is to be added to the Egyptian series, an addition which will cause a complete re-arrangement of this part of the collection.]

**First Egyptian Room.** The first wall-cases contain an extensive collection of small figures of the Egyptian gods in various materials. 1. Ameura (Jupiter) and Chons (Hercules); 2. Muth, Munt-ra; 3. Ptah (Vulcan); 4. Bast or Pasht (Diana); 5. Ma (Truth), Ra (the Sun); 6. Athor; 7-9. Osiris; 10, 11. Isis; 12, 13. Various deities. Cases 14-19. Sacred animals: jackal, cat, baboon, lion, owl, ibis, crocodile, snakes. Cases 22-28.

Statuettes of kings and officials. Cases 29, 30. Pillows or head-rests in wood and clay. Cases 31-39. Chairs and seats of different kinds. Cases 40-47. (in the middle). Stamped **bricks**, painted table, model of a house. Cases 48-53. Slices of calcareous **stone** with inscriptions and drawings. Cases 54-59. Pectoral plates, **network of** beads. — Table-case A. Hieratic **inscriptions and ornaments. Case** I. Fragments of inlaid figures. Case D. Glazed tiles from Tell-el-Yehûdiyeh. Case E. Ancient glass of various periods. Case G. Articles of attire, among which is a large wig. Case H. Scarabæi, rings, seals, and necklaces.

Second **Egyptian Room.** Wall-cases 48-53. Alabaster vases; 54-57. Glazed vases; 58-69. Painted vases; 70-72. Bronze vases; 73, 74. Food, fruit, seeds; 75-80. Boxes, spoons, weapons, and household utensils; 81. Tools; 82-85. Musical instruments, toys, and implements of spinning; 86-91. Sepulchral tablets and boxes; 92-99. Jugs of the Ptolemaic period and various objects of the Greek and Roman periods. — Table-case C. Inscriptions on bronze and terracotta, lamps, etc.; in Compartment 105, terracotta lamps from Palestine. Table-case B. Egyptian objects of the period of the Greek and Roman dominion, including two 'Portraits of Græco-Egyptian females (in Compartment 95), which are the oldest known portraits on wood. Table-case J. Bronze weapons and pottery. Table-case K. Mummy bandages and linen, bronze instruments of music, and sepulchral jars. Table-case F. Objects in bone and ivory, chiefly of the Roman period.

Third **Egyptian Room.** Wall-cases 100-133. Painted mummies, in an upright position; Cases 134-137. Sepulchral tablets; Case 138. (below) Coffin and mummy of a Græco-Egyptian child, with portrait on the outer bandages; Cases 139-140. Remains of mummies, partly under glass. Cases 143-150. Large collection of figures dedicated to the dead, composed of wood, alabaster, stone, or glass, and usually bearing a religious motto, and the name and rank of the deceased. Cases 151-154. Sepulchral vases. Cases 155-160. Sepulchral figures of deities used as cases to hold embalmed portions of the body, rolls of papyrus, and other objects. Cases 161-167. Mummies of animals. The Floor-cases contain a °Collection of mummies and coffins.

**Assyrian Room.** 1st Pier-case. Inscribed tablets, terracotta cylinders, and other Babylonian antiquities. 2nd Pier-case. Cylinders and other Assyrian antiquities. 3rd Pier-case. Assyrian and Babylonian antiquities, chiefly of the Parthian period. Table-case A. contains some fine bronze platings from the large gates of Shalmaneser II. (859-824 B.C.), discovered by Mr. Rassam in 1878, at Balawat in Mesopotamia; they are about 21 ft. high, and bear cuneiform inscriptions and figures in delicate repoussé sculpture, representing the campaigns against Ararat and Karkemish (pontoon bridges), Tyre and Sidon paying tribute, etc. Table-case D. contains necklaces and Parthian pottery; and the other smaller cases contain gems, seals, and engraved stones. Wall-cases 43-48. Glazed bricks and ceiling ornaments from Nineveh, Babylon, and Nimroud; 49-59. Parthian pottery; 60-67. Assyrian bronzes; 74-78. Bronze vessels, some with Hebrew inscriptions; 79-84. Bronze and stone tablets with Himyaritic or Sabæan inscriptions from Amran in Arabia.

We have now reached what used to be the *Refreshment Room* but which now forms the American Room of the Ethnographical Department (see p. 254). It is adjoined by a Staircase descending to the King's Library (p. 236). In the meantime we pass through the ante-room at the head of the staircase, and enter the SECOND NORTH GALLERY, consisting of a series of smaller rooms parallel with those just described and chiefly containing a selection of *Prints*, arranged so as to illustrate the growth and development of the Art of Engraving.

The room we first enter contains two cabinets filled with Christian antiquities. In that to the right is a Bridal Casket and a collection of silver objects found at Rome in 1793, including statuettes personifying Alexandria, Rome, Constantinople, and Antioch. In the cabinet to the left are bronze and terracotta lamps, chiefly from the East. — The walls of this and the following rooms are hung with a selection (frequently changed) of prints, drawings, engravings, and etchings.

**Second Coin Room.** English, Scottish, Irish, and American coins. Greek coins. General view of the coinage of Southern Asia subsequent to the Greek invasion of India. General view of the coinage of the United Kingdom down to the currency of the present day.

**First Coin Room.** French, Dutch, German, and Italian medals, some of the last by the great masters of the Renaissance. Large medals with Portrait-heads by Vittore Pisano. The case opposite contains gold and silver money current before the Christian era, from Greece, Asia Minor, and Magna Græcia. English medals.

The following two rooms are devoted entirely to the exhibition of engravings and other reproductions of paintings by eminent foreign and British masters, which are changed from time to time.

We now regain the head of the staircase (Pl. 19) descending to the Egyptian galleries (p. 247) and enter the rooms to the left, which contain the vases and other small objects of Hellenic art.

**First Vase Room.** The arrangement of the painted terracotta vases in the cases of this room affords an instructive survey of the development of the art of vase-painting. Cases 1-13. Archaic vases from Rhodes, with simple linear patterns. Cases 14-21. Vases from Athens, with intricate geometric patterns. Cases 22-39. Vases from Cyprus, resembling the last, but some with figures. Cases 40, 41. Vases from various Hellenic localities, with figures of animals. Cases 42, 43. Vases from Corinth and Corcyra. Cases 44-51. Vases from the Greek settlements in Lower Italy. Cases 52-64. Vases from Rhodes. The two huge vases in the centre of the room are also from Rhodes. The two smaller vases to the right, with dark figures on a white ground, are interesting examples of the first attempts to combine figure-painting with the older geometrical ornamentation. A table-case in this room contains interesting small objects of the Mycenæ period.

**Second Vase Room.** The vases in this room are almost entirely of Greek design and fabric, and are in most cases adorned with black figures on a red ground. Cases 7-15 contain the oldest vases and also terracotta figures. Cases 28-32 contain vases with black figures on a white ground. The finest vases are in the middle of the room. The —

**Third Vase Room** contains the vases of the best period, adorned with human and animal forms. To the right are several large vases adorned with groups of great beauty. At the top of one of the cases is an Athenian 'Lekythos', with a painting of Electra at the grave of Agamemnon, executed with wonderful delicacy (in several colours). The —

**Fourth Vase Room** contains vases of the period of the decline of the art (end of 4th and beginning of the 3rd cent. B.C.). — The

**Bronze Room** contains Greek and Roman bronzes. Cabinet 1-11. Candelabra. Cabinet 12-19. Armour. Cabinets 20-30. Vessels of various kinds. Cabinets 31-43. Rich collection of bronze statuettes (chiefly Roman or Græco-Roman), arranged according to the different groups of gods and heroes: 31, 32. Venus and Cupid; 33-35. Jupiter, Pluto, Hecate, Neptune, Minerva, Mars, Vulcan, Apollo, and Diana; 36-39. Bacchus, Silenus, etc.; 40, 41. Hercules and Mercury; 42, 43. Heroes (Atys, Harpocrates). Cabinets 44-47 contain a selection of larger bronzes: 'Venus putting on her sandals, from Patras; 'Youthful Bacchus; Apollo with the chlamys; Jupiter in a sitting posture, with sceptre and thunderbolt (from Hungary); busts of Lucius Verus and Claudius; Meleager. Cabinets 48, 49. Statuettes of Fortune, Victory, the Seasons, etc.; 50-53. Figures of Lares and actors, allegorical lamps, and other objects; 54, 55. Roman chair of state (bisellium) inlaid with silver, figure-head of an ancient galley, tripods, etc.;

56-60. Candelabra and lamps. — On a **circular table in** the centre of the room is a 'Head of a goddess, of heroic size, from Armenia. — The large case near the middle of the room contains several fine works: 'Boy playing at morra, from Foggia; Silenus carrying a cask, the base of a candelabrum; Hercules, **from** Bavay in France; ' Philosopher (?), found at Brindisi (identical **with a statue** in the Villa Borghese); 'Statuette of Pomona; 'Winged **head (perhaps of** Hypnos, the god of sleep), Perugia; head of a **man, from Cyrene; head** of a man (perhaps Homer), from Constantinople; **Venus** arranging **her** hair; Mercury with wallet and caduceus, found at Huis **in** France. — Adjacent **is a small** case with bronzes from Paramythia in **Epirus** (4th cent. B.C.): **Dione (?); one of the** Dioscuri; Venus; Jupiter **with** his left hand **outstretched; Jupiter with** his right hand outstretched; Apollo bending **his bow. — A table-case** contains **several** select bronzes: the bronzes **of Siris, two shoulder-pieces** of Greek armour, from Magna Græcia; figures and **animals in** relief, embossed in silver, for the decoration of a chariot; **mirror with** Menelaus laying hold of Helen (Cervetri); another mirror, **with an** alto-relief of **Venus and Adonis at** the foot (Locri); **youthful** heroic figure in a sitting posture, from Tarentum; group of Boreas **and Orithyia from** Calymnos; iron sword in a bronze scabbard, found at Mayence. — **The** following **are** exhibited singly in small cases: Hercules **with the apples** of the Hesperides, **from** Phœnicia; **'Marsyas; leg of a colossal figure,** apparently **a warrior, from** Magna **Græcia. — The** other **table-cases** contain **weapons, knives,** figures of **animals, bracelets, brooches, fibulæ,** armlets, **pins, locks, keys, and other small bronze articles.**

We next reach the new —

**Etruscan Room, which** contains **archaic bronzes, works in terracotta, pottery, burial urns, cists, and reliefs. Most of the Etruscan sarcophagi and other heavy objects are** now **placed in the basement,** see p. 240. **Many of the finest bronzes are in a large detached case, including a** ' Lebes', **with an engraved frieze representing Hercules driving away the oxen** of **Cacus; at the back are chariot races and mock combats; on the lid, Hercules carrying off Auge (or Pluto and Proserpine?); round the rim are four mounted Amazons (from Capua). Female figure in long drapery, from Sessa; 'Amphora, the handles composed of men bending backwards, with sirens at their feet, from Vulci; Hercules taming the horses of Diomede, from Palestrina; Ceres sitting in a waggon, from Amelia,** in **Etruria; Peleus struggling with Atalanta, also from the lid of a cist.** Noteworthy **bronzes in other cases are Hercules with the lion's hide,** 'Mars in richly **ornamented armour, and a bearded head, all from the** Lake of **Falterona; female figure in voluminous drapery, with archaic** inscription; **Etruscan helmet with inscription, belonging to Hiero I., King** of Syracuse, **from Olympia; 'Cist with engraved frieze, representing the** sacrifice **of captive Trojans at the funeral pile of Patroclus, and a Satyr and** Mænad **on the lid, from Palestrina. To the left of the entrance is a large terracotta sarcophagus, with life-size male and female figures, modelled in the round; the contents of the inscriptions have recently raised suspicion that this is a modern imposture. In a large case on the** other side **Sarcophagus cover, with the half-recumbent** figure **of a woman holding a mirror. The same case contains several cists, urns, and other** figures. **To the right, Cists with funeral and feasting scenes, in low** relief. To **the left is** a **case with arms and armour. — Some of the** wall-cases **to the left contain** bronzes, **and others archaic** Etruscan pottery. — In wall-cases **126-135 are** antiquities from **the Polledrara** Tomb, near Vulci (ca. B.C. 600). **— The S.** section **of** this room, **containing** Roman mosaics, **terracotta** reliefs, etc., may **be regarded as an annex** of the Terracotta Room (p. 222). **Among the** objects exhibited **here are six mural** paintings from the tombs **of the** Nasones, **near** Rome. **In the S.E.** corner, adjoining the entrance **to the** Medal Room, **is a mummy from the** Fayoum, **with a** portrait on panel (comp. p. 150).

**Medal** and **Gold Ornament Rooms** (closed, admission **by ringing the bell). The collection of medals, gold ornaments, coins, and gems preserved here is very** complete and extremely valuable, being probably the finest in Europe. The famous **"Portland Vase** is also kept here. It was exhibited to the public down to 1845, when it was broken to pieces by a madman named Lloyd. It was afterwards, however, skilfully reconstructed. The vase, which is about 1 ft. in height, is of dark blue glass, adorned with beautifully cut reliefs in opaque white glass, and was found in a tomb at Rome in the early part of the 17th century. It came for a time into the possession of Prince Barberini, whence it is also called the 'Barberini Vase', and is now the property of the Duke of Portland. The subject of the reliefs is a matter of dispute; some authorities maintain that they represent the metamorphosis of Themis into a snake, others Alcestis' delivery from Hades; the Museum Guide describes them as the meeting of Peleus and Thetis, and Thetis consenting to be the wife of Peleus. The bottom, which has been detached, is adorned with a bust of Paris.

The next room, formerly containing the Museum Collection of Glass, has recently been fitted up to hold the **Terracotta Antiquities.** (The numbering of the cases begins at the end farthest from the Etruscan Room.) To the right are the Greek and Græco-Phœnician Terracottas, to the left are the Græco-Roman Terracottas. Probably the most generally interesting are the exquisite little figures from Tanagra (Cases 16-22; to the right).

The **Central Saloon**, at the top of the Great Staircase, contains the **Prehistoric Antiquities**, including the *Greenwell Collection of Antiquities from British Barrows* (not yet finally arranged).

The whole remaining portion of the upper story was formerly occupied by the collections of natural history (now at South Kensington; see p. 273), which surpass in extent all similar collections in the world, except, perhaps, those of Paris. The rooms formerly devoted to the botanical collections are now occupied by the **Anglo-Saxon** and **Anglo-Roman Antiquities.**

**Anglo-Saxon Room.** On the N. side are the antiquities found in England, consisting of cinerary urns, swords and knives (some inscribed), three matrices of seals (the only Anglo-Saxon seals extant), runic caskets of whale's bone, a runic cross, silver ornaments, bronze articles, etc. Opposite is a collection of foreign Teutonic antiquities of similar date, the most noticeable of which are the contents of a Livonian grave.

**Anglo-Roman Room.** The series begins with four leaden coffins and numerous smaller objects found in graves, including the contents of the four large sarcophagi in the Roman Gallery on the ground-floor, and several cists of marble, lead, and glass. Tomb of tiles. Vessels of glass, pewter, and metal. Bronze figures, among which are three of Mars, several good statuettes found in the valley of the Thames, and a fine figure of an archer. Then silver votive ornaments. Sculptures, including a figure of Luna, the finest piece of Roman sculpture found in Britain. Building materials, tiles, bricks, drain-pipes. The S. side of the room is devoted to pottery, and at the N. end is a mosaic pavement found on the removal of the old East India House in Leadenhall Street. In the middle of the room are a colossal bronze bust of Hadrian from the Thames valley, a fine figure of an emperor from Suffolk, and an interesting bronze helmet. The table-cases contain brooches, trinkets, moulds for coins, and implements of various kinds.

The **Mediæval Room**, entered from the Prehistoric Saloon, contains the mediæval objects, excepting the glass and pottery.

**Mediæval Room.** Cases 1-6. Arms and armour; 7-10. Oriental and Venetian metal-work; 11. Irish bells and crozier (1050); 12-14. Metal-work; 15, 16. Astrolabes and clocks, including a time-piece in the form of a ship, made for the emperor Rudolph II. (1576-1612); 17-20. Eccle-

siastical metal-work and Limoges enamels; 21, 22. Paintings from St.
Stephen's Chapel at Westminster (1356); 23-26. Ivory carvings; 27, 28.
Carvings in wood, among which is a set of panels from a Coptic church
near Cairo; 29, 30. Caskets of ivory, wood, and leather; 31-32. Monumental brasses and stone slabs. Table-case A. contains historical relics,
including an ivory hat which belonged to Queen Elizabeth, the punchbowl of Robert Burns, the Lochbuy brooch, and quadrants belonging to
various English monarchs. In Table-case B. are objects illustrating magic,
talismans, locks and keys, spoons, and knives. Table-cases C, D. Matrices
of English seals and signet rings. Table-case E: Enamels, including a
plaque representing Henry of Blois, Bishop of Winchester and brother
of King Stephen (1139-1146). Table-case F: Carvings in ivory and other
materials. Table-case G: Matrices of foreign seals. Table-case K: Watches.
Table-case L: Objects used in games; curious set of chessmen of the 13th
cent., from the island of Lewis in the Hebrides, made of walrus tusk.

The **Asiatic Saloon** contains collections illustrating Buddhist mythology (Cases 1-26), Hindoo mythology (119-128), **Jain mythology** (116-118),
and Shamanism (114,115). Cases 31-96 contain Oriental porcelain and
pottery. Cases 97-110. Works of **art from China;** 27-30. Japan; 111-113.
India and Persia.

From the Asiatic Saloon we turn to the right into the new
rooms of the WHITE BUILDING (see p. 234), which contains the
collections of *Glass and Pottery* and also the **Department of Prints
and Drawings.** The latter contains an unrivalled collection of
original drawings, engravings, and etchings. Hitherto the use of
this collection has been practically restricted to students, who
receive tickets on application to the Principal Librarian (see below),
but the spacious new rooms now built for it include a fine Exhibition Gallery (see below). Foreigners and travellers may obtain
access to the *Students' Rooms* on giving in their names. Comp. the
Handbook to the 'Department', by Louis Fagan (3s. 6d.).

We first enter the —

English Ceramic Ante-Room, containing pottery and porcelain chiefly
bought from Mr. Willett or presented by Mr. Franks. Cases 1-8. Early
English Pottery (11-15th cent.); 9-20. Glazed Ware of the 16-18th cent.;
21-26. English Pottery, chiefly from Staffordshire; 27-32. Pavement Tiles
(13-16th cent.); 33. Fulham Stoneware (17th cent.); 35-46. English Porcelain
(that in the last four cases inferior); 47-50. Liverpool Tiles, transferprinted, by Sadler. The table-case contains a collection of so-called
'Chelsea Toys'.

Glass and Ceramic Gallery, including the valuable Slade Collection
of Glass. Cases 1, 2. English Delft, chiefly made at Lambeth in the 17-
18th cent.; 3. Dutch and German Delft; 8. Italian Pottery; 9-23 Italian
Majolica; 24-26. Spanish Pottery; 27-30. Rhodian and Damascus Ware;
32, 33. Persian Pottery; 31, 35. French Pottery; 37-45. Antique Glass,
chiefly of the Roman period; 46-54. Venetian Glass; 55-58. German Glass;
59-61. Oriental Glass; 62. French Glass; 63. English Glass; 64-66. Wedgwood and other Staffordshire Wares and Bristol Delft. The table-cases
contain Wedgwood medallions, antique, German, Dutch, and Flemish
glass; English engraved glass, etc. Another case contains a terracotta bust
of Mme. du Boccage (1766), a plaster cast of Flaxman's 'Shield of Achilles',
models by Michelangelo (apparently designs for the Medici tombs in San
Lorenzo, Florence), a terracotta model by Giovanni da Bologna, and some
portrait-medallions in wax.

The Print and Drawing Exhibition **Gallery is at** present occupied by a
Collection of Japanese and Chinese Paintings, purchased from Mr. William
Anderson in 1881 (special catalogue 2d.). The collection is divided into
two series, each of which is arranged in historical order, and affords an
admirable **survey of** the pictorial art of China and Japan.

We now return to the Asiatic **Saloon** and begin our inspection of the extensive and interesting **Ethnographical Collection**, which is arranged topographically and occupies the whole of the EAST GALLERY. The Asiatic Section is first entered; then follow the Oceanic, African, and American Sections, each containing a great variety of objects illustrating the habits, dress, warfare, handicrafts, etc., of the less civilised inhabitants of the different quarters of the globe.

On the N. side of the spacious entrance hall, facing the entrance door, is a passage leading to the *__Reading Room__, constructed in 1855-57 at a cost of 150,000*l*; it is open from 9 a.m. to 7 or 8 p.m. (closed on the first four days of March and October). This imposing circular hall, covered by a large dome of glass and iron (140 ft. in diameter, or 1 ft. larger than the dome of St. Peter's at Rome, and 106 ft. high), has ample accommodation for 360 readers or writers. Around the superintendent, who occupies a raised seat in the centre of the room, are circular cases containing the *General Catalogue* for the use of the readers (in about 2000 vols.) and various special catalogues and indexes. On the top of these cases lie printed forms (white for books, green for MSS.) to be filled up with the name and 'press-mark' (*i. e.* reference, indicated in the catalogue by letters and numerals, to its position in the book-cases) of the work required, and the number of the seat chosen by the applicant at one of the tables, which radiate from the centre of the room like the spokes of a wheel. The form when filled up is put into a little basket, placed for this purpose on the counter. One of the attendants will then procure the book required, and send it to the reader's seat. About 20,000 vols. of the books in most frequent request, such as dictionaries, encyclopædias, histories, periodicals, etc., are kept in the reading-room itself, and may be used without any application to the library officials; while coloured plans, showing the positions of the various categories of these books, are distributed throughout the room. Every reader is provided with a chair, a folding desk, a small hinged shelf for books, pens, and ink, a blotting-pad, and a peg for his hat. The reader will probably find the arrangements of the British Museum Reading Room superior to those of most public libraries, while the obliging civility of the attendants, and the freedom from obtrusive supervision and restrictions are most grateful. The electric light has been introduced into the Reading Room and Galleries. — In the year 1858, the first after the opening of the New Reading Room, the number of readers amounted to 190,400, who consulted in all 877,897 books or an average of 3000 a day. In 1888 there were 188,432 readers, or 622 per day. A *Description of the Reading Room* may be had from the officials (1*d.*).

Persons desirous of using the Reading Room must send a written application to the Principal Librarian, specifying their names, rank or profession, and address, and enclosing a recommendation from some well-known householder in London. The applicant must not **be** under **21 years of age.** The permission, which is granted without limit **of term, is not transferable and is** subject to withdrawal. The Reading Room tickets entitle to the use of the new *Newspaper Room* (comp. p. 236). It is possible for strangers to **get permission to use the Reading Room for a single day** by **personal application at the office of the Principal Librarian, to** the left **of the First Græco-Roman Room. Tickets for visitors to the** Reading Room are obtained on the right side of the entrance hall. Visitors are **not allowed to walk through the Reading Room, but** may view it from the **doorway. — The Libraries contain a collection of** books and manuscripts, rivalled in extent by the National Library of Paris alone. The number of printed books is about 1,590,000, and it increases at the rate of about 30,000 volumes per annum.

## 23. St. James's Palace and Park. Buckingham Palace.

The site of **St. James's Palace** (Pl. R, 22; *IV*), an irregular brick building at the S. end of St. James's Street, was originally occupied by a hospital for lepers, founded previously to 1190. In 1532 the building came into the possession of Henry VIII., who erected in its place a royal palace, said to have been designed by *Holbein*. Here Queen Mary died in 1558. Charles I. slept here the night before his execution, and walked across St. James's Park to Whitehall next morning (1649). The palace was considerably extended by Charles I., and, after Whitehall was burned down in 1691, it became the chief residence of the English kings from William III. to George IV. In 1809 a serious fire completely destroyed the eastern wing, so that with the exception of the interesting old brick gateway towards St. James's Street, the Chapel Royal, and the old Presence Chamber, there are few remains of the ancient palace of the Tudors. The state rooms are sumptuously fitted up, and contain a number of portraits and other works of art. The initials HA above the chimney-piece in the Presence Chamber are a reminiscence of Henry VIII. and Anne Boleyn. It is difficult to obtain permission to inspect the interior. The guard is changed every day at 10.45 a m., when the fine bands of the Grenadier, Coldstream, or Fusilier Guards play for $1/4$ hr. in the open court facing Marlborough House. Though St. James's Palace is no longer the residence of the sovereign, the British court is still officially known as the 'Court of St. James's'.

On the N. side, entered from Colour Court, is the *Chapel Royal*, in which the **Queen** and **some of** the highest nobility have seats. Divine service **is** celebrated **on** Sundays at 10 a. m., 12 noon, and 5.30 p. **m. A limited** number of strangers are admitted to the two latter **services by tickets** obtained from the Lord Chamberlain; for the **service at 10 no ticket is required. —** The marriage of Queen

Victoria with Prince Albert, and those of some of their daughters, were celebrated in the Chapel Royal.

Down to the death of Prince Albert in 1861, the Queen's **Levées** and **Drawing Rooms** were always held in St. James's Palace. Since then, however, the drawing-rooms have taken place at Buckingham Palace, but the levées are still held here. A levée **differs from** a drawing-room in this respect, that, at the former, gentlemen only are presented to the sovereign, while at the latter it is almost entirely ladies who are introduced. Richly **dressed** ladies; gentlemen, magnificent in gold-laced uniforms; **lackeys in** gorgeous liveries, knee-breeches, silk stockings, and powdered **hair**, and bearing enormous bouquets; well-fed coachmen with carefully curled wigs and three-cornered hats; splendid carriages and horses, **which** dash along **through the** densely packed masses of spectators; and a mounted band of **the Life** Guards, playing in front of the palace; — such, so far as **can** be **seen by** the spectators who crowd the adjoining streets, windows, **and balconies, are the** chief ingredients in the august ceremony of a 'Queen's Drawing Room'. A notice of the drawing-room, with the names of the ladies presented, appears next day in the newspapers.

In the life of **a** young English lady of the higher ranks her presentation **at Court is an epoch of no** little **importance, for after** attending her first **drawing-room, she is** considered 'out', and enters on **the** round **of** balls, concerts, and other gaieties, which often play so large a part in her life.

On the W. side of St. James's Palace lies *Clarence House*, the residence, since 1874, of the Duke of Edinburgh and his consort, the Grand Duchess Marie of Russia. — *Marlborough House*, **on the** E. side of the palace, see p. 220.

**St. James's Park** (Pl. R, 21, 22, 25, 26; *IV*), which **lies to the S. of St. James's Palace, was** formerly **a** marshy meadow, **belonging to St.** James's Hospital for Lepers. Henry VIII., on the **conversion of the hospital into a palace,** caused the marsh to be **drained, surrounded with a** wall, **and** transformed into a deer-park **and riding-path. Charles II.** extended the park by 36 acres, **and had it laid out in pleasure-grounds by** *Le Nôtre*, **the celebrated French landscape gardener. Its walks, etc.,** were all constructed **primly and neatly in straight lines, and the** strip of water received **the appropriate name of 'the** canal'. The present form of St. James's **Park was imparted to it** in 1827-29, during the reign of George IV., by *Nash*, **the architect (see below). Its** beautiful clumps of trees, its winding **expanse of water enl**ivened by water-fowl, and the charming **views it affords of the stately buildings arou**nd it, combine to make **it the most attractive of the London parks. In** 1857 **the bottom** of **the lake was levelled so as to give it a uniform** depth of **3-4** ft. **The new suspension bridge, across the centre of it,** forms the most **direct communication for pedestrians between St.** James's Street **and** Queen's **Square, Westminster, Birdcage Walk on the S.** side of the park, **and Westminster Abbey.**

The broad avenue, **planted with rows of** handsome trees, on the N. side of the **park, is called the** *Mall*, from the game of 'paille maille' once played here **(comp. p. 218). At the E.** extremity, near *Carlton House* **Terrace, is the flight of** steps mentioned at p. 219, leading to **the York Column (p. 219).** — *Birdcage Walk*, on the S.

side of the park, is so named from the aviary maintained here as early as the time of the Stuarts.

At the E. end of Birdcage Walk is *Storey's Gate*, leading to Great *George Street* and *Westminster*. In *Petty France*, to the S. of Birdcage Walk, Milton once had a house. — A battalion of the Royal Foot Guards is quartered in *Wellington Barracks*, built in 1834, on the S. side of Birdcage Walk; the interior of the small chapel is very tasteful (open Tues., Thurs., & Frid., 11-4). The *Government Offices* (p. 183), the *India* and *Foreign Offices*, and beyond them the *Horse Guards* and *Admiralty*, lie on the E. side of St. James's Park. In an open space called the *Parade*, between the park and the Admiralty, are placed a Turkish cannon captured by the English at Alexandria, and a large mortar, used by Marshal Soult at the siege of Cadiz in 1812, and abandoned there by the French. The carriage of the mortar is in the form of a dragon, and was made at Woolwich.

**Buckingham Palace** (Pl. R, 21; *IV*), the Queen's residence, rises at the W. end of St. James's Park. The present palace occupies the site of *Buckingham House*, erected by John Sheffield, Duke of Buckingham, in 1703, which was purchased by George III. in 1761, and occasionally occupied by him. His successor, George IV., caused it to be remodelled by Nash in 1825, but it remained empty until its occupation in 1837 by Queen Victoria, whose town residence it has since continued to be. The eastern and principal façade towards St. James's Park, 360 ft. in length, was added by *Blore* in 1846; and the large ball-room and other apartments were subsequently constructed. The palace now forms a large quadrangle. The rooms occupied by Her Majesty are on the N. side.

A portico, borne by marble columns, leads out of the large court into the rooms of state. We first enter the *Sculpture Gallery*, which is adorned with busts and statues of members of the royal family and eminent statesmen. Beyond it, with a kind of semicircular apse towards the garden, is the *Library*, where deputations, to whom the Queen grants an audience, wait until they are admitted to the royal presence. The ceiling of the magnificent *Marble Staircase*, to the left of the vestibule, is embellished with frescoes by Townsend, representing Morning, Noon, Evening, and Night.

On the first floor are the following rooms: *Green Drawing Room*, 50 ft. long and 33 ft. high, in the middle of the E. side; *Throne Room*, 66 ft. in length, sumptuously fitted up with red striped satin and gilding, and having a marble frieze running round the vaulted and richly decorated ceiling, with reliefs representing the Wars of the Roses, executed by Baily from designs by Stothard; *Grand Saloon*; *State Ball Room*, on the S. side of the palace, 110 ft. long and 60 ft. broad; lastly the *Picture Gallery*, 180 ft. in length, containing a choice, though not very extensive collection of paintings.

PICTURE GALLERY. The enumeration begins to the right. Carracci, Christ in the Garden; 182. *Frans Hals*. Portrait of a man, dated 1636;

## 23. BUCKINGHAM PALACE.

180. *Dujardin*, Three peasants by a wall; 172. *G. Schalcken*, Girl with a candle; °174. *Rembrandt*, Portrait of himself; 170. *Teniers*, Scholars at table; 171. *Dujardin*, Shepherd boy and cattle; 176. *Teniers*, Peasants dancing (dated 1645); °168. *A. Cuyp*. Evening scene, with figures; 165. *N. Berchem*, Shepherdess wading through a river (1650); °164. *Rembrandt*, Lady with a fan (dated 1641), the counterpart of a picture in Brussels; 163. *Rubens*, The Falconer; 159. *Isaac van Ostade*. Scene in a village street; 157. *Jan Steen*, Card-players. — °154. *Rembrandt*. Adoration of the Magi (dated 1657). a celebrated work.

'The impasto of the light on this picture is remarkably bold, being of a beautiful golden tone, rich and mellow'. — *Vosmaer*.
²155. *Van Dyck*. Madonna and Child with St. Catharine; °152. *A. van Ostade*, Boors talking (1650); °149. *Rubens*, Landscape; 150. *Rubens*, St. George and the Dragon; 147. *A. van Ostade*. Boors smoking (1665); ²148. *Metsu*, Lady with a champagne glass; 145. *Van Dyck*, Charles I. on horseback; 141. *F. Mieris*, Woman selling grapes (dated; erroneously attributed to G. Dou); 135. *A. Cuyp*, Cavalier; 140. *Cuyp*. Harbour; 136. *Pieter de Hooghe*, Woman spinning; °134. *Claude Lorrain*, Europa; 132. *Metsu*, Concert; 133. *A. van de Velde*, Scene on the beach (dated 1666); °129. *Hobbema*, Mill (dated 1665); 131. *Rembrandt*. Portrait of an old man. °126. *Rubens*. Pythagoras (the fruit by *Snyders*); 118. *Wouwerman*, Horsefair; 110. *Cuyp*, Lady and gentleman riding in a wood; 116. *Rubens*. Pan and Syrinx; °113. *Paul Potter*, Cattle (dated 1640); 109. *Teniers*, Rocky landscape; 107. *Jan Steen*, Violinist and card players; 104. *W. van de Velde*, Calm (1659); °103. *J. Steen*, Woman pulling on her stockings (1663); 106. *Cuyp*, Grey horse; 100. *J. van Ostade*, Village street (dated 1643).

We now pass into the DINING ROOM. which contains a series of portraits of English sovereigns, several being by *Gainsborough*. In an adjoining room is *Sir Frederick Leighton's* Procession in Florence with the Madonna of Cimabue. We then return to the —

PICTURE GALLERY. and examine the works on the opposite wall. 98. *A. van der Werff*, Lady in a swoon; 91. *Backhuisen*, Rough sea; 92. *Teniers*. Camp scene (dated 1647); 88. *Berchem*, Shepherds at a ford; 89. *Cuyp*, Stag-hunt; 98. *Teniers*, Peasants dancing; °86. *A. Cuyp*. Ducks on a lake; 83. *Jan Steen*. Interior; °84. *A. van de Velde*. Cattle pasturing; 82. *Cuyp*. Cattle and shepherds by a canal; 72. *Rubens*. The Pensionary John of Oldenbarneveld visited by his son after his condemnation; °67. *A. van de Velde*. Landscape with shepherds (1659); °68. *Paul Potter*. Cavalier in front of a hut (1651); °64. *J. Steen*. Family scene; 62. *Hobbema*, Landscape; °59. *J. van Ruysdael*, Evening scene with windmill, a masterpiece; 57. *Wouwerman*, Hay harvest; 54. *A. van Ostade*, Reading the papers (1650); 56. *J. Steen*. Brawl of peasants beside a canal (1672); °52. *A. van de Velde*. Hunting in a forest; 50. *Van Dyck* (?). Three cavaliers, a sketch for the finished picture in the Berlin Museum; 51. *Van Dyck*, Virgin and Child; 48. *A. van Ostade*. Peasants sitting round the fire; °45. *N. Maes*. Girl in a listening attitude stealing down a winding staircase (of a radiant golden tone). — °°41. *Rembrandt*, 'Noli me tangere' (morning light; dated 1638).

Rembrandt's friend, Jeremias de Decker, dedicated a sonnet to the praise of this picture.

°°40. *Terburg*. Lady writing a letter, with an attendant, the *chef-d'oeuvre* of this great master of scenes of refined domestic life; °34 *Rubens*. Assumption of the Virgin. sketch for the picture at Brussels; 29. *A. van Ostade*, Family scene (1668); 28. *W. van de Velde*. On the beach; °30. *Rembrandt*. Burgomaster Pancras and his wife, painted in 1645; 26. *F. Mieris*, Boy blowing soap-bubbles (1663); 22. *P. de Hooghe*, Card-players (1658). one of the artist's masterpieces; 23. *Cuyp*. Evening scene; 18. *Dou*, Mother nursing her child, very minute in the details; 14. *P. Potter*, Farm scene (dated 1615). — °10. *Rembrandt*, A ship-builder, occupied in making a drawing of a ship, is interrupted by his wife, who has just come into the room with a letter (dated 1633).

'The momentary nature of the simple action, the truth of the heads, the wonderful clearness of the full bright sunlight, and the conscientious execution, render the picture extremely attractive' — *Waagen*. It was purchased by George IV., when Prince of Wales, for 500*l*.

7. *Teniers*, Peasants dancing; 2. *A. van Ostade*, Backgammon players (1670); *\*Titian*, A summer storm amid the Venetian Alps, an effective rendering of unusual natural phenomena (painted about 1534).

Permission to visit the Picture Gallery may sometimes be obtained (during the Queen's absence only) from the Lord Chamberlain on written application.

The Gardens at the back of the Palace contain a summer-house decorated with eight frescoes from Milton's 'Comus', by Landseer, Stanfield, Maclise, Eastlake, Dyce, Leslie, Uwins, and Ross.

The ROYAL MEWS (so called from the 'mews' or coops in which the royal falcons were once kept), or stables and coach-houses (for 40 equipages), entered from Queen's Row, to the S. of the palace, are shown on application to the Master of the Horse. The magnificent state carriage, designed by Sir W. Chambers in 1762, and painted by Cipriani (cost 7660*l*.), is kept here.

To the N., between Buckingham Palace and Piccadilly, lies the GREEN PARK, which is 60 acres in extent. Between this and the Queen's private gardens is *Constitution Hill*, leading direct to *Hyde Park Corner* (p. 260). Three attempts on the life of the Queen have been made in this road.

## 24. Hyde Park. Kensington Gardens and Palace. Holland House.

Park Lane, a street about 1/2 M. in length, connecting the W. end of Piccadilly with Oxford Street, forms the eastern boundary of Hyde Park (Pl. R, 14, etc.), which extends thence towards the W. as far as Kensington Gardens, and covers an area of 390 acres. Before the dissolution of the religious houses, the site of the park belonged to the old manor of Hyde, one of the possessions of Westminster Abbey. The ground was laid out as a park and enclosed under Henry VIII. In the reign of Elizabeth stags and deer were still hunted in it, while under Charles II. it was devoted to horse-races. The latter monarch also laid out the 'Ring', a kind of corso, about 350 yds. in length, round an enclosed space, which soon became a most fashionable drive. The fair frequenters of the Ring often appeared in masks, and, under this disguise, used so much freedom, that in 1695 an order was issued denying admission to all whose features were thus concealed.

At a later period the park was neglected, and was frequently the scene of duels, one of the most famous being that between Lord Mohun and the Duke of Hamilton in 1712, when both the principals lost their lives. Under William III. and Queen Anne a large portion of the park was taken to enlarge Kensington Gardens; and, finally, Queen Caroline, wife of George II., caused the *Serpentine*, a sheet of artificial water, to be formed. The Serpentine was originally fed by the *Westbourne*, a small stream coming from that ancient region of fountains, *Bayswater*, to the N.; but it is now supplied from the Thames.

Hyde Park is one of the most frequented and lively scenes in London. It is surrounded by a handsome and lofty iron railing, and provided with nine carriage-entrances, besides a great number of gates for pedestrians, all of which are shut at midnight. On the S. side are *Kensington Gate* and *Queen's Gate*, both in Kensington Road, near Kensington Palace; *Prince's Gate* and *Albert Gate* in Knightsbridge; and *Hyde Park Corner* at the W. end of Piccadilly. On the E. side are *Stanhope Gate* and *Grosvenor Gate*, both in Park Lane. On the N. side are *Cumberland Gate*, at the W. end of Oxford Street, and *Victoria Gate*, Bayswater. The entrances most used are Hyde Park Corner at the S.E., and Cumberland Gate at the N.E. angle. At the latter rises the MARBLE ARCH, a triumphal arch in the style of the Arch of Constantine, originally erected by George IV. at the entrance of Buckingham Palace at a cost of 80,000*l*. In 1850, on the completion of the E. façade (p. 257), it was removed from the palace, and in the following year was re-erected in its present position. The reliefs on the S. are by *Baily*, those on the N. by *Westmacott*; the elegant bronze gates well deserve inspection. The handsome gateway at HYDE PARK CORNER, with three passages, was built in 1828 from designs by *Burton*. The reliefs are copies of the Elgin marbles (p. 241). The *Green Park Arch*, opposite, at the W. end of the *Green Park* (p. 259), erected in 1846, was removed in 1883, in the course of improvements made at Hyde Park Corner, and has been rebuilt on Constitution Hill. The *Equestrian Statue of Wellington*, by *Wyatt*, with which it was disfigured, has been re-erected at Aldershot Camp, while another equestrian statue of the Duke, in bronze, by *Boehm*, has been erected in Wellington Place, opposite Apsley House. At the corners of the red granite pedestal are figures of a grenadier, a Highlander, a Welsh fusilier, and an Inniskillen dragoon, all also by Boehm. *Apsley House* (p. 267), the residence of the Duke of Wellington, lies directly to the E. of Hyde Park Corner. The house next it is that of *Baron Rothschild*, and that at the W. corner of Park Lane is occupied by the *Duke of Cambridge*.

To the N. of Hyde Park Corner rises another monument to the 'Iron Duke', consisting of the colossal figure known as the *Statue of Achilles*, which, as the inscription informs us, was erected in 1822, with money subscribed by English ladies, in honour of 'Arthur, Duke of Wellington, and his brave companions in arms'. The statue, by *Westmacott*, is cast from the metal of 12 French cannon, captured in France and Spain, and at Waterloo, and is a copy of one of the Dioscuri on the Monte Cavallo at Rome. No carts or waggons are allowed to enter Hyde Park, and cabs are admitted only to one roadway across the park near Kensington

Gardens. The finest portion of the park, irrespectively of the magnificent groups of trees and expanses of grass for which English parks stand pre-eminent, is that near the Serpentine, where, in spring and summer, during the 'Season', the fashionable world rides, drives, or walks. The favourite hour for carriages is 5-7 p.m., and the fashionable drive is the broad, southern avenue, which leads from Hyde Park Corner to the left, past the Albert Gate. Equestrians, on the other hand, appear, chiefly from 12 to 2 p.m., but also later in the afternoon, in *Rotten Row*, a track exclusively reserved for riders, running parallel to the drive on the N., and extending along the S. side of the Serpentine from Hyde Park Corner to Kensington Gate, a distance of about 1½ M. The scene in this part of Hyde Park, on fine afternoons, is most interesting and imposing. In the Drive are seen unbroken files of elegant equipages and high-bred horses in handsome trappings, moving continually to and fro, presided over by sleek coachmen and powdered lacqueys, and occupied by some of the most beautiful and exquisitely dressed women in the world. In the Row are numerous lady and gentlemen riders, who parade their spirited and glossy steeds before the admiring crowd sitting or walking at the sides. It has lately become 'the thing' to walk by the Row on Sundays, and on a fine day the 'Church Parade', between morning service and luncheon (*i.e.* about 1-2 p.m.), is one of the best displays of dress and fashion in London. — The drive on the N. side of the Serpentine is called the *Ladies' Mile*. The Coaching and Four-in-hand Clubs meet here during the season, as many as thirty or forty drags sometimes assembling. The flower-beds adjoining Park Lane and to the W. of Hyde Park Corner are exceedingly brilliant, and the show of rhododendrons in June is deservedly famous. At the S. end of Park Lane is a handsome *Fountain* by Thorneycroft, adorned with figures of Tragedy, Comedy, Poetry, Shakspeare, Chaucer, and Milton, and surmounted by a statue of Fame. In Hamilton Gardens, a little farther to the S., near Hyde Park Corner (p. 260), is a statue of *Lord Byron* (d. 1824), erected in 1879. The district between Park Lane and Bond Street (p. 225) is known as MAYFAIR, and is one of the most fashionable in London.

A refreshing contrast to this fashionable show is afforded by a scene of a very unsophisticated character, which takes place in summer on the Serpentine before 8 a.m. and after 8 p.m. At these times, when a flag is hoisted, a crowd of men and boys, most of them in very homely attire, are to be seen undressing and plunging into the water, where their lusty shouts and hearty laughter testify to their enjoyment. After the lapse of about an hour the flag is lowered, as an indication that the bathing time is over, and in quarter of an hour every trace of the lively scene has disappeared. — Pleasure-boats may be hired on the Serpentine.

In winter the Serpentine, when frozen over, is much frequented by skaters. To provide against accidents, the *Royal Humane Society*, mentioned at p. 146, has a 'receiving-house' here, where attendants and life-saving apparatus are kept in readiness for any **emergency**. The bottom of the Serpentine was cleaned and levelled in 1870; the average depth in the centre is now 7 ft., **and towards the edges** 3 ft. At the point where the Serpentine **enters** Kensington Gardens it is crossed by a five-arched bridge, constructed by *Sir John Rennie* in 1826.

On the W. **side of the** park **is a** powder magazine. **Reviews**, **both** of regular troops and volunteers, sometimes take **place in Hyde Park**. The Park **is also a** favourite rendezvous of organised **crowds**, holding 'demonstrations' in favour or disfavour of **some political** idea or measure. The Reform Riot of 1866, when quarter of a mile of the park-**railings was torn** up and 250 policemen were seriously injured, **is perhaps the** most historic of such gatherings; and **a very large one, to protest** against the Irish Crimes Bill, was held on Easter Monday, 1887. The **wide** grassy expanse adjoining the Marble Arch is also the favourite haunt of Sunday lecturers of all kinds.

To the W. of Hyde Park, and separated from it by a sunk-fence, lie **Kensington Gardens** (Pl. R, 10, etc.), with their pleasant walks and expanses of turf (carriages not admitted). Many of the majestic old trees have, unfortunately, had to be cut down. Near the Serpentine are the new flower gardens; at the N. extremity is a sitting figure of Dr. Jenner (d. 1823), by *Marshall*. The *Broad Walk* on the W. side, 50 ft. in width, leads from Bayswater to Kensington Road. The *Albert Memorial* (p. 270) rises on the S. side. The handsome wrought-iron gates opposite the Memorial were those of the S. Transept of the Exhibition Buildings of 1851, which stood a little to the E., on the ground between Prince's Gate and the Serpentine, and was afterwards removed and re-erected as the Crystal Palace at Sydenham (see p. 305).

Kensington **Palace** (Pl. R, 6), an old royal residence, built in part by William III., was the scene of the death of that monarch and his consort, Mary, of Queen Anne and her husband, Prince George of Denmark, and of George II. Here, too, Queen Victoria was born and brought up, and here she received the news of the death of William IV. and her own accession. The interior contains nothing noteworthy. Kensington Palace was till lately the London residence of the Princess Louise and her husband the Marquis of Lorne, and is now occupied by the Prince and Princess of Teck (the latter first cousin to the Queen), and by **various** annuitants and widows belonging to the aristocracy. The palace has a chapel of its own, in which regular Sunday services are held.

The space to the W. of Kensington Palace is now occupied by rows of fashionable residences. Thackeray died in 1863 at *No. 2 Palace Green*, the second house to the left in Kensington Palace Gardens (Pl. R, 6) as we enter from Kensington High Street. Among his previous London residences were 88 St. James's Street, 13 (now 16) Young Street, Kensington (where 'Vanity Fair', 'Pendennis', and 'Esmond' were written), and 36 Onslow Square (re-numbered). *Holly Lodge*, the home of Lord Macaulay, **where he died** in 1859, is in a lane leading off Campden Hill Road, a little farther to the W. The next house is *Argyll Lodge*, the London **residence of the Duke of Argyll.**

Farther to the W., on a hill lying between Uxbridge Road, on the N., and Kensington Road on the S., stands Holland House (Pl. R, 1), built in the Tudor style by *John Thorpe*, for Sir Walter Cope, in 1607. The building soon passed into the hands of Henry Rich, Earl of Holland (in Lincolnshire), son-in-law of Sir Walter Cope, and afterwards, on the execution of Lord Holland for treason, came into the possession of Fairfax and Lambert, the Parliamentary generals. In 1665, however, it was restored to Lady Holland. From 1716 to 1719 it was occupied by Addison, who had married the widow of Edward, third Earl of Holland and Warwick. The lady was a relative of Sir Hugh Myddelton (see p. 100). In 1762 it was sold by Lord Kensington, cousin of the last representative of the Hollands, who had inherited the estates, to Henry Fox, afterwards Baron Holland, and father of the celebrated Charles James Fox. The house is now the property of Lady Holland, widow of the fourth Lord Holland of the Fox line; but the reversion is said to have been sold to Lord Ilchester, a descendant of a brother of Henry Fox. The demesnes of Holland House have recently been much curtailed by laying out sites for building.

Since the time of Charles I., Holland House has frequently been associated with eminent personages. Fairfax, Cromwell, and Ireton held their deliberations in its chambers; William Penn, who was in great favour with Charles II., was daily assailed here by a host of petitioners; and William III. and his consort Mary lived in the house for a short period. During the first half of the 19th cent. Holland House was the rallying point of Whig political and literary notabilities of all kinds, such as Moore, Rogers, and Macaulay, who enjoyed here the hospitality of the distinguished third Baron Holland. The house contains a good collection of paintings and historical relics. Compare Princess Lichtenstein's 'Holland House'.

Along the N. side of Hyde Park and Kensington Gardens runs the Uxbridge Road, leading to Bayswater and Notting Hill. Near the Marble Arch (Pl. R, 15) is the *Cemetery of St. George's*, Hanover Square (open 10-4, on Sun. and holidays 2-4), containing the grave of Laurence Sterne (d. 1768; near the middle of the wall on the W. side). Mrs. Radcliffe, writer of the 'Mysteries of Udolpho', is said to be buried below the chapel. The rows of houses on this road, overlooking the park, contain some of the largest and most fashionable residences in London.

## 25. Private Mansions around Hyde Park and St. James's.

*Grosvenor House. Stafford House. Bridgewater House. Dudley House. Lansdowne House. Apsley House. Bath House. Dorchester House. Hertford House. Devonshire House.*

The English aristocracy, many of the members of which are enormously wealthy, resides in the country during the greater part of the year; but it is usual for the principal families to have a mansion in London, which they occupy during the season, or at other times when required. Most of these mansions are in the vicinity of Hyde Park, and many of them are worth visiting, not only on account of the sumptuous manner in which they are fitted up, but also for the sake of the treasures of art which they contain.

Permission to visit these private residences, for which application must be made to the owners, is often difficult to procure, and can in some cases be had only by special introduction. During winter it is customary to pack away the works of art in order to protect them against the prejudicial influence of the atmosphere.

**Grosvenor House** (Pl. R, 18; *I*), Upper Grosvenor Street, is the property of the *Duke of Westminster*, and is open to the public daily from May to July by tickets obtained on written application to the Duke's secretary. The pictures are arranged in the private rooms on the ground-floor, and catalogues are provided.

Room I. (*Dining Room*). To the left: 2. *West*, Death of General Wolfe at Quebec in 1759; 5. *Albert Cuyp*, Moonlight scene; 8. *Sustermans*, Portrait of a lady; 12. *Claude Lorrain*, Roman landscape; *17. *11. *Rembrandt*, Portraits of Nicolas Burghem and his wife (dated 1647); 15. *Rubens*, Landscape; 18, 19. *Claude*, Landscapes; 21. *Adrian van de Velde*, Hut with cattle and figures (1658); 23. *Rembrandt*, Portrait of a man with a hawk; 24. *Wouverman*, Horse fair; 25. *Hogarth*, The distressed poet; 28. *Claude*, Landscape; 30. *Cuyp*, Sheep (an early work); *26. *Claude*, Sermon on the Mount; *31. *Rembrandt*, Portrait of a lady with a fan; *34. *Berchem*, Large landscape with peasants dancing (1656); 88. *Sustermans*, Portrait.

Room II. (*Saloon*). To the left: *40. *Rembrandt*, The Salutation. 'A delicate and elevated expression is here united with beautiful effects of light. This little gem is distinguished for its marvellous blending of warm and cold tints'. — *Vosmaer*.

Above. *Cuyp*, River scene; *41. *G. Dou*. Mother nursing her child; *42. *Paul Potter*. Landscape near Haarlem (1647); 45. *N. Poussin*, Children playing; *46. *Hobbema*, Wooded landscape, with figures by *Lingelbach*; *Andrea del Sarto*, Portrait; *53. *Murillo*, John the Baptist; 59. *Canaletto*, Canal Grande in Venice; 66. *Parmigiano*, Study for the altarpiece in the National Gallery (No. 33; p. 160); 67. *N. Poussin*, Holy Family and angels; 69. *Giulio Romano*. St. Luke painting the Virgin; *72. *Murillo*. Infant Christ asleep; **70. *Hobbema*. Wooded landscape, with figures by *Lingelbach* (a counterpart of the picture opposite); 75. *Garofolo* (?), Holy Family.

Room III. (*Small Drawing Room*). To the left: 92. *Van Dyck*, Virgin and Child with St. Catharine; *91. *Reynolds*, Portrait of Mrs. Siddons as the Tragic Muse (1784); 89. *Andrea del Sarto*, Holy Family; 83. *Teniers*, Château of the painter with a portrait of himself; *77. *Gainsborough*, The 'Blue Boy', a full-length portrait of Master Buthall.

Room IV. (*Large Drawing Room*). To the left: *95. *Rembrandt* (or *A. Brouwer*?), Landscape with figures; 112. *Paul de Koning*, Landscape; 110.

*Giovanni Bellini* (or, more probably, an early imitator of *Lorenzo Lotto*). Madonna and saints; 107. *School of Bellini*, Circumcision of Christ; 106. *Titian*(?), The Woman taken in adultery; 105. *Rubens*, Portrait of himself and his first wife, Elisabeth Brandt, as Pausias and Glycera (the flowers by *Jan Brueghel*); *101. *Velazquez*, Don Balthazar Carlos, Prince of Asturias, a sketch; 99. *Poussin*, Landscape with figures; 97. *Turner*, Conway Castle.

Room v. (*Rubens Room*). To the left: 113. Israelites gathering manna; *114. **Abraham** and **Melchisedek**; 115. The four Evangelists, three of a series of nine pictures painted by *Rubens* in Spain in the year 1628.

vi. Corridor: 116. *Murillo*, Landscape with Jacob and Laban; Sketches of Egyptian scenes.

vii. Ante-Room. To the left: 119. *Fra Bartolommeo* (?), Holy Family; 125. *Domenichino*, Landscape.

The *Vestibule* contains a Terracotta Bust by *Alessandro Vittoria*.

**Stafford House, or Sutherland House** (Pl. R, 22; *IV*), in St. James's Park, between St. James's Palace and the Green Park, the residence of the *Duke of Sutherland*, is perhaps the finest private mansion in London, and contains a good collection of paintings, which is shown to the public on certain fixed days in spring and summer. Application for admission should be made to the Duke's secretary.

We begin to the right, in the large gallery: 73. *Zurbaran*, Madonna with the Holy Child and John the Baptist (1653); 67. *Annibale Carracci*, Flight into Egypt; *62. *Murillo*, Return of the Prodigal Son; 61. Ascribed to *Raphael*, Christ bearing the Cross (a Florentine picture of little value); 59. *Parmigiano*, Betrothal of St. Catharine; 58. 54. *Zurbaran*, 88. Cyril and Martin; 57. *Dujardin*, David with the head of Goliath; 53. *Murillo*, Abraham entertaining the three angels; 51. After *Dürer*, Death of the Virgin; 48. *Paul Delaroche*, Lord Strafford, on his way to the scaffold, receiving the blessing of Archbishop Laud (1838). — 47. Ascribed to *Correggio*, Mules and mule-drivers.

This work is described as having been painted by Correggio in his youth, and is said to have served as a tavern-sign on the Via Flaminia near Rome. In reality it is an unimportant work of a much later period.

Opposite: 42. *Tintoretto*, Venetian senator; 36. *Rubens*, Coronation of Maria de' Medici, design in grisaille upon wood for the painting in the Louvre; 33. *Honthorst*, Christ before Caiaphas; 30. *Murillo*, Portrait; *27. *Van Dyck*, Portrait of the Earl of Arundel; 25. *L. Carracci*, Holy Family; 23. *Parmigiano*, Portrait; 22. *Guercino*, Pope Gregory and Ignatius Loyola; *19. *Moroni*, Portrait; 18. Ascribed to *Titian*, Mars, Venus, and Cupid; 15. *Zurbaran*, St. Andrew; 5. *A. Cano*, God the Father.

The pictures in the private apartments are not exhibited.

**Bridgewater House** (Pl. R, 22; *IV*), in Cleveland Row, by the Green Park, to the S. of Piccadilly, is the mansion of the *Earl of Ellesmere*, and possesses one of the finest picture-galleries in London. The most important works are hung in the private rooms. Admission to the large picture hall is granted for Wednesdays and Saturdays, on application supported by some person of influence.

On the walls of the Staircase: *A. Carracci*, Copy of Correggio's 'Il Giorno' at Parma; *N. Poussin*, The Seven Sacraments, a celebrated series of paintings; *Veit*, Mary at the Sepulchre; *Pannini*, Piazza di S. Pietro at Rome.

Gallery. To the right of the entrance: *Guido Reni*, Assumption of the Virgin, a large altarpiece, nobly conceived and carefully finished. To the left: 156. *G. Coques*, Portrait; 225. *Stoop*, Boy with grey horse; 142. *Brekelencamp*, Saying grace; 31. Ascribed to *Sebastian del Piombo*, Entombment; 125. *Bassano*, Last Judgment; 263. *P. van Slingeland*, The kitchen (1685); 213. *N. Berchem*, River scene; 247. *Metsu*, Fish-woman; *126. *A. van Ostade*, Man with wine-glass (1677); 137. *Arg de Vous*, Young man in a library; 209. *N. Berchem*, Landscape; 17. *Titian*, Diana and her

nymphs interrupted at the bath by the approach of Actæon, painted in 1559; 136. *Rembrandt*, Portrait; 247. *J. van Ruysdael*, Bank of a river; °166. *A. van Ostade*, Skittle-players (1676); 258. *W. van de Velde*, Rough sea (1656); 212. *N. Berchem*, Landscape; °196. *Ruysdael*, Bridge; °65. *Paris Bordone*, Portrait of a man (high up); °281. *J. Wynants*, Landscape, with figures by *A. van de Velde* (1669). — °°19. *Titian*, The Venus of the shell.'
'Venus Anadyomene rising — **new-born** but full-grown — from the sea, and wringing her hair... Titian never gave more perfect rounding with so little shadow'. — *Crowe and Cavalcaselle*. This work, painted some time after 1520, has unfortunately suffered from attempts at restoration.
135. *Van der Heyde*, Draw-bridge; 222. *A. Brouwer*, Peasants at the fireside; 171. *Van Huysum*, Flowers (1723-24); 177. *A. van Ostade*, Portrait; 242. *Metsu*, Lady caressing her lap-dog. — °18. *Titian*, Diana and Callisto, companion to No. 17.
'Titian was too much of a philosopher **and naturalist to** wander into haze or supernatural halo in a scene altogether of **earth'**. — *C. & C.*
284. *A. van der Neer*, Moonlight **scene**; 233. *Netscher*, Lady washing her hands; 154. *A. von Ostade*, Backgammon players; 130. *Teniers*, The alchemist; °141. *W. van de Velde*, Naval piece (an early work).
On the opposite wall: °153. *Jan Steen*, The school-room, a large canvas; 190. *Wynants*, Landscape; 182. *Isaac van Ostade*, **Village** street; 168. *Rembrandt*, Mother with sons praying; 280. *Paul Potter*, Cows; 111. *Netscher*, A fashionable lady; °183. *Isaac van Ostade*, Village street; 191. *J. Steen*, The fishmonger; 267. *Cuyp*, Ruin; °90. *Lorenzo Lotto*, Madonna with saints, an early work (hung high); 109. *Salomon Koning*, The philosopher's study; 214. *W. Mieris*, The violinist; 244. *G. Dou*, The violinist (1637); 165. *Wynants*, Landscape; °129. *A. Brouwer*, Landscape, surrounded with a border of fruit and flowers by *D. Seghers*; °194. *Metsu*, The stirrup-cup (an early work); 257. *Ruysdael*, Landscape; °201. *Pynacker*, Alpine scene with waterfall; °195. *Hondecoeter*, The raven detected, illustrating the well-known fable; 257. *Hobbema*, Landscape; °174. *Rubens*, Free copy with altered arrangement of Raphael's frescoes in the Villa Farnesina at Rome, the landscapes by some other painter.
The following masterpieces on the ground-floor are not shown to visitors. In LADY ELLESMERE'S SITTING ROOM: °°*Raphael*, Madonna and Child, the 'Bridgewater Madonna' (copy in the National Gallery); °35. *Raphael*, Holy Family ('La Vierge au palmier'); °°29. *Titian*, Holy Family (an early work, ascribed to *Palma Vecchio*); °11. *Luini*, Head of a girl (assigned to *Leonardo da Vinci*); °77. *Palma Vecchio*, The three periods of life (after Titian's painting in the Palazzo Doria at Rome). The DRAWING ROOM and LORD ELLESMERE'S SITTING ROOM contain a number of admirable works of the Dutch school, including the fine °Girl at work, by *N. Maes*.

**Dudley House** (Pl. R, 19; *I*), Park Lane, the mansion of the *Earl of Dudley*, also contains a fine collection of paintings, particularly of the Italian schools, and is one of the most sumptuously furnished houses in London. Admission is granted almost daily from February to July on application, enclosing an introduction, to the Earl's secretary.

The ENTRANCE HALL and STAIRCASE are embellished with modern statuary in marble.

The most important works in the PICTURE GALLERY (on the first floor) are as follows. To the left: °°*Raphael*, The Graces, a youthful work, in good preservation; *Correggio*, The Magdalene (copy); °*A. van de Velde*, Scene in the Roman Campagna (1630); Landscapes by *Cuyp* and *Salvator Rosa*; Ascribed to *Titian*, Recumbent Venus; *Rembrandt*, Portrait; *Peruzzi* (?), Nativity; *Andrea del Sarto*, Pietà (replica of original in Vienna); *Raphael* (? formerly assigned to *Giulio Romano*), Holy Family, freely retouched; *Titian*, Madonna **and** Child; °*Mieris*, Interior; *Leonardo da Vinci*(?), Holy Family, sadly damaged; *Perino del Vaga*, Adoration of the Child Christ; *Bonifazio*, Holy Family, and other works; °*Raphael*, Crucifixion, with the Virgin, Mary Magdalene and SS. Jerome and John, painted about

1500, in the style of Perugino, for the Dominican Church of Citta di Castello; *Fra Angelico*, Last Judgment. At the end of the room *Correggio*, Cherubs, two fragments of the frescoes which formerly embellished the choir of the church of S. Giovanni at Parma; *Fr. Francia*, Holy Family; *Giovanni Bellini*, Madonna and Child; *Carlo Crivelli*, Madonna and Child with saints; Miniatures ascribed to *Mantegna*; *Ercole Grandi*, The Israelites gathering manna; *Karel Fabritius*, Portrait of Abraham de Notte (1640); *Lorenzo di Credi*, Madonna and Child.

In the private rooms (not accessible): *Murillo*, Six scenes from the story of the Prodigal Son. Death of St. Clara; *Zurbaran*, Annunciation. Also valuable works of *Velazquez*, *Claude Lorrain*, *Greuze*, and others.

**Lansdowne House** (Pl. R, 22; *I*), Berkeley Square, the residence of the *Marquis of Lansdowne*, contains a valuable picture-gallery and a collection of Roman sculptures. Admission only by introduction to the Marquis of Lansdowne, the works of art being distributed throughout the private apartments. The ancient sculptures form probably the most extensive private collection out of Rome. Most of them were discovered at Hadrian's Villa by Gavin Hamilton. It was while living here, as librarian to Lord Shelburne, that **Priestley discovered oxygen**.

SCULPTURES. Statue of Mercury, replica of the misnamed Antinous of the Belvedere; Youthful Hercules; Juno enthroned; Bacchus; Diomede with the palladium; Jason untying his sandals; Wounded Amazon; Marcus Aurelius as Mars; Statue of an emperor; Numerous reliefs, funereal columns, etc. Woman asleep, by *Canova*, his last work; Child soliciting alms, by *Rauch*.

PICTURES. In the *Ante-Room*: *Tidemand* and *Gude*, Norwegian landscape; *Gonzales Coques*, Portraits of an architect and his wife; *Sir Thomas Lawrence*, Portrait of Lord Lansdowne. — In *Lord Lansdowne's Sitting-Room*: *Rembrandt*, The last-painted portrait of himself (about 1665); *Reynolds*, Lady Ilchester; *Master of Treviso* (assigned to *Giorgione*). Concert; Landscapes by *Both* and *Isaac van Ostade*. — In the *Library*: *Van Dyck*, Henrietta Maria, wife of Charles I.; *Rembrandt's School*, Two portraits; *Luini*, St. Barbara. — In the *Drawing Room*: *Rembrandt*, Portrait of a lady (1642); *B. van der Helst*, Portrait of a lady (1640); *Guercino*, The Prodigal Son; *Murillo*, The Conception; *Velazquez*, Portrait of himself; *Velazquez*, Portrait of Olivarez; *Cuyp*, Portrait of a young girl; *C. Dolci*, Madonna and Child. — In the *Front Drawing Room*: Sebastian del Piombo, Portrait of Federigo da Bozzolo; *Gainsborough*, Portrait of a lady.

**Apsley House** (Pl. R, 18; *IV*), Hyde Park Corner, the residence of the *Duke of Wellington*, was built in 1785 for Earl Bathurst, Lord High Chancellor of England, and in 1820 purchased by Government and presented to the Duke of Wellington, as part of the nation's reward for his distinguished services. A few years later the mansion was enlarged, and the external brick facing replaced by stone. The site is one of the best in London, and the interior is very expensively fitted up. It contains a picture-gallery, numerous portraits and statues, and a great many gifts from royal donors. Admission only through personal introduction to the Duke.

On the STAIRCASE: *Canova's* colossal Statue of Napoleon I.

PICTURE GALLERY (on the first floor). To the right: *Velazquez*, Peasants at a bridge; *Parmigiano*, Betrothal of St. Catharine; *Velazquez*, The master of the feast (an early work); *Marcello Venusti*, Annunciation; *Velazquez*, Quevedo, poet and satirist; *Velazquez*, Portrait of Pope Innocent X. (repetition of the painting in the Doria Gallery at Rome); *Correggio*, Christ in Gethsemane (copy in the National Gallery); *Watteau*, Court festival; *Wouwerman*, Equestrian scene; *Claude*, Palaces at sunset; *Rubens*, Holy Family; *Spagnoletto*, Allegorical picture; *Wouwerman*, Starting for the chase; *Velazquez*, Two boys; *Murillo*, St. Catharine; several large and well-executed copies of *Raphael* (Bearing of the Cross, etc.).

The Sitting Room of the Duchess contains some admirable examples of the art of the Netherlands: °*P. Potter*, Deer in a wood; °*A. Cuyp*, Cavalier with grey horse; *A. van Ostade*, Peasants gaming; *Jan Steen*, Family scene. The smokers; *Van der Heyde*, Canal in a town; *N. Maes*, The Milk-seller; *Wouwerman*, Camp scene; °*Lucas van Leyden*, Supper; *N. Maes*, The listener. — In the Corridor: *J. Victor*, Horses feeding; *Jan Steen*, Peasants at a wedding feast.

**Bath House** (Pl. R, 22; *IV*), 82 Piccadilly, at the corner of Bolton Street, the mansion of Lord Ashburton, contains one of the finest picture-galleries in London, although several masterpieces were destroyed by fire a few years ago. The pictures are exhibited on written application, enclosing an introduction to Lord Ashburton.

Dining Room. °*Rubens*, Wolf-hunt, with a portrait of the artist as a huntsman (early but very important work); *Rembrandt*, Portrait of Jansenius (dated 1661); *Rubens*, Rape of the Sabine women, and Reconciliation of the Romans and Sabines; Portraits by *Velazquez* and *Bronzino*.

Drawing Room. °*A. van de Velde*, Sheep in a pasture (dated 1663); *A. Cuyp*, Landscape with shepherds; °*Cuyp*, Flight into Egypt; °*N. Maes*, Girl sewing (1655); *Rembrandt*, Sitting figure of a man; *Dujardin*, The mill; *Terburg*, Concert; *Rembrandt*, Portrait of Lieven van Coppenol, the celebrated writing-master; *Rembrandt*, Portrait of a man (a round picture); °*Velazquez*, Stag-hunt; *Jan Steen*, Boors playing skittles; *A. van Ostade*, Family at breakfast; *Metsu*, Woman reading at a window; *Cuyp*, Portrait of himself; Three works by *A. van Ostade*; Landscape by *Isaac van Ostade*; *Rembrandt*, Portrait; *J. van Ruysdael*, Two landscapes.

Lady Ashburton's Sitting Room. °°*Correggio*, SS. Peter, Margaret, Martha, and Anthony of Padua, an early work, painted in 1517 for S. Maria della Misericordia at Correggio; *Van Dyck*, Portrait of the Duke of Nassau; °*Rembrandt*, Portraits of a man and woman, companions, and each dated 1641; °°*Luini* (ascribed to Leonardo da Vinci), Christ and John the Baptist as children; °°*Murillo*, St. Thomas of Villa Nueva distributing alms. — In the Ante-Room, Mercury by *Thorvaldsen*.

**Dorchester House** (Pl. R, 18; *IV*), the residence of R. S. Holford, Esq., a handsome edifice in Park Lane, contains a good collection of pictures, shown in spring and summer to visitors provided with an introduction. Among the finest works of art are —

Room I. *Velazquez*, Portrait of the Duke Olivarez; *G. Camphuisen* (ascribed to *Paul Potter*), Goats at pasture (dated 1617); *A. van Ostade*, Interior (1661); *Cornelis de Vos*, Portrait of a lady; °*Ruysdael*, Landscape with view of Haarlem; °*Velazquez*, Life-size portrait of Philip IV.

Room II. °*Lorenzo Lotto*, Portrait; °*Gaud. Ferrari*, Mary, Joseph, and a cardinal; *Titian*, Portrait; °*Andrea del Sarto*, Holy Family; °*Cuyp*, View of Dordrecht; *Tintoretto*, Portrait; *Luini* (?), Flora; *Fra Angelico*, Six saints.

Room III. °*Bronzino*, Leonora, consort of Cosimo I.; *Tintoretto* (ascribed to *Bassano*), Conversation piece of three figures; °*Rembrandt*, Portrait of Martin Looten (dated 1632); °*Hobbema*, Margin of a forest (1663); °*Paolo Veronese*, Portrait of the Queen of Cyprus; *Titian*, Holy Family with John the Baptist; *Dosso* (?), Portrait of the Duke of Ferrara; *Adr. van Ostade*, Street in a village; °*Van Dyck*, Portrait of the Marchesa Balbi.

**Hertford House** (Pl. R, 20; *I*), Manchester Square, the residence of *Sir Richard Wallace*, contains, in a fine gallery built for its reception, the famous *Hertford Collection*, long on view at Bethnal Green Museum (p. 128). Besides a very choice gallery of pictures, the collection includes specimens of gold and silver workmanship, Renaissance and rococo furniture, majolica, porcelain, bronzes, and art-treasures of every description. It is rarely shown to strangers, but admission may sometimes be obtained in spring or summer on Wed., 11-1, by cards obtained on application to the private secretary of the owner.

Almost the whole of the FURNITURE of the exhibition rooms and the private apartments was brought from Versailles and other royal châteaux of France.

The **PICTURE GALLERY** is justly esteemed the finest private collection in England. It contains 13 genuine specimens of *Rembrandt*; and *Velazquez* and *Murillo*, **Rubens** and *Van Dyck* are also represented by masterpieces. The collection of modern French paintings is more important than that of the Luxembourg at Paris, including 25 masterpieces by *Meissonier*, 13 by *Delaroche*, 31 by *Decamps*, and 5 by *Ary Scheffer*. Among the Italian pictures are the 'Vierge au Lys' by *Leonardo da Vinci* and good works of *Canaletto* and *Guardi*. The English school is represented by *Reynolds* ('Portrait of Nelly O'Brien), *Lawrence*, *Stanfield*, *Landseer*, *Bonington*, and others.

Some of the other private art-collections of London, to which access can be gained only through personal introduction, must be mentioned more briefly.

**Devonshire House** (Pl. R, 22; *IV*), Piccadilly, between **Berkeley Street** and Stratton Street, the London residence of the *Duke of Devonshire*, contains fine portraits by **Jordaens, Reynolds**, *Tintoretto, Dobson, Lely*, and *Kneller*. In the library are the 'Kemble Plays', a valuable collection of English dramas, including the first editions of Shakspeare, formed by John Philip Kemble; and a fine collection of gems.

The *Earl of Northbrook's Collection*, at 4 Hamilton Place, Piccadilly, formed out of the famed *Baring Gallery*, is especially notable for its numerous and admirable examples of the Quattrocentists (Mantegna, **Crivelli**, Antonello da Messina, etc.), and also contains *Holbein's* fine portrait of his master, Hans Herbster of Strassburg (1516), and important works by **Jan van Eyck**, Cranach, Luini, Mazzolini, Garofalo, Seb. del Piombo, Murillo, Zurbaran, Velazquez, Rembrandt, Bol, Dou, Steen, Ruysdael, Cuyp, **Rubens**, etc.

The collection of *Lady Eastlake*, 7 Fitzroy Square, is notable for its select examples of the Quattrocentists of N. Italy (Bellini, Cima da Conegliano, Ghirlandajo, Caroto, etc.).

*J. Malcolm, Esq.*, of Poltalloch, 7 Great Stanhope St., possesses an extremely valuable collection of *Drawings*, including one hundred and forty-six by Italian masters (large cartoon by Michael Angelo, drawings by Raphael, **Leonardo da Vinci, Michael Angelo**, etc.), fifty by French, **Flemish**, and German masters (Dürer, Holbein, **Rubens, Van Dyck**), and sixty-two of the Dutch school (Cuyp, Ostade, Rembrandt, etc.).

## 26. Albert Memorial. Albert Hall. Horticultural Society's Gardens. Natural History Museum.

To the S. of Kensington **Gardens**, between Queen's Gate and Prince's Gate, near the site of the Exhibition of 1851, **rises the \*Albert Memorial** (Pl. R, 9), a magnificent monument **to Albert, the late Prince Consort** (d. 1861), **erected by the English nation at a** cost **of 120,000*l*.**, **half** of **which was defrayed by voluntary** contributions. On a spacious **platform, to which granite steps ascend on each** side, rises a **basement, adorned with reliefs in marble, representing artists of every period** (169 figures). **On the S. side** are Poets **and Musicians, and on the E. side** Painters, by *Armstead*; on the **N. side Architects, and on the W. Sculptors**, by *Philip*. **Four projecting pedestals at** the angles support marble groups, representing **Agriculture, Manufacture,** Commerce, **and** Engineering. In the **centre of the basement sits the** colossal **bronze-gilt figure of Prince Albert, wearing the robes of the** Garter, 15 ft. high, by *Foley*, under a Gothic canopy, borne by four clustered granite columns. The canopy terminates **at the top in a** Gothic spire, rising in three stages, and surmounted by a **cross.** The whole monument, designed by *Sir G. G. Scott* (d. 1878), is 175 ft. in height, and is gorgeously embellished with a profusion of bronze and marble statues, gilding, coloured stones, and mosaics. **At** the corners of the steps leading **up to the basement are pedestals** bearing allegorical marble figures **of the quarters of the globe: Europe** by *Macdowell*, **Asia by** *Foley*, **Africa by** *Theed*, **America by** *Bell*. The canopy bears, in blue mosaic **letters** on a gold ground, the inscription: 'Queen Victoria and Her **People to the memory of Albert,** Prince Consort, as a tribute of their **gratitude for a life** devoted to the public good.'

On the opposite side of Kensington Road stands the **\*Royal Albert Hall** *of Arts and Sciences* (Pl. R, 9), **a vast amphitheatre in** the Italian Renaissance style, destined for concerts, scientific and art assemblies, and **other similar uses.** The building, which was con**structed in** 1867-71 from designs by *Fowke* and *Scott*, is oval in form (measuring **270 ft. by** 240 ft., **and** 810 ft. in circumference), and can **accommodate 8000** people comfortably. The cost of its erection amounted to 200,000*l*., of which 100,000*l*. was contributed by the public, 50,000*l*. came from **the** Exhibition of 1851, and about 40,000*l*. was defrayed by the sale of the boxes. The exterior **is tastefully ornamented in coloured** brick and terracotta. The terracotta **frieze**, **which runs** round the whole building above the gallery, was executed by *Minton & Co.*, and depicts **the** different **nations of the globe. The** *Arena* is 100 ft. long by 70 **broad, and has space for 1000 persons. The** *Amphitheatre*, **which adjoins it, contains 10 rows of seats, and holds** 1360 **persons. Above it are three rows of boxes, those in the lowest row being constructed for** 8 **persons each, those in the centre or** 'grand tier' for 10, and those in the upper tier for 5 persons. Still higher is the *Balcony* with 8 rows of seats (1800 persons), and lastly, above the balcony, is the *Picture Gallery*, adorned with scagliola columns, containing accommodation for an audience of 2000, and affording a good survey of the interior. It communicates by a number of doors with the *Outer Gallery*, which encircles the whole of the Hall, and commands a fine view of the Albert Memorial. The ascent to the gallery is facilitated by two 'lifts', one on each side of the building (1*d*.). The *Organ*, built by Willis, is one of the largest in the world; it has 8000 pipes, and its bellows are worked by two steam engines. (The organ is occasionally played about 4 p.m., when notice is given in the daily papers; small fee.)

A subway, lined with white glazed tiles, has been constructed under the Exhibition Road from the S. Kensington railway station to the Albert Hall, with branches to the Natural History Museum and South Kensington Museum.

The Albert Hall stands nearly on the former site of Gore House, which has given its name to *Kensington Gore*, the high road from Knightsbridge to Kensington. Although less famous than Holland House, it possessed fully as much political and social influence at the beginning of the present century. It was for many years the residence of William Wilberforce, around whom gathered the leaders of the anti-slavery and other philanthropic enterprises. It was afterwards the abode of the celebrated Lady Blessington, who held in it a kind of literary court, which was attended by the most eminent men of letters, art, and science in England. Louis Napoleon, Brougham, Lyndhurst, Thackeray, Dickens, Moore, Landor, Bulwer, Landseer, and Count D'Orsay were among her frequent visitors. During the exhibition of 1851 Gore House was used as a restaurant, where M. Soyer displayed his culinary skill; and it was soon afterwards purchased with its grounds by the Commissioners of the Exhibition, for 60,000*l*.

On the W. side of the Albert Hall is the *Royal College of Music*, incorporated by royal charter in 1883 for the advancement of the science and art of music in the British Empire. The Prince of Wales is the president and Sir George Grove the director of the college, which provides a thorough musical education in the style of the Continental Conservatoires. Upwards of fifty scholarships and exhibitions are open to the competition of students. The teaching staff consists of 11 professors and 30 teachers; and in the first year of its existence the college was attended by 150 pupils, including several from the Colonies and the United States. Adjacent is the *Alexandra House*, a home for female students, projected by the Princess of Wales and erected in 1886 at the cost of Sir Francis Cook. A little to the E. of the Albert Hall is *Lowther Lodge*, a very satisfactory example of Norman Shaw's modern-antique style.

Immediately to the S. of the Albert Hall, in South Kensington, lay the Gardens of the *Royal Horticultural Society*, which was founded in 1804 for the promotion of scientific gardening. The gardens have, however, lately been chosen as the site of the Imperial Institute (p. 232), and a new road has been constructed through them from Prince's Gate (Exhibition Road) to Queen's Gate. The flower-shows of the Society, formerly held here, are now held in the Drill Hall of the London Scottish Rifle Volunteers, James Street, Victoria, or at the Society's Experimental Gardens at Chiswick. The latter are open on week-days from 9 to sunset, and in summer on Sun. also from 1 to sunset.

## 26. IMPERIAL INSTITUTE.

The **Imperial Institute of the United Kingdom, the Colonies,
and India**, the foundation-stone of which was laid by Queen Victoria in 1887, as the national memorial of Her Majesty's Jubilee,
is a huge Renaissance edifice by *Mr. T. E. Colcutt*, with a frontage
600 ft. in length, surmounted by a large central tower (280 ft.
high), with smaller towers at the corners. In addition to the main
building there are to be a Conference Hall, to the N., 100 ft. long
and 60 ft. wide, and Exhibition Galleries covering two acres of
ground. The building will probably be completed in 1891; its estimated cost is about 170,000*l*.

The main objects of the Institute, which is supported by funds subscribed by the people of the British Empire, are: — 1. The formation and exhibition of collections **representing** the important raw materials and manufactured products **of the** Empire and of other countries, so maintained as to illustrate the development of agricultural, commercial, and industrial progress **in the Empire**, and the comparative advances made in other countries. — 2. **The establishment or promotion of** commercial museums, sample-rooms, **and intelligence offices in London and** other parts of the Empire. — 3. **The collection and dissemination of** information relating **to trades and industries and to emigration.** — 4. **Exhibitions** of special branches of industry **and commerce, and of the work of artizans** and of apprentices. — 5. **The promotion of technical and commercial** education, and of the industrial **arts and sciences.** — 6. **The furtherance of** systematic colonization. — 7. **The promotion of conferences and lectures in** connection with the general **work of the Institute, and the facilitating of** commercial and friendly intercourse **among the inhabitants of the different parts** of the British Empire.

The buildings which enclose the (former) Horticultural Society's
Gardens on three sides were used, from 1861 to 1874, for the *International Exhibition*, which took place annually from April to September, and consisted of specimens of the art and industry of
different nations. The exhibition buildings, consisting of two-storied
galleries running along the W. and E. sides of the Horticultural
Gardens, are tastefully built of red brick in the Italian Renaissance
style, and adorned with an elegant balustrade and other terracotta
decorations. The gallery on the S. side is older. There are two
entrances in *Prince's Gate* (*Exhibition Road:* see below), and another (comp. p. 289) from *Queen's Gate* on the W. side, while they
may also be reached from the Albert Hall. The S. and W. Galleries now contain collections connected with S. Kensington Museum
(see p. 288), while the E. Gallery is devoted to the *India Museum*
(Pl. R, 9; see p. 289). In Exhibition Road, to the N. of the India
Museum, is the Central Institution of the *City and Guilds of London Institute* (p. 74). Connected with the Institute is *Finsbury Technical College*, Tabernacle Row, City. Adjacent is the *Royal School of Art Needlework*, open to visitors from 10 to 5 or 6 (Sat. 10-2).

The Eastern Gallery also contains the *National School of Cookery*
(entrance in Exhibition Road; on view 2-4), an institution for
teaching the **economical preparation of articles** of food suitable to
smaller households, **and for training** teachers for branch cookery
schools, of which there **are now several** in London and other towns.

## 26. NATURAL HISTORY MUSEUM.

On the opposite side of Exhibition Road, at the corner of Cromwell Road, is the *South Kensington Museum* (p. 275).

The large and handsome building to the S. of the International Exhibition Galleries, occupying a great part of the site of the Exhibition of 1862, is the new \*Natural History Museum, containing the natural history collections of the British Museum. It was built in the Romanesque style in 1873-80, from a design by Mr. Waterhouse, and consists of a central structure, with wings flanked by towers 192 ft. high. The extreme length of the front is 675 ft. The whole of the external façades and the interior wall-surfaces is covered with terracotta bands and dressings, producing a very pleasing effect. The Museum is open daily from 10 to 4, 5, or 6 p.m. according to the season (closed on Sundays, Good Friday, and Christmas Day); on Mon. and Sat., from May 1st to July 16th, it is open till 8 p.m., and from July 18th to Aug. 29th, till 7 p.m. General guide 2d. In 1888 the Natural History Collections were visited by 372,802 persons.

We first enter the GREAT HALL, 170 ft. wide and 72 ft. high, with a skeleton of the cachalot, or sperm-whale (*Physeter macrocephalus*), 59 ft. long, in the centre. The adjoining glass-cases contain groups illustrating albinism, the variation of species under the influence of domestication (pigeons), and the crossing of what outwardly appear to be quite distinct species. On each side of the whale is a section of the trunk of an enormous tree, on one of which (a Douglas pine from British Columbia), 533 years old, are marked some of the dates of great events with which it was contemporaneous, beginning with the battle of Poictiers in 1356. The alcoves round the hall are devoted to the Introductory or Elementary Morphological Collection (still incomplete), 'designed to teach the most important points in the structure of the principal types of animal and plant life, and the terms used in describing them'. The W. side of the gallery round the hall contains a very interesting collection of birds with their nests, eggs, and young, as in nature; while in the E. gallery is the *Gould Collection of Humming Birds* (special catalogue 2d.). A room on the ground-floor, behind the great staircase, contains the British Zoological Collection.

The \*Geological and Palæontological Collection occupies the basement of the E. wing (to the right). The S.E. GALLERY, 280 ft. long and 50 ft. wide, contains fossil remains of animals of the class Mammalia. In the first *Pier-case* to the right are placed human and animal remains, with implements of flint and bone, chiefly from the caves of France; among them is the skull of the great sabre-toothed tiger. *Table-case 1* also contains skulls and other remains of the prehistoric cave-dwellers, as well as bone-needles, harpoons of reindeer-antler, carved bones, etc. In the *Pier-case* between the first two windows is a fossilised human skeleton, found in the limestone rock on the coast of Guadeloupe, West Indies. *Table-cases 2* and *3* contain the remains of extinct carnivorous animals, including a fine collection of bones of the great cave-bears. The following cases on this side are devoted to the Ungulata or hoofed animals, such as the rhinoceros, hippopotamus, palæotherium, horse, pig, and the great family of ruminants. Among the most prominent objects are the skull and lower jaw of the Rhinoceros leptorhinus from the Thames Valley, the sivatherium, a gigantic Indian antelope, and the heads and horns of the extinct wild ox of Great Britain. To this class belong the skeletons of the gigantic Irish elk (*Cervus* or *Megaceros hibernicus*) in the central passage.

Most of the cases on the left side of the gallery are occupied by the very complete collection of the molar teeth and other remains of the Proboscidea, or elephants, including the mastodon, mammoth, and twelve other species. In one case is a fragment of the woolly skin of the Siberian mammoth. Closely allied to this species was the Ilford mammoth, found in the valley of the Thames, the skull and tusks of which are exhibited in the **middle** of the gallery. On a stand close by is the skeleton of Steller's sea-cow (*Rhytina*), an extinct species, found in the peat deposits of Behring's Island, Kamschatka. On a separate stand near the beginning of the gallery is a perfect skeleton of the mastodon, found in Missouri, to one side of which are the skulls of a dinotherium (lower jaw a plaster reproduction), from Epplesheim in Hesse-Darmstadt, and of a mastodon from Buenos Ayres. — At the end of the gallery we enter the *Pavilion*, which contains the fossil Birds, Marsupialia, and Edentata. Among the first are remains **of the** dinornis, or moa, **an extinct** wingless **bird of New** Zealand. *Table-case 13* contains specimens **of the** oldest **fossil birds as** yet discovered, in which the tail is an elongation of the back-bone. Other cases contain remains of the gigantic extinct kangaroo of Australia (six **times larger** than its living representative), and of some of the diminutive **mammals of** the earliest geological period. In the centre is the skeleton of a megatherium from Buenos Ayres, a huge extinct animal, the bony frame-work of which is almost identical with that of the existing sloth. Its colossal **strength is** indicated by the **form of** its bones, with their surfaces roughened for the attachment of **powerful** muscles and tendons. Adjacent is a cast of a gigantic extinct **armadillo** (*Glyptodon clavipes*) from Buenos Ayres, beside which the skeleton of a living species is placed for comparison.

In **the corridor** leading to the N. from **the** end of the **gallery is** placed a plaster cast of a plesiosaurus. The passage leads to —

GALLERY D, **which is** devoted to the fossil Reptiles. In *Wall-case 1* and *Table-cases 1 & 2* are remains **of** the pterodactyles **or** flying lizards, while on the left is a large collection of icthyosauria. At the **end** of the gallery is a cast of a gigantic **Indian tortoise.**

The various galleries extending to the N. **of the** reptile gallery, **each** about 140 ft. long, contain the fossil Fishes and Invertebrate Animals.

We now return to the entrance-hall and enter the S.W. GALLERY, to the left, which contains the Ornithological Collection. The mounting of the specimens of the glass-cases in **the** middle of the floor is extremely skillful. The Pavilion at the **end of the** gallery contains the ostriches, emus, and cassowaries.

The parallel gallery to the N. contains the **Collection** of Corals, while the galleries at right angles to this are devoted to the Fishes, Insects, **Reptiles, and Shells.** A staircase, descending from the westernmost of the passages connecting the Bird and Coral Galleries, leads to the basement of the W. wing, which is occupied by the **Cetacean Collection,** including the skeleton of a common rorqual or fin-whale (*Balaenptera musculus*), 68 ft. long.

We now again return to the Great Hall and ascend the large flight of steps at the end of it to the first floor. On the first landing-place is a statue of *Charles Darwin* (d. 1882), by *Boehm*. To the right, above the geological department, is the **Mineralogical Collection,** which contains a most extensive array of minerals, meteorites, etc. A notice at the door gives instruction as to the best order in which to study the specimens here. To **the right and left of the entrance are** cases containing different varieties **of marble and granite.** Among the most remarkable **objects** in the other cases are a unique crystalline mass of Rubellite from Ava (Case 33), a magnificent **crystal of light red silver ore from** Chili **(Case** 8), **and** the unrivalled groups of topazes and agates (Cases 25 & 14). In Case **13 is a** piece of jasper, the veining in which bears a singular resemblance to a **well-known portrait of Geoffrey Chaucer.** Among the larger objects in the room at **the** E. end of the gallery is the Melbourne meteorolite, the heaviest known (3½ tons).

The gallery in the **W. wing of the first floor, above the** Bird Gallery, contains the **Mammalian Collection. The most** interesting section is that devoted to the various **species** of monkeys; close to the entrance are the **anthropoid apes.** In the **middle** of the gallery are the seals and walruses; **farther** on, the giraffes, **elephants, and** hippopotami.

The 'Botanical Collection is exhibited on the second floor of the E. wing. It includes specimens of plants of all kinds, polished tablets of different kinds of wood, specimens of fruit and seeds, etc. Among the most interesting herbaria are those of Sir Hans Sloane, founder of the British Museum (see p. 233; about 1750), John Ray, Sowerby (English plants), and Sir Joseph Banks (1820), the last including the collection of Ceylon plants made by Hermann and described by Linnæus. The botanical drawings by *F. Bauer*, some of which are exhibited to the public in cases, form the finest collection of the kind in the world, remarkable both for scientific accuracy and artistic beauty.

The second floor of the W. wing is devoted to the Osteological Collection, with a very extensive collection of skulls. At the top of the staircase (second floor) is a sitting figure of *Sir Joseph Banks* (d. 1820), the botanist, by Chantrey, brought from the British Museum in 1886. Adjacent is the *Refreshment Room*.

The Natural History Museum faces *Cromwell Road*, a street of palatial residences, about 1 M. in length, and so called because Henry, son of the Protector, resided in a house which once stood here.

## 27. South Kensington Museum.
### India Museum.

The **South Kensington Museum** (Pl. R, 9), in Brompton, to the S. of Hyde Park, at the corner of Exhibition Road and Cromwell Road, 1 M. to the W. of Hyde Park Corner, is most easily reached by the Metropolitan Railway. The station (p. 37) is only a few hundred yards to the S.W. either of the principal entrance in Cromwell Road, or of the N.W. entrance in Exhibition Road. The Museum is open gratis on Mondays, Tuesdays, and Saturdays from 10 a.m. to 10 p.m.; on Wednesdays, Thursdays, and Fridays, 10 a.m. to 4, 5, or 6 p.m. according to the season, charge 6d. Tickets, including admission to the libraries, etc., 6d. per week, 1s. 6d. per month, 3s. per quarter, 10s. per year. In the middle of the building is a restaurant (p. 282), to the right and left of which are lavatories for ladies and gentlemen.

The Museum, which was opened in 1857, is one of the subdivisions of the Science and Art Department of the Committee of Council on Education, which is under the control of the Lord President of the Council for the time being, assisted by a Vice President. The object of the Department is the promotion of art and science by means of the systematic training of competent teachers, the foundation of schools of art, public examinations and distribution of prizes, the purchase and exhibition of objects of art, and the establishment of art libraries. It is carried on at an annual expense of about 450,000*l.*, defrayed by the national exchequer. Several other institutions in England, Scotland, and Ireland are administered by the Department. Among its professors, directors, and examiners are numbered many of the chief English *savants;* and the tangible results of its teaching and influence are seen in the progress of taste and knowledge in the fine arts and natural science throughout the kingdom. The Museum was visited in 1888 by 897,225 persons, and the total number of visitors since its opening in 1857 has been 27,352,935. The director is Sir Philip Cunliffe Owen, K.C.B., K.C.M.G., C.I.E. — **Bethnal Green Museum** (p. 128) is a branch of the South Kensington Museum, established for the benefit of the great industrial population of the E. End, and maintained at an annual cost of 8000*l*.

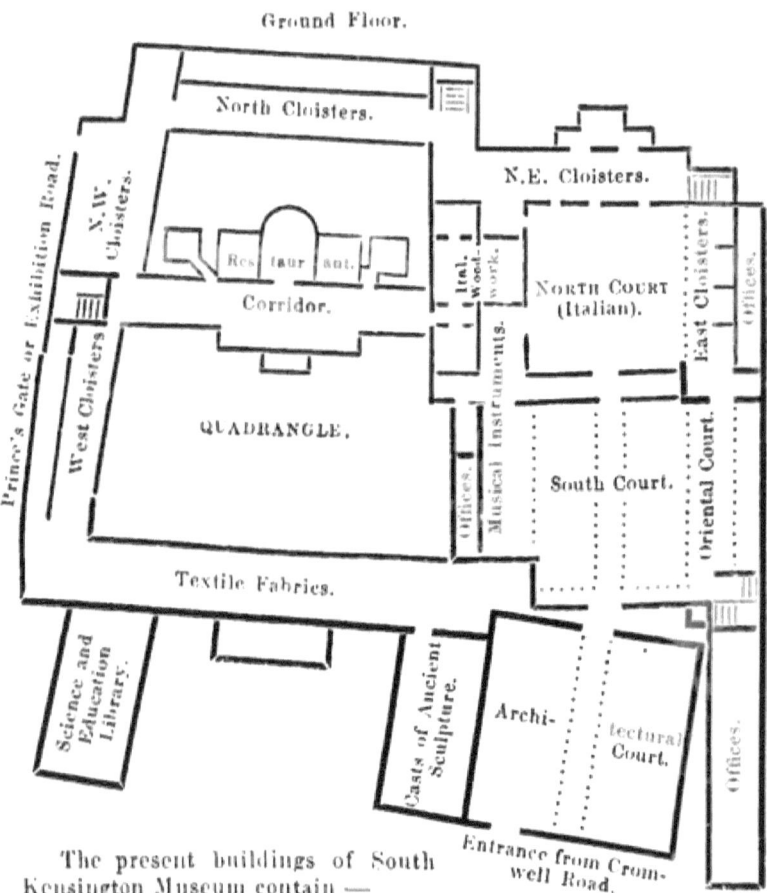

Ground Floor.

The present buildings of South Kensington Museum contain —

1. The MUSEUM OF ORNAMENTAL OR APPLIED ART, a collection of 20,000 modern and mediæval works of art, and plaster casts or electrotype reproductions of celebrated ancient and modern works, partly belonging to the Museum and partly on loan.

2. The NATIONAL GALLERY OF BRITISH ART, or Picture Gallery, on the upper floor.

3. The ART LIBRARY, consisting of 70,000 vols. and a collection of 240,000 drawings, engravings, and photographs.

4. The SCIENCE AND EDUCATION LIBRARY, containing 66,000 volumes.

5. The **NATIONAL** ART TRAINING SCHOOL, in which drawing, painting, and modelling are taught.

6. The NORMAL **SCHOOL** OF SCIENCE, for the training of teachers and others.

The **Art Collection, which both in value and** extent is **one** of the **finest in the world, is at** present exhibited **in** three large courts **roofed with glass, and in** the galleries surrounding and diverging **from them, including a new wing opened in 1884. A** large central **structure in the Renaissance style, designed by** Fowke, is now in **course of construction. A building in Exhibition Road for the** Science Schools, chiefly of terracotta, with fine sgraffito decorations, **has recently been completed. The Museum** is largely **indebted for its rapid progress to the generosity of** private individuals in **lending the most costly treasures of art for** public **exhibition (Loan Collection); but Government has also** liberally **expended considerable sums in the acquisition of valuable objects of art. All the articles in the museum are provided with a notice of their** origin, **the names of the artist and (if on loan) owner, and (when** acquired by pur**chase) a statement of their cost. The following is** necessarily **but a limited list of the chief objects of** interest permanently belonging **to the institution; and of** the numerous plaster casts **only** such are **mentioned as are not usually met with** in other collections. The arrangement is frequently altered. Even a superficial glance at all **the** different **departments of the** museum occupies **a whole day; but it is far more** satisfactory, as well as less fatiguing, to pay **repeated visits.** Guide-books, catalogues, and photographs are sold at stalls close **to the entrance** of the Architectural Court.

In the grounds at the PRINCIPAL ENTRANCE (temporary) in Cromwell **Road is a sitting statue** of Sir Jamsetjee Jeejeebhoy by Marochetti.

Inside the **building we first find ourselves in the Architectural Court,** measuring **135 ft. each way. It is** divided into two portions by an arcade (17 ft. broad) running down the centre, and is devoted to full-size **plaster and other reproductions, chiefly** of large architectural works, along with a **few original** objects. In entering **we** pass under a fine *Rood Loft, of alabaster and marble, from the Cathedral of Bois-le-Duc, North Brabant (1625). — Immediately in front is a cast of **the** Monument of Sir Francis **Vere** in Westminster Abbey (p. 216), behind which is the original plaster model of a statue of Cromwell by John Bell. In the middle of the room is a copy, in two parts, of Trajan's Column, the original of which was erected at Rome in A. D. 114. The reliefs represent Trajan's war with the Dacians, and include 2500 human figures, besides animals, chariots, etc. Farther on is a plaster cast of the Bronze Lion of Brunswick, the original **of which is said to have been** brought from Constantinople in 1166 by Henry the Lion. — To the right of the entrance is the competition sketch model for the Wellington Monument in St. Paul's, in painted plaster of Paris, by *Alfred Stevens*. Adjacent are original models of various figures and groups forming part of the design. The composition is pleasing, though in a decorative rather than in a monumental style. — To the left: **Copy** of the Chapter House Door in Rochester Cathedral (see *Baedeker's Great Britain*). Cast of a portion of Rosslyn Chapel, near Edinburgh, with the column known as the 'Prentice's Pillar (1446). Cast of the angle of the Cloisters of San Juan de los Reyes at Toledo (15th cent.), an admirable example of Spanish Gothic. Cast of the Tabernacle in the church of St. Leonhard at Léau, in Belgium, executed by Cornelis de Vriendt in 1554, and one of the finest works of the Flemish Renaissance. — To the right, cast of the Schreyer Monument, outside the St. Sebaldus Church at Nuremberg, one of Adam Krafft's masterpieces, executed in 1492 (Crucifixion, Entombment, Resurrection). Cast of Choir-stalls, in carved oak, from the Cathedral of Ulm, by Jörg Syrlin (about 1470). — By the end-wall: \***Cast of the** Puerta della Gloria or portal of the Cathedral of Santiago de **Compostella**, Spain, by Maestro Mateo, an imposing work in the early-Romanesque style (end of the 12th cent.). In the lunette is a colossal figure of Christ. — To the left, an original **Alhacena** or **cupboard** from Toledo (14th century). — This section of the court also contains casts of **works by Jean Cousin (1501-90), Jean** Goujon (1515-72), etc.

In the **CENTRAL PASSAGE** are five wrought-iron screens made by **Huntington Shaw for H**ampton **Court** Palace (1695; see p. 320).

**EASTERN SECTION** of the Court. On the entrance-wall **is the cast of a** Chimney-piece from the Palais de Justice at Bruges, by Lancelot Blondeel, a fine specimen **of** Flemish work of the 16th century. Above is a cast of Thorwaldsen's frieze representing **the Triumphal Entry of Alexander the Great into Babylon. In front, to the left, is a cast of the choir-screen of the ch**urch of St. Michael, **Hildesheim, a** Romanesque work **of the end** of the 12th century. — Behind the last, Cast of the shrine of St. Sebaldus, Nuremberg, the masterpiece of Peter Vischer (1519). — On the other side are ori**ginal sculptures and casts from Mexico and Honduras. — In the** middle of the room **are** casts of two celebrated **Pulpits in Pisa, by** Niccolò (1260) and Giovanni Pisano (1302-1311). — To the right, by the wall, the **original Monument of** Marquis Malaspina from Verona (1536). — At **the N. end is** a series of casts of the masterpieces of Michael Angelo, including the colossal statue of David, **backed by** a **cast of the** great doorway of S. Petronio, Bologna. — Numerous casts of other large objects formerly in different parts of **the** Museum have been transferred to this court. The entrance on **the W.** side leads to the Collection **of Casts** of classical sculptures (p. 280). We now descend the steps at the end of the Central Passage into the —

## 27. SOUTH KENSINGTON MUSEUM.

**South Court**, which is also divided into an eastern and a western half by an arcade (above it the Prince Consort Gallery, p. 287). — On the upper part of the walls of these two departments, in sunken panels, are portraits in mosaic of the 35 following famous artists (beginning on the left, at the S. angle of the W. section):

1. Leonardo da Vinci, painter (d. 1519); 2. Raphael Sanzio, painter (d. 1520); 3. Torregiano, sculptor (d. 1522); 4. Peter Vischer, artist in metal (d. 1529); **5.** Bernardino Luini, painter (d. 1530); 6. Lancelot Blondeel, Flemish painter, sculptor, and architect (d. 1560); 7. Velazquez de Silva, painter (d. 1660); 8. Maestro Giorgio of Gubbio, potter (d. 1552); 9. Hans Holbein the Younger, painter (d. 1543); 10. Michael Angelo Buonarotti, painter and sculptor (d. 1564); 11. Titian, painter (d. 1576); 12. Bernard Palissy, potter (d. 1590); 13. Inigo **Jones, architect** (d. 1652); 14. Grinling Gibbons, carver in wood (d. 1721); **15. Sir Christopher** Wren, architect (d. 1723); 16. William Hogarth, painter **(d. 1764)**; 17. Sir Joshua Reynolds, painter (d. 1792); 18. W. Mulready, painter **(d. 1863)**; 19. John van Eyck, painter (d. 1441); 20. **Phidias**, sculptor **(d.** 432 B.C.); **21. Apelles**, painter (d. 332 B.C.); 22. **Niccolò Pisano**, sculptor (d. 1280); 23. Giovanni **Cimabue**, painter (d. 1300); 24. **William Torel**, goldsmith (d. 1300); 25. **Jean Goujon**, sculptor (d. 1572); **26. William of** Wykeham, **Bishop** of Winchester, architect (d. 1404); 27. **Giotto, painter** (d. 1336); **28.** Lorenzo **Ghiberti**, sculptor (d. 1455); 29. Fra **Giovanni Angelico da Fiesole**, painter (d. 1455); 30. Donatello, sculptor **(d. 1466); 31. Benozzo** Gozzoli, painter (d. 1478); 32. **Luca della** Robbia, **sculptor (d. 1481); 33. A.** Mantegna, painter (d. 1506). **34. Giorgione**, painter **(d. 1511); 35. Fra Beato** Giacomo d'Ulma, painter on **glass (d. 1517).**

In the northern lunette of the E. section of the court is a fine \*Fresco by *Sir Frederick Leighton*, representing the 'Arts of War' or the application of human skill to martial **purposes** (best seen from the gallery upstairs). The corresponding \*Fresco in the S. lunette, by the same artist, illustrates the 'Arts of Peace'.

The Court contains an **extremely** valuable \*\*Collection **of small** objects of art in metal, **ivory, amber,** agate, **jade, and** porcelain, many of which are **lent to the Museum** by **private owners.** The W. half of **the** court **is devoted to European objects, while** the E. half contains works **of art from China and Japan.**

**The** Western **Section contains Ivory Carvings,** Gold and Silver Work, and Loan Collections. On the walls and in the cases at the S. end are several hundred ivory carvings, affording a complete and highly instructive survey of **the development** of this mediæval art (scientific catalogue by *Westwood*). Among these belonging to the Museum are some works of world-wide celebrity, such as the figure of a \*Muse of the 4th cent., probably the finest early ivory carving extant. There are **also** a few Consular diptychs, some of which were used at a later period as book-covers. Among the latest specimens are six \*Panels by François du Quesnoy, surnamed Il Fiamingo, with processions of children. Then, bishops' croziers, tankards, caskets, combs, etc. The best works of other collections are here represented by admirable casts in fictile ivory. — Other cases contain a valuable collection of silversmith's work, ecclesiastical vessels, jewellery, personal ornaments, clocks and watches, carvings in amber, engraved crystal, snuff-boxes, etc. Among the single objects of greatest importance are the 'Gloucester candlestick' (early 12th cent.), a *Byzantine crystal ewer of the 9th or 10th cent., a *Cup in repoussé work, attributed to Jamnitzer, but probably by an imitator, an Astronomical Globe made at Augsburg for the Emp. Rudolf II. in 1584, a Mirror and a Table in damascened work (Milan), etc. At the N. end are cases of weapons remarkable for their curious construction or artistic decoration.

The CENTRAL PASSAGE contains an admirable collection of rings, arranged according to countries and destined uses (wedding, mourning, motto, charm, iconographic, etc.); cameos, gems, precious stones; bracelets, earrings, necklaces of various nations; and a collection of military and naval medals and other decorations. In one case is a large and varied collection of precious stones bequeathed by the *Rev. Chauncy Hare Townshend*. This passage also contains collections of gold and silver plate and jewellery lent by Mr. *J. Dunn-Gardner*, of arms and armour lent by Mr. *D. M. Currie*, and of ecclesiastical objects lent by *Lord Zouche*. In one of the cases is an elaborately carved violin lent by the *Earl of Warwick*, bearing the date 1579 but believed to be much older.

The WEST ARCADE of this court contains fans and numerous examples of musical instruments (comp. p. 282).

The GALLERY beginning at the S.W. corner of the S. Court contains embroideries and articles of silk and damask. On the N. wall are three pieces of Flemish tapestry dating from 1507, with scenes from the visions of Petrarch's 'Trionfi'. In a frame is an exquisite example of Flemish tapestry in silk and gold and silver thread, representing the Adoration of the Infant Saviour. The cases by the windows contain the *Museum Collection of Ancient and Modern Lace*.

The large room to the left, at the beginning of this gallery, contains the extensive *Collection of Casts of Classical Sculptures* (special catalogue 6d). The corresponding room at the other end of the gallery is now devoted to the *Science and Education Library*.

The staircase at the E. end of the gallery ascends to the new and spacious ART LIBRARY, opened in 1884. The staircase walls are hung with pictures, including six fine Works by *G. F. Watts*.

EAST SECTION of the South Court. **Collection of Chinese and Japanese porcelain, enamels, lacquer-work, bronzes, and metal works, unrivalled for completeness and value. In front of the N. wall is a colossal bronze figure (Japanese) of a *Bodhisattva, or sacred being destined to become a Buddha. A case in front of this contains an admirably-executed bronze *Eagle, with extended wings, by a Japanese metal-worker named Miyôchin Munéharu (purchased for 1000*l*.). In glass-cases at the S. end of the court are a large Chinese lantern and models of three Chinese villas, sent by the Emperor of China to Josephine, wife of Napoleon, but captured by the British. Among the 400 pieces of Oriental jade, amber, and crystal bequeathed to the Museum in 1882 by *Mr. Arthur Wells*, the most valuable is a green and white writing-box decorated with rubies and worth at least 1400*l*. Here also is the fine collection of Chinese porcelain lent by *Mr. G. Salting*.

## 27. SOUTH KENSINGTON MUSEUM. 281

East Arcade. Oriental textile fabrics, armour, weapons, porcelain, **enamel, carved** work, furniture, etc., including great part of the Museum Collection of Chinese Pottery and Porcelain. — At the S. end is a *Parisian Boudoir of the time of Louis XVI., originally belonging to the Marquise de Scrilly, Maid of Honour to Marie Antoinette (bought for 2100l.). The paintings are by Natoire and Fragonard, the chimney-piece by Clodion, the metal work by Gouthière.

In the South Arcade are the Royal Treasures from Abyssinia, including robes worn by King Theodore, Moorish Saddles, Ashantee Jewellery, **etc.**

Leaving the S. Court, we next enter the **North Court**, devoted to **Italian art, comprising numerous** original sculptures of the Italian Renaissance.

**Over the S.** doorway is placed a marble *Cantoria or singing gallery from the church of S. Maria Novella at Florence, by *Baccio d'Agnolo* (1500).

East Section. The following **are the most noteworthy objects in this part of the** court. Several works by *Michael Angelo* and his school, including an unfinished statuette of St. Sebastian and a *Cupid (guaranteed by documents) by the master himself, and a **statue of Jason**, probably executed by a pupil — *Christ in the **sepulchre, a bas-relief** by *Donatello* (bought for 1000l.). — Life-size **figure of the V**irgin, with worshippers, formerly the tympanum **of** a doorway at S. Maria della Misericordia, Venice, attributed to **Bartolommeo** Bono (15th cent.). — Case containing small models in **wax** and terracotta by Italian sculptors of the 16th cent., including twelve ascribed **to Michael Angelo**. — Tabernacle, **ascribed to** *Desiderio da Settignano*, a pupil of *Donatello*. — **Altar or shrine of a** female saint, from Padua, by a pupil of *Donatello*. — Tabernacle from the **church of S.** Giacomo at Fiesole, **by Andrea Ferrucci** (c. 1490). — *Terracotta **figures of Italo-Greek** workmanship (B. C. 200), found **near Canosa in S. Italy**. — *Bronze busts of Popes Alexander VIII. **and Innocent X., attributed to** *Bernini*. — Collection of Italian bronzes of the **14-17th** centuries. In the 1st case are **the famous** *Martelli **Bronze,** a mirror-cover by *Donatello*, **and two** large **medallions** attributed to the celebrated medallist *Sperandio* (15th cent.).

By the pillars to **the** right are **some ad**mirable busts of the early **Renaissance.** *Giov. di San Miniato, by *Antonio Rossellino*, signed and dated 1456, with strongly marked characteristics; Portrait of a man, a vigorous work of the school of Donatello; *Marble bust of a Roman emperor, crowned with laurel, a masterpiece of the Lombard sch**ool, of** extraordinarily careful execution.

**The E. Arcade** contains a collection of European tapestry and textile fabrics, including the superb *Syon Cope, from the monastery of Syon at Isleworth, English embroidery of the 13th century.

At the N. end of the court are the tribune and the high-altar of the conventual church of S. Chiara at Florence, **the latter by** *Leonardo del Tasso* (about 1520).

WEST SECTION. Collection of glazed terracotta works, chiefly by *Luca* and *Andrea della Robbia* of Florence (15-16th cent). Those **in white** or uncoloured enamel are the oldest, while the coloured pieces date from the first decade of the 16th century. Among the most interesting specimens are twelve *Medallions representing the months, ascribed to *Luca della Robbia*; large medallion executed **by** *Luca della Robbia* for the Loggia de' Pazzi, with the **arms of King René of Anjou in the centre**; Adoration of the Magi, with a portrait of Perugino (looking over the shoulder of the king **in the** green robe and turban); Virgin and Child, by *Andrea della Robbia*. — **Collection of Florentine terracotta busts**, chiefly by or in the style of *Donatello*, including one of Savonarola (burned at Florence **in 1498**). — Extensive collection of Italian *Majolica*. — **This court also contains examples** of Italian **art in** carved furniture, **tarsia work, etc.** In fact it now represents the Italian section of the Museum.

Part of the WEST ARCADE (see also p. 280) is occupied by a valuable collection of *Musical Instruments*: Harpsichord which belonged to Händel; **German finger-organ, said to** have once belonged to Martin Luther; **Spinet of pear-tree wood, carved and adorned** with ebony, ivory, lapis lazuli, and marble, by *Annibale de' Rossi* of Milan (1577); virginal of richly gilt leather, stated to have been **the property of Elizabeth of the Palatinate**; harpsichord inscribed 'Hieronymus Bononiensis faciebat, Romæ MDXXI'.

The NORTH ARCADE contains Italian and other glass vessels, antique pottery, terracotta figurines from **Tanagra, etc.**

The **Fernery,** which forms a pleasant object at the windows of this arcade, was fitted up to enable the art-students to draw from plants at all seasons.

To the W. of the North Court are **three new Rooms**, formerly occupied by the Art Library. The first two of these are devoted to *Italian Woodwork* and *Furniture*, including several fine marriage coffers ('cassoni'); the third room contains specimens of *Spanish Art*, some ancient *Mural Decorations* from Puteoli, and a reproduction of the *Wolf of the Capitol*.

From the last-mentioned room a CORRIDOR leads to the *Refreshment Rooms* (p. 275). This passage contains a number of modern marble statues and original models. The windows contain interesting specimens of stained glass, partly from German churches. At the end of the corridor is a highly decorated staircase leading **to the** Keramic Gallery (p. 287). On this staircase is a memorial tablet with portrait of *Sir Henry Cole, K.C.B.* (d. 1882), the first Director of the Museum. We turn to the left into the —

**West Cloisters,** which, along with the **North West Cloisters,** to the right, contain the *Museum Collection of Furniture*. The walls are covered with **wood-carvings, tapestry,** casts, and paintings.

The N.W. Cloisters also contain some old state carriages and sedan chairs. At the N.W. corner of the North West Cloisters is the door opening on Exhibition Road, on the opposite side of which are the Exhibition Galleries (p. 288) and the India Museum (p. 289). We turn to the right into the —

**North** Cloisters, which contain a unique collection of Persian **earthenware, tiles, carpets,** works in metal, etc., including the **Persian Textiles** presented to the Museum by the Shah of Persia. In a case at the E. end are several interesting monumental tablets, with Persian inscriptions. Here also is a "*Mimbar*', or **pulpit**, from a mosque **at Cairo, of** carved **wood** inlaid with ivory **and** ebony, and **still bearing traces** of painting (1480).

In the angle **between the N. and N.W.** Cloisters is a Room from Damascus (1756), **fitted** up **with its original** carpets and furniture; **on the** walls are **Arabic** inscriptions. Adjacent is a similar room, together with **lattice** windows *(Meshrebiyehs)* from Cairo.

We now reach a broad flight **of steps leading to the upper floor,** which contains **the —**

\*National Gallery of British Art, a valuable and representative collection **of** English paintings. **It includes** the collections given or bequeathed by *Messrs. Sheepshanks, Parsons, Forster, W. Smith,* and **others,** and the pictures lent by the *Royal Academy.* It also contains **the famous** *Cartoons* **of** *Raphael*, formerly in Hampton Court. Before **entering any of the** rooms, **we** notice, **at the** top of the stairs by **which we have just ascended, some** original cartoons of the frescoes **in the Houses of Parliament, and an original** model of a group of the **Graces, by** *Baily*.

Rooms I, VIII, VII, IV **(see Plan,** p. 285) contain the \**Historical Collection* **of** *British Water-colour Drawings*, of great **interest to the student and lover of art.**

Room I. Water-colour paintings by *F. Wheatley, P. Sandby, W. Payne, E. Dayes,* and other **masters of the close of last century.** The screens in the middle of the **room bear a collection** of studies in oil, water-colour, and pencil, by *John Constable* **(p. 174).**

Room II. Collection lent **by the Royal Academy** (pictures purchased with the *Chantrey Fund*). To the **left,** *John Collier,* The last voyage of Henry Hudson; *Watts,* Psyche; *J. M. Strudwick,* A golden thread; *Wyllie,* Toil. Glitter, Grime, and **Wealth**; *Small,* **The** last **match**; *Pettie,* The vigil; *E. Poynter,* A visit to Æsculapius; *J. C. Hook,* **The stream**; *F. Inchoe,* **Harmony**; *Colin Hunter,* Their only **harvest**; *Seymour Lucas,* After Culloden; *W. Hunt,* Dog in the **manger**; *J. Brett,* Britannia's realm; *E. Parton,* **The waning of the year**; *Marcus Stone,* 'Il y a toujours un autre'; *Val. Prinsep*, **Ayesha**; *J. R. Reid,* Toil and pleasure; *J. Farquharson*, **The** joyless **winter day**; *H. Moore,* Cat's paw off the land; *W. Q. Orchardson,* Napoleon **on board** the Bellerophon; *W. Hilton,* Christ crowned with thorns; *A. C. Gow*, Cromwell at Dunbar; *F. W. Fenner,* Death of Amy Robsart; *D. Murray,* My love has gone a-sailing. In the centre of the room: \***Athlete** struggling with a python, in bronze, by *Sir Fred. Leighton*, Presi**dent of the** Royal Academy; a Mounted Indian attacked by a serpent, also in bronze, by *Thos. Brock*; Teucer, by *Hamo Thorneycroft*; Folly, by *E. Onslow Ford*; The Prodigal Son, in marble, by *W. Calder Marshall*.

Room III. Forster Collection. On the wall, to the left. Original drawings of portraits of literary men, by *Maclise*; Illustrations of Jerrold's

'Men of Character', by W. M. Thackeray. Then, water-colours and drawings by Stanfield, Turner, Cattermole, Stothard, Cipriani, Maclise, and Gainsborough. Frans Hals, Man with a jug; Gainsborough, His daughters; Reynolds, Portrait. — To the right: Drawings by Maclise, Leech, Landseer, and Count d'Orsay. Then, Boxall, Walter Savage Landor; Frith, Charles Dickens; Maclise, Macready as 'Werner'; Maclise, Scene from Jonson's 'Every Man in his Humour', with portrait of Forster; Watts, Thomas Carlyle; Wynfield, Death of Cromwell. The glass-cases in the middle of the room contain autographs of Charles II., Cromwell, Addison, Burns, Pope, Johnson, Byron, Keats, etc.; the MSS. of several of Dickens's novels, including the unfinished 'Edwin Drood', with the last words he wrote; three sketch-books of Da Vinci, which the master used to carry at his belt; chair, desk, and Malacca cane of Oliver Goldsmith. Small model of a curious Chinese Temple, with a grotto. — The door to the right leads to the Keramic Gallery (p. 287); that on to the left to —

Room IV. Continuation of the Collection of Water-colours, including specimens of Rossetti, Cattermole, Hunt, Sidney Cooper, Albert Moore, etc. A set of screens here bear a series of water-colours illustrating the Coronation of George IV. (1821). The case contains a collection illustrating the history of engraving on wood.

Room V. Dyce Collection. Pictures. To the left: West, Saul and the Witch of Endor; Janssens, Dr. Donne; Halls, Edmund Kean as Richard III.; Worlidge, Garrick as Tancred; Unknown Artist, Kemble as Coriolanus; Loutherbourg, Garrick as Don John; Richardson the Elder, Portrait of Pope. To the right: G. Romney, Serena; Unknown Painter, John Milton; Reynolds, Portrait. The room also contains books (fine editions of the classics), drawings, and miniatures. — The door to the right leads into the reading-room of the Dyce and Forster Library (open daily, 10 to 4, 5, or 6), containing 18,000 vols and a collection of drawings in portfolios (catalogue on the table).

Room VI. Dyce Collection. Books, Engravings, and Autographs of eminent men. — We now return through Rooms V. and IV. to —

Room VII, Collection of Water-colours, chiefly landscapes and architectural subjects.

Room VIII. Water-colours, chiefly of the beginning of the present century, including examples of Turner, J. Crome (1769-1821), the founder of the English school of landscape-painters, etc. On the screens is the rest of the Constable Collection (see p. 283).

We next turn to the right into the North Gallery, or Raphael Room, containing the marvellous cartoons executed by the great painter for Pope Leo X., in 1515 and 1516, as copies for tapestry to be executed at Arras in Flanders. Two sets of tapestry were made from the drawings, one of which, in a very dilapidated condition, is preserved in the Vatican; the other, after passing through the hands of many royal and private personages, is now in the Old Museum at Berlin. The cartoons were originally ten in number, but three, representing the Stoning of St. Stephen, the Conversion of St. Paul, and St. Paul in prison at Philippi, have been lost (represented here by copies). The cartoons rank among Raphael's very finest works, particularly in point of conception and design. The cartoons here are as follows, beginning to the right on entering: —

 Christ's Charge to Peter.
 Death of Ananias.
 Peter and John healing the Lame Man.
 Paul and Barnabas at Lystra.
Then, on the opposite wall: —
 Elymas the Sorcerer struck with blindness.
 Paul preaching at Athens.
 The Miraculous Draught of Fishes.

The room also contains copies of other works by Raphael and a very fine 'Altar-piece (lent by the Duke of Castro) which he painted for the Convent of St. Anthony at Perugia about 1505 (contemporary with the Ansidei Madonna, p. 151). In the centre of the room are some Italian 'Cassoni' (coffers) in carved wood. At the E. end of the hall we turn to the right, and reach the three rooms occupied by the SHEEPSHANKS COLLECTION.

**Room A.** To the left: *Leslie*, 114. Florizel and Perdita; 171. *Redgrave*, Ophelia weaving garlands; *Leslie*, 109. Scene from the 'Taming of the Shrew'; 115. Autolycus; 118. 'Le Malade imaginaire'; 111. 'Who can this be?'; 128. Griselda; 117. 'Les Femmes savantes'; 122. Queen Catharine and Patience; 127. Portia; 116. 'Le Bourgeois Gentilhomme'; 112. 'Who

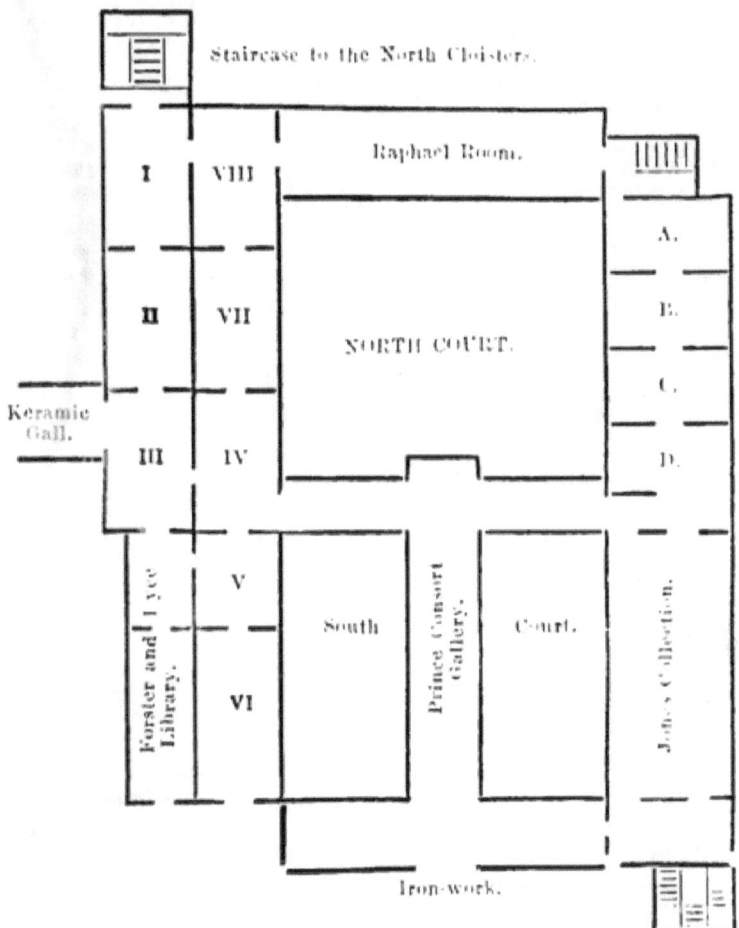

can this be from?'; 125. The toilette. 35. *Constable*, Hampstead Heath; 172. *Redgrave*, Bolton Abbey; 58. *Cope*, L'Allegro; 132. *L*     *Sa*   Panza; 66. *Danby*, Calypso's Island; 210. *Turner*, East Cowes C      t of Wight; 59. *Cope*, Il Penseroso; 11. *Callcott*, Dort (a     no    236. *Wilkie*, The refusal (Duncan Gray); 215. *Uwins*, Italian mothe  her child the tarantella; 208. *Turner*, Venice; 71. *Frith*, H a     troducing the bailiffs to Miss Richmond as his friends; 211.  *F*    S  cion; 207. *Turner*, Line-fishing off Hastings; 10. *Callcott*, S  o    and V  Page; 209. *Turner*, St. Michael's Mount, Cornwall; 225. *W*      Contrary winds; 166. *Newton*, Portia and Bassanio     *Callcott*     B  l     Abbey

31. *Seaford*, Coast of Sussex; 71. *Eastlake*, Italian contadina and her children; 113. *Leslie*, Uncle Toby and Widow Wadman (comp. p. 175); 108. *Lee*, Distant view of Windsor; 211. *Turner*, Vessel in distress off Yarmouth; 187. *G. Smith*, Children gathering wild flowers; 28. *Collins*, Hall Sands, Devonshire; 170. *Redgrave*, Throwing off her weeds; 81. *Horsley*, The contrast, **Youth and Age**. — The cases in the centre of the room contain a collection of fine enamels and **miniatures**.

**Room B**. To the left: 64. *Creswick*, Scene on the Tummel, Perthshire; *Lance*, Fruit; 126. *Wilson*, Coast-scene; 1403. *Morland*, Interior of a stable; 64. *Crome*, Woody landscape. *Gainsborough*, 91. Queen Charlotte; 136. Daughters of George III. *Linnell*, 1407. Driving cattle; 134. Milking time. *Wilson*, 105. **Landscape**; 246. Evening. *Mulready*, 147. The sailing-match; 152. Portrait of Mr. Sheepshanks; 111. First love; 162. Portrait of a little girl; 143. Open your mouth and shut your eyes! 144. Brother and sister; 148. The butt — shooting a cherry; 263. Mother teaching her son; 140. Giving a bite; 139. The fight interrupted; 138. Seven ages of man; 142. Interior with portrait of Mr. Sheepshanks; 145. Choosing the wedding **gown**. 107. *Lee*, Gathering seaweed; 222. *Webster*, Village choir; 103. *C. Landseer*, **Temptation** of Andrew Marvell; 33. *Constable*, Cathedral of Salisbury; 15. *Callcott*, Sunny morning; 197. *Stothard*, Shakspeare's principal characters; 219. *Webster*, Sickness and health; 62. *Creswick*, A summer's afternoon; 167. *Redgrave*, Cinderella; 110. *Leslie*, Characters from the 'Merry Wives of Windsor'; 85. *Jackson*, Portrait of **Earl** Grey; 225. *Wilkie*, The broken jar; *189. *Stanfield*, Market-boat on the Scheldt; 221. *Webster*, Returning from the fair; 188. *Stanfield*, Near Cologne; 220. *Webster*, Going to the fair. — The frames in the centre contain several hundred drawings and **sketches by** Mulready.

Room C. To the left: *261. *De Wint*, Woody landscape; 242. *Howard*, Peasants of Subiaco; 34. *Constable*, Dedham Mill; 258. *De Wint*, Cornfield; 249. *Monamy*, Old East India Wharf at London Bridge; 220. *Ward*, Bulls fighting; 9. *Callcott*, Brisk gale; *88. *E. Landseer*, The drover's departure, a scene in the Grampians; 176. *Roberts*, Gate at Cairo; *190. *Stanfield*, Sands near Boulogne. *E. Landseer*, 96. Sancho Panza and Dapple; 92. The 'Twa Dogs'; 101. Young roe-deer and rough hounds; 93. The old shepherd's chief mourner ('one of the most perfect poems or pictures', says Mr. Ruskin, 'which modern times have seen'); 87. Highland breakfast; 94. A Jack in office; 102. The eagle's nest; 90. A fireside party; 91. 'There's no place like home'; 89. The dog and the shadow; 95. Tethered rams; 100. Comical dogs; 99. Suspense. *Webster*, A village school; *Maccallum*, Sherwood Forest; 234. *Chalon*, **Hastings** — fishing-boats making for shore in a breeze; 164. *Mulready Junior*, Interior; 64. *Crome*, Woody landscape.

Room D. and the adjacent long GALLERIES contain the superb **Collection of French furniture**, porcelain, miniatures, bronzes, paintings, and sculptures of the 18th cent., bequeathed to the Museum by Mr. **John Jones** (d. 1882), officially valued at 250,000*l*. Special handbook, with numerous illustrations, 1*s*.

Room D. Between the exits, Magnificent armoire with inlaid work by *André Boule* or *Buhl*, the court cabinet-maker of Louis XIV. In a glass-case to the right, *Golden plaque, with three exquisite enamelled figures, in low relief. The rest of this room contains numerous articles of furniture and ornaments of admirable workmanship.

The LEFT GALLERY contains the remainder of the furniture, nearly all of the best period of French art in this department. Among the most interesting pieces are an Escritoire à toilette, in light-coloured wood, which is said to have belonged to Marie Antoinette, **and was** probably executed by *Riesener*; two escritoires by *David*; a writing-table and **a small** round table with Sèvres plaque, both belonging to Marie Antoinette (the two valued at upwards of 5000*l.*); cabinet of black boule (purchased by Mr. Jones for 3500*l.*); a **marqueterie** cabinet inlaid with Sèvres plaques, etc.

RIGHT GALLERY. Collection of Sèvres, Oriental, Dresden, and Chelsea **porcelain**. — Collection of miniatures, including *Portraits of Louis XIV. by *Petitot*. — Sculptures, among which are busts of Marie **Antoinette** and the Princess de Lamballe, in the style of *Houdon*. — The pictures on the walls include examples of *Gainsborough*, **Landseer, Linnell, Mulready**, and other English artists. The foreign works are mostly school-copies, but there is a genuine, signed work by *Crivelli* (Madonna).

The lunettes in the galleries contain decorative paintings to illustrate the different branches of Art Studies. At the S. end of the Gallery is a staircase leading down to the Oriental Court (the E. section of the S. Court, p. 280).

We now return to Room D., and turn (to the left) into the Gallery, which separates the N. from the S. Court, passing Leighton's great fresco described at p. 279. The balcony on our right, from which we look down into the N. court, is the singing gallery, mentioned at p. 281. Opposite it is the *\*Prince Consort* Gallery, which contains a rich selection of small mediæval works of art, arranged in glass-cases.

The case under the archway contains small plaques and reliquaries of enamel. The next case, standing in advance of the others, holds ancient enamelled works, the most important of which are a *Shrine in the form of a church with a dome (Rhenish Byzantine of 12th cent., bought for 2142*l.*), a *Triptych of champlevé enamel (German, 13th cent.), and an *Altar-cross of Rhenish Byzantine work with enamel medallions (12th cent.) The following cases contain examples of ancient and modern enamels, especially some fine *Limoges Enamels* of the 15th, 16th, and 17th centuries. The most valuable objects are the oval *Portrait of the Cardinal de Lorraine (bought for 2000*l.*) and the large *Casket, enamelled on plates of silver, with a band of dancing figures, ascribed to *Jean Limosin* (16th cent.). One case is devoted to English enamels (Bilston and Battersea). To the right, at the end of the gallery, are three cases containing specimens of *Bookbinding*.

The W. portion of the Gallery contains a few unimportant oil-paintings, and also a fresco of *Perugino*, successfully transferred to canvas.

The Gallery of the *Architectural Court*, reached by a few steps at the S. end of the Prince Consort Gallery, contains the collection of Ornamental Ironwork, of Italian, French, German, and English origin, balconies, window-gratings, lamps, etc.

The *\*Keramic Gallery*, entered from Room III. of the picture galleries (p. 283), contains an admirable collection of earthenware, porcelain, and stoneware. We first reach the collection of

## 27. SOUTH KENSINGTON MUSEUM.

English pottery of the 17th and 18th cent.; Wedgwood china; Chelsea, Worcester, and Derby china; enamelled earthenware. The following cases contain the *Collection of English Pottery* given to the Museum by Lady Charlotte Schreiber, including fine examples of most of the older wares. This is succeeded by a collection of German and Flemish stoneware, including several large German stoves. Adjoining are specimens of French earthenware of the 16th cent., including 5 pieces of the famous Henri-Deux ware (in a small case by itself); choice collection of Palissy ware; Sèvres porcelain; Dresden china; Italian porcelain, including 3 pieces of the rare Florentine porcelain of the 17th cent., probably the earliest porcelain made in Europe; Persian, Arabian, and Rhodian glazed pottery; some Hispano-Moresco (Spanish) ware. At the end are a few cases containing ancient terracottas from Cyprus, Greece, Rome, and S. Italy. The windows on the right, in grisaille, designed by *W. B. Scott*, represent scenes connected with the history of pottery. From the opposite windows a good view is obtained of the new buildings of the Museum.

[At present the examples of art manufactures of modern date (1851 and onwards) are deposited in the Exhibition Galleries.]

At the W. end of the Keramic Gallery is the staircase mentioned at p. 282, leading to the Refreshment Rooms.

---

Opposite the W. entrance of the Museum, in Exhibition Road, is the entrance to the **Exhibition Galleries** (p. 272), which contain various objects for which there is no room in the Museum (adm. free, daily, from 10 to 4, 5, or 6).

We first enter the S. GALLERY, containing the *Collection of Electrotypes and other Reproductions of Works of Art*, part of which is exhibited upstairs. Other rooms upstairs contain the *Collections of Modern Objects* and *Naval Models*. On the ground-floor we next reach the *Collection of Machinery and Inventions*, including many interesting objects from the late Patent **Office Museum**, now incorporated with the South Kensington Museum.

Among the chief objects of interest from the Patent Museum are the following, which are scattered throughout the galleries.

The original *Hydraulic Press*, made by Joseph Bramah and patented in 1795. — Engine of Bell's *Comet*, the first steamboat that ever plied in European waters. Bell's ingenious project for applying steam-power to navigation was received with neglect by the various European governments, but at once excited attention in the United States, where the first experiments were made in 1805. It was not till 1812 that the *Comet* was advertised to ply on the Clyde for the conveyance of passengers and goods'. — Stephenson's first locomotive, the *Rocket*, constructed to compete in the trial of locomotives on the Liverpool and Manchester Railway in 1829, where it gained the prize of 500*l*. — Adjacent, '*Puffing Billy*', the first locomotive engine ever constructed, in use at the Wylam Collieries from 1813 to 1862. — The *Sans Pareil*, by Hawksworth of Darlington, another competitor at the above-mentioned trial. — Cornish Pumping Engine, formerly in operation at Soho near Birmingham, to which James Watt in 1777 applied for the first time his separate condenser and air-pump (patented 1769). Hislop's **Winding** and Pumping Engine, patented

1790) and **erected for** raising **coals** about 1795. — Watt's first Sun and Planet Engine, erected at Soho in 1788. — Clock of Glastonbury Abbey, constructed by one **of the** monks in 1325, and showing the phases of the moon. — Swiss striking clock of 1348. — Clock with stone weights, from Aymestrey Church, Herefordshire.

The *Historical Collection of Telegraphic Apparatus* beginning with Bain's chemical telegraph, **the** first instrument of the kind ever used in England (1846), is interesting. Here also are the electrical machine used by Benjamin Franklin **in his** experiments, a collection **of chronometers,** and other **scientific instruments.**

Beyond the Machinery Department, in the S. part of the W. Gallery, we reach the *Museum of Economic Fish Culture*, where a State Barge, 270 years old, is exhibited.

The W. Gallery is here intersected by the new Imperial Institute Road (p. 272), which we cross in order to reach the N. half of the gallery, containing the *Collections of Scientific Apparatus used in Education and Research,* comprising much that is of great value and interest to students. Here also is the *Anthropometric Laboratory,* established by Mr. F. Galton.

The rooms to the right of the entrance to the Exhibition Galleries contain a *\*Collection of Objects from Palestine,* lent by the Palestine Exploration Fund.

Among the most interesting are: Mediæval and other glass of Arabian manufacture; large collection of early Christian lamps, found in or near Jerusalem. Seal of Hagai, son of Shebniah, found at Jerusalem, 22 ft. below the present surface of the ground, in a shaft sunk to the S. of the Temple area; the engraved characters are in Hebrew of the transition period. Stone weights, with inscriptions, chiefly from excavations made by Mr. Robinson. Plaster casts of ideographic inscriptions from Hamath. Models of Jerusalem and Mt. Sinai. Various fragments with inscriptions. Fragments of carved and ornamented stones from early Christian churches, chiefly from the neighbourhood of Jericho (4th cent.). Three well-preserved sepulchral chests with interesting ornamentation, probably of ante-Christian origin.

The *National Portrait Gallery,* formerly exhibited here, is now at Bethnal Green (see p. 129).

The **\*India Museum** (Pl. R, 9), in the E. Exhibition Gallery (comp. p. 272), was placed in 1880 under the management of the authorities of South Kensington Museum, who have considerably extended and improved it, so that it now ranks among the most interesting exhibitions in London. The museum is open free, daily, Sundays excepted, from 10 to 4, 5, or 6 according to the season. The entrance is in Exhibition Road, in the centre of the building.

We first reach a court containing original and reproduced examples of Hindoo architecture, including the stone front of a house from Bulandshah, the façade of a shop in Cawnpore, **and the** large façade of a dwelling-house from Ahmedabad, in teak wood, carved and painted (17th cent.). Over the archway is a large and splendid specimen of carved and perforated sandal wood. Round the hall are ranged carved windows, doorways, balconies, etc., and reproductions of antique specimens.

The objects in the next court illustrate Mogul art and architecture. To the right is an inlaid Marble Colonnade from Agra. A series of cases to the left contain 'loot' from Burmah, including King Theebaw's royal robes. Farther on is a plaster cast of the Eastern Gateway of the great Buddhist Tope at Sanchi, in the territory of the Begum of Bhopal; the original was built about the beginning of our era. Adjacent is a model of the huge domed tope to which the gate belongs, erected about B.C. 500; at the sides, marble **figures of** Buddha. On the walls are glazed tiles **and** carpets. Cast **of** the throne pillar in the private Hall of Audience **in** Akbar Khan's palace at Fáthpúr Sikrí, near Agra (16th cent.).

We now ascend a few steps, and turn to the right into the long **galleries**, containing textile fabrics.

[The staircase immediately to the right leads to the upper galleries, in which **are** placed the collections of furniture, carvings, lacquer-work, arms, pottery, jewellery, and bronzes.]

FIRST SECTION. On the walls, Indian carpets. Cases with figure-models of Indian divinities, handicraftsmen, agriculturalists, etc. Plaster casts of architectural details and sculptures. Architectural models. Ethnological Collection from Yarkund.

SECOND SECTION. On the walls, cotton carpets from the Deccan.

THIRD SECTION. Tents and canopies used at the Durbar held on the occasion of the proclamation **of** the Queen as Empress of India at Delhi, Jan. 1877. Embroidery, **brocades**, state carpets and canopies; peasant dresses from the Punjab, turbans, caftans.

FOURTH SECTION. Embroidered shawls **from** Delhi; garments decorated with beetles' wings; fine muslins from Dacca. Cases with specimens of the wild silks **of** India, lent by Thos. Wardle, Esq. On the walls, embroidered coverlets and printed chintzes.

FIFTH SECTION. On the right, **saddles and** trappings. On the left, male and female **costumes**.

We now ascend the **staircase, the** walls of which are hung with photographs of Indian scenery, costumes, etc. Then, in the Upper Gallery: —

FIRST SECTION. The first **cases** contain Indian works in metal, arranged according to countries. The most interesting are the brass vessels with reliefs from Thibet; the Bidri work from Purneah (in the N.W. Provinces); objects in dark metal, damascened with silver, from the Deccan; bells from Burmah and Tanjore. Among the most valuable pieces are the large Ewer, with enamels of Indian scenery, in Bidri work (on a separate stand); Samovar, of tinned copper, from Cashmere (18th cent.); Bowl and stand, **in** pierced silver, from Ahmedabad; Ancient silver patera (5th **or** 6th cent. A. D.), found **at** Badakshan, with representations resembling **those of classical antiques** (worship **of** Bacchus?). The next cases contain Hindoo sacred **figures,** and **brass and** marble idols and vessels used in the worship **of Buddha**. Among these is **a** figure of "Buddha as Siddhartha **before** his **conversion** taking part **in** a grand procession, an extremely interesting **'Lotah' of** about 20-30 A. D., found in a Buddhist cell (No. 2910); **also a Siamese figure** of Buddha (19th cent.), of gilt metal decorated **with glass** spangles. — **On** the walls are native paintings on talc. — Many **of the** most interesting objects in this room are often removed for loan **to** provincial museums.

SECOND SECTION. Jewellery and articles **in** jade, crystal, gold, and silver. — On the **walls:** Ornaments. In the **cases** to the right. Works **in** silver and other **metals.** Cases in the centre: Bracelets and necklaces; 'Ankus', or elephant **goad,** of gold, richly ornamented with a spiral band of diamonds, and set **with** rubies (from Teypore); necklace of tiger-claws; carvings in jade. — **To the** right Golden throne of the Maharajah Runjeet Singh, with three **velvet** cushions. Adjacent, Model illustrating the way in which Hindoo females wear jewelry. — To the right: Case with silver filigree work. Then, Golden relics from Rangoon, discovered in levelling a Buddhist temple, consisting of three 'Charifas' or relicshrines, a tassel, a leaf-scroll, a bowl with cover, a small cup, a helmet, and a jewelled belt (dated the year 516, i.e. 1454-55 A.D.). Buddhist Reliquary in gold (said to date from B.C. 500), with interesting figures, resembling later Christian works. — To the left Indian crystal vessels, right, niellos; left, Kuftgari and enamel work. — By the walls: Ornaments of various kinds.

THIRD SECTION. By the walls: Arms and Armour, arranged according to provinces; the swords in the cases to the left are particularly interesting. — On the right: 'Howdah', with embroidered covering. Opposite, 'Palanquin', of ivory, with representations of battles and beautiful ornamentation. — To the left: Weapons from Afghanistan. — In the centre: Bronze gun from **Burmah**, in the form of a dragon. — On the wall to the right is the **banner of** Ayoub Khan, captured at the battle of Candahar in 1880.

FOURTH SECTION. Pottery and Tiles, arranged by provinces. The most important are **the** manufactures of the N.W. Provinces (left), Sinde (right), and Madras (left). — **By the** walls: Glazed tiles, chiefly from Sinde.

FIFTH SECTION Wood and Ivory Carvings. Mosaics. Lacquer Work; Musical Instruments, Carvings in Marble and Stone. — 4th Case to the left: Models of tombs and vessels in soapstone. — 5th Case on the right Wind Instruments. — 4th, 6th, and 7th Cases to the right: String Instruments. — In the centre: Tiger devouring an English officer, a barbaric mechanical toy that belonged to Tippoo Sahib. — To the left: Drums and other musical instruments. — In the centre: Bedstead from Theebaw's Palace, Mandalay; swinging bedstead of painted wood, from Sinde. — Wooden articles, **lacquered**, the ornamentation of which is more striking than the forms. — Wood and Ivory Mosaics, of great delicacy of execution. — Furniture made of ivory and various kinds of wood. On the walls is a fine collection of 274 water-colour drawings of Indian scenery, costumes, customs, etc., by *Wm. Carpenter*.

The lofty building to the E. of South Kensington Museum is the Roman Catholic *Church of the Oratory*, Brompton (see p. 52), the finest modern example in London of the style of the Italian Renaissance. The façade is still unfinished. The interior is remarkable for its lofty marble columns and the domed ceiling of concrete vaulting. In the Lady Chapel are a superb altar and reredos, inlaid with precious stones, brought from Brescia and valued at 12,000*l*. The various chapels are embellished with mosaics and carvings, and it is intended to cover all the walls with mosaics. The choir-stalls are beautifully carved in Italian walnut, the floor is of rich marquetry, and the altar-rail is formed of *gialto antico* marble. The two seven-branched candlesticks of gilt bronze are accurate copies of the Jewish one on the Arch of Titus.

## 28. Belgravia. Chelsea. Kensal Green Cemetery.
*Millbank Prison. Chelsea Hospital. Royal Military Asylum.*

The southern portion of the West End, commonly known as **Belgravia**, and bounded by Hyde Park, the Green Park, Sloane Street, and Pimlico, consists of a number of handsome streets **and** squares (*Belgrave Square, Eaton Square, Grosvenor Place*, etc.), all of which have sprung up within the last few decades. It derives its general name from Belgrave Square, the centre of West End pride and fashion. Like *Tyburnia*, to the N., and *Mayfair* to the E. of Hyde Park, it is one of the most fashionable quarters of the town. At Pimlico on the S.E. stands *Victoria Station*, the extensive West End terminus of the London, Chatham, and Dover Railway, and of the London and Brighton Railway (p. 34), whence Victoria Street, opened up not many years ago through a wilderness of purlieus, leads N.E. to Westminster; Vauxhall Bridge Road S.E. to Vauxhall Bridge; Buckingham Palace Road and Commercial Road S.W. to Chelsea Bridge and Battersea Park (p. 299).

On the Thames, near Vauxhall Bridge, to the E. of Pimlico, and between Chelsea and Westminster, rises **Millbank** Penitentiary (Pl. G, 25), a huge mass of buildings, built and arranged from designs by *Jeremy Bentham* (d. 1832). It is about to be discontinued as a prison.

*Vauxhall Bridge*, constructed by Walker in 1816, is 800 ft. long, and consists of nine iron arches. The river is crossed farther up by the *Victoria Railway Bridge*, used for the various lines of railway converging at Victoria Station, and by the elegant *Chelsea Suspension Bridge*, built in 1858, both of which are at the E. end of Battersea Park (p. 299). — A little to the S. of Vauxhall Bridge is *Kennington Oval*, a cricket-ground second only to Lord's in public favour and in interest.

**Chelsea**, now a suburb of London, was for many ages before it was swallowed up, a country village, like Kensington, with many distinguished residents. It appears in Domesday Book as *Chelched*, i.e. 'chalk hythe', or wharf. The extensive building on the N. bank of the Thames, a little to the W. of Chelsea Bridge, is **Chelsea Hospital** (Pl. G, 18, 14), an institution for old and invalid soldiers, begun in the reign of Charles II. by *Wren*, on the site of a theological college (the name 'college' being sometimes still applied to the building), but not completed till the time of William and Mary. The hospital, consisting of a central structure flanked by two wings, and facing the river, has accommodation for 540 pensioners. In addition to these about 70,000 out-pensioners annually obtain relief, varying from 1½d. to 3s. 7½d. a day, out of the invested funds of the establishment, which is also partly supported by a grant from Parliament. The annual expenses are about 28,000l.

The centre of the quadrangle in front of the hospital is occupied by a bronze statue of Charles II., by *Grinling Gibbons*. The hospital (small fee to pensioner who acts as cicerone) contains a chapel with numerous flags, 13 French eagles, and an altarpiece by *Sebastian Ricci*, representing the Ascension of Christ. In the dining-hall is an equestrian portrait of Charles II., by *Verrio*. Visitors may attend the services in the chapel on Sun., at 11 a.m. and 3.30 p.m. The gardens are open to the public.

To the N. of the hospital lies the **Royal Military Asylum** (Pl. G, 13, 17), founded in 1801 by the Duke of York, and consequently often called the *Duke of York's School*, an institution in which about 500 orphans of soldiers are annually maintained and educated. The building has a Doric portico. Friday, from 10 to 4, is the best day to visit the school. — In Chelsea Bridge Road, near the hospital, are the largest and finest of all the *Barracks* for the Foot Guards, with accommodation for 1000 men.

To the S.E., on part of the ornamental grounds of Chelsea Hospital, there stood in the reigns of George II. and George III, a place of amusement named the *Ranelagh*, which was famous beyond any other place in London as the centre of the wildest and showiest gaiety. Banquets, masquerades, fêtes. etc., were celebrated here in the most extravagant style. Kings and ambassadors, statesmen and literati, court beauties, ladies of fashion, and the *demi-monde* met and mingled at the Ranelagh as they now meet nowhere in the metropolis. Its principal building, the Rotunda, 185 ft. in diameter, not unlike in external appearance to the present Albert Hall, was erected in 1740, by William Jones. Horace Walpole describes it as 'a vast amphitheatre, finely gilt, painted, and illuminated into which everybody that loves eating, drinking, staring, or crowding is admitted for twelve pence'. This haunt of pleasure-seekers was closed in 1805, and every trace of it has long been obliterated.

To the S.W. of the hospital lies the Chelsea *Botanic Garden*, presented by *Sir Hans Sloane* to the Society of Apothecaries, on condition that 50 new varieties of plants grown in it should be annually furnished to the Royal Society, until the number so presented amounted to 2000. It is famed for its fine cedars. Tickets of admission (gratis) may be obtained in Apothecaries' Hall, Water Lane, Blackfriars (p. 115).

*Chelsea Old Church (St. **Luke**'s), which stands by the river, at the corner of Cheyne Walk and Church Street (Pl. G, 1), is one of the most interesting churches in London. It was originally built in the reign of Edward II. (1307-27), but in its present form it dates mainly from about 1660, though some older work remains in the chancel and its side-chapels. Among the numerous monuments it contains are those of Lord Bray and his son (1539); several of the Lawrence family, mentioned by H. Kingsley in 'The Hillyars and the Burtons'; the sumptuous monument of Lord and Lady Dacre (1594-5); the Duchess of Northumberland (d. 1555; mother-in-law of Lady Jane Grey and grandmother of Sir Philip Sidney); Lady Jane Cheyne (d. 1669), a large monument by Bernini, the only work now remaining that he did for England; and Sir Hans Sloane (d. 1753; see below). Sir Thomas More built the chapel on the S. side of the chancel, and erected a monument to himself, which is now in the chancel. In all probability his remains are in this church, except his head, which is at Canterbury (see *Baedeker's Great Britain*). In the churchyard are buried, though their monuments have disappeared, *Shadwell*, poet laureate (d. 1692), Henry Sampson Woodfall, printer of the celebrated Letters of Junius (d. 1805), and John Cavalier, the Huguenot leader (d. 1740). In the church are the 'Vinegar Bible', Foxe's Book of Martyrs (2 vols.), and two other books, chained to a desk. The keys of the church may be had from the *Rev. R. H. Davies*, 178 Oakley Street.

The past associations of Chelsea are full of interest. Sir Thomas More resided in Chelsea, near the river and Battersea Bridge, in Beaufort

House, which has now disappeared, and where he was often visited by Erasmus. Sir Hans Sloane, lord of the manor of Chelsea, lived at the manor house there, and made the collection which formed the beginning of the British Museum (see p. 233). His name is commemorated in Sloane Street, Sloane Square, etc. Bishop Atterbury, Dean Swift, and Dr. Arbuthnot all resided in Church Street. Sir Richard Steele resided not far off. Mrs. Somerville lived at Chelsea Hospital, where her husband was physician. Leigh Hunt lived in Cheyne Row, and the same unpretending street for many years contained the residence of Thomas Carlyle (No. 24, formerly No. 5; indicated by a memorial tablet), who died here in 1881. George Eliot (Mrs. Cross; d. 1880) lived and died in Cheyne Walk. Turner, the great landscape-painter, died in obscure lodgings at Chelsea in 1851.

A little to the W. was Little Chelsea, now West Brompton, where the famous Earl of Shaftesbury of the 'Characteristics' resided in Shaftesbury House. This mansion, in which Locke wrote part of his 'Essay on the Human Understanding', and Addison parts of the 'Spectator', has been converted into a workhouse.

Skirting the Thames, a little to the W. of Chelsea Hospital, is the *Chelsea Embankment* (p. 114), on which, opposite Cheyne Row, is a *Statue of Thomas Carlyle* (d. 1881), by Boehm. The embankment passes the elegant *Albert Suspension Bridge*, and *Battersea Bridge* (new bridge in progress), and leads to the site of *Cremorne Gardens*, so named from their original owner, Lord Cremorne, and formerly a very popular place of recreation, but closed in 1877 and now almost covered with buildings.

**Kensal Green Cemetery.** The majority of the cemeteries of London are uninteresting, owing to the former English custom of burying eminent men within the walls of churches. This cemetery, however,, on the N.W. side of London, forms an exception, and will repay a visit. It is most easily reached by omnibus from Edgware Road. We may also travel by the Metropolitan Railway to Notting Hill or Westbourne Park Station (p. 334), each of which is about $3/4$ M. to the S. of the cemetery; or by the North London Railway viâ Hampstead Heath to Kensal Green Station, $1/2$ M. to the north.

Kensal Green Cemetery, laid out in 1832, covers an area of about 60 acres, and contains about seventy thousand graves. It is divided into a consecrated portion for members of the Church of England, and an unconsecrated portion for dissenters. Most of the tombstones are plain upright slabs, but in the upper part of the cemetery, particularly on the principal path leading to the chapel, there are several monuments handsomely executed in granite and marble, some of which possess considerable artistic value. Among the eminent people interred here are — Brunel, the engineer; Sidney Smith, the author; Mulready, the painter; Kemble, the actor; Sir Charles Eastlake, the painter and historian of art; Buckle, the historian; Leigh Hunt, the essayist; Sir John Ross, the arctic navigator; Thackeray, the novelist; John Leech, the well-known illustrator of 'Punch'; Gibson, the sculptor; Mme. Tietjens, the great singer; Charles Mathews, the actor; John Owen, the social reformer. Adjoining the grave of the last is the Reformers' Memorial. — Cardinal Wiseman is interred in the Roman Catholic Cemetery, adjacent to Kensal Green.

*Highgate Cemetery* (p. 328) to the N., and *Norwood Cemetery* to the S. of London, are worth visiting for the sake of the excellent \*Views they afford. *Abney Park Cemetery*, near Stoke Newington, is much used as a burying-ground by Nonconformists.

# III. THE SURREY SIDE.

## 29. St. Saviour's Church.

*Barclay and Perkins' Brewery. Guy's Hospital. Southwark Park.*

The 'Surrey Side' of the metropolis, with a population of about 750,000 souls, has in some respects a character of its own. It is a scene of great business life and bustle from Lambeth to Bermondsey, but its sights, institutions, and public buildings are few. That part of it immediately opposite the City, from London Bridge to Charing Cross, is known as 'the Borough', a name which it rightly enjoys over the heads of such newly created boroughs as Greenwich or the Tower Hamlets, seeing it has returned two members to Parliament for more than 500 years. We note a few of its objects of interest.

Mention must be made, in the first place, of **St Saviour's Church** (Pl. R, 38; *III*), one of the oldest churches in London, situated opposite the London Bridge Station, in Wellington Street, which runs S. from London Bridge. The church, which was built in the 13th cent. by Gifford, Bishop of Winchester, belonged originally to the old Augustinian Priory of St. Mary Overy, but was converted into a parish church by Henry VIII. in 1540. Of this original building, which was cruciform in shape, and constructed in the Early English style, nothing now remains but the interesting choir, transept, and Lady Chapel. The nave was taken down in 1840, and replaced by an incongruous new structure. Above the cross is a low quadrangular tower, flanked by corner-towers.

The trials of reputed heretics under Queen Mary in 1555 took place in the beautiful *Lady Chapel*, which is flanked with aisles, and lies north and south. The chapel and choir were restored in 1820 and 1832, with only partial success. The altar-screen in the choir was erected by Fox, Bishop of Winchester, in the early years of the 16th century.

The most interesting monument in the church is that of the the poet *John Gower* (1325-1402), the friend of Chaucer. It consists of a sarcophagus with a recumbent marble figure of the poet, whose head rests upon his three principal works, the *Speculum meditantis*, *Vox clamantis*, and *Confessio amantis*, while his feet are supported by a lion. In the Lady Chapel is the monument of Lancelot Andrews, Bishop of Winchester (d. 1625). *Massinger* and *Fletcher*, the dramatists, *Edmund Shakspeare*, a player, brother of the poet, and *Lawrence Fletcher*, who was a lessee, along with

Shakspeare and Burbage, of the Globe and Blackfriars Theatres, are also buried here. — On the river, near St. Saviour's, once stood Winchester House, the residence of the bishops of Winchester, and the Globe Theatre just mentioned. — The central station of the *Metropolitan Fire Brigade* is in Southwark Bridge Road.

In Park Street, near St. Saviour's, is situated **Messrs. Barclay, Perkins, and Co.'s Brewery** (Pl. R, 38; *III*), partly on the former site of the Globe Theatre. This is one of the most extensive establishments of the kind in London, and is well worthy of a visit, on account both of its great size and its admirable arrangements.

The brewery covers an area of about 12 acres, forming a miniature town of houses, sheds, lofts, stables, streets, and courts. At the entrance stand the Offices, where visitors, who readily obtain an order to inspect the establishment on application by letter, enter their names in a book. The guide who is assigned to the visitor on entering, and who shows all the most interesting parts of the establishment, expects a fee of one shilling. In most of the rooms there is a very oppressive and heady odour, particularly in the cooling-room, where the carbonic acid gas lies about a foot deep over the fresh brew. Visitors are recommended to exercise caution in accepting the guide's invitation to breathe this gas.

In spite of the vast dimensions of the boilers, vats, fermenting 'squares', and other apparatus, none but the initiated will have any idea of the enormous quantity of liquor brewed here in the course of a year. About 200,000 quarters of malt are annually consumed, and the yearly duty paid to government by the firm amounts to the immense sum of 180,000*l*. The head brewer receives a salary of 1000*l*. per annum. The originator of the brewery was Dr. Johnson's friend Thrale, after whose death it was sold to Messrs. Barclay and Perkins. Dr. Johnson's words on the occasion of the sale, which he attended as an executor, though often quoted, are worthy of repetition: 'We are not here to sell a parcel of boilers and vats, but the potentiality of growing rich beyond the dreams of avarice.' Two vats are shown, each of which can contain 3300 barrels of liquor. The water used in brewing is supplied by Artesian wells, sunk on the premises.

The stables contain about 150 horses, many of which are bred in Yorkshire. They are used for carting the beer in London.

The brewing trade in London has become a great power within the last twenty or thirty years, and is felt to have a serious bearing upon the results of parliamentary and municipal elections. It is no longer a merely manufacturing trade, but promotes the consumption of its own goods by the purchase or lease of drinking-houses, where its agents are installed to conduct the sale. These agents are nominal tenants and are possessed of votes, and their number and influence are so great, that the power of returning the candidate who favours the 'trade' is often in their hands. All the great brewers are now understood to be extensive proprietors of public houses.

To the S. of London Bridge Station is Guy's Hospital (Pl. G, 42), founded in 1721 by Guy, the bookseller, who had amassed an immense fortune by speculation in South Sea stock. The institution contains 710 beds, and relieves 5000 in-patients and above 80,000 out-patients annually. The yearly income of the hospital is 40,000*l*.

The court contains a brazen, and the chapel a marble statue of the founder (d. 1724), the latter by *Bacon*. Sir Astley Cooper, the celebrated surgeon, to whom a monument has been erected in St. Paul's (see p. 86), is buried here.

**Southwark Park** (Pl. R, 49, G, 49, 53), in Rotherhithe (p. 67), farther to the S., recently laid out by the Metropolitan Board of Works at a cost of more than 100,000*l*., covers an area of 62 acres, and is in the immediate neighbourhood of the extensive *Surrey Docks* (p. 128).

Among other interesting associations connected with this locality the following may be noticed. The name of *Park Street* reminds us of the extensive Park of the Bishops of Winchester, which occupied the river side from Winchester House to Holland House. In the fields to the S. of this park were the circuses for bull and bear baiting, so popular in the time of the Stuarts. Edward Alleyne was for many years the 'Keeper of the King's wild beasts' here, and amassed thereby the fortune which enabled him to found Dulwich College (see p. 312). — Richard Baxter often preached in a church in Park Street, and in Zoar Street there was a chapel in which John Bunyan is said to have ministered. — *Mint Street* recalls the mint existing here under Henry VIII. — In High Street there stood down to 1875 the old *Talbot* or *Tabard Inn*, the starting-point of Chaucer's 'Canterbury Pilgrims'. — The *White Hart*, 63 Borough High Street (see p. 15), mentioned by Shakspeare in 'Henry VI'. (Part II., iv. 8) and by Dickens in the 'Pickwick Papers' (as the meeting-place of Mr. Pickwick and Sam Weller), and the *George* (rebuilt after a fire in 1676), are interesting specimens of old-time inns, with galleries round their inner courts. — The *Marshalsea Gaol*, the name of which is familiar from 'Little Dorrit', stood near St. George's Church, Southwark.

## 30. Lambeth Palace. Bethlehem Hospital. Battersea Park.

*St. Thomas's Hospital. St. George's Cathedral.*

On the right bank of the Thames, from Westminster Bridge to Vauxhall Bridge, stretches the new *Albert Embankment* (p. 114). On it, opposite the Houses of Parliament, stands **St. Thomas's Hospital** (Pl. R, 29; *IV*), a spacious edifice built by *Currey* in 1868-71, at a cost of 500,000*l*. It consists of seven four-storied buildings in red brick, united by arcades, and is in all 590 yds. long. The number of in-patients annually treated at the hospital is 6000, of out-patients over 60,000. Its annual revenue is 39,000*l*. Professional visitors will be much interested in the admirable internal arrangements (admission on Tuesdays at 10 a. m.). The hospital was formerly in a building in High Street, Southwark, which was sold to the South Eastern Railway Company in 1862 for 296,000*l*.

**Lambeth Palace** (Pl. R, 29; *IV*), above the hospital, at the E. end of *Lambeth Bridge* (built in 1862), has been for over 600 years the London residence of the Archbishops of Canterbury. It

## 30. BETHLEHEM HOSPITAL.

can only be visited by the special permission of the archbishop (apply to the chaplain). The *Chapel*, 72 ft. long and 26 ft. broad, built in 1245 by Archbishop Boniface in the Early English style, is the oldest part of the building. The screen and windows were placed here by Archbishop Laud. The '*Lollards' Tower*' (properly the *Water Tower*), adjoining the W. end of the chapel, so called because the Lollards, or followers of Wycliffe, were supposed to have been imprisoned and tortured here, is an old, massive, square keep, erected by Archbishop Chicheley in 1434. A small room in the upper part of the tower, 13½ ft. long, 12 ft. wide, and 8 ft. high, called the 'prison' and forming part of a staircase-turret more than 200 years older than the time of Chicheley, still contains several inscriptions by prisoners, and eight large rings fastened in the wall, to which the heretics were chained. The Earl of Essex, Queen Elizabeth's favourite (1601), Lovelace, the poet (1648), and Sir Thomas Armstrong (1659), were also confined here. The name of Lollards' Tower, applied to what is really a group of three buildings distinct in character and architecture, dates only from the beginning of the 18th century. The real Lollards' Tower was the S.W. tower of old St. Paul's Cathedral, as mentioned in Stow's Survey of London (1598). — The *Hall*, 92 ft. long and 40 ft. broad, was built by Archbishop Juxon in 1663, and has a roof in the style of that of Westminster Hall, with Italian instead of Gothic details. — The *Library*, established by Archbishop Bancroft in 1610, consists of 30,000 vols. and 2000 MSS., some of which, including the Registers of the official acts of the archbishops from 1274 to 1744 in 41 vols., are very valuable. It is at present kept in the hall, and is accessible daily, except Saturdays, between 10 a.m. and 3 p.m. (in summer, 5 p.m; closed from Sept. 1st to Oct. 15th). — The *Guard Chamber*, 60 ft. long, and 25 ft. broad, contains portraits of the archbishops since 1533, including Archbishop Laud, by *Van Dyck*; Herring, by *Hogarth*; Secker, by *Sir Joshua Reynolds*; Sutton, by *Sir William Beechey*; Howley, by *Shee*; and a portrait of Archbishop Warham, after *Holbein* (1504), a copy of the original in the Louvre. The dining-room contains portraits of Luther and his wife. The massive brick gateway, flanked by two towers, was erected by Cardinal Morton in the end of the 15th century. — See 'Lambeth Palace and its Associations', by *Rev. J. Cave-Browne* (2nd ed., 1883), and 'Art Treasures of the Lambeth Library', by the librarian, *S. W. Kershaw* (1873).

**Bethlehem Hospital** (Pl. R, 33; popularly corrupted into *Bedlam*), a lunatic asylum, is situated at the point where Lambeth Road, leading E. from Lambeth Palace, joins St. George's Road.

The hospital was founded in Bishopsgate Street by Sheriff Simon Fitz-Mary in 1246, but was presented by Henry VIII. to the city of London in 1547, and converted into a madhouse. The building in Bishopsgate Street was taken down in 1675, and a new hospital built in Moorfields, to replace which the present building in St. George's Fields, Lambeth, was begun in 1842. The cost of construction of the hospital, which has a frontage 900 ft. long, was 122,000l.; the architect was Lewis, but the dome was added by *Smirke*. The establishment can accommodate 40 patients, and is fitted up with every modern convenience, including hot air and water pipes, and various appliances for the amusement of the hapless inmates, including billiards. Professional men, who are admitted by cards obtained from one of the governing physicians, will find a visit to the hospital exceedingly interesting. — There are also extensive lunatic asylums at *Hanwell* (p. 334), 7½ M. to the W. of London, on the Great Western Railway, and *Colney Hatch*, 6½ M. to the N. of London, on the Great Northern Railway.

Near the hospital, at the corner of St. George's Road and Westminster Bridge Road, stands the principal Roman Catholic church in London, **St. George's Cathedral** (Pl. R, 33), begun by *Pugin* in the Gothic style in 1840, and completed, with the exception of the tower, in 1848.

In Newington Butts, a little to the E., near the well-known inn, the Elephant and Castle (p. 78), is the *Tabernacle* of the popular preacher Mr. Spurgeon, built in the classic style, and accommodating 6000 persons (comp. p. 51). — An elegant Nonconformist chapel, called *Christchurch*, has been erected in Westminster Bridge Road, partly with American contributions, for the congregation of the late celebrated *Rowland Hill*, of Surrey Chapel. The beautiful tower and spire are a memorial of President Lincoln.

*Doulton's Pottery Works*, on the Albert Embankment, above Lambeth Palace, have obtained a high artistic reputation and are well worth a visit.

**Battersea Park** (Pl. G, 14, 15, 18, 19), at the S.W. end of London, on the right bank of the Thames, opposite Chelsea Hospital, was laid out in 1852-58 at a cost of 312,890l., and is 185 acres in extent. It is most conveniently reached by taking a steamboat to Battersea Park Pier. At the lower end of the park is the elegant *Chelsea Bridge*, leading to Pimlico, and ½ M. distant from the Sloane Square and Victoria stations of the Metropolitan Railway. From the upper end of the park the *Albert Suspension Bridge* crosses to the Chelsea Embankment. Near the S.E. angle of the park are *Battersea Park Station* of the West London Extension and the *Battersea Park Road Station* of the Metropolitan Extension (see p. 34). The principal attraction of the extensive pleasure-grounds, which are provided with an artificial sheet of water, groups of trees, etc., is the *Sub-tropical Garden*, 4 acres in extent, containing most beautiful and carefully cultivated flower-beds and tropical plants, which are in perfection in August and September. Near the N. entrance is a convenient refreshment-room, and in the vicinity there is a good restaurant. On the S. side of the park is the *Albert Palace* (p. 43).

*Dives' Flour Mills*, Battersea, to the E. of the parish-church of St. Mary, occupy the site of the manor-house of Henry St. John, Viscount Bolingbroke (1678-1751). The W. wing still remains, containing the cedar-wainscotted room, overlooking the Thames, in which Pope wrote the 'Essay on Man'. Bolingbroke and his wife are buried in the church. Their monument, in the N. gallery, is adorned with their medallions by Roubiliac and bears epitaphs written by Bolingbroke himself. The E. window contains ancient stained glass, relating to the St. John family.

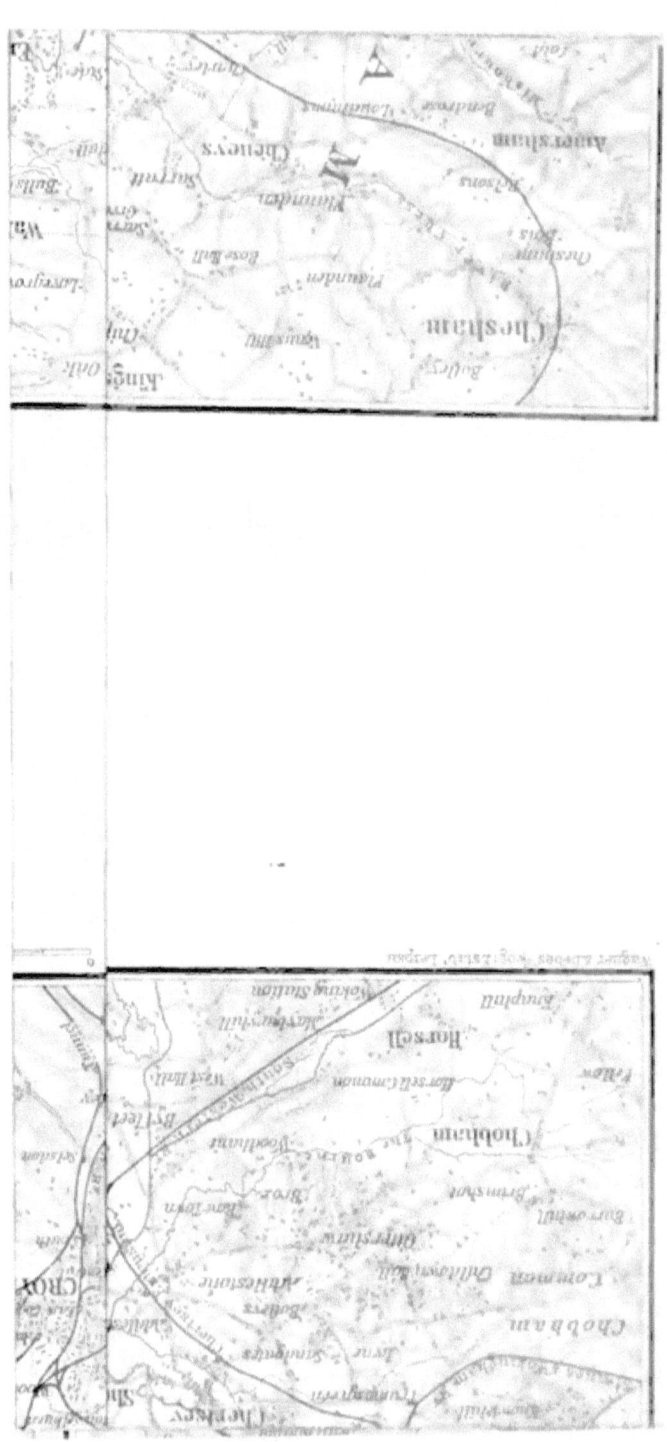

# EXCURSIONS FROM LONDON.

### 31. Greenwich Hospital and Park.

**Greenwich**, situated on the Thames. 6 M. below London Bridge, may be reached **either by the** *South Eastern Railway* from Charing Cross Station, in **24 min. (trains every** 20 min.; fares 1s., 9d., 6d.; stations, *Waterloo Junction*, *Cannon* **Street**, **London** Bridge, Spa **Road**, *Deptford*, **Greenwich**); **by the London**, Chatham, and Dover *Railway* from Victoria, **Holborn Viaduct, or Ludgate** Hill in 30-35 **min.**; **by** *Tramway* **from** Blackfriars Bridge **or** Westminster Bridge; **or by Steamboat**, in $3\frac{1}{4}-1\frac{1}{4}$ **hr.** according **to the** state of the tide (every $\frac{1}{2}$ **hr.; fares** 6d. **and** 4d.**; piers**, Westminster, Charing Cross, Waterloo, Temple, Blackfriars, **St. Paul's**, London Bridge, Cherry Gardens, Thames Tunnel, Globe Stairs, **Limehouse**, West **India** Dock, Commercial Dock, Millwall, Greenwich). **The last route is preferable** in fine weather. — The traveller may **combine a** visit to *Blackwall* (East India Docks, see p. 128) with the excursion to Greenwich; trains **of the** *Blackwall Railway* run in 20 min. (fares 6d., **4d.**) **to** Blackwall, **whence** a steamboat plies every $\frac{1}{2}$ hour to Greenwich, **in** 20 **minutes**.

**Greenwich. Hotels:** THOS. QUARTERMAINE'S SHIP TAVERN; TRAFALGAR **HOTEL** (**both very expensive**; fish-dinner from about 7s.); CROWN AND SCEPTRE. **Connected with** the Ship Tavern is a **restaurant, called the *SHIP STORES**, which is cheaper; dinner 3-4s. **At the close of the** parliamentary session the Cabinet **Ministers and some other members of the** Government usually meet **to partake of a banquet at Greenwich, known** as the *Whitebait Dinner*, **from the whitebait, a small fish not** much more than an **inch in length, for which Greenwich is famous, and** which is considered **a great delicacy. It is eaten with** cayenne pepper, lemon **juice, and brown bread and butter. Pop. of** Greenwich (1881) 131,264.

*Greenwich Hospital (Pl. G, 70) occupies **the site of** an old royal palace, built in 1433 by Humphrey, Duke of Gloucester, and called by him Placentia or Plaisance. In it Henry VIII. and his daughters, Mary and Elizabeth, **were born**, and here Edward VI. died. During the Commonwealth the palace was removed. In 1667 Charles II. **began to rebuild it,** but he only completed the wing **which is named after him.** Twenty years later, after the accession of William III., the building was resumed, and in 1694 the palace was converted into a hospital for aged and disabled sailors. The number of inmates accommodated in the hospital reached its highest point (2710) in 1814, but afterwards decreased considerably. In 1865 the number was 1400, and of these nearly 1000 took advantage of a resolution of the Admiralty, which gave the pensioners the option of remaining in the hospital or of receiving an out-door pension, and chose the latter alternative. The revenue of the hospital now amounts to about 160,000l. per annum, being derived mainly from landed property; and upwards of 9000 seamen and marines derive benefit from it in one form or another. The funds also support Greenwich Hospital School (p. 303). The hospital is now partly used as a *Royal Naval College*, for the instruction of naval officers; but many of the suites of rooms are at present unoccupied. The expenses of the college and the maintenance of the building are defrayed by votes of Parliament.

The building consists of four masses or sections. On the side next the river are the W. or KING CHARLES BUILDING, with the library, and the E. or QUEEN ANNE BUILDING, which now contains a naval museum. These are both in the Corinthian style. Behind are the S.W. or KING WILLIAM BUILDING, and the S.E. or QUEEN MARY BUILDING, each furnished with a dome in Wren's style. The *River Terrace*, 890 ft. long, is embellished with two granite obelisks, one in commemoration of the marine officers and men who fell in the New Zealand rebellion of 1863-64; and the other (of red granite) in honour of *Lieutenant Bellot*, a French naval officer, who lost his life in a search for Franklin. The quadrangle in the centre contains a marble statue of *George II.*, in Roman costume, by Rysbrack; an Elizabethan gun found in the Medway and supposed to have belonged to a ship sunk by the Dutch in 1667; and a gun which was on board the 'Victory' at Trafalgar (1805). In the upper quadrangle is a colossal bust of *Nelson*, by Chantrey. — On the S.W. side is the *Seamen's Hospital*, for sailors of all nationalities, transferred hither in 1865 from the *Dreadnought*, an old man-of-war stationed in the Thames.

The Painted Hall (see below) is open to the public daily from 10 to 4. 5, or 6 (on Sun. after 2 p.m.), and the Chapel and Royal Museum are open daily, except. Sun. and Frid., at the same hours.

The chief feature of the King William section is the PAINTED HALL, 106 ft. long, 50 ft. broad, and 50 ft. high, containing the *Naval Gallery* of pictures and portraits which commemorate the naval victories and heroes of Great Britain. The paintings on the wall and ceiling were executed by *Sir James Thornhill* in 1707-27. The *Descriptive Catalogue* (price 3d.) supplies brief biographical and historical data.

The VESTIBULE contains, amongst other pictures, Portraits of Columbus and Andrea Doria (from Italian originals), Vasco da Gama (from a Portuguese original), Duquesne by *Steuben*, and the Earl of Sandwich by *Gainsborough*; statues of Admirals St. Vincent, Howe, Nelson, and Duncan; a memorial tablet to Sir John Franklin and his companions, executed by *Westmacott* (on the left); and a painting of the turret ship 'Devastation at a naval review in honour of the Shah of Persia (1873), by *E. W. Cooke* (to the right). — The Hall. The four corners are filled with marble statues: to the left of the entrance, Adm. de Saumarez, by *Steele*; to the right, Capt. Sir William Peel, by *Theed*; to the left of the exit, Viscount Exmouth, by *Macdowell*; to the right, Adm. Sir Sidney Smith, by *Kirk*. The numbering of the pictures begins in the corner to the right. Among the most conspicuous are the following: *Loutherbourg*, 11. Destruction of the Spanish Armada in 1588; 28. Lord Howe's victory at Ouessant; 26. *Briggs*, George III. presenting a sword to Lord Howe in commemoration of the victory at Ouessant in 1794; 34. *Drummond*, Battle of Camperdown (1797); 46. *Chambers* (after *Ben. West*), Battle of La Hogue, 1692; 53. *Zoffany*, Death of Captain Cook in 1779; 80. *Davis*, Death of Nelson in 1805; 86. *Turner*, Battle of Trafalgar; 91. *Arnold* Battle of Aboukir; 98. *Jones*, Battle of St. Vincent; 107. *Allan*, Nelson boarding the San Nicholas, 1797. Among the most interesting portraits are: 10. Hawkins, Drake, and Cavendish, a group after *Mytens*; 21. St. Vincent; 29. Hood; 37. Bridport, by *Reynolds*; 50. George, Duke of Cumberland, by *Kneller*; 52. Cook, by *Dance*; 51. James II., by *Lely*; 56. Sir James Clark Ross; 63. Adm. Kempenfelt; 77. Sir Charles Napier; 85. Nelson; 87. Collingwood; 88. Capt. G. Duff; 104. Monk, Duke of Albemarle, by *Lely*; 109. Sir W. Penn, by *Lely*. — In the Upper Hall are busts of (left) Rivers, Goodenough, William IV., Sir Joseph Banks, Blake, Adam, Liardet, Tschitchagoff (a Russian admiral), and Vernon. The upper hall also contains glass-cases with relics of Nelson, including the coat and waistcoat he wore at Trafalgar, when he received his death wound; the coat he wore at the battle of the Nile; his watch; his pig tail, cut off after death; an autograph letter; and a Turkish gun and sabre presented to him after the battle of the Nile. — The Nelson Room (to the left of the upper hall) contains pictures by West and others in honour of the heroic Admiral, a series of portraits of his contemporaries, portraits of General Barrington by *Reynolds* and Admiral Hope (d. 1881) by *Hodges*; the silken hangings of Nelson's hammock, etc.

In the S.E. or Queen Mary edifice is the Chapel, which contains an altarpiece by *West*, representing the shipwreck of St. Paul, and monuments of Adm. Sir R. Keats, by *Chantrey*, and Adm. Sir Thomas Hardy, by *Behnes*.

The Royal Naval Museum, in the W. or King Charles wing and the E. or Queen Anne wing (admission free), contains models of ships, rigging, and various apparatus; relics of the Franklin expedition; mementoes of Nelson; a model of the Battle of Trafalgar; a number of paintings and drawings, etc.

At the *Royal Naval School*, lying between the hospital and Greenwich Park, 1000 children of English seamen are educated (800 boys and 200 girls).

To the S. of Greenwich is *Greenwich Park (Pl. G, 3), 174 acres in extent, laid out during the reign of Charles II. by the celebrated *Le Nôtre*. The park, with its fine old chestnuts and hawthorns (in blossom in May) and herds of tame deer, is a favourite resort of Londoners of the middle classes on Sundays and holidays, particularly on Good Friday, Easter Monday, and Whitsun-Monday. A hill in the centre, 180 ft. in height, is crowned by the famous Greenwich *Royal Observatory* (no admission), from the meridian of which English astronomers make their calculations. The correct time for the whole of England is settled here every day at 1 p.m. ; a large coloured ball descends many feet, and the time is telegraphed hence to the most important towns throughout the country. A standard clock (with the hours numbered from 1 to 24) and various standard measures of length are fixed just outside the entrance, *pro bono publico*. The terrace in front of the observatory and the other elevated portions of the park command an extensive and varied view over the river, bristling with the masts of vessels all the way to London, over the Hainault and Epping Forests, backed by the hills of Hampstead, and over the plain extending to the N. of the Thames and intersected by docks and canals.

On the S. and S.E., Greenwich Park is bounded by *Blackheath*, where Wat Tyler and Jack Cade once assembled the rebellious 'men of Kent', grown impatient under hard deprivations, for the purpose of attacking the metropolis, and where belated travellers were not unfrequently robbed in former times. Blackheath is now much frequented by golfers.

## 32. Woolwich.

**Woolwich**, also situated on the Thames, 9 M. below London, may be reached by a steamboat of the Victoria Steamboat Company (fares 6d. and 4d.); or by the *North Kent Railway* (stations, *New Cross*, *St. John's*, *Lewisham*, *Blackheath*, *Charlton*) from Charing Cross, Cannon Street, or London Bridge; or, lastly, by the *Great Eastern Railway* from Liverpool Street or Fenchurch Street. A free ferry, opened in March, 1889, connects Woolwich with North Woolwich. Pop. (1881) 80,782.

The ROYAL ARSENAL, one of the most imposing establishments in existence for the manufacture of materials of war, is shown on Tuesdays and Thursdays between 10 and 12, and 2 and 4, by tickets, obtained at the War Office, Pall Mall. Foreigners must receive special permission by application through their ambassador. The chief departments are the *Gun Factory*, established in 1716 by a German named Schalch (the new Woolwich guns are not cast, but formed of wrought-iron bars); the *Laboratory* for making cartridges and projectiles; and the *Gun-carriage and Waggon Department*. The arsenal covers an area of 100 acres, and affords employment to 10,000 men. The magazines, which extend along the Thames for nearly a mile, contain enormous stores of war materials.

To the W. of the arsenal, and higher up the slope, lie the *Royal Marine Barracks*, eight buildings connected by a corridor, and containing a battalion of marines. Still higher up, opposite Woolwich Common, are the *Royal Artillery Barracks*, 1200 ft. in length, with accommodation for 4000 men and 1000 horses. In front of the building are placed several pieces of ordnance from India and the Crimea, including a cannon $16^{1}/_{2}$ ft. long, cast in 1677 for the Emperor Aurungzebe, and 'looted' at Bhurtpore; four Florentine guns of 1750; and specimens of armour-plating penetrated by shots.

The *Royal Military Academy*, established in 1719, and transferred in 1806 to the present building on Woolwich Common, trains cadets for the Engineers or Artillery.

On the N.W. side **of the Common** stands the *Royal Military Repository*, or *Rotunda* (113 ft. in diameter), built by Nash in 1814, containing **a military museum, with models of fortifications and designs and specimens of** modern **artillery (open to the public** daily **from 10 to 5).**

The *Dockyard*, established by Henry VIII. in 1532, has been **closed since 1st Oct., 1869.** — The extensive *Telegraphic Works* of *Siemens Brothers*, where submarine cables are made, are worth visiting (special **card of admission necessary**, to be procured only at the London office, 12 Queen Anne's Gate, by visitors provided with an introduction).

About 1½ M. to the S. of Woolwich Common rises *Shooter's Hill*, **a conspicuous eminence, commanding an** extensive and charming **view of the richly-wooded plains of Kent.**

## 33. The Crystal Palace at Sydenham.

**Trains for the** Crystal Palace leave *London Bridge Station* (p. 35), **Ludgate Hill Station (p. 34),** *Holborn Viaduct Station* (p. 34), and **Victoria Station (p. 33) nearly** every ¼ hr. Fares from each of these **stations, 1s. 3d., 1s., and 7d.;** return-tickets **2s., 1s. 6d.,** 1s. **Admission to the Palace 1s.; annual** season-ticket 21s. Return-tickets **including the price of admission are issued at** the railway stations, **and cost (on the 1s. days) 2s.** 6d., **2s., and 1s. 6d.** On the dates of **the Saturday concerts** in winter **and other special occasions,** duly **advertised in the** newspapers **beforehand, the prices are raised.** Children **under 12** years of **age pay half-price. Trains also run from** all **stations on the North London Railway, but by** a very circuitous **route, viâ Hampstead Heath, Willesden Junction,** and Kensington; and **visitors will do better to book through from** the stations of the Metropolitan lines. The **Palace is opened** at 10 a.m., and **closed at** 7.30 p.m. in winter (except on nights **when the** interior of the Palace is illuminated) and **at 10 p.m.** in summer, when illuminated **garden fêtes are a great feature (comp. p.** 311).

A hasty visit to the Palace and gardens, including **the** journey **there and back,** occupies **at least half-a-day. Meals** may be taken **at the Palace, where there are good restaurants with** various charges, **from the Third** Class Refreshment Rooms **in the** S. Basement **upwards. Refreshments may be obtained at** any of the counters distributed **throughout the building, and there are** also public and private **dining-rooms** in three or four different parts of the Palace.

BAEDEKER. London. 7th Edit.

## 33. THE CRYSTAL PALACE AT SYDENHAM.

**The Palace also** contains a library and reading-room (adjoining the transept in the N.E. section, admission 1*d.*), letter-boxes, lavatories, railway time-tables, shoe-blacks, a hair-cutting room, and other conveniences. If fatigued, the visitor may hire a wheel-chair and attendant at the rate of 1*s.* 6*d.* an hour.

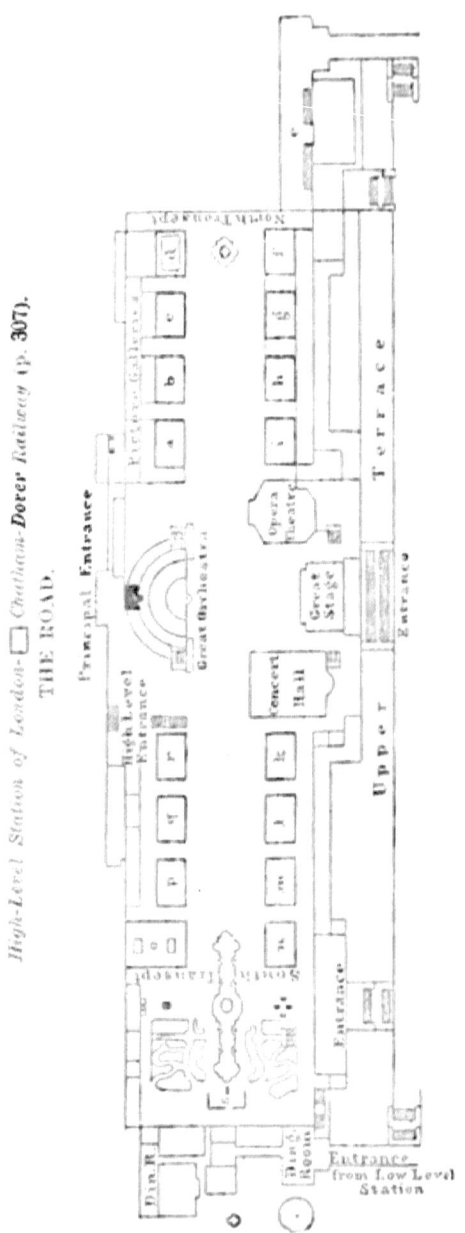

The Crystal Palace at Sydenham, designed by *Sir Joseph Paxton*, consists entirely of glass and iron. It was constructed mainly with the materials of the first great Industrial Exhibition of 1851, and was opened in 1854. It is composed of a spacious central hall or nave, 1608 ft. long, with lateral sections, two aisles, and two transepts. (A third transept at the N. end was burned down in 1866.) The central transept is 390 ft. long, 120 ft. broad, and 175 ft. high; the S. transept is 312 ft. long, 72 ft. broad, and 110 ft. high. The two water-towers at the ends (Pl. kk) are 282 ft. in height. The cost of the whole undertaking, including the magnificent garden and grounds, and much additional land outside, amounted to a million and a half sterling.

ENTRANCES. (1.) The *Low Level Station* of the Brighton and South Coast Railway, and of the South London Line (London Bridge, **Crystal** Palace, Wandsworth, Victoria Station), is on the S.E. side **of the Palace,** and connected with it by a glass gallery. We pay **at the entrance of the gallery,** which also communicates directly with **the garden and terrace of the Palace.** — (2.) From the *High Level Station* of the London, Chatham, and Dover Line (Victoria Terminus **or Holborn** Viaduct Station), on the W. side of the Palace, we pass **through the subway to the right,** and ascend the staircase, where **we observe the notice 'To the Palace only',** leading direct to the W. **portion of the Palace. If we leave the subway** on the right, and **ascend the stairs past the booking-office, we reach a broad** road at **the top, on the other side of which is the principal entrance in the central transept (Pl. bb).** — Those who approach from Dulwich (p. 312) alight at Sydenham Hill Station, 1/2 M. from the Palace.

The Crystal **Palace is of such vast extent, that in** our limited **space we can only give a brief outline of its arrangements.** A **fuller description will be found in the official** *Guide*, which is sold **at the Palace (price 1s.; smaller guide-books** 2d., programme for **the day 2d.). The chief objects of interest are most conveniently visited in the** following **order (comp. Plan).**

Approaching from the **Low Level Station (see above) through the glass arcade,** 720 ft. in length, we first enter the *S. Transept*, whence, **opposite the great partition** (Pl. s), we **obtain a** good general survey **of the** Palace (better still from **the gallery** above **the partition).** The effect produced by the **contrast between** the green foliage of the plants, distributed along the whole of the nave, and the white **forms of the statuary to which they form a background, is most pleasing. Behind the statues are the richly-coloured façades of the courts, and high above is the light and airy glass vaulting of the roof. The whole presents, at a single** *coup d'œil*, **a magnificent and unique view of the art and culture of nations which are widely** separated from **each other in time and space.**

In order **to obtain a general idea of the arrangements of the** Palace we **walk to the opposite end of the nave, and then** visit **the various courts, beginning with the Egyptian Court on the** N.W. **side of the central transept.**

In the SOUTH TRANSEPT **we first observe, in** recesses in the partition mentioned **above (adjoining which** are refreshment rooms, **see p. 305), a series of plaster casts of** the statues **of** English **monarchs in the Houses of Parliament** (see p. 185). The equestrian **statue of** Queen Victoria in the middle of the transept is by **Marochetti. A** little beyond it **is** a water-basin containing the ***Crystal Fountain* (by** Osler), which once adorned the original Crystal **Palace of 1851** in Hyde Park, and is now embellished with **aquatic plants and ferns.** The casts from modern sculptures are arranged **for the most part** in the S. nave and transept, and those from the antique in the N. half of the building. On the left (W.) of the **Central Transept** is the great *Händel Orchestra*, which can accommodate 4000 persons, and has a diameter (216 ft.) twice as great as the dome of St. Paul's. In the middle is the powerful organ, with 4384 pipes, built by Gray & Davison at a cost of 6000 *l.* and worked by hydraulic machinery (a performance usually given in the afternoon; organist, Mr. A. J. Eyre). Opposite, at the garden end of the transept, is the *Great Stage*. The *Concert Hall*, on the S. side of the stage, can accommodate an audience of 4000. An excellent orchestra plays here daily (at present on Mon. at 12.30 and 4. Tues. and Thurs. at 12.30, Wed. at 3.30, and Frid. at 4), and admirable concerts are given every Saturday from October to April (conductor, Mr. August **Manns**). The *Opera House*, on the N., opposite the Concert Hall, accommodates 2000 persons, and is used for plays and pantomimes as well as for operas.

On each side of the nave is a range of so-called \*Courts, containing copies of the architecture and sculpture of the most highly civilised nations, from the earliest period to the present day, arranged in chronological order.

**Egyptian Court** (Pl. a), with imitations of ancient Egyptian architecture. The small room with the fluted columns is a reproduction of the rock tomb of Beni Hassan. Adjoining it is the pillared Hall of Karnak; behind, in the recess, the tomb of Abû Simbel in Nubia. The chamber situated next the nave, with **the avenue of lions in front** of it, **is a model of a** temple of the period of the Ptolemies (B.C. 300). On the wall to the left are pictorial representations from **the great Temple** of Ramses III. at Thebes; on the right, **the storming of a fortress and a battle.**

The **Greek Court** (Pl. b) **contains** portions of Greek buildings and casts of Greek sculpture. In the centre of the front room **are two copies of the Venus of Milo,** one showing the pose of the original figure as set up in the Louvre in 1820, the **other the amended pose of the statue as re-erected** after the Franco-German War. The contents of this room also include the Laocoon, the Genius of Death, the Ludovisi Mars, the Discus-thrower, and the Vatican Ariadne. The *Atrium* to the W. of this contains a model of the Acropolis, while the Gallery at the back reveals casts of the Elgin marbles in the British Museum, the Niobe group, etc.

The **Roman Court** (Pl. c) contains casts of the most celebrated objects **of art of the Roman period: the** Apollo Belvedere, the Diana of Versailles, **the Venuses of** Arles, Florence, and Naples (Kallipygos), busts **of the** Emperors, etc. In the centre are models of the Pantheon **and the Colosseum** at Rome, restored, and of the Roman Forum in **its present condition.** — Adjoining is a cabinet with views of Pompeii.

Next comes the **Alhambra Court** (Pl. d), a copy of part of the Alhambra, the Moorish palace at Granada. Approaching from the

## 33. THE CRYSTAL PALACE AT SYDENHAM.

nave, we first enter the *Court of the Lions*, and then the *Hall of Justice*, whence we pass into the *Hall of the Abencerrages* (in the centre). To the right and left are smaller apartments. This **court was injured by the** fire of 1866, but has been restored.

**The North Transept,** which once formed a palm-house of **imposing dimen**sions, was destroyed by fire on 31st Dec. 1866, and has not been restored. This end **of the** Palace, like the other, **boasts** of a handsome *Fountain **with a basin** of aquatic plants. **From this part of the building** a staircase descends to the right by **the buffet into the** *Aquarium (Pl. e), **which contains** an admirable **collection of salt-water and shell fish. There is a skating rink** in **the same part of the palace.**

We now proceed past the North Transept to the E. side of the nave, where we first enter the Byzantine and Romanesque Court (Pl. f), with specimens of architecture and sculpture of various **dates from the 6th to the 13th** century. At the entrance is a **fragment of a cloister from the Church** of St. Maria im Capitol at Cologne; **in the centre a fountain from the Abbey** of Heisterbach in the Seven **Mountains. Also the Fontevrault effigies;** a piece of **sculpture from** the Baptistery of **St. Mark at Venice;** above, an **arcade** from the church **at Gelnhausen;** Norman portal from the church of Kilpeck, in **Herefordshire; the** doors of the cathedral of Hildesheim, of 1015; also **those of Ely Cathedral, and of the church of** Shobden, Herefordshire.

The following three **Mediæval Courts (Pl. g)** contain copies of **buildings, ornaments, and monuments of the Gothic** period (12th-**16th cent.). The first** is devoted **to German Gothic,** the second to English, **and the third to** French. The English Court is particularly **rich and interesting.** The *Norman-Romanesque Style*, with its **semicircular, horse-shoe arches and indented columnar** ornamentation, the *Early English Style* **(13th cent.), the** *Decorated* or *Developed Gothic* (14th cent.), the *Perpendicular* or *Late Gothic*, and the *Tudor Style* are **all represented in this court by** numerous **reproductions** of original **buildings.**

The adjacent Renaissance Court (Pl. h) contains, at the W. entrance, **an arched gateway from the Hôtel** du Bourgtheroulde at **Rouen** (beginning **of the 16th cent.); in the** centre, a fountain from **the Château de Gaillon in Normandy;** **two** fountains from the Doge's Palace at Venice; altar from the Certosa, near Pavia (1473); opposite, the celebrated **doors of** the Baptistery at Florence, by L. r. Ghiberti (1420); **statues and reliefs by Donatello,** Della Robbia, etc.

The adjoining Elizabethan Vestibule contains architectural specimens of the English Renaissance of the time of Queen Elisabeth (end of the 16th, and beginning of the 17th cent.), chiefly from Holland **House,** Kensington, and a number of monuments **from** Westminster Abbey (p. 193) and the Temple Church (p. 130).

The **Italian** Court (Pl. i), the last hall of this department, represents part of the Palazzo Farnese at Rome, which was completed under the direction of Michael Angelo. The loggia or arcade on the S. side contains copies of Raphael's celebrated frescoes in the Vatican; also a number of works by Michael Angelo, including the monument of Giuliano de' Medici with the celebrated figures of Day and Night. Opposite, by the N. arcade, is the monument of Lorenzo de' Medici. The Pietà, and the colossal Moses in the division behind, rank among Michael Angelo's finest works. — The ITALIAN VESTIBULE recalls the Casa Taverna at Milan, and contains an excellent model of St. Peter's at Rome.

On the S. side of the Central Transept, which we now traverse, begin the *Industrial Courts*, most of the objects in which are for sale. We first observe, next to the Concert Hall, the FRENCH COURT (Pl. k), now used as an afternoon tea room; then a COURT (Pl. l) containing scientific instruments and books; next, the FABRICS COURT (Pl. m); and then the GLASS AND CHINA COURT (Pl. n). Behind these four courts is the *Carriage Department*, where vehicles of every description are exhibited.

We have now again reached the South Transept. Among the shrubberies around the water-basin mentioned at p. 307 are groups of figures representing the different races of mankind, stuffed animals, and other objects. On the W. side is the POMPEIAN COURT, which is intended to represent a Roman house of the reign of Titus, having been carefully copied, both in form and pictorial decoration, from a building excavated at Pompeii a few years ago. The pavement at the entrance shows the figure of a dog in mosaic, with the inscription 'Cave canem', such as was frequently found in Roman houses. A small passage (passing small rooms for porters and slaves on the right and left) leads to the 'atrium', or public reception court, with a rectangular water-basin ('impluvium') in the centre, and 'cubicula' or dormitories around it. Next comes the 'tablinum', which contained the art treasures of the house. Beyond is the 'ambulatorium' and the garden, round which are dining and dressing rooms, the sleeping chamber of the master of the house, the kitchen, and other rooms.

Two of the three courts between the Roman House and the Central Transept are devoted to industrial products.

The MANUFACTURING COURT (Pl. q) shows interesting processes of manufacture, including a steam loom for ornamental weaving.

The ENTERTAINMENT COURT (Pl. r) is used for small entertainments, lectures, etc.

Ascending now to the GALLERY, by a staircase near the Central Transept (W. side), we reach the collection of OIL AND WATERCOLOUR PAINTINGS, which includes some fine modern works. On the opposite side of the Orchestra we observe the PORTRAIT GALLERY, consisting of a series of busts of eminent men of all nations. The N. portion of the same (E.) gallery is occupied by a Museum.

The South-Eastern and South Galleries are filled with stalls for the sale of trinkets, toys, millinery, confectionery, and knickknacks of all sorts. The Palace also possesses a gymnasium, the Würtemberg collection of stuffed animals, a camera obscura, and many other attractions of which it is needless to give an exhaustive list.

The chief exit from the Crystal Palace into the *Gardens is in the S. basement, below the Central Transept; they may also be entered from the covered arcade leading to the Palace from the Low Level Station (p. 307), or by any one of the small side-doors in different parts of the building. The Gardens, covering an area of 200 acres, and laid out in terraces in the Italian and English styles, are tastefully embellished with flower-beds, shrubberies, fountains, cascades, and statuary. The numerous seats offer grateful repose after the fatigue of a walk through the Palace. At the head of the broad walk is a monument to Sir Joseph Paxton, surmounted by a colossal bust by *Woodington*. The FOUNTAINS are the finest in the world. The two large fountains in the lower basin throw their jets to a height of 280 ft., and the central jet in the upper basin reaches a height of 150 ft. On the occasion of a 'grand display of the fountains', which only takes place at rare intervals, 120,000 gallons of water are thrown up per minute. A great display of fireworks (by Messrs. C. T. Brock & Co.) takes place every Thursday evening in summer, often attracting 10-20,000 visitors. The *GEOLOGICAL DEPARTMENT in the S.E. portion of the park, by the Great Pond, is extremely interesting and should not be overlooked. It contains full-size models of antediluvian animals, — the Megalosaurus, Ichthyosaurus, Pterodactyl, Palæotherium, Megatherium, and the Irish Elk (found in the Isle of Man) — together with the contemporaneous geological formations. — The N.E. part of the park is laid out as a CRICKET GROUND, and on summer afternoons the game attracts numerous spectators. The *Lawn Tennis Courts* are also here. At the end of the N. terrace are a bear-pit, monkey-house, and aviaries; and the gardens also contain open-air gymnasia, 'roller coaster' and 'switchback' railways, an archery-ground, swings, etc. Near the Rosery is a *Panorama of the Battle of Tell el-Kebir*, by Philippoteaux (adm. 6d.). The S. great fountain-basin is spanned by a facsimile, on a scale of one-fourth, of the Tower Bridge (p. 112).

The highest *Terrace*, the balustrade of which is embellished with 26 marble statues representing the chief countries and most important cities in the world, affords a magnificent view of the park and of the rich scenery of the county of Kent. The prospect is still more extensive from the platform of the N. Tower, which rises to a height of 282 ft. above the level of the lowest basins, and is ascended by a winding staircase; it extends into six counties and embraces the whole course of the Thames.

## 34. DULWICH.

In the London Road, Forest Hill, about 1¼ M. from the Crystal Palace and the same distance from the Dulwich Gallery (see below), is the *Surrey House Museum*, a private collection belonging to Mr. F. J. Horniman, which is open to visitors on previous application by letter to the curator (no fees). The collections include objects of natural history, china and porcelain, ethnographical curiosities, historical relics, carved furniture, etc.; and visitors are also admitted to the pleasant grounds and to the view-tower. The Museum is about 3 min. walk from *Lordship Lane*, on the London, Chatham, & Dover Railway, and 5 min. walk from *Forest Hill*, on the London, Brighton, & South Coast Railway.

## 34. Dulwich.

A little to the N. of the Crystal Palace, at a distance of 5 M. from London, lies **Dulwich College**, in the village of the same name, a large charitable and educational institution, famous for its valuable *Picture Gallery*. This collection was formed by *Noël Desenfans*, a picture-dealer in London, by desire of Stanislaus, King of Poland, but in consequence of the partition of Poland it remained in the possession of the collector. It was afterwards acquired by *Sir P. J. Bourgeois*, the painter (d. 1811), who bequeathed it to God's Gift College at Dulwich, which was founded by Alleyne, the actor, a friend of Shakspeare. Along with the pictures Bourgeois left 12,000*l*. for their maintenance and the erection of a suitable building to contain them. The Picture Gallery is open daily, Sundays excepted, from 10 to 5 in summer (till 7 in June, July, & Aug.), and from 10 to 4 in winter (free).

Dulwich is most conveniently reached from Victoria Station, in 20 min., or Ludgate Hill Station, in 25-30 min. (fares 9*d*., 7*d*., 5*d*.; return-tickets, 1*s*., 10*d*., 8*d*.). We leave the station by a flight of steps on the E., at the foot of which we turn to the right. After proceeding for about 100 paces we observe in front of us the *New College*, a handsome red brick building in the Renaissance style. Here we take the broad road to the left (Gallery Road), and in 5 min. more reach, on the right, the entrance to the Gallery, indicated by a notice on a lamp-post. The scenery around is very pleasing, and the excursion an interesting one.

This collection possesses a few excellent Spanish works by *Velazquez* (1599-1660) and (more especially) his pupil *Murillo* (1618-1682), and also some good examples of the **French** school (particularly *N. Poussin*, 1594-1665, and *Watteau*, 1684-1721); while, among Italian schools, later masters only (such as the Academic school of the Carracci at Bologna) are represented. The small pictures catalogued as by Raphael have been, unfortunately, freely retouched. The glory of the gallery, however, consists in its admirable collection of Dutch paintings, several masters being excellently illustrated both in number and quality. For instance, no collection in the world possesses so many paintings by *Albert Cuyp* (1605-1672), the great Dutch landscape and animal painter, as the Dulwich Gallery (seventeen, two of which, Nos. 189 and 68, are doubtful). The chief power of Cuyp, who has been named the Dutch Claude, lies in his brilliant and picturesque treatment of atmosphere and light. Similar in style are the works of the brothers *Jan* and *Andrew Both*, also well represented in this gallery, who resided in Italy and imitated Claude. Andrew supplied the figures to the landscapes of his brother Jan (Utrecht, 1610-1656). The ten examples of *Philip Wouwerman* (Haarlem, 1620-1668), the most eminent Dutch painter of battles and **hunting scenes**, include specimens of **his early** manner (Nos. 65 and 156), **as well as others** exhibiting the brilliant effects of his later period. Among the **fine examples** of numerous other masters, two genuine works by *Rembrandt* (1607-1669) are conspicuous (Nos. 189 and 206). About twenty **pictures here were formerly assigned** to *Rubens* (1577-1641), but traces of an inferior hand are visible in most of them. Among the works of Flemish masters the large canvasses of Rubens' rival *Van Dyck* (†, †† 1641), and those of *Teniers the Elder* (Antwerp, 1582-1649) and *Teniers the Younger* (1610-1694), call for special notice. The specimens of the last-named, one of the most prominent of all genre painters, will in particular well repay examination. — Catalogue, by J. P. Richter and J. Sparkes.

Room I. On the left: 334. *Bolognese School*, St. Cecilia; 9. *Cuyp*, Landscape **with cattle**; 5. *Cuyp*. Cows and sheep, an early work; 89. *W. von Romeyn* (Utrecht, pupil of Berchem; d. 1662), Landscapes with figures; *30, 199. 205, 41. *Jan* and *Andrew Both*, **Landscapes** with figures and cattle; 16, 15. *Bartolommeo Breenberg* (of Utrecht, settled in Rome; d. 1610. Small landscapes; 14. *Corn. Poelemburg* (Utrecht; d. 1666), Dancing nymph; 112. *Adrian van der Neer* (Amsterdam; d. 1691). Moonlight scene; 153. *61. *Teniers the **Younger**, Landscapes with figures; 52. *Teniers the Elder*, Cottage and figures; '64, '63. *Wouwerman*, Landscapes.

104. *Corn. Dusart* (Haarlem. d. 1704). Old building, with figures.
'A remarkably careful and choice picture by this scholar of Adrian van Ostade, who approaches **nearest to his master in the glow** of his colouring'. — *Waagen*.

107. *Adrian van Ostade* (Haarlem; d. 1685), Interior of a cottage with **figures**; *36. *Both*, Landscape; 84. *Teniers the Younger*, Cottage with figures; 85. *Brekelenkamp*, Old woman **eating porridge**; 72. *Adrian van de Velde* (Amsterdam; d. 1672), Landscape **with cattle**; 86. *Teniers the Younger*, Cottage **with figures**; *106. *Gerard Dou*, Lady playing on a keyed instrument; 319. *Le Brun*, Horatius Cocles **defending the bridge**; 50. *Teniers the Younger*, Guard-room; 329 *Spanish School*, Christ bearing the cross; *111. *Cuyp*, Interior of a riding-school. — The room to the left of R. I. contains the *Cartwright Collection of Portraits*.

Room II. On the left: 93. *Wouwerman*. View near Scheveningen, **early work**; 113. *Willem van de Velde the Younger* (Amsterdam; d. 1707). Calm; 156. *Cuyp*, Two horses; *125. 173, 126. *Wouwerman*, Landscapes **with figures**; 124. *Van Dyck*, Charity; 229. *Karel du Jardin* (Amsterdam, pupil of Berchem, painted at Rome; d. 1678), Smith shoeing an ox; *131. *Meindert Hobbema* (Amsterdam; d. 1709), Landscape with a water-mill; 130. *Adam Pynacker* (of Pynacker, near Delft, settled in Italy; d. 1673), Landscape with sportsmen; 135. *Van Dyck*, Virgin and Infant Saviour (repetitions at Dresden and elsewhere); 137. *Wouwerman*, Farrier and an old **convent** (engraved under the title 'Le Colombier du Maréchal'); 139. *Teniers the Younger*, A château with the family of the proprietor. 141. *Cuyp*, Landscape with figures; *144. *Wouwerman*, Halt of travellers. *166. *W. van de Velde*, Brisk gale off the Texel.
'A warm evening light, happily blended with the delicate silver **tone of the master**, and of the most exquisite finish in all the parts, makes **this one** of **his most charming** pictures.' — *W*.

*147. *Jan Weenix* (Amsterdam, 1640-1719, son and pupil of *Jan Baptist Weenix*), Landscape with accessories, dated 1664; *1. *Adrian Brouwer* (Haarlem, pupil of F. Hals, d. 1640), Interior of an ale-house, a genuine specimen of a scarce master; 151. *Ruysdael*, Waterfall painted in an unusually broad manner; 190. *A. van Ostade*, Boors making merry.

astonishing depth, clearness, and warmth of colour'; 12. 11. *Jan Wynants* (Haarlem, d. 1677), Landscapes; 140. *Jan van Huysum* (Amsterdam, d. 1749), Flowers; 460. *Nic. Berchem* (Haarlem, d. 1683), Wood scene; 168. School of *Rubens*, Samson and Delilah; \*163, \*\*169. *Cuyp*, Landscapes with cattle and figures; 182. *Rubens*, Portrait; 176. *Unknown Master*, **Landscape with cattle**; 159. *Salvator Rosa* (Naples and Rome; d. 1673), **Landscape; 178.** *Unknown Master of Haarlem*, Landscape with figures; **358.** *Gainsborough*, **Portrait of** Thomas Linley; 116. *Teniers the Younger*, **Winter-scene.**

Room III. On the left: \*60. *Teniers the Younger*, Sow and pigs; 191. *Adrian van der Werff* (court painter to the Elector Palatine; d. 1722), Judgment of Paris; 241. *Ruysdael*, **Landscape** with mills.

194. *Velazquez*, Portrait of the **Prince of Asturias**, son **of Philip IV.,** a copy of the original at Madrid.

*Antoine Watteau* (Paris, d. 1721), \*210. Le bal champêtre; \*197. La fête champêtre. 277. **German School**, **Salvator Mundi**; 200, 209. *Berchem*, Landscapes; \*205. **Rembrandt**, **A girl at a window**; \*196. *Jan van der Heyde* (Amsterdam, d. 1712), Landscape, figures by *A. van de Velde*; 213. After *Van Dyck*, **Portrait**; 145. **Cuyp**, **Winter scene**; 225. *Wouwerman*, **Landscape**.

**359.** *Sir Thos. Lawrence* (d. 1830), Portrait of Wm. Linley, the author; 183. *Northcote*, Sir P. J. Bourgeois (p. 312); 150. *Pynacker*, Landscape with figures; **238.** *G. Schalcken*, Ceres at the old woman's cottage, from Ovid; 239, **243.** *Cuyp*, Landscapes near Dort, with cattle; 212. *Van Dyck*, Lady Venetia Digby, taken after death; 226. *Italian Master*, Venus gathering apples in the garden of the Hesperides; \*189. *Rembrandt*, Portrait, early work, painted in 1632; 186. *W. van de Velde*, Calm.

Room IV. On the left: \*248. *Murillo*, Spanish flower-girl; 252. *Charles le Brun* (pupil of N. Poussin; d. 1690), Massacre of the Innocents; \*244. *Claude*, **Landscape**, with Jacob and Laban ('one of the most genuine Claudes I know', writes Mr. Ruskin); 278. *Wynants* (ascribed to *Ruysdael*), Landscape, with **figures by** *A. van de Velde*; 269. *Gaspar Poussin* (pupil of N. Poussin; d. 1675), **Destruction of** Niobe **and her** children; \*275. *Claude Lorrain* (d. 1682), Italian seaport; 271. *Salvator Rosa*, Soldiers gaming ('very spirited, and **in a** deep glowing tone'); 270. *Claude*, Embarkation of St. Paula at Ostia.

\*283. *Murillo*, Two Spanish peasant boys and a negro boy.

'Very natural **and** animated, defined in **the** forms, and painted in a golden warm tone'. — *W.*

\*286. *Murillo*, **Two** Spanish **peasant** boys. *N. Poussin*, 291. Adoration **of the Magi; 295.** Inspiration **of a poet.** 335. *Annibale Carracci* (Bologna; **d. 1609), Virgin, Infant** Christ, **and St.** John *N. Poussin*, 300. Education **of Jupiter; 305. Triumph of** David; 315. Rinaldo and Armida, from Tasso; 310. **Flight** into Egypt. \*306, \*307. **Raphael**, 88. Antony of Padua and Francis **of** Assisi (retouched); 337. *Carlo* **Dolci** (Bologna, d. 1686), Mater **Dolorosa;** \*83. *Cuyp*, Landscape **with** figures (bright and calm sunlight); **365.** *Antonio Belucci* (d. 1726), **St.** Sebastian with **Faith and Charity;** 309. *Velazquez*, Portrait of Philip IV. of Spain.

Room V. On the left: 327. *Andrea del Sarto* (d. 1530), Holy Family (repetition **of a picture in** the Pitti Palace at Florence, and ascribed by Mr. Crowe to Salviati); 287. **Umbrian School,** Virgin and Child; 331. *Guido Reni* (d. 1642), **St. John in the wilderness**; 336. *N. Poussin*, Assumption of the Virgin; 240. **Van Dyck (ascribed to** *Rubens*), **The** Graces; 343. After *Cristofano Allori* (d. 1621), **Judith with** the head of Holofernes; 339. *G. Reni*, St. Sebastian; 333. **Paolo Veronese** (d. 1583), Cardinal blessing a donor; 317 *Murillo*, La Madonna **del Rosario;** 349. *Domenichino*, Adoration of the Shepherds; 351. *Rubens*, **Venus, Mars,** and Cupid, **a late** work; 355. School of *Rubens*, Rubens's mother.

Room VI. On the left: 110, 111. **Vernet**, Landscapes; 361. *Gainsborough*, Samuel Linley; 46. *Teniers* **the** *Elder*, Landscape with shepherd and sheep; 53, 89. *Loutherbourg*, Landscapes; 366. **Gainsborough**, **Mrs.** Moodey and her two children; 310. Sir *Joshua Reynolds* (d. 1792), Mrs. Siddons as the Tragic Muse, painted in 1789. — \*1. *Gainsborough*, Portraits of Mrs. Sheridan and Mrs. Tickell, the daughters of Thomas Linley.

Mrs. Tickell sits on a bank, while Mrs. Sheridan stands half behind her. Waagen characterises this work as one of the best specimens of the master, and Mrs. Jameson says: 'The head of Mrs. Sheridan is exquisite, and, without having all the beauty which Sir Joshua gave her in the famous St. Cecilia, there is even more mind.'
215. *Wilson*, Tivoli; 113. *Reynolds*, Mother and sick child; 31. *Teniers the Elder*, Landscape, with the Magdalene.

'102. *Daniel Seghers* (Antwerp; d. 1661). Flowers encircling a bas-relief. **'A very** admirable picture of this master, so justly celebrated in his **own times, and** whose red **roses still** flourish in their original beauty, **while those of the later painters,** De Heem, Huysum, and Rachel Ruysch, **have more or less changed. The vase is** probably by Erasmus Quellinus' — *Waagen*.

355. *Teniers the Elder*, Landscape, with the repentant Peter; 3 *. *Gainsborough*, Son of Thomas Linley.

Dulwich **College, a separate building, contains** other old portraits. In the chapel **is the tomb of Alleyne, the founder.** — About 5 min. walk beyond **the Picture Gallery is the \*Greyhound Inn.**

## 35. Hampton Court. Richmond. Kew.

These places are **frequently visited on a Sunday, as the Palace** of Hampton **Court, with its fine picture-gallery, is almost the only resort of the kind in or about London which is not closed on that day.**

One of the best ways to make this excursion is to go to Hampton **Court by** railway; to walk through **Hampton Court** Gardens and **Bushy** Park to **the** Teddington **station; to take the train** thence to **Richmond,** and **to return to London, viâ Kew, on the top of an omnibus; or,** if **time permit, we may return by steamboat** from Kew **(1½-2 hrs. ; fare to Chelsea 1s., thence to London Bridge 3d.).** Some **of the coaches mentioned at p. 32 pass through Hampton** Court. **Omnibuses, chars-a-bancs, and brakes ply frequently on** Sun. **afternoon from Charing Cross, Piccadilly,** etc., **to Kew (**1s.**), Richmond (1s. 6d), and Hampton Court (2s.** 6d.**).**

Another pleasant round, involving more walking, is as follows: by **train to Richmond; drive viâ Strawberry Hill to** Teddington; walk through **Bushy Park** to Hampton **Court and through Richmond** Park to Richmond **then back** to London **by train.**

RAILWAY. **We may travel by the** *South Western* Railway from *Waterloo Station* **to** *Hampton Court*; or by the *North London Railway* **from** *Broad Street*, **City (**comp. p. 34**)** to *Kew*, *Richmond*, **and** *Teddington* (p. 321); or by the *Metropolitan District Railway* **from** the *Mansion House*, *Charing Cross*, *Victoria*, *Westminster*, or *Kensington* to *Richmond*, and thence to *Teddington*.

The SOUTH WESTERN RAILWAY (from Waterloo Station to Hampton Court ¾ hr.; fares 2s., 1s. 6d., 1s. 3d.) runs for a considerable **distance on a viaduct above the streets of London.** Vauxhall, **the first station, is still within the town; but we emerge from its** precincts near *Clapham Junction*, the second station. The first **glimpse of the** pretty scenery traversed by the line is obscured after **passing through the** long cutting beyond Clapham. The landscape, **bordered on** the N. **by** gently sloping hills, and dotted with groups of magnificent trees and numerous comfortable-looking country-houses, affords a charming and thoroughly English picture. — 7½ M. *Wimbledon* lies a little to the S. of *Wimbledon Common*, where the great volunteer rifle-shooting competition was held annually down to 1889 (henceforth to be at Bisley, near Woking). *Wimbledon House* was once occupied by Calonne, the French minister, and afterwards by the Duc d'Enghien, who was shot at Vincennes in 1804. About ¾ M. from the station is a well-preserved fortified camp of cruciform shape, probably of Saxon origin.

Beyond Wimbledon a line diverges to the left to *Epsom*, near which are *Epsom Downs*, where the great races, the 'Derby' and the 'Oaks', take place annually in May or June (see p. 46). Before reaching (10 M.) *Coombe-Malden*, we pass, on a height to the right, *Coombe House*, formerly the property of Lord Liverpool, who in 1815, when Prime Minister, entertained the Emperor of Russia, the King of Prussia, and the Prince Regent here. About 2 M. beyond (12 M.) *Surbiton* the branch-line to Hampton Court diverges to the right from the main line, passing *Thames Ditton*, pleasantly situated in a grassy neighbourhood.

On arriving at **Hampton Court** (*Castle, Prince of Wales*, at the station; *Mitre*, beyond the bridge; *King's Arms, Greyhound*, first-class inns, at the entrance to Bushy Park; *Park Cottage; Queen's Arms*, D. from 1s. 6d.), we turn to the right, cross the bridge over the Thames, which commands a charming view of the river, and follow the broad road to the Palace on the right. The Palace is open to the public gratis daily, except Fridays, from 10 to 6, from 1st April to 1st October, and from 10 to 4 in winter; Sundays, 2-6 or 2-4 p. m. The Gardens are open daily until dusk.

The Palace was originally built by *Cardinal Wolsey*, the favourite of Henry VIII., in red brick with battlemented walls, on the site of a property mentioned in Domesday Book, and was afterwards presented by him to the King. It was subsequently occupied by Cromwell, the Stuarts, William III., and the first two monarchs of the house of Hanover. Since the time of George II., Hampton Court has ceased to be a royal residence, and it is now inhabited by various pensioners of the Crown. The buildings to the left on entering from the W. are used as barracks for a cavalry guard.

The Palace comprises three principal courts, the *Entrance Court*, the *Clock Court*, and the *Fountain Court*. Above the entrance to the central or *Clock Court* are seen the armorial bearings of Wolsey, with his motto 'Dominus mihi adjutor'. The court is named from the curious *Astronomical Clock*, originally constructed for Henry VIII., and recently repaired and set going again. On the towers of the archways between the different courts are terracotta medallions of Roman emperors (the best being that of Nero), obtained by Wolsey from the sculptor, *Joannes Maiano*. From the S. side of this court we pass through an Ionic colonnade, erected by Wren, to the *King's Grand Staircase*, adorned with allegorical paintings by *Verrio*. Umbrellas and sticks are left at the foot of it. The names of the rooms are written above the doors, on the inside; we always begin with the pictures on the left. Visitors are required to pass from room to room in one direction only. The gallery is rich in Italian pictures, especially of the Venetian school, but the names attached to them are often erroneous. The following list pays no regard to the names on the pictures themselves. Comp. *E. Law's* 'History of the Palace in Tudor Times' (1885) and 'Historical Guide to the Pictures at Hampton Court' (1881). The 'Illustrated Guide' (1889; 1s.) is an abridgment of the latter.

ROOM I. *(The Guard Chamber)*. The walls are tastefully decorated with trophies and large star-shaped groups of pistols, guns, lances, and other modern weapons. The best of the pictures are: 9. *Canaletto*, Coloseum and Arch of Constantine at Rome; 20. *Zucchero*, Queen Elizabeth's porter; several battle-pieces by *Rugendas*.

ROOM II. *(The King's First Presence Chamber)* contains the canopy of the throne of King William III. The wood-carving above the chimney piece and doors is by *Grinling Gibbons*; the candelabrum dates from the reign of Queen Anne. The upper row of portraits are the so-called 'Hampton Court Beauties', or ladies of the court of William and Mary, painted by *Sir Godfrey Kneller*, after the model of the 'Windsor Beauties' of Charles II.'s Court, by *Sir Peter Lely*, formerly in Windsor Castle, and now in Room VI. of this gallery. The following pictures may also be remarked: 29. *Kneller*, William III. landing at Torbay, a large allegorical work; 35, 36. *Denner*, Portraits; 39, 52. *Schiavone*, Frieze-like landscapes with figures; 57. *Kneller*, Peter the Great; 58. *Unknown Master*, Portraits of Villiers, Duke of Buckingham, and his family; 60. *Unknown Painter*, Man's head; 64. Good Dutch copy, in the style of *Mabuse*, of a sketch by *Leonardo da Vinci*, Infant Christ and St. John; 66. *De Bray*, History of Marc Antony and Cleopatra, the figures being portraits of the artist's family.

ROOM III. *(The Second Presence Chamber)*. On the left: 69. *Tintoretto*, Esther before Ahasuerus; 72. *Leandro Bassano*, Sculptor; 73. *Bonifazio Veronese*, Diana and Actæon in a fanciful landscape, one of the artist's masterpieces; 78. *Jacopo Bassano*, Dominican; 79. Copy from *Titian*, Holy Family; \*80. *Dosso Dossi*, Portrait of a man, well preserved; 83. *Van Dyck*, Equestrian portrait of Charles I.; \*90. *Velazquez*, Consort of Philip IV. of Spain; \*91. *Tintoretto*, Knight of Malta; \*97. *Dosso Dossi*, Holy Family; 98. (above the mantelpiece) *Van Somer*, Christian IV. of Denmark; 104. *Pordenone*, His own family (dated 1524).

ROOM IV. *(The Audience Chamber)*. On the left: 117. *Giov. B. Busi* (? or of his school; forged signature). Portrait of himself; 113. *Titian* (?), Ignatius Loyola; \*114. *Lorenzo Lotto*, Portrait; \*115. *Palma Vecchio*, Holy Family; 130. *Unknown Artist*, Portrait; 125. *Giorgione* (?), Portrait; 128. *Honthorst*, Elizabeth, Queen of Bohemia, wife of Frederick V. of the Palatinate (above the mantelpiece); 138. *Savoldo*, Warrior in armour; 141. *Fialetti*, Venetian senators; \*144. Wrongly ascribed to *Lor. Lotto*, Family concert; \*148. *Lotto*, Portrait of Andrea Ordini, a sculptor; 149. *Titian*, Portrait of an unknown gentleman.

ROOM V. *(The King's Drawing Room)*. On the left: 153. *J. Bassano*, Boaz and Ruth; 175. *Schiavone*, Judgment of Midas; 182. *Master of Treviso*, Lawyer; 183. *Dosso*, St. William taking off his armour.

ROOM VI. *(King William the Third's Bedroom)* contains the bed of Queen Charlotte. The clock in the corner to the left of the bed goes for a year without re-winding; though in good repair it is no longer wound up. On the walls are the 'Beauties' of the Court of Charles II., chiefly painted by *Lely* (comp. Room II.), including 184. Duchess of York (afterw.

the mantel-piece); 195. Duchess of Richmond, who was the original of the 'Britannia' on the reverse of the British copper coins; 196. Marie d'Este (?, misnamed Nell Gwynne); all three by *Lely*. The ceiling by *Verrio*.

ROOM VII. *(The King's Dressing Room)*. Ceiling paintings by **Verrio**, representing Mars, Venus, and Cupid. No. 212. *Salv. Rosa*, Brigand scene; 224. *Girol. da Treviso*, Marriage of the Virgin.

ROOM VIII. *(The King's Writing Closet)*. On the left: 235. *Bordone* (? **more** probably Palma Vecchio), Lucretia, **injured** by repainting; *Artemisia Gentileschi*, 227. Sibyl, 226. Her own portrait. The mirror above the chimney-piece **here** is placed at such an angle as to reflect the whole suite of rooms.

ROOM IX. *(Queen Mary's* **Closet)**. On the left: 251. ***Giulio Romano***, Holy Family; 267. *Dutch Master*, **Sophonisba**.

ROOM X. *(The Queen's* **Gallery)** is **a hall, 69 ft.** long and 260 ft. broad, with **tapestry** representing **scenes from the life** of Alexander the Great, after **Le Brun**.

ROOM XI. *(The Queen's* Bedroom) contains Queen Anne's bed, and has a **ceiling painted by** *Thornhill*, representing Aurora rising from the sea. To **the left: *276. *Correggio*,** Holy Family, with St. Jerome on the left, a small and **admirable work of** the painter's early period. *L. Giordano*, 278. Offerings **of the** Magi; 288, 292. Myth of Cupid and Psyche, **in** 12 small pictures. *307. *Francesco Francia*, Baptism of Christ.

ROOM XII. *(The Queen's Drawing Room)*, **with** ceiling painted by *Verrio*, representing Queen Anne **as** the Goddess of Justice. The windows command a fine view of the gardens and canal (³/₄ **M**. long). The pictures **are** all by *West*: above the door, 309. Duke of Cumberland and his two **sisters,** when children; 314. Peter denying his Master; 320. Death of **General** Wolfe (duplicate of the original in Grosvenor House); 321. Queen **Charlotte**; 322. Prince of Wales and Duke of York.

ROOM XIII. *(The Queen's Audience Chamber)*. On the left: 329. *P. Snayers*, **Battle of** Forty; *334. *Palamedes*, Embarking from Scheveningen. *Holbein*, 259. (?) Countess of Lennox, mother of Lord Darnley; *340. Henry VIII. and his family; 342. Meeting of Henry VIII. and Francis I. of France, at the Field of the Cloth of Gold. 798. *Mytens*, Portrait of the dwarf Sir Jeffery Hudson (immortalised in Scott's 'Peveril of the Peak').

ROOM XIV. *(The Public Dining Room)*. **On** the left: 354. *Beechey*, George III. reviewing the 10th Dragoons, the Prince of Wales on the **right and the Duke** of **York** on the left; 560. *Zucchero*, Mary, Queen of Scots; **361.** *Knapton*, Family of Frederick, Prince of Wales (the boy with the plan **on his knee** is George III.); above the fire-place, 663. *Van Dyck*, Cupid **and** Psyche; 363. *Sir* **T.** *Lawrence*, **F. von** Gentz; 365. *Walker*, Portrait of himself; 366. *Gainsborough*, Jewish **Rabbi**; 369. *Michael Wright*, John Lacy, **comedian, in** three characters; 376. *Dobson*, Portrait of himself **and his wife. We proceed in a** straight direction; the door **to** the left leads to **the Queen's Chapel, etc.** (see below).

ROOM **XV.** *(The Prince of Wales's Presence Chamber)*. On **the** left. 380. *N. Poussin*, **Nymphs and** Satyrs. *Rembrandt*, 381. **Rabbi**; 382. Dutch lady. *385. *Mabuse*, **Adam** and Eve; 404. *Heemskerck*, Quakers' meeting.

ROOM XVI. *(The Prince of Wales's Drawing Room)*. On the left: 407. *Van Belchamp*, Louis XIII. of France; 411. *Pourbus*, Mary de' Medici; 413. *Greuze*, Louis XVI. of France; 423. *Claude Lorrain*, Sea-port; 418. *Pourbus*, Henry IV. **of** France; 429. **Greuze**, Madame de Pompadour; **above,** 428. *Mignard*, **Louis XIV.,** as **a** youth.

ROOM XVII. *(The* **Prince of** *Wales's Bedroom)* contains tapestry representing the Battle of Solebay (1672), and **a few** portraits.

**We** now return to Room XIV. *(Public* **Dining** *Room)*, and pass **through the door on** the right, indicated **by notices** pointing the 'Way Out'.

QUEEN'S PRIVATE CHAPEL. On **the left:** *463. *Hondecoeter*, Birds; 464. *Snyders*, Still-life; *De Heem*, *467, **469.** Still-life pieces. — The CLOSET adjoining the chapel contains nothing of much interest. The PRIVATE DINING ROOM contains three **bright** red **beds,** and some portraits, including **one of the Duchess of Brunswick, sister** of George III., by *Angelica*

*Kaufmann* (502). Adjoining it is a second Closet with 12 saints by *Fab* (506).

Queen's Private Chamber. In the centre, 16. *Unknown Flemish or German Master*, Triptych with the Crucifixion in the centre, the Bearing of the Cross to the left, the Resurrection to the right, and the Ecce Homo on the exterior, of admirable colouring. The King's Private Dressing Room contains some poor copies of various well-known works and a bust of a negro. We then pass through George II.'s Private Room, with fruit and flower pieces, and a dark corner room into the —

South Gallery, where Raphael's famous cartoons, now at South Kensington (p. 284), were formerly preserved. It is divided into five sections by partitions, and contains the most valuable smaller pictures of the collection. Section I.: *561. *Janet*, Queen Eleanor of France; 563. *Holbein* (?), Henry VIII., as a youth; 576. *Van Orley*, Death of Adonis; 579. *Hemmessen*, St. Jerome; 581. *Mazzolini of Ferrara*, Turkish warrior; 578. *Schoreel*, Virgin and Child. SS. Andrew and Michael. — Section II. 588. *Cranach*, The Judgment of Paris; *610. *Holbein*, Reskemeer(?) with hands beautifully painted); *589. *Dürer*, Portrait; *590. School of *Van Eyck*, Head of a young man; *595. *Mabuse*, Children of Christian II. of Denmark; Gil. *Remée* (Antwerp; d. 1678), Henry VII. and his queen Elizabeth. Henry VIII. and his queen Jane Seymour, copy of a fresco by *Holbein* in Whitehall, which was burned with that palace; 600. *L. Cranach*, St. Christopher and other saints; 602. *Lucas v. Leyden*, Joseph in prison. *Holbein*: 643. Frobenius (the famous printer); *608. The artist's parents. 676. School of *Frans Hals*, Portrait; 629, 637. Gonzales Coques, Portraits; 631. *Hendrik Pot*, Play scene (the actor here is supposed to be Charles I.); 638. *Van Dyck*, Dying saint. — Section III.: 654. After *Rubens*, Venus and Adonis; 657. *Verdussen*, Windsor Castle; 662. *Molenaer*, Dutch merry-making; 666. Ascribed to *Holbein*, Face at a window, misnamed Will Somers, court jester of Henry VIII.; 680. *Rottenhammer*, Judgment of Paris; 684. *Wilkens*, Flower-piece (1665). — Section IV.: 698. *Everdingen* (?), Landscape; 707. *Janssen*, Villiers, Duke of Buckingham; 710. *Dutch Master*, Portrait (described by the Catalogue as a portrait of Raphael by himself); 734. *P. Brill*, Landscape; 731. *J. B. Weenix*, Dead game. — Section V.: 744. *Roestraeten*, Still-life (the earthenware jug very fine); 745, 754. *W. van de Velde*, Sea-pieces (sketches); *746. *Wynants*, Landscape; 748. *Brueghel the Elder*, Slaughter of the Innocents, thoroughly Dutch in conception; 751. *Holbein*, Landscape; 769. James I., copy of a painting by an unknown artist in Ham House. Above, opposite the window, 704. *Snyders*, Boar-hunt.

We now pass through a small, dark chamber on the right, and enter the last long gallery, called the —

**Mantegna Gallery**, which contains the gem of the whole collection, the Triumphal Procession of Cæsar, by *Mantegna* (Nos. 813-811), extending the whole length of the wall, and protected by glass. The series of pictures, painted in distemper upon linen, is in parts sadly defaced, and has also been retouched. Mantegna began the work, which was intended for stage-scenery, in 1485, and finished it in 1490-92. The series was purchased by Charles I. along with the rest of the Duke of Mantua's collection, and valued by the Parliament after the king's death at 1000l. It was rescued by Cromwell, along with Raphael's cartoons.

*Section* I. Beginning of the procession with trumpeters, standard-bearers, and warriors; on the flag-poles paintings of the victories of Cæsar. — II. Statues of Jupiter and Juno in chariots, bust of Cybele, war-like instruments. — III. Trophies of war; weapons, urns, tripods, etc. — IV. Precious vessels and ornaments; oxen led by pages; train of musicians. — V. Elephants bearing fruit, flowers, and candelabra. — VI. Urns, armour, etc. borne in triumph. — VII. Procession of the captives; men, women, and children, and mocking figures among the populace. — VIII. Dancing musicians, standard-bearers with garlands; among them a soldier of the German Legion, bearing a standard with the she-wolf of Rome. — IX. *Julius Cæsar*, with sceptre and palm-branch, in a triumphal car; behind him Victoria; on his standard the legend, 'Veni, vidi, vici'.

'With a stern realism, which was his virtue, Mantegna multiplied illustrations of the classic age in a severe and chastened style, balancing his composition with the known economy of the Greek relief, conserving the dignity of sculptural movement and gait, and the grave marks of the classic statuaries, modifying them though but slightly with the newer accent of Donatello. ... His contour is tenuous and fine **and** remarkable for a graceful and easy flow; his clear lights, shaded with grey, are blended with extraordinary delicacy, his colours are bright and variegated, yet thin, spare, and of gauzy substance.' — *Crowe* and ***Cavalcaselle***.

The Mantegna Gallery also contains a few other paintings, including portraits of Jane Shore, mistress of Edward IV. (No. 793; immediately to the right of the door by which we enter) and of Christian, Duke of Brunswick, in his youth (No. 569; by *Honthorst*).

We now pass the top of the (QUEEN'S STAIRCASE, embellished with ceiling-paintings by *Vick*, and a large picture by *Honthorst*, representing Charles I. and his wife as Apollo and Diana, and reach two other rooms, which contain the remainder of the pictures.

ROOM I. (*The Queen's Guard Chamber*). On the left: 811. *Ciro Ferri*, Triumph of Bacchus; 815, 816. Portraits of Giulio Romano and Michael Angelo; 818. *Milani*, Portrait of a child; 819. Portrait of Tintoretto; 824. *Kneller*, John Locke; 839. *Battoni*, Pope Benedict XIV.; 842. Frederick the Great; 846. *Kneller*, Sir Isaac Newton; 850. *Romanelli*, after *Guido Reni*, Triumph of Venus, with Bacchus and Ariadne; 862. *Lely*, Portrait of himself. The wrought-iron railings, generally ascribed to Huntington Shaw (p. 278), are two of twelve formerly in the gardens. — We now pass through a small *Ante-Room* into —

ROOM II. (*The Queen's Presence Chamber*), with sea-pieces: 871. *Zucchero*, Adoration of the Shepherds; 873. *Post*, View in the West Indies. *W. van de Velde*, 879. British ship engaged with three Spanish vessels; 880. Close of the same action. 884. *James*, View on the Thames, comprising old London Bridge; 898, 899. *Huggins*, Battle of Trafalgar. *W. van de Velde*, 902. British fleet attacking the French fleet in a harbour; 910. Burning of a fleet 887. *S. van Ruysdael*, River in Holland; 912. *W. van de Velde*, Boats attacking the Dutch fleet in a harbour. Here also are two pieces of timber from Nelson's flag-ship, the *Victory*.

The *Great Hall*, 106 ft. in length, 40 ft. in breadth, and 60 ft. in height, begun by Henry VIII. immediately after the death of Wolsey, and completed in 1536, contains a handsome high-pitched timber roof with pendants, good stained-glass windows (mostly modern), and fine tapestry representing scenes from the life of Abraham. The room at the end has a modern portrait of Wolsey over the chimney-piece.

A door to the right, at the foot of the staircase where umbrellas have been left, leads to the gardens, to reach which we pass through a small court, emerging at the E. façade of the Palace.

The \*Garden in front of the Palace is laid out in the French style, and embellished with tasteful flower-beds and shady avenues. In the private garden, on the S. side of the Palace, is exhibited a vine of the Black Hamburgh variety, planted in 1768, the stem of which is 38 in. in circumference, and the branches of which spread over an area of 2200 sq. ft. The yield of this gigantic vine amounts annually to 1200 or 1300 bunches of grapes, weighing about $3/4$ lb. each. — The old *Tennis Court*, opening from the garden to the N. of the Palace, is still used.

The *Maze* (adm. 1*d*.), or labyrinth, in the so-called *Wilderness* to the N. of the Palace, may be successfully penetrated by keeping invariably to the left, *except the first time* we have an option, when we keep to the **extreme** right; in coming out, we keep to the *right*, till we reach **the same place**, when we turn to the *left*. Opposite, between Hampton Court and Teddington, is *Bushy Park*, a royal domain of about **11,000 acres**, entered by four gates: viz., the one **here**, one near **Teddington**, one at Hampton Wick (p. 315), and **one at Hampton village**. Its white-thorn trees in blossom are very **beautiful, but its chief glory is in the end of spring** or in early summer, **when the horse-chestnuts are in full bloom**, affording a sight quite unequalled **in England** (usually announced in the London papers). These majestic **old trees, planted by William III.** and interspersed **with limes, form a triple avenue, of more than a mile** in length, from **Hampton Court to Teddington**. Near the Hampton Court end of the avenue **is a curious basin with carp and** gold-fish. The deer in the **park, never being molested, are** so tame that they scarcely exert themselves **to get out of the way of visitors**. They even thrust their **heads in at the open windows of the** houses that **look on the park, insisting on being fed. The residence of the ranger is a sombre red brick house, screened off by railings**, near **one** margin **of the** park.

Travellers provided with a return-ticket of the North London **Railway walk** through Bushy Park to Teddington station, whence **London is reached** via Richmond in $^3/_4$ hr. On leaving Hampton Court by the *Lion Gates*, **near the Maze**, we see the entrance to **Bushy Park** immediately opposite. **We turn to the left on** quitting **the** park. The road almost immediately forks, when we keep to the right, and then take the **second turning on the right**, leading to ($1^1/_4$ M.) *Teddington Station*. **The train from Teddington** to London passes *Strawberry Hill* (p. **315**), Richmond, Willesden Junction, and *Dalston*. The walk from **Teddington to (3 M.)** Richmond is very picturesque (fine cedars). **Carriage from** Hampton Court to Teddington 2s. 6d., to **Richmond 6s.** Waggonettes ply through Bushy Park between Hampton **Court** and Teddington (fare 3d.); omnibus to Richmond and Kew, **see p. 315.**

**Richmond** (*\*Star and Garter*, with fine view from the terrace, expensive; *Queen's*, opposite; *\*Talbot Hotel*; *Roebuck*; several **tea-gardens and coffee-houses**; 'Maids of honour', a favourite **kind of cake) may be reached direct from London by the** South **Western Railway** (N. Entrance, p. 35) or Underground Railway every half-hour, by a Richmond omnibus **(fare 1s.)**, or, in summer, by the **steamboat. It is a** small **town on the** right bank of the Thames, **charmingly situa**ted on the slope **of a** hill. Ascending the broad **main street of the** town to the right, we reach, **at the top** of the hill, **a fine park, terrace,** and avenue, commanding a beautiful \*View. Pretty walks also wind along the opposite **bank** of the Thames, and the grounds formerly belonging to the Duke of Buccleuch were opened as a public garden in May, 1887. Pop. (1881) 19,068.

The original name of the place was *Sheen* ('beautiful'), which still survives in the neighbouring *East Sheen*. Edward I. possessed a palace here, which was rebuilt in 1499 by Henry VII., the founder of the Tudor dynasty, who named it Richmond, after his own title. Henry VIII. and his daughter Elizabeth often held their courts in this palace, and the latter died here in 1603. In 1648 the palace was demolished by order of Parliament, and all that now remains of it is a stone gateway in Richmond Green.

Richmond is a favourite summer-resort, both of Londoners and strangers; and its large park, 2255 acres in area, and 8 M. in circumference, is frequented in fine weather by crowds of pedestrians, horsemen, and carriages. Large herds of deer here also add to the charms of the park. *Pembroke Lodge* in this park was the seat of Lord John Russell (d. 1878). — The small church of Richmond contains the tombs of James Thomson, the poet of the 'Seasons' (p. 202), and Edmund Kean, the famous actor (d. 1833).

From Richmond we may take the omnibus (6d. outside) or tramway (2d.; from the N. end of the town) to **Kew** (*Star and Garter; Kew Gardens Hotel*, close to Kew Gardens Station, R. & A. 3s., B. 2s., also 'pension'), the beautiful **\*Botanic Gardens** of which are open gratis daily from noon (on Sundays from 1 p.m.) till sunset; the hothouses are open daily from 1 p.m. — Kew is reached from London direct by steamboat, omnibus (comp. pp. 28 and 37), or railway (South Western Railway, N. entrance, or North London Railway, Broad Street Station, or Underground Railway, from Mansion House). The present Keeper of the gardens is Dr. W. T. Thiselton Dyer, whose predecessors were the distinguished botanists Sir Joseph D. Hooker and Sir William J. Hooker.

Kew has two railway-stations, *Kew Bridge Station* on the left, and *Kew Gardens Station* on the right bank of the Thames. Leaving the first of these, we cross the Thames to *Kew Green*, and thence proceed to the right to the principal entrance of the Gardens, near which is *Kew Cottage*. From Kew Gardens station a short road leads direct to the new Lichfield Gate, which is visible from the station. Visitors may not bring eatables into the Gardens, or pluck even the wild flowers. Smoking is strictly prohibited in the houses, but is permitted both in the Gardens and in the Arboretum (p. 323).

The path to the right on entering by the principal gate leads straight to *Kew Palace*. To the left lie the *Botanic Gardens*, with numerous hothouses, where the ferns, orchids, and cacti are particularly interesting. By the pond, at the S. end of the Gardens, are the *\*Palm House* (362 ft. long, 100 ft. broad, and 66 ft. high), where the temperature is kept at 80° Fahr., and the *Water Lily House*. A little to the N. of the artificial piece of water is the *Tropical House*, containing the tank for the Victoria Regia, which flowers in August. There are also three *Botanical Museums* in different parts of the Gardens. To the S. and W. of the Botanic Gardens proper, and separated from them by a wire-fence, lies the *Arboretum*, covering an area of 178 acres, which extends to the Thames, and is intersected in every direction by shady walks and avenues. In the N. part is a small *American Garden*, with magnolias and fine azaleas (best about the end of May). On the path leading from the pond towards the Richmond Gate, the elegant *North Gallery*, the gift of Miss North, was opened in 1882. It contains, in geographical sequence, a most interesting collection of tropical flowers, etc., sketched by Miss North in their native localities (catalogue 3d.). The *Winter Garden*, or *Temperate House*, built in 1805 at a cost of 35,000l., is designed for keeping plants of the temperate zone during winter. The central portion is 212 ft. long, 137 ft. wide, and 60 ft. high; with the wings the total length is 582 ft. At the S. extremity of the Arboretum is the *Pagoda*, rising in ten stories to a height of 165 ft., the summit of which, in clear weather, commands the environs for 30 M. round (no admission). Near the Pagoda is a *Refreshment Pavilion* (tea, ices, etc.). Both the Gardens and the Arboretum contain a number of small ornamental *Temples*.

Opposite the Pleasure Grounds, on the left bank of the Thames, lies *Brentford* (p. 325), the official county town of Middlesex. Its name often occurs in English literature; thus the 'two kings of Brentford on one throne' are mentioned by Cowper and in the 'Rehearsal'. Adjacent is *Sion House*, a place of great historic interest, which was a nunnery in the 15th cent., and is now the property of the Duke of Northumberland.

A footpath on the right bank of the Thames leads through *Old Richmond Park*, with the *Kew Observatory*, to Richmond.

## 36. The Thames from London Bridge to Hampton Court.

STEAMBOATS are sometimes advertised to ply in summer, tide permitting, from **London Bridge** to *Hampton Court* (22 M. in 2-3 hrs.; fare 1s. 6d., return 2s. 6d.); but they are seldom able to proceed farther than Kew. By embarking at *Chelsea* or *Battersea Park* the traveller may shorten the trip by about 1 hour. The scenery, after London is fairly left behind, is of a very soft and pleasing character, consisting of luxuriant woods, smiling meadows, and picturesque villas and villages. The course of the river is very tortuous. The words right and left in the following description are used with reference to going upstream.

ROWING AND SAILING BOATS may be hired at Richmond, Kingston, Hampton Wick, and several other places on the river, the charges varying according to the season, the size of the boat, etc. (previous understanding advisable). The prettiest part of the river near London for short boating excursions is the stretch between Richmond and Hampton Court. A trifling fee, which may be ascertained from the official table posted at each lock (3d.-1s. for rowing-boats), has to be paid for passing the locks. Rowing-boats going upstream generally keep near the bank to escape the current. Boats pass each other to the right, but a boat overtaking another one keeps to the left.

The prominent objects on both banks of the Thames between London Bridge and Battersea Bridge have already been pointed out in various parts of the Handbook, so that nothing more is required here than a list of them in the order in which they occur, with references to the pages where they are described: — *South Eastern Railway Bridge*, **Southwark Bridge** (p. 117), *St. Paul's Cathedral* (right; p. 81), *London, Chatham, and Dover Railway Bridge* (p. 113), *Blackfriars Bridge* (p. 112), *Victoria Embankment* (right; p. 113), the *City of London School* (right; p. 114), the *Temple* (right; p. 136), with the new *Law Courts* (p. 139) **appearing above it**, **Somerset House** (right; p. 142), *Waterloo* **Bridge** (p. 143), *Cleopatra's Needle* (p. 144), *Charing Cross Railway Bridge*, *Montague House* (right; p. 184), *Westminster Bridge* (p. 192), **Houses** *of Parliament* (right; p. 184), *Westminster Abbey* (right; p. 193), *Albert Embankment* (left; **p. 114**), *St. Thomas's Hospital* (left; p. 297), *Lambeth Palace* (left; p. 297), *Lambeth Bridge* (p. 297), *Millbank Penitentiary* (right; p. 292), *Vauxhall Bridge* (p. 292), *London, Chatham, and Dover Railway Bridge* (*Victoria*, p. 292), *Chelsea Suspension Bridge* (p. 281), *Battersea Park* (left; p. 299), **Chelsea Hospital** (right; p. 294), *Albert Bridge* (p. 299), *Battersea Bridge* (p. 294).

A little way above Battersea we reach —

L. **Wandsworth** (railway-station, see p. 335), an outlying suburb of London, containing a large number of factories and breweries. The scenery now begins to become more rural in character, and the dusky hues of the great city give place to the green tints of meadow and woodland. About 1 M. above Wandsworth the river is spanned by *Putney Bridge*, erected in 1886, connecting **Fulham**, on the right, with **Putney**, on the left.

R. **Fulham** is principally noted for containing a country residence of the Bishops of London, who have been lords of the manor from very early times. The Episcopal Palace, which stands above the bridge, dates in part from the 16th century. Its grounds contain some fine old trees, and are enclosed by a moat about 1 M. in circumference. In the library are portraits of *Sandys*, Archbishop of York, *Laud*, *Ridley* the martyr, and other ecclesiastics, chiefly Bishops of London. The first bishop who is known with certainty to have resided here was Robert Seal, in 1241. A handsome, but somewhat incongruous, chapel was added to the palace in 1867. *Fulham Church* has a tower of the 14th cent., and contains the tombs of numerous Bishops of London. In a house at the N. end of Fulham, on the road to Hammersmith, Richardson wrote 'Clarissa Harlowe'.

L. **Putney** (railway-station, p. 335) is well known to Londoners as the starting-point for the annual boat-race between Oxford and Cambridge universities (p. 48), which takes place on the river between this village and Mortlake (p. 325).

Thomas Cromwell, Wolsey's secretary, and afterwards Earl of Essex, was the son of a Putney blacksmith; and Edward Gibbon, the historian, was born here in 1737. In 1806 William Pitt died at Bowling Green House, on the S. side of the town, near Putney Heath, where, eight years before, he had engaged in a duel with George Tierney. Lord Castlereagh and George Canning also fought a duel on the heath in 1809. The tower of Putney Church is about 400 years old.

*Beautiful walk from Putney over Putney Heath, through the village of Roehampton (1½ M. to the S.) and Richmond Park, to (4 M.) Richmond.

The fine old house, called *Barnes Elms*, which we now soon observe on the left, was granted by Queen Elizabeth to Sir Francis Walsingham, who entertained his sovereign lady here on various occasions. It was afterwards occupied by Jacob Tonson, the publisher, who built a room here for the famous portraits of the Kit-Cat Club, painted for him by Sir Godfrey Kneller (p. 320).

On the opposite bank, a little farther on, formerly stood *Brandenburgh House*, built in the time of Charles I.; it was once inhabited by Fairfax the Parliamentary general, by Queen Caroline, consort of George IV, who died here in 1821, and by various other notabilities.

R. Hammersmith (railway-station), now a town of considerable size, but of little interest to strangers. The *Church of St. Paul*, consecrated in 1631, containing some interesting monuments, a ceiling painted by Cipriani, and an altarpiece carved by Grinling Gibbons, was pulled down in 1882 to make room for a new and larger edifice. The town contains numerous Roman Catholic inhabitants and institutions. Hammersmith is connected by a suspension-bridge, opened in 1887, with the cluster of villas called *Castelnau*.

R. Chiswick (railway-station, p. 335) contains the gardens of the Horticultural Society (p. 271). Opposite Chiswick lies *Chiswick Eyot*.

In *Chiswick House*, the property of the Duke of Devonshire, Charles James Fox died in 1806, and George Canning in 1827. It was built by the Earl of Burlington, the builder of Burlington House, Piccadilly (p. 220), in imitation of the Villa Capra at Vicenza, one of Palladio's best works. The wings, by Wyatt, were added afterwards. — The churchyard contains the grave of Hogarth, the painter (d. 1764), who died in a dwelling near the church, now called Hogarth House.

L. *Barnes* (railway-station, p. 335), a village with a church partly of the 12th cent., freely restored, and possessing a modern, ivy-clad tower. At the next bend lies —

L. Mortlake (rail. stat., p. 335), with a church occupying the site of an edifice of the 14th cent.; the tower dates from 1543. In the interior is a tablet to *Sir Philip Francis* (d. 1818), now usually identified with *Junius*. Mortlake is the terminus of the University Boat Race course (comp. p. 324).

The two famous astrologers, Dee and Partridge, resided at Mortlake, where Queen Elizabeth is said to have consulted the first-named. *Pleasant walk through (S.) East Sheen to Richmond Park.

L. *Kew* (p. 322) has a railway-station on the opposite bank, with which a stone bridge connects it. Picturesque walk to Richmond.

R. *Brentford* (p. 323), near which is *Sion House* (p. 323).

R. Isleworth (rail. stat.), a favourite residence of London merchants, with numerous villas. The woods and lawns on the banks of the river in this neighbourhood are particularly charming. The course of the stream is from N. to S. We now pass under a railway-bridge, and then a stone bridge, the latter at —

L. *Richmond* (see p. 321); boats may be hired here (p. 323).

L. *Petersham* (Dysart Arms), with a red brick church, in a quaint classical style, dating from 1505. Close to the church is *Ham House*, also of red brick, with its back to the river, the meeting-place of the Cabal during its tenancy by the Duke of Lauderdale.

A little farther from the river stands **Sudbrook** *House*, built by the Duke of Argyll (d. 1743), and now a hydropathic establishment. It is immortalised by Scott in the 'Heart of Midlothian', as the scene of the interview between Jeanie Deans and the Duke.

On the opposite bank of the Thames is —

R. **Twickenham** (*Railway; King's Head; Albany*), with a great number of interesting historical villas and mansions. The name most intimately associated with the place is that of Pope, whose villa, however, has been replaced by another, while his grotto is also altered. Near the site of Pope's villa stands *Orleans House*, a building of red brick, once the residence of Louis Philippe and other members of the Orleans family, and now used by the Orleans Club (p. 75) as a pleasant country resort for members, their families, and their friends. Farther up the river, about $1/2$ M. above Twickenham, is *Strawberry Hill*, Horace Walpole's famous villa; it was long the residence of the late Countess Waldegrave, who collected here a great many of the objects of art which adorned it in Walpole's time. Among other celebrities connected with Twickenham are Henry Fielding, the novelist, and Kitty Clive, the actress. *Eel Pie Island* (Inn), opposite Twickenham, is a favourite resort of picnic parties.

R. *Teddington* (p. 324), with the first lock on the Thames and a new foot-bridge (opened in 1889).

L. **Kingston** (*Griffin; Sun; Railway*; rail. stat., p. 336), an old Saxon town, where some of the early kings of England were crowned. In the market-place, surrounded by an ornamental iron railing, is the *Stone* which is said to have been used as the king's seat during the coronation ceremony. The names of those believed to have been crowned here are carved on the stone. The *Town Hall* is an imposing edifice, built in 1840. The *Church of All Saints* is a fine cruciform structure, dating in part from the 14th century. Kingston is united with *Hampton Wick* on the other bank, by a stone bridge, constructed in 1827. It is surrounded by numerous villas and country-residences, and is a favourite resort of Londoners in summer.

Rowing and sailing boats may be hired either at Kingston or Hampton Wick. — Pleasant walks to *Ham Common*, and through *Bushy Park* to (2 M.) *Hampton Court*.

Steaming past *Surbiton*, the southern suburb of Kingston, and *Thames Ditton* (p. 316), on the left, we now arrive at the bridge crossing the river at —

**Hampton Court**, see p. 316. (The village of *Hampton* lies on the right, about 1 M. farther up.)

## 37. Hampstead. Highgate.

The visitor should go to *Hampstead* by omnibus (p. 31) or train (North London Railway, from Broad Street), and walk thence to *Highgate*.

The two hills of Hampstead and Highgate, lying to the N. of London, are well worth visiting for the extensive views they command of the metropolis and the surrounding country.

The village of **Hampstead** ('home-stead'), has been long since **reached** by the ever advancing **suburbs of London**, from which it **can now scarcely be** distinguished. It is an ancient place, known **as early as the time of the Romans; and** various Roman antiquities **have been found in the neighbourhood,** particularly at the mineral **wells. These wells (in Well Walk, to the E.** of the High Street) **were discovered or re-discovered about 1620, and** for a time **made Hampstead a fashionable spa; the old well-house is** now used as **a church. Well Walk also contains the** house in **which John Keats and his brother lodged in 1817-1818, and at** the bottom **of John Street, near Hampstead Heath Station, is** Lawn Bank (then called **Wentworth Place), where Keats lived with** his friend **Charles Brown in 1818-20. Part of 'Endymion' was** written in the **first of these, and much of Keats's finest work, including parts of 'Hyperion' and the 'Eve of St. Agnes', was done at Lawn** Bank. Leigh **Hunt long lived in a cottage in the Vale of** Health. The parish **church of** *St. John* **dates from 1747, and with its square** tower **forms a conspicuous object in the view** from many **parts of London. In the churchyard are** buried *Sir James Mackintosh* (d. 1832), *Joanna Bailie* (d. 1851), her sister *Agnes* (d. 1861, aged 100 years), **and** *Constable*, the painter (d. 1837), **who has** left many painted **memorials of his love** for Hampstead (see, *e.g.*, his pictures of **Hampstead in the National Gallery, p. 174). The well-known Kit-Cat Club, which numbered Addison, Steele, and Pope among its** members, **held its first meetings in a tavern at Hampstead.**

*Hampstead **Heath** (430 ft. above* the sea-level) is one of **the** most open and picturesque **spots** in the immediate neighbourhood of London, and is **a favourite** and justly valued resort of **holiday-makers and a**ll who **appreciate pure** and invigorating air. **The heath is about 240 acres in extent. Its** wild and irregular **beauty, and picturesque alternations of hill** and hollow, make it **a refreshing contrast to the trim elegance of** the Parks. The heath **was once a notorious** haunt of highwaymen. Some years ago the **lord** of the manor began **to lay out** the heath for building purposes; **but fortunately his intention was frustrated,** and the heath purchased **by the Me**tropolitan Board **of Works for the** unrestricted **use of the public.** Parliament Hill, **to** the S.E. of the heath proper **has also been** acquired for the public. Near the ponds at the S.E. **corner of the h**eath, the Fleet Brook (p. 134) takes its rise. The **garden of the** *Bull and Bush Inn*, **on** the N. margin of the heath, **contains a holly planted by Hogarth,** the **painter; and** 'Jack

*Straw's Castle*, on the highest part of the heath, is another interesting old inn. On public holidays Hampstead Heath is generally visited by 25-50,000 Londoners and presents a gay and characteristic scene of popular enjoyment.

The *View is extensive and interesting. On the S. lies London, with the dome of St. Paul's and the towers of Westminster rising conspicuously from the dark masses of houses; while beyond may be discerned the green hills of Surrey and the glittering roof of the Crystal Palace at Sydenham. The varied prospect to the W. includes Harrow-on-the-Hill (p. 332; distinguishable by the lofty spire on an isolated eminence), and, in clear weather, Windsor Castle itself. To the N. lies a fertile and well-peopled tract, studded with numerous villages and houses and extending to Highwood Hill, Totteridge, and Barnet. To the E., in immediate proximity, we see the sister hill of Highgate, and in clear weather we may descry the reach of the Thames at Gravesend.

We leave Hampstead Heath at the N. end, near 'Jack Straw's Castle', and follow the road leading to the N.E. to Highgate. We soon reach, on the left, the '*Spaniards' Inn*', the gathering point of the 'No Popery' rioters of 1780, and described by Dickens in 'Barnaby Rudge'. The stretch of road between 'Jack Straw's Castle' and this point is perhaps the most open and elevated near London, affording fine views to the N.W. and S.E. The road then leads between *Caen Wood*, with its fine old oaks, on the right, and *Bishop's Wood* on the left. Caen Wood or Ken Wood House, was the seat of the celebrated judge, Lord Mansfield, who died here in 1793. Bishop's Wood once formed part of the park of the Bishops of London. We now pass the grounds of *Caen Wood Towers* on the right, and reach *Highgate*.

There is also a pleasant path leading past the Ponds and through the fields from Hampstead to Highgate.

**Highgate**, which is situated on a hill about 30 ft. lower than Hampstead Heath, is one of the healthiest and most favourite sites for villas in the outskirts of London. The view which it commands is similar in character to that from Hampstead, but not so fine. The new church, built in the Gothic style in 1833, is a handsome edifice, and, from its situation, very conspicuous. The Highgate or North London *Cemetery, lying on the slope of the hill just below the church, is very picturesque and tastefully laid out. The catacombs are in the Egyptian style, with cypresses, and the terraces afford a fine view. *Michael Faraday*, the great chemist (d. 1867; by the E. wall), *Lord Lyndhurst* (d. 1863), and *George Eliot* (d. 1880) are buried here. *Samuel Taylor Coleridge* (d. 1834) is interred in a vault below the adjacent Grammar School, which, founded in 1565, was lately rebuilt in the French Gothic style. The *Whittington Almshouses* at the foot of the hill were established by the famous Lord Mayor of that name, and are popularly supposed to occupy the very spot where he heard the bells inviting him to return. Close by is the stone on which he is said to have rested, now forming part of a lamp-post; it is needless to say that its identity is more than doubtful. The *Highgate Gravel Pit Wood*, 70 acres in extent, was opened as a public park in 1886.

Many of the walks around Highgate are picturesque and interesting. Among the houses in the vicinity we may mention *Holly Lodge*, the residence of Baroness Burdett Coutts; *Cromwell House*, said to have been built for Cromwell's son-in-law, General Ireton, and now a Convalescent Hospital for Children; *Lauderdale House*, where Nell Gwynne lived; and the third house to the right in the 'Grove', where Coleridge died. *Arundel House*, where the great Lord Bacon died, has disappeared.

Highgate used to be notorious for a kind of mock pilgrimage made to it for the purpose of 'swearing on the horns.' By the terms of his oath the pilgrim was bound never to kiss the maid when he could kiss the mistress, never to drink small beer when he could get strong, etc. 'unless he liked it best'. Some old rams' heads are still preserved at the inns. Byron alludes to this custom in 'Childe Harold'. Canto I.

Highgate station, on the Great Northern Railway, lies to the E. of the town, and is daily passed by numerous trains. Cable Tramway up Highgate Hill, see p. 32. About 2 M. off, on the elevated ground to the E. of *Muswell Hill* and N. of *Hornsey*, is the **Alexandra Palace**, an establishment resembling the Crystal Palace, with a large park, theatre and concert hall, panorama, etc.

## 38. Epping Forest. Waltham Abbey. Rye House.

*Great Eastern Railway* to (12 M.) *Loughton*, in 1 hr. (fares 2s. 1d., 1s. 7d., 1s. 1/2d.). From Loughton, which may also be reached from *Chalk Farm* and other stations of the *North London Railway* (via *Dalston Junction*), on foot, through *Epping Forest*, to (5 M.) *Waltham Abbey*. From Waltham Abbey to (6 M.) *Rye House* by railway. From Rye House back to (19 M.) London by railway (fares 3s. 8d., 2s. 10d., 1s. 7d.).

We may start either from Fenchurch Street Station (p. 34) or from *Liverpool Street Station* (p. 33). The first stations after Liverpool Street are *Bishopsgate*, *Bethnal Green* (p. 128), *Old Ford*, and *Stratford*, where the train joins the North London line. Then *Leyton* and *Leytonstone*. At (8 M.) *Snaresbrook* is an *Infant Orphan Asylum*, with accommodation for 300 children (to the left of the line). 8¾ M. *George Lane*; 9¾ M. *Woodford*, 3 M. from Chingford (see below); 11 M. *Buckhurst Hill*. Then (12 M.) Loughton (*Railway Hotel*), within a few hundred paces of the Forest.

Another route to Epping Forest is by the Great Eastern Railway from Liverpool Street, viâ *Walthamstow*, to (9 M.) *Chingford* (fares 1s. 5d., 1s. 1d., 10d.), which may also be reached from the North London Railway viâ *Dalston Junction* and *Hackney* or viâ *Gospel Oak*. Chingford (*Royal Forest Hotel*, D. 1s. 6d.), which lies 2 M. to the W. of Buckhurst Hill, about 4½ M. to the S.W. of Waltham Abbey, and 2½ M. to the S. of *High Beach* (see below), is perhaps the best starting point from which to visit the most attractive parts of the Forest. Open conveyances of various kinds run from Chingford station and from the Royal Forest Hotel to High Beach (6d. each). Waltham Abbey, Chigwell, Epping, and other points of interest; the best conveyance is the four-horse coach starting at the hotel. On an eminence to the W. of Chingford is an obelisk, due N.

from Greenwich Observatory, and sometimes used in verifying astronomical calculations.

**Epping Forest**, along with the adjoining *Hainault Forest*, at one time extended almost to the gates of London. In 1793 there still remained 12,000 acres unenclosed, but these have been since reduced to about 5500 acres. The whole of the unenclosed part of the Forest was recently purchased by the Corporation of London, and was opened by Queen Victoria in May, 1882, as a free and inalienable public park and place of recreation. One of the finest points in the Forest, if not the very finest, is *High Beach*, an elevated tract covered with magnificent beech-trees, about $1^1/_2$ M. from Loughton. Tennyson was living here when he wrote 'The Talking Oak' and 'Locksley Hall'. There is an inn here, called the 'King's Oak', which is much resorted to by picnic parties. About $2^1/_2$ M. farther, on the northern verge of the Forest, stands *Copped Hall*, a magnificent mansion in the midst of an extensive park. The town of *Epping*, with 2300 inhab., lies 2 M. to the E. of this point. Near *Buckhurst Hill* (p. 329) is the *Roebuck Inn*, and there is also a small inn (the *Robin Hood*) at the point where the road from Loughton joins that to High Beach.

On the high-road between Loughton and Epping lies *Ambresbury Bank*, an old British camp, 12 acres in extent, and nearer Loughton is another similar earthwork. Tradition reports that it was here that Boadicea, Queen of the Iceni, was defeated by Suetonius, on which occasion 80,000 Britons are said to have perished. — A good map of Epping Forest, price 2d., may be obtained of H. Sell, 10 Bolt Court, Fleet Street. Good handbooks to the Forest are those of *E. N. Buxton* (Stanford; 1s. 6d.) and *Percy Lindley* (6d.).

**Waltham Abbey** lies on the river Lea, about 2 M. from the W. margin of the forest, and 6 M. to the W. of Copped Hall. The abbey was founded by the Saxon king Harold, and after his death in 1066 became his burial-place. The nave of the old abbey has been restored, and now serves as the parish-church. The round arches are specimens of very early Norman architecture, and may even have been built before the Conquest. Adjoining the S. aisle is a fine Lady Chapel, in the decorated style. The tower is modern.

The station lies $^3/_4$ M. to the W. of the abbey; and $^1/_4$ M. beyond the station stands *Waltham Cross*, one of the crosses which Edward I. erected on the different spots where the body of his queen Eleanor rested on its way from Nottinghamshire to London. The cross has been well restored. Another of these monuments, that at Charing Cross, has been already mentioned (see p. 145). At one of the entrances to *Theobalds Park*, near Waltham Cross, stands the re-erected *Temple Bar* (comp. p. 140).

The railway journey from Waltham Abbey to Rye House occupies 20 minutes. The intermediate stations are *Cheshunt* and *Broxbourne*; at the latter is the Crown Inn, with an extensive garden, which, in the rose season, presents a beautiful sight.

The river *Lea*, near which the line runs, is still, as in the days of its old admirer Isaac Walton, famous for its fishing; and the various stations on this line are much frequented by London anglers. Nearly the whole of the river is divided into 'swims', which are either private property, or confined to subscribers. Visitors, however, can obtain a day's fishing by payment of a small fee (at the inns). The free portions of the river do not afford such good sport.

**Rye** House, a favourite summer-resort for schools, clubs, societies, and workshop picnics. was built in the reign of Henry VI.: it belonged, with the manor, to Henry VIII., and afterwards passed into private hands. It is now a tavern. There are still some remains of the old building, particularly the embattled Gate House. As many as 1000 school children or excursionists have dined in Rye House at one time. The grounds are large and beautiful, affording abundant open air amusements ('*Guide*', price 3d.). The fishing near Rye House, both in the Lea and the New River, is very good.

Rye House gave its name in 1683 to the famous 'Rye House Plot', which had for its object the assassination of Charles II. and the Duke of York, as they travelled that way. The supposed conspiracy, which was headed by Rumbold, then owner of the manor. is said to have failed on account of the premature arrival of the King and his brother. It led to the execution of Rumbold, Algernon Sidney, Lord William Russell, etc. Whether a conspiracy, however, existed at all, is doubtful.

FROM RYE HOUSE TO (6 M.) HERTFORD, railway in 15 minutes. First station *St. Margaret's*. In the vicinity, on a branch of the Lea, is the pleasant little village of *Amwell*. On a small island in the stream is a monument to *Sir Hugh Myddelton*, who conducted the New River water to London (comp. p. 100). — Next stat. *Ware*, a busy market-town of 5270 inhabitants, with a considerable trade in malt and corn. At the inn called the 'Saracen's Head' was till lately exhibited the Great Bed of Ware, which measures 12 ft. both in length and breadth. The bed and its trappings now form part of the attractions of the Rye House. It is alluded to by Shakspeare (*Twelfth Night*, iii. 2). — Then **Hertford** (*Salisbury Arms; Dimsdale Arms; White Hart*), the capital of the shire of that name, situated on the S. bank of the Lea. It contains the remains of a castle of the 10th cent., and also a castle erected in the reign of the first Charles, now used as a school. The preparatory school in connection with Christ's Hospital is at Hertford (comp. p. 92). In the vicinity are various hand some country-seats. Among these are (S.W.) *Bayfordbury*, with the Kit Cat portraits (p. 325); *Balls Park*, the seat of the Marquis of Townshend and *Brickendonbury*. — On the W. is *Panshanger*, for many years the residence of Lord Palmerston, now the seat of Earl Cowper, with a good collection of pictures, of which the following are the most important "*Raphael*, Two Madonnas; *Fra Bartolommeo*, Holy Family; *Andrea del Sarto*, Three pictures illustrating the story of Joseph; *Sebastian del Piombo*, The Fornarina. Admission is granted on previous application by letter. The famous Panshanger Oak, one of the largest oaks in England, stands on the lawn to the W. of the house.

## 39. St. Albans.
### *Harrow. Luton. Dunstable.*

*Midland Railway*, from St. Pancras, 20 M., in 0¾-1 hr. (fares 2s. 8d., 1s. 7½d., no second class); *North Western Railway*, from Euston Square, 21 M., in ¾-1¼ hr. (fares 2s. 8d., 2s., 1s. 7½d.); or *Great Northern Railway*, from King's Cross, 23½ M. in ¾-1¼ hr. (fares 2s. 8d., 2s., 1s. 7½d.). Our chief description applies to the first-mentioned route, for which

through-tickets may be obtained at any of the Metropolitan Railway
stations. — During the summer months a four-horse *Coach* runs to St.
Albans four times a week, starting at 11 a.m. from Hatchett's, Piccadilly,
and, for the return journey, from the Peahen, St. Albans, at 4 p.m.
(2½ hrs.; fare 6s., return 10s.). The drive is picturesque and pleasant.

The first stations on the Midland Railway are *Camden Road,
Kentish Town*, *Haverstock Hill*, *Finchley Road*, and *West End*,
where we leave London fairly behind us and enter the open country.
Hampstead here lies on the right and Willesden on the left, while
the spire of Harrow church, also on the left, may be descried in
the distance. Then *Child's Hill*, and (5½ M.) *Welsh Harp*, with
an artificial lake, formed as a reservoir for the Regent Canal. It
contains abundance of fish, and attracts large numbers of anglers
(who for permission to fish apply at the inn, 'Old Welsh Harp';
day-tickets 1s. and 2s. 6d.). It is also a favourite resort of skaters
in winter. — 6 M. *Hendon*, with a picturesque ivy-grown church.
— 8 M. *Mill Hill*, with a Roman Catholic Missionary College and
a Congregationalist College. *Sir Stamford Raffles* died here in
1826; and *William Wilberforce* lived here, and built the Gothic
*Church of St. Paul* (1836).

About 1 M. to the W. lies *Edgware*, and a little more remote is
*Whitchurch*. While Händel was chapel-master to the Duke of Chandos at
Canons, a magnificent seat in this neighbourhood, now demolished, he
acted as organist in the church of Whitchurch (1718-1771). The church
still contains the organ on which he played, and also some fine wood-
carving. A blacksmith's shop in Edgware is said to be the place
where Händel conceived the idea of his 'Harmonious Blacksmith'.

11 M. *Elstree*, a picturesque village in Hertfordshire, which
we here enter. Good fishing may be obtained in the Elstree
reservoir. — 14 M. *Radlett*. — 20 M. St. Albans, p. 333.

If the *London and North Western Railway* route be chosen, the traveller
is recommended to visit, either in going or returning, Harrow on the
Hill *(King's Head; Railway)*, one of the stations on that line (the station
being 1 M. from the town). The large public school here, founded in 1571,
is scarcely second to Eton, and has numbered Lord Byron, Sir Robert Peel,
Sheridan, Spencer Perceval, Viscount Palmerston, and numerous other
eminent men among its pupils. The older portion of the school is in the
Tudor style. The chapel, library, and speech-room are all quite modern.
The panels of the great school-room are covered with the names of the boys,
including those of Byron, Peel, and Palmerston. The number of scholars
is now about 500. Harrow church has a lofty spire, which is a conspicuous
object in the landscape for many miles round. The churchyard commands
most extensive *View*. A flat tombstone, on which Byron used to lie, a
when a boy, and compose his juvenile poems, is still pointed out. — A
visit to Harrow alone is now most easily accomplished by the extension
of the Swiss Cottage branch of the Metropolitan Railway (from Baker
Street in ½ hr.; fares 1s. 5d., 1s., 8½d.). Beyond Harrow this line goes
on to *Pinner, Rickmansworth*, and *Chesham*.

The traveller who is equal to a walk of 10 M., and is fond of
natural scenery, may make the excursion to St. Albans very pleasantly
as follows. By railway from King's Cross *(Great Northern Railway)* to (9 M.)
*Barnet*; thence on foot, viâ (1 M.) *Chipping Barnet* and (5 M.) *Elstree* (see
above), to (10 M.) *Watford*, a station on the London and North Western Railway; and from Watford by rail to (7 M.) *St. Albans*. If the traveller means
to return by the Great Northern Railway, he should take a return-ticket
to Barnet. — Near *Hatfield*, the first station on this line in returning
from St. Albans, is *Hatfield House*, the seat of the Marquis of Salisbury,

a fine mansion built in the 17th cent. on the site of an earlier palace, in which Queen Elizabeth was detained in a state of semi-captivity before her accession to the throne (comp. *Baedeker's Great Britain*).

**St. Albans** (*Peahen*, *George*, both near the Abbey, unpretending) lies a short distance to the E. of the site of *Verulamium*, the most important town in the S. of England during the Roman period, of which the fosse and fragments of the walls remain. Its name is derived from St. Alban, a Roman soldier, the proto-martyr of Christianity in our island, who was executed here in A.D. 304. Holmhurst Hill, near the town, is supposed to have been the scene of his death. The Roman town fell into ruins after the departure of the Romans, and the new town of St. Albans began to spring up after 795, when Offa II., King of Mercia, founded here, in memory of St. Alban, the magnificent abbey, of which the fine church and a large square gateway are now the only remains. Pop. (1881) 10,930.

The *Abbey Church is in the form of a cross, with a tower at the point of intersection, and is one of the finest and largest churches in England. It was raised to the dignity of a cathedral in 1877, when the new episcopal see of St. Albans was created. It measures 550 ft. in length, (being the second longest church in England, coming after Winchester), by 175 ft. in breadth across the transepts; the fine Norman *Tower* is 145 ft. high. The earliest parts of the existing building, in which Roman tiles from Verulamium were freely made use of, date from the 11th cent. (ca. 1080); the *Choir* was built in the 13th cent. and the *Lady Chapel* in the 14th century. An extensive restoration of the building, including a new E.E. W. *Front*, with a large Dec. window, is nearing an end. St. Albans, 320 ft. above the sea, lies higher than any other English cathedral. See Froude's 'Annals of an English Abbey'.

The fine **Interior** (adm. 6d.; tickets procured at the booksellers in the town or from the verger) has recently been restored with great care. The Nave, the longest Gothic nave in the world, shows a curious intermixture of the Norman, E.E., and Dec. styles; and the change of the pitch of the vaulting in the S. aisle has a singular effect. The *Stained Glass Windows* in the N. aisle date from the 15th century. In the N. Transept some traces of old fresco-painting have been discovered, and the ceiling of the Choir is also coloured. The *Screen* behind the altar in the presbytery is of very fine mediæval workmanship, and has lately been restored and fitted with statues. Many of the chantries, or mortuary chapels of the abbots, and other monuments deserve attention. The splendid brass of *Abbot de la Mare* is best seen from the aisle to the S. of the Presbytery. In the *Saint's Chapel* are the tomb of Duke Humphrey of Gloucester (d. 1447), brother of Henry V., and the shrine of St. Alban. A door at the N. end of the transept leads to the *Tower*, the top of which commands a magnificent View.

The *Gate*, the only remnant of the conventual buildings of the abbey, stands to the W. of the church. It is a good specimen of the Perp. style. It was formerly used as a gaol, and is now a school.

About $3/4$ M. to the W. of the abbey stands the ancient Church of **St. Michael**, which is interesting as containing the tomb of the great Lord Bacon, Baron Verulam and Viscount St. Albans, who died at Gorhambury House here in 1626. The monument is by Rysbrack

To reach the church we turn to the left (W.) on leaving the cathedral and descend to the bridge over the Ver. The keys are kept by Mr. Monk, shoemaker (to the left, between the bridge and the church). The present *Gorhambury House*, the seat of the Earl of Verulam, 1½ M. to the W. of St. Michael's, is situated in the midst of a beautiful park, and contains a good collection of portraits.

St. Albans was the scene of two of the numerous battles fought during the Wars of the Roses. The scene of the first, which ushered in the contest, and took place in 1455, is now called the *Key Field*; the other was fought in 1461 at *Barnard's Heath*, to the N. of the town, just beyond St. Peter's Church.

From St. Albans to (10 M.) Luton by railway in 20-30 minutes. This excursion is particularly recommended to all who are interested in manufacturing industries. — First stat. *Harpenden*, near which, on the right of the line, is *Harpenden Lodge*. The train here passes from Hertfordshire into Bedfordshire. — *Chiltern Green*. On the right, *Luton Hoo Hall*, a very fine mansion. — Then (10 M.) Luton (*George; Red Lion; Midland*), a busy town of 24,000 inhab., famous for its manufacture of straw-hats. The straw-plait hall, market, and factories are all most interesting. Admission to one of the last establishments may usually be obtained on application. The *Parish Church*, with its fine embattled tower, possesses a chapel founded in the reign of Henry VI. (1422-61) and contains a curious font.

**Dunstable** (*Sugar Loaf; Red Lion; Railway*), 5 M. from Luton by a local line, contains 4000 inhab., and also possesses large straw-plait bonnet and basket manufactories. Dunstable larks are famous for their size and succulence, and are sent to London in great quantities. The *Church* is a fine specimen of Norman architecture, dating in part from the time of Henry I. (1100-1135). Charles I. slept at the Red Lion Inn while on his way to Naseby.

## 40. Windsor. Eton.

**Windsor** is reached by the *Great Western Railway*, from Paddington Station (21 M. in 35-65 min.; fares 3s. 9d., 2s. 10d., 1s. 9½d.; return-tickets, available for 8 days, 5s. 6d., 4s. 3d., available from Sat. to Mon., 4s. 6d., 3s. 6d.); or by the *South Western Railway*, from Waterloo Station, N. side (25½ M. in 1¼ hr.; same fares).

Great Western Railway. The first station is *Royal Oak*, where, by a clever piece of engineering, the rails for local trains are carried under those for through trains, by a descent and then an ascent. The second station, called *Westbourne Park*, near which *Kensal Green Cemetery* (p. 294) lies on the right, is still within the precincts of the town. The next stations are *Acton*, *Ealing*, *Castle Hill*, and *Hanwell*, at which last, on the left, is the extensive *Middlesex County Lunatic Asylum*, with a fine park and accommodation for 1000 inmates. At *Southall* a branch-line diverges on the left to *Brentford*. Next come *Hayes*, *West Drayton* (branch-lines to *Uxbridge*, a busy little town, prettily situated on the Colne, 3 M. to the N., and to *Staines*, p. 335), *Langley*, and *Slough*, where the **branch** to Windsor diverges to the left from the main Great Western line. (Passengers who are not in a through Windsor carriage change here.)

*Sir William Herschel* (d. 1822) and *Sir John Herschel* (d. 1871), the celebrated astronomers, made many of their important discoveries in their observatory at Slough.

A pleasant ramble, through picturesque scenery, may be made from Slough to (2 M.) *Stoke Poges* and (3 M.) *Burnham Beeches*. The churchyard at Stoke Poges is the scene of Gray's famous 'Elegy', and now contains the poet's grave. A monument to his memory has been erected in the adjacent *Stoke Park*, a fine property which once belonged to the descendants of William Penn. Sir Edward Coke entertained Queen Elizabeth at Stoke Poges in 1601. At a little distance is *Beaconsfield*, with a house (named *Gregories*) once occupied by *Edmund Waller* (d. 1687) and *Edmund Burke* (d. 1797), of whom the one lies buried in the churchyard, and the other in the church. It furnished the title of *Benjamin Disraeli, Earl of Beaconsfield* (d. 1881), who lived at *Hughenden*, 8 M. to the W., and is buried in a vault near the church. The beeches at Burnham, the finest in England, have been secured as a public resort by the Corporation of London (see 'Burnham Beeches', by F. G. Heath; 1s.).

Before reaching Windsor the train crosses the Thames, passing Eton College (p. 341) on the right. The station is on the S.W. side of the town, in George Street, about $1/4$ M. from the Castle.

SOUTH WESTERN RAILWAY. Route to *Clapham Junction*, see p. 315; the branch-line to Richmond and Windsor diverges here to the right from the main South Western line, and approaches the Thames at *Wandsworth* station (p. 324). We next pass *Putney* (p. 324), *Barnes* (p. 325; branch-line to *Chiswick*, p. 325, and *Kew Bridge*, p. 322), *Mortlake* (p. 325), and *Richmond* (p. 321). The line skirts Richmond Park, crosses the Thames by a bridge of three arches, and reaches *Twickenham* (p. 326; on the left a branch-line to *Teddington*, p. 321, *Hampton Wick*, p. 315, and *Kingston*, p. 326). Next stations, *Feltham*, with a large reformatory for youthful criminals, *Ashford*, and *Staines*, a picturesque old town, deriving its name from the 'stones' which once marked the limits of the jurisdiction of London in this direction.

A branch of the South Western Railway runs hence to the left to *Virginia Water* (p. 342), *Ascot* (p. 342), and *Reading*. Near *Egham*, the first station beyond Staines on this line, is the plain of *Runnimede*, where King John signed the Magna Charta in 1215 (see p. 57). Above the town rises *Cooper's Hill* (view), celebrated in Denman's well-known poem; on it stands the *Royal Indian Engineering College*. Beyond Egham is *Mt. Lee*, on the top of which is the large **Holloway College for Women**, erected and endowed by Mr. Holloway (of the 'Pills') at a cost of 1,000,000l. The buildings, which are very handsome and elaborate, have accommodation for 300 students.

Our train runs in a N.W. direction. Stations *Wraysbury* and *Datchet* (Manor House; Stag). On the left rise the large towers of Windsor Castle, round the park of which the train describes a wide circuit. Before reaching Windsor we cross the Thames, on the N. bank of which lies Eton College (p. 342). The station lies in Thames Street, on the N.E. side of the town, near the bridge over the Thames, and $1/2$ M. from the Castle.

HOTELS AT WINDSOR (pop. in 1881, 19,080): *White Hart*, said to be expensive; *Castle*; *Great Western*; *Bridge House* (well spoken of), *Christopher*, at Eton.

The wards of Windsor Castle and the northern terrace are al-

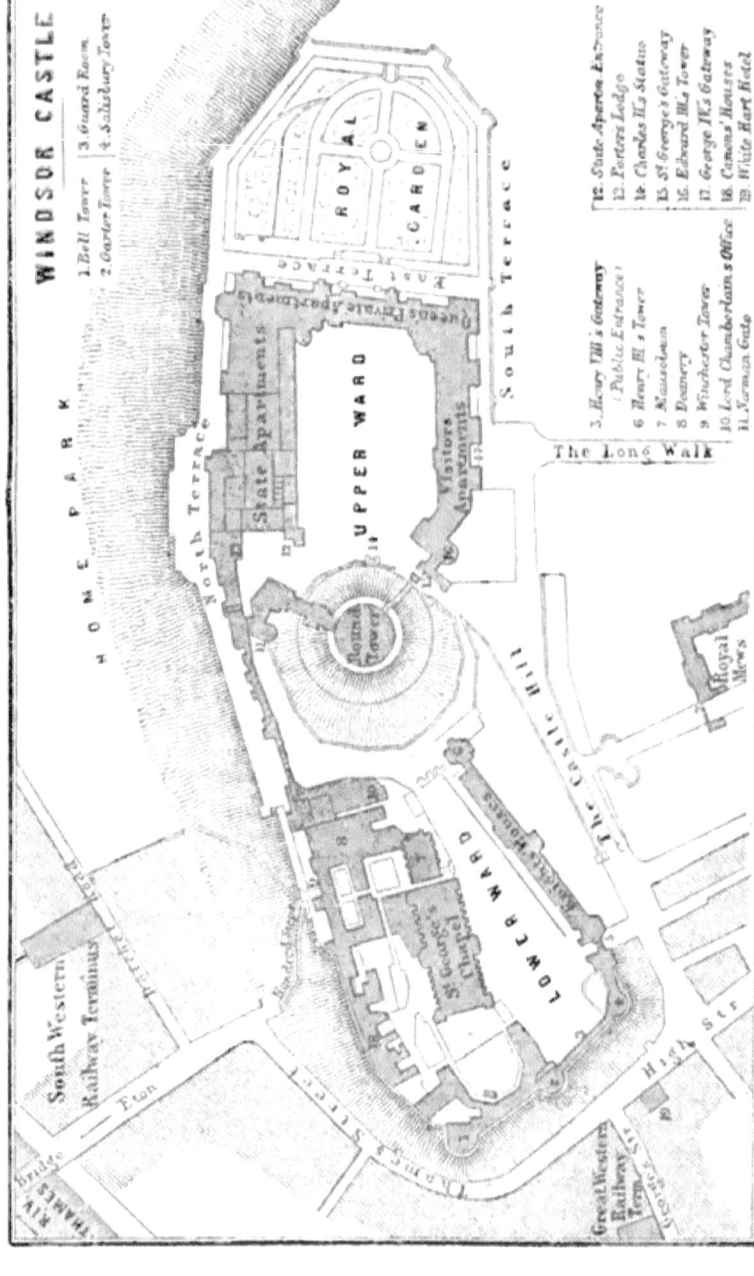

ways open to the public; admission to the eastern terrace is granted on Saturdays and Sundays only, from 2 to 6 p.m., in the absence of the Queen. (The Guards' band usually plays here on Sundays.) The State Apartments are shown (in the absence of the Queen) on Mondays, Tuesdays, Thursdays, and Fridays, from 1st April to 31st Oct., 11-4; from 1st Nov. to 31st March, 11-3. St. George's Chapel is open daily, except Wednesday, from 12.30 to 4; divine service is celebrated on Sundays at 11 a.m. and 5 p.m.; on weekdays, at 10.30 a.m. and 4.30 p.m. The *Albert Chapel* is open every Wednesday, Thursday, and Friday, 12-3 p.m., without tickets. The best days for a visit to Windsor are therefore Thursday and Friday. Tickets of admission for the State Apartments are obtained in the Lord Chamberlain's office at the castle. The Private Apartments of the Queen are shown only by a special order from the Lord Chamberlain, which it is difficult to obtain.

*Windsor* (originally *Windleshore*, from an Anglo-Saxon root, in allusion to the winding course of the Thames here), an estate presented by Edward the Confessor to the monks of Westminster Abbey, was purchased by William the Conqueror for the purpose of erecting a castle on the isolated hill in its centre. The building was extended by Henry I. and Henry II.; and Edward III., who was born at Windsor, caused the old castle to be taken down, and a new one to be erected on its site, by *William of Wykeham*, the art-loving Bishop of Winchester.

Under succeeding monarchs Windsor Castle was frequently extended; and finally George IV. began a series of extensive restorations under the superintendence of *Sir Jeffrey Wyattville*. The restoration, completed in the reign of Queen Victoria at a total cost of 900,000*l*., left Windsor Castle one of the largest and most magnificent royal residences in the world.

The Castle consists of two courts, called the *Upper* and *Lower Wards*, surrounded by buildings; between the two rises the *Round Tower* (see below). We first enter the Lower Ward from the *Castle Hill* by *Henry VIII.'s Gateway*. On the N.W. side of the ward, opposite the entrance, stands \*St. George's Chapel, or chapel of the Knights of the Order of the Garter, begun in 1474, in the late-Gothic style, by Edward IV. on the site of a chapel of Henry I., and completed by Henry VIII.

The Interior, which is richly adorned in the Perpendicular style, possesses a handsome, fan-shaped, vaulted roof. To the right of the entrance is a cenotaph of the Prince Imperial, with a recumbent figure in white marble, erected by the Queen. The large W. window contains old stained glass, the subjects of which refer to the Order of the Garter. In the S.W. corner is *Beaufort Chapel*, adjoining which, below the modern window at the end of the S. aisle, is the tomb of the Queen's father, the Duke of Kent, consisting of an alabaster sarcophagus with the recumbent marble effigy of the Duke, designed by Sir G. G. Scott (d. 1878), and executed by *Boehm*. Opposite, at the end of the N. aisle, is the monument of Princess Charlotte, designed by *Wyatt*. The richly-adorned \*Choir contains the stalls of the Knights of the Garter,

BAEDEKER. London 7th Edit.

with their coats of-arms and banners. At the E. end, above the altar, is a fine stained glass window to the memory of Prince Albert, erected from designs by Sir *G. G. Scott*. The reredos below the window, sculptured in alabaster marble, is very fine. The subjects are the Ascension, Christ appearing to his Disciples, and Christ meeting Mary in the Garden. To the left, adjoining the altar, is the monument of Edward IV., consisting of an iron gate between two battlemented towers, and said to have been executed by the Antwerp painter *Quintin Matsys*. Among the numerous other monuments in the chapel we may mention the plain marble tombstone of Henry VI. and the handsome monument erected by Queen Victoria to her aunt, the Duchess of Gloucester (d. 1857), both in the S. part of the retro-choir, and the statue of Earl Harcourt (d. 1830), on the N. side of the retro-choir. The vault in the middle of the choir contains the remains of Henry VIII., his wife Jane Seymour, and Charles I. — A subterranean passage leads from the altar to the royal *Tombhouse* under the Albert Chapel, situated on the E. side of St. George's Chapel, in which repose George III., George IV., William IV., and other royal personages. (Divine service, etc., see p. 337.)

The *Albert Chapel* (Pl. 7), adjoining St. George's Chapel on the E., was originally erected by Henry VII. as a mausoleum for himself; but, on his ultimate preference of Westminster, it was transferred for a similar use to Cardinal Wolsey. On the fall of that prelate it reverted to the Crown, and was subsequently fitted up by James II. as a Roman Catholic chapel. An indignant mob, however, broke the windows and otherwise defaced it, and 'Wolsey's Chapel', as it was called, was doomed to a century of dilapidation and neglect, after which George III. constructed the royal tomb-house beneath it. Queen Victoria then undertook the restoration of the chapel in honour of her deceased husband, Prince Albert, and has made it a truly royal and sumptuous memorial.

The interior, beautified with coloured marble, mosaics, sculpture, stained glass, precious stones, and gilding, in extraordinary profusion and richness, must certainly be numbered among the finest works of its kind in the world, though, it must be owned, rather out of harmony with the Gothic architecture of the building. The ceiling, which resembles in form that of St. George's Chapel, is composed of Venetian enamel mosaics, representing in the nave, angels bearing devices relating to the Prince Consort; in the chancel, angels with shields symbolical of the Passion. The false window at the W. end is of similar workmanship, and bears representations of illustrious personages connected with St. George's Chapel. At the sides of the W. entrance are two marble figures — the Angels of Life and Death. The walls are decorated with a series of pictures of scriptural subjects inlaid with coloured marbles, by *Triqueti*, in which 28 different kinds of marble have been introduced. Above each scene is a white marble medallion of a member of the royal family, by *Miss Susan Durant*, while between them are bas-reliefs, emblematical of the virtues. Round the edges of the pictures are smaller reliefs in white and red marble, and other ornamentation. Below the marble pictures is a dark green marble bench; and the floor, which is very handsome, is also of coloured marbles. Most of the modern stained-glass windows exhibit ancestors of the Prince Consort; those in the chancel are filled with scriptural subjects. The reliefs of the reredos, which was designed by *Sir G. G. Scott*, and is inlaid with coloured marble, malachite, porphyry, lapis lazuli, and alabaster, have for their subject the Resurrection. In the centre of the nave stands the *Cenotaph* of the Prince, by Triqueti, consisting of a handsome sarcophagus, enriched with reliefs, bearing the recumbent figure of Prince Albert in white marble. The restoration was superintended by *Sir G. G. Scott*, the architect. Near the W. door is a cenotaph with a recumbent figure.

in white marble, of the Duke of Albany (d. 1884), in the dress of the Seaforth Highlanders. The mosaics were executed by Salviati. The length of the chapel is 68 ft., its breadth 28 ft., and its height 59 ft.

The **Round Tower**, or *Keep*, used as a prison down to 1660, rises on the E. side of the Lower Ward, on an eminence 42 ft. high, surrounded on three sides by a deep moat. The scarps are embellished by beds of flowers. The battlements, 80 ft. above the ground (entrance from the Upper Ward, near the Norman Gate, Pl. 11), command a charming **View of the country round Windsor, embracing, in clear weather, parts of no fewer than twelve counties. The bell, weighing 17 cwt., was brought from Sebastopol. The tower is not perfectly symmetrical, measuring 102 ft. by 95 ft.; admission gratis, 11-4. (The custodian points out the principal places in the environs, in which case he expects a trifling fee.)

On the N. side of the tower is the vaulted *Norman Gateway* (Pl. 11), flanked by pinnacled towers, and leading to the Upper WARD. Opposite, by the *Porter's Lodge* (Pl. 13), is the entrance to the State Apartments (Pl. 12), which lie on the N. side of the large *Quadrangle*. On the E. are the *Queen's Private Apartments*. *George IV's Gateway* (Pl. 17), in the middle of the S. side, at the end of the Long Walk (p. 342), is the principal entrance to the palace, and is used by royal carriages only. At the foot of the tower, on its E. side, is a bronze statue of Charles II. (Pl. 14), with reliefs on the pedestal by *Grinling Gibbons*.

The **State Apartments** are usually shown in the following, though sometimes in the reverse, order. They contain many good pictures; but the barriers, which leave a narrow passage only for the public, and the hurried manner in which the rooms are shown, render it difficult for visitors to see them satisfactorily. The vestibule contains a good portrait of Sir Jeffrey Wyattville, the architect (see p. 337), by Lawrence.

The QUEEN'S AUDIENCE CHAMBER. The ceiling is decorated with paintings by *Verrio*. The walls are hung with tapestry, representing the story of Esther and Mordecai, with portraits of Prince Frederick Henry and William II. of Orange, by *Honthorst*, and an old portrait of Mary, Queen of Scots, by *Janet*.

The QUEEN'S PRESENCE CHAMBER has also a ceiling painted by Verrio, and is hung with tapestry continuing the story of Esther and Mordecai. The carvings are by Grinling Gibbons.

The GUARD CHAMBER contains suits of old armour; four bronze cannon captured in India; above the mantelpiece, a silver shield inlaid with gold, under glass, presented by Francis I., of France to Henry VIII and said to be the work of *Benvenuto Cellini*; a colossal bust of Nelson by *Chantrey*, on a pedestal formed of a piece of the mast of the 'Victory', on board which Nelson was shot, with a hole made by a ball at that battle; busts of Marlborough, after *Rysbrack*, and Wellington by *Chantrey*.

ST. GEORGE'S HALL, 200 ft. long and 34 ft. wide, has a ceiling adorned with the armorial bearings of the Knights of the Garter since 1362. On the walls are portraits of the English kings from James I. to George IV., by *Van Dyck*, *Lely*, *Kneller*, *Lawrence*, etc. At the E. end is the carved oak throne, a copy of the coronation chair in Westminster Abbey.

The GRAND RECEPTION ROOM, originally meant for a ball room, is magnificently decorated in the rococo style, and is hung with tapestry representing the story of Jason and Medea. At the N. end are a vase of malachite, the gift of the Emperor Nicholas of Russia, and two granite vases, presented by King Frederick William III. of Prussia.

The THRONE ROOM contains pictures by *West* (Establishment of the Order of the Garter), and portraits by *Lawrence*, *Gainsborough*, and others.

The WATERLOO CHAMBER, or GRAND DINING ROOM, 98 ft. long by 47 ft. broad, in the Elizabethan style, is filled with portraits of Wellington, Blucher, Castlereagh, Metternich, Pope Pius VII., Emperor Alexander, Canning, W. von Humboldt, and others associated with the events of 1813-15, painted by *Lawrence*, *Beechey*, *Pickersgill*, *Wilkie*, etc. The carvings are by *Grinling Gibbons*.

The GRAND VESTIBULE, 46 ft. long, 28 ft. broad, and 46 ft. high, is decorated with armour and banners, and contains two bronze cannon from Seringapatam; a brass gun from Borneo; a curious root in the shape of a dragon; and a statue of Queen Victoria, by *Boehm*.

The GRAND STAIRCASE, with *Chantrey's* statue of George IV.

The STATE ANTE-ROOM, originally the 'King's Public Dining Room', contains carving by *Grinling Gibbons*, allegorical ceiling-paintings by *Verrio*, and a portrait of George III. after *Reynolds* (on glass, above the chimney-piece).

In the SMALL VESTIBULE are five historical paintings by *West*, being scenes from the reign of Edward III.

The RUBENS ROOM contains eleven pictures by *Rubens*.

The COUNCIL CHAMBER contains 35 valuable works by *Carlo Maratta*, *Parmeggianino*, *Guido Reni*, *Guercino*, *Correggio*, *Andrea del Sarto*, *Leonardo da Vinci*, *Garofalo*, *Carlo Dolci*, *Annibale Carracci*, *Domenichino*, *Rembrandt*, *Teniers*, *Peter Neefs*, *Holbein*, *G. Poussin*, *Claude Lorrain*, *Lely*, and *Kneller*.

The KING'S CLOSET is hung with pictures by the painters already named, and also by the Netherlandish masters *Brueghel*, *Wouwerman*, *Westermann*, *Mierevelt*, *A. van de Velde*, *Rubens*, *Steenwyk*, and *Jan Steen*.

The QUEEN'S CLOSET is hung with 30 works by old masters.

The QUEEN'S STATE DRAWING ROOM contains several large landscapes by *Zuccarelli*, and portraits of George I., George III., Frederick Prince of Wales (father of George III.), and the Duke of Gloucester.

The OLD BALL ROOM, or VAN DYCK ROOM, is exclusively devoted to portraits by that master. The best are those of Henry, Count de Berg; Charles I. and his family; Mary, Duchess of Richmond; Henrietta Maria, wife of Charles I. (four portraits); Lady Venetia Digby; George, second Duke of Buckingham, and his brother Lord Francis Villiers; Children of Charles I.; Head of Charles I. from three different points of view, painted as an aid in the execution of a bust; Lucy, Countess of Carlisle; Charles II. when a boy; Portrait of the master himself; The three eldest children of Charles I.; Charles I. on horseback. — There are also in this room two small bronzes of the Laocoon and Prometheus Bound, and some valuable cabinets, the best of which is a magnificent specimen of ormolu work by Gouthière.

The *Small Vestibule*, *Throne Room*, *Rubens Room*, *Council Chamber*, *King's Closet*, and *Queen's Closet* are shown only to those furnished with a special order from the Lord Chamberlain.

Those who are fortunate enough to gain admittance to the *Private Apartments* will enjoy one of the greatest artistic treats that England has to offer. The rooms are most sumptuously fitted up, and contain a magnificent collection of Chelsea, Oriental, and Sèvres china, mediæval and Oriental cabinets, gold and silver plate, pictures, etc. In the *Library* is a valuable collection of drawings and miniatures by *Holbein*, *Leonardo da Vinci*, *Raphael*, and *Michael Angelo*.

The *N. Terrace*, 625 yds. in length, is always open to the public, and commands a charming view; the *E. Terrace* is open on Saturdays and Sundays only, from 2 to 6 (see p. 337). From the latter, which affords an admirable view of the imposing E. façade of the castle, broad flights of steps descend into the *Flower Garden*, which is tastefully laid out, and embellished with marble and bronze statues, and a fountain in the centre.

The *Royal Stables*, or *Mews*, on the S. side of the castle, built at a cost of 70,000l., are open daily from 1 to 3 p.m. Tickets of admission are obtained at the entrance from the Clerk of the Mews (small fee to groom who conducts the visitors round).

The *Town Hall* of Windsor contains some good portraits, an ancient mayor's chair in carved oak, and a marble bust of Charles Knight (1791-1873), a native of Windsor. The Parish Church, High Street, has some quaint monuments, carved railings by Grinling Gibbons, and mosaics by Salviati. The Garrison Church (Holy Trinity) contains numerous military memorials.

On the left bank of the Thames, 10 min. to the N. of Windsor Bridge, is **Eton College**, one of the most famous of English schools, founded in 1440 by Henry VI. The number of pupils on the foundation, who live at the college, and wear black gowns, is about 70; the main portion of the establishment consists of the *Oppidans*, numbering more than 900, who live at the residences of the masters, or in the authorised 'Dames' houses, in the town, but under the jurisdiction of the college. The Eton boys, in their short jackets, broad collars, and tall hats, represent a large section of the youthful wealth and aristocracy of England.

The school buildings enclose two large courts, united by the archway of the clock tower. The centre of the *Outer Quadrangle*, or larger court to the W., is occupied by a bronze statue of Henry VI.; on its N. side is the *Lower School*; on the W., the *Upper School*, the hall of which contains marble busts of English monarchs and of distinguished Etonians, including Chatham, Fox, Canning, Peel, and Wellington. The *Chapel* on the S. side, a handsome Gothic building, is decorated internally with wood-carving, stained-glass windows, and mosaics; in the antechapel is a marble statue of Henry VI. The *Inner Quadrangle* is bounded in part by the dining-hall of the students who board at the college, and by the library, containing a rich collection of classical and Oriental MSS. A new *Quadrangle*, including a museum and a chapel for the Lower School, was erected in 1888-89. Those who desire to see the school should apply to Mr. Osborn, Clerk to the Head Master, at the School Office. The chapel is in the charge of Mr. Oakley. The *Playing Fields* should be visited. Comp. Maxwell Lyte's 'History of Eton College' (1875). See also the amusing little book entitled 'A Day of My Life at Eton'.

To the N. and E. of Windsor lies the Home Park, or smaller park, surrounded on three sides by the Thames, and about 4 M. in circumference. A carriage-road leads through it to the village of *Datchet* (p. 336), situated on the left bank of the Thames, 1 M. to the E. of Windsor. *Herne's Oak*, celebrated in Shakspeare's 'Merry Wives of Windsor', formerly stood by the roadside in 1863.

however, the old tree was destroyed by lightning, and a young oak planted in its place by the Queen. Opposite Datchet is the small royal country-seat of *Adelaide Lodge*; and farther S. is *Frogmore Lodge*, once the seat of the Queen's mother, the Duchess of Kent (d. 1861). Its grounds contain the Duchess's tomb, the magnificent mausoleum erected by the Queen to her husband, Prince Albert (d. 1861), and a cenotaph of Princess Alice (d. 1878).

The **Great Park**, 1800 acres in extent, lies to the S. of Windsor, and is stocked with several thousand fallow deer. The *Long Walk*, a fine avenue of elms, leads from *George IV's Gateway* (p. 325), in a straight line of nearly 3 M., to *Snow Hill*, which is crowned by a statue of George III., by *Westmacott*. At the end of this avenue is a road to the left, which passes *Cumberland Lodge*, and leads to *Virginia Water* (\*Wheatsheaf Hotel; carriage from Windsor and back 7-9s.), an artificial lake, formed in 1746 by the Duke of Cumberland, the victor at Culloden, in order to drain the surrounding moorland. The views from various points around the lake are very pleasing. There is a station of the South Western Railway (p. 35) about 1½ M. from Virginia Water; and in summer a coach runs daily to Virginia Water from Piccadilly (see p. 32). — *Queen Anne's Ride*, another avenue, running almost parallel with the Long Walk, leads to the right to *Ascot* (p. 336), the scene of the fashionable *Ascot Races* in June, on the occasion of which some members of the Royal Family usually drive up the course in state (comp. p. 46).

## 41. Gravesend. Chatham. Rochester.

NORTH KENT RAILWAY from Charing Cross, Cannon Street, and London Bridge, to *Gravesend* (24 M., in 1-1½ hrs.; fares 3s. 6d., 2s. 8d., 2s. 2d); thence to *Strood*, *Rochester*, and *Chatham* in 10-20 min. more (fares 5s., 3s. 6d., 2s. 6d); or to Strood by rail, and thence across the Medway to Rochester and Chatham. The return journey may be made by the LONDON, CHATHAM, AND DOVER RAILWAY, which runs *viâ* Bromley and Beckenham to Victoria. Holborn Viaduct, Ludgate Hill, and King's Cross (in 1hr. 5 min. to 1¾ hr.; fares 5s., 3s. 6d., 2s. 6d.).

During the summer months *Gravesend* may also be reached by a Thames STEAMBOAT from London Bridge (2½ hrs.; fares 1s. 6d., 1s.).

A pleasant way of making this excursion is as follows: by river to Gravesend, and thence on foot by *Cobham Hall* (p. 346) to (7 M.) *Rochester* and *Chatham*, the return journey being effected by the London, Chatham, and Dover Railway. A whole day will thus be occupied.

As far as Gravesend, we describe both the river and the railway route.

A. THE THAMES FROM LONDON BRIDGE TO GRAVESEND.

The scenery of the Thames below London contrasts very unfavourably with the smiling beauties of the same river higher up; yet the trip down to Gravesend has attractions of its own, and may be recommended as affording a good survey of the vast commercial traffic of London. The appearance of the Thames just below London

Bridge has already been described (p. 110), and the names of the wharves as far as Greenwich and Woolwich will be found in Route **31**. The principal objects seen on the banks thus far are the *Monument* (left; p. 110), *Billingsgate* (left; p. 111), *Custom House* (left; p. 112), *Tower* (left; p. 117). *St. Katherine's Docks* (left; p. 126), *London Docks* (left; p. 126), *Wapping* (left; p. 127), *Rotherhithe* (right; p. 67), *Surrey Docks* (right; p. 128), *Commercial Docks* (right; p. 128), *Deptford* (right; p. 68), *West India Docks* (left; p. 128), *Greenwich Hospital* (right; p. 301), *Isle of Dogs* (left; p. 128), *Blackwall Station* (left; p. 301), *East India Docks* (left; p. 128), *Victoria Docks* (left; p. 128), *Woolwich*, with its dock-yard and arsenal (right; p. 304), *North Woolwich* (left). Just above London Bridge we cross the *City of London Subway* (p. 126), below the Custom House we cross the *Tower Subway* (p. 126), and by the Surrey Docks we pass over the *Thames Tunnel* (p. 127). The different docks are frequented by different classes of vessels. Thus in the London Docks we see ships bound for the Cape, the Mediterranean, India, and China. Most of the ships in the Commercial Docks are engaged in the timber trade with Sweden and Norway. The Victoria Docks are devoted to steamships plying to America and the Black Sea. The West India Docks contain the stately merchantmen which bring the wealth of the West Indies to this country, while the East India Docks are filled with merchant and passenger vessels sailing between England and India, China, Australia, and New Zealand.

The banks of the Thames below Woolwich are very flat and marshy, recalling the appearance of a Dutch landscape. Shortly after leaving Woolwich, we enter a part of the river called *Barking Reach*, where, at Barking Creek on the N., and Crossness on the S. bank, are situated the outlets of London's new and gigantic system of drainage. The pumping-house at Crossness is a building of some architectural merit, with an Italian tower (visitors admitted on application at the office). Passing through *Halfway Reach* and *Erith Reach*, with *Erith Marshes* on our right, we next arrive at —

R. *Erith*, a village pleasantly situated at the base of a wooded hill, with a picturesque, ivy-clad, old church. — On the opposite bank of the river, 2 M. lower down, lies —

L. *Purfleet* (Royal Hotel, fish-dinners), the seat of large Government powder magazines, capable of containing 60,000 barrels of powder. Opposite is the mouth of the small river Darent. The training-ship *Cornwall* is moored in the Thames at Purfleet. — Three miles below Purfleet, on the same side, is —

L. *West Thurrock* (Old Ship), with the Saxon church of St. Clement, one of the most ancient in England. There are still some remains of an old monastery. The Essex bank here forms a sharp promontory, immediately opposite which, in a corresponding indentation, lies —

R. *Greenhithe* (Pier; White Hart), a pretty little place, with a number of villas. Some training-ships lie in the river here, and it is also a yachting station. A little way inland is *Stone Church*, supposed to have been built by the architect of Westminster Abbey, and restored by Mr. Street; it contains some fine stone-carving and old brasses. Just beyond Greenhithe the eye is attracted by the conspicuous white mansion of *Ingress Abbey*, at one time occupied by the father of Sir Henry Havelock. — Then —

L. *Grays Thurrock*, near which are some curious caves. — Next, 3 M. lower, —

R. *Northfleet*, with chalk-pits, cement factories, and a fine old church containing some monuments and a carved oak rood-screen of the 14th century. Northfleet also possesses a college for indigent ladies and gentlemen, and a working-man's club, the latter a large red and white brick building. An electric tramway runs, between 2 and 11 p.m., from Northfleet station (S. E. R.) to the top of Northfleet Hill (1*d*.), where it connects with a horse-tramway to Rosherville and Gravesend (through-fare 2*d*.). We now observe, on the Essex bank, opposite Gravesend, the low bastions of —

L. *Tilbury Fort*, originally constructed by Henry VIII. to defend the mouth of the Thames, and since extended and strengthened. It was here that Queen Elizabeth assembled and reviewed her troops in anticipation of the attack of the Armada (1588), appearing in helmet and corslet, and using the bold and well-known words: 'I know I have the body of a weak, feeble woman, but I have the heart and stomach of a king, and of a king of England too!' The large docks at *Tilbury* (Tilbury Grand Hotel) were opened in 1886.

R. *Gravesend*, see below.

### B. London to Gravesend by Rail.

On quitting London Bridge station the train first traverses the busy manufacturing districts of *Bermondsey* and *Rotherhithe*; in the churchyard of the latter is buried Prince Lee Boo (d. 1784), son of the king of the Pellew Islands, who in 1783 treated the shipwrecked crew of the Antelope with great kindness. The train then stops at (3 M.) *New Cross*, *St. John's*, and (6 M.) *Lewisham Junction*. It next passes through a tunnel, about 1 M. in length, and arrives at (7 M.) *Blackheath* (p. 304). Then (9 M.) *Charlton*, close to the station of which is the old manor-house of the same name. We next pass through two tunnels, and reach (10 M.) *Woolwich Dockyard*, followed immediately by *Woolwich Arsenal*. — 11¼ M. *Plumstead*, with Plumstead Marshes on the left. — 13 M. *Abbey Wood*, a small village of recent origin, with pleasant surroundings, and some scanty remains of *Lesnes Abbey*, an Augustinian foundation of the 12th century. — Close to (14 M.) *Belvedere* lies

Belvedere House, the seat of Lord Sayes. — (15½ M.) *Erith*, see p. 343. The **train** crosses the river Cray, and reaches —

17 M. **Dartford** *(Bull; Victoria)*, a busy town of 11,000 inhab., with a large paper-mill, a machine and engine factory, a gunpowder factory, and the City of London Lunatic Asylum. The first paper mill in England was erected here at the end of the 16th century. Foolscap paper takes its name from the crest (a fool's cap) of the founder, whose tomb is in the church. Dartford was the abode of the rebel Wat Tyler (p. 96).

Another route from London to Dartford passes the interesting little town of (9 M.) **Eltham** *(Greyhound; Chequers)*, prettily situated among trees, with the villas of numerous London merchants. About ¼ M. to the N. of the station lie the remains of *Eltham Palace*, a favourite royal residence from Henry III. (1216-72) to Henry VIII. (1509-1547). Queen Elizabeth often lived here in her childhood. The palace is popularly known as *King John's Barn*, perhaps because the king has been confounded with John of Eltham, son of Edward II., who was born here. Part of the old moat surrounding the palace is still filled with water, and we cross it by a picturesque old bridge. Almost the only relic of the building is the fine *Banqueting Hall* (key kept in the adjacent lodge), somewhat resembling Crosby Hall in London in general style and dating like it from the reign of Edward IV. (1461-83). The hall was long used as a barn, and some of its windows are still bricked up. The Roof is of chestnut. Adjoining the hall on the left is the *Court House*, a picturesque gabled building, formerly the buttery of the Palace.

There were originally three Parks attached to Eltham Palace, one of which, the *Middle Park*, has attained some celebrity in modern days as the home of the Blenkiron stud of race-horses, which produced the Derby winners, Gladiateur and Blair Athole. The *Great Park* has been built over. — The *Church* of Eltham was rebuilt in 1871; in the churchyard are buried *Bishop Horne* (d. 1792), the commentator on the Psalms, and *Doggett*, the comedian, founder of 'Doggett's Coat and Badge' (p. ). *Van Dyck* was assigned summer-quarters at Eltham during his stay in England (1632-41), probably in the palace.

A visit to Eltham may be conveniently combined with one to Greenwich (p. 301), which is reached by a pleasant walk of 4 M. across Blackheath (p. 304) and Greenwich Park; or to Woolwich (also 4 M.), reached viâ Shooter's Hill (p. 305). Another pleasant walk may be taken to (3 M.) *Chiselhurst*.

Beyond Dartford we cross the Darent, pass (20 M.) *Greenhithe* (p. 345) and *Northfleet* (p. 344), and reach —

24 M. *Gravesend*.

**Gravesend** *(Clarendon Hotel; Old Falcon; New Falcon; Nelson)*, a town with 25,000 inhab., lying on the S. bank of the Thames, at the head of its estuary, has greatly increased in size in recent years, and is much resorted to by pleasure-seekers from London. The newer parts of the town are well built, but the streets in the lower quarter are narrow and crooked. Gravesend possesses two good piers. On the W. side, towards Northfleet, are *Rosherville Gardens* (see p. ), a favourite resort, where music, dancing, archery, and other amusements find numerous votaries. The parish-church was built in the reign of Queen Anne, on the site of an earlier church which had been burned down in 1520. Pocahontas (d. 1617), the Indian princess who married John Rolfe, is interred in the chancel (see *Doyle's* 'English in America', 1882). *Windmill Hill*, at the back of the town, now almost covered with the buildings of the increasing suburbs, commands a fine view of the Thames, Shooter's Hill (p. 305), London, with the hills of Highgate and Hampstead beyond, and (to the S.) over the county of Kent, with Cobham Hall (see below) and Springhead as conspicuous points.

Pleasant excursion to \*Cobham Hall, the seat of the Earl of Darnley, in the midst of a magnificent park (fine rhododendrons, in bloom in June), 7 M. in circumference, lying about 4 M. to the S. of Gravesend. (Tickets of admission to the house, which is open to visitors on Fridays from 11 to 4 only, may be obtained at Caddel's Library, King Street, Gravesend, and High Street, Rochester, price 1s.; the proceeds are devoted to charitable purposes.) The central portion of this handsome mansion was built by *Inigo Jones* (d. 1653); the wings date from the 16th century. The interior was restored during the present century. The fine collection of pictures includes a \*Portrait of Ariosto and \*Europa and the Bull by *Titian*, \*Tomyris with the head of Cyrus by *Rubens*, and examples of Van *Dyck*, *Lely*, *Kneller*, and other masters. — The *Parish Church* of Cobham contains some fine old brasses.

The pedestrian may extend his walk, through the famed woods of Cobham Park, and down the valley of the Medway, to *Strood*, a suburb of Rochester, a walk of about 7 M. in all from Gravesend. — The direct road from Gravesend to (6 M.) *Rochester* runs viâ \*Gadshill and the old village of *Chalk*. Gadshill, which commands a splendid view, is famous as the scene assigned by Shakspeare to the encounter of Sir John Falstaff with the 'men in buckram', commemorated by an inn bearing the name of the worthy knight. Nearly opposite is the picturesque house in which Charles Dickens resided, and where he died in 1870 (comp. *Baedeker's Great Britain*).

The railway from Gravesend to (7 M.) Strood passes only one station, called *Higham*, 3½ M. from which is Cowling Castle, built in the time of Richard II., and now a picturesque ruin. Beyond Higham the train penetrates a tunnel, 1¼ M. in length, and enters the station of *Strood*, a suburb of Rochester, on the opposite bank of the river Medway. Some of the North Kent trains go no farther in this direction, but others cross the Medway, and proceed to Rochester and Chatham, which practically form one town, surrounded by fortifications defending the entrance to the river.

**Rochester** *(Crown; Victoria & Bull; King's Head)*, to the N. of Chatham, a very ancient city, with a pop. of 21,590, a fine Norman *Castle*, and an interesting *Cathedral*, is described at length in *Baedeker's Great Britain*.

**Chatham** *(Sun; Mitre)*, with 46,806 inhab., on the E. bank of the Medway, below Rochester, is one of the chief naval arsenals and military stations in Great Britain. See *Baedeker's Great Britain*.

# INDEX.

Abbey Wood 344.
Abney Park Cemetery 294.
Academy of Arts, Royal 45. 221.
— of Music, Royal 224.
'Achilles' Statue 260.
Acton 334. 37. 34.
Addison Road 37.
Addresses 71.
Adelphi Theatre 41. 144.
Admiralty 183.
Agricultural Hall 43. 45.
Albany, The 222.
Albert Embankment 114. 297.
— Hall 43. 270.
— Memorial 270.
— Palace 43. 299.
— Statues of Prince 94. 105. 270.
— Suspension Bridge 294. 299.
Aldersgate St. Stat. 36. 98.
Aldgate Station 36. 107.
Aldridge's 27.
Ale 12.
Alexandra House 271.
— Palace 329. 43.
— Park 33.
Alhambra Theatre 43. 223.
Allan Wesleyan Library 98. 17.
All Hallows, Barking, Church of 125.
All Hallows, Staining, Tower of 107.
All Saints' Church 225.
All Souls' Church 225.
Almack's 43. 220.
Alsatia 135.
Ambresbury Bank 330.
American Banks 50.
— Exchange 50.
— Newspapers 18.
— Reading-rooms 17.
Amusements 43.
Amwell 334.
Angling 47.

Anne, Statue of Queen 82.
Antiquarian Society 222.
Apothecaries' Hall 115.
Apsley House 267. 260.
Aquarium, Royal 44. 218
Aquatics 48.
Arcade, the Royal 26.
Archery Society 229.
Architectural Museum 217.
Argyll Lodge 263.
Armourers' Hall 102.
Army and Navy Club 74. 219.
— Stores 27.
Arrival 5.
Art Collections, Private 264-269.
Arthur's Club 220. 74.
Artillery Barracks(Woolwich) 304.
Artillery Company, Hon. 98.
Art-Needlework, School of 272.
Arts, Society of 144.
Ascot Races 46. 342.
Ashford 336.
Astronomical Society 222.
Athenæum Club 219.
Athletic Sports 47.
Auctions 71.
Audit Office 143.
Austin Friars 104.
Avenue Theatre 42.

Badminton Club 220. 71.
Baker Street Bazaar 26.
— — Station 36. 229.
Balham 31.
Baltimore to Liverpool 3.
Bank of England 103.
—, National Provincial 106.
—, Coutts's 146.
Bankers 50.
Bankers' Clearing House 104.
Banknotes 4.
Baptist Chapels 51.

Barber-Surgeons' Court Room 94.
Barclay's Brewery 296.
Barking Reach 313.
Barnard's Inn 94. 139.
Barnes 325.
— Elms 325.
Barnet 332. 33.
Barnsbury 31.
Bartholomew Fair 26.
Bath House 268.
Baths 48.
Battersea Bridge 294.
— Park 29. 34.
— — Station 289.
— — Road Station 289.
Baynard's Castle 115.
Bayswater 294.
— Station 37.
Bazaars 26.
Beaconsfield 335.
—, Statue of Lord 192.
Beckenham 33. 31.
Bedford 4.
— Coffee House 180.
— Square 226.
—, Statue of the Duke of 226.
Beefsteak Club 184.
Beer 12.
Belgravia 291.
Bellot, Statue of Lieut. 302.
Belvedere 344.
Bennet's Hill St. 116.
Bentinck's Statue 224.
Bentley Priory 32.
Berkeley Square 225.
Bermondsey 67. 344. 34.
Bethlehem Hospital 298.
Bethnal Green 67. 329. 33.
— — Museum 128.
Bible Society, British and Foreign 146.
Bicycling 48.
Billiard Rooms 45.
Billingsgate 26. 144. 15.
Birdcage Walk 266.
Birmingham 4.

Bishopsgate Station 36.
329.
Bishop's Road 37.
— Wood 328.
Blackfriars Bridge 112.
— — Station 113.
— Metrop. Railw. Station 37. 115.
Blackheath 304. 344. 33.
Blackwall 128. 301.
Bloomsbury Square 226
Blue Coat School 91.
Board of Trade 183.
— — Works 69.
Boarding Houses 10.
Boating 48. 323.
Boat Races 48.
Bodegas 12.
Bolt Court 135.
Bond Street 225.
Boodle's Club 220. 74.
Books on London 80 b.
Borough, the 295. 109.
*Boston to Liverpool* 3.
— *to Queenstown* 3.
Botanic Gardens 232.
Botanical Society 229.
Bow Church 102.
— Station 34.
— Street Police Court 179.
Boxing 48.
Brandenburgh House 325.
Breakfast 6.
Brentford 323. 325. 331.
Bridewell 115.
Bridgewater House 265.
Britannia Theatre 42.
British Museum 233:
  Anglo-Roman and Anglo-Saxon Rooms 252.
  Assyrian Gallery 245.
  Bronze Room 250.
  Coin Rooms 250.
  Egypt. Antiquities 247.
  Elgin Room 241.
  Etruscan Room 251.
  Hellenic Room 243.
  King's Library 236.
  Library 235. 255.
  Manuscripts 235.
  Medal Room 251.
  Mediæval Room 253.
  Print Room 253. 236.
  Reading Room 254.
  Sculpture Gallery 238.
  Vase Rooms 250.
Brixton 34.
Broad Sanctuary 217.
Broad St. Stat. 34.
Bromley 33. 34.
Brompton Oratory 291.
— Station 37. 34.

Brondesbury 37. **34.**
Brooks' Club 74. **220.**
Brook Street 225.
Broxbourne 330.
Brunel's Statue **113.**
Buckhurst Hill **329.** 330.
Buckingham Palace 257.
Bunhill **Fields Cemetery** 98.
Burgoyne's Statue **219.**
Burlington Arcade **26. 220.**
— House 220.
Burnham Beeches 335.
Burns's Statue 113.
Bushy Park 324.
Byron's Statue 261.

Cabs **28. 6.**
Caen **Wood** 328.
Cafés **16.** 15.
Camberwell **34.**
Cambridge Hall of Varieties 44.
Camden Road **332. 33.**
— Town **227. 31.**
Campbell, Statue of Colin **219.**
*Canada* 2.
Canning's Statue **192.**
Cannon Street **116.**
— — Station **33. 117.**
— — Metrop. Station 37. **117.**
Canonbury 34.
— Tower 227.
Canterbury Hall **43.**
Carlton Club 74. 219
— House Terrace 256. 219.
Carlyle's Statue 294.
Castelnau **325.**
Castle Hill **334.**
Catholic Apostolic Churches **227. 51.**
Cattle Market **27.**
Cavendish **Square 224.**
Cemeteries:
  Abney Park **294.**
  Bunhill Fields **98.**
  Highgate 328.
  Kensal Green **294.**
  Norwood **294.**
  St. George's, Hanover Sq. **263.**
Central Crim. Court 93.
Central House for Nurses for the Poor 232.
Central London Meat **Market 96. 26.**
Chalk **346.**
Chalk Farm Station **229. 31.**
Chancellor of the Exchequer's Office 183.

Chancery. Court **of 139.**
Chancery Lane **67. 136.** 135.
Channel, Passage of the 5.
Chapels, Baptist 51.
—, Congregationalist **51.**
—, Independent 51.
—, Methodist 51.
—, Swedenborgian **51.**
—, Unitarian 52.
Charing **Cross 147.**
— — Bridge **145.**
— — Hospital **145.**
— — Road 147.
— — Station 33. **145.**
— — Metrop. Railw. Station 37. **145.**
Charities 72
Charles I.'s **Statue 147.**
Charles II., Statues of **104.** 292.
Charlton 344.
Charterhouse **97.**
Chatham 346.
Cheapside 104.
**Chelsea** 68. 292. 31.
— Botanic Gardens 293.
— Bridge 299.
— Embankment **114. 294.**
— Hospital 292.
— Old Church 293.
— Suspension Bridge 292.
Chemical Society 222.
Chesham 37. 332.
Cheshunt 330.
Chester 4.
Chesterfield House 225.
Child's Bank 140.
— Hill 332.
Chiltern Green **334.**
Chingford 329.
Chipping Barnet 332.
Chislehurst 345.
Chiswick 325.
Christchurch 299.
Christie and Manson's Auction Rooms 220.
Christ's Hospital 91.
Churches 50:
  All Hallows, Barking 125.
  — — Staining **107.**
  — Saints' **225.**
  — Souls' **225.**
  Bow **101.**
  Brompton Oratory 291.
  Catholic Apostolic 227. 51.
  Christchurch 299.
  City Temple 93.
  Dutch 104.
  Ely Chapel 94.
  Foreign 52.

Churches:
- Hanover Chapel 224.
- Irvingite 51. 227.
- Marylebone 225.
- Presbyterian 52.
- Roman Catholic 52.
- St. Alphage's 96.
- — Andrew's 93.
- — — Undershaft 107.
- — Bartholomew's 95.
- — Bride's 134.
- — Catherine Cree's 107.
- — Clement Danes 141.
- — Dunstan's in the West 135.
- — Etheldreda's 52. 94.
- — George's 224.
- — — Cathedral 299.
- — Giles, Cripplegate 96.
- — — in the Fields 226.
- — Helen's 106.
- — James's 222.
- — —, Curtain St. 98.
- — John's 97.
- — Jude's 108.
- — Luke's, Chelsea 293.
- — Magnus the Martyr 111.
- — Margaret's 191.
- — Martin's in the Fields 146.
- — Mary le Bow 101.
- — — le Strand 142.
- — — Undercroft 191.
- — — Woolnoth 109.
- — — the Virgin 226.
- — Mary's 136.
- — —, Battersea 299.
- — Michael's 107.
- — Olave's 108.
- — Pancras' 227.
- — —, Old 227.
- — Paul's Cathedral 81.
- — —, Cov. Gard. 180.
- — Peter's 107.
- — Saviour's 295.
- — Sepulchre's 93.
- — Stephen's 102.
- — Swithin's 117.
- Savoy 144.
- Temple 136.
- Trinity 108.

Cigars 2. 21.
Circulating Libraries 17.
Circus 44.
City, The 68. 81.
- — Companies 69.
- — of London School 114.
- — of London and Southwark Subway 126.
- — and Guilds of London Institute 73. 272.

City Temple 93.
Civil Service Supply Association 27. 144.
Clapham Junction 315. 34.
Clapton 33.
Clarence House 256.
Clearing House, Bankers' 101.
Clement's Inn 139. 141.
Cleopatra's Needle 114.
Clerkenwell 67. 98.
Clothworkers' Hall 108.
Clubs 73.
Coaches 32.
Coaching Club 261.
Coal Exchange 112.
Coals 69. 112.
Cobham Hall 346.
Cocoa Tree Club 220.
Coffee-houses 16.
College of Arms 116.
— of Music, Royal 271.
— of Physicians, Royal 147.
— of Surgeons, Royal 177.
Colne, the 334.
Colney Hatch 299.
Colonial Institute 75.
— Office 184.
Columbia Market 27.
Comedy Theatre 42.
Commerce of London 69.
Commercial Docks 128.
Commissionnaires 55.
Concerts 43.
Confectioners 16.
Congregational Memorial Hall 134.
Congregationalist Chapels 51.
Conservative Club 74. 220.
— —, National 218. 75.
Constitution Hill 259.
Constitutional Club 147. 74.
Consulates 49.
Cookery, School of 272.
Coombe House 316.
— -Malden 316.
Co-operative System 27.
— Working-Societies 28.
Cooper's Hill 336.
Corn Exchange 108.
Cornhill 107.
Corporation Art Gallery 100.
County Council, London 69.
— Lunatic Asylum 334.
Court Theatre, Royal 45.

Coutts's Bank 145.
Covent Garden Market 26. 180.
— Theatre 40. 179.
Coventry Street 223.
Cowling Castle 346.
Crane Court 135.
Craven St. 145.
Cremorne Gardens 294.
Crewe 1.
Cricket 47.
Crimean Monument 218.
Criminal Court Ceo. 93.
Criterion Theatre 41.
Crockford's 220.
Cromwell Road 275.
Crosby Hall 106.
Crown Jewels 122.
Croydon 34. 46.
Crystal Palace 13. 349.
34.
Cumberland, Statue of the Duke of 224.
Curtain Theatre 98.
Custom House 2. 112.
Cycling 48.

Dalston 106. 134. 324. 34. 329.
Dartford 33. 345.
Datchet 336.
Denmark Hill 34.
Deptford 68. 27. 304. 33.
— Road 36.
Derby 4.
—, the 46.
— Statue of Lord 132.
Devonshire Club 220. 71.
— House 269.
Diary 80.
Dinner 12.
— parties 71.
Directories 71.
Disposition of Time 78.
Dives' Flour Mills 224.
Divine Service 50.
Docks 126.
Doctors' Commons 116.
Doggett's Coat and Badge 48. 345.
Dorchester House 268.
Doré Gallery 45. 226.
Dorking 32.
Doulton's Pottery Works 289.
*Dover* to *Calais* 5.
— to *Ostend* 5.
Downing Street 183.
Drainage System 30.
Drapers' Garden 108.
— Hall 104.
Drawing Rooms 268.

Drury Lane Theatre 40.
142. 180.
Dudley Gallery 45.
— House 266.
Duke of York's School
292.
Dulwich 312. 34.
— College 312.
— Gallery 312.
Dunstable 334.
Dutch Church 104.

Ealing 334. 37.
Earl's Court 37.
East End 67.
— India Co.'s House 107.
— — Docks 128.
— — Museum 184. 289.
— Sheen 322.
Edgware 332. 33.
— Road 225.
— Station 37.
Education Office 183.
Eel Pie Island 326.
Egham 336.
Egyptian Hall 41. 220.
Eleanor's Cross 145.
Elephant and Castle 29.
78. 299.
Elephant and Castle
Market 27.
— — Theatre 42.
Elephant Tavern 107.
Elizabeth, Statues of
Queen 101.
Elstree 332.
Eltham 345.
Ely Chapel 91.
— Place 93.
Embankment Gardens
113. 145.
Embassies 49.
Empire Theatre 223. 43.
Entertainments 39.
Epping Forest 330. 33
Epsom 316. 46.
Erith 33. 313. 345.
Ethical Societies 52.
Eton 341.
Euston Sq. Stat. 33. 227.
Evans's 180.
Exchange, Royal 104.
Exeter Hall 113.
Exhibition Galleries 288.
Exhibitions of Pictures
45.
Expenses 1.

Farringdon St. Market
27.
— — Station 36. 94.
Feltham 336.
Fenchurch St. 107.

Fenchurch St. Stat. 34.
108.
Fetter Lane 135.
Finchley Road 37. 332. 34.
Finsbury 68.
— Technical College 272.
Fire Brigade 70. 296.
Fishing 47.
Fish Markets 26. 96. 111.
Fishmongers' Hall 111.
Flaxman Museum 227.
Fleet Brook 93. 134.
— Prison 131.
— Street 134.
Floral Hall 179.
Flower Market 26. 180.
— Shows 232.
Flushing to Amsterdam 5.
Flys 28.
Folkestone to Boulogne 5.
Foreign Cattle Market
27.
— Churches 52.
— Office 184.
Foresters' Hall 43.
Forest Hill 35.
Foundling Hospital 228.
Four-in-hand Club 261.
Fox-hunting 47.
Fox's Statue 226.
Franklin's Statue 219.
Frere's (Sir Bartle) Statue
113.
French Hospice 134.
Friends' Meeting Houses
51.
Fruit Market 26. 180.
Fulham 324.

Gadshill 346.
Gaiety Theatre 41. 143.
Gallery, National 147.
—, National Portrait 129.
Galleries, Picture 15. 264.
269.
Games 47.
Gardens, Botanic 232.
—, Chelsea Botanic 293.
—, Public 43.
—, Zoological 229.
Garrick Club 180. 74.
— Theatre 41.
Gas-lighting 66. 68.
Gates of London, Old 63.
General Hints 71.
Geographical Society 222.
Geological Museum 222.
— Society 222.
George Lane 329.
George II., Statue of 302.
George III., Statues of
99. 218. 143.
George IV.'s Statue 116.

German Hospital 106. 72.
— Reed's Entertainment
44.
Gipsy Hill 34.
Glasgow 3.
Globe Theatre 41. 141.
Gloucester 4.
— Road Station 37.
Goldsmiths' Hall 100.
Gordon's Statue 146.
Gore House 271.
Gorhambury House 334.
Gospel Oak 34. 329.
Gough Sq. 135.
Government Offices 183.
184.
Gower Street 226.
— Station 36. 227.
Grand Theatre 42. 227.
Grantham 5.
Gravesend 33. 345.
Gray's Inn 139.
— Thurrock 314.
Great Eastern Railway
Market 27.
— Fire 65. 81. 110.
Greenhithe 344.
Green Park 259.
— Arch 260.
Greenwich 68. 301.
— Hospital 301.
— Park 303.
— Railway 33.
Gresham College 100.
Grill Rooms 42.
Grocers' Hall 102.
Grosvenor Gallery 45.
— House 261.
— Square 225.
Grub Street 96.
Guards' Club 74. 220.
Guildford 32.
Guildhall 98.
— Library 99.
— Museum 100.
— School of Music 114.
Guilds 72.
Gunnersbury 37. 34.
Guy's Hospital 296.
Gymnastics 47. 48.

Hackney 68. 134. 33. 34.
329. 233.
Haggerston 134. 34.
Hainault Forest 330.
Halfway Reach 313.
Halifax to Liverpool 4.
Ham Common 326.
— House 326.
Hammersmith 325. 37. 34.
Hampstead 327. 68.
— Heath 327. 34.

# INDEX. 351

Hampton Court 316. 31. 326.
— Wick 326.
Hanover Chapel 221.
— Square 224.
Hansoms 28.
Hanwell 334. 299.
Harcourt House 221.
Harpenden 334.
Harrow 332. 37.
Hartshorn Lane 117.
*Harwich to Antwerp* 5.
— *to Hamburg* 5.
— *to Rotterdam* 5.
Hatfield 332.
Havelock's Statue 116.
Haverstock Hill 332. 33.
Hayes 334.
Haymarket 218.
— Theatre 40. 218.
Hendon 332. 33.
Hengler's Circus 44.
Henley Regatta 48.
Henry VIII.'s Statue 91.
Heralds' College 116.
Herbert of Lea, Statue of Lord 219.
Her Majesty's Theatre 40. 218.
Hereford 4.
Herne Hill 34.
Herne's Oak 341.
Hertford 331.
— House 268.
Higham 346.
High Beech 330.
Highbury 227. 34.
Highgate 328. 33.
High Holborn 228.
Hill's (Rowland) Statue 105.
Hints, General 71.
Historical Sketch of England 57.
— — of London 62.
Holborn 94. 228.
— Viaduct 93.
— — Station 34. 93.
Holland House 263.
Holloway 227.
— College 336.
Holly Lodge 263.
Holy Well 142.
Home Office 184.
Homerton 134. 31.
Honor Oak 34.
Hornsey 329. 33.
Horse Guards 183.
— Markets 27.
— Races 46.
Horticultural Society 271.

Hospice for French Protestants 134.
Hospitals 72.
Hotels 6.
Houndsditch 67. 108.
Hounslow 35.
Houses of Parliament 184.
Hughenden 335.
Humane Society, Royal 116. 262.
Hungerford Market 145.
Hunting 47.
Huskisson's Statue 105.
Hyde Park 259.
Hyde Park Corner 260.

Imperial Institute 272.
— Theatre 42.
Independent Chapels 51.
India Museum 289.
— Office 184.
Ingress Abbey 344.
Inland Revenue Office 143.
Inns of Chancery 139. 94.
— of Court 67. 136.
International Exhibition 272.
— Hall 43.
Ironmongers' Hall 107.
Irvingite Churches 227.51.
Isle of Dogs 128.
Isleworth 325. 34.
Islington 227. 34.
Italian Opera, Royal 40. 179.

James II.'s Statue 184.
Jenner's Statue 262.
Jewish Synagogues 51.
Jewry, Old 192.
Junior Athenæum Club 220. 74.
— Army and Navy Club 220. 74.
— Carlton Club 219. 74.
— United Service Club 224. 74.
Justice, Royal Courts of 139.

Kempton Park Races 46.
Kennel Club 74.
Kennington Oval 292. 47.
Kensal Green 34.
— — Cem. 294. 332.
Kensington Gardens 262.
— Gore 271.
— High Street Station 37. 34.
— Museum 275.
— Palace 262.

Kentish Town 327. 33. 31. 332.
Kew 322. 325.
— Botanic Gardens 323
— Bridge Station 322. 34.
— Gardens 37. 322. 34.
— Observatory 324.
— Palace 322.
Kilburn 37.
Kingsbury 37
King's College 142.
— Cross Station 33. 225.
— — Metrop. Railw. Station 36.
Kingsland 108.
Kingston on Thames 326. 34.
King Street 192.
King William Street 109.
Kit-Cat Portraits 125. 334.

Ladies' Mile 261.
Lady Guide Association 55.
Lambeth 66. 297.
— Bridge 297.
— Palace 297. 17.
Langley 334.
Lansdowne House 267.
Latimer Road 37.
Law Courts, New 141.
Lawn Tennis 48.
Lawrence's (Lord) Statue 219.
Lea, The 17. 330.
Leadenhall Market 27. 107.
— Street 107.
Leathersellers' Hall 106.
Leicester Square 223.
Lesnes Abbey 344.
Levees 256.
Lewisham 344. 68. 33.
Leyton 329.
Leytonstone 329.
Libraries 17.
Life Boat Institution 144.
Lincoln's Inn 148.
Linnæan Society 223.
*Liverpool to London* 4.
Liverpool Street Station 31.
Lloyd's 105.
Lodgings 10.
Lombard Street 107.
London Bridge 108. 34.
— — Station 36.
— Chatham and Dover Railway Bridge 114.
— County Council 60.
— Crystal Palace 36. 280.
— Docks 126.
— Institution Library 17.

London Pavilion 43.
— Stone 117.
— University 222.
— Wall 63. 96.
London to Antwerp 5.
— to Boulogne 5.
— to Bremerhafen 5.
— to Calais 5.
— to Dover 5.
— to Folkestone 5.
— to Hamburg 5.
— to Harwich 5.
— to Newhaven 5.
— to Ostend 5.
— to Queenborough 5.
— to Rotterdam 5.
Long Shore 67.
Lord Mayor's Show 71.
Lord's Cricket Ground 47. 233.
Lordship Lane 34.
Loughborough 34.
Loughton 329.
Lower Thames St. 109. 111.
Lowther Arcade 26. 115.
— Lodge 271.
Ludgate Hill 115.
— — Station 34. 115.
Luton 334.
Lyceum Theatre 40. 113.
Lyric Theatre 41.

Maiden Lane 180.
Mall, The 296.
Mansion House 102.
— — Station 37. 117.
Marble Arch 260.
Marine Barracks (Woolwich) 304.
Markets 26.
Mark Lane 108.
— — Station 36. 118.
Marlborough Club 220.
— House 220.
— Road 37. 232.
Marshalsea Gaol 297.
Marylebone 68. 228.
— Church 225.
— Park 228.
— Theatre 42.
— Workhouse 233.
Matlock 4.
Mayfair 261. 291.
Meat Market, Central 96. 26.
Medical Examination Hall 113.
Mercers' Hall 102.
Merchant Taylors' Hall 105.
— — School 97.

Mermaid Tavern 101.
Methodist Chapels 51.
Metropolitan Board of Works 69.
— Cattle Market 24.
— Fire Brigade 296. 70.
— Improvements 70.
— Meat Market 26. 96.
— Music Hall 44.
— Police District 68.
— Railways 36.
Mews, Royal 259.
Mildmay Park 34.
Mile End Road 108.
Military Academy (Woolwich) 305.
— Asylum 292.
— Repository (Woolwich) 305.
Millbank Penitentiary 292.
Mill Hill 332.
Mill's Statue 113.
Millwall Docks 128.
Mincing Lane 107.
Ministerial Offices 183. 184.
Minories 67. 108.
Mint, Royal 125.
— Street 297.
Missionary Society's Museum, London 98.
Mitre Court 135.
Money 1.
— Changers 50.
— Order Office 90.
Montague House 184.
Monument, The 110. 109
— Station 38. 109.
—, Crimean 218.
Moore and Burgess Minstrels 44.
Moorgate Station 36.
Mortlake 325.
Museum, Royal Architectural 217.
—, Bethnal Green 128.
—, British 233.
—, Geological 222.
—, Guildhall 100.
—, India 289.
—, London Missionary Society 98.
—, Military (Woolwich) 305.
—, Natural History 273.
—, Naval (Greenwich) 303.
—, Patent Office 288.
— of Royal College of Surgeons 177.
—, Soane 178.
—, South Kensington 275.

Museum, Surrey House 312.
—, United Service 182.
Music Halls 43.
—, Guildhall School of 114.
—, Royal Academy of 224.
—, Royal College of 274.
Musical Union 43.
Muswell Hill 329.

Napier's Statue 146.
National Gallery 147.
— Liberal Club 147. 74.
— Portrait Gallery 129.
— Provincial Bank 106.
— School of Cookery 272.
Natural History Museum 273.
Naval and Military Club 220. 75.
Naval Museum (Greenwich) 303.
Naval School (Greenwich) 303.
Neasden 37.
Nelson's Column 115.
New College 233.
New Court 117.
New Cross 344. 36. 33.
New Gallery 45.
Newgate Prison 92.
— Street 91.
Newhaven to Dieppe 5.
Newmarket Races 46.
New Oxford Street 236.
Newspapers 17.
New University Club 220. 75.
New York to Glasgow 3. 4.
— — to Liverpool 2. 3. 4.
— — to London 3.
— — to Queenstown 3.
— — to Southampton 3.
New Zealand Chambers 107.
Niagara, Panorama 45.
Norbury 34.
Northfleet 344.
Northumberland House 146.
Norwood 34.
— Cemetery 294.
Notting Hill 37. 294.
— — Gate Station 37.
Novelty Theatre 42.

Oaks, the 46.
Observatory, Royal 303.
Old Ford 329. 33.
— Jewry 102.
Olympia 44.
Olympic Theatre 42. 144.

Omnibuses 29.
Opéra Comique 41.
Opera House 40. 218.
—, Royal Italian 40. 179.
Ophthalmic Hospital 145.
Oratory, the 291.
Oriental Club 221. 75.
Orleans House 326.
Outram's Statue 113.
Oxford 4.
— House 108.
— Music Hall 44.
— Street 225.
— and Cambridge Club 75. 220.
Oyster Shops 15.

Paddington Station 33.
Palace of Westminster 184.
Pall Mall 218.
Palmerston's Statue 192.
Panoramas 45. 311. 329.
Panshanger 331.
Pantheon 226.
Panyer Alley 91.
Parade, the 257.
Paragon Theatre of Varieties 44.
Parcels Companies 55.
— Post 51.
Park Street 297.
Parliament, Houses of 184.
Parliament Hill 327.
Passports 2.
Patent Office Museum 288.
Paternoster Row 67. 90.
Pavilion Theatre 42.
Peabody's Statue 105.
Peckham Rye 33. 34.
Peel, Statues of Sir Robert 90. 192.
Pembroke Lodge 322.
Penge 35.
People's Palace 108.
Peterborough 5.
Petersham 326.
Petty France 257.
Philadelphia to Liverpool 3. 4.
Philharmonic Concerts 43.
Physicians, Royal College of 147.
Piccadilly 220.
— Hall 45.
Picture Galleries (public) 45.
Picture Galleries (private) 264.

Pindar's House, Sir P. 106.
Pinner 37. 332.
Pitt's Statue 224.
Playhouse Yard 113.
Plumstead 344.
Plymouth to London 5.
Policemen 68. 71.
Polytechnic Institution 224.
Pool, the 110.
Poplar 34.
Popular Concerts 43.
Population 66. 68. 69.
Port, the 126. 110.
Portland Place 225.
— Road Station 36. 229.
Portland to Liverpool 3.
Portman Square 225.
Portrait Gallery, National 129.
Post Office 53.
— —, General 53. 90.
— — Directory 71.
— — Orders 54.
— — Savings Banks 90.
Postal Districts 54.
— Orders 54.
— Regulations 51. 53.
— Traffic 90.
Poultry 102.
— Market 26. 96.
Praed Street Station 37.
Preliminary Ramble 76.
Presbyterian Churches 52.
Primrose Hill 233.
Prince of Wales Theatre 24. 223.
Prince's Hall 43.
Princess's Concert Room 43.
— Theatre 43. 226.
Printing House Sq. 115.
Poisons 92. 292.
Private Apartments 10.
— Picture Galleries 264.
Privy Council Office 183.
Provincial Bank 106.
Prussia House 219.
Public Gardens 43.
— Houses 12.
— Offices 183. 184.
Purfleet 343.
Putney 324.
— Bridge 37. 324.

Quakers' Meeting Houses 51.
Quadrant, the 224.
Queen Victoria 61.

Queen Victoria Street 102. 115.
Queenborough to Flushing 5.
Queen's Road Station 37. 24.
— Tobacco Pipe 127.
— Warehouse 127.
Queenstown 3.
Races 46.
Rackets 47.
Radlett 332.
Raikes's Statue 113.
Railways 32.
Raleigh Club 221. 75.
Ranelagh, the 293.
Reading 336.
Reading Rooms 17.
Record Office 135.
Reform Club 75. 219.
Regalia 122.
Regattas 48.
Regent Circus 222. 224.
— Street 224.
Regent's Canal 128.
— Park 228.
Registrar General's Office 143.
Restaurants 11. 12.
Richard Coeur de Lion's Statue 192.
Richmond 324. 34. 37.
Rickmansworth 37. 332.
Rochester 33. 34. 336.
Rolls Buildings 136.
— Chapel 136.
Roman Bath 142.
— Catholic Churches 52.
— Remains 63.
Rosherville Gardens 44. 345.
Rotherhithe 67. 344. 35.
Rotten Row 261.
Routes to and from London 2.
Royal Academy 221. 45.
— Aquarium 44. 218.
— Architectural Museum 217.
— Colonial Institute 76.
— Exchange 104.
— Family 61.
— Geographical Society 222.
— Humane Society 146.
— Institution 75.
— Mews 250.
— Military Asylum 302.
— Mint 125.
— Oak 37. 294.
— Society 224.

Royalty Theatre 42.
Rugby 4.
Runnimede 336.
Russell Square 226.
Rye House 331.

Sacred Harmonic Society 43.
Saddlers' Hall 102.
Sadler's Wells Theatre 42.
St. Albans 332. 333.
— Alphage's Church 96.
— Andrew's Church 93.
— Andrew's Undershaft 107.
— Bartholomew's 95.
— — Hospital 94.
— Bride's 134.
— Catherine Cree's 107.
— Clement Danes 141.
— Dunstan's 135.
— Etheldreda's 52. 94.
— George's Cathedral 299.
— — Church 224.
— — Club 224.
— — Hall 43.
— Giles, Cripplegate 96.
— — in the Fields 226.
— Helen's Church 106.
— James's Church 222.
— — —, Curtain St. 98.
— — Club 220.
— — Hall 43. 223.
— — Palace 255. 220.
— — Park 256.
— — — Station 37.
— — Square 219.
— — Street 220.
— — Theatre 40. 220.
— John's 344.
— — Church 97.
— — Gate 97.
— — Wood Road 37. 233.
— — — — Stat. 229.
— Jude's 108.
— Katherine's Docks 126
— — Hospital 232.
— Magnus the Martyr's Church 111.
— Margaret's Church 191
— — Station 331.
— Martin's Church 146.
— Mary le Bow 101.
— — le Strand 142.
— — Undercroft 191.
— — the Virgin 226.
— — Woolnoth 109.
— Mary's Church 136.
— — —, Battersea 299.
— — Station 36.
— Michael's 107.

St. Olave's 108.
— Pancras' 227.
— —, Old 227.
— — Station 33. 227.
— Paul's Cathedral 81.
— — Church 180.
— — Churchyard 89.
— — Station 34. 116.
— Peter's 107.
— Peter ad Vincula, Chapel of 123.
— Peter's College 217.
— Saviour's Church 295.
— Sepulchre's 93.
— Stephen's 102.
— Swithin's Church 117.
— Thomas's Hospital 297.
Salters' Hall 117.
Sanctuary, Broad 217.
Sandown Races 46.
Sanger's Amphitheatre 42.
Savile Club 220. 75.
Savoy Chapel 144.
— Palace 144.
— Theatre 41. 144.
School Board, London 70.
—, — Office of 113.
— of Art Needlework 272.
— of Cookery 272.
Scotland Yard 183.
Seamen's Hospital 301.
Season 1.
Serjeants' Inn 136.
Serpentine 259. 261.
Sevenoaks 32.
Shadwell 36. 34.
— Market 27.
Shaftesbury Avenue 147.
— Theatre 41.
Shakspeare's Statue 223
Shepherd's Bush 32. 37.
Shoe Lane 135.
Shooter's Hill 305.
Shops 19.
Shoreditch 68. 106. 134.
Siemens' Telegraphic Works 305.
Sion College 17. 114.
Sion House 323.
Skinners' Hall 117.
Sloane Square Station 37.
Slough 334.
Smithfield 26. 95.
Snaresbrook 329.
Snow Hill 342.
Soane Museum 178.
Societies 73.
Society, Antiquarian 221.
— Archery 229.
— of Arts 144. 73.

Society, Astronomical 221.
— Chemical 221.
— Geographical 222.
— Geological 221.
— Horticultural 271.
— Humane 146. 262.
— Linnæan 221.
— Royal 221.
Soho Bazaar 26. 226.
— Square 226.
Somerset House 142.
Southall 334.
Southampton to London 5.
South Eastern Railway 33.
— Kensington Museum 275.
— — Station 37. 275.
— London Palace of Amusements 44.
Southwark 66. 67.
— Bridge 117.
— Park 297.
Spa Road 33.
Spitalfields 67.
Sports, Athletic 47.
Spurgeon's Tabernacle 299. 51.
Stafford House 265.
Staines 336.
Stamford Bridge 47.
Standard Theatre 42.
Staple Inn 94. 139.
Stationers' Hall 90.
Statistics 66.
Statue of Achilles 260.
— of Prince Albert 94. 270. 105.
— of Queen Anne 82.
— of Lord Beaconsfield 192.
— of Duke of Bedford 226.
— of Lieut. Bellot 302.
— of Lord Bentinck 224.
— of Brunel 113.
— of Burgoyne 219.
— of Burns 113.
— of Byron 261.
— of Colin Campbell 219.
— of Canning 192.
— of Carlyle 294.
— of Charles I. 147.
— of Charles II. 104. 292.
— of Duke of Cumberland 224.
— of Lord Derby 192.
— of Queen Elizabeth 104. 135.
— of Fox 226.
— of Franklin 219.
— of Sir Bartle Frere 113.
— of George II. 302.
— of George III. 99. 143. 218.

Statue of George IV. 146.
— of General Gordon 146.
— of Havelock 146.
— of Henry VIII. 94.
— of Lord Herbert 219.
— of Rowland Hill 105.
— of Huskisson 105.
— of James II. 181.
— of Jenner 262.
— of Lord Lawrence 219.
— of J. S. Mill 113.
— of Sir C. Napier 146.
— of Nelson 146.
— of Gen. Outram 113.
— of Palmerston 192.
— of Peabody 105.
— of Sir R. Peel 90. 192.
— of William Pitt 224.
— of Robt. Raikes 113.
— of Richard Coeur de Lion 192.
— of Shakspeare 223.
— of Geo. Stephenson 227.
— of Tyndale 113.
— of Queen Victoria 104.
— of Wellington 105. 260.
— of William III. 219.
— of William IV. 109.
— of Duke of York 219.
Steel Yard 117.
Steamboats 2. 38.
Steinway Hall 43.
Stephenson's Statue 227.
Stepney 35.
Stock Exchange 104.
Stockwell 34.
Stoke Poges 335.
Stone Church 344.
Store Street Hall 43.
Storey's Gate 257.
Stout 12.
Strand 141.
Strand Theatre 41. 142.
Stratford (Essex) 329. 33.
Strawberry Hill 326. 321.
Streatham Hill 34.
Strood 346.
Subways 126.
Sudbrook House 326.
Surbiton 316. 326.
Surgeons, College of 177.
Surrey Docks 128.
— House Museum 312.
— Side 295.
— Theatre 42.
Sutherland House 265.
Swedenborgian Chapels 51.
Swimming Clubs 49.
Swiss Cottage 37. 233.
Sydenham 305. 34.
Synagogues 51.

Tabard Inn 297.
Tabernacle, the 299.
Tattersall's 27.
Teddington 321. 326.
Telegraph Office 91.
Telegraphs 54.
Telephones 55.
Temperance Hotels 10.
Temple 136.
— Bar 140. 330.
— Church 136.
— Gardens 137.
— Station 37.
Tennis 47. 48.
Terminus Hotels 7.
Terry's Theatre 41.
Thames, the 66. 323. etc.
— Ditton 316. 326.
— Embankment 70. 113.
— Tunnel 127.
Theatres 39.
Theobalds Park 330.
Thorney Isle 193.
Thornton Heath 34.
Tilbury Fort 344. 33.
— Docks 128.
Time 2.
Times Office 115.
Tobacco 2. 21.
— Dock 127.
Toole's Theatre 41.
Topography 66.
Tottenham Court Road 226.
Tower 117.
— Bridge 112.
— Hamlets 68.
— Hill 124.
— Subway 126.
Toxopholite Society 229.
Toynbee Hall 108.
Trafalgar Square 145.
Tramways 32.
Travellers' Club 75. 219.
Treasury 183.
Trinity Church 108.
— College 73. 225.
— House 124.
Trocadero 43.
Turf Club 230. 75.
Turnham Green 37.
Tussaud's Waxwork Exhibition 44. 232.
Twickenham 326. 35.
Tyburn 229.
Tyburnia 229. 291.
Tyndale's Statue 113.

Underground Railways 36.
Union Club 75. 117.
Unionist Club 75. 230.
Unitarian Chapels 52.

United Service Club 75. 218.
— Museum 182.
University Boat Race 48. 324.
— Club 75. 218.
— College 226.
— Hospital 227.
— Sports 47.
Uxbridge 334.
— Road 37.

Vaudeville Theat. 44. 144.
Vauxhall 315. 35.
— Bridge 282.
Vegetable Market 26. 180.
Vegetarian Restaurants 15.
Verulamium 333.
Veterinary College 227.
Victoria and Albert Docks 128.
— Coffee Music Hall 43.
— Embankment 113.
— Park 133.
— — Station 134. 34.
— Railway Bridge 282.
— Station 33. 294.
— — (Metrop.) 37.
—, Statue of Queen 104.
Virginia Water 342. 32.
Visits 71.

Waltham Abbey 330.
— Cross 330.
Walthamstow 329.
Wandsworth 324. 34.
Wapping 127. 36.
War Office 219.
Ware 334.
Warwick 4.
— Lane 92.
Watergate 145.
Waterloo Bridge 113.
— Place 218.
— Station 36.
— Steps 219.
Watford 332.
Wellington Barracks 253.
Wellington, Statues of 105. 260.
Welsh Harp 332.
Westbourne, the 39.
— Park 37. 334.
West Brompton 37.
— Drayton 334.
— End 67. 441.
— — (Station) 332.
— Lane 34.
— Hampstead 37.
— India Docks 128.
Westminster 68.
— Abbey 184.

Westminster Bridge 192.
— — Metrop. Railway Station 37.
— Column 217.
— Hall 189.
— Hospital 218.
— Palace 184.
— School 217.
— Town Hall 217.
West Thurrock 343.
Whitchurch 332.
White's Club 75. 220.
Whitebait 301.
Whitechapel 67. 108.

Whitechapel Station 36.
Whitehall 180.
Willesden Green 37.
— Junction 321. 34.
Will Office 143.
Will's Coffee House 179.
William III., Statue of 219.
William IV., Statue of 109.
Williams' Library 17.
Willis's Rooms 43. 220.
Wimbledon 316. 37. 35.
Windmill Hill 316.

Windsor 334. 336. 337. 35.
Wine 12. 25.
Wine Office Court 135.
Woodford 329.
Woolwich 304. 33.
— Arsenal 304. 344.
— Dockyard 305. 314.
Worcester 4.
Wraysbury 336.

York Column 219.

Zoological Gardens 229.
— Society 229.

# ALPHABETICAL LIST
## OF
# EMINENT PERSONS MENTIONED IN THE HANDBOOK.

The following is a list of distinguished persons mentioned in the Handbook in connection with their birth, death, residence, burial-place, and the like. It does not profess to give the names of architects and other artists where mentioned in connection with their works, nor does it enumerate the subjects of the portraits in the National Portrait Gallery and elsewhere.

Abercromby, Sir Ralph 86.
Aberdeen, Earl of 197.
Abernethy 95.
Addison 97. 201. 208. 210. 218. 263. 294. 327.
Adelaide, Queen 220.
Aiton, Sir Robt. 207.
Albert, Prince 270. 338.
Aldrich 217.
Alleyne 312. 297.
André 200.
Andrews, Bp. 295.
Anne, Queen 82. 208. 262.
Anne of Denmark (wife of James I.) 142.
Arbuthnot 294.
Argyll, Duke of 202. 226.
Arundel, Earl of 123. 111.
Ascham, Roger 93.
Askew, Anne 124.
Atterbury 294.

Bacon, Lord 139. 329. 333.
Bailie, Joanna 327.
Balfe 198.
Baliol 124.
Barham 89.
Barrow 97. 201.
Barry, Sir Chas. 201.
Baxter 144. 297.
Beaconsfield, Lord 93. 181. 192. 196. 335.
Beaumont 101.
Becket 102. 112.
Bell, Dr. And. 201.
Bennet, W. Sterndale 198.
Bentinck 224.
Berkeley, Bishop 180.
Blackstone 97.
Blake, Adm. 192.
Blake, Wm. 95.

Blessington, Lady 271.
Blow, John 198.
Boleyn, Anna 123. 182.
Bolingbroke 299.
Booth 98. 203.
Boswell 435.
Bourne, Vincent 217.
Boyle 224.
Bradshaw 190.
Brougham, Lord 139. 271.
Bruce, David 124.
Brunel 113. 199. 294.
Buckingham, Duke of 145. 209.
Buckland, Wm. 200.
Buckle 294.
Bulwer Lytton 206. 271.
Bunyan 98. 297.
Burdett Coutts, Baroness 27. 131. 329.
Burgoyne 219.
Burke 336.
Burleigh, Lord 143.
Burney 198.
Burns 113. 202.
Busby 208.
Butler, Sam. 180. 203.
Buxton, Sir T F. 198.
Byron 222. 225. 329. 332.

Cade, Jack 117. 304.
Calamy 114.
Calonne 316.
Camden 92. 201.
Campbell 202.
Canning 192. 196. 222. 325. 341.
Carlyle 294.
Cartwright 217.
Casaubon 204.
Castlereagh 197. 324.
Catharine of Arragon 113.

Catharine of Braganza 142.
Catharine Howard, Queen 123.
Cave 97. 15.
Cavendish, Lord F. 192.
Caxton 194.
Chapman 226.
Charles I. 117. 182. 190. 255. 338.
Charles II. 208. 225. 304. 194. 292.
Chatham, Lord 196. 344.
Chaucer 111. 114. 203. 297.
Chesterfield 225.
Child 225.
Churchill 217.
Clarence, Duke of 123.
Claypole, Eliz. 209.
Clive, Lord 225.
Clive, Kitty 326.
Clyde, Lord 201. 219.
Cobbett 135.
Cobden 197.
Cobham 124. 190.
Coke 336.
Coleman, Geo. 217.
Coleridge, S. T. 95. 202. 328. 329.
Collingwood 86. 88.
Congreve, Wm. (the poet) 200.
Congreve, Sir W. 114.
Constable 327.
Cooper, Sir Astley 86. 88.
Coode 197.
Cornwallis 86.
Coverdale, Miles 114.
Cowley 203. 217.
Cowper 203. 217.
Crabbe 180. 328.
Cranmer 124. 219.

Cromwell, Henry 275.
Cromwell, O. 96. 182. 190.
192. 209. 263. 316.
Cromwell, Thos. 123. 139.
324.
Cruikshank, Geo. 89.
Cumberland, Duke of
234. 342.

Darwin, Chas. 198.
Davy 216. 221. 229.
Defoe 92. 98.
Denman 336.
Derby, Earl of 192.
Dibdin 227.
Dickens, Chas. 94. 202.
271. 297. 328. 346.
Disraeli, Ben., see Beaconsfield.
Dodsley 218.
Donne 85. 101.
D'Orsay, Count 271.
Douglas, Gavin 114.
Drayton 135. 203.
Dryden 110. 179. 203. 217.
Dudley, Guildford 123.
144.
Dyck, Van 143. 345.
Dyer 92. 217.

Eastlake 294.
Edinburgh, Duke of 125.
Edward the Confessor
193. 213. 217. 337.
Edward I. 212. 322. 330.
Edward III. 212. 337.
Edward V. 210. 120.
Edward VI. 209. 301.
Eleanor, Queen 145. 147.
211. 330.
Eliot, George 294. 328.
Elizabeth, Queen 123. 182.
209. 217. 301. 322. 325.
333. 336. 344.
Ellenborough, Lord 97.
Elmsley 217.
Enghien, Duc d' 316.
Erskine, Lord 139.
Essex, Earl of 124. 144.
190. 298.

Fairfax 263.
Falstaff 109. 346.
Faraday 328.
Farquhar 116.
Fawcett, Hen. 289.
Fawkes, Guy 190.
Fielding 326.
Flaxman 227.
Fletcher, Giles 217.
Fletcher, John 101. 296.
Foote 180.

Fox, Charles 197. 199.
226. 325. 341.
Foxe 96.
Francis, Sir Philip 325.
Franklin, Ben. 95. 145.
Franklin, Sir John 214.
219.
Frere 89. 113.
Frobisher 96.
Froude 217.

Gainsborough 218.
Garrick 180. 204.
Gaunt, John of 94.
Gay 202.
George, Prince, of Denmark 208. 220. 262.
George I. 301
George II. 209. 302. 316.
George III. 218. 99. 113.
338.
George IV. 146. 338.
Gibbon 217. 324.
Gibbons, Grinling 81. 87.
Gibson 294.
Gladstone 125.
Godolphin 200.
Goldsmith 89. 135. 137
138. 202. 227.
Gordon, General 87. 146.
Gower 295.
Grabe 201.
Grattan 197.
Gray 107. 203. 336.
Gresham 100. 105. 106.
Grey, Lady Jane 123.
124.
Grote 97. 204.
Gwynne, Nell 140. 146. 329.

Hackluyht 217.
Hale 139.
Halifax, Earl of 197. 210.
Hallam, Henry 85.
Halley 221.
Handel 202. 225. 228. 332.
Hardy, Sir Thos. 199.
Harrington 192.
Harvey 94.
Hastings, Warren 190.
197. 217.
Hatton, Sir Chris. 214.
Havelock 97. 146. 344.
Heber 85. 139.
Henrietta Maria, Queen
112.
Henry I. 337.
Henry II. 337.
Henry III. 211. 217.
Henry IV. 216.
Henry V. 210. 211.
Henry VI 123. 124.
Henry VII. 207. 209. 322.

Henry VIII. 94. 182. 245
301. 316. 322. 338.
Herbert, Geo. 200. 217.
Herbert, Lord 219.
Herschel, Sir John 198.
336.
Herschel, Sir Wm. 221.
336.
Hill, Sir Rowland 105.
210.
Hogarth 95. 107. 180. 223.
225. 228. 325. 328.
Holbein 143. 192. 255.
Holland, Lord 199. 263
Hone 135.
Hooker (theologian) 137.
Hooker, Sir Joseph 322.
Hooker, Sir Wm. 322.
Horne, Bp. 345.
Horner, Francis 197.
Horrocks 199.
Howard, John 85.
Howe, Adm. 86.
Hunt, Leigh 92. 294. 327.
Hunter 177. 199. 223.

Ireton 190. 263. 329.
Irving, Edw. 227.
Irving, Wash. 95.

James I. 209.
James II. 181.
Jeffreys 124.
Jenner 262.
Jersey, Lady 225.
John, King 336.
John, King (of France)
124. 144.
Johnson, Samuel, 85. 89.
135. 138. 140. 144. 143.
296.
Jones, Inigo 81. 142.
Jones, Sir Wm. 86. 89.
Jonson, Ben 101. 138.
147. 199. 203. 217.

Katherine of Valois 207.
Kean 322.
Keats 327.
Keble 200.
Kemble 215. 294.
Kempenfelt 216.
Kenrick 140.
Kingsley 200.
Kneller 180. 204.
Kynaston 180.

Lamb, Chas. 92. 107.
Landor 271.
Landseer, Sir E. 89. 274.
Lansdowne, Marquis of
199.
Laud 107. 124. 145.
Lauderdale 326.

Lawrence, Lord 200. 201. 219.
Lawrence, Sir Thos. 89.
Leech 97. 294.
Lely 180.
Leopold of Belgium 220.
Lewes, Sir G. C. 197.
Liverpool, Lord 316.
Livingstone 201.
Locke 217.
Longfellow 203.
Louis Philippe 326.
Lovat 124. 190.
Lovelace 97. 135. 298.
Lyell 199.
Lyndhurst 271. 328.
Lytton, Bulwer 206. 271.

Macaulay, Lord 201. 222. 263.
Macaulay, Zachary 199.
Mackintosh 199. 327.
Maine, Sir H. S. 92.
Mansel 87.
Mansfield, Lord 139. 197. 328.
Marlborough, Duke of 124. 220.
Marvell 226.
Mary I. 209. 301.
Mary II. 208. 263.
Mary, Queen of Scots 208.
Mason 203.
Massinger 295.
Mathews, Chas. 294.
Maurice, F. D. 139. 200.
May, Sir T. Erskine 192.
Melbourne 87.
Middleton 92.
Mill 113.
Milman 84. 85. 89.
Milton, John 91. 95. 96. 101. 135. 182. 192. 203. 267.
Monk 208.
Monmouth, Duke of 124.
Montagu, Lady Mary Wortley 224.
Montagu, Mrs. 225.
Montpensier, Duc de 209.
Moore, Sir John 86.
Moore, Thos. 263. 271.
More, Sir Thos. 101. 106. 123. 139. 190. 293.
Mulready 294.

Napier, Adm. 85.
Napier, Sir Chas. 85. 146.
Napier, Gen. Wm. 87.
Napoleon III. 271.
Nelson, Lord 86. 88. 115. 302. 303.
Newcastle, Duke of 196.

Newton, Sir Isaac 135. 143. 198. 224. 234.
Newton, John 89.
Norfolk, Duke of 97.
North, Lord 97. 192.
Northumberland, Duke of 124.

Oates, Titus 92.
Oldcastle 190.
Opie 89.
Otway 124.
Outram 113. 200. 201.
Overbury 124.
Owen, John 294.

Palmerston 192. 196. 331. 332.
Paoli 201.
Parr, Old 203.
Peabody 105.
Peel, Sir Robt. 90. 184. 192. 197. 332. 341.
Penn, Wm. 93. 124. 125. 112. 263. 336.
Pepys 106. 140.
Perceval, Spencer 198. 332.
Peter the Great 112. 125. 141. 223.
Philippa, Queen 211.
Phillips 203.
Picton 87. 88.
Pindar, Peter 180.
Pitt, Wm. 139. 197. 193. 224. 324.
Pocahontas 315.
Pollock, Sir Geo. 201.
Pope 300. 326. 327.
Priestley 267.
Prior 203. 217.
Purcell 198.

Radcliffe, Mrs. 263.
Raffles, Sir T. S. 198. 229. 230. 332.
Raglan, Lord 217.
Raikes 113.
Raleigh 120. 121. 191.
Randolph 140.
Rennie 89. 110. 117.
Reynolds 87. 89. 223.
Richard I. 192.
Richard II. 120. 212.
Richard III. 120. 123.
Richardson, Sam. 92. 135. 324.
Rodney 87.
Rogers 263.
Ross, Sir John 204.
Roubiliac 146.
Howe 202. 217.
Rupert, Prince 140.

Russell, Earl 199. 217.
Russell, Lord John 332.
Russell, Lord Wm. 124. 330.

Sackville 135.
St. Evremont 303.
St. John 299.
Sale 112.
Schomberg 218.
Scott, Sir G. G. 294.
Selden 135. 139.
Seymour, Lord Adm. 123.
Shadwell 303. 293.
Shaftesbury, First Earl of 139. 294.
Shaftesbury, Seventh Earl of 199. 224.
Shakspeare, Edm. 295.
Shakspeare, Wm. 98. 100. 101. 106. 135. 143. 202. 223. 297. 346.
Sharp, Granville 302.
Sheppard, Jack 92.
Sheridan 223. 332.
Shirley 223.
Shovel, Sir Cloudesly 201.
Shrewsbury, Talbot, Earl of 296.
Siddons, Mrs. 215.
Sidney, Algernon 334.
Simpson, Sir James 215.
Skelton 192.
Sloane, Sir Hans 293. 294.
Smith, Jas. 146.
Smith, Capt. John 93.
Smith, Sydney 82. 294.
Somerset, Protector 123. 112. 190.
Somerville, Mrs. 294.
South 203.
Southampton, Earl of 124.
Southey 202. 217.
Speed 96.
Spenser, Edm. 192. 203.
Stanhope, Earl 332.
Steele 97. 294. 327.
Stephenson, Robt. 198. 204.
Sterne 263.
Stillingfleet 92.
Stow 107.
Strafford 124. 190.
Stratford de Redcliffe 196.
Street 294.
Surrey, Earl of 144.
Swift 294.
Sydenham, Dr. 192.

Tait, Abp. 333.
Telford 215.

Temple, Sir Rich. 200.
Tennyson 330.
Thackeray 97. 201. 262. 271. 294.
Thirlwall 97. 201.
Thomson 202. 322.
Tierney 199. 324.
Tietjens, Mme. 294.
Tillotson 139.
Tonson 325.
Toplady 217.
Turner 86. 89. 171. 176. 294.
Tyler, Wat 96. 111. 304. 345.
Tyndale 81. 113.

Usher 139.

Wade, Gen. 200.
Wales, Prince of 125.
Wallace, Wm. 96. 124. 190.

Waller 376.
Walpole, Hor. 225. 326.
Walsingham 325.
Walton, Isaac 135. 330.
Warwick 92. 123.
Watt, Jas. 210. 221.
Watts, Dr. 98. 200.
Wellington, Duke of 86. 88. 105. 121. 260. 267. 341.
Wesley, Chas. 200. 217. 225.
Wesley, John 200.
Wesley, Susannah 98.
West, Ben. 89.
Whittington, Rich. 91. 102. 328.
Wilberforce, Wm. 198. 332.
Wild, Jonathan 93.
William I. 120. 337.

William III. 208. 262. 263. 302. 316.
William IV. 338.
William of Wykeham 337.
Wiseman, Card. 294.
Wither, Geo. 92. 144.
Wolcot 180.
Wolfe 121. 214.
Wolsey 113. 181. 316. 338.
Woodfall 293.
Worde, Wynkin de 135.
Wordsworth 200.
Wren, Sir C. 84. 84. 89. 217. 221.
Wyatt 124. 190.
Wycherley 180.
Wycliffe 81.

York, Duke of 219.
Young 216.

# INDEX OF STREETS

AND

# PLAN OF LONDON.

## CONTENTS.

1. List of the principal streets, public buildings, etc., of London.
2. General Plan of London, showing the limits of the special plans.
3. Large Plan of London, in three sections.
4. Four Special Plans of the most important quarters of London.
5. Railway Plan of London and its suburbs.

This cover may be detached from the rest of the book by severing the yellow thread which will be found between pp. 38 and 39 of the list of streets.

## List of the Principal Streets, Squares, Public Buildings, etc.
### with Reference to the accompanying Plans.

The large Map of London, on the scale of 1:24,200, is divided into three sections, of which the uppermost is coloured brown, the central red, and the lowest gray. Each section contains numbered squares. In the accompanying index the capital letters **B, R, G**, following the name of a street or building, refer to the different sections, while the numbers correspond with those of the squares in each section. When the name required is also to be found on one of the special plans, this is indicated by an italicised Roman numeral. Thus, Adam Street, Adelphi, will be found on the red section, square 30; and also on the second special map.

The numbering of the squares is so arranged, that squares in different sections bearing the same number adjoin each other. Thus, square 16 on the brown section finds its continuation towards the S. in square 16 on the red section.

The squares will also be useful for calculating distances, each side of a square being exactly half a mile, while the diagonals if drawn would be 1,244 yards.

Names, to which *Great*, *Little*, *Old*, *New*, *Upper*, *Lower*, or *Saint* are prefixed, are to be sought for under these prefixes.

The following abbreviations are used: *ave.*, avenue; *ch.*, church; *cres.*, crescent; *ct.*, court; *ea.*, east; *grdns.*, gardens; *grn.*, green; *gro.*, grove; *gt.*, great; *hl.*, hill; *ho.*, house; *la.*, lane; *nth.*, north; *pk.*, park; *pl.*, place; *rd.*, road; *sq.*, square; *st.*, street; *sta.*, station; *sth.*, south; *ter.*, terrace; *tn.*, town; *wd.*, wood; *we.*, west.

| | B | R | G | | B | R | G |
|---|---|---|---|---|---|---|---|
| Abbey grdns., St. John's wd. | 11 | | | Adam street, Adelphi | | 11 | |
| Abbey road., St. John's wood | 7 | | | Adam street, New Kent road | | | 37 |
| Abbey st., Bethnal green road | 48 | | | Adam street, Rotherhithe | | | |
| Abbey street, Bermondsey | | 41 | | Adam st. ea., Manchester sq | I | | |
| Abbeyfield road, New road, Rotherhithe | | | 49 | Adam's mews, Sth. Audley street | I | 19 | |
| Abbotts road, Kilburn | 6 | | | Adam's pl., Borough High st | | | 37 |
| Abchurch la., King William street | | 43 | | Adamson road, Belsize park | 10 | | |
| Abercorn pl., St. John's wood | 11 | | | Addington sq., Camberwell | | | 35 |
| Aberdeen pk., Highbury gro. | 37 | | | Addington street, Lambeth | | | 28 |
| Aberdeen pk. rd., Highbury | 37 | | | Addle hl., Doctors' comm. | | II | 20 |
| Aberdeen pl., St. John's wood | 12 | | | Addle st., Wood st., Cheapside | | II | |
| Abersham road, Shacklewell | 45 | | | Adelaide road, Hampstead | 14 | | |
| Abingdon road, Kensington | | 1 | | Adelaide street, Strand | | II | 22 |
| Abingdon st., Westminster *IV* | | 25 | | Adelphi Strand | | II | |
| Abingdon villas, Kensington | | 1 | | Adelphi terrace, Strand | | II | |
| Acacia road, St. John's wood | 11 | | | Adelphi theatre, opposite Adam street, Strand | | II | 22 |
| Academy, Royal, Burlington house, **Piccadilly** | I | 22 | | Admiralty, Whitehall | | IV | |
| Acorn st., Brunswick square | | 13 | | Ager Street, Strand | | II | 30 |
| Acton street, Gray's inn road | 32 | | | Agnes street, Waterloo road | | | |
| Ada st., Broadw., Lond. fields | 51 | | | | | | |

BAEDEKER, London. 7th Edit.

# LIST OF THE PRINCIPAL STREETS,

| | B | R | G | | B | R | G |
|---|---|---|---|---|---|---|---|
| Ainger rd., Regent's pk. rd. | 14 | | | Alfred street, Bow road | 64 | | |
| Air street, Piccadilly . . I | | 23 | | Alfred street, Colebrook row | 35 | | |
| Albany, Piccadilly. . . I | | 22 | | Alfred street, Lower Wandsworth road | | | 20 |
| Albany road, Camberwell | | | 42 | | | | |
| Albany street, Regent's pk. | 24 | 24 | | Alfred street, Whitehorse la. | | 60 | |
| Albemarle st., Piccadilly I | | 22 | | Alhambra theatre . . . . I | | 27 | |
| Albert bridge, Battersea. | | | 14 | Alice st., Bermondsey New road | | | 41 |
| Albert embankment . . IV | | 29 | 29 | | | | |
| Albert gate, Knightsbridge | | 18 | | Allcroft road, Kentish town | 17 | | |
| Albert hall, Kensington rd. | | 9 | | Allen street, Holloway road | 38 | | |
| Albert place, Kensington | | 5 | | Allen street, Kensington rd. | | 1 | |
| Albert road, Bow | 59 | | | Allen street, Lambeth . . . | | 29 | |
| Albert road, Glo'ster gate | 19 | | | Allendale road, Camberwell | | | 40 |
| Albert road, Kilburn park | 3 | | | Allerton street, Hoxton . . | 44 | | |
| Albert road, Battersea | | | 15 | Allhallows ch., Gt. Tower street . . . . . . . . III | | 39 | |
| Albert road, Queen's road, Dalston | 46 | | | Allhallows lane . . . . III | | 38 | |
| Albert road, St. John's wood | 7 | | | Allington street, Vauxhall bridge road . . . . IV | | 21 | |
| Albert square, Clapham rd. | | | 31 | | | | |
| Albert street, Cambridge rd. | 56 | | | All Saints' church, Margaret street . . . . . . . . I | | 24 | |
| Albert street, Homerton | 53 | | | | | | |
| Albert street, London road | | 33 | | All Saints' road, Westbourne park | | 4 | |
| Albert st., Mile End New tn. | | 48 | | | | | |
| Albert st., Mornington cres. | 23 | | | Allsop pl., Upper Baker st. | | 20 | |
| Albert street, Pentonville | 35 | | | All Souls' church, Langham place . . . . . . . . I | | 24 | |
| Albion gro., Barnsbury | 30 | | | | | | |
| Albion place, London wall II | | 36 | | Alma road, Blue Anchor rd. | | | 45 |
| Albion place, St. John's lane | | 36 | | Alma road, Old Ford road | 56 | | |
| Albion road, Belsize road | 10 | | | Alma st., Kentish town rd. | 21 | | |
| Albion road, Clapham . . | | | 24 | Alma street, New North rd. | 43 | | |
| Albion road, Dalston | 46 | | | Almorah road, Islington . . | 42 | | |
| Albion road, Hackney | 54 | | | Alpha road, Park road | | 16 | |
| Albion road, Holloway | 33 | | | Alpha terrace, Blenheim st., Chelsea | | | 14 |
| Albion square, Queen's road, Dalston | 46 | | | Alscot road, Bermondsey | | | 45 |
| Albion st., Caledonian road | 31 | | | Alvey st., Walworth common | | | 44 |
| Albion street, Hyde park | | 15 | | Alvington st., Shacklewell | 45 | | |
| Albion street, Rotherhithe | | 53 | | Alwyne lane, Canonbury . | 38 | | |
| Albion terrace, Kensington | | 3 | | Alwyne road, Canonbury | 38 | | |
| Aldenham st., St. Pancras | 27 | | | Amberley rd., Maida hill | | 8 | |
| Aldermanbury . . . . III | | 39 | | Amelia street, Walworth | | | 37 |
| Alderminster road, Bermondsey | | | | Amersham vale, New Cross road | | | 59 |
| Alderney road, Globe road | | 56 | 45 | Amhurst road, Shacklewell | 45 | | |
| Alderney st. | | | 21 | Amhurst road, Hackney | 49 | | |
| Aldersgate street . . . III | | 40 | | Ampton st., Gray's inn road | 32 | | |
| Aldersgate street station | | 40 | | Amwell street, Claremont sq. | 36 | | |
| Aldgate station . . . . III | | 48 | | Anchor street . . . . . . | | 48 | |
| Aldgate High street . . III | | 48 | | Anderson walk, Lambeth | | | 29 |
| Aldred road, Walworth | | | 34 | Andrews road, Mare street, Hackney | 54 | | |
| Aldrich road, Kentish town | 21 | | | | | | |
| Aldridge road villas, Westbourne park | | 4 | | Angel court, Throgmorton street . . . . . . . . III | | 43 | |
| Alexander square, Brompton | | | 13 | Angel place, Boro' High st. | | 37 | |
| Alexander st., Westbrne. pk. | | 8 | | Angel street, St. Martin's-le-Grand . . . . . . . III | | 39 | |
| Alexandra road, Kilburn pk. | 3 | | | | | | |
| Alexandra rd., St. John's wd. | 6 | | | Angell road, Brixton | | | 30 |
| Alfred place, Bedford sq. I | | 28 | | Angler's lane, Kentish town road | 21 | | |
| Alfred place, Old Kent road. | | | 41 | | | | |
| Alfred rd., Westbourne grn. | | 4 | | Ann street, Bethnal green | 52 | | |
| Alfred street, Barnsbury. | 29 | | | Ann st., Union sq., Islington | 39 | | |

## SQUARES, PUBLIC BUILDINGS, etc. 3

### B R G

| | |
|---|---|
| Annis road, Victoria park 58 | Ashburnham rd., King's rd. . . 11 |
| Anthony st., St. Georges east . 51 | Ashbury rd., Shaftesbury pk. . . 30 |
| Antill road, Bow . . . . 60 | Ashby road. New Cross . . . 60 |
| Appleby road, London fields 50 | Ashby road. Islington . . . 38 |
| Appleby street, Kingsland rd. 47 | Ashcroft road. Grove road 60 |
| Approach rd., Victoria pk. 55 | Ashford street, Hoxton . . 44 |
| Apsley house, Piccadilly *IV* . 18 | Ashmore place, Clapham rd. . . 30 |
| Aquarium & winter garden. | Ashmore road, Harrow rd. 4 |
|   Tothill street . . . . *IV* . 25 | Ashwell road. Roman road 59 |
| Arabella row, Pimlico . *IV* . 21 | Aske street, Hoxton . . . 44 |
| Arbour square, Commercial | Astey's row, Essex road . . 38 |
|   road east . . . . . . . 55 | Astley st., Old Kent road . . 16 |
| Arbour street, east & west, | Aston road. Cornwell road. |
|   Commercial road east . . . 55 |   Notting hill . . . . . . 4 |
| Arch street, Poplar row, New | Aston st., Limehouse fields . 59 |
|   Kent road . . . . . . . 37 | Asylum road, Old Kent road . 51 |
| Archer street, Camden town 23 | Athenæum club, Pall mall *IV* . 26 |
| Archer st., Gt. Windmill st. *I* . 27 | Aubin street, Waterloo rd. . 29 |
| Archer street, Notting hill . 3 | Aubrey road. Notting hill . 2 |
| Archibald street, Campbell | Auckland road, Bow . . . 59 |
|   road. Bow . . . . . . . 64 | Auckland street, Upper Ken- |
| Arden street. Nine Elms . . 23 |   nington lane . . . . . . 30 |
| Argyle square, Euston road 32 | Augusta street, Poplar. . . 63 |
| Argyle street. Euston road 32 | Augustus street, Cumberland |
| Argyll place, Regent street *I* . 23 |   market . . . . . . . 24 |
| Argyll road, Kensington . . 1 | Austinfriars, City . . . *III* . 43 |
| Argyll street, Oxford street *I* . 23 | Austin road. Lower Wands- |
| Arlington sq., New Nord rd. 39 |   worth road . . . . . . . 20 |
| Arlington street, Islington 39 | Austin street, Shoreditch . 48 |
| Arlington street, Mornington | Austral st. . . . . . . . 33 |
|   crescent . . . . . . . . 23 | Avenue road. Camberwell . 39 |
| Arlington st., Piccadilly *IV* . 22 | Avenue road, Regent's park 10 |
| Arlington st., Sadler's wells 36 | Avery row, Grosvenor st. *I* . 23 |
| Armagh road, Old Ford . . 63 | Avondale sq.. Old Kent rd. . 16 |
| Army & Navy club, Pall mall | Aylesbury st., Clerkenwell . 36 |
|   *IV* . 22 | Aylesford st., Thames bank . 26 |
| Army & Navy stores . . *IV* . 21 | Ayliff street, Harper street . 37 |
| Arnold road, Bow road . . 64 | Azenby sq., Lyndhurst road . 18 |
| Artesian road, Bayswater . . 3 | |
| Arthur mews, London street, | Baalzephon st., Bermondsey . 11 |
|   Paddington . . . . . . 11 | Baches row, Hoxton . . . 44 |
| Arthur road, Wells street . 54 | Back Church lane, Commer- |
| Arthur st., Camberwell road . 35 |   cial road . . . . . . . 47 |
| Arthur street, Chelsea . . . 9 | Back hill. Leather lane . . 36 |
| Arthur st., Gray's inn road 32 | Back alley, Bow . . . . 64 |
| Arthur street. Lower Wands- | Bacon street, Brick lane. . . 48 |
|   worth road . . . . . . 20 | Bagshot street, Albany road . 42 |
| Arthur street. Oxford street . 27 | Bainbridge street, Oxford |
| Arthur st., Trevor square . 13 |   street . . . . . . *I. II* . 27 |
| Arthur street east, London | Baker street, Lloyd square 36 |
|   bridge . . . . . . *III* . 12 | Baker street, Portman sq. *I* . 20 |
| Artillery lane, Bishopsgate | Baker st. bazaar, Baker st. *I* . 20 |
|   street . . . . . . *III* . 44 | Balaclava rd., Blue Anchor rd. . 45 |
| Artillery row, Westminster *IV* . 21 | Baldwin street, City road. 40 |
| Artillery st., Horselydown . 44 | Baldwin's gardens, Leather |
| Arundel square, Barnsbury 34 |   lane . . . . . . . *II* . 36 |
| Arundel t., Stoke Newington 44 | Bale street, Stepney . . . 50 |
| Arundel street. Strand . *II* . 31 | Ballance road, Homerton . 58 |
| Ascham reet, Kentish town 21 | Ball's Pond road . . . . 44 |
| Ash gro., Mare st., Hackney 51 | Balms rd., De Beauvoir town 43 |
| Ash street, New Kent road . 37 | Baltic street St. Luke's. . 40 |

1*

## LIST OF THE PRINCIPAL STREETS,

| | B | R | G |
|---|---|---|---|
| Banbury rd., South Hackney | 54 | | |
| Bancroft road, Mile end | 56 | 56 | |
| Bank of England ... *III* | | 43 | |
| Bank buildings, Lothbury *III* | | 43 | |
| Bankside, Southwark ... *III* | | 38 | |
| Banner street, St. Luke's | | 40 | |
| Barbara street, Barnsbury | 29 | | |
| Barbican | | 40 | |
| Barchester street, Poplar New town | | 67 | |
| Barclay & Perkin's Brewery *III* | | 38 | |
| Barclay road, Walham green | | | 3 |
| Barclay street, Aldenham st. | 27 | | |
| Barlow street, Walworth | | | 41 |
| Barnard's inn, Holborn *II* | | 36 | |
| Barnet grove, Hart's lane, Bethnal green | 48 | | |
| Barnham street, Tooley st. | | 41 | |
| Barnsbury grove, Holloway | 30 | | |
| Barnsbury road, Islington | 35 | | |
| Barnsbury square, Islington | 34 | | |
| Barnsbury street, Islington | 34 | | |
| Baroda pl. | | 55 | |
| Baroness road, Hackney rd. | 48 | | |
| Barrett's grove, Stoke Newington | 41 | | |
| Barrosa place, Chelsea | | | 9 |
| Barrow hill rd., Portland tn. | 15 | | |
| Bartholomew close | | 40 | |
| Bartholomew lane, Bank *III* | | 43 | |
| Bartholomew road, Kentish town road | 22 | | |
| Bartholomew road north, Kentish town road | 21 | | |
| Bartholomew villas, Kentish town | 21 | | |
| Basing road, Westbourn pk. | | | 4 |
| Basinghall street ... *III* | | 39 | |
| Bassett street, Kentish town | 17 | | |
| Bateman's buildings, Soho *I* | | 27 | |
| Bateman's row, Shoreditch | 44 | | |
| Bath house ... *IV* | | 22 | |
| Bath place, Copenhagen st. | 31 | | |
| Bath place, Peckham | | | 47 |
| Bath street, Newgate st. *III* | | 39 | |
| Bath st., Old st., City road | 40 | | |
| Bath street, Tabernacle sq. | 44 | | |
| Bath terrace, Union road | | | 37 |
| Battersea bridge | | | 11 |
| Battersea bridge road | | | 15 |
| Battersea park | | | 19 |
| Battersea park pier | | | 18 |
| Battersea park railway pier, Victoria railway bridge | | | 18 |
| Battersea pk. railway station | | | 18 |
| Battersea railway station, High street | | | 12 |
| Battersea rise | | | 19 |
| Battersea park road | | | |

| | B | R | G |
|---|---|---|---|
| Battle bridge road, King's cross road | | 27 | |
| Baxendale st., Barnet grove | 48 | | |
| Baxter road, Essex road, Islington | | 42 | |
| Bayham st., Camden town | 23 | | |
| Bayswater ter., Paddington | | 7 | |
| Beak street, Regent street *I* | | 23 | |
| Beale road, Old Ford road | 59 | | |
| Bear gardens, Southwark | | 38 | |
| Bear lane, Southwark street | | 34 | |
| Bear street, Leicester sq. *II* | | 27 | |
| Beatrice road, Bermondsey | | | 49 |
| Beauchamp st., Leather la. *II* | | 36 | |
| Beaufort buildings, Strand *II* | | 31 | |
| Beaufort gardens, Brompton | | 13 | |
| Beaufort street, Chelsea | | | 10 |
| Beaumont sq. Mile end road | | 56 | |
| Beaumont st., Marylebone *I* | | 20 | |
| Beckway street, East street, Walworth | | | 44 |
| Bedford gardens, Kensington | | 2 | |
| Bedford pl., Russell sq. *II* | | 28 | |
| Bedford row, Holborn *II* | | 32 | |
| Bedford sq., Bloomsbury *I* | | 28 | |
| Bedford sq. ea., Commercial road east | | 51 | |
| Bedford street, Ampthill sq. | 24 | | |
| Bedford street, Bedford row | | 32 | |
| Bedford street, Strand *II* | | 27 | |
| Bedfordbury, Covent gdn. *II* | | 27 | |
| Beech street, Barbican | | 40 | |
| Beer la., Low. Thames st. *III* | | 42 | |
| Belgrave mews ea. Chapel st. | | 17 | |
| Belgrave road, Pimlico | | | 21 |
| Belgrave rd., St. John's wd. | 7 | | |
| Belgrave square ... *IV* | | 17 | |
| Belgrave street, Commercial road east | | 59 | |
| Belgrave street, King's cross | 32 | | |
| Belgrave street, Pimlico *IV* | | 21 | |
| Belham st., Camberwell pk. | | | 39 |
| Belitha villas, Barnsbury pk. | 30 | | |
| Bell lane, Wentworth st. *III* | | 48 | |
| Bell street, Edgware rd. | | 16 | |
| Bell yard, Temple bar *II* | | 35 | |
| Belmont st., Chalk farm rd. | 18 | | |
| Belsize avenue, Belsize pk. | 9 | | |
| Belsize crescent, Belsize pk. | 9 | | |
| Belsize lane, Hampstead | 9 | | |
| Belsize park, Hampstead | 9 | | |
| Belsize pk. gdns., Hampstead | 13 | | |
| Belsize road, Finchley road | 6 | | |
| Belsize square, Hampstead | 9 | | |
| Belvedere road, Lambeth | | 30 | |
| Bemerton st., Caledonian rd. | 30 | | |
| Ben Jonson road, Stepney | | 60 | |
| Benjamin st., Cowcross st. *II* | | 36 | |
| Bennet's hill, Doctors' commons ... *III* | | 39 | |
| Bentham road, Wick road | | | |

| | | |
|---|---|---|
| Bentinck st. Manchester sq. *I* | 19 | Blackheath road . . . . . . . 68 |
| Bentinck street, Soho . . *I* | 23 | Blackheath railway station, |
| Benwell road, Highbury . | 33 | Blackheath hill . . . . . 68 |
| Benyon rd., Southgate rd. | 43 | Blackman street, Borough . 37 |
| Beresford st., Walworth rd. | 38 | Blackwall . . . . . . . . 70 |
| Berkeley rd., Regent's pk. rd. | 18 | Blackwall railway station . 70 |
| Berkeley square . . . . *I* | | Blake's road, Peckham grove . 43 |
| Berkeley st., Piccadilly *I, IV* | 22 | Blakesley street, Commercial |
| Bermondsey New road . . | 22 | road east . . . . . . . 51 |
| Bermondsey street . . . . | 41 | Blandford square . . . . . 16 |
| Bermondsey wall . . . . | 49 | Blandford st., Portman sq. *I* . 20 |
| Bernard st., Regent's pk. rd. | 18 | Blantyre street, Chelsea . . 40 |
| Bernard street, Russell sq. . | 28 | Blenheim road, St. John's |
| Berners road, Islington . . | 35 | wood . . . . . . . . 41 |
| Berners street, Oxford st. *I* | 24 | Blenheim st. Cale st. Chelsea . 13 |
| Berwick st., Oxford st. . *I* | 23 | Blenheim st. New Bond st. *I* . 23 |
| Berwick street, Pimlico . | 21 | Blenheim street. Oxford st. *I* . 23 |
| Bessborough street, Pimlico | 25 | Blenheim ter., St. John's |
| Beta place, St. John's wood | 16 | wood . . . . . . . . . 7 |
| Bethlehem hospital, Lam- | | Blomfield place, Harrow rd. . 8 |
| beth road . . . . . . . . | 33 | Blomfield road, Edgware rd. . 8 |
| Bethnal green museum, Cam- | | Blomfield street, Dalston . 46 |
| bridge road . . . . . . | 52 | Blomfield st., Harrow road . 8 |
| Bethnal green junction sta., | | Blomfield st., London wall |
| Three Colt lane . . . . . | 51 | *III* . . . . . . . . . 44 |
| Bethnal green road . . . . | 52 48 | Blomfield terrace, Pimlico . 17 |
| Bevenden street, Hoxton | 44 | Bloomsbury market . . . 32 |
| Bevis marks, St. Mary Axe | | Bloomsbury place . . . *II* . 32 |
| *III* | 43 | Bloomsbury square . . *II* . 32 |
| Bible society . . . . . *II* | 35 | Bloomsbury street . . . *II* . 27 |
| Bidborough street, Judd st. | 28 | Blount street, Salmon's lane . 59 |
| Billingsgate market . . *III* | 42 | Blue Anchor la., Bermondsey . 45 |
| Billiter street, Fenchurch | | Blue Anchor yd. . . . . . . 47 |
| street . . . . . . . *III* | 43 | Blue Anchor road . . . . . 45 |
| Bina road, Old Brompton . | 5 | Bluecross st., Leicester sq. *I* . 26 |
| Binfield road, Clapham road | 28 | Blundell st., Caledonian rd. . 30 |
| Bingfield st., Caledonian rd. | 30 | Blythe st., Bethnal green rd. . 52 |
| Birchin lane, Cornhill *III* | 43 | Board of Trade, Whitehall |
| Birchington road, Kilburn | 2 | gardens . . . . . . . *IV* . 26 |
| Bird street, Oxford street *I* | 19 | Board of Works, Spring |
| Bird st., West sq., Lambeth | 33 | gardens . . . . . . . *IV* . 26 |
| Birdcage walk, St. James's | | Boleyn road . . . . . . . . 41 |
| park . . . . . . . . *IV* | 21 | Bolingbroke road, Church |
| Bird-in-bush road, New Peck- | | street, Battersea . . . . . 11 |
| ham . . . . . . . . . . | 47 | Bolsover street . . . . . . 24 |
| Birkbeck Institution . . *II* | 35 | Bolton road, Notting hill . 3 |
| Bishop's road, Hackney . . | 55 | Bolton road, St. John's wood 7 |
| Bishop's rd., North Brixton | 35 | Bolton row, Mayfair . . *IV* . 22 |
| Bishop's road, Paddington | 7 | Bolton street, Kennington . 34 |
| Bishop's road, Victoria pk. | 55 | Bolton street, Piccadilly *IV* . 22 |
| Bishopsgate st. rail. station | 44 | Boltons (The), W. Brompton . 5 |
| Bishopsgate st. within *III* | 43 | Bond street, Pentonville . 36 |
| Bishopsgate st. without *III* | 44 | Bond street, New . . . *I* . 23 |
| Blackfriars bridge . . . *II* | 34 | Bond street, Old . . . . *I* . 22 |
| Blackfriars pier, Blackfriars | | Bond street, Vauxhall . . . 26 |
| bridge . . . . . . . *II* | 35 | Bonner's road, Victoria pk. . 55 |
| Blackfriars railway bdg. *II* | 35 | Bonny street, Camden town . 22 |
| Blackfriars railway sta. *II* | 35 | Boodle's club, St. James's |
| Blackfriars road . . . . *II* | 34 | street . . . . . . . . *IV* . 22 |
| Blackheath avenue . . . . | 71 | Bookham street, Hoxton . 44 |
| Blackheath hill . . . . . | 68 | Boomfield road, Clapham . 28 |

# LIST OF THE PRINCIPAL STREETS,

| Street | B | R | G |
|---|---|---|---|
| Booth street, Spitalfields | | 48 | |
| Borough High street | | 38 | |
| Borough rd. railway station | | | 37 |
| Borough road, Southwark | | 33 | |
| Boscobel gardens, St. John's wood | | 16 | |
| Boscobel pl., St. John's wood | | 16 | |
| Boston place, Dorset square | | 16 | |
| Boston street, Dorset square | 16 | | |
| Boston street, Hackney rd. | 17 | | |
| Botanic gardens, Inner circle, Regent's park | | 20 | |
| Botolph lane, Lower Thames street | | 42 | |
| Boundary la., Camberwell rd. | | | 38 |
| Boundary rd., St. John's wd. | 10 | | |
| Boundary rw., Blackfriars road | | 33 | |
| Boundary street, Shoreditch | 18 | | |
| Bourdon st. I, IV | | 18 | |
| Bouverie st., Fleet st. II | | 3 | |
| Bow churchyard, Cheapside III | | 39 | |
| Bow common, Middlesex | | 64 | |
| Bow common lane | | 64 | |
| Bow junction railway sta., Fairfield road | 64 | | |
| Bow lane, Cheapside. III | | 39 | |
| Bow lane, Poplar | | 63 | |
| Bow rail. statn., Avenue rd. | 64 | | |
| Bow road, Mile end | | 64 | |
| Bow street, Covent garden | | 31 | |
| Bowling grn. la., Clerkenwell | | 36 | |
| Bowling green street, Kennington road | | 30 | |
| Boxworth grove, Barnsbury | 35 | | |
| Boyle street, Savile row I | | 23 | |
| Boyson road, Walworth | | | 38 |
| Bradley street, Sth. Lmbth. | | | 27 |
| Brady st., Whitechapel rd. | | 52 | |
| Bramah road, Brixton | | | 35 |
| Branch place, Hoxton | 13 | | |
| Brandon road, York road | 26 | | |
| Brandon street, Walworth | | | 37 |
| Bread street, Cheapside III | | 39 | |
| Brecknock road | 25 | | |
| Brewer street, Golden sq. I | | 23 | |
| Brewer st. Pancras road | 27 | | |
| Brewer street, Pimlico. IV | | 21 | |
| Brewery rd., Caledonian rd. | 30 | | |
| Brick court, Temple | | 35 | |
| Brick lane, Spitalfields III | | 48 | |
| Brick street, Park lane, Piccadilly IV | | 18 | |
| Bricklayers' Arms station | | 44 | |
| Bride street, Holloway | 30 | | |
| Bridewell place, New Bridge station II | | 35 | |
| Bridge road, Battersea | | 44 | |
| Bridge street, Homerton | 53 | | |
| Bridge st., Westminster IV | | 25 | |

| Street | B | R | G |
|---|---|---|---|
| Bridgewater ho., St. James's park IV | | 22 | |
| Bridgewater st., Somers town | 27 | | |
| Bridport pl., New North road | 43 | | |
| Bright street, Bromley | | 67 | |
| Brill row, Somers town | 27 | | |
| Brindley st., Westbourne grn. | 4 | | |
| Bristol gardens, Warwick rd. | 8 | | |
| Britannia rd., Walham green | | 7 | |
| Britannia row, Islington | 39 | | |
| Britannia street, Hoxton | 40 | | |
| Britannia st., Gray's inn rd. | 32 | | |
| British museum II | 28 | | |
| British street, Bow road | 64 | | |
| Britten st., Blenheim street | | | 13 |
| Brixton road | | | 32 |
| Broad court, Long acre | | 31 | |
| Broad Sanctuary, Westminster IV | | 25 | |
| Broad street, Bloomsbury II | | 27 | |
| Broad street, Golden sq. I | | 23 | |
| Broad street, Lambeth | | 29 | |
| Broad st. railway sta. III | | 44 | |
| Broad street, Ratcliff | | 55 | |
| Broadley ter., Blandford sq. | 16 | | |
| Broadwall, Stamford street | | 34 | |
| Broadway, Deptford | | | 63 |
| Broadway, Ludgate hill II | | 35 | |
| Broadway, Westminster IV | | 25 | |
| Broke road, Dalston | 47 | | |
| Bromehead st., Commercial road east | | 51 | |
| Bromley railway station, St. Leonard's street | | 68 | |
| Bromley street, Commercial road east | | 55 | |
| Brompton crescent | | | 13 |
| Brompton road | | 13 | |
| Brompton square | | 13 | |
| Brondesbury park, Kilburn | 3 | | |
| Brondesbury villas, Kilburn | 3 | | |
| Brook street, Bermondsey New road | | 41 | |
| Brook st., Grosvenor sq. I | | 19 | |
| Brook street, Lambeth | | | 33 |
| Brook street, Ratcliffe | | 55 | |
| Brooke street, Holborn II | | 36 | |
| Brookfield rd., Victoria pk. | 58 | | |
| Brook's mews, Davies st. I | | 23 | |
| Brooksby street, Islington | 34 | | |
| Brooksby's walk, Homerton | 53 | | |
| Brook's club, St. James's st. IV | | 22 | |
| Broom's alley, Fulham | | 8 | |
| Broomhouse lane, Fulham | | 4 | |
| Brougham road, Dalston | 51 | | |
| Brougham st., Queen's rd. | | | 20 |
| Brown st., Bryanston sq. | | 15 | |
| Brown street, Grosvenor sq. I | | 19 | |
| Brown's lane, Brick lane | | 48 | |
| Brownlow road, Dalston | 47 | | |

| | | | | |
|---|---|---|---|---|
| Brownlow st., Drury la. *II* | | 31 | Bushey hill, Peckham road | 44 |
| Brownlow st., Haggerstone | 47 | | Buttesland steet, East road. | |
| Brownl. st., High Holborn *II* | | 32 | Hoxton | 44 |
| Bruce road, Bromley | | 68 | Byron street, St. Leonard's | |
| Brunel street, Vauxhall | | 30 | road. Bromley | 67 |
| Brunswick gardens,Campden | | | Bywater street, King's road | 13 |
| hill | | 2 | Cable street, Wellclose sq. | 51 |
| Brunswick chapel | *I* | 15 | Cadogan pier | 11 |
| Brunswick rd., Ea. Ind. rd. | | 67 | Cadogan place, Sloane street | 13 17 |
| Brunswick sq., Camberwell | | 43 | Cadogan street, Sloane street | 13 |
| Brunswick sq., Foundling h. | 32 | 32 | Cadogan ter., Sloane street | 13 |
| Brunswick street, Hackney | 54 | | Cale street, Chelsea | 9 |
| Brunswick st., Hackney rd. | 47 | | Caledonia st., King's cross | 31 |
| Brunswick st., Southwark | | 31 | Caledonian road, Holloway | 30 |
| Brunswick street, Poplar | | 70 | Callow street, Fulham road | 10 |
| Brunswick yard, City road | 4 | | Camberwell grove | 44 |
| Brushfield street, Bishops- | | | Camberwell square | 39 |
| gate street | | 44 | Camberwell New road | 35 |
| Bruton st., New Bond st. *I* | | 23 | Camberwell railway station, | |
| Bryan street, Caledonian rd. | 31 | | Station road | 10 |
| Bryanston square | | 16 | Camberwell road | 39 |
| Bryanston st., Portman sq. *I* | | 15 | Cambridge gdns., Kilburn | 3 |
| Brydges street, Strand. *II* | | 31 | Cambridge circus . *I, II* | 27 |
| Buckingham gate,Pimlico *IV* | | 21 | Cambridge club, Old Bond | |
| Buckingham palace *IV* | | 21 | street *I* | 23 |
| Buckingham palace road *IV* | | 21 17 | Cambridge house *IV* | 22 |
| Buckingham road, De Beau- | | | Cambridge pl., Paddington | 11 |
| voir town | 42 | | Cambridge rd., Kilburn pk. | 4 |
| Buckingham st., Fitzroy sq. | | 24 | Cambridge road, Mare street | 52 52 |
| Buckingham st., Strand *II* | | 26 | Cambridge sq., Upper South- | |
| Buckland cres., Belsize pk. | 10 | | wick street | 15 |
| Buckland st., New North rd. | 43 | | Cambridge st., Edgware rd. | 15 |
| Bucklersbury, Cheapside *III* | | 39 | Cambridge street, Pimlico | 12 |
| Buck's row,Whitechapel rd. | | 52 | Cambridge ter., Edgware rd. | 11 |
| Budge row, Cannon st. *III* | | 39 | Cambridge ter., Regent's pk. | 21 |
| Bull & Mouth street, *III* | | 39 | Camden cots., Camden town | 22 |
| Bulstrode st., Welbeck st. *I* | | 20 | Camden grove, Peckham | |
| Bunhill row, Chiswell street | 40 40 | | grove | 43 |
| Burcham street, Bromley | | 63 | Camden park road | 25 |
| Burdett road, Limehouse | | 60 | Camden road, Camden town | 22 |
| Burdett road railway station | | 64 | Camden sq., Camden town | 36 |
| Burleigh street, Strand. *II* | | 31 | Camden st., Bethnal grn. rd. | 52 |
| Burlington arcade, Picca- | | | Camden street, Camden town | 22 |
| dilly *I* | | 22 | Camden st., Islington green | 35 |
| Burlington grdns., Old Bond | | | Camden town railway sta., | |
| street *I* | | 22 | Great College street | 72 |
| Burlington rd., Westbourne | | | Camelia st., South Lambeth | 27 |
| park | | 4 | Camera square, Chelsea | 10 |
| Burne street, Edgware road | | 16 | Camilla road, Bermondsey | 49 |
| Burnett street, Vauxhall | | 30 | Camomile st., Bishopsgate *III* | 43 |
| Burr street, St. Katharine's | | | Campbell road, Bow road | 64 64 |
| docks | | 46 | Campden grove, Kensington | 2 |
| Burton crescent, Euston road | 28 | | Campden hill, Kensington | 2 |
| Burton road, Brixton road | | 36 | Campden hill rd., Kensington | 2 |
| Bury court, St. Mary Axe *III* | | 43 | Campden ho. rd., Kensington | 2 |
| Bury place, Oxford street | | 32 | Campden street, Kensington | 2 |
| Bury street, Bloomsbury *II* | | 28 | Canal road, Kingsland road | 43 |
| Bury street, Jermyn st. *IV* | | 22 | Canal road, Mile end road | 60 |
| Bury st., Sydney st., Chelsea | | 9 | Canfield gardens, Kilburn | 6 |
| Busby place, Osney crescent | 25 | | Canning pl., Kensington gate | 5 |
| Bush lane, Cannon street *III* | | 39 | Cannon row, Parliament st *IV* | 25 |

## LIST OF THE PRINCIPAL STREETS,

| | B | R | G |
|---|---|---|---|
| Cannon street..... *III* | . | 39 | |
| Cannon st. railway bdg. *III* | . | 38 | |
| Cannon st. railway sta. *III* | . | 39 | |
| Cannon street road, Commercial road east.... | | | 51 |
| Canonbury grove, Islington | 38 | | |
| Canonbury junction station, Douglas road north... | 37 | | |
| Canonbury lane...... | 38 | | |
| Canonbury pk. — nth & sth. | 38 | | |
| Canonbury place...... | 38 | | |
| Canonbury road...... | 38 | | |
| Canonbury square, Islington | 38 | | |
| Canonbury street..... | 38 | | |
| Canrobert street...... | 52 | | |
| Cantelows rd., Camden sq. | 26 | | |
| Canterbury road, Ball's Pond road............. | 44 | | |
| Canterbury rd., Kilburn pk. | 3 | | |
| Canterbury terrace, Kingsbury road......... | 44 | | |
| Canton street, East India dock road......... | | | 63 |
| Capland street, Lisson grove | 12 | | |
| Carburton st.,Gt.Portland st. | | 24 | |
| Cardigan road, Old Ford . | 63 | | |
| Cardigan st., Kennington la. | | | 30 |
| Carey lane, Foster lane *III* | . | 39 | |
| Carey street, Lincoln's inn *II* | . | 31 | |
| Carey street, Westminster . | | | 25 |
| Carlisle place, Victoria street | . | 21 | 24 |
| Carlisle street, Lambeth *IV* | | 29 | |
| Carlisle st., Portman market | 12 | 12 | |
| Carlisle street, Soho.... *I* | . | 27 | |
| Carlos street, Grosvenor squ. *I* | | 19 | |
| Carlton club, Pall mall *IV* | . | 26 | |
| Carlton gardens, Pall mall | . | 26 | |
| Carlton grove, Low. Wandsworth road...... | | | 16 |
| Carlton grove, Queen's road | | | 54 |
| Carlton hill, St. John's wood | 7 | | |
| Carlton house ter., Pall mall | . | 26 | |
| Carlton road, Kentish town | 17 | | |
| Carlton road, Kilburn park | 3 | | |
| Carlton rd., Mile end Old tn. | 56 | | |
| Carlton road, Notting hill . | . | 4 | |
| Carlton road, Warden road, Kentish town .... | 17 | | |
| Carlyle square, Chelsea... | | | 10 |
| Carnaby street, Golden sq. *I* | . | 25 | |
| Caroline mews, Bedford sq. | . | 28 | |
| Caroline place, Marlboro' road, Chelsea...... | | | 13 |
| Caroline place, Mecklenburgh square...... | . | 32 | |
| Caroline street, Bedford sq. *I* | . | 28 | |
| Caroline street, Coleshill st. | | | 17 |
| Caroline street, Lambeth . | . | . | 29 |
| Carpenter st., Berkeley sq. *I* | . | 18 | |
| Carter la., Doctors' coms. *III* | . | 39 | |

| | B | R | G |
|---|---|---|---|
| Carter street, Brick lane, Spitalfields....... | . | . | 48 |
| Carter street, Walworth road | . | . | 38 |
| Carteret st., Westminster *IV* | . | 21 | |
| Cartwright st., Royal Mint st. | . | . | 46 |
| Cassland rd., South Hackney | 54 | | |
| Castle la., High st., Battersea | . | . | 16 |
| Castle road, Kentish town . | 22 | | |
| Castle street, City road.. | . | 44 | |
| Castle street, Long acre *II* | . | 27 | |
| Castle st. east, Oxford st. *I* | . | 23 | |
| Catharine st., Caledonian rd. | 31 | | |
| Cathcart hill, Junction road | 21 | | |
| Cathcart rd., West Brompton | . | . | 6 |
| Catherine street, City road . | | 44 | |
| Catherine street, East India dock road........ | . | . | 63 |
| Catherine street, Jonathan street, Lambeth.... | . | . | 29 |
| Catherine street, Limehouse fields........... | . | . | 59 |
| Catherine street, Strand *II* | . | 31 | |
| Cator street, Peckham road | . | . | 47 |
| Causton st., Vauxhall bdg. rd. | . | . | 25 |
| Cavendish place, Cavendish square........ *I* | . | 24 | |
| Cavendish rd., St. John's wd. | 11 | | |
| Cavendish sq., Oxford st. *I* | . | 23 | |
| Cavendish st., New North road | 43 | | |
| Cavendish st., Queen's cres. | 17 | | |
| Caversham road, Kentish tn. road............. | 21 | | |
| Caversham street, Chelsea . | . | . | 11 |
| Caxton street, Westmnstr. *IV* | . | 21 | |
| Cecil street, Strand.. *II* | . | 31 | |
| Celbridge pl., Westbourne pk. | . | 8 | |
| Central London Ophthalmic hospital, Calthorpe street | 32 | | |
| Central street, St. Luke's . | 40 | | |
| Chadwell st., Myddelton sq. | 36 | | |
| Chadwick road, Peckham . | . | . | 48 |
| Chalcot cres., Regent's park | 18 | | |
| Chalcot ter., Regent's park | 18 | | |
| Chalk Farm railway station, Regent's park road . | 18 | | |
| Chalk Farm rd., Camden tn. | 18 | | |
| Chalk Farm station.... | 18 | | |
| Chalton street, Somers town | 28 | | |
| Chamber street, Goodman's fields........ *III* | . | 47 | |
| Champion gro., Denmark hill | . | . | 44 |
| Champion hill, Camberwell | . | . | 44 |
| Champion park...... | . | . | 40 |
| Chancery lane..... *II* | . | 35 | |
| Chandos st., Cavendish sq. *I* | . | 24 | |
| Chandos st., Covent grdn. *II* | . | 26 | |
| Chandos street, Stratford . | 69 | | |
| Change alley, Cornhill *III* | . | 43 | |
| Chapel place, Montpelier st. | . | 13 | |
| Chapel row, Exmouth street | 36 | | |
| Chapel royal, St. James's *II* | . | 22 | |

## SQUARES, PUBLIC BUILDINGS, etc. 9

| | B | R | G | | B | R | G |
|---|---|---|---|---|---|---|---|
| Chapel royal, Whitehall *IV* | . | 26 | | Chenies mews, Bedford sq. | . | 28 | |
| Chapel royal Savoy, Savoy street . . . . . . . . *II* | . | 31 | | Chenies place, Pancras road | 28 | | |
| | | | | Chenies st., Tottenham court road . . . . . . . . . . *I* | . | 28 | |
| Chapel st., Belgrave sq. *IV* | . | 17 | | | | | |
| Chapel street, Edgware road | . | 16 | | Chepstow place, Westbourne grove . . . . . . . . . . | . | 3 | |
| Chapel street, Pentonville . | 35 | | | | | | |
| Chapel street, Somers town | 28 | | | Chepstow villas, Ledbury rd. | . | 3 | |
| Chapel st., Sth. Audley st. *I* | . | 18 | | Cherry garden pier . . . . | . | 49 | |
| Chapter street, Vauxhall bdg. road . . . . . . . . . . | . | 25 | | Cherry garden st., Bermondsey wall . . . . . . . . . | . | 47 | |
| Charing cross . . . . . *IV* | . | 26 | | Cherry tree ct., Aldersgate st. | . | 10 | |
| Charing cross hospital, Agar street . . . . . . . . *II* | . | 26 | | Chesham place, Belgrave sq. | . | 17 | |
| | | | | Chesham street, Belgrave sq. | . | . | 17 |
| Charing cross pier, Victoria embankment . . . . . *IV* | . | 30 | | Cheshire street, Bethnal grn. | . | 52 | |
| | | | | Chester mews, Regent's pk. | 24 | | |
| Charing cross railway sta. *IV* | . | 30 | | Chester place, Bedford square | . | 17 | |
| Charing cross road . . . *II* | . | 27 | | Chester place, Hyde park sq. | . | 11 | |
| Charing cross terminus & hotel . . . . . . . . . . *II* | . | 26 | | Chester place, Regent's park | 20 | | |
| | | | | Chester square, Pimlico *IV* | . | 17 | 17 |
| Charing cross theatre, King William street . . . . *II* | . | 26 | | Chester st., Belgrave sq. *IV* | . | 17 | |
| | | | | Chester st., Kennington road | . | . | 33 |
| Charles lane, St. John's wd. | 15 | | | Chester terrace, Eaton square | . | . | 17 |
| Charles square, Pitfield st. | 44 | | | Chester terrace, Regent's pk. | 24 | | |
| Charles street, Berkeley sq. *I* | . | 18 | | Chesterfield ho., Curzon st. *IV* | . | 18 | |
| Charles street, City road . | 10 | | | Chesterfield st., Argyle sq. | 32 | | |
| Charles street, Drury lane *II* | . | 31 | | Chesterfield st., Mayfair *IV* | . | 18 | |
| Charles st., Hampstead road | 24 | | | Cheyne walk, Chelsea . . . | . | . | 10 |
| Charles st., Hatton garden *II* | . | 36 | | Chichester road, Harrow rd. | . | 8 | |
| Charles street, Islington . . | 42 | | | Chichester road, Kilburn pk. | 3 | | |
| Charles street, Portland town | 15 | | | Chichester street, Pimlico . | . | . | 22 |
| Charles street, St. James's square . . . . . . *I, IV* | . | 26 | | Chicksand street, Spitalfields | . | 48 | |
| | | | | Child's place, Temple bar . | . | 35 | |
| Charles st., Westminster *IV* | . | 25 | | Chilton street, Bethnal green | 48 | | |
| Charles street, Whitechapel | . | 55 | | Chilworth st., Paddington . | . | 11 | |
| Charlesworth st. . . . . . | 33 | | | Chippenham rd., Harrow rd. | 8 | 4 | |
| Charlotte street, Bedford square . . . . . *I, II* | . | 28 | | Chislett rd., West Hampstead | 6 | | |
| | | | | Chiswell street, Finsbury sq. | . | 40 | |
| Charlotte st., Caledonian rd. | 31 | | | Chrisp street, Poplar . . . | . | 67 | |
| Charlotte st., Fitzroy sq. *I* | . | 24 | | Christ church, Newgate *III* | . | 39 | |
| Charlotte street, Curtain rd. | 44 | | | Christ church, Wandsworth | . | . | 28 |
| Charlotte st., Old Kent rd. | . | 46 | | Christchurch street, Chelsea | . | . | 14 |
| Charlton place, Islington . . | 35 | | | Christ's hospital . . *II. III* | . | 39 | |
| Charlton st., Marylebone *I* | . | 24 | | Christian street, Commercial road east . . . . . . . | . | 54 | |
| Charlwood st., Belgrave rd. | . | 21 | | | | | |
| Charrington st., Oakley sq. | 27 | | | Christie road, Victoria park | 58 | | |
| Charterhouse . . . . . *II* | . | 40 | | Christopher st., Finsbury sq. | . | . | 41 |
| Charterhouse square . . *II* | . | 40 | | Chryssell road, Brixton road | . | . | 35 |
| Charterhouse street, City *II* | . | 36 | | Chumleigh st., Camberwell | . | . | 42 |
| Chatham place, Hackney . | 54 | | | Church pl., Paddington grn. | . | 12 | |
| Cheapside . . . . . . . *III* | . | 39 | | Church road, Battersea . . | . | . | 44 |
| Chelsea barracks . . . . . | . | . | 17 | Church road, High street, Homerton . . . . . . . . | . | 57 | |
| Chelsea basin, Chelsea . . | . | . | 17 | | | | |
| Chelsea bridge road . . . . | . | . | 18 | Church road, Islington . . | 42 | | |
| Chelsea embankment . . . | . | . | 14 | Church row, Bethnal grn. rd. | 48 | | |
| Chelsea hospital, Queen's road east . . . . . . . . | . | . | 14 | Church street, Bethnal green | 48 | | |
| | | | | Church st., Camberwell grn. | . | . | 39 |
| Chelsea pier, Battersea bdg. | . | . | 10 | Church street, Chelsea . . | . | . | 10 |
| Chelsea railway sta., Harriet street, Fulham road . . . | . | . | 7 | Church street, Deptford . . | . | . | 63 |
| | | | | Church street, Greenwich . | . | . | 66 |
| Chelsham road, Clapham . | . | 28 | | Church street, Horselydown | . | 41 | |
| Cheltenham terrace, Chelsea | . | 13 | | Church street, Islington . . | 35 | | |

# LIST OF THE PRINCIPAL STREETS,

| Street | B | R | G | Street | B | R | G |
|---|---|---|---|---|---|---|---|
| Church street, Kensington | | 2 | | Clement's lane, Lombard st. | | | |
| Church street, Lisson grove | | 12 | | *III* | | 43 | |
| Church street, Rotherhithe | | 49 | | Clement's rd., Drummond rd. | | | 49 |
| Church street, Smith square, Westminster *IV* | | 25 | | Cleopatra's needle *II* | | 30 | |
| Church street, Soho *I* | | 27 | | Clephane road, Islington | | 38 | |
| Church street, Spitalfields | | 48 | | Clerkenwell clo., Clerkenwell | | 36 | |
| Church street, Trinity sq., Boro' | | 37 | | Clerkenwell green | | 36 | |
| Church street, Waterloo rd. | | 34 | | Cleve rd., West Hampstead | 6 | | |
| Churchill road, Homerton | 53 | | | Cleveland gdns., Bayswater | | 7 | |
| Churton street, Pimlico | | | 21 | Cleveland rd., Downham rd. | 42 | | |
| Circus place, Finsbury circus *III* | | 44 | | Cleveland road, St. James's *IV* | | 22 | |
| Circus road, Haverstock rd. | 17 | | | Cleveland square, Bayswater | | 7 | |
| Circus rd., St. John's wood | 12 | | | Cleveland st., Fitzroy sq. *I* | | 24 | |
| Circus street, Marylebone rd. | | 16 | | Cleveland st., Mile end road | | 56 | |
| Cirencester st., Harrow road | | 8 | | Clifden road, Lower Clapton | 53 | | |
| City garden road, City road | 40 | | | Clifford st., New Bond st. *I* | | 23 | |
| City gardens, City road | 40 | | | Clifford's inn, Fleet street *II* | | 35 | |
| City liberal club *III* | | 43 | | Clift street, New North road | 43 | | |
| City road | 40 | 44 | | Clifton gardens, Maida hill | 12 | 8 | |
| Civil Service club *IV* | | 22 | | Clifton road, Asylum road | | | 51 |
| Clanricarde gardens, Notting hill | | 3 | | Clifton road, Camden town | 25 | | |
| Clapham road | | | 31 | Clifton road, Maida vale | | 8 | |
| Clapton road, Clapton | 53 | | | Clifton road, New Cross | | | 59 |
| Clapton square, Clapton | 53 | | | Clifton road, St. John's wood | 7 | | |
| Clare market, Strand *II* | | 31 | | Clifton road, Shacklewell | 45 | | |
| Clare street, Clare market *II* | | 31 | | Clifton rd. ea., St. John's wd. | 11 | | |
| Claremont sq., Pentonville | 36 | | | Clifton street, Clapham | | | 28 |
| Clarence gdns., Regent's pk. | 24 | | | Clifton street, Finsbury | | 44 | |
| Clarence place, Clapton | 49 | | | Clifton villas, Camden sq. | 25 | | |
| Clarence house *IV* | | 22 | | Clinger street, Hoxton | 43 | | |
| Clarence road, Bow | 64 | | | Clinton road, Grove road | 60 | | |
| Clarence road, Hackney | 49 | | | Clipstone st., Fitzroy sq. *I* | | 24 | |
| Clarence road, Kentish town | 22 | | | Cloak lane, Queen street, Cheapside *III* | | 39 | |
| Clarence street, Rotherhithe | | 53 | | Cloudesley road, Islington | 35 | | |
| Clarence street, St. Peter's street, Islington | 39 | | | Cloudesley sq., Liverpool rd. | 35 | | |
| Clarence street, York road, City road | 39 | | | Cloudesley st., Cloudesley sq. | 35 | | |
| Clarence ter., Regent's park | 16 | | | Clyde street, West Brompton | | | 6 |
| Clarendon gdns., Maida vale | 12 | 12 | | Clydesdale road, Notting hill | | 3 | |
| Clarendon place, Hyde park gardens | | 15 | | Coal yard, Drury lane | | | 31 |
| Clarendon road, Kensington | | 5 | | Coal Exchange, Lower Thames street *III* | | 42 | |
| Clarendon sq., Somer's town | 28 | | | Cobham road, Stratford | 60 | | |
| Clarendon street, Harrow rd. | | 8 | | Coborn road, Bow road | 60 | | |
| Clarendon street, Pimlico | | | 21 | Coborn street, Bow road | 64 | | |
| Clarendon st., Somer's town | 27 | | | Cobourg road, Old Kent road | | | 46 |
| Clarges street, Piccadilly *IV* | | 22 | | Cobourg row, Tothill fields *IV* | | | 21 |
| Clark st., Commercial rd. ea. | | 51 | | Coburg street, Clerkenwell | 36 | | |
| Claverton street, Lupus st. | | | 21 | Cochrane st., St. John's wd. | 11 | | |
| Clay street, Crawford street *I* | | 20 | | Cock lane, Smithfield | | 36 | |
| Clayland's road, South Lambeth | | | 30 | Cock & Castle lane, Stoke Newington | 45 | | |
| Clayton st., Caledonian road | 30 | | | Cockspur st., Charing cross *IV* | | 26 | |
| Clayton street, Kennington | | | 30 | Colchester street, Pimlico | | | 22 |
| Cleaver street, Kensington | | | 34 | Colchester st., Whitechapel *III* | | 47 | |
| Clement's inn, Strand *II* | | 31 | | Coldharbour lane | | | 40 |

## SQUARES, PUBLIC BUILDINGS, etc.    11

| | B | R | G | | B | R | G |
|---|---|---|---|---|---|---|---|
| Colebrooke row, Islington . | 35 | | | Connaught pl., Edgware rd. | | 15 | |
| Coleherne rd., West Bromp- | | | | Connaught sq., Edgware rd. | | 15 | |
| ton . . . . . . . . . . . . | | | 6 | Conservative club,St.James's | | | |
| Coleman st., Bunhill row *III* | | 39 | | street . . . . . . . . . . | | 22 | |
| Coleman street, Gresham st. | | 40 | | Constitution hill . . . . *IV* | | 17 | |
| Coleman st., New North road | 39 | | | Cooper's rd., Old Kent road | | 46 | |
| Coleshill street, Eaton sq. . | | 17 | | Cooper's row, Trinity square | | 47 | |
| College of Arms & Heralds' | | | | Copenhagen street, Islington | 31 | | |
| College, Queen Victoria | | | | Corbet's lane, New road, | | | |
| street . . . . . . . . *III* | | 39 | | Rotherhithe . . . . . . . | | 53 | |
| College avenue, Homerton | 53 | | | Cordova road, Grove road | 60 | | |
| College cres., Belsize park | 10 | | | Cork st., Burlington grdns. *I* | | 22 | |
| College hill, Upper Thames | | | | Corn Exchange, Mark la. | | | |
| street . . . . . . . . *III* | | 39 | | . . . . . . . . . . . *III* | | 43 | |
| College lane, Homerton . . | 53 | | | Cornhill . . . . . . . *III* | | 43 | |
| College place, King's road, | | | | Cornwall gardens, South | | | |
| Chelsea . . . . . . . . . | | 13 | | Kensington . . . . . . | | 5 | |
| College road, Haverstock hl. | 18 | | | Cornwall road, Lambeth . | | 34 | |
| College st., Camberwell gro. | | 44 | | Cornwall road, Victoria park | 55 | | |
| College street, Camden tn. | 22 | | | Cornwall road, Westbourne | | | |
| College st., Dowgate hl. | | | | park . . . . . . . . . . . | | 4 | |
| . . . . . . . . . . . . *III* | | 39 | | Cornwall street, Moore park, | | | |
| College street, Fulham road | | 13 | | Fulham . . . . . . . . . | | 7 | |
| College street, Homerton . | 53 | | | Cornwall street, Pimlico . . | | 22 | |
| College st. west, Camden tn. | 23 | | | Cornwall ter., Regent's pk. | | 21 | |
| College ter., Barnsbury st. | 34 | | | Corporation la., Clerkenwell | 36 | | |
| Collier street, Pentonville | 31 | | | Corunna street, Battersea . | | 23 | |
| Collingham pl., Cromwell rd. | | 5 | | Cottage grove, Mile end rd. | 60 | | |
| Collingham road,Kensington | | 5 | | Cottage row, Bermondsey . | | 45 | |
| Collingwood street, Birkbeck | | | | Cotton street, Poplar . . . | | 63 | |
| street, Cambridge road . | | 52 | | Courland gro., Sth. Lambeth | | 28 | |
| Collingwood st., Blackfriars | | | | Courtfield gdns., Collingham | | | |
| road . . . . . . . . . . . | | 34 | | road . . . . . . . . . . . | | 5 | |
| Collingwood st., Shoreditch | 48 | | | Courtnell street, Bayswater | | 3 | |
| Colonial office, Downing st. | | | | Courts of justice (new) *II* | | 31 | |
| . . . . . . . . . . . . *IV* | | 26 | | Cousin lane, Upper Thames | | | |
| Columbia market . . . . . | 48 | | | street . . . . . . . . *III* | | 39 | |
| Columbia road, Hackney rd. | 48 | | | Covent garden . . . . . *II* | | 31 | |
| Colverstone cres., Kingsland | 45 | | | Covent garden market . *II* | | 31 | |
| Colville gardens, Notting hl. | | 3 | | Covent garden theatre, Bow | | | |
| Colville road . . . . . . . | | 3 | | street . . . . . . . . *II* | | 31 | |
| Colville square, Notting hill | | 3 | | Coventry st., Haymarket *I* | | 27 | |
| Colville terrace, Colville sq. | | 3 | | Cow cross st., St. John st. *II* | | 36 | |
| Commercial Docks, Rother- | | 53 | | Cowley road, Brixton road | | 35 | |
| hithe . . . . . . . . . . | | 53 | | Cowper street, City road | 41 | | |
| Commercial docks pier . . | | 57 | | Crampton street, Newington | | | |
| Commercial road, Lambeth | 31 | 47 | | butts . . . . . . . . . . | | 37 | |
| Commercial road, Peckham | | 17 | | Cranbourn street, Leicester | | | |
| Commercial road, Pimlico . | | | | square . . . . . . *I. II* | | 27 | |
| Commercial road east *III* | | 51 | | Crane grove . . . . . . . | 33 | | |
| Commercial street, White- | | | | Cranley place, Onslow sq. . | | 9 | |
| chapel . . . . . . . *III* | | 48 | | Cranmer road, Brixton road | | 35 | |
| Comptown mews, Canon- | | | | Craven court, Strand . . . | 31 | | |
| bury road . . . . . . . . | 34 | | | Craven hill, Bayswater . . | | 7 | |
| Compton road, Canonbury | 38 | | | Craven bl. gdns., Bayswater | | 7 | |
| Compton st., Brunswick sq. | 28 | | | Craven place, Kensington rd. | | 5 | |
| Compton street, Goswell rd. | 36 | | | Craven st., East rd., City rd. | 44 | | |
| Compton st., St. Paul's road | 41 | | | Craven street, Strand . *IV* | | 26 | |
| Compton ter., Canonbury sq. | 34 | | | Craven terrace, Bayswater | | 11 | |
| Conder st., Limehouse fields | | 59 | | Crawford st., Camberwell . | | 40 | |
| Conduit street, Regent st. *I* | | 23 | | Crawford st., Marylebone *I* | | 16 | |

## LIST OF THE PRINCIPAL STREETS,

| Street | B | R | G |
|---|---|---|---|
| Crawshay road, Brixton | | | 35 |
| Creek road, Deptford | | | 63 |
| Cremorne gardens | | | 11 |
| Cremorne road, Chelsea | | | 10 |
| Cremorne pier | | | 11 |
| Cripplegate buildings, London wall | | | *III* 40 |
| Crispin street, Spitalfields | | 48 | |
| Criterion, Piccadilly | *I* | 26 | |
| Crogsland rd.,Chalk farm rd. | 18 | | |
| Cromer st., Gray's inn road | 32 | | |
| Cromwell cres. | | | 1 |
| Cromwell pl.,Sth.Kensington | | | 9 |
| Cromwell road, S. Kens'tn | | 9 | 5 |
| Cromwell rd., West | | | 1 |
| Cropley st., Wenlock st. | 32 | | |
| Crosby hall, Bishopsg. st. | *III* | 43 | |
| Crozier street, Lambeth | *IV* | 29 | |
| Cross st., Ball's Pond rd. | 42 | | |
| Cross street, Blackfriars rd. | | 31 | |
| Cross street, Essex road | | 38 | |
| Cross st., Hatton garden | *III* | 36 | |
| Crown street, Soho | *I* | 27 | |
| Crown street, Wyndham rd. | | | 39 |
| Crowndale rd.,Camden town | 23 | | |
| Crucifix la.. Bermondsey st. | | 41 | |
| Crutched friars, Mark la. | *III* | 43 | |
| Cubitt's town, Isle of Dogs | | | 69 |
| Cubitt town pier | | | 69 |
| Cubitt tn. rail.sta.,Wharf rd. | | | 66 |
| Culford rd., De Beauvoir tn. | 42 | | |
| Culvert road, Battersea | | | 16 |
| Cumberland mkt., Regent's park | 24 | | |
| Cumberland gate | *I* | 15 | |
| Cumberland place, College place, Chelsea | | | 13 |
| Cumberland st., Hackney rd. | 17 | | |
| Cumberland st., St. George's road, Pimlico | | | 24 |
| Cumberland ter., Regent's pk. | 24 | | |
| Cumming street, Pentonville | 31 | | |
| Cunard street, Albany road | | | 42 |
| Cunningham place, St.John's wood | 12 | | |
| Currie street, Everet street, Nine Elms | | | 26 |
| Cursitor street | *II* | 35 | |
| Curtain road, Shoreditch | 11 | 44 | |
| Curzon street, Mayfair | *IV* | 18 | |
| Custom ho., Lower Thames street | *III* | 42 | |
| Cutler st., Houndsditch | *III* | 43 | |
| | | | |
| Dacre st., Westminster | *IV* | 25 | |
| Dagmar road, Peckham rd. | | | |
| Dale road, Kentish town | 17 | 11 | |
| Daleham gdns. | 9 | | |
| Dalston green | 45 | | |
| Dalston junction railway station, Dalston lane | 49 | | |

| Street | B | R | G |
|---|---|---|---|
| Dalston lane, Hackney | 49 | | |
| Dalston lane, Kingsland | 45 | | |
| Danes inn, Strand | *II* | 31 | |
| Daneville road, Camberwell | | | 40 |
| Dante rd., Newington butts | | | 33 |
| Danvers street, Paulton sq., Chelsea | | | 10 |
| Darby st., Royal Mint st. | | 46 | |
| Darnley rd., Hackney | | 54 | |
| Dartmouth st., Westm. | *IV* | 25 | |
| Darwin street | | | 41 |
| Dashwood road, New road | | | 23 |
| Date street, Richard street | | | 38 |
| David street,York pl., Baker street | *I* | 20 | |
| Davies st., Berkeley sq. | *I* | 19 | |
| Dawes lane, Fulham | | | 3 |
| Dawson place, Prince's sq. | | | 3 |
| Deacon street,Walworth rd. | | | 37 |
| Deale st. Mile end New town | | 48 | |
| Dean st., Commercial rd.east | | 51 | |
| Dean street, Fetter lane | | 35 | |
| Dean street, Park lane | | 18 | |
| Dean street, Soho square | *I* | 27 | |
| Dean's yard,Westminster | *IV* | 25 | |
| De Beauvoir crescent | 43 | | |
| De Beauvoir road | 42 | | |
| De Beauvoir square | 42 | | |
| De Crespigny park, Camberwell | | | 40 |
| D'Eynsford road, Waterloo street, Camberwell | | | |
| Delahay st., Westminster | *IV* | 25 | 39 |
| Delamere cres., Harrow rd. | | | 8 |
| Delancy street, Camden tn. | 23 | | |
| Delanne street, Kennington park road | | | 34 |
| Delhi street, Copenhagen st. | 31 | | |
| Dempsey street, Stepney | | 55 | |
| Denbigh street, Belgrave rd. | | | 24 |
| Denman road., Peckham rd. | | | 48 |
| Denman st., Haymarket | *I* | 27 | |
| Denman street, London bdg. | | | 42 |
| Denmark hill, Camberwell | | | 40 |
| Denmark hill railway stat., Champion park | | | 40 |
| Denmark rd., Camberwell | | | 40 |
| Denmark rd., Kilburn park | 3 | | |
| Denmark street, Coldharbour lane | | | 40 |
| Denmark street, Pentonville | 35 | | |
| Denmark street, St. Giles (or Soho) | *I* | 27 | |
| Dennett's road, Queen's rd., Peckham | | | 56 |
| Denver st., Marlborough rd. | | | 13 |
| Deptford High street | | | 63 |
| Deptford High street railway station | | | 63 |
| Deptford station | | | 53 |
| Deptford Lower road | | | 53 53 |

## SQUARES, PUBLIC BUILDINGS, etc. 13

| | B | R | G | | B | R | G |
|---|---|---|---|---|---|---|---|
| Derby rd., De Beauvoir tn. | 42 | | | Douglas plane,Queen's road, | | | |
| Derby rd., Victoria pk. rd. | 55 | | | Bayswater | | 7 | |
| Derby street, Liverpool st., | | | | Douglas road, Canonbury | 38 | | |
| King's cross | | 32 | | Douglas street, Deptford | | | 63 |
| Derbyshire st., Bethnal grn. | 52 | | | Douglas street, Vincent sq. | | | 27 |
| Devas street, Bromley | | 68 | | Dulton's pottery works, | | | |
| Deverell st., Great Dover st. | | 37 | | Lambeth | | | 29 |
| Devon's road, Bromley, | | | | Dove row | 47 | 22 | |
| Middlesex | 68 | 64 | | Dover street, Piccadilly. I | | 39 | |
| Devonshire house. . . IV | | 22 | | Dowgate hl., Cannon st. III | | | |
| Devonshire place, Upper | | | | Dowlas street, Wells street | | 18 | 41 |
| Kennington lane | | | 30 | Down street, Piccadilly IV | | | |
| Devonshire road, Hackney | 51 | | | Downham road | | 42 | |
| Devonshire road, South | | | | Downing st., Whitehall IV | | 26 | |
| Lambeth | | | 27 | Down's pk. rd.. Shacklewell | 45 | | |
| Devonshire square . . III | | 44 | | Draycott pl., Pavilion road | | | 13 |
| Devonshire street, Bishops- | | | | Draycott street. Cadogan ter- | | | |
| gate III | | 44 | | race, Chelsea | | | 13 |
| Devonshire st., Cambridge | | | | Driffield road. Bow | 59 | | |
| road, Mile end | 56 | 56 | | Drummond cres.. Euston sq. | 28 | | |
| Devonshire street, Islington | 39 | | | Drummond rd.. Bermondsey | | 49 | 53 |
| Devonshire st., Lisson gro. | | 16 | | Drummond st., Euston sq. | 28 | | |
| Devonshire st., Mile end . | 39 | | | Drury court, Drury lane II | | 31 | |
| Devonshire street, Newing- | | | | Drury lane II | | 31 | |
| ton causeway | | 37 | | Drury Lane theatre . . II | | 31 | |
| Devonshire street, Portland | | | | Duchess st.. Portland pl. I | | 29 | |
| place I | | 20 | | Duck lane, Victoria st. IV | | 24 | |
| Devonshire st., Queen sq. II | | 32 | | Ducksfoot lane, Upper Tha- | | | |
| Devonshire ter., Bayswater | | 11 | | mes street III | | 43 | |
| Digby road, Homerton . . | 53 | | | Dudley gro., Paddington gn. | | 12 | |
| Digby walk, Globe road. . | 56 | | | Dudley house I | | 19 | |
| Distaff lane, Cannon st. III | | 39 | | Duke street, Adelphi . . II | | 26 | |
| Dock street, Royal Mint st. | | 47 | | Duke street, Aldgate . III | | 43 | |
| Dockley rd.. Blue Anchor la. | | 45 | | Duke street, Brushfield st. | | 44 | |
| Dockhead, Bermondsey . . | | 45 | | Duke st., Grosvenor sq. II | | 19 | |
| Doctor street, Walworth | | | | Duke street, Lincoln's inn | | | |
| common | | | 38 | fields II | | 31 | |
| Doctors' commons. . . III | | 39 | | Duke st., Little Britain III | | 40 | |
| Dod street. Burdett road . | | 63 | | Duke street. London bridge | | 42 | |
| Doddington grove, Ken- | | | | Duke street.Manchester sq. I | | 19 | |
| nington | | | 31 | Duke st., New Oxford st. II | | 28 | |
| Doddington grove, Lower | | | | Duke street, Portland pl. I | | 24 | |
| Wandsworth road | | | 20 | Duke st., St. James's sq. IV | | 22 | |
| Doré gallery, New Bond st. I | | 23 | | Duke street, Stamford st. | | 31 | |
| Dorchester house . . IV | | 18 | | Duke street, Union street . | | 18 | |
| Dorchester pl.. Blandford sq. | | 16 | | Duke street. Westminster | | | |
| Dorchester st.. New North rd. | 43 | | | bridge road | | | 33 |
| Doris street, Lambeth . . . | | | 29 | Duke's terrace, Malden rd. | | | |
| Dorrington st., Leather la. II | | 36 | | Duncan road, London fields | 47 | | |
| Dorset place, Clapham road | | | 31 | Duncan street. Islington | 51 | | |
| Dorset pl., Pall mall ea. I | | 26 | | Duncan street. London fields | 35 | | |
| Dorset rd., South Lambeth | | | 31 | Duncan street, Whitechapel | 54 | 47 | |
| Dorset square, Marylebone | | 16 | | Duncan terrace, Islington . | | | |
| Dorset street, Baker st. I | | 20 | | Duncannon street. Strand II | 35 | 26 | |
| Dorset street, Essex road, | | | | Dunlace road, Lower Clap- | | | |
| Islington | 42 | | | ton | | | |
| Dorset street, Spitalfields | | 48 | | Dunston st.. Kingsland road | 53 | | |
| Dorset st., Vauxhall bdg. rd. | | | 25 | Durham street, Hackney rd | 47 | | |
| Doughty mews. Foundling h. | | 32 | | Durham street. King's road, | 52 | | |
| Doughty st., Mecklenburgh | | | | Chelsea | | | 14 |
| square | | 32 | | Durham street, Strand II | | 30 | |

## LIST OF THE PRINCIPAL STREETS,

| | B | R | G | | B | R | G |
|---|---|---|---|---|---|---|---|
| Durham street, Upper Kennington lane . . . . . . | | . . | 30 | Edward st., Shepherdess walk | 40 | | |
| Durham ter., Westbourne park . . . . . . . . . . | | . | 8 | Edward street, Stepney . . . | | . . | 60 |
| Durham villas, Phillimore gardens . . . . . . . . . . | | . | 1 | Edwardes sq., Kensington . | | . | 1 |
| | | | | Eel brook com., Fulham . | | . . | 3 |
| | | | | Egbert road. Primrose hill | 18 | | |
| | | | | Egleton road, Grace street, Bromley . . . . . . . . . | 68 | | |
| Eagle street, Red Lion st. *II* | . | 32 | | Egyptian hall, Piccadilly *IV* | | . | 22 |
| Eagle st., Shepherdess walk | 10 | | | Eland road, Lavender hill | | . . | 16 |
| Eagle wharf road, New North road . . . . . . . . . . | 39 | | | Elcho street, Bridge road, Battersea . . . . . . . . . | | . . | 15 |
| Eardley cres. W. Brompton | | . . | 1 | Elder walk, Essex road . . | 39 | | |
| Earl road, Upper Grange rd. | | . . | 45 | Eleanor rd., Richmond road | 50 | | |
| Earl street, Holywell street, Millbank . . . . . . . . | | . . | 25 | Eldon road, Victoria road | | . | 5 |
| | | | | Eldon street, Finsbury *III* | | . | 44 |
| Earl street, London road . | | . . | 33 | Eleanor road north, Richmond road . . . . . . | 50 | | |
| Earl st. east, Lisson grove | | . | 16 | | | | |
| Earl's court, West Brompton | | . . | 1 | Elephant & Castle . . . . | | . . | 37 |
| Earl's court gardens, Old Brompton . . . . . . . . | | . | 5 | Elgin road, Harrow road . | 8 | | |
| | | | | Elgin road, Maida vale . . | | . | 4 |
| Earl's court station . . . . | | . | 5 | Eli street, Kingsland road | 47 | | |
| Earl's court road . . . . . | | 1 | 1 | Eliza place, Sadler's walk | 36 | | |
| Earl's court square . . . . | | . | 5 | Elizabeth street, Eaton sq. | | . . | 17 |
| East lane, Bermondsey wall | | . | 45 | Elizabeth street, Hackney rd. | 52 | | |
| East road, City road | 44 | | | Elizabeth street, Hans place | | . | 13 |
| East Smithfield, Tower bl. *II* | | . | 46 | Elizabeth street, Walworth common . . . . . . . . . | | . . | 38 |
| East street, Hoxton street | 44 | | | | | | |
| East street, Kennington road | | . . | 29 | Elizabeth terrace, Islington | 35 | | |
| East st., Manchester sq. *I* | | . | 20 | Ellen st., Back church lane | | . | 47 |
| East street, Red Lion sq. | | . | 32 | Ellesmere street, Poplar . . | | . | 67 |
| East street, Walworth road | | . | 37 | Ellington street, Holloway | 33 | | |
| East Ferry rd., Isle of Dogs | | . | 65 | Elliot road, Brixton . . . . | | . . | 35 |
| East India docks . . . . . | | . | 71 | Elliott's street, St. George's road, Lambeth . . . . . | | . . | 33 |
| East India docks pier . . . | | . | 70 | | | | |
| East India dock rd., Poplr. | | . | 63 | Ellis street, Sloane street | | . | 17 |
| East Surrey street, Peckham | | . | 47 | Elm place, West Brompton | | . . | 9 |
| Eastbourne ter., Paddington | | . | 11 | Elm street, Gray's inn road | | . | 32 |
| Eastcheap, Gracechurch st. *III* | | . | 43 | Elm tree road, St. John's wd. | 12 | | |
| | | | | Elmore street, Essex road | 38 | | |
| Eastfield st., Limehouse fields | | . | 59 | Elsted st., East st., Walworth | | . . | 41 |
| Easton street, Exmouth st. | 36 | | | Elvaston pl., Sth. Kensington | | . | 5 |
| Eaton lane, Victoria road, Pimlico . . . . . . . *IV* | | . | 21 | Elwood st. . . . . . . . . | 34 | | |
| Eaton place, Eaton sq. *IV* | | . | 17 | 17 | Ely pl., Charterhouse st. *II* | | . | 36 |
| Eaton square, Pimlico . *IV* | | . | 17 | 17 | Ely place, Holborn hill *II* | | . | 36 |
| Eaton terrace, St. John's wd. | 11 | | | Emerson st., Bankside *III* | | . | 38 |
| Ebury square, Pimlico . . | | . | 17 | Emery street, Battersea . . | | . . | 13 |
| Ebury street, Pimlico . *IV* | | . | 17 | 17 | Emmett street, Poplar . . . | | . | 62 |
| Eccleston square, Pimlico . | | . | 21 | Emperor's gate, South Kensington . . . . . . . . . | | . | 5 |
| Eccleston street, Pimlico *IV* | | . | 17 | 17 | Endell street, Long acre *II* | | . | 27 |
| Edbrook rd., St. Peter's pk. | 8 | | | Endsleigh st., Tavistock sq. | 28 | | |
| Edgware road . . . . . . | 2 | 10 | | Enfield road north, De Beauvoir town . . . . . . . | 42 | | |
| Edith grove, Fulham road | | . | 6 | | | | |
| Edith st., Great Cambdg. st. | 47 | | | Enfield road south . . . . | 42 | | |
| Edith terrace, King's road | | . | 6 | Englefield road . . . . . . | 42 | | |
| Edmund rd., New Church rd. | | . | 39 | England's la., Haverstk. hl. | 13 | | |
| Edward st., Bethnal green | 48 | | | Ennismore gardens, Prince's gate . . . . . . . . . . | | . | 9 |
| Edward st., Blackfriars road | | 34 | | | | | |
| Edward st., Deptford High st. | | . | 59 | Ernest street, Regent's park | 24 | | |
| Edward st., Hampstead rd. | 24 | | | Ernest st., White Horse lane | | . | 56 |
| Edward st., Kingsland road | 44 | | | Erskine road, Primrose hill | 18 | | |

## SQUARES, PUBLIC BUILDINGS, etc. 15

### B R G  B R O

| | | |
|---|---|---|
| Esher street, Upper Kennington lane | | 30 |
| Essex road, Islington | 38 | |
| Essex street, Bethnal green | 52 | |
| Essex street, Islington | 39 | |
| Essex street, Kingsland road | 41 | |
| Essex st., Mare st., Hackney | 51 | |
| Essex st., Mile end Old town | 56 | |
| Essex street, Strand .. //  | 31 | |
| Essex villas, Phillimore grdns. | 1 | |
| Ethelburga street, Bridge rd. | | 15 |
| Eton avenue, Hampstead | 10 | |
| Eton road, Haverstock hill | 14 | |
| Eton street, Gloucester road | 18 | |
| Euston grove, Euston sq. | 28 | |
| Euston road | 28, 24 | |
| Euston square | 28 | |
| Euston sq. railway station | 28 | |
| Euston street | 28 | |
| Evans st., Poplar New town | 63 | |
| Evelina road | | 52 |
| Evelyn st., New North rd. | 43 | |
| Everett st., Brunswick sq. | 28 | |
| Eversholt street, Oakley sq. | 23 | |
| Ewer street, Southwark | 38 | |
| Exchange (Royal) buildings /// | 43 | |
| Exeter hall, Strand .. // | 31 | |
| Exeter street, Chelsea | 13 | |
| Exeter street, Strand . // | 31 | |
| Exhibition road, South Kensington | 9 | |
| Exmouth st., Clerkenwell | 36 | |
| Exmouth street, Commercial road east | 55 | |
| Exmouth street, Mare street, Hackney | 50 | |
| Eyre street hill, Leather la. | 36 | |
| Fair street, Horselydown | 41 | |
| Fair street, Stepney | 55 | |
| Fairclough st.. Back Chrch. la. | 47 | |
| Fairfax road, Finchley road, Hampstead | 10 | |
| Fairfield road, Bow | 64 | |
| Fairfoot road, Bow | 64 | |
| Falcon road, Battersea | | 12 |
| Falcon sq., Aldersgate st. /// | 39 | |
| Falkland road, Kentish tn. | 21 | |
| Falmouth rd., New Kent rd. | 37 | 37 |
| Fann street, Aldersgate st. | 40 | |
| Faraday street, Walworth | 42 | |
| Farm lane, Walham green | | 2 |
| Farm street, Berkeley sq. / | 18 | |
| Farringdon market .. // | 35 | |
| Farringdon road .. // | 36, 34 | |
| Farringdon st., Fleet st. // | 35 | |
| Farringdon street station // | 36 | |
| Fashion st., Spitalfields /// | 48 | |
| Faunce st., Kennington pk. | | 31 |
| Fawcett st., West Brompton | | 6 |

| | | |
|---|---|---|
| Featherstone buildings, // | | 32 |
| Featherstone st., City road | 40 | |
| Felix street, Hackney road | 51 | |
| Fellowes road, Hampstead | 14 | |
| Fellows st.— North & South, Kingsland road | 47 | |
| Fen court, Fenchurch street | | 43 |
| Fenchurch street . . . /// | | 43 |
| Fenchurch street railway station . . . . . /// | | 43 |
| Fendall street, Orange road | | 41 |
| Fenelon road, Kensington | | 1 |
| Fentiman's rd., Clapham rd. | | 20 |
| Ferdinand pl., Chalk farm rd. | 18 | |
| Ferdinand st., Chalk farm rd. | 18 | |
| Fern street, Bromley | | 64 |
| Fernhead road, Harrow rd. | 1 | |
| Ferntower road, Highbury New park | | 37 |
| Fetter lane, Holborn hill // | | 35 |
| Finborough road, West Brompton | | 6 |
| Finch lane, Cornhill . /// | | 43 |
| Finch street, Whitechapel | | 48 |
| Finchley road, Hampstead | 10 | |
| Finchley road, Walworth | | 34 |
| Finchley New road | | 10 |
| Finsbury avenue, Crown st. | | 44 |
| Finsbury circus, London wall /// | | 43 |
| Finsbury market | | 44 |
| Finsbury pavement .. /// | | 44 |
| Finsbury square, City road | | 44 |
| Fish street hill . . . /// | | 43 |
| Fisher st., Red Lion sq. // | | 32 |
| Fitzjohn's avenue | 9 | |
| Fitzroy hall . . . . . . . / | | 24 |
| Fitzroy road, Regent's park | 18 | |
| Fitzroy square | | 24 |
| Fitzroy street, Fitzroy sq. / | | 24 |
| Fleet la., Farringdon st. // | | 35 |
| Fleet street, City . . . // | | 35 |
| Fleming road, Walworth | | 34 |
| Fleming st., Kingsland rd. | 43 | |
| Fleur-de-lis st., Spitalfields | | 48 |
| Flint st., East st., Walworth | | 44 |
| Flint st., Poplar New town | | 67 |
| Flood street, Chelsea | | 14 |
| Florence street, Upper st. | 34 | |
| Flower & Dean st., Spitalfields | | 48 |
| Foley street, Great Titchfield street . . . . . . . / | | 24 |
| Folly lane, Bridge road, Battersea | | 11 |
| Fopstone rd., Earl's Court rd | | 1 |
| Ford road, Old Ford | 59 | |
| Ford street, Old Ford | 59 | |
| Fore street, Cripplegate /// | | 40 |
| Foreign cattle mkt., Deptford | | 62 |
| Forest road, Dalston | 46 | |

## 16 LIST OF THE PRINCIPAL STREETS,

| | B | R | G | | B | R | G |
|---|---|---|---|---|---|---|---|
| Formosa street, Maida hill | . | 8 | | Garway rd., Westbourne gr. | . | 7 | |
| Forston st., New North rd. | 39 | | | Gascoyne road, Victoria pk. | 58 | | |
| Fort road, Bermondsey | . | . | | Gate street, Lincoln's inn | | | |
| Fort street, Spital square | . | 44 | 45 | fields . . . . . . . . . . II | . | 31 | |
| Fortune grn. la., Hampstead | 1 | | | Gayhurst rd., London fields | 50 | | |
| Foster lane, Cheapside III | . | 39 | | Gaywood street, London rd. | . | 33 | |
| Foulis terrace, Fulham rd. | . | . | | Gee street, Goswell road | . | 40 | |
| Foundling hospital, Guilford street . . . . . . . . . | . | 32 | 9 | Gee st., Upper Seymour st. General Post Office . . III | 27 | . | 39 |
| Fountain court, Strand II | . | 31 | | Geological Museum . . . I | . | 22 | |
| Foxley road, North Brixton | . | . | 35 | George 1st's statue . . . I | . | 19 | |
| Frampton park road . . . | 54 | | | George st., Blackfriars rd. | . | 34 | |
| Francis st., Barnsbury rd. | 35 | | | George street, Camberwell | . | . | 39 |
| Francis street, Battersea . | . | . | | George street, Euston sq. | 24 | | |
| Francis st., Tothill fields IV | . | 11 | | George st., Grosvenor sq. I | . | 19 | |
| Francis street, Tottenham court road . . . . . . I | . | 21 28 | | George street, Hanover sq. I George st., Langham pl. I | . . | 23 24 | |
| Francis street, Vauxhall st. | . | . | | George street, London fields | 51 | | |
| Franklin row, Pimlico road | . | 29 | | George st., Manchester sq. I | . | 20 | |
| Frazier street, Lower marsh, Lambeth . . . . . . . . | . | 18 34 | | George st., Mansion ho. III George st., Old Montague st. | . . | 39 48 | |
| Frederick pl., Mile end road | 60 | | | George st., St. Giles's . II | . | 27 | |
| Frederick place, Newington butts . . . . . . . . . . . | . | . | | George street, Tower hill . George street, Vauxhall . . | . . | 46 . | 29 |
| Frederick st., Caledonian rd. | 30 | 33 | | George yard, London st. . | . | 43 | |
| Frederick st., Gray's inn rd. | 32 | | | George's road, Holloway . | 29 | | |
| Frederick st., Hampstead rd. | 24 | | | Georgiana st., Camden tn. | 22 | | |
| Frederick st., Portland town | 15 | | | Gerald Road, Pimlico . . . | . | . | 17 |
| Freeling st., Caledonian rd. | 30 | | | German hospital, Dalston | 45 | | |
| Freeschool st., Horselydown | . | 42 | | Gerrard street, Islington . | 39 | | |
| French R. Cath. Chapel I | . | 20 | | Gerrard street, Soho . . I | . | 27 | |
| Friar st., Blackfriars road | . | 33 | | Gertrude street, Chelsea . . | . | . | 10 |
| Friday street, Cheapside III | . | 39 | | Gibraltar walk, Bethnal grn. | 48 | | |
| Friendly place, Mile end rd. | . | 56 | | Gibson square, Islington . | 35 | | |
| Frith street, Soho square I | . | 27 | | Gifford st., Caledonian rd. | 30 | | |
| Frognal . . . . . . . . . . | 9 | | | Gilbert road, Lower Kennington lane . . . . . . | . | . | 33 |
| Fulham place, Harrow rd. | . | 12 | | |||
| Fulham park . . . . . . . | . | . | | Gilbert st., Museum st. II | . | 28 | |
| Fulham road, Brompton . | . | . | 3 | Gilbert st., Grosvenor sq. I | . | 19 | |
| Fuller st., Bethnal green . | 48 | 10 | | Gilbert's st., Clare market | . | 31 | |
| Furnival's inn, Holborn II | . | 36 | | Gill street, Limehouse . . | . | 63 | |
| Furnival street, Holborn II | . | 35 | | Gilston rd., W. Brompton . | . | . | 6 |
| | | | | Giltspur st., W. Smithfield II | . | 40 | |
| Gaiety theatre, Strand II | . | 31 | | Glaskin road, Hackney . . | 54 | | |
| Gainsford st., Richmond rd. | 35 | | | Glasshouse st., Regent st. I | . | 23 | |
| Gainsborogh rd. . . . . . | 61 | | | Glasshouse st., Royal Mint street . . . . . . . . . . | . | 47 | |
| Gainsford st., Horselydown | . | 45 | | |||
| Gainsford street, Kentish town road . . . . . . . . | 21 | | | Glasshouse street, Vauxhall Glenarm rd., Lower Clapton | . 58 | . | 29 |
| Gallery of Illustration. Regent street . . . . . . I | . | 26 | | Glengall gro., Old Kent rd. Glengall rd., Isle of Dogs. | . 65 | . | 46 |
| Galway street, City road . | 40 | | | Glengall rd., Old Kent rd. | . | . | 46 |
| Garden row, London road | . | 33 | | Globe road, Mile end . . . | 56 | 56 | |
| Gardener's road, Grove rd. | 59 | | | Globe theatre, Newcastle street, Strand . . . . II | . | 31 | |
| Garford street, Poplar . . | . | 62 | | |||
| Garlick hill, Upper Thames street . . . . . . . . . . | . | 39 | | Gloucester cres., Regent's park . . . . . . . . . . | 22 | | |
| Garnault place, Clerkenwell | 36 | | | Gloucester crescent, Westbourne park . . . . . . . | | 8 | |
| Garrick club, Garrick st. II | . | 27 | | |||
| Garrick st., Covent grdn. II | . | 27 | | Gloucester gate, Regent's pk. | 19 | | |
| Garrick theatre . . . . II | . | 27 | | Gloucester gro., Old Bromptn. | . | . | 9 |

## SQUARES, PUBLIC BUILDINGS, etc. 17

| | B | R | G | | B | R | G |
|---|---|---|---|---|---|---|---|
| Gloucester mews east, Portman square . . . . . *I* | . | 20 | | Gracechurch st., Cornhill *III* | . | 43 | |
| Gloucester mews we., Hyde park . . . . . . . . . *I* | . | 16 | | Grafton rd., Kentish town road . . . . . . . . . | 21 | | |
| Gloucester pl., Lancaster gate | . | 11 | | Grafton street, Fitzroy sq. | . | 24 | |
| Gloucester pl., Portman sq. *I* | . | 20 | | Grafton street, Mile end. | . | 56 56 |
| Gloucester rd., Glo'str. gate | 18 | | | Grafton st., New Bond st. *I* | . | 23 | |
| Gloucester road station . . | . | . | 5 | Graham rd., Dalston . . | 46 | | |
| Gloucester rd., Peckham gro. | . | . | 43 | Graham street, City road | 39 | | |
| Gloucester road, Kensington gate . . . . . . . . | . | 5 | 5 | Graham street, Pimlico | . | . | 17 |
| Gloucester sq.. Hyde park | . | 11 | | Granby st., Hampstead rd. | 23 | | |
| Gloucester street, Albert embankment . . . . . | . | . | 29 | Grand Junction road, Paddington . . . . . . . . . | . | 11 | |
| Gloucester st., Camden tn. | 23 | | | Grand Surrey docks, Rotherhithe . . . . . . . . | . | . | 57 |
| Gloucester st., Clerkenwell | 36 | | | Grange rd., Bermondsey | . | 41 | |
| Gloucester st., Hackney rd. | 51 | | | Grange road, Camden town | 22 | | |
| Gloucester st., Haggerston | 47 | | | Grange rd., Canonbury pk. | 37 | | |
| Gloucester st., Hoxton st. | 44 | | | Grange road, Dalston . . | 46 | | |
| Gloucester street, Pimlico | . | . | 21 | Grange road, Peckham road | . | . | 11 |
| Gloucester st., Portman sq. *I* | . | 19 | | Grange street, Hoxton . . | 43 | | |
| Gloucester st., Queen sq. *II* | . | 32 | | Grange walk, Bermondsey | . | 41 | |
| Gloucester street, Lambeth | . | 33 | | Granville pl., Portman sq. *I* | . | 19 | |
| Gloucester ter., Hyde park | . | 11 | | Gravel lane, Houndsditch . | . | 47 | |
| Gloucester ter.. Kensington | . | 2 | | Gravel lane, Southwark. . | . | 34 | |
| Gloucester ter., Regent's pk. | 19 | | | Gray street, Blackfriars rd. | . | 33 | |
| Godfrey st., Cale st., Chelsea | . | . | 13 | Gray st., Manchester sq. *I* | . | 19 | |
| Godliman street, Doctors' commons . . . . . *II* | . | 39 | | Gray's inn, High Holborn *II* | . | 32 | |
| Golden lane, Barbican . . | . | 40 | | Gray's inn road . . . . *II* | 32 | 32 | |
| Golden square, Regent st. *I* | . | 23 | | Gray's inn sq., Gray's inn *II* | . | 32 | |
| Goldhurst terrace . . . . | 6 | | | Grayshott rd., Lavender hl. | . | . | 20 |
| Goldington cres., St. Pancras | 27 | | | Great Alie st., Goodman's fields . . . . . . . *IV* | . | 47 | |
| Goldington street, Bedford New town . . . . . . | 27 | | | Great Arthur st., Golden la. | . | 40 | |
| Goldney road, Harrow road | 8 | | | Great Barlow street, Marylebone. . . . . . . . *I* | . | 20 | |
| Goldsmith road, Peckham. | . | . | 47 | Great Bell alley, Moorgate street . . . . . . . *III* | . | 39 | |
| Goldsmith st., Wood st. *III* | . | 39 | | Great Bland st., Gt. Dover st. | . | 37 | |
| Goldsmiths' row, Hackney road . . . . . . . . . | 47 | | | Great Cambridge street, Hackney road . . . . . | 47 | | |
| Goodge street, Tottenham court road . . . . . *I* | . | 24 | | Great Castle st., Regent st. *I* | . | 23 | |
| Goodman's fields, Withechapel . . . . . . . . | . | 47 | | Great Chapel street, Oxford street, Soho . . . . . *I* | . | 27 | |
| Goodman's yd., Minories *III* | . | 47 | | Great Chapel street, Westminster . . . . . . *IV* | . | 25 | |
| Gordon place, Gordon sq. | 28 | 28 | | | | | |
| Gordon square . . . . . | 28 | 28 | | Great Chart street, Hoxton | 44 | | |
| Gordon street, Gordon sq. | 28 | | | Great College st.. Camden tn. | 22 | | |
| Goring street, London fields | 51 | | | Great College street, Westminster . . . . . . *IV* | . | 25 | |
| Gossett st., Bethnal grn. rd. | 48 | | | | | | |
| Goswell road . . . . . . | 36 | 40 | | Great Coram street, Brunswick square . . . . . | 28 | | |
| Gough street, East India rd. | . | 63 | | | | | |
| Gough street, Gray's inn rd. | 32 | 32 | | Great Cumberland place. . | . | 15 | |
| Goulston st., Whitechapel *III* | . | 47 | | Great Dover st., Southwark | . | 37 | |
| | | | | Great Earl street, Seven dials *II* | . | 27 | |
| Government offices, Downing street . . . . . *IV* | . | 26 | | Great Eastern street. . . | 44 | 44 | |
| Gower place, Euston square | 28 | | | Great Eastern terminus, Liverpool street . . *III* | . | 44 | |
| Gower street, Bedford sq. *I* | 28 | 28 | | | | | |
| Gower's walk, Whitechapel | . | 47 | | Great George street, Westminster . . . . . . *IV* | . | 25 | |
| Grace street, Bromley. . . | 68 | | | | | | |

BAEDEKER, London. 7th Edit.      11

# LIST OF THE PRINCIPAL STREETS,

| | B | R | G |
|---|---|---|---|
| Great Guildford street, Borough . . . . . . *III* | . | 38 | |
| Great Hermitage street, Wapping . . . . . . . . | . | 50 | |
| Great Hunter street, Gt. Dover street . . . . . | . | 42 | |
| Great James st., Bedford row | . | 32 | |
| Great James st., Hoxton . | 43 | | |
| Great James st., Lisson gro. | . | 16 | |
| Great Marlborough street *I* | . | 23 | |
| Great Maze pnd., Southwk. | . | 42 | |
| Great Mitchell st.. St. Luke's | 40 | | |
| Great New st., Fetter la. *II* | . | 35 | |
| Great Newport st., Soho *II* | . | 27 | |
| Great Northern terminus, King's cross . . . . . . . | 32 | | |
| Great Ormond st., Queen sq. | . | 32 | |
| Great Pearl st., Spitalfields | . | 48 | |
| Great Percy st., Amwell st. | 32 | | |
| Great Peter street, Westminster . . . . . . . *IV* | . | 25 | |
| Great Portland street . . *I* | . | 24 | |
| Great Prescot street, Goodman's fields . . . . . *III* | . | 47 | |
| Great Pulteney street, Golden square . . . . . . *I* | . | 23 | |
| Great Quebec st., Montagu sq. | . | 16 | |
| Great Queen street, Lincoln's inn . . . . . *II* | . | 31 | |
| Great Queen street, Westminster . . . . . . . *IV* | . | 25 | |
| Great Russell st., Bloomsbury . . . . . . *I, II* | . | 28 | |
| Great Saffron hill, Hatton wall . . . . . . . . . *II* | . | 36 | |
| Great St. Andrew street, Seven dials . . . . *II* | . | 27 | |
| Great St. Helen's, Bishopsgate . . . . . . . *III* | . | 43 | |
| Great St. Thomas street, Bow lane . . . . . *III* | . | 39 | |
| Great Scotland yard, Charing cross . . . . . . *IV* | . | 26 | |
| Great Smith street, Westminster . . . . . *IV* | . | 25 | |
| Great Stanhope street . *IV* | . | 18 | |
| Great Suffolk st., Borough | . | 37 | |
| Great Sutton st., Clerkenwell | . | 40 | |
| Great Titchfield street, Oxford street . . . . . *I* | . | 24 | |
| Great Tower street, Tower hill . . . . . . . *III* | . | 42 | |
| Great Trinity lane, Cannon street west . . . . *III* | . | 39 | |
| Great Western terminus, Paddington . . . . . . | . | 11 | |
| Great Western ter., Westbourne park . . . . . | . | 4 | |
| Great White Lion street, Seven dials . . . *II* | . | 27 | |
| Great Wild st., Drury la. *II* | . | 31 | |

| | B | R | G |
|---|---|---|---|
| Great Winchester street *III* | . | 43 | |
| Great Windmill street, Haymarket . . . . . *I* | . | 27 | |
| Greek street, Soho square *I* | . | 27 | |
| Green Bank, Wapping . . . | . | 50 | |
| Green park, St. James's *IV* | . | 22 | |
| Green st., Bethnal green . | 56 | | |
| Green st., Grosvenor sq. *I* | . | 19 | |
| Green street, Leicester sq. *I* | . | 27 | |
| Green street, Malboro' road, Chelsea . . . . . . . . | . | 13 | |
| Green Man street, Essex rd. | 38 | | |
| Greenwich hospital . . . . | . | 70 | |
| Greenwich naval asylum . | . | 70 | |
| Greenwich observatory . . | . | 71 | |
| Greenwich park . . . . . | . | 71 | |
| Greenwich pier . . . . . . | . | 66 | |
| Greenwich railway station, London road . . . . . . | . | 67 | |
| Greenwich road . . . . . . | . | 67 | |
| Greenwood road, Dalston . | 49 | | |
| Grenville street, Guilford st. | . | 32 | |
| Gresham st., Old Jewry *III* | . | 39 | |
| Gresham street west, Wood street . . . . . . . *III* | . | 39 | |
| Gresse st. . . . . . . . *I* | . | 28 | |
| Greville pl., Kilburn priory | 7 | | |
| Greville road, Kilburn . . | 7 | | |
| Greville street, Holborn *II* | . | 36 | |
| Greycoat street, Westminster *IV* | . | 25 | |
| Grey Eagle st., Spitalfields | . | 48 | |
| Greystoke place, Fetter la. | . | 35 | |
| Griffin st., York rd., Lambeth | . | 29 | |
| Groombridge road, Hackney | 54 | | |
| Grosvenor cres., Belgrave square . . . . . . . . | . | 17 | |
| Grosvenor gardens, Pimlico | . | 17 | |
| Grosvenor gate, Hyde park *I* | . | 18 | |
| Grosvenor house . . . . *I* | . | 18 | |
| Grosvenor mews, Grosvenor street . . . . . . . . *I* | . | 23 | |
| Grosvenor park, Camberwell | . | 38 | |
| Grosvenor place, Hyde park corner . . . . . . . *IV* | . | 17 | |
| Grosvenor road, Pimlico . | . | 22 | |
| Grosvenor road, Highbury New park . . . . . . | 37 | | |
| Grosvenor gallery, New Bond street . . . . . *I* | . | 23 | |
| Grosvenor rd. rail. station | . | 18 | |
| Grosvenor square . . . *I* | . | 19 | |
| Grosvenor street, Camberwell road . . . . . . | . | 38 | |
| Grosvenor st., Comrcl. rd. ea. | . | 55 | |
| Grosvenor street, New Bond street . . . . . . . *I* | . | 19 | |
| Grove end rd., St. John's wd. | 12 | | |
| Grove lane, Camberwell . | . | 44 | |
| Grove park square, Camberwell grove . . . . . . | . | 44 | |

## SQUARES, PUBLIC BUILDINGS, etc. 19

| | B | R | G | | B | R | G |
|---|---|---|---|---|---|---|---|
| Grove place, Hackney... | 49 | | | Hampton st., Walworth rd. | | | 37 |
| Grove place, Lisson grove | . | 16 | | Hanniker road, Stratford | | | |
| Grove pl., Southampton st. | . | . | 43 | New town | 69 | | |
| Grove road, Falcon lane | . | . | 16 | Hanover ch., Regent st. | *I* | . | 23 |
| Grove rd., St. John's wood | 12 | | | Hanover square | *I* | . | 23 |
| Grove st., Deptford | . | . | 57 | Hanover st., Hanover sq. | *I* | . | 23 |
| Grove street, Hackney... | 54 | | | Hanover street, Islington | 39 | | |
| Grove street road, Hackney | 58 | | | Hanover street, Kentish tn. | 17 | | |
| Guards' club, Pall mall *IV* | . | 22 | | Hanover street, Long acre | . | 27 | |
| Guildford rd., Sth. Lambeth | . | . | 27 | Hanover street, Pimlico | . | . | 24 |
| Guildford street, Lambeth | . | 29 | | Hanover st., Walworth road | . | . | 37 |
| Guildhall, King st., Cheapside . . . . . . . . . *III* | . | 39 | | Hanover ter., Regent's park | 16 | | |
| | | | | Hans place, Sloane street | . | . | 13 |
| Guildhall School of Music *II* | 35 | | | Hanway street, Oxford st. | *I* | . | 27 |
| Guilford road, Poplar... | 66 | | | Harcourt street, Marylebone | . | . | 16 |
| Guilford st., Russell square | 32 | | | Harcourt house, Cavendish | | | |
| Gun la., West India dock rd. | 63 | | | square . . . . . . . . *I* | . | . | 23 |
| Gun street, Spitalfields... | 48 | | | Hardinge street, Commercial | | | |
| Gunter's gro., We. Brompton | | | 6 | road east | . | . | 55 |
| Gurney st., Walworth road | . | 37 | | Hardington street, Portman | | | |
| Gutter lane, Cheapside *III* | . | 39 | | market | . | . | 12 |
| Guy's hospital, St. Thomas's | | | | Hare street, Bethnal green | . | . | 48 |
| street, Borough . . . . | . | 42 | | Hare walk, Kingsland road | 43 | | |
| Guy street, Bermondsey... | . | 44 | | Harewood pl., Hanover sq. *I* | . | 23 | |
| Gwynne road, Battersea... | | | 12 | Harewood square, Dorset sq. | . | . | 16 |
| Gye street, Vauxhall... | . | 30 | | Harewood st., Harewood sq. | . | . | 16 |
| | | | | Harford street, Stepney | . | . | 69 |
| Haberdasher street, Hoxton | 44 | | | Harley rd., St. John's wood | 10 | | |
| Hackford road, Brixton.. | . | 31 | | Harley street, Bow road | . | 64 | |
| Hackney downs junction | | | | Harley st., Cavendish sq. *I* | . | 20 | |
| railway station . . . . | . | 45 | | Harleyford road, Vauxhall | . | . | 30 |
| Hackney rail. sta., Church | | | | Harling street, Albany road, | | | |
| street . . . . . . . . . | 49 | | | Camberwell | . | . | 42 |
| Hackney road . . . . . . | 48 | | | Harman st., Kingsland rd. | 43 | | |
| Hadley street, Kentish town | 22 | | | Harmood st., Chalk Frm. rd. | 22 | | |
| Haggerston rail. sta., Lee st. | 47 | | | Harp lane, Lower Thames | | | |
| Haggerston rd., Kingsland rd. | 46 | | | street . . . . . . . . *III* | . | . | 42 |
| Hague st., Bethnal green rd. | 52 | | | Harrington gardens, Gloucester road . . . . . . . | | | 5 |
| Haines st., Battersea road | . | 23 | | |
| Halfmoon cres., Islington | 31 | | | Harrington road, South | | | |
| Halfmoon st., Piccadilly *IV* | . | 22 | | Kensington . . . . . . | | | 9 |
| Half Nichols st., Shoreditch | 48 | | | Harrington sq., Hampstd. rd. | 23 | | |
| Halkin street, Grosvenor | | | | Harrington st., Hampstd. rd. | 24 | | |
| place . . . . . . . . *IV* | . | 17 | | Harrison st., Gray's inn rd. | . | 32 | |
| Halkin st. west, Belgrave sq. | . | 17 | | Harrow alley, Houndsditch | . | 43 | |
| Hall place, Paddington.. | . | 12 | | Harrow road | . | . | 8 |
| Hall road, St. John's wood | 12 | | | Harrow street, Lisson gro. | . | . | 16 |
| Hall street, City road... | 36 | | | Hart st., Bloomsbury square | . | . | 28 |
| Halliford street, Islington. | 38 | | | Hart street, Bow street | . | . | 27 |
| Halsey street, Chelsea... | . | . | 13 | Hart st., Grosvenor sq. *I* | . | 19 | |
| Halton road, Islington... | 38 | | | Hartham road, Camden rd. | 29 | | |
| Hamilton pl., Piccadilly *IV* | . | 18 | | Hartland road, Chalk farm | 22 | | |
| Hamilton road, Grove road | 60 | | | Hartley street, Green street | 56 | | |
| Hamilton st., Camden town | 22 | | | Hart's la., Bethnal green rd. | 48 | | |
| Hamilton terrace, St. John's | | | | Harvey road, Camberwell | . | . | 39 |
| wood . . . . . . . . | 12 | | | Harwood road, Fulham . | . | . | 3 |
| Hammond st., Kentish tn. | 21 | | | Hassard street, Hackney rd. | 48 | | |
| Hampden street, Harrow rd. | . | 4 | | Hastings street, Burton crcs. | 28 | | |
| Hampstead rd., Hampstead | 13 | | | Hatcham, Surrey . . . . | . | . | 56 |
| Hampstead rd., Tottenham | | | | Hatcham New town, Old | | | |
| court road . . . . . . | 24 | | | Kent road . . . . . . | . | . | 50 |

II *

# LIST OF THE PRINCIPAL STREETS,

| | B | R | G |
|---|---|---|---|
| Hatcham park road, New Cross | | . 55 | |
| Hatfield street, Goswell rd. | . 40 | | |
| Hatfield street, Stamford st. | . 34 | | |
| Hatton garden, Holborn hill . . . . . . . . . . *II* | | . 36 | |
| Hatton wall, Hatton garden | | . 36 | |
| Havelock street . . . . . . | 31 | | |
| Havelock road . . . . . . | 54 | | |
| Haverstock grove, **Haverstock hill** . . . . . . . . | 13 | | |
| Haverstock hill . . . . . . | 18 | | |
| Haverstock **road**, **Haverstock park** . . . . . . | 17 | | |
| Haverstock **street, City rd.** | 40 | | |
| Havil **street, Camberwell** | | . 43 | |
| Hawley cres., **Camden tn.** | 22 | | |
| Hawley road, Kentish **town** | 22 | | |
| Haydon street, Minories *III* | . 47 | | |
| Hayles st., St. George's **rd.** | | . 33 | |
| Haymarket, St. James's *I* | . 26 | | |
| **Haymarket theatre**, Haymarket . . . . . . . . . *I* | . 26 | | |
| **Hayne street, Long lane** . | . 40 | | |
| **Hay's lane, Tooley street** . | . 42 | | |
| **Hay's street** . . . . . . *I* | . 22 | | |
| Heath road, Hampstead . . | | . 20 | |
| Heath **street**, Commercial road east . . . . . . . . | | . 55 | |
| **Heaton** place, Stratford . . | 69 | | |
| **Heddon** street, Regent **st.** *I* | . 23 | | |
| **Helmet** row, Old street, **St. Luke's** . . . . . . . . . | 40 | | |
| **Hemingford rd., Barnsbury** | 30 | | |
| **Hemsworth street, Hoxton** | 43 | | |
| **Heneage st., Spitalfields** . . | . 48 | | |
| **Hengler's circus, Argyll street** . . . . . . . . . *I* | . 23 | | |
| Henley **street**, Battersea road east . . . . . . . . | . 20 | | |
| Henrietta **street**, Brunswick **sq.** . . . . . . . . | 32 | | |
| Henrietta **street**, Cavendish square . . . . . . . *I* | . 19 | | |
| Henrietta **street**, Covent garden . . . . . . . *II* | . 27 | | |
| Henrietta street, Manchester square . . . . . . . . *I* | . 19 | | |
| Henry street, Bermondsey **st.** | . 41 | | |
| Henry street, Gray's **inn rd.** | . 32 | | |
| Henry street, Hampstead rd. | 24 | | |
| Henry street, **Pentonville** . | 31 | | |
| Henry st., Portland town . | 15 | | |
| Henry street, St. Luke's . | 40 | | |
| Henry street, Upper **Kennington lane** . . . . . . | | . 30 | |
| Herbert street, Hackney rd. | 47 | | |
| Herbert st., New North rd. | 40 | | |
| Hercules bldgs., Lambeth | . 29 | | |
| Hereford grdns., Park la. *I* | . 19 | | |
| Hereford **road, Paddington** | . | | |

| | B | R | G |
|---|---|---|---|
| Hereford sq., Old Brompton | . | . | 9 |
| Hereford st., Lisson grove. | . | 16 | |
| Her Majesty's theatre, Opera arcade, Haymarket . *IV* | . | 26 | |
| Herme st., Paddington grn. | . | 12 | |
| Hermes street, Pentonville | 31 | | |
| Hertford rd., De Beauvoir tn. | 42 | | |
| Hertford house, Manchester square . . . . . . . . . *I* | . | 20 | |
| Hertford house, Piccadilly *IV* | . | 22 | |
| Hertford street, Mayfair *IV* | . | 18 | |
| Hewlett road, Roman road | 59 | | |
| Heygate st., Walworth rd. | . | . | 37 |
| High Holborn . . . . . *II* | . | 32 | |
| High street, Aldgate . *III* | . | 47 | |
| High street, Battersea . . . | . | . | 12 |
| High street, Bloomsbury . . | . | 27 | |
| High street, Borough . . . | . | 38 | |
| High street, Bromley . . . | 68 | | |
| High street, Camberwell . | . | . | 40 |
| High street, Camden town | 23 | | |
| High street, Deptford . . . | . | . | 63 |
| High street, Homerton . . | 58 | | |
| High street, Islington . . . | 35 | | |
| High street, Kensington . . | . | 5 | |
| High street, Kingsland . . | . | 45 | |
| High street, Lambeth . . . | . | . | 20 |
| High street, Marylebone *I* | . | 20 | |
| High street, Notting hill . | . | 2 | |
| High street, Peckham . . . | . | . | 47 |
| High street, Poplar . . . . | . | 66 | |
| High street, St. Giles's *I. II* | . | 27 | |
| High street, St. John's wood | 11 | | |
| High street, Shadwell . . . | . | 55 | |
| High street, Shoreditch . . | . | 44 | |
| High street, Vauxhall . . . | . | . | 30 |
| High street, Wapping . . . | . | 50 | |
| High st., Whitechapel *III* | . | 47 | |
| Highbury crescent. . . . . | 33 | | |
| Highbury grove . . . . . . | 37 | | |
| Highbury new park . . . . | 47 | | |
| Highbury pl., Holloway rd., | 38 | | |
| Highbury railway station, Holloway road . . . . . | 34 | | |
| Highbury terrace, Highbury crescent . . . . . . . . . | 33 | | |
| Highgate road, Kentish tn. | 21 | | |
| Hilgrove road, Finchley rd. | 10 | | |
| Hill place street, Upper North street, Poplar . . . | . | 63 | |
| Hill road, St. John's wood | 11 | | |
| Hill street, Berkeley sq. . *I* | . | 18 | |
| Hill street, Blackfriars rd. | . | 33 | |
| Hill street, Finsbury . . . | . | 44 | |
| Hill street, Knightsbridge . | . | 13 | |
| Hill street, Peckham . . . | . | . | 47 |
| Hill street, Walworth road | . | . | 38 |
| Hilldrop crescent, Holloway | 25 | | |
| Hilldrop road, Camden rd. | 25 | | |
| Hillfield road, Hampstead | 1 | | |

## SQUARES, PUBLIC BUILDINGS, etc.   21

| | B | R | G | | B | R | G |
|---|---|---|---|---|---|---|---|
| Hillmarten road, Camden rd. | 29 | | | Horseshoe alley, Wilson st., Finsbury | | | 44 |
| Hills place, Oxford street *I* | | 23 | | Horseshoe yard, New Bond street *I* | | 23 | |
| Hind street, Poplar | | 63 | | | | | |
| Hinde st., Manchester sq. *I* | | 19 | | Horticultural gardens, South Kensington | | | 9 |
| Hindle street, Shacklewell | 45 | | | | | | |
| Hindon street, Pimlico | | | 24 | Horton road, Wilton road | | 50 | |
| Hobart place, Eaton sq. *IV* | | 17 | | Hosier la., West Smithfield *II* | | 36 | |
| Hobury street, Chelsea | | | 10 | | | | |
| Holborn *II* | | 36 | | Houghton st., Clare market *II* | | 31 | |
| Holborn **circus** *II* | | 36 | | Houndsditch *III* | | 43 | |
| Holborn **theatre** *II* | | 32 | | Houses of Parliament *IV* | | 25 | |
| Holborn **viaduct** *II* | | 34 | | Howard street, Strand *II* | | 34 | |
| Holborn viaduct station *II* | | 35 | | Howard st., Wandsworth rd. | | | 27 |
| Holford **square**, Pentonville | 32 | | | Howey st., Bridge rd., Batt. | | | 15 |
| Holland grove, **Cranmer rd.** | | | 35 | Howland street, Fitzroy sq. *I* | | 24 | |
| Holland house, Kensington | | 1 | | Howley place, Belvidere rd. | | 30 | |
| Holland **park**, Notting hill | | 1 | | Howley place, Harrow road | | 12 | |
| Holland park road, Kensington road | | 1 | | Hows street, Kingsland road | 47 | | |
| Holland **road**, Kensington | | 2 | | Hoxton square | 44 | | |
| Holland road, Brixton | | | 36 | Hoxton street | 44 | | |
| Holland st., Blackfriars rd. | | 31 | | Huggin lane, Wood street, Cheapside *III* | | 39 | |
| Holland street, Brixton **rd.** | | 31 | | | | | |
| Holland st., Horseferry **rd.** *IV* | | 24 | | Hugh street, St. George's road, Pimlico | | | 24 |
| Holland street, Kensington | | 2 | | Hungerford pier, Victoria embankment *IV* | | 30 | |
| Hollen st., Wardour st. *I* | | 27 | | | | | |
| Holles st., Cavendish sq. *I* | | 24 | | Hungerford road, Holloway | 25 | | |
| Holles st., Clare market *II* | | 34 | | Hunt street, Pelham street | | 48 | |
| Hollingsworth st., Holloway | 29 | | | Hunter street, Brunswick sq. | 32 | | |
| Hollington road, Wyndham road | | | 39 | Huntingdon st., Caledonian road | | 30 | |
| Holloway road | 33 | | | Huntingdon st., Hoxton st. | 44 | | |
| Holly road, Dalston | 46 | | | Huntley street, Tottenham court road | | | 28 |
| Hollybush gardens, Bethnal green | 52 | | | Hyde park | | | 14 |
| Hollywood road, **West** Brompton | | | 6 | Hyde pk. barracks, Knights bridge | | | 13 |
| Holyoak **road**, Dante road | | | 33 | Hyde park corner, Hyde park *IV* | | 18 | |
| Holywell **lane**, Shoreditch | | 44 | | Hyde park grdns., Hyde pk. | | 11 | |
| Holywell row, Curtain **road** | | 44 | | Hyde park gate, Kensington | | 5 | |
| Holywell street, Strand *II* | | 34 | | Hyde park place, Oxford street *I* | | 15 | |
| Home office, New Government build., Whitehall *IV* | | 26 | | | | | |
| Homer road, Victoria park | 58 | | | Hyde park square | | 15 | |
| Homer row, Crawford street | | 16 | | Hyde park st., Hyde pk. sq. | | 15 | |
| Homer street, Crawford st. | | 16 | | Hyde pk. ter., Bayswater rd. | | 15 | |
| Homer street, Westminster bridge road | | 29 | | Hyde place, Westminster | | | 25 |
| | | | | Hyde road, Battersea | | | 11 |
| Homerton | 53 | | | Hyde road, Hoxton | 43 | | |
| Honey lane, Cheapside *III* | | 39 | | | | | |
| Horace st., South Lambeth | | 27 | | Idol lane, Gt. Tower street | | 42 | |
| Horney lane, Neckinger road | | 45 | | Ifield road, West Brompton | | | 6 |
| Hornton street, Kensington | | 1 | | Imperial Institute | | 9 | |
| Horse Guards, Whitehall *IV* | | 26 | | India off., St. James's pk. *IV* | | 26 | |
| Horseferry rd., Westminster *IV* | | 25 | 25 | Ingleton street, Brixton road | | | 32 |
| | | | | Ingrave street, Battersea | | | 13 |
| Horseferry branch rd., Commercial road east | | 59 | | Inkerman road, Kentish tn. | 24 | | |
| | | | | Inner circle, Regent's park | 29 | | |
| Horselydown lane, Shad Thames | | 46 | | Inner Temple *II* | | 36 | |
| | | | | Inverness **gardens** | | | 2 |

## LIST OF THE PRINCIPAL STREETS,

| Street | B | R | G |
|---|---|---|---|
| Inverness road, Bishop's road | . | 7 | |
| Inverness terrace | . | 7 | |
| Inville road, Walworth | . | . | 42 |
| Ion square, Hackney road | 48 | | |
| Ironmonger lane, Cheapside III | | 39 | |
| Ironmonger row, Old street | 40 | | |
| Isle of Dogs | . | . | 65 |
| Islington High street | 35 | | |
| Islington railway stat. | 33 | | |
| Islip st., Kentish town road | 21 | | |
| Iverson road, Edgware road, Kilburn | 1 | | |
| Ivy lane, Hoxton | 43 | | |
| Ivy lane, Newgate street | . | 39 | |
| Jacob st., Mill st., Dockhead | . | 45 | |
| Jamaica level, Bermondsey | . | 49 | 49 |
| Jamaica road, Bermondsey | . | 45 | |
| Jamaica street, Commercial road east | . | 55 | |
| James grove, Commercial road, Peckham | . | . | 47 |
| James street, Bethnal green | 56 | | |
| James street, Buckingham gate IV | 21 | | |
| James street, Clapham | . | . | 28 |
| James street, Commercial road east | . | 55 | |
| James st., Covent garden II | . | 31 | |
| James street, Essex road | 38 | | |
| James street, Haymarket I | . | 26 | |
| James street, Kennington | . | . | 35 |
| James street, Kensington sq. | . | . | 5 |
| James street, Lambeth | . | 29 | |
| James street, Lambeth walk | . | . | 29 |
| James street. Oxford street I | . | 19 | |
| James st., Westbourne ter. | . | 11 | |
| Jardin street, Albany road | . | . | 42 |
| Jeffrey street, Camden town | 22 | | |
| Jeffries road, Clapham road | . | . | 28 |
| Jeremiah street, East India dock road | . | . | 67 |
| Jermyn st., St. James's I, IV | . | 22 | |
| Jewin court, Jewin street | . | 40 | |
| Jewin st., Red Cross st., City | . | 40 | |
| Jewry street, Aldgate III | . | 47 | |
| Jockey fields II | . | 32 | |
| John st., Adelphi, Strand II | . | 30 | |
| John street, Edgware road | . | 16 | |
| John st., Gt. Suffolk st. Boro' | . | 37 | |
| John st., High street, Stoke Newington | 45 | | |
| John street, Kingsland road | 47 | | |
| John street, Minories III | . | 47 | |
| John street, Old Ford road | 50 | | |
| John street, Old Kent road | . | 41 | |
| John street, St. John's wood | 15 | | |
| John street, Spitalfields | . | 48 | |
| John street, Wilmington sq. | 36 | | |
| John st. nth., Marylebone rd. | . | 16 | |
| John st. west, Thornhill sq. | 34 | | |
| John Campbell road, High street, Kingsland | 45 | | |
| Johnson st., Commercial road east | . | . | 55 |
| Johnson street, Camden tn. | 27 | | |
| Joiner street, Westminster bridge road | . | 33 | |
| Joiners street, Tooley street | . | 42 | |
| Jonathan st., Vauxhall walk | . | . | 29 |
| Jubilee place, King's road, Chelsea | . | . | 43 |
| Jubilee street, Commercial road east | . | 55 | |
| Judd street | 38 | | |
| Junior United Service club I | . | 26 | |
| Junior Athenæum club, Piccadilly IV | . | 26 | |
| Junior Carlton club, Pall mall IV | . | 26 | |
| Keetons road, Rotherhithe | . | . | 49 |
| Kempsford gardens, Richmond rd., West Brompton | . | . | 1 |
| Kempsford rd., Lower Kennington lane | . | . | 33 |
| Kender street, New Cross | . | . | 55 |
| Kenilworth road, Roman road | 59 | | |
| Kennett road, Harrow road | 4 | | |
| Kennington oval | . | . | 30 |
| Kennington park | . | . | 34 |
| Kennington park gardens, Royal road | . | . | 34 |
| Kennington park road | . | . | 34 |
| Kennington road, Lambeth | . | 33 | 33 |
| Kensington gardens | . | 10 | |
| Kensington gardens square | . | 7 | |
| Kensington gate | . | 5 | |
| Kensington gore, Kensington | . | 9 | |
| Kensington High street | . | 5 | |
| Kensington museum, Cromwell road | . | 9 | |
| Kensington palace | . | 6 | |
| Kensington palace gardens | . | 10 | |
| Kensington pk. grdens., Ladbrooke square | . | 3 | |
| Kensington park road | . | 3 | |
| Kensington road | . | 1 | |
| Kensington square | . | 5 | |
| Kensington station | . | 5 | |
| Kent street, Borough | . | . | 37 |
| Kentish town road | 22 | | |
| Kenton street, Brunswick sq. | 28 | | |
| Keppel street, Chelsea | . | . | 13 |
| Keppel street, Russell square I, II | . | 28 | |
| Kerbey st., East India dock | . | . | 67 |
| Kilburn lane, Kilburn | 4 | | |
| Kildare gardens, Bayswater | . | 3 | |

| | | | | |
|---|---|---|---|---|
| Kildare terrace, Bayswater | . | 7 | Knowsley road, Latchmere road | . . 16 |
| Kilton street, Lower Wandsworth road | . | 19 | | |
| King square, Goswell road | 40 | | Lacey street, Mostyn road | 64 |
| King street, Baker street *I* | . | 20 | Ladbroke grove | . 2 |
| King street, Cale st., Chelsea | . . | 13 | Ladbroke grove road | . 3 |
| King street, Camden town | 23 | | Ladbroke road, Notting hill | . 2 |
| King street, Cheapside *III* | . | 39 | Ladbroke square, Notting hl. | . 3 |
| King st., Covent garden *II* | . | 27 | Lady Lake's grn..Mile end rd. | . 52 |
| King street, Drury lane *II* | . | 31 | Lamb lane, Mare street, Hackney | 50 |
| King street, Golden square *I* | . | 23 | | |
| King street, Goswell road | . | 36 | Lambeth bridge . . . . *IV* | . . 25 |
| **King st., Grosvenor square** *I* | . | 19 | Lambeth High street | . . 29 |
| | | | Lambeth Lower marsh . . | . 29 |
| **King street, High st., Kensington** | . | 5 | Lambeth Palace . . . *IV* | . 29 |
| | | | Lambeth Palace rd. . . *IV* | . 29 |
| King st., Lee **st., Kingsland** | 47 | | Lambeth pier, Albert embankment . . . . *IV* | . . 29 |
| King street, Long **acre** . . *II* | . | 27 | | |
| King street, Moor street . . | . | 27 | Lambeth road, Southwark | . 33 |
| King st., St. James's sq. *IV* | . | 22 | Lambeth st., Little Alie st. | . 47 |
| King street, Snow hill *II* | . | 36 | Lambeth Upper marsh . . . | . 29 |
| King street, Whitehall . *IV* | . | 25 | Lambeth walk, Lambeth . | . 29 |
| King Edward st., Blackfriars | . | 35 | Lamb's Conduit st., Foundling hosp. | . . 32 |
| King Edward street, Lambeth road | . | 33 | Lamb's passage, Chiswell st. | . 40 |
| King Edward **st., New**gate street . . . . . . . *III* | . | 39 | Lammas rd., Hackney common | . 54 |
| King Edward's road . . . . | . | 55 | Lanark villas, Edgware rd. | . 12 |
| **King** Henry street, Stoke Newington | . | 41 | Lancaster gate, Hyde park | . 7 |
| | | | Lancaster road, Belsize pk. | 9 |
| **King** Henry's road, Adelaide road, Hampstead | . | 14 | Lancaster rd., Notting hill | . 4 |
| | | | Lancaster street, Boro' road | . 33 |
| King Henry's walk, **Stoke** Newington | . | 41 | Lancelot pl., Brompton road | . 13 |
| | | | Lancing street, Euston sq. | 28 |
| King William street, London bridge . . . . . . . *III* | . | 43 | Landseer st., Lower Wandsworth road | . . 19 |
| King William st., **Strand** *II* | . | 26 | Langford pl., St.John's wood | 11 |
| King's road, Chelsea . . . | . . | 10 | Langford rd., Kentish town | 17 |
| King's road, Hoxton **street** | 43 | | Langham place, Regent st. *I* | . 24 |
| King's road, Peckham . . . | . . | 51 | Langham st., Marylebone *I* | . 24 |
| King's Bench walk, Temple *II* | . | 35 | Langley street, Long acre *II* | . 27 |
| | | | Langton road, Camberwell New road | . . 35 |
| King's college, Strand . *II* | . | 31 | | |
| King's college hospital, Portugal st., Lincoln's inn *II* | . | 31 | Langton street, King's road | . . 10 |
| | | | Lansdowne house . . . . *I* | . 22 |
| King's cross railway station | 32 | | Lansdowne place, Russell sq. | . 32 |
| King's cross road . . . . . | 32 | | Lansdowne rd..London fields | 50 |
| Kingsbury road, Ball's pond | 41 | | Lansdowne rd., South Lambeth | . 27 |
| Kingsgate st., High Holborn *II* | . | 32 | Lant street, Southwark . . | . 37 |
| Kingsland basin, Kingsland | 43 | | Lark row, Cambridge road | 55 |
| Kingsland road . . . . . . | 44 | | Larkhall lane, Clapham . . | . . 28 |
| Kingsleigh st., Shaftesbury park | . . | 16 | Latchmere grove, Battersea | . 16 |
| | | | Latchmere road, Battersea | . . 16 |
| Kinnerton st., Knightsbridge | . | 17 | Laurel street, Queen's road | 46 |
| Kirby st., Hatton garden *II* | . | 36 | Laurence Pountney lane, Upper Thames street *III* | . 43 |
| Kitto road . . . . . . . . | . . | 56 | |
| Knightrider street, Doctors' commons . . . . . . *III* | . | 39 | Lausanne road, Nunhead . | . 56 |
| | | | Lavender grove, Queen's rd. | 46 |
| Knightsbridge barracks . . | . | 13 | Lavender road | . 12 |
| Knightsbridge grn., Hyde pk. | . | 13 | Lawford road, Kentish town | 21 |

## 24 LIST OF THE PRINCIPAL STREETS,

| | B | R | G |
|---|---|---|---|
| Lawn road, Haverstock hill | 13 | | |
| Lawrence la., Cheapside *III* | | 39 | |
| Lawrence st., Cheyne walk | | | 10 |
| Lawrence street, St. Giles *I* | | 27 | |
| Lawson street, Gt. Dover st. | | 37 | |
| Layard **rd.**, Blue Anchor rd. | | | 49 |
| Laystall st., Liquorpond st. | | 36 | |
| Leadenhall market, Leadenhall street | | *III* | 43 |
| Leadenhall street . . . *III* | | 43 | |
| Leader st., Marlborough rd. | | | 13 |
| Leamington rd. villas, Westbourne park | | 4 | |
| Leather lane, Holborn hill *II* | | 36 | |
| Lebanon street, Walworth common | | | 42 |
| Ledbury road, Notting hill. | 3 | | |
| **Lee** street, Kingsland . . . | 47 | | |
| Leek street, **King's cross** rd. | 32 | | |
| Leete st., King's rd., **Chelsea** | | | 13 |
| Lefevre road, Tredegar road | 63 | | |
| Leicester place, Leicester square . . . . . . . *I* | | 27 | |
| Leicester **square** . . . . *I* | | 27 | |
| Leicester **st.**, Leicester sq. *I* | | 27 | |
| Leigh street, Burton crescent | 28 | | |
| Leighton grove, Kentish **tn.** | 25 | | |
| Leighton road, Kentish town | 21 | | |
| Leinster gardens, Bayswater | | 7 | |
| Leinster road, Kilburn park | 4 | | |
| **Leinster** square, Bayswater | | 7 | |
| **Leipsic road,** Camberwell **New road** . . . . . . . | | | 39 |
| Leman **st.**, Whitechapel *III* | | 47 | |
| Lenthall **street. Dalston** . . | 46 | | |
| Leonard **st., Tabernacle walk** | 44 | | |
| Lesly street, Barnsbury . . | 29 | | |
| Lessada street, Grove **road** | 60 | | |
| Lever street, Goswell **road** | 40 | | |
| Leverton st., Kentish town | 21 | | |
| Lewis st., Kentish town road | 22 | | |
| Lewisham road, Greenwich | | | 68 |
| Lewisham road, New Cross | | | 60 |
| Lewisham rd. **railway sta.** | | | 64 |
| Lewisham st., **Westminster** *IV* | | 25 | |
| Lexham rd., Earl's **court rd.** | | 1 | 1 |
| Lexington street . . . . . *I* | | 23 | |
| Leyton road, Stratford . . | 69 | | |
| Leyton sq. . . . . . . . . | | | 16 |
| Lichfield street, Soho *I, II* | | 27 | |
| Lillie road, Fulham . . . . | | | 2 |
| Lillington st., Westminster | | | 21 |
| Lime street passage, Leadenhall street . . . . . *III* | | 43 | |
| Lime str. sq., Lime str. *III* | | 43 | |
| Limehouse pier . . . . . . | | | 62 |
| Limehouse railway station, Three Colt street . . . . | | | 63 |
| Limerston street, Chelsea . | | | 10 |
| Lincoln street, Mile end road | 64 | | |
| Lincoln's inn . . . . . . *II* | | 31 | |
| Lincoln's inn fields. . . *II* | | 31 | |
| Linden green, High street, Notting hill . . . . . . . | | 3 | |
| Linford st., Battersea fields | | | 23 |
| Lingham st., Stockwell green | | | 28 |
| Linsey st., Blue Anchor lane | | | 45 |
| Linton st., New North road | 39 | | |
| Lion street, New Kent road | | | 37 |
| Lisle street, Leicester sq. *I* | | 27 | |
| Lisson grove . . . . . . . | | 16 | |
| Lisson st., Marylebone road | | 16 | |
| Litcham st., Kentish town | 17 | | |
| Little Albany st., Regent's park . . . . . . . . . | | 24 | |
| Little Alie st., Whitechapel *III* | | 47 | |
| Little Argyle street, Regent street . . . . . . . . *I* | | 23 | |
| Little Britain, Aldersgate street . . . . . . . *III* | | 39 | |
| Little Cadogan pl., Sloane st. | | 17 | 17 |
| Little Cambridge st., Hackney road . . . . . . . | 47 | | |
| Little Camden st., Camden town . . . . . . . . . | | 23 | |
| Little Chapel street, Wardour street . . . . . . . . *I* | | 27 | |
| Little Charlotte st., Blackfriars road . . . . . . | | | 34 |
| Little Compton street, Soho *I* | | 27 | |
| **Little** Dean street, Dean st., Soho . . . . . . . . *I* | | 27 | |
| Little **Earl** street, Seven dials . . . . . . . . *II* | | 27 | |
| Little Grove st., Lisson grove | | 16 | |
| Little Guilford street, Brunswick square . . . . . | | | 28 |
| Little James street, Gray's inn road . . . . . . . | | 32 | |
| Little Marylebone street . . | | 20 | |
| Little Newport street, Long acre . . . . . . . . . *I* | | 27 | |
| Little Northampton street, Goswell road . . . . . | 36 | | |
| Little Portland st., Regent street . . . . . . . . *I* | | 24 | |
| Little Pulteney st., Soho *I* | | 27 | |
| Little Queen st., High Holborn . . . . . . . . *II* | | 32 | |
| Little Queen street, Westminster . . . . . . . *IV* | | 25 | |
| Little Russell st.,Bloomsbury *II* | | 28 | |
| **Little** Saffron hill . . . . . | | 36 | |
| **Little** St. Andrew street, **Upper** St. Martin's lane *II* | | 27 | |
| Little Store **street**, Bedford square . . . . . . . *I* | | 28 | |
| Little Sutton st.,Clerkenwell | | | 40 |

## SQUARES, PUBLIC BUILDINGS, etc. 25

Little Titchfield street, Great Portland street . . . . *I* . 24
Little Torrington street, Torrington square . . . . . 28
Littl**e** Tower hill . . . *III* . 46
Little Tower st., Eastcheap . 43
Little White Lion street, Seven dials . . . . . . 27
Li**tt**le Wild **st., Great Wild** street . . . . . *III* . 31
L**itt**le Winchester **st., Lon**don wall . . . . . *III* . 43
Livermore road, Dalston . 46
Liverpool road . . . . . 31
Liverpool street station *III* . 44
Liverpool street, King's cross 32
Liverpool st., Bishopsgate within . . . . . . *II* . 44
Liverpool street, Walworth . . 38
Lizard street, Radnor street 40
Lloyd square, Pentonville . 36
Loampit hill . . . . . . . 64
Loddiges road, Hackney . . 54
Lodge place, Grove road . 12
Lodge rd., Park rd., Regent's park . . . . . . . . . 46
Lombard road, Battersea . . . 13
Lombard street, Fleet st. *II* . 35
**Lombard** st., Mansion ho. *III* . 43
Lombard street, Southwark bridge road . . . . . . 37
London, Brighton & South Coast terminus, Victoria . . 21
London bridge . . . . *III* . 42
London bridge pier . . *III* . 42
London bdg. railway sta. *III* . 42
London, Chatham & Dover terminus, Holborn viad. *II* . 35
London **Central meat market** *II* . 36
**London** Commercial Sale rooms, Mincing lane *III* . 43
**London** Crystal Palace ba**zaar, Great** Portland **st.** *I* . 23
**London docks,** Wapping . . 50
**London Fever** hospital, Liverpool road . . . . . . . 35
London fields, Hackney . 50
London **fields railway sta.,** Grosvenor place . . . . . 50
London hospital, **Mount st.** east, Whitechapel **road .** . 52
London lane, Mare street . 50
London & North Western terminus, Broad street . . . 44
London & South Western terminus, Waterloo . . . 30
London street, Greenwich . .
London street, London road . 33
London street, Norfolk sq . 11 67

London street, Ratcliff cross . 59
London university, Burlington gardens . . . . . . *I* . 22
London street, Tottenham court road . . . . . . . 24
**London** wall, Moorfields *III* . 40
**Long** acre, Drury lane . *II* . 27
**Long** lane, Bermondsey . . 41
**Long** lane, West Smithfield . 40
**Long street,** Kingsland road 48
**Long walk,** Berm**o**ndsey sq. 41
Longfellow rd., Mile end rd. 60
Longnor road, Bancroft road 60
Longridge road, Earl's ct. rd. . 1
**Lonsdale road, Notting hill** . 3
**Lonsdale square, Islington** 34
**Lord's cricket ground, St. John's wood road** . . . 12
**Lorn road, Brixton road** . . . 32
**Lorrimore road,** Walworth . . 38
**Lorrimore** square, Walworth . 34
**Lorrimore st**reet, Walworth . . 38
**Lothbury,** Coleman st. *III* . 39
**Lothian road,** Camberwell New road . . . . . . . 35
**Loudoun** rd., **St.** John's **wd.** 11
**Lough**borough junction railway **sta.,** Coldharbour **la.** . . 36
Loughborough road, **Brixton** road . . . . . . . . . 36
Loughborough street, **Upper** Kennington lane . . . . 30
Love lane, Bow . . . . . . 68
Love lane, Eastcheap . *III* . 42
Love lane, Wood street. Cheapside . . . . . . *III* . 39
Lovegrove st., Old Kent rd. . . 46
Loveridge road . . . . . 1
Lower Berkeley st., Portman square . . . . . . . . *I* . 19
Lower Belgrave st., Pimlico *IV* . 17
Lower Calthorp st., Gray's inn road . . . . . . 32
Lower Chapman st., Cannon street road . . . . . . 54
Lower Clapton road . . . . 53
Lower East Smithfield . . . 46
Lower George st., Sloane sq. . . 17
Lower Grosvenor st., Grosvenor street . . . . *IV* . 21
Lower James street, Golden square . . . . . . . *I* . 23
Lower John street, Golden square . . . . . . . *I* . 23
Lower Kennington lane . . . 33
Lower marsh, Lambeth . . . 29
Lower Phillimore pl., Kensington . . . . . . . . 4
Lower Seymour st., Portman square . . . . . . . *I* . 19

## LIST OF THE PRINCIPAL STREETS,

| | B | R | G |
|---|---|---|---|
| Lower Thames street . *III* | . | 42 | |
| Lower Whitecross street . | . | 40 | |
| Lower William st., High street, Portland town . . | 15 | | |
| Lowndes place . . . . . . | | 47 | |
| Lowndes square, Sloane st. | . | 17 | |
| Lowther arcade, West Strand *II* | . | 26 | |
| **Luard** street, Caledonian rd. | 31 | | |
| Lucas road, Walworth . . | . | . | 34 |
| Lucas street, Commercial road east . . . . . . . . | . | 55 | |
| Lucas **street, Rotherbithe** . | . | . | 58 |
| **Lucey rd., Blue Anchor lane** | . | . | 45 |
| Lucretia street, Lambeth . | . | . | 33 |
| **Ludgate circus** . . . . . *II* | . | 35 | |
| **Ludgate hl., St. Paul's church yard** . . . . . . . . *II* | . | 35 | |
| **Ludgate hill railway station, New Bridge street** . . *II* | . | 35 | |
| **Luke street, Deal street** . . | | 48 | |
| **Luke street, Finsbury** . . . | | 44 | |
| **Luke st., Mile end New town** | | 47 | |
| **Lupus street, Pimlico** . . . | . | . | 22 |
| **Lyall pl., Eaton pl., Pimlico** | . | . | 17 |
| Lyall **road, Roman rd., Bow** | 60 | | |
| Lyall **st., Eaton pl., Pimlico** | . | 17 | 17 |
| Lyceum **theatre, Wellington street. Strand** . . . . *II* | . | 31 | |
| Lyme street, **Camden town** | 22 | | |
| **Lyndhurst grove, Peckham** | . | . | 48 |
| **Lyndhurst rd., Hampstead** . | 9 | | |
| **Lynton** rd., **Bermondsey** . . | . | . | 45 |
| **Lyon** street, **Caledon. road** | 30 | | |
| | | | |
| **Macclesfield** street, **Soho** *I* | . | 27 | |
| Macclesfield st. nth., City **rd.** | 40 | | |
| Macclesfield st. sth., City **rd.** | 40 | | |
| Maddox street, Regent **st.** *I* | . | 23 | |
| Magdalen st., Bermondsey | . | 42 | |
| Maida hill . . . . . . . . . | . | 12 | |
| Maida vale . . . . . . . . | 8 | | |
| Maiden lane, Cheapside *III* | . | 39 | |
| Maiden la., Covent garden *II* | . | 31 | |
| Maidenhead ct., Aldersgate street . . . . . . . . *III* | . | 40 | |
| Maidstone st., Hackney road | 47 | | |
| Maitland park road, Haverstock hill . . . . . . . . | . | 17 | |
| **Maitland pk. villas, Haverstock** hill . . . . . . . | . | 17 | |
| Malden road, Prince **of Wales** road . . . . . . . . | . | 17 | |
| Mall, The, Kensington . . | . | 2 | |
| Mall, The, St. James's . . | . | 26 | |
| Maltby street, Bermondsey | . | 45 | |
| Malvern road, Dalston . . | 46 | | |
| Malvern road, Kilburn park | 4 | | |
| Manchester rd., Isle of Dogs | . | 65 | |
| Manchester square, Marylebone . . . . . . . . . *I* | . | 19 | |

| | B | R | G |
|---|---|---|---|
| Manchester st., Gray's inn rd. | 32 | | |
| Manchester street, Manchester square . . . . . . *I* | . | 20 | |
| Mann st., Walworth common | . | . | 42 |
| Manning street, Bermondsey | . | 41 | |
| Manor lane, Rotherhithe . . | . | . | 53 |
| Manor place, Amhurst road, Hackney . . . . . . . . | 49 | | |
| Manor place, Walworth road | . | . | 37 |
| Manor road, Blue Anchor rd. | . | . | 49 |
| Manor road, Wells street . | 54 | | |
| Manor street, Chelsea . . . | . | . | 14 |
| Manor street, Old Kent road | . | . | 50 |
| Mansell st., Goodman's fields *III* | . | 47 | |
| Mansfield pl., Kentish town | 21 | | |
| Mansfield st., Kingsland rd. | 47 | | |
| Mansfield st., Portland pl. *I* | . | 24 | |
| Mansion house . . . . *III* | . | 39 | |
| Mansion house place . *III* | . | 39 | |
| Mansion house station, Mansion house . . . . . *III* | . | 39 | |
| Mansion house st., Lower Kennington lane . . . . | . | . | 33 |
| Mape st., Bethnal green rd. | 52 | | |
| Mapes lane, Edgware road | 2 | | |
| Maplin street, Mile end road | 60 | | |
| Marble arch . . . . . . . *I* | . | 19 | |
| Marchmont st., Brunswick sq. | 28 | | |
| Mare street, Hackney . . . | 50 | | |
| Margaret st., Cavendish sq. *I* | . | 23 | |
| Margaret street, Haggerston | 47 | | |
| Margaret street, Wells street | 54 | | |
| Margaret st., Wilmington sq. | 36 | | |
| Margareta terrace, Chelsea | . | . | 14 |
| Maria street, Kingsland road | 47 | | |
| Marigold street, Bermondsey | . | 47 | |
| Mark lane, Fenchurch st. *III* | . | 43 | |
| Mark lane station . . . *III* | . | 42 | |
| Mark street, Curtain road | . | 44 | |
| Market street, Bermondsey | . | 41 | |
| Market street, Borough road | . | 33 | |
| Market street, Caledonian rd. | 30 | | |
| Market street, Edgware road | . | 12 | |
| Market street, Mayfair . . . | . | 18 | |
| Market street, Soho . . . *I* | . | 27 | |
| Markham square, Chelsea . | . | . | 13 |
| Markham street, Chelsea . | . | . | 13 |
| Marlborough house, Pall mall *IV* | . | 22 | |
| Marlborough hill, St. John's wood . . . . . . . . . | 11 | | |
| Marlborough pl., Harrow rd. | . | 8 | |
| Marlborough road, Chelsea | . | . | 13 |
| Marlborough road, Dalston | 47 | | |
| Marlborough rd., Old Kent rd. | . | . | 46 |
| Marlborough road, Peckham | . | . | 47 |
| Marlborough rd., St. John's wood . . . . . . . . . | 7 | | |
| Marlborough street, Blackfriars road . . . . . . . | . | . | 34 |

## SQUARES, PUBLIC BUILDINGS, etc. 27

| | B | R | G | | B | R | G |
|---|---|---|---|---|---|---|---|
| Marloes road, Kensington | | . | 5 | Middlesex st., Whitechapel | | | |
| Marquess road, Canonbury | 38 | | | *III* | . | | 47 |
| Marquis road, Camden town | 26 | | | Middleton road, Holloway | 25 | | |
| Marshall street, Golden sq. | | . | 23 | Middleton road, Kingsland | 46 | | |
| Marshall street, Southwark | | . | 33 | Midland road, Euston rd. | . | 28 | |
| Marsham st., Westminster *IV* | | . | 25 | Midland terminus, St. Pancras, Euston road | | 28 | |
| Martha street, Cable street | 51 | | | | | | |
| Martha street, Queen's road | 47 | | | Mildmay park, Stoke Newington | | | 44 |
| Martin's la., Cannon st. *III* | | . | 39 | | | | |
| Mary street, Arlington square | 39 | | | Mildmay grove north, Stoke Newington | | | 44 |
| Mary street, Kingsland road | 43 | | | | | | |
| Maryland road, Harrow rd. | 8 | | 4 | Mildmay grove south, Stoke Newington | | | 44 |
| Marylebone High street | | . | 20 | | | | |
| Marylebone lane *I* | | . | 19 | Mildmay rd., Stoke Newington | 41 | | |
| Marylebone workho., Great Marylebone street *I* | | . | 20 | Mildmay street, Stoke Newington | | | 44 |
| Marylebone road | | . | 16 | Mile end road | | 60 | 56 |
| Mason street, Old Kent road | | . | 44 | Miles street, South Lambeth | . | . | 26 |
| Matilda st., St. George's east | 52 | | | Milford lane, Strand *II* | | . | 31 |
| Matilda street, Thornhill sq. | 31 | | | Milk street, Cheapside *III* | | . | 39 |
| Maude grove, Fulham road | | . | 6 | Mill lane, Hampstead | | 1 | |
| Maude road, Peckham road | | . | 44 | Mill lane, Tooley street | | . | 42 |
| Mawbey st., South Lambeth | | . | 27 | Mill row, Kingsland road | . | 43 | |
| Maxwell road, Fulham | | . | 7 | Mill street, Dockhead | | . | 45 |
| Maygrove road, Edgware rd. | 1 | | | Mill street, Hanover sq. *I* | . | 23 | |
| Mayville street, Kingsland | 44 | | | Mill street, Lambeth walk | . | . | 29 |
| Maze Pond, Southwark | | . | 42 | Mill yard, Leman street | . | 47 | |
| Meade's place, Newington causeway | | . | 37 | Millard road, Back road | . | 44 | |
| | | | | Millbank | . | . | 25 |
| Meadow rd., S. Lambeth | | . | 30 | Millbank Penitentiary, Millbank | . | . | 25 |
| Mecklenburgh square, Gray's inn road | 32 | | | Millbank st., Westminster *IV* | . | 25 | |
| Medical Examination Hall *II* | | . | 30 | Mill hill pl., Welbeck st. *I* | . | 19 | |
| | | | | Millman street, Bedford row | . | 32 | |
| Medburn street, Camden tn. | 27 | | | Millman's row, King's road | | . | 10 |
| Median road, Clapton | 53 | | | Millwall, Poplar | . | 61 | |
| Medway road, Roman road | 60 | | | Millwall docks | . | 65 | 65 |
| Medway st., Westminster *IV* | | . | 25 | Millwall dock railway station, Glengall road | . | 65 | |
| Meetinghouse la., Peckham | | . | 51 | | | | |
| Melbourne sq., Brixton rd. | | . | 36 | Millwall junction railway sta. | . | 66 | |
| Melbury ter., Harewood sq. | | . | 16 | Millwall pier | . | 61 | |
| Melton street, Euston square | 28 | | | Milner square, Islington | . | 34 | |
| Menotti street | 52 | | | Milner street, Chelsea | . | . | 13 |
| Mercer street, Long acre *II* | | . | 27 | Milner street, Islington | . | 34 | |
| Meredith street, Clerkenwell | 36 | | | Milton place, Dorset square | . | 16 | |
| Mermaid court, Borough High street | | . | 37 | Milton road, Old Ford road | 59 | | |
| | | | | Milton st., Cripplegate *III* | . | 40 | |
| Merrow st., Walworth road | | . | 38 | Milton street, Dorset sq. | . | 16 | |
| Methley st., Milverton street | | . | 34 | Milton street, Finsbury | . | 40 | |
| Metropolitan Board of Works, Spring gardens *IV* | | . | 26 | Mina road, Old Kent road | . | . | 42 |
| | | | | Mincing la., Fenchurch st. *III* | . | 43 | |
| Metropolitan cattle market | 29 | | | Minerva street, Hackney rd | 52 | | |
| Metropolitan District railway, Mansion house *III* | | . | 39 | Minories *III* | . | 47 | |
| | | | | Mint street, Borough | . | 37 | |
| Metropolitan meat & poultry market, Smithfield *II* | | . | 36 | Mint street, Tower hill *III* | . | 45 | |
| | | | | Mintern street, Hoxton | . | 43 | |
| Michael's grove, Brompton | . | 13 | | Minto street, Bermondsey | . | 44 | |
| Middle Temple lane *II* | | . | 35 | Mitre court, Cheapside *III* | . | 39 | |
| Middlesex hospital, Charles street, Goodge street *I* | | . | 24 | Mitre street, Aldgate *III* | . | 43 | |
| | | | | Modbury ter., Queen's cres. | 17 | | |
| Middlesex st., Somers town | 27 | | | Molyneux st., Edgware road | . | 10 | |

## LIST OF THE PRINCIPAL STREETS,

| Street | B | R | G |
|---|---|---|---|
| Moneyer street, East road | 44 | | |
| Monkwell st., Wood st. *III* | . | 40 | |
| Monmouth road, Bayswater | . | 7 | |
| Monnow rd., Blue Anchor rd. | . | . | 45 |
| Montagu mews north, Montagu square | . | . | . |
| Montagu pl., Montagu sq. *I* | . | 16 | |
| Montagu square *I* | . | 16 | |
| Montagu street, Upper Berkeley street *I* | . | . | . |
| Montague close, Boro' | . | 19 | |
| Montague ho., Whitehall *IV* | . | 42 | |
| Montague ho., Portman sq. *I* | . | 26 | |
| Montague pl., Russell sq. *I.II* | . | 19 | |
| Montague road, Dalston | . | 28 | |
| Montague st., Russell sq. *II* | 45 | | |
| Montague street, Spitalfields | . | 28 | |
| Monteith rd., Old Ford road | 48 | | |
| Montpelier pl., Montpelier st. | 59 | | |
| Montpelier road, Peckham | . | 13 | |
| Montpelier row, Brompton rd. | . | . | 51 |
| Montpelier sq., Brompton rd. | . | 13 | |
| Montpelier st., Montpelier sq. | . | 13 | |
| Montpelier street, Walworth | 24 | | |
| Monument station *III* | . | . | 38 |
| Monument yard, Fish street hill *III* | . | 43 | |
| **Moor lane, Fore street, Cripplegate** *III* | . | . | 43 |
| Moor st., Crown st., Soho *I* | . | 40 | |
| Moore street, Chelsea | . | 27 | |
| Moore park road, Fulham | . | . | 13 |
| Moorgate railway station | . | . | 7 |
| Moorgate street *III* | . | 40 | |
| Moreton place, Moreton st. | . | 39 | |
| Moreton st., Belgrave road | . | . | 21 |
| Moreton ter., Belgrave road | . | . | 21 |
| Morgan street, Tredegar sq. | 60 | . | 21 |
| Morgan's lane, Southwark | . | 42 | |
| Morning lane, Hackney | 53 | | |
| Mornington crescent, Hampstead road | . | 23 | |
| Mornington road, Bow road | 64 | | |
| Mornington rd., Regent's pk. | . | 23 | |
| Morpeth road, Victoria pk. | 55 | | |
| Morpeth street, Green street | 56 | | |
| Morpeth ter., Victoria st. *IV* | . | . | 21 |
| Morris road, Poplar | . | 68 | |
| Mortimer crescent, Kilburn | . | . | . |
| Mortimer rd., DeBeauvoirtn. | 42 | | |
| Mortimer road, Kilburn | . | 7 | |
| Mortimer st., Cavendish sq. *I* | . | 24 | |
| Morton rd., New North road | 38 | | |
| Morville street, Bow | 61 | | |
| Moscow road, Bayswater | . | 7 | |
| Mostyn road, Stockwell | . | . | 36 |
| Mostyn rd., Tredegar road | 64 | | |
| Motcomb street, Belgrave sq. | . | 17 | |
| Mount Pleasant, Gray's inn rd. | . | 36 | |
| Mount row, Berkeley sq. *I* | . | 19 | |
| Mount street, Berkeley sq. *I* | . | 18 | |

| Street | B | R | G |
|---|---|---|---|
| Mount street, Bethnal green | 48 | | |
| Mount st., New rd., Whitechapel road | . | . | 52 |
| Mountford road, Norfolk rd., Dalston | . | . | 45 |
| Munster square, Regent's pk. | 24 | | |
| Munster street, Regent's pk. | 24 | | |
| Murray street, Camden sq. | 26 | | |
| Murray st., New North rd. | 40 | | |
| Museum st., Bloomsbury *II* | . | 28 | |
| Myddelton sq., Pentonville | 36 | | |
| Myddelton st., Clerkenwell | 36 | | |
| Myddleton pl., Sadler's wells | 36 | | |
| Mylne street, Claremont sq. | 36 | | |
| Myrtle street, Dalston | . | 46 | |
| Myrtle street, Hoxton | . | 44 | |
| **Nailour** st., Caledonian rd. | 30 | | |
| Napier street, Hoxton | 39 | | |
| Narrow street, Ratcliff cross | . | 58 | |
| Nassau street, Middlesex hospital *I* | . | 24 | |
| Nassau street, Soho *I* | . | 27 | |
| National Gallery, Trafalgar square *I* | . | 26 | |
| Natural History museum, Cromwell road | . | 9 | |
| National Liberal club *IV* | . | 26 | |
| Navarino road, Dalston | 49 | | |
| Naylor's yard, Silver street | . | 23 | |
| Neate street, Coburg road, Old Kent road | . | . | 42 |
| Neckinger road, Bermondsey | . | 45 | |
| Nelson sq., Blackfriars road | . | 34 | |
| Nelson street, Bethnal green | 52 | | |
| Nelson st., Commercial rd. ea. | . | 51 | |
| Nelson street, Greenwich | . | . | 70 |
| Nelson street, Hackney road | 48 | | |
| Nelson street, Long lane | . | 44 | |
| Nelson st., Wyndham road | . | . | 39 |
| Neptune street, Church st., Rotherhithe | . | 53 | |
| Neptune st., South Lambeth | . | . | 27 |
| Netherwood street, Kilburn | 2 | | |
| Netley st., Hampstead road | 24 | | |
| Neville street, Onslow sq. | . | . | 9 |
| Neville street, Vauxhall | . | . | 30 |
| New Bond st., Oxford st. *I* | . | 23 | |
| New Bridge st., Blackfriars *II* | . | 35 | |
| **New Broad st.**, London wall *III* | . | 44 | |
| **New** Burlington house, Piccadilly *I* | . | 22 | |
| New Burlington street, Regent street *I* | . | 23 | |
| New Cavendish street, Portland place *I* | . | 24 | |
| New Church rd., Camberwell | . | . | 39 |
| New Church road, Wells st. | 54 | | |
| New Church st., Bermondsey | . | 45 | |

## SQUARES, PUBLIC BUILDINGS, etc. 29

| | B | R | G | | B | R | G |
|---|---|---|---|---|---|---|---|
| New Compton st., Soho *I, II* | . | 27 | | Nichols row, Bethnal grn. rd. | 48 | | |
| New Cross railway station | . | . | 59 | Nichols square, Hackney rd. | 48 | | |
| New Cross road | . | . | 59 | Nightingale lane, St. Katherine's docks | | . | 46 |
| New cut, Lambeth | . | 34 | | | | | |
| New Gloucester st., Hoxton | 44 | | | Nile street, Hoxton | 44 | | |
| New Government offices *IV* | . | 26 | | Nine Elms lane, Vauxhall | . | . | 26 |
| New Gravel lane, Wapping | . | 50 | | Nine Elms pier, Nine Elms la. | . | . | 26 |
| New inn, Wych st., Strand *II* | . | 31 | | Nine Elms station | . | . | 26 |
| New inn street, **Curtain rd.** | 44 | | | Noble street, Cheapside *III* | . | 39 | |
| **New Kent road** | . | . | 37 | Noble street, Falcon sq. *III* | . | 39 | |
| **New King street**, Deptford | . | . | 62 | Noble street, Goswell road | 40 | | |
| **New King's road**, Fulham | . | . | 4 | Noble street, Spafields | . | 36 | |
| **New Lambeth street** | . | . | 29 | Noel street, Islington | . | 35 | |
| **New Nichols st.,** Shoreditch | 48 | | | Noel street, Soho . . *I* | . | 23 | |
| **New North road** | 39 | | | Norfolk cres., Edgware road | . | 15 | |
| **New North st.,** Red Lion sq. | . | 32 | | Norfolk road, Dalston lane | 45 | | |
| **New Ormond st.,** Queen sq. | . | 32 | | Norfolk road, Islington | . | 42 | |
| **New Oxford street** . . *II* | . | 27 | | Norfolk road, St. John's wd. | 11 | | |
| **New Palace yard**, Westminster . . *IV* | . | 25 | | Norfolk row, Church street, Lambeth | . | . | 30 |
| **New Peter st.**, Westminster | . | 25 | | Norfolk sq., Sussex gardens | . | 11 | |
| **New Quebec street**, Portman square . . *I* | . | 19 | | Norfolk st., Cambridge rd. | . | 52 | |
| **New road**, Rotherhithe | . | . | 53 | Norfolk street, Essex road | 38 | | |
| **New road**, Wandsworth rd. | . | . | 23 | Norfolk street, Globe road | 56 | | |
| **New rd.,** Whitechapel road | . | 51 | | Norfolk street, Park lane *I* | . | . | 19 |
| **New sq.,** Lincoln's inn . *II* | . | 31 | | Norfolk street, Strand . *II* | . | 31 | |
| **New st.,** Bath st., City road | 40 | | | Norfolk terrace, Bayswater | . | 3 | |
| **New st.,** Bishopsgate st. *III* | . | 44 | | Norman road, Old Ford | . | 60 | |
| **New street**, Borough road | . | 33 | | Norman street, Chelsea | . | . | 13 |
| **New street**, Brompton | . | 13 | | Norman's buildgs., St. Luke's | 40 | | |
| **New street,** Covent garden *II* | . | 27 | | North Bank, Regent's park | 16 | | |
| **New street,** Dorset square | . | 16 | | North End road, Fulham | . | . | 2 |
| **New street,** Golden square *I* | . | 23 | | North row, Grosvenor sq. *I* | . | . | 19 |
| **New st.,** Kennington pk. rd. | . | . | 34 | North st., Limehouse fields | 60 | | |
| **New street**, New road, Whitechapel | . | 51 | | North street, Maida hill | . | 12 | |
| | | | | North st., Manchester sq. *I* | 29 | | |
| | | | | North street, Mare street | 51 | | |
| **New street,** Portland town | 15 | | | North street, Pentonville | 31 | | |
| **New street,** Vincent square | . | . | 25 | North street, Sloane street | . | 13 | |
| **New Tothill street**, Westminster . . . *IV* | . | 25 | | North street, Smith sq. *IV* | . | 25 | |
| | | | | North street, Walworth | . | . | 37 |
| New Weston st., Bermondsey | . | 41 | | North Audley st., Oxford st. | . | 19 | |
| New York st., Bethnal green | 52 | | | North Wharf rd., Paddington | . | 11 | |
| Newcastle street, Farringdon street . . . . *II* | . | 35 | | Northampton rd., Clerkenwell | 36 | | |
| Newcastle street, Strand *II* | . | 31 | | Northampton square, Goswell road | 36 | | |
| Newcastle st., Whitechapel | . | 47 | | Northampton street, Goswell road | 36 | | |
| Newgate prison, Old Bailey *II* | . | 35 | | | | | |
| Newgate street . . *II, III* | . | 39 | | Northampton st., Islington | 38 | | |
| Newington butts | . | . | 33 | Northport st., New North rd. | 43 | | |
| Newington causeway | . | 37 | | Northumberland alley, Fenchurch street | . | . | 43 |
| Newington green road | . | 41 | | | | | |
| Newland street, Pimlico | . | . | 17 | Northumberland avenue *IV* | . | 26 | |
| Newman street, Oxford st. *I* | . | 24 | | Northumberland place, Artesian road | . | 3 | |
| Newnham st., Edgware road | . | 16 | | | | | |
| Newton rd., Westbourne gro. | . | 7 | | Northumberland street, Marylebone . . . *I* | . | 20 | |
| Newton st., Cavendish | 43 | | | | | | |
| Newton st., High Holborn *II* | . | 31 | | Northumberland st., Strand *IV* | . | 26 | |
| Nicholas la., Lombard st. *III* | . | 43 | | | | | |
| Nicholas street, Hoxton | 48 | | | Northwick ter., Maida hill | 12 | | |
| Nicholas st., Mile end road | . | 56 | | Notting hill, High street | . | . | 2 |

## LIST OF THE PRINCIPAL STREETS,

| | B | R | G |
|---|---|---|---|
| Notting hill gate station | | 2 | |
| Notting hill grove | | 2 | |
| Notting hill square | | 2 | |
| Nottingham pl., Marylebone | | 20 | |
| Nottingham st., Marylebone *I* | | 20 | |
| Nutford place, Edgware rd. | | 15 | |
| Oakden st., Kennington road | | | 33 |
| Oakley road, Southgate rd. | 42 | | |
| Oakley square | | 23 | |
| Oakley street, Chelsea | | 14 | |
| Oakley street, Westminster bridge road | | | 33 |
| Oakley street, Bethnal green | 48 | | |
| Oat lane, Noble st., Falcon square *III* | | 39 | |
| Ocean street, Stepney | | | 60 |
| Ockenden road, Essex road | 42 | | |
| Office of Works & Public buildings, Whitehall *IV* | | 26 | |
| Offord rd., Caledonian road | 39 | | |
| Old Bailey, Newgate street *II* | | | |
| Old Bethnal Green road | | 52 | |
| Old Bond st., Piccadilly *I* | | 22 | |
| Old Broad street, Threadneedle street *III* | | 13 | |
| Old Brompton road | | | 5 |
| Old Burlington street *I* | | 23 | |
| Old Castle st., Bethnal grn. | 48 | | |
| Old Castle st., Whitechapel | | 47 | |
| Old Cavendish street *I* | | 23 | |
| Old Change, Cheapside *III* | | 39 | |
| Old Church road, Commercial road east | | 55 | |
| Old Compton street, Soho *I* | | 27 | |
| Old Ford railway station, Old Ford road | | | 63 |
| Old Ford railway station, Coborn road | | | 60 |
| Old Ford road, Bow | 57 | | |
| Old Gravel lane, Wapping | | 50 | |
| Old Jewry, Cheapside *III* | | 39 | |
| Old Kent road | | | 41 |
| Old Kent rd. railway sta. | | | 51 |
| Old King street, Deptford | | | 62 |
| Old Montague street, Whitechapel | | 48 | |
| Old Nichols st., Shoreditch | 48 | | |
| Old Palace yard, Westminster *IV* | | 25 | |
| Old Pye st., Westminster *IV* | | 25 | |
| Old Quebec street, Portman square *I* | | 19 | |
| Old Rochester row *IV* | | 21 | |
| Old St. Pancras road | | 27 | |
| Old square, Lincoln's inn *II* | | 31 | |
| Old street, St. Luke's | 40 | 40 | |
| Old Swan pier *III* | | 42 | |
| Olympic theatre, Wych st. *II* | | 31 | |
| Omega place, St. John's wood | 16 | | |
| Onslow crescent, Brompton | | | 13 |

| | B | R | G |
|---|---|---|---|
| Onslow grdns., We. Brompton | | | 9 |
| Onslow square, Brompton | | | 9 |
| Onslow vils., We. Brompton | | | 9 |
| Opéra Comique, Holywell st. *II* | | 31 | |
| Orange street, Borough | | | 38 |
| Orange st., Leicester square *I, II* | | 26 | |
| Orange st., Red Lion sq. *II* | | 32 | |
| Orb street, Walworth | | | 37 |
| Orchard place, Clarence rd., Clapton | 49 | | |
| Orchard street, Essex road | 42 | | |
| Orchard st., Portman sq. *I* | | 19 | |
| Orchard st., Westminster *IV* | | 25 | |
| Ordnance rd., St. John's wd. | 11 | | |
| Oxford st., Marlborough rd. | | | 13 |
| Oriel road, Homerton | 57 | | |
| Oriental club, Hanover sq. *I* | | 23 | |
| Orme square, Bayswater rd. | | 7 | |
| Ormonde ter., Primrose hill | 15 | | |
| Orsett street, Vauxhall st. | | | 29 |
| Orsett ter., Gloucester gdns. | | 8 | |
| Orwell road, Bow | 64 | | |
| Osborn pl., Whitechapel *III* | | 48 | |
| Osborne pl., South Lambeth | | | 31 |
| Oseney cres., Kentish town | 25 | | |
| Osnaburgh street | 24 | 24 | |
| Osprey street, Rotherhithe | | | 53 |
| Ossery road, Old Kent road | | | 46 |
| Ossington street, Bayswater | | 7 | |
| Ossulston st., Somers town | 28 | | |
| Otto st., Kennington park | | | 34 |
| Outram st., Copenhagen st. | 31 | | |
| Oval, Hackney road | 51 | | |
| Oval, Kennington | | | 30 |
| Oval road, Clapham road | | | 30 |
| Ovington square, Brompton | | 13 | |
| Ovington street, Chelsea | | | 13 |
| Owen street, King's road | | | 7 |
| Owen st., St. John st. road | 36 | | |
| Owen's row, St. John st. rd. | 36 | | |
| Oxenden street *I* | | 26 | |
| Oxford mansions, Oxford st. *I* | | 23 | |
| Oxford road, Islington | 38 | | |
| Oxford road, Kilburn park | 7 | | |
| Oxford square, Edgware rd. | | 15 | |
| Oxford street *I* | | 19 | |
| Oxford street, Whitechapel | | 52 | |
| Oxford ter., Edgware road | | 15 | |
| Oxford & Camb. club, Pall mall *IV* | | 22 | |
| Packington street, Essex rd. | 39 | | |
| Paddington green | | 12 | |
| Paddington railway station | | 11 | |
| Paddington recreation ground | 8 | | |
| Paddington st., Marylebone *I* | | 20 | |
| Page street, Westminster | | | 25 |
| Pakenham st., King's Cross rd. | 32 | | |
| Palace gardens, Kensington | | 6 | |

## SQUARES, PUBLIC BUILDINGS, etc. 31

| | B R G | | B R G |
|---|---|---|---|
| Palace gate, Kensington | . 5 | Parliament square... *IV* | . 25 |
| Palace street, Pimlico . *IV* | . 21 | Parliament street ... *IV* | . 25 |
| Pall Mall ........*IV* | . 22 | Parnell road, Tredegar road | 63 |
| Pall Mall East ... *I, IV* | . 27 | Parr street, New North road | 39 |
| Palm street, Grove road . | 60 | Parson's green, Fulham ... | . . 3 |
| Palmer place, Holloway rd. | 33 | Paternoster row, St. Paul's | . 39 |
| Palmer's passage, Little Chapel street .... *IV* | . 21 | Patriot sq., Cambridge rd. | 52 |
| Palmerston road, Kilburn . | 2 | Patshull road, Kentish tn. | 21 |
| Palmerston terrace, Lower Wandsworth road.... | . 19 | Paul street, Finsbury ... | 44 44 |
| | | Paulet road, Camberwell . | . . 36 |
| Pancras lane, Queen st. *III* | . 39 | Paul's alley, Paternoster rw. | . 40 |
| Panton street, Haymarket *I* | . 26 | Paulton square, Chelsea... | . . 10 |
| Panyer alley, Paternoster row .........*III* | . 39 | Pavilion road, Chelsea .. | . 13 13 |
| | | Payne street. ....... | 31 |
| Paradise place, Hackney . | 51 | Peabody buildings . *III* | . 38 |
| Paradise place, Essex road | 39 | Peacock st., Newington butts | . . 33 |
| Paradise road, Clapham rd. | . . 28 | Pear Tree st., Goswell rd. | 10 |
| Paradise street, Chelsea.. | . 14 | Pearson st., Kingsland road | 47 |
| Paradise street, Finsbury . | . 41 | Peckham gro., Camberwell | . . 13 |
| Paradise street, Gray's inn road .......... | 32 | Peckham park, Hill street | . . 17 |
| | | Peckham park road .... | . . 17 |
| | | Peckham road. ....... | . . 13 |
| Paradise street, Lambeth . | . 29 | Peckham rye stat., Rye la. | . . 18 |
| Paradise st., Marylebone *I* | . 20 | Peckwater st., Kentish tn. | 21 |
| Paradise street, Rotherhithe | . 19 | Peel road, Kilburn park . | 4 |
| Paragon, New Kent road . | . . 41 | Peel street, Kensington . | . 2 |
| Paragon road, Hackney .. | 50 | Peerless street, Bath street | 40 |
| Paris street, Lambeth . *IV* | . 29 | Pelham crescent, Brompton | . . 9 |
| Parish street, Horselydown | . 41 | Pelham street, Brompton . | . . 9 |
| Park crescent, Regent's park | 21 | Pelham st..Mile end New tn. | . 48 |
| Park crescent, Stockwell . | . . 32 | Pembridge gardens. High street, Notting hill ... | . 3 |
| Park crescent mews west, Marylebone road .... | 24 | Pembridge place, Bayswater | . 3 |
| | | Pembridge sq., Bayswater | . 3 |
| Park grove, Lower Wandsworth road ....... | . 19 | Pembridge villas, Westbourne grove ...... | . 3 |
| Park lane, Dorset square . | 16 | | |
| Park lane, Hyde park *I, IV* | . 18 | Pembroke gardens, Kensington .......... | . 1 |
| Park pl., St. James's street *IV* | . 22 | Pembroke mews, Chapel st. | . 17 |
| Park place, Paddington .. | . 12 | Pembroke road, Kensington | . 1 1 |
| Park road, Bridge road .. | . . 15 | Pembroke road, Kilburn pk. | 3 |
| Park road, Chelsea .... | . . 10 | Pembroke sq., Kensington | . 1 |
| Park road, Dalston .... | 46 | Pembroke st., Bingfield st. | 30 |
| Park road, Haverstock hill | 13 | Pembury grove, Clapton .. | 49 |
| Park road, Regent's park | 15 | Pembury road, Clapton .. | 49 |
| Park side street, Lower Wandsworth road ... | . . 20 | Pennington st., St. George's east .......... | . 50 |
| Park sq. east, Regent's pk. | . 21 | Penrose st., Walworth rd. | . . 38 |
| Park sq. west, Regent's park | . 20 | Penshurst rd., Sth. Hackney | 54 |
| Park st., Borough market | . 38 | Penton place, Kennington park road ........ | . . 33 |
| Park street, Camden town | 23 | | |
| Park street, Dorset square | . 16 | Penton pl., Pentonville rd. | 32 |
| Park st., East rd., City rd. | 44 | Penton street, Pentonville | 35 |
| Park st., Grosvenor sq. *I* | . 19 | Pentonville road ...... | 32 |
| Park street, Limehouse ... | . 62 | Penywern road, Earl's ct.. | . . 1 |
| Park st., Victoria park rd. | 58 | People's Palace ....... | . 60 |
| Park village east & west, Regent's park ..... | 23 | Pepys road, New Cross rd. | . . 56 |
| | | Percival street, Clerkenwell | 36 |
| Park walk, Chelsea ... | . 10 | Percy road, Kilburn park . | 4 |
| Parker street, Drury la. *II* | . 31 | Percy street, Lambeth... | . 30 |
| Parliament, houses of . *IV* | . 25 | Percy st., Tottenham ct. rd. *I* | . 28 |

## LIST OF THE PRINCIPAL STREETS,

| Street | B | R | G | Street | B | R | G |
|---|---|---|---|---|---|---|---|
| Peter street, Southwark bridge road | . | 38 | | Poplar railway station, East India dock road | . | 66 | |
| Peter street, Wardour street, Soho | . | 27 | / | Porchester road | . | 8 | |
| Peterborough rd., King's rd. | . | . | 7 | Porchester sq., Bishop's rd. | . | 8 | |
| Petherton road, Highbury | 37 | | | Porchester st., Edgware rd. | . | 15 | |
| Phelp st., Walworth common | . | 38 | | Porchester ter., Edgware road | . | 7 | |
| Phene street, Chelsea | . | 14 | | Porson street, Nine elms | . | . | 23 |
| Philip la., London wall /// | . | 40 | | Porteus road, Paddington | . | 12 | |
| Philip st., Back Church la. | . | 47 | | Portland bazaar, Langham place | . | 24 | |
| Phillimore pl., Kensington | . | 1 | | Portland pl., Park cresc. / | . | 24 | |
| Phillimore ter., Kensington road | . | 1 | | Portland street, Commercial road east | . | 55 | |
| Phillip street, Queen's rd. | . | . | 20 | Portland street, Soho / | . | 23 | |
| Phillip st., Victoria st. IV | . | 21 | | Portland street, Walworth | . | . | 38 |
| Phillip st., Kingsland road | 43 | | | Portman Epis. Chapel / | . | 20 | |
| Philpot lane, Fenchurch street /// | . | 43 | | Portman square / | . | 19 | |
| Philpot street, Commercial road east | . | 51 | | Portman street, Oxford st. / | . | 19 | |
| | | | | Portobello road, Notting hl. | . | 3 | |
| Phœnix place, Phœnix st. | 32 | | | Portpool lane, Gray's inn road // | . | 36 | |
| Phœnix street, Soho . . / | . | 27 | | | | | |
| Phœnix street, Somers town | 28 | | | Portsdown road | . | 8 | |
| Piazza, Covent garden . // | . | 31 | | Portsea pl., Connaught sq. | . | 15 | |
| Piccadilly IV | . | 22 | | Portsmouth street, Lincoln's inn // | . | 31 | |
| Piccadilly circus / | . | 26 | | Portugal st., Grosvenor sq. / | . | 18 | |
| Piccadilly place, Picadilly | . | 22 | | Portugal st., Lincoln's inn // | . | 31 | |
| Pickering place, Queen's rd. | . | 7 | | Pott st., Bethnal green road | 52 | | |
| Pickle Herring st., Tooley st. | . | 42 | | Potter's fields, Tooley street | . | 42 | |
| Pigott st., East India dock rd. | . | 63 | | Poultry, Cheapside . . /// | . | 39 | |
| Pilgrim st., Ludgate hill // | . | 35 | | Powell street east, King sq. | 40 | | |
| Pilgrim street, Upper Kennington lane | . | 30 | | Powell street west, King sq. | 40 | | |
| Pimlico pier, Grosvenor rd. | . | 26 | | Powis gardens, Powis sq. | . | 4 | |
| Pimlico road | . | 17 | | Powis sq., Westbourne pk. | . | 3 | |
| Pitfield street, Hoxton | 44 | | | Pownall road, Dalston | 47 | | |
| Pitman st., Wyndham rd. | . | 39 | | Praed st., Paddington | . | 11 | |
| Pitt street, Bethnal green | 52 | | | Pratt street, Camden town | 23 | | |
| Pitt street, Commercial rd., Camberwell | . | 47 | | Prebend st., Camden town | 22 | | |
| Pitt street, Fitzroy sq. . / | . | 28 | | Prebend st., New North rd. | 29 | | |
| Pitt street, St. George's rd. | . | 33 | | President st. east, King sq. | 40 | | |
| Platt street, Somers town | 27 | | | President st. west, King sq. | 40 | | |
| Playhouse yard, Water lane | . | 35 | | Preston st., Mile end New town | . | 48 | |
| Pleasant place, West square | . | 33 | | Preston's road, Poplar | . | 66 | |
| Plough street, Whitechapel | . | 47 | | Primrose hill, Regent's pk. | 14 | | |
| Plumber street, Hoxton | 44 | | | Primrose hl. rd., Hampstead | 14 | | |
| Poet's road, Highbury New park | 37 | | | Prince Edward's st., Kingsland | . | 41 | |
| Poland street, Oxford st. / | . | 23 | | Prince of Wales's crescent, Camden town | . | 18 | |
| Pollen street, Hanover sq. / | . | 23 | | | | | |
| Polytechnic, Regent street / | . | 23 | | Prince of Wales rd., Battersea | . | . | 19 |
| Pomeroy st., Old Kent rd. | . | 55 | | Prince of Wales road, Kentish town | . | 18 | |
| Pond place, Chelsea | . | 9 | | | | | |
| Ponsonby street, Millbank | . | 25 | | Prince of Wales terrace, Kensington | . | 5 | |
| Pond street, Belgrave square | . | 13 | | | | | |
| Poole st., New North road | 43 | | | Prince's grdns., S. Kensington | . | 9 | |
| Popham rd., New North rd. | 38 | | | Prince's gate, Hyde park | . | 9 | |
| Poplar High street | . | 66 | | Princes road, Bermondsey | . | 45 | |
| Poplar railway station, Brunswick street | . | 67 | | Princes rd., Lambeth walk | . | . | 29 |
| | | | | Princes square, Bayswater | . | 7 | |

## SQUARES, PUBLIC BUILDINGS, etc. 33

|  | B | R | G |
|---|---|---|---|
| Princes st., Bedford **row** *II* | . | 32 | |
| Princes st., Cavendish sq. *I* | . | 23 | |
| Princes street, Drury la. *II* | . | 31 | |
| Princes street, Hanover sq. | . | 23 | |
| Princes street, Kingsland rd. | 47 | | |
| Princes street, Lambeth | . | 34 | |
| Princes street, Lothbury *III* | . | 39 | |
| Princes street, Spitalfields | . | 48 | |
| Princes st., Westminster *IV* | . | 25 | |
| Princes street, Wilson street, Finsbury | . | 44 | |
| Princess street, Edgware rd. | . | 12 | |
| Princess ter., Regent's park | 18 | | |
| Princess's theatre, Castle street, Oxford street . *I* | . | 23 | |
| Printing ho. sq., Water la. | . | 35 | |
| Priory grove, Clapham | 2 | . | 28 |
| Priory park road, Kilburn | | | |
| Priory rd., Wandsworth rd. | . | . | 27 |
| Pritchard's rd., Hackney rd. | 51 | | |
| Pro-Cathedral | . | 4 | |
| Provost rd., Haverstock hl. | 18 | | |
| Provost street, Plumber st., City road | 40 | | |
| Prussia house . . . . . *IV* | . | 26 | |
| Pudding lane, Eastcheap | . | 43 | |
| Pulteney st., Barnsbury rd. | 31 | | |
| Punderson gardens, Bethnal green road | 52 | | |
| Pyrland road, Highbury New park | 37 | | |
| Quadrant road, Islington | 38 | | |
| Quaker street, Spitalfields | . | 48 | |
| Quebec institution . . . *I* | . | 20 | |
| Queen sq., Bloomsbury *II* | . | 32 | |
| Queen street, Brompton rd. | . | 13 | |
| Queen street, Camden tn. | 23 | | |
| Queen street, Cheapside *III* | . | 39 | |
| Queen street, Edgware road | . | 16 | |
| Queen street, Goswell road | 36 | | |
| Queen st., Grosvenor sq. *I* | . | 19 | |
| Queen street, Kingsland rd. | 47 | | |
| Queen street, Mayfair | . | 18 | |
| Queen street, Seven dials *II* | . | 27 | |
| Queen street, Soho . . . *I* | . | 27 | |
| Queen street place, Upper Thames street | . | 39 | |
| Queen Anne street, Cavendish square . . . . *I* | . | 20 | |
| Queen Anne's gate, Westminster . . . . . *IV* | . | 25 | |
| Queen Elizabeth street, Horselydown | . | 45 | |
| Queen Margaret's grove, Stoke Newington | 41 | | |
| Queen Victoria street *III* | . | 39 | |
| Queen's acres, Haverstock hl. | 17 | | |
| Queen's gardens, Bayswater | . | 7 | |
| Queen's gate | . | 9 | |
| Queen's gate gardens | . | 5 | 9 |
| Queen's gate place | . | 5 | |
| Queen's gate terrace | . | 5 | |
| Queen's Head st., Essex rd. | 39 | | |
| Queen's rd., Wandsworth rd. | . | . | 29 |
| Queen's road, Bayswater | . | 7 | |
| Queen's road, Dalston | . | 46 | |
| Queen's road railway station, Peckham | . | . | 51 |
| Queen's road, Peckham | . | . | 51 |
| Queen's rd., St. John's wood | 41 | | |
| Queen's road east, Chelsea | . | . | 17 |
| Queen's road west, Chelsea | . | . | 14 |
| Queen's theat., Longacre. *II* | . | 31 | |
| Queen's ter., St. John's wd. | 41 | | |
| Queensborough ter., Bayswater | . | 7 | |
| Queensbury st., Islington | . | 38 | |
| Quex road, Kilburn | . | 2 | |
| Radnor pl., Gloucester sq. | . | 11 | |
| Radnor st., Bath st., City rd. | 40 | | |
| Radnor street, Chelsea | . | . | 14 |
| Radnor street, Sth. Lambeth | . | . | 27 |
| Raglan street, Kentish tn. | 21 | | |
| Rahere street, Goswell rd. | 40 | | |
| Railway street, York road, King's cross | 31 | | |
| Randall street, Bridge road, Battersea | . | . | 15 |
| Randolph cresc., Maida vale | 8 | | |
| Randolph grdns., Kilburn pk. | 7 | | |
| Randolph road, Maida hill | 3 | | |
| Ranelagh grove, Pimlico | . | . | 17 |
| Ranelagh rd., Thames bank | . | . | 21 |
| Rathbone pl., Oxford st. *I* | . | 28 | |
| Raven row, Whitechapel rd. | . | 52 | |
| Ravenscroft st., Hackney rd. | 48 | | |
| Ravensdon street, Kennington park road | . | . | 34 |
| Rawlings st., Cadogan st. | . | . | 13 |
| Rawstorne street, St. John street road | 36 | | |
| Ray street, Clerkenwell | . | 36 | |
| Rayment road, Grove road | 60 | | |
| Raymond build..Gray's inn*II* | . | 32 | |
| Raymouth road, Blue Anchor road | . | . | 49 |
| Record office (Public).Chancery lane . . . . . *II* | . | 35 | |
| Rectory grove, Clapham | . | . | 24 |
| Rectory sq., Whitehorse la. | . | 56 | |
| Red Lion passage, Red Lion street | . | 28 | |
| Red Lion square, High Holborn . . . . . *II* | . | 32 | |
| Red Lion street, Clerkenwell green | . | 36 | |
| Red Lion street, High Holborn . . . . . *II* | . | 32 | |
| Red Lion yard, Old Cavendish street . . . *I* | . | 24 | |

BAEDEKER, London. 7th Edit. III

| Street | B | R | G |
|---|---|---|---|
| Redcliffe grdns., W. Brompton | | | 6 |
| Redcliffe sq., West Bromptn. | | | 6 |
| Redcliffe street, Redcliffe sq. | | | 6 |
| Redcross st., Cripplegate *III* | | 40 | |
| Redcross street, Southwark | | 38 | |
| Redhill st., Regent's park | 24 | | |
| Redman's row, Stepney grn. | | 56 | |
| Redmead lane, Wapping | | 50 | |
| Redworth st., Kennington rd. | | | 33 |
| Reeve's mews, Grosvenor sq. | | 19 | |
| Reform club, Pall mall *IV* | | 26 | |
| Regency street | | | 25 |
| Regent circus, Oxford st. *I* | | 23 | |
| Regent square, Gray's inn rd. | 32 | | |
| Regent street | | 23 | |
| Regent street, Chelsea | | | 13 |
| Regent street, City road. | 40 | | |
| Regent st., Lambeth walk | | | 29 |
| Regent street, Limehouse | | 70 | |
| Regent's park | 19 | | |
| Regent's pk. road, Regent's park | 18 | | |
| Regent's row, Queen's road | 47 | | |
| Remington street, City rd. | 40 | | |
| Renfrew road, Lower Kennington lane | | | 33 |
| Retreat place, Hackney | 54 | | |
| Rheidol terrace, Islington | 39 | | |
| Rhodeswell rd., Limehouse | | 59 | |
| Rhyl st., Weedington road | 17 | | |
| Ricardo st., Poplar New tn. | | 67 | |
| Richard st., Liverpool rd. | 35 | | |
| Richardson st., Bermondsey | | 41 | |
| Richmond cres., Islington | 30 | | |
| Richmond grove, Barnsbury | 35 | | |
| Richmond rd., Caledonian rd. | 31 | | |
| Richmond road, Dalston. | 46 | | |
| Richmond rd., Westbourne grove | | | 3 |
| Richmond st., Edgware rd. | 12 | | |
| Richmond st., St. George's rd. | | | 33 |
| Richmond street, St. Luke's | 40 | | |
| Richmond street, Soho *I* | | 27 | |
| Richmond st., Southwark | | | 33 |
| Richmond. st. Thornhill sq. | 30 | | |
| Richmond ter., Whitehall *IV* | | 26 | |
| Ridinghouse st., Regent st. *I* | | 24 | |
| Ridley road, Dalston | 15 | | |
| Riley street, King's road | | | 10 |
| Riley street, Russell street | | 41 | |
| Risinghill st. | 31 | | |
| River st., Essex rd., Islington | 38 | | |
| River st., Myddelton square | 36 | | |
| River street, York road, King's cross | 31 | | |
| Riverhall st., South Lambeth | | | 27 |
| Robert street, Adelphi *II* | | 30 | |
| Robert st., Grosvenor sq. *I* | | 19 | |
| Robert street, Hampstead rd. | 24 | | |
| Robert st., High st., Hoxton | 44 | | |
| Robert street, King's road, Chelsea | | | 9 |
| Robin Hood lane, East India dock road | | 67 | |
| Robinson rd., Victoria park | 56 | | |
| Rochester pl., Camden road | 22 | | |
| Rochester rd., Camden town | 22 | | |
| Rochester row *IV* | | 21 | 21 |
| Rochester sq., Camden town | 26 | | |
| Rochester ter., Camden town | 22 | | |
| Rockingham street, Newington causeway | | 37 | |
| Rodney rd., New Kent road | | | 37 |
| Rodney street, Pentonville | 31 | | |
| Roland gdns., Brompton rd. | | | 9 |
| Rollo street, Lower Wandsworth road | | | 20 |
| Rolls buildings, Fetter la. *II* | | 35 | |
| Rolls chapel, Chancery la. *II* | | 35 | |
| Rolls road, Bermondsey | | | 45 |
| Rolls yard, Chancery la. *II* | | 35 | |
| Roman road, Barnsbury | 29 | | |
| Roman road, Bow | 59 | | |
| Romney st., Westminster *IV* | | | 26 |
| Rood la., Fenchurch st. *III* | | 43 | |
| Ropemaker street, Finsbury | | 40 | |
| Roseberry street, Dalston | 46 | | |
| Rosemary road, Peckham | | | 47 |
| Rosetta st., South Lambeth | | | 27 |
| Roslyn park | 9 | | |
| Rosoman street, Clerkenwell | 36 | | |
| Rotherfield street, Islington | 38 | | |
| Rotherhithe New road | | | 50 |
| Rotherhithe street | 54 | | |
| Rotherhithe wall | 54 | | |
| Rotten row *IV* | | 13 | |
| Rouel road, Bermondsey | | | 45 |
| Roupell street, Cornwall rd. | 34 | | |
| Royal Academy, Burlington house, Piccadilly *I* | | 22 | |
| Royal Academy of Music *I* | | 23 | |
| Royal avenue, Chelsea | | | 13 |
| Royal Catholic chapel *I* | | 20 | |
| Royal College of Surgeons, Lincoln's inn fields *II* | | 31 | |
| Royal Exchange, Cornhill *III* | | 43 | |
| Royal Exchange buildings | | 43 | |
| Royal hospital, Greenwich | | | 70 |
| Royal mews, Pimlico | | 21 | |
| Royal Military asylum, King's road | | | 13 |
| Royal Mint st., Minories *III* | | 47 | |
| Royal Naval asylum, Greenwich | | | 70 |
| Royal Oak railway station, Celbridge place | 8 | | |
| Royal Ophthalmic hospital, Bloomfield street *III* | | 44 | |
| Royal road, Walworth | | | |
| Royal street, Carlisle street | | 29 | |

## SQUARES, PUBLIC BUILDINGS, etc. 35

| | B | R | G | | B | R | G |
|---|---|---|---|---|---|---|---|
| Royal victualling yard, Deptford | | | 61 | St. Edmund's terrace, Regents park | | 15 | |
| Royalty theatre, Dean st. *I* | | 27 | | St. Ethelburga, Bishopsgate | *III* | | 43 |
| Rudolph road, Kilburn pk. | 7 | | | St.George's cathedral (R.C.), Westminster bridge road | | | 33 |
| Rupert street, Haymarket *I* | | 27 | | St. George's church, Bloomsbury | *II* | | 28 |
| Rupert street, Whitechapel | | 47 | | | | | |
| Rushton street, Hoxton | 43 | | | | | | |
| Rushton st., New Nth. rd. | 39 | | | St. George's church, Hanover square | *I* | | 23 |
| Russell square, Bloomsbury | | 28 | | | | | |
| Russell st., Bermondsey st. | | 41 | | St. George's barracks *I* | | | 26 |
| Russell st., Covent garden *II* | | 31 | | St. George's hall, Langham place | *I* | | 24 |
| Russell street, Lower Wandsworth road | | | 19 | | | | |
| Russian greek chapel *I* | | 20 | | St. George's hospital, Hyde park corner *IV* | | | 17 |
| Russia lane, Bethnal green | 55 | | | | | | |
| Rutland gate, Knightsbridge | | 13 | | St. George's road, Battersea fields | | | 23 |
| Rutland mews,Rutland gate, Knightsbridge | | 13 | | St. George's rd., Camberwell | | | 12 |
| Rutland st., Hampstead rd. | 24 | | | St. George's road, Pimlico *I* | | | 21 |
| Rutland st., Kingsland road | 47 | | | St. George's rd..Regent's pk. | 18 | | |
| Rutland street, Pimlico | | | 21 | St. George's rd., Southwark | | 33 | 33 |
| Rutland st., South Lambeth | | | 27 | St. George's row, Ebury bdg. | | | 21 |
| Rutland st., Victoria park | 55 | | | St. George's square, Pimlico | | | 26 |
| Rutland street, Whitechapel | | 51 | | St. George's street, Battersea | | | 19 |
| Ryder street, St. James's *IV* | | 22 | | St. George's street, London docks | | | 50 |
| Rye lane, Peckham | | | 48 | St. George's ter., Hyde pk. | | 15 | |
| Sable street, Halton road | 38 | | | St. Giles in Fields, High street, St. Giles *II* | | 27 | |
| Sackville street, Piccadilly *I* | | 22 | | | | | |
| St. Alban's place *I* | | 26 | | St. Helen's, Bishopsgate *III* | | 43 | |
| St. Alban's rd., Kensington | | 5 | | St. Helen's place, Bishopsgate street *III* | | 43 | |
| St. Alban's street, Lambeth | | | 29 | | | | |
| St. Andrew's ch., Holborn *II* | | 36 | | St. James's church, Piccadilly *I* | | 22 | |
| St. Andrew's street, Holborn circus *II* | | 35 | | | | | |
| St. Andrew's street, Wandsworth road | | | 24 | St. James's grove, Lower Wandsworth road | | | 16 |
| St. Ann st., Orchard st. *III* | | 39 | | St. James's hall, Piccadilly *I* | | 22 | |
| St. Ann's court, Dean st. *I* | | 27 | | St. James's palace, Pall mall *IV* | | 22 | |
| St. Ann's st., Westm. *IV* | | 25 | | | | | |
| St. Anne's church, Dean st. *I* | | 27 | | St. James's park, Westminster *IV* | | 25 | |
| St. Augustine's road, Camden town | | 26 | | St. James's road, Holloway | 29 | | |
| | | | | St. James's rd., Old Kent rd. | | | 49 |
| St. Augustine's & Faith church, Old Change *III* | | 39 | | St. James's rd., Victoria pk. | 55 | | |
| St. Bartholomew's hospital, West Smithfield *II, III* | | 10 | | St. James's square *IV* | | 22 | |
| | | | | St. James's st., Clerkenwell | | 36 | |
| St. Bene't place, Gracechurch street *III* | | 43 | | St. James's st., Islington | 39 | | |
| | | | | St. James's st., Pall mall *IV* | | 22 | |
| St. Botolph ch., Aldgate *III* | | 47 | | St. James's theatre, King street, St. James *IV* | | 22 | |
| St. Bride street, Fleet st. *II* | | 35 | | | | | |
| St. Bride's ch., Fleet st. *II* | | 35 | | St. John street, Islington | 39 | | |
| St. Clement Danes church, Strand *II* | | 34 | | St. John street, West Smithfield *II* | | 36 | |
| St. Clement's inn, Strand *II* | | 34 | | St. John st. rd., Clerkenwell | 36 | | |
| St. David st., Falmouth rd. | | 37 | | St. John's lane, Clerkenwell | | 36 | |
| St. Dunstan's hill, Lower Thames street | | 42 | | St. John's road, Deptford New town | | | 64 |
| St. Dunstan's-in-the-east ch., Great Tower st. *III* | | 42 | | St. John's road, Hoxton | 43 | | |
| | | | | St. John's sq., Clerkenwell | | 36 | |
| St. Dunstan's-in-the-west, Fleet street *II* | | 35 | | St. John's st., Smith's sq. | | 25 | |
| | | | | St. John's wood park | | 10 | |

III

## LIST OF THE PRINCIPAL STREETS,

| | B | R | G |
|---|---|---|---|
| St. John's wood road | 12 | | |
| St. John's wood terrace | 11 | | |
| St. Jude's st., Ball's Pond rd. | 41 | | |
| St. Julian's road, Kilburn | 2 | | |
| St. Katherine Cree, Leadenhall street | III | | 43 |
| St. Katherine's, Regent's pk. | 19 | | |
| St. Katherine's wharf. III | | | 46 |
| St. Katherine's docks. III | | | 46 |
| St. Leonard street, Bow | 68 | | |
| St. Leonard's road | | | 67 |
| St. Leonard's ter., Chelsea hospital | | | 13 |
| St. Luke's road, Westbourne park | | | 4 |
| St. Magnus the Martyr, Fish street hill | III | | 42 |
| St. Margaret's church, Broadway, Westminster | IV | | 25 |
| St. Margaret's church, Lothbury | III | | 43 |
| St. Mark's church | I | | 19 |
| St. Mark's rd., Camberwell | | | 35 |
| St. Mark's st., Goodman's fields | III | | 47 |
| St. Martin-in-the-Fields church. Trafalgar sq. | II | | 26 |
| St. Martin's lane, Trafalgar square | II | | 27 |
| St. Martin's-le-Grand. | III | | 39 |
| St. Martin's place, Trafalgar square | II | | 26 |
| St. Martin's street, Leicester square | I | | 26 |
| St. Mary Aldermary church, Bow lane | | | 63 |
| St. Mary-at-hill, Eastcheap | III | | 42 |
| St. Mary Axe, Leadenhall street | III | | 43 |
| St. Mary-le-Bow church, Cheapside | III | | 39 |
| St. Mary-le-Strand church. Strand | II | | 31 |
| St. Mary Magdalene church, Bermondsey street | | | 41 |
| St. Mary Woolnoth church, Lombard street | III | | 43 |
| St. Mary's church, Temple | II | | 35 |
| St. Mary's road, Canonbury | 38 | | |
| St. Mary's road, Queen's rd. | | | 52 |
| St. Mary's sq., Kennington rd. | | | 33 |
| St. Marylebone ch., Marylebone road | | | 16 |
| St. Matthias road, Stoke Newington | 41 | | |
| St. Michael's ch., Chester sq. | | | 17 |
| St. Michael's ch., Cornhill | III | | 43 |
| St. Olave's church, Tooley street | III | | 43 |
| St. Pancras ch., Euston sq. | 25 | | |

| | B | R | G |
|---|---|---|---|
| St. Pancras goods station, Agar town | | | 27 |
| St. Patrick's terrace, Falmouth road | | | 37 |
| St. Paul's cathedral | III | | 39 |
| St. Paul's church, Covent garden | II | | 31 |
| St. Paul's churchyard | III | | 39 |
| St. Paul's cres., Camden road | 26 | | |
| St. Paul's pl., St. Paul's rd. | 41 | | |
| St. Paul's pier, Up. Thames street | II, III | | 39 |
| St. Paul's road, Bow | | | 61 |
| St. Paul's road, Camden sq. | 26 | | |
| St. Paul's road, Islington | 37 | | |
| St. Paul's road, Walworth | | | 34 |
| St. Paul's station, Blackfriars | II | | 35 |
| St. Peter street, Hackney rd. | 52 | | |
| St. Peter street, Islington | 38 | | |
| St. Peter's ch., Cornhill | III | | 43 |
| St. Peter's ch., Pimlico | IV | | 24 |
| St. Peter's rd., Mile end rd. | | | 56 |
| St. Petersburgh place, Bayswater | | | 7 |
| St. Philipp's rd., Kingsld. rd. | 16 | | |
| St. Saviour's church, London bridge | III | | 38 |
| St. Sepulchre church, Snow hill | II | | 35 |
| St. Stephen's church, Walbrook | III | | 39 |
| St. Stephen's road, Bow | | | 59 |
| St. Stephen's road, Westbourne park | | | 4 |
| St. Stephen's square, Westbourne park | | | 4 |
| St. Swithin's lane, King William street | III | | 43 |
| St. Swithin's, London Stone church, Cannon street | III | | 43 |
| St. Thomas's church and school | I | | 19 |
| St. Thomas's hospital, Albert embankment | IV | | 29 |
| St. Thomas's place, Hackney | 54 | | |
| St. Thomas's ch., Borough | III | | 42 |
| St. Thomas square, Hackney | 50 | | |
| St. Thomas's street, Boro' | | | 33 |
| St. Thomas street east, Boro' | | | 42 |
| St. Thomas street, Islington | 39 | | |
| St. Vincent st., Charles st. | | | 55 |
| Sale street, Edgware road | | | 16 |
| Salisbury ct., Fleet st. | II | | 35 |
| Salisbury lane, Bermondsey wall | | | 45 |
| Salisbury st., Lisson grove | 12 | | 12 |
| Salisbury street, Strand | II | | 30 |
| Salmon lane, Limehouse | | | 59 |
| Sancroft st. | | | 29 |
| Sandringham road, Dalston | 45 | | |

## SQUARES, PUBLIC BUILDINGS, etc. 37

| | B R G | | B R G |
|---|---|---|---|
| Sandwich st., Burton cres. | 28 | Shepherd's st., Spitalfields | 48 |
| Sandy's row, Bishopsgate | | Shepperton road | 39 |
| street | 44 | Sherborne la., King William | |
| Sanger's Amphitheatre IV | 29 | street III | 43 |
| Sarah street, Burdett road | 63 | Sherborne pl., Blandford sq. | 16 |
| Savage gardens, Tower hill | 43 | Sherborne st., Blandford sq. | 16 |
| Savile row, Burlington | | Sheridan street, Commercial | |
| gardens I | 23 | road east | 54 |
| Saville place, Lambeth walk | 29 | Sherwood st., Golden sq. I | 23 |
| Saville street, Langham st. I | 24 | Shipton street, Hackney rd. | 48 |
| Savona street, Nine elms | 23 | Shirland rd., St. Peter's pk. | 8 |
| Savoy church, Strand II | 34 | Shoe lane, Fleet street II | 35 |
| Savoy street, Strand II | 34 | Shoemaker street II | 35 |
| Saxon rd., St. Stephen's rd. | 60 | Shore road, Hackney | 55 |
| Scarborough st., Goodman's | | Shoreditch High street | 44 |
| fields III | 47 | Shoreditch railway station | 48 |
| Scarsdale villas, Kensington | 1 | Short's gardens, Drury la. II | 27 |
| Scotland yard, Whitehall IV | 26 | Shouldham st., Bryanston sq. | 16 |
| Scrutton st. | 44 | Shrewsbury rd., Westbourne | |
| Seabright st., Hackney road | 52 | park | 3 |
| Seagrave road, Fulham | 2 | Shrubland grove, Dalston | 46 |
| Sebbon street, Canonbury sq. | 38 | Shrubland road, Dalston | 47 |
| Sedan street, Walworth | 42 | Sibella road, Clapham | 27 |
| Seething lane, Tower hill III | 43 | Sidmouth st., Gray's Inn rd. | 32 |
| Sekforde street, Clerkenwell | 36 36 | Sidney square, Commercial | |
| Selborne road, Camberwell | 40 | road east | 54 |
| Selby street, Bethnal green | 52 | Sidney street, City road | 36 |
| Selwood place, Queen's elm | 9 | Sidney st., Upper North st. | 63 |
| Selwood terrace, Fulham rd. | 9 | Sidney street, York road | 34 |
| Senior road, Harrow road | 8 | Sigdon road, Hackney | 49 |
| Selwin road, Plaistow | 60 | Silver street, Golden sq. I | 23 |
| Serjeants' inn, Chancery la. II | 35 | Silver street, Stepney | 56 |
| Serjeants' inn, Fleet st. II | 35 | Silver street, Wood st. III | 39 |
| Serle st., Lincoln's inn fields | 34 | Simpson st., South Lambeth | 27 |
| Sermon la., Doctors' com. III | 39 | Simpson street, York road | 12 |
| Sermon la., White Conduit st. | 35 | Sion College II | 35 |
| Seven Dials II | 27 | Skidmore street, Mile end | 64 |
| Seville st. | 13 | Skinner street, Clerkenwell | 36 |
| Seward street, Goswell road | 40 | Skinner street, Somers town | 25 |
| Sewardstone rd., Victoria pk. | 55 | Sloane square, Chelsea | 17 |
| Seymour pl., Bryanston sq. | 16 | Sloane street, Chelsea | 13 17 |
| Seymour place, Fulham road | 6 | Sloane terrace, Chelsea | 17 |
| Seymour st., Portman sq. I | 15 | Smedley st. | 29 |
| Shacklewell la., Kingsland rd. | 45 | Smith sq., Westminster IV | 25 |
| Shacklewell road | 45 | Smith street, Chelsea | 44 |
| Shad Thames, Horselydown | 46 | Smith street, Kennington pk. | 34 |
| Shadwell railway station, | | Smith st., Northampton sq. | 36 |
| Sutton street east | 54 | Smith street, Peckham | 47 |
| Shaftesbury avenue I, II | 27 | Smith street, Stepney | 56 |
| Shaftesbury street, Hoxton | 39 | Smith terrace, Smith street | 44 |
| Shalcomb street, King's road | 10 | Smithfield West, Giltspur st. | 40 |
| Sharple's Hall st., Regent's | | Smyrk's road, Old Kent rd. | 42 |
| Park road | 18 | Snow hl., Holborn viaduct II | 36 |
| Sharstead st., Kensington pk. | 34 | Snow's fields, Bermondsey | 44 |
| Shawfield street, King's road | 44 | Soane's museum, Lincoln's | |
| Sheffield ter., Campden hill | 2 | inn fields | 34 |
| Shellwood rd., Latchmere rd. | 10 | Society of Brit. Artists I | 26 |
| Shepherd street, Mayfair IV | 22 | Soho bazaar, Oxford street I | 25 |
| Shepherdess walk, Hoxton | 40 | Soho square I | 27 |
| Shepherd's lane, Homerton | 53 | Soho street, Soho sq. I | 27 |
| Shepherd's market, Mayfair | 18 | Somerset house, Strand II | 34 |

## LIST OF THE PRINCIPAL STREETS,

| | B | R | G | | B | R | G |
|---|---|---|---|---|---|---|---|
| Somerset place, Strand *II* | . | 31 | | Spencer road, Park road, Battersea | . | 7 | 15 |
| Somerset st., Portman sq. *I* | . | 19 | | Spencer st., Canonbury sq. | 38 | | |
| Somerville road, Queen's rd. | . | . | 56 | Spencer street, Commercial road east | . | . | 54 |
| South Audley street, Grosvenor square ... *I, IV* | . | 18 | | Spencer street, Goswell road | 36 | | |
| South Bank, Regent's park | 16 | | | Spicer street, Brick lane, Spitalfields | . | . | 48 |
| South Bermondsey, Bermondsey New road ... | . | . | 49 | Spital street, Pelham street | . | . | 48 |
| South Bruton mews, Bruton street ........ *I* | . | 23 | | Spitalfields market ... | . | . | 48 |
| South cres., Bedford sq. *I* | . | 28 | | Spring grdns., Charing cross | . | . | 60 |
| South grove, Bow road .. | 60 | | | Spring gro., South Lambeth | . | . | 27 |
| South Island pl., Brixton rd. | . | 31 | | Spring place, South Lambeth | . | . | 27 |
| South Kensington station . | . | . | 9 | Spring street, Farringdon rd. | 38 | | |
| South Kensington museum | . | 9 | | Spring street, Paddington . | . | . | 14 |
| South Lambeth road ... | . | . | 31 | Spring street, Portman sq. *I* | . | . | 20 |
| South Molton lane, Grosvenor square ..... *I* | . | 19 | | Spurstowe road, Hackney . | 49 | | |
| South Molton st., Oxford st. *I* | . | 19 | | Squirries st., Bethnal grn.rd. | 52 | | |
| South pl., Finsbury .... | . | 14 | | Stable yard, St. James's palace ........ *IV* | . | 22 | |
| South square, Gray's inn *II* | . | 32 | | Stacey street, Soho . *I. II* | . | 27 | |
| South street, Bethnal green | 48 | | | Stafford house...... *IV* | . | 22 | |
| South street, Blackheath rd. | . | . | 67 | Stafford road, Roman road | 59 | | |
| South street, Camberwell . | . | . | 43 | Stafford street, Lisson grove | . | 16 | |
| South st., Finsbury .... | . | 44 | | Stafford st., Old Bond st. *I* | . | 22 | |
| South st., Grosvenor sq. *I* | . | 18 | | Stafford terrace, Phillimore gardens, Kensington ... | . | 1 | |
| South st., Manchester sq. *I* | . | 20 | | Stainsby road, Poplar ... | . | . | 63 |
| South st., New North road | 39 | | | Stamford road, De Beauvoir town | 42 | | |
| South street, Walworth .. | . | . | 42 | Stamford st., Blackfriars rd. | . | . | 34 |
| South Wharf rd., Paddington | . | 12 | | Standard st., New Kent rd. | . | . | 37 |
| Southampton build., Chancery lane........ *II* | . | 32 | | Stanford road, Fulham . . | . | . | 7 |
| Southampton rd., Maitld. rd. | 17 | | | Stangate st., Upper Marsh | . | . | 29 |
| Southampton row, Russell square ........ *II* | . | 32 | | Stanhope gardens, South Kensington | . | . | |
| Southampton st., Bloomsbury | . | 32 | | Stanhope st., Clare mkt. *II* | . | 31 | |
| Southampton st., Camberwell | . | . | 43 | Stanhope street, Euston road | 24 | | |
| Southampton st., Strand *II* | . | 34 | | Stanhope st., Victoria gate | . | 11 | |
| Southampton ter., Islington | 34 | | | Stanhope terrace, Hyde pk. gardens ....... | . | 11 | |
| Southboro' rd., Sth. Hackney | 55 | | | Stanley cres., Kensington pk. | . | . | 3 |
| Southgate grove, Kingsland | 42 | | | Stanley gardens, Belsize pk. | 13 | | |
| Southgate road ...... | 42 | | | Stanley gardens, Kensington park | . | . | 3 |
| Southsea ho., Threadneedle street ....... *III* | . | . | 43 | Stanley park rd., King's rd. | . | . | 7 |
| Southville street, Wandsworth road ....... | . | . | 27 | Stanley place, Stanley street | . | . | 21 |
| Southwark & Vauxhall waterworks reservoirs ... | . | . | 48 | Stanley rd., Ball's Pond rd. | 41 | | |
| Southwark bridge ... *III* | . | 38 | | Stanley road, Hackney . . | 54 | | |
| Southwark bridge rd., Boro' | . | 37 | | Stanley street, Hoxton . . | 40 | | |
| Southwark park ..... | . | 19 | 49 | Stanley street, London street | . | 11 | |
| Southwark street ... *III* | . | 38 | | Stanley street, Queen's road | . | . | 20 |
| Southwell gardens, S. Kensington ........ | . | 5 | | Stanmore street, Pancras rd. | 27 | | |
| Southwick cres., Oxford sq. | . | 15 | | Staple street, Long lane .. | . | 41 | |
| Southwick place, Hyde Park square ........ | . | 14 | | Star corner, Bermondsey . | . | 41 | |
| | | | | Star street, Edgware road | . | 16 | |
| Southwick street, Oxford sq. | . | 15 | | Station road, Camberwell . | . | . | 40 |
| Spa road, Bermondsey ... | . | 45 | 45 | Stationers' hall, Ludgate hill ........... *II* | . | 35 | |
| Spanish pl., Manchester sq. *I* | . | 20 | | Steeles road, Haverstock hill | 14 | | |
| Spencer house .... *IV* | . | 22 | | Steinway Hall ..... *I* | . | 19 | |

## SQUARES, PUBLIC BUILDINGS, etc. 39

| | B | R | G |
|---|---|---|---|
| Stephen street, Tottenham court road ...... *I* | | 28 | |
| Stepney green, Mile end road | | 56 | |
| Stepney rail., Whitehorse st. | | 59 | |
| Steward street, Artillery st. | | 44 | |
| Steward street, Isle of Dogs | | 65 | |
| Stewart's grove, Fulham rd. | | | 9 |
| Stewart's la., Battersea fields | | | 23 |
| Stock Exchange, **Capel court** *III* | | 43 | |
| Stock orchard st.,**Caledonian road** ........... | 29 | | |
| Stockbridge **ter.**, **Victoria st.** | | 21 | |
| Stockwell **green** ...... | | | 32 |
| Stockwell **park road** .... | | | 32 |
| Stockwell **road** ...... | | | 32 |
| Stoke Newington road... | 45 | | |
| Stonecutter st., Farringdon st. | | 35 | |
| Stonefield street, Islington | 35 | | |
| Stonefield ter., Stonefield **st.** | 35 | | |
| Stoney lane, Tooley **street** | | 42 | |
| Stoney street, Borough . . | | 38 | |
| Store street, Bedford **sq.** *I* | | 28 | |
| Storey's gate, St. George street ........ *IV* | | 25 | |
| Storks road, Bermondsey | | 48 | 49 |
| Strand (The) ...... *II* | | 31 | |
| Strand theatre, Surrey **st.** *II* | | 31 | |
| Strand lane, Strand .. *II* | | 31 | |
| Stratford central **railway sta.** | 70 | | |
| Stratford **market railway sta.**, High **street**.... | 70 | | |
| Stratford High street .. | 71 | | |
| Stratford **pl.**, Camden **town** | 26 | | |
| Stratford road, Kensington | | 1 | |
| Stratford road ...... | 67 | | |
| Stratton street, Piccadilly *IV* | | 22 | |
| Streatham st., Bloomsbury *II* | | 28 | |
| **Strutton grnd.**, Westminster *IV* | | 25 | |
| Studley **road**, **Clapham road** | | 28 | |
| **Subway**, Tower **hill** .... | | 42 | |
| **Suffolk lane**, Upper Thames street ....... *III* | | 39 | |
| Suffolk street, Cambridge **rd.** | | 52 | |
| Suffolk street, Halliford **st.** | 38 | | |
| Suffolk street, Pall **mall** *I* | | 26 | |
| Suffolk st., Upper North **st.** | | 63 | |
| Sumner place, Onslow **sq.** | | | 9 |
| Sumner **road**, **Commercial road**, **Peckham** ..... | | 47 | |
| Sumner st., Southwark *III* | | 38 | |
| **Sunderland** terrace, Westbourne park ...... | | 8 | |

| | B | R | G |
|---|---|---|---|
| Sussex place, Kensington . | | 5 | |
| Sussex place, Regent's park | 16 | | |
| Sussex square, Hyde park | | 11 | |
| Sussex street, Stainsby road | | 63 | |
| Sussex st., St. George's road | | | 23 |
| Sutherland gardens .... | 8 | 8 | |
| Sutherland place, Bayswater | | 3 | |
| Sutherland sq., Walworth rd. | | | 38 |
| Sutherland street, Pimlico | | | 21 |
| Sutton place, Homerton | 53 | | |
| Sutton street, Soho ... *I* | | 27 | |
| Sutton street, York road | | 40 | |
| **Sutton** street east ..... | | 55 | |
| **Swallow** street, Piccadilly *I* | | 22 | |
| **Swan lane**, Rotherhithe . | | 53 | |
| **Swan lane**, **Upper** Thames **street** ....... *III* | | 42 | |
| Swan pier, London bridge *III* | | 42 | |
| Swan place, Old Kent road | | | 41 |
| Swan street, Minories . *III* | | 13 | |
| Swan street, Shoreditch .. | | 17 | |
| Swan street, Trinity square | | 37 | |
| Swinton st., Gray's inn road | 32 | | |
| Swiss Cottage railway sta., Belsize road ....... | 10 | | |
| **Sydney** place, Pelham cres. | | | 9 |
| **Sydney** road, Homerton .. | 57 | | |
| **Sydney** street, Fulham road | | | 9 |
| **Symon's** street, Sloane sq. | | | 13 |
| Tabernacle **row**, City road | 44 | | |
| Tabernacle wk., Finsbury | 44 | 44 | |
| Tachbrook st., Belgrave rd. | | | 21 |
| Tait street ........ | | 51 | |
| Talbot road, Westbourne pk. | | 3 | |
| Talfourt road, Peckham rd. | | | 44 |
| Tanner's hill, Deptford .. | | | 64 |
| Tarling street, Commercial road east ...... | | 51 | |
| Tavistock crescent, Westbourne **park** ...... | | 4 | |
| Tavistock mews, Litt. Coram street ........ | 28 | | |
| **Tavistock pl.**, Tavistock sq. | 28 | | |
| **Tavistock road**, Westbourne **park** ....... | | 4 | |
| Tavistock square ..... | 28 | | |
| Tavistock st., Bedford sq. *I* | | 28 | |
| Tavistock st., Covent garden *II* | | 31 | |
| Taviton street, Gordon sq. | 28 | | |
| Templar road, Homerton . | 53 | | |
| Temple (The), Fleet st. *II* | | 35 | |
| Temple church(St.Mary's)*II* | | 35 | |
| Temple lane, Whitefriars *II* | | 35 | |
| Temple station ..... *II* | | 31 | |
| Temple pier, Victoria embankment ...... *II* | | 35 | |
| Temple st., Hackney road | 62 | | |
| Temple street, Queen's road | 46 | | |
| Temple st., St. George's road | | | 43 |
| Sussex pl., Hyde pk. gardens | | 11 | |

| Street | B | R | G |
|---|---|---|---|
| Temple st., Whitefriars *II* | | 35 | |
| Temple mill rd. | 64 | | |
| Tennison street, York road, Lambeth | | 30 | |
| Tennyson street, Queen's rd. | | | 20 |
| Tenter st., Little Moorfields | | 40 | |
| Tenter street, Spitalfields *III* | | 48 | |
| Tenter street, Goodman's fields *III* | | 47 | |
| Tenterden st., Hanover sq. *I* | | 23 | |
| Terrace road, Well street | 54 | | |
| Tetley street, Poplar | | 67 | |
| Thames subways | | 42 | |
| Thames tunnel | | 50 | |
| Thanet street, Burton cres. | 28 | | |
| Thayer st., Manchester sq. *I* | | 20 | |
| The Mall, Kensington | | 2 | |
| Theberton street, Islington | 35 | | |
| Theobald's road *II* | | 32 | |
| Theobald's st., New Kent rd. | | 37 | |
| Thistle gro., West Brompton | | 5 | |
| Thistle grove lane, West Brompton | | 9 | |
| Thomas street, Brick lane | | 48 | |
| Thomas st., Commercial rd. | | 51 | |
| Thomas st., Grosvenor sq. *I* | | 19 | |
| Thomas st., Kennington pk. | | 31 | |
| Thomas st., Kingsland road | 48 | | |
| Thomas street, Limehouse | | 63 | |
| Thomas street, Old Kent rd. | | 41 | |
| Thomas street, Stamford st. | | 34 | |
| Thorne rd., South Lambeth | | 27 | |
| Thornhill road, Islington | 34 | | |
| Thornhill sq., Caledonian rd. | 30 | | |
| Thornton street, Dockhead | | 45 | |
| Thrawl street Spitalfields | | 48 | |
| Threadneedle street *III* | | 43 | |
| Three Colt st., Limehouse | | 63 | |
| Three Cranes lane, Upper Thames street *III* | | 39 | |
| Throgmorton avenue *III* | | 43 | |
| Throgmorton street *III* | | 43 | |
| Thurloe place, South Kensington | | 9 | |
| | | 9 | |
| Thurloe square | | 42 | |
| Thurlow street, Walworth | | 24 | |
| Thurlow st., Wandsworth rd. | | | |
| Tilson road, Peckham | | 43 | |
| Times office, Printing house square *II* | | 35 | |
| Tindall street, Camberwell New road | | 35 | |
| Titchborne st., Edgware rd. | | 15 | |
| Titchfield rd., St. John's wd. | 15 | | |
| Tiverton street, Newington causeway | | 37 | |
| Tomlin's grove, Bow road | 64 | | |
| Tonbridge st., Euston road | 28 | | |
| Tooley street, Southwark *III* | | 42 | |
| Torriano avenue, Camden tn. | 25 | | |
| Torrington place | | 28 | |

| Street | B | R | G |
|---|---|---|---|
| Torrington square, Bloomsbury *I* | | 28 | |
| Torrington st., Torrington sq. *I* | | 28 | |
| Tothill st., Westminster *IV* | | 25 | |
| Tottenham court road *I* | | 28 | |
| Tottenham rd., Southgate rd. | 42 | | |
| Tottenham st., Fitzroy sq. *I* | | 24 | |
| Totty street, Roman road | 60 | | |
| Tower of London *III* | | 46 | |
| Tower bridge *III* | | 46 | |
| Tower hill *III* | | 42 | |
| Tower hill (Little), Tower hill *III* | | 46 | |
| Tower street, Westminster bridge road | | 33 | |
| Townsend st., Old Kent rd. | | | 41 |
| Townshend rd., St. John's wd. | 15 | | |
| Toynbee Hall *III* | | 47 | |
| Tracey street, Kennington | | | 29 |
| Trafalgar road, Greenwich | | | 70 |
| Trafalgar road. Haggerston | 46 | | |
| Trafalgar road, Old Kent rd. | | | 46 |
| Trafalgar square, Charing cross *II, IV* | | 26 | |
| Trafalgar square, Chelsea | | | 9 |
| Trafalgar street | | | 38 |
| Tranton rd., Blue Anchor la. | | 49 | |
| Travellers' club, Pall mall *IV* | | 26 | |
| Treadway st. | 52 | | |
| Treasury, Whitehall *IV* | | 26 | |
| Tredegar road | 64 | | |
| Tredegar square, Bow road | 60 | | |
| Tregunter rd., W. Brompton | | | 6 |
| Treherne rd., North Brixton | | | 35 |
| Trevor sq., Knightsbridge | | 13 | |
| Trigon road, South Lambeth | | | 34 |
| Trinity house, Tower hill *III* | | 47 | |
| Trinity square, Southwark | | 37 | |
| Trinity sq., Tower hill *III* | | 43 | |
| Trinity street, Blackman st. | | 37 | |
| Trinity street, Liverpool rd. | 35 | | |
| Trott st., High st. Battersea | | | 11 |
| Trump street, Cheapside *III* | | 39 | |
| Tudor grove, Well street | 50 | | |
| Tudor road, Hackney | 54 | | |
| Tudor st., New Bridge st. *II* | | 35 | |
| Tufton st., Westminster *IV* | | 25 | |
| Tuilerie street, Hackney rd. | 47 | | |
| Turin street, Bethnal grn. rd. | 48 | | |
| Turk street, Bethnal green | 48 | | |
| Turnee sq., Hoxton street | 43 | | |
| Turner street, Commercial road east | | 51 | |
| Turner's road, Limehouse | 64 | | |
| Turnmill st., Clerkenwell | | 36 | |
| Turnville street, Bethnal green road | 48 | | |
| Tussaud's waxworks, Baker street *I* | | 20 | |

| | | | |
|---|---|---|---|
| Tweed street, Nine elms | . . | 23 | |
| Twyford st., Caledonian rd. | 31 | | |
| Tyers street, Lambeth | . . | 29 | |
| Tyler street, Carnaby st. I | 23 | | |
| Tyneham rd., Lavender hl. | . . | 20 | |
| Type street, Chiswell street | 40 | | |
| Tysoe st., Wilmington sq. | 36 | | |
| Tyssen street, Bethnal green | 18 | | |
| | | | |
| Ufton grove, Southgate rd. | 42 | | |
| Ufton road north, Kingsland | 42 | | |
| Ufton road south, Kingsland | 42 | | |
| Underwood street, Mile end | . | 48 | |
| Union grove, Clapham | . . | . . | 28 |
| Union road, Albion road Holloway | . . | 33 | |
| Union road, Clapham | . . | . . | 28 |
| Union road, Millpond street | . | 19 | |
| Union road, Newington causeway | . . | 37 | |
| Union sq., New North rd. | 39 | | |
| Union st., Berkeley sq. IV | . | 18 | |
| Union street, Boro' | . . . | 38 | |
| Union street, Clapham | . . | . . | 28 |
| Union street, East road | . | 44 | |
| Union st., Kennington rd. | . . | . . | 29 |
| Union street, Kingsland rd. | 48 | | |
| Union street, London road | . | 33 | |
| Union street, Middlesex hospital | . . . I | 24 | |
| Union street, Pimlico road | . . | . . | 17 |
| Union st., Whitechapel rd. | . | 51 | |
| United Service, Pall mall IV | . | 26 | |
| United Service institution (museum), Whitehall yard IV | . | 30 | |
| University college, Gower st. | 28 | | |
| University College hospital, University st., Gower st. | . | 28 | |
| University street, Tottenham court road | . . | 24 | |
| Upper Baker st., Regent's pk. | . | 20 | |
| Upper Barnsbury street | . . | 34 | |
| Upper Bedford pl., Russell square | . . | . . | 28 |
| Upper Belgrave street, Pimlico IV | . | 17 | |
| Upper Berkeley street. . I | . | 15 | |
| Upper Bland street, Gt. Dover street | . | 37 | |
| Upper Brook street, Grosvenor square . . . . I | . | 19 | |
| Upper Charles street, Goswell road | . . | . . | 36 |
| Upper East Smithfield III | . | 46 | |
| Upper Eccleston street. Pimlico IV | . | 17 | |
| Upper Garden street, Westminister | . . | . . | 24 |
| Upper George street, Edware road | . . | 15 | |

| | | | |
|---|---|---|---|
| Upper Glo'ster place, Dorset square | . . | . . | 16 |
| Upper Gower mews, Torrington place | . . | . . | 28 |
| Upper Grange road, Bermondsey | . . | . . | 15 |
| Upper Grosvenor street . . | . . | . . | 19 |
| Upper Hamilton terrace, St. John's wood | . . | . . | 7 |
| Upper Homerton road. . . | . . | 53 | |
| Upper James street, Golden square . . . . . . . I | . . | 23 | |
| Upper James street, Oval road, Camden town . . | . . | . . | 22 |
| Upper John st., Golden sq. I | . . | 23 | |
| Upper John street, Hoxton | 11 | | |
| Upper Kennington lane . . | . . | . . | 30 |
| Upper Manor street, Chels. | . . | . . | 13 |
| Upper Marylebone street I | . . | 24 | |
| Upper North street, East India dock road | . . | . . | 63 |
| Upper Ogle street, Upper Marylebone street . . . I | . | 24 | |
| Up. Park rd., Haverstock hl. | 13 | | |
| Up. Park st., Liverpool rd. | 34 | | |
| Upper Phillimore gardens . | . | 1 | |
| Up. Prebstr. st., Edgware rd. | . | 15 | |
| Upper Rathbone place . I | . | 28 | |
| Upper Rupert street, Leicester square . . . . . I | . | 27 | |
| Up. Russell st., Bermondsey | . | 44 | |
| Upper St. Martin's lane II | . | 27 | |
| Upper Smith street, Northampton square | . . | . . | 36 |
| Upper Spring street, Marylebone . . . . . . I | . . | 20 | |
| Upper street, Islington . . | 34 | | |
| Upper Thames street . III | . | 39 | |
| Upper Vernon st., Pentonville | 32 | | |
| Upper Westbourne terrace | . | 8 | |
| Upper Weymouth street, Marylebone I | . | 20 | |
| Upper Whitecross street . | . | 40 | |
| Upper William street, Portland town | . . | 15 | |
| Upper Wimpole street . I | . | 20 | |
| Upper Winchester street, Caledonian road | . . | 34 | |
| Upper Woburn place, Tavistock square | . . | 28 | |
| Upton road, Kilburn . . . | . . | 6 | |
| Usher road, Bow | . . | 63 | |
| Uxbridge road railway stat. | . | 2 | |
| Uxbridge street, Kensington | . | 2 | |
| Uxbridge street, Newington causeway | . . | 37 | |
| | | | |
| Valentine place, Blackfriars road | . . | 33 | |
| Varden street, New road, Whitechapel | . . | 51 | |

## LIST OF THE PRINCIPAL STREETS,

| Street | B | R | G |
|---|---|---|---|
| Vassal road, Camberwell New road | | | |
| New road | | 35 | |
| Vaudeville theatre, Strand (opposite Salisbury st.) *II* | | 31 | |
| Vauxhall bridge | | 26 | |
| Vauxhall bridge rd. . . *IV* | | 24 | |
| Vauxhall High street . . | | 30 | |
| Vauxhall pier, Millbank . | | 25 | |
| Vauxhall railway station . | | 30 | |
| Vauxhall street, Lambeth | | 30 | |
| Vauxhall walk | | 29 | |
| Vere street, Clare market *II* | | 31 | |
| Vere street, Oxford street | | 19 | |
| Verney rd., St. James's rd. | | 50 | |
| Vernon place, Bloomsbury square *II* | | 32 | |
| Vernon road, Roman road | 63 | | |
| Vernon st., King's cross rd. | 32 | | |
| Verona street, York road . | | 12 | |
| Verulam street, Gray's inn road *II* | | 36 | |
| Vestry road, Peckham rd. | | 43 | |
| Viaduct st., Bethnal grn. rd. | 52 | | |
| Viceroy rd., Sth. Lambeth | | 27 | |
| Victoria embankment *II, IV* | | 34 | |
| Victoria grove, Fulham rd. | | 6 | |
| Victoria grove, Kensington | | 5 | |
| Victoria park | 59 | | |
| Victoria park railway station, Wick lane | 62 | | |
| Victoria park road | 55 | | |
| Victoria park square, Green street, Bethnal green | | 56 | |
| Victoria place, Bayswater | | 3 | |
| Victoria railway bridge . . | | 18 | |
| Victoria railway station *IV* | 21 | 21 | |
| Victoria road, Battersea . | | 19 | |
| Victoria road, Holloway. . | 33 | | |
| Victoria road, Kensington | | 5 | |
| Victoria road, Kentish tn. | 22 | | |
| Victoria road, Kilburn . . | | 2 | |
| Victoria rd., Rye la., Peckham | | 48 | |
| Victoria square, Pimlico *IV* | | 21 | |
| Victoria st., Westminster *IV* | | 21 | |
| Vigo street, Regent street *I* | | 21 | |
| Villa street, Walworth com. | | 12 | |
| Villiers street, Strand *II* | | 26 | |
| Vincent sq., Westminster | | 21 | |
| Vincent street, Shoreditch | 48 | | |
| Vincent st., Westminster | | 25 | |
| Vincent terrace, City road | 35 | | |
| Vine street, Minories *III* | | 47 | |
| Vine street, Regent street *I* | | 23 | |
| Vine street, Tooley street | | 12 | |
| Vine st., York rd., Lambeth | | 30 | |
| Virginia row, Bethnal grn. | 48 | | |
| Vivian road, Old Ford . . | 59 | | |
| Vyner street, Cambridge rd. | 51 | | |
| Wakefield st., Gray's inn rd. | 32 | | |
| Walbrook, Mansion ho. *III* | | 39 | |

| Street | B | R | G |
|---|---|---|---|
| Walbrook street, Hoxton . | 39 | | |
| Walcot square, Lambeth . | | 33 | |
| Walham gro., Walham grn. | | 3 | |
| Walker street, Poplar . . . | | 67 | |
| Wallace rd., Canonbury . . | 37 | | |
| Walnut Tree walk, Lambeth | | 29 | |
| Walpole street, King's road, Chelsea | | 13 | |
| Walter street, Bethnal grn. | 56 | | |
| Wallerton road, Harrow rd. | 4 | | |
| Walton place, Queen street, Brompton | | 13 | |
| Walton street, Chelsea . . | | 13 | |
| Walworth road | | 37 | |
| Wandsworth road | | 24 | |
| Wandsworth rd. rail. station | | 24 | |
| Wansey st., Walworth rd. | | 37 | |
| Wapping, High street . . | | 50 | |
| Wapping station | | 50 | |
| War office, Pall mall . *IV* | | 22 | |
| Warburton rd., Hackney . | 50 | | |
| Ward st., Princes st., Lambeth | | 29 | |
| Warden road, Kentish tn. | 17 | | |
| Wardour street, Soho . . *I* | | 27 | |
| Warley street, Bethnal grn. | 56 | | |
| Warner place, Hackney rd. | 52 | | |
| Warner road, Camberwell New road | | 40 | |
| Warner street, Clerkenwell | | 36 | |
| Warner st., New Kent rd. | | 44 | |
| Warren street, Fitzroy sq. | | 24 | |
| Warren street, Pentonville | 35 | | |
| Warrington cres., Maida vale | 8 | | |
| Warwick grdns., Kensington | | 1 | |
| Warwick la., Newgate st. *II* | | 39 | |
| Warwick place, Gray's inn | | 32 | |
| Warwick road, Kensington | | 1 | |
| Warwick road, Maida hill | 8 | 8 | |
| Warwick road north, Clifton gardens | | 8 | |
| Warwick square, Pimlico . | | 21 | |
| Warwick st., Belgrave rd. | | 21 | |
| Warwick st., Golden sq. *I* | | 23 | |
| Warwick st., Kensington | | 1 | |
| Water lane, Homerton . . | 53 | | |
| Water lane, Lower Thames street *III* | | 42 | |
| Water street, Strand . *II* | | 34 | |
| Waterford road, Fulham . | | 7 | |
| Waterloo bridge . . . *II* | | 39 | |
| Waterloo pier . . . . *II* | | 30 | |
| Waterloo pl., Pall mall *IV* | | 26 | |
| Waterloo rd., Bishop's rd. | 15 | | |
| Waterloo road | | 33 | |
| Waterloo railway sta., Waterloo road | | 34 | |
| Waterloo st., Camberwell | | 39 | |
| Waterman's Alley | | 35 | |
| Watling street . . . *III* | | 39 | |
| Waverley pl., St. John's wd. | 11 | | |
| Waverley rd., Harrow rd. | | 4 | |

## SQUARES, PUBLIC BUILDINGS, etc. 43

| | B R G | | B R G |
|---|---|---|---|
| Wayford street, Battersea | 16 | West India docks | 62 |
| Webber row, Blackfriars rd. | 33 | West India dock pier | 61 |
| Webber st., Blackfriars road | 33 | West India dock rail. sta. | 62 |
| Wedderburn rd. | 9 | West India dock road | 63 |
| Weedington road, Prince of Wales road | 17 | West India dock road railway station | 63 |
| Welbeck st., Cavendish sq. | 20 | West London & Westminster Cemetery | 6 |
| Well street, Jewin street. Aldersgate ... III | 40 | West Smithfield ... II | 36 |
| Well street, South Hackney | 54 | West Strand ... II | 25 |
| Well street, Wellclose sq. | 47 | Westbourne gro. Bayswater | 3 |
| Wellclose square | 47 | Westbourne park | 8 |
| Wellesley rd., Kentish tn. | 17 | Westbourne park crescent | 8 |
| Wellesley street, Stepney | 56 | Westbourne park railway station. Great Western rd. | 4 |
| Wellington barracks, Birdcage walk ... IV | 21 | Westbourne park road | 8 |
| Wellington road, Bridge road, Battersea | 11 | Westbourne park villas | 8 |
| Wellington rd., Camberwell | 40 | Westbourne place, Eaton sq. | 17 |
| Wellington road, St. James's road | 29 | Westbourne rd., Barnsbury | 29 |
| Wellington road, St. John's wood | 1 | Westbourne rd. east, Liverpool road | 33 |
| Wellington rd. so., Bow rd. | 61 | Westbourne st., Victoria gate | 11 |
| Wellington row. Bethnal grn. | 18 | Westbourne street. Pimlico | 17 |
| Wellington square. Chelsea | 13 | Westbourne terrace, Sussex gardens | 11 |
| Wellington street. Blackfriars road | 33 | Westbourne terrace north, Westbourne green | 8 |
| Wellington st., Camden tn. | 22 | Westbourne terrace road, Paddington | 8 |
| Wellington street. Chelsea | 11 | Westcroft rd. | 6 |
| Wellington street. Holloway | 20 | Western ter. Notting hill | 3 |
| Wellington street. Islington | 34 | Westminster abbey, Old Palace yard ... IV | 25 |
| Wellington st., Kingsland rd. | 34 | Westminster bridge ... IV | 29 |
| Wellington street. New Kent road ... III | 37 | Westminster bridge rd. IV | 29 |
| Wellington st., Pentonville | 34 | Westminster bridge sta. IV | 25 |
| Wellington street, Shacklewell lane | 45 | Westminster hospital. Princes street. Victoria st. IV | 25 |
| Wellington street, Strand II | 31 | Westminster pier, Victoria embankment ... IV | 29 |
| Wellington st., Victoria park | 56 | Westminster school ... IV | 25 |
| Wells place, Camberwell | 13 | Westminster Town Hall IV | 25 |
| Wells street, Camberwell | 13 | Westmoreland pl., Bayswater | 3 |
| Wells street, Oxford st. I | 24 | Westmoreland pl., City rd. | 40 |
| Wenlock basin, Wenlock rd. | 39 | Westmoreland rd., Camberwell | 13 |
| Wenlock road, City road | 39 | Westmoreland road, Bayswater | 4 |
| Wenlock street, Shepherdess walk | 39 | Westmoreland road, Walworth | 8 |
| Wentworth street, Whitechapel ... III | 47 | Westmoreland street. Kingsland road | 47 |
| Werrington st., Oakley sq. | 23 | Westmoreland street. Marylebone ... I | 23 |
| West sq., St. George's road | 33 | Westmoreland st., Pimlico | 22 |
| West street, Bethnal green | 56 | Weston street, Pentonville | 32 |
| West st., Mare st.. Hackney | 54 | Weston street, Tooley street | 42 |
| West st., Mile end Old town | 56 | Wetherby road, South Kensington | 5 |
| West street. Soho | 27 | | |
| West street, Well street. | 54 | | |
| West Brompton railway sta. | 2 | | |
| West Cromwell road | 1 | | |
| West end railway station | 5 | Weymouth mews, Portland place ... I | 24 |
| West Ferry road. Millwall | 61 | | |
| West Ham lane | 51 | | |

## LIST OF THE PRINCIPAL STREETS,

| | B | R | G |
|---|---|---|---|
| Weymouth st., Gr. Portland street | | *1* | 20 |
| Weymouth st., Hackney rd. | 47 | | |
| Weymouth st., New Kent rd. | | | 37 |
| Weymouth ter., Hackney rd. | 47 | | |
| Wharf road, City road | 40 | | |
| Wharf road, Pancras road | 28 | | |
| Wharfdale rd., King's cross | 31 | | |
| Wharton street, Lloyd sq. | 32 | | |
| Whetstone park, Lincoln's inn fields | | *II* | 32 |
| Whiskin street, Clerkenwell | 36 | | |
| Whitcomb street, Leicester square | | *I* | 27 |
| White st., Bethnal grn. rd. | 52 | | |
| White street, Borough | | | 37 |
| White st., Little Moorfields | | | 40 |
| White Conduit st., Islington | 35 | | |
| White Hart st., Drury lane | *II* | | 31 |
| White Hart st., Kennington | | | 33 |
| White Horse la., Mile end rd. | | | 56 |
| White Horse street, Commercial road east | | | 59 |
| White Horse street, Piccadilly | | *IV* | 22 |
| White Lion street, Norton Folgate | | | 48 |
| White Lion st., Pentonville | 35 | | |
| Whitechapel (High st.) *III* | | 47 | |
| Whitechapel road | | | 52 |
| Whitechapel station | | | 52 |
| Whitecross street, Borough | | | 38 |
| Whitefriars | | *II* | 35 |
| Whitefriars st., Fleet st. | *II* | | 35 |
| Whitehall | | *IV* | 26 |
| Whitehall gardens | | *IV* | 26 |
| Whitehall place | | *IV* | 26 |
| Whitehall stairs | | *IV* | 30 |
| Whitehead's grove, Chelsea | | | 13 |
| White's club, St. James's street | | *IV* | 22 |
| White's ground, Bermondsey | | | 41 |
| White's row, Spitalfields | | | 48 |
| Whitfield st., Fitzroy sq. | *I* | | 21 |
| Whitmore road, Hoxton | 43 | | |
| Whitmore street, Hoxton | 43 | | |
| Wick lane, Old Ford | 58 | | |
| Wick road, Homerton | 58 | | |
| Wickham st., Jonathan st. | | | 29 |
| Wicklow st., King's cross rd. | 32 | | |
| Widegate st., Bishopsgate st. | | | 41 |
| Wigmore street, Cavendish square | | *I* | 19 |
| Wilcox rd., South Lambeth | | | 27 |
| Wild court, Gt. Wild street | | | 31 |
| Wilfred St. | | *IV* | 21 |
| Wilkes place, Hoxton street | 44 | | |
| Wilkes street, Spitalfields | | | 48 |
| Wilkin st., Weedington rd. | 17 | | |
| William street, Adelphi, Strand | | *II* | 30 |
| William street, Curtain road | 44 | | |
| William street, Hart's lane | 48 | | |
| William street, High street Lambeth | | | 29 |
| William street, Lisson grove | | | 16 |
| William street, Lowndes sq. | | | 13 |
| William street, Marylebone lane | | *I* | 20 |
| William street, New Bridge street | | *II* | 35 |
| William street, Regent's pk. | 24 | | |
| William street, Regent st., Lambeth | | | 29 |
| William street, St. Peter street, Islington | | | 39 |
| William st., Stepney green | | | 56 |
| William street north, Caledonian road | 31 | | |
| Willingham ter., Kentish tn. | 21 | | |
| Willis road, Prince of Wales' road | 21 | | |
| Willis street, Poplar | | | 67 |
| Willis's rooms, King st. | *IV* | | 22 |
| Willow walk, Bermondsey | | | 41 |
| Willow bdg. rd., Canonbury | 38 | | |
| Wilmer gardens, Hoxton | 43 | | |
| Wilmington sq., Spafields | | | 36 |
| Wilmot place, Rochester rd. | 22 | | |
| Wilmot st., Bethnal grn. rd. | 52 | | |
| Wilmot street, Russell sq. | | | 28 |
| Wilson road, Peckham road | | | 44 |
| Wilson st., Finsbury la. | *II* | | 31 |
| Wilson street, Finsbury sq. | | | 44 |
| Wilton cres., Belgrave sq. | | | 17 |
| Wilton place, Knightsbridge | | | 17 |
| Wilton road, Dalston | 50 | | |
| Wilton road, Pimlico | | | 21 |
| Wilton street, Grosvenor place | | *IV* | 17 |
| Wilton street, Earl st., Westminster | | | 25 |
| Wiltshire road, Brixton | | | 36 |
| Wimbourn st., N. North rd. | 39 | | |
| Wimpole st., Cavendish sq. | *I* | | 20 |
| Winchester gardens, Belsize park | | | 9 |
| Winchester rd., Adelaide rd. | 10 | | |
| Winchester street, Borough market | | | 38 |
| Winchester street, Pentonville road | 31 | | |
| Winchester street, Pimlico | | | 21 |
| Windmill lane, Deptford Lower road | | | 57 |
| Windmill st., Canterbury pl. | | | 34 |
| Windmill st., Finsbury sq. | | | 44 |
| Windmill st., Lambeth rd. | | | 34 |
| Windmill street, Tottenham court road | | *I* | 28 |
| Windsor pl., Denmark hill | | | 40 |
| Windsor street, Essex road | 39 | | |

| | | | |
|---|---|---|---|
| Windsor terrace, City road | 10 | Wynyatt street, Goswell road | 36 |
| Winsley street, Oxford st. *I* | . 23 | | |
| Winter gardens & aquarium, | | Yalding rd., Blue Anchor rd | . . 15 |
| Tothill street . . . . *IV* | . 25 | Yardley street, Exmouth st. | 36 |
| Woburn place, Russell sq. | . 28 | Yatton street . . . . . . . . | . 68 |
| Woburn square, Bloomsbury | . 28 | Yeoman's row, Brompton . | . 13 |
| Wolsey road, Kingsland . | 41 | York bldgs., Adelphi, Strand | |
| Wood street, Cheapside *III* | . 39 | | *II* . 26 |
| Wood street, Exmouth st. | 36 | York gate, Regent's park . | . 39 |
| Wood st., Millbank st. *IV* | . 25 | York place, Adelphi . . *II* | . 30 |
| Wood street, Prince's road, | | York place, Baker street *I* | . 39 |
| Lambeth . . . . . . . . | . . 29 | York place, Offord road . . | 30 |
| Woodbridge st., Clerkenwell | 36 | York road, Battersea . . . | . . 12 |
| Woodchester st., Harrow rd. | . 8 | York road, King's cross . | 31 |
| Woodchurch rd. . . . . . . | 6 | York rd., Westminster bdg. | |
| Woodfield rd., Harrow road | . 4 | road . . . . . . . . . . | . 29 |
| Woodland street, Dalston | 16 | York road railway station | . . 13 |
| Woodstock st., Oxford st. *I* | . 19 | York square, Commercial | |
| Wootton st., Cornwall road | . 34 | road east . . . . . . . | . 59 |
| Worcester street, Pimlico . | . . 22 | York street, Baker street . | . 16 |
| Worcester street, Southwark | . 38 | York street, Blackfriars road | 34 |
| World's end passage, King's | | York st., Commercial rd. ea. | . 51 |
| road . . . . . . . . . . | . . 10 | York street, Globe road . . | 56 |
| Wormwood st., Bishopsgate | | York street, Hackney road | 17 |
| street . . . . . . . . *III* | . 43 | York st., St. James's sq. *IV* | . 22 |
| Worship st., Norton Folgate | . 44 | York street, Walworth road | . . 37 |
| Wright's lane, Kensington | . 5 | York street, Westminster *IV* | . 21 |
| Wright's rd., St. Stephen's rd. | 59 | York st., York rd., Lambeth | . 29 |
| Wrotham rd., Camden town | 26 | York terrace, Regent's park | . 29 |
| Wych street, Drury lane *II* | . 31 | Young street, Kensington . | . 5 |
| Wye st., York rd., Battersea | . 13 | | |
| Wyndham rd., Camberwell | . . 39 | Zoar street, Blackfriars . . | 38 |
| Wyndham street, Bryanston | | Zoological gardens, Regent's | |
| square . . . . . . . . . . | . 16 | park . . . . . . . . . . | 19 |

Leipsic, Printed by Breitkopf & Hartel.

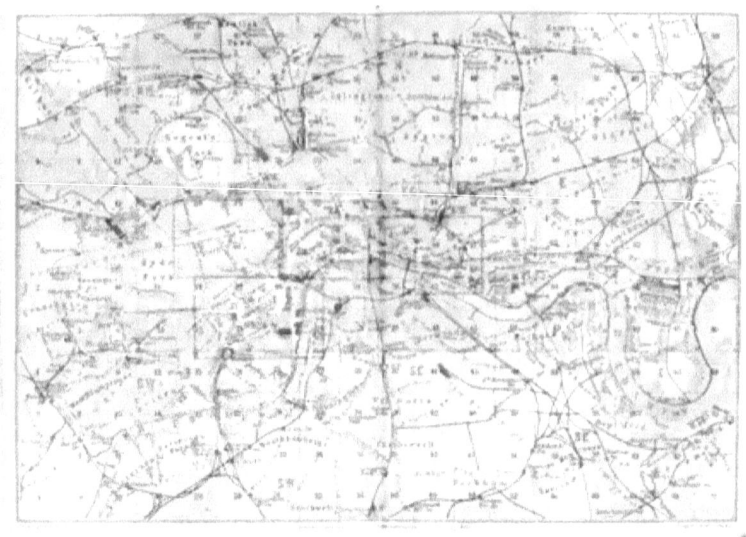

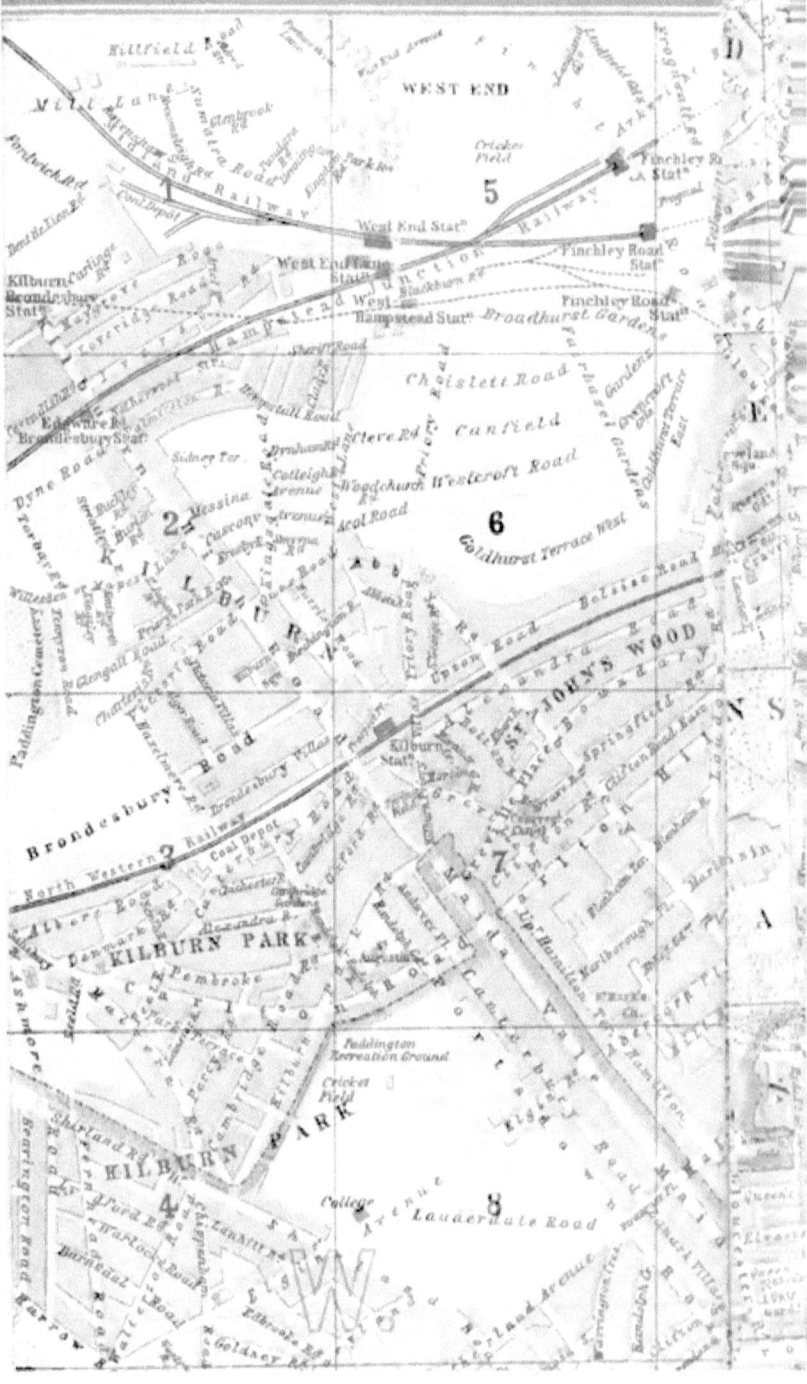

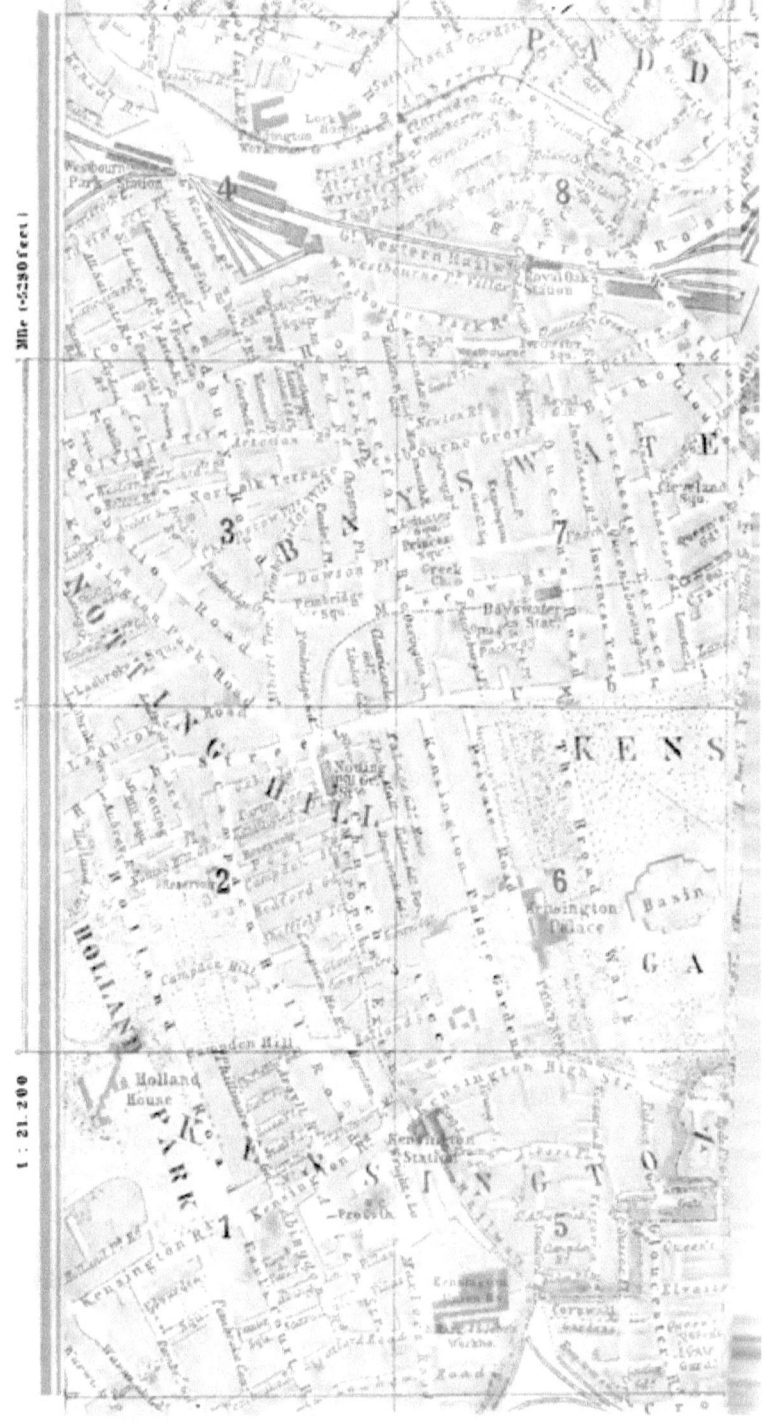

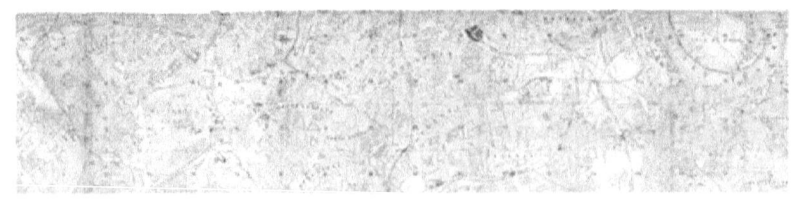

I. THE WEST END FROM BAKER STREET TO SOHO.

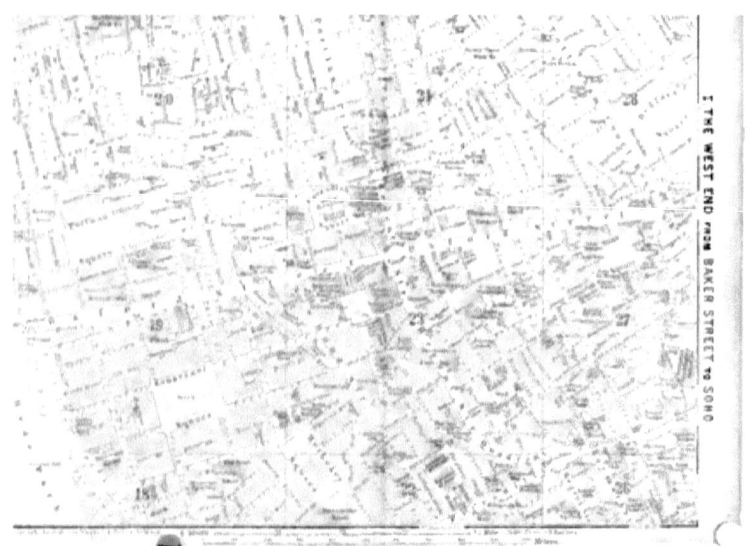

I. THE WEST END FROM BAKER STREET TO SOHO.

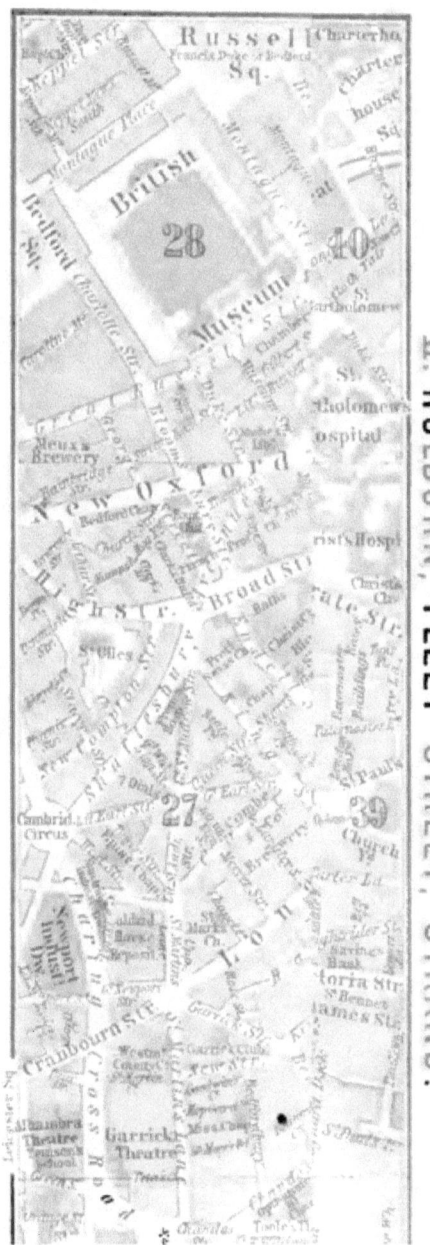

II. HOLBORN, FLEET STREET, STRAND.

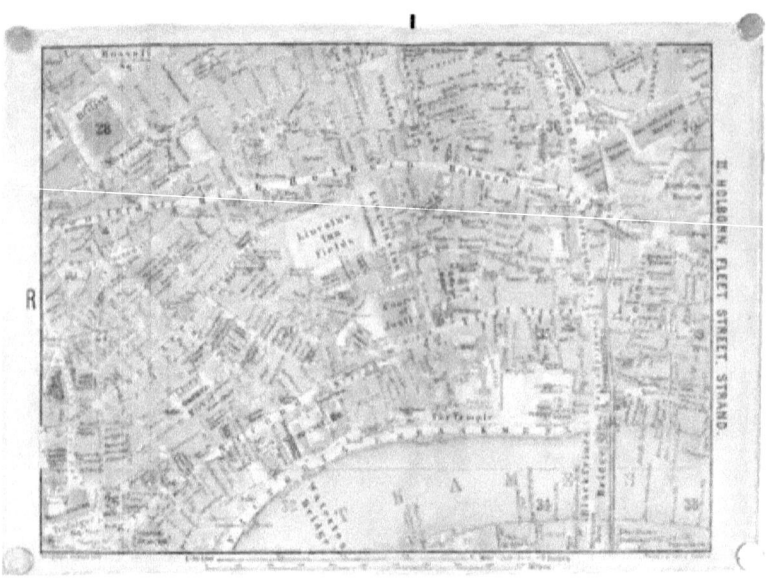

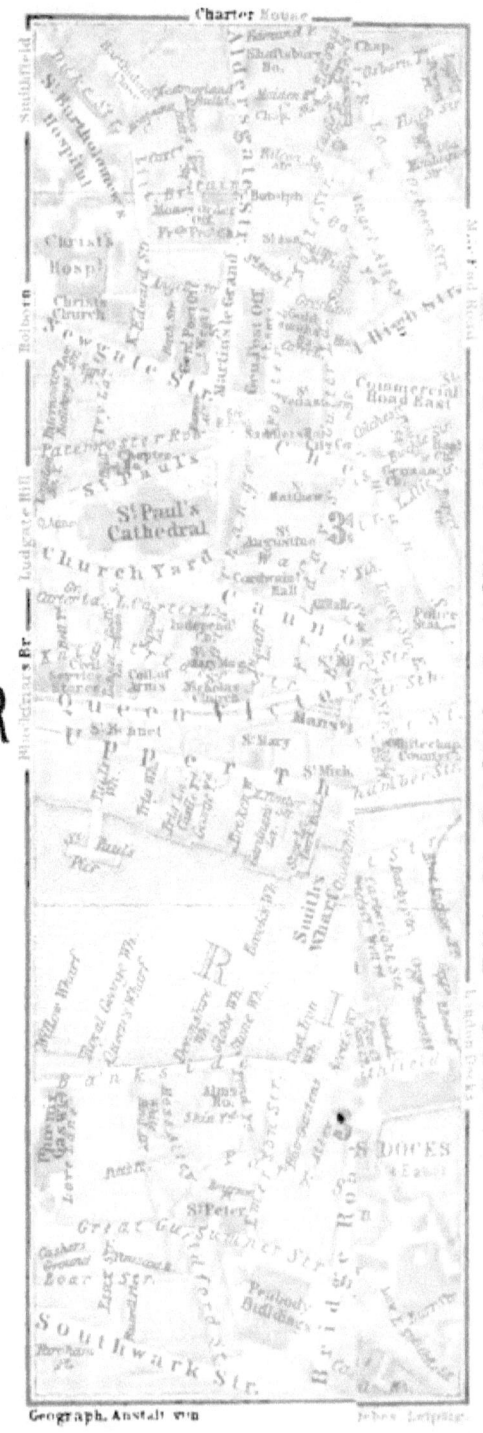

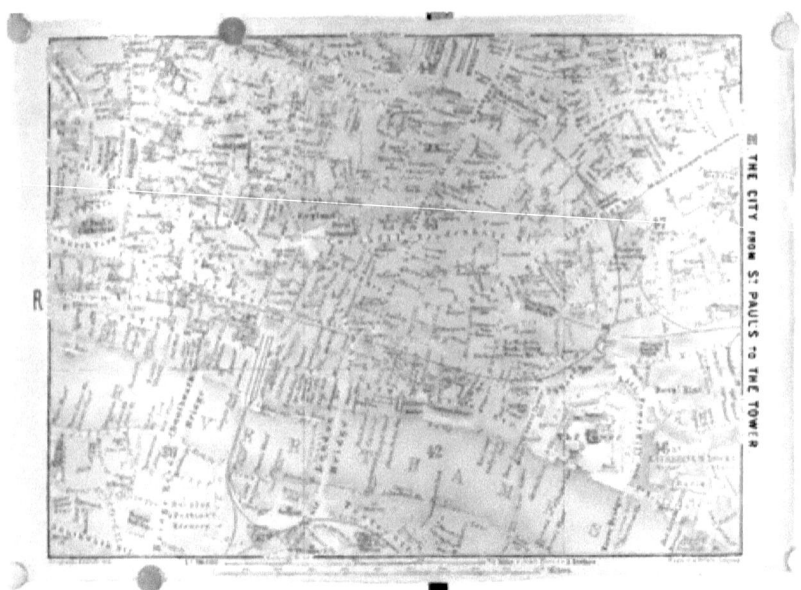

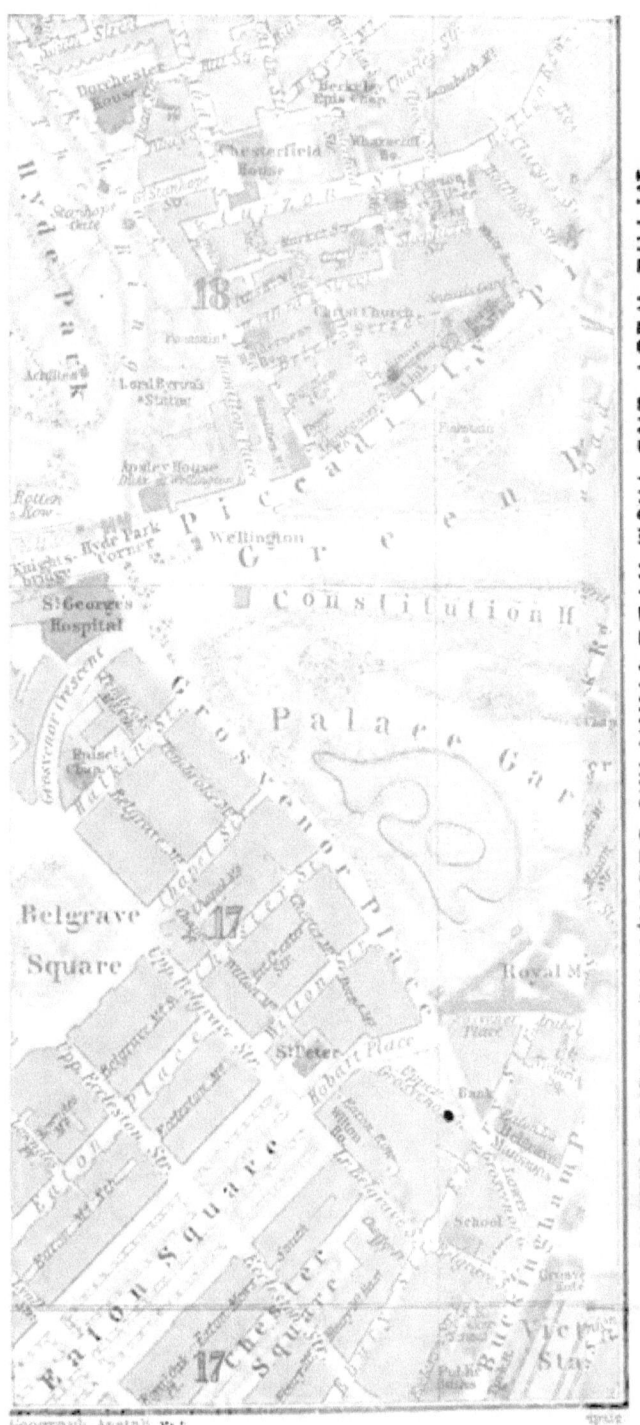

IV. THE WEST END FROM HYDE PARK AND BELGRAVIA TO THE THAMES.

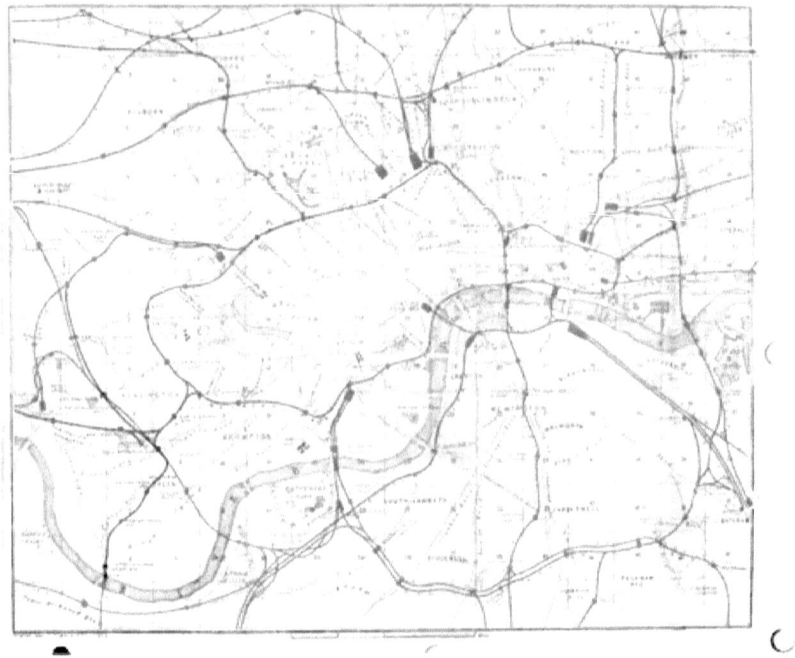

LEIPSIC: KARL BAEDEKER.

1889.

www.ingramcontent.com/pod-product-compliance
Lightning Source LLC
Chambersburg PA
CBHW022138300426
44115CB00006B/238